# Chinese Femininities/
# Chinese Masculinities

ASIA: LOCAL STUDIES/GLOBAL THEMES

Jeffrey N. Wasserstrom, Kären Wigen, and Hue-Tam Ho Tai, Editors

# Chinese Femininities/ Chinese Masculinities

*A Reader*

Edited by Susan Brownell
and Jeffrey N. Wasserstrom

FOREWORD BY

Thomas Laqueur

UNIVERSITY OF CALIFORNIA PRESS

Berkeley   Los Angeles   London

University of California Press
Berkeley and Los Angeles, California

University of California Press, Ltd.
London, England

Library of Congress Cataloging-in-Publication Data

Chinese femininities, Chinese masculinities : a reader / edited by Susan
Brownell and Jeffrey N. Wasserstrom ; foreword by Thomas Laqueur.
   p.    cm.
  ISBN 978-0-520-22116-1
  1. Sex role—China.   2. Femininity—China.   3. Masculinity—China.
I. Brownell, Susan.  II. Wasserstrom, Jeffrey N.

HQ1075.5.C6 C47   2002
305.3'0951—dc21                           2001005079

14  13  12  11  10  09  08
10  9  8  7  6  5  4

# CONTENTS

# ILLUSTRATIONS

# FOREWORD

*Thomas Laqueur*

No one who reads the essays in this collection will fail to hear the mighty resonance of gender in Chinese culture over the past three centuries. From the legal control of masculinity and the adjudication of chastity in the seventeenth century, to the politics of marriage and the family in the nineteenth and early twentieth centuries, to the present, when national minorities are represented as pretty girls performing local rituals for Han tourists, the range and depth of this collection is remarkable. Two vignettes, chosen almost at random, are exemplary of its historical and ethnographic riches, of the ways in which finely drawn details about gender and sexuality open up great questions of culture and politics. The first, recounted by Janet Theiss, involves an eighteenth-century murder. Fan Zhaoer, the twenty-three-year-old only son of a prosperous lower-gentry family, stabbed to death his nineteen-year-old wife, Gao Shi, with her sewing shears. She had often teased him about the fact that "his stalk [was] small," but he usually took her banter as an edgy marital joke. One day she accused him of delaying her from having a son and thus ruining her life; presumably a small stalk made conceiving a male heir less likely. He says he got a little angry. Then one night, with his "chaste widow" mother asleep in the next room and a few glasses of wine in his belly, Fan Zhaoer could take it no more. He had hoped for marital intimacy with his wife; he made some jokes to that effect; his wife was not amused. "Such a useless thing as yours! Why bother to afflict people's daughters!" How, he responded, did she know so much about comparative penis sizes: "Whose stalk have you seen that's bigger?" She was furious, it seems, because he had impugned her chastity. But, at the same time, she threatened to be unchaste; she would marry someone else when he died. And so it went back and forth until he cracked and in his fury thrust her scissors into her breast.

The second vignette is about men; this book understands that even if our Western ancestors understood masculinity as relatively fixed and unproblematic, contemporary scholars need not follow suit. This story does not involve marital relations, and it is from a slightly earlier time, the mid–seventeenth century, when male hairstyle was a matter of life and death. The conquering Manchu required every Han Chinese man to shave the front of his head as a sign of submission to the new dynasty; lack of a tonsure could result in the unceremonious loss of a head. One day in 1653, troops arrested two traveling players for having full heads of hair and accused them of rebellion. Their defense—the facts of which were supported by witnesses in their home village—was that they were opera singers who performed female roles. They were genuinely confused as to whether they counted as male and were thus appropriate bearers of the sign of submission; one actually had had himself tonsured and then had let his hair grow back. The two kept their heads.

Neither incident is itself of special significance and both could safely be excluded, one might think, from all but the most detailed histories of the centuries in which they played their tiny parts. But in another register the murder of a young wife and the escape from death by male actors who failed to bear the mark of the loyal male are almost impossibly freighted with meaning. Layer upon layer emerges from the story of Fan Zhaoer and Gao Shi's troubled marriage. It is about how the norms of an aristocratic culture of chastity became a part of daily life; it was a matter of life and death for arrivistes like Fan Zhaoer, only one or two generations removed from the common class. It is about how the official chastity cult of the Yuan dynasty (1279–1368), with its rules on remarriage, its guides to widow suicide, and its system of plaques, monuments, and money for virtuous female behavior, survived the early Manchu attack on it (and related customs like footbinding) to become, in the seventeenth and eighteenth centuries, even more central to defining individual status in society and in relation to the state. And it opens up new questions of cultural history: How did a young woman of good upbringing like Gao Shi learn so much sexual word play? The microhistory of marital sex gone wrong becomes a synecdoche for a vast system of power, prestige, and politics.

And as for the humble and despised actors, they too seem to take on near-mythic significance: they are excused from bearing the sign of submission to the new political order. Biology is clearly not legal destiny in a world in which social place means more than the configuration of the genitals. (One of the stories this collection tells is how what we would take to be categories of sexual identity emerged only as China adapted a Western politics of gender to its particular conditions. There was, we learn, no generic category "woman" until a neologism was created by Republican-era reformers.) But more important, this collection attests to how deeply the categories "male" and "masculine" were imbricated with the legitimacy of the Chinese world order. To be part of the new Manchu order was to be a man with a partially shaved head; to be a male actor playing a woman was somehow to be an exemplary outsider. And the general abolition of dishonorable status was understood through the prism of rehabilitating specifically the status of women in that category.

In a general sense this collection argues that no political or economic or social history is possible without a cultural history: a history of the meanings of things, actions, events, movements, gestures, clothes, and accomplishments, among much else. And it argues, moreover, that there can be no cultural history without a history of gender. In some measure these claims are internal to the history of China: twentieth-century male bandits and rebel workers recapitulate older, elite tensions between the ideal of the warrior male and the ideal of the man of cultivation and learning. (After the sixteenth century few European rulers or aristocrats were completely illiterate, but only a handful had even the slightest pretension to any personal artistic or intellectual standing. No conflict here.) Thus the nature and organization of Shanghai politics are in some immediate sense comprehensible only in a specific historicist context of traditions of masculinity. Mediterranean societies certainly valued female chastity, and Mediterranean families felt dishonored by lapses of virtue, but nothing remotely like the Chinese state-supported cult of chastity existed in the West. Even the cult of the virgin saints does not come close. Thus the seemingly private, familial quality of a wife's or daughter's virtue is at the same time public. Or put differently, the ambiguous nature of the public-private divide is registered powerfully in the domain of gender.

Of course, the claim that a general history of culture is refracted through a history of gender is not peculiar to China nor to the authors and editors represented in this volume. It was made by thinkers of the Scottish Enlightenment and, in one way or another, by almost all the major social theorists of the next century. Chinese men and women, as they came in contact with the West, took up these arguments in their thoughts and deeds. Progress, as the thinkers of the Scottish Enlightenment argued, was measured by progress in the status of women: the more advanced the society, the more educated its women—and the more extensive and polite the relations between the sexes. For better or for worse the development of capitalism—and, with it, economic and military advances—seemed linked to individualism and liberty in all realms, including that of gender: freedom from the extended family was a key element of freedom more generally, as was the ability to choose a mate and to dress, wear one's hair, or make up one's face as one pleased. The private, again and again, was rendered public and political even as its distinctiveness was maintained. Beginning in the middle of the nineteenth century, Chinese political reformers—men and women—took these intellectual imports onboard. Thus the Chinese past, present, and future came to be articulated through what was taken to be a sort of universal history of gender. The prostitution or seclusion of women, a life of leisured, refined literary learning for men: all came to have different meanings— and called for new political responses—when regarded by Chinese thinkers through the lens of Western historicism.

Finally, the essays and introductions in this book will be of great interest to historians of other places—Europe, Latin America, Southeast Asia, the Middle East, Africa—because they demonstrate so pointedly the importance of gender in understanding the great transformations of modernity. Nationalism is translated into masculinity not just in Shanghai but also in Calcutta. The right to marry whom one pleases is a major sticking point today for the Universal Declaration of Human Rights—just as it was in early-twentieth-century China—because it is perceived as striking so deeply at the foundations of an established social order: the freedom to dress as one pleases and the claim to a gendered corporeal integrity have been and continue to be immensely fraught elements in the politics of modernity. Manifestly, if one is to understand Chinese history of the last three centuries, one has to pay attention to gender. And, because the essays in this volume give evidence of the sheer scale, ambition, and weightiness of this history, they serve as models for rethinking world history more generally. Taken together, they tell a tale that is so variegated, complex, and fascinating that students of other times and places will want to follow its leads.

# Introduction:
# Theorizing Femininities
# and Masculinities

*Susan Brownell and Jeffrey N. Wasserstrom*

The last two centuries have witnessed tremendous upheavals and transformations in every aspect of Chinese culture and society, from national politics to everyday life. At the level of everyday life, some of the most obvious and remarkable of these transformations have affected, or occurred in, the realm of gender. What are the links between broad political and economic trends and trends in notions about gender? Have elite and popular visions of the differences between the sexes tended to overlap or diverge? How have gender distinctions related to other kinds of distinctions, such as ones associated with ethnicity, class, and generation? How have images of the ideal female and male changed over time? Alternately, have there been changes in categories of the abnormal—that is, those categories defined by images of women and men who must be viewed with suspicion due to their failure to conform to the codes of proper femininity or masculinity?

In this book, we explore questions of this sort while treating gender as more than simply a collection of roles, symbols, and behaviors that are always attached to two incommensurable sexes. The authors of the following chapters approach gender as an important organizing principle of an entire worldview. As such, it certainly shapes understandings of sex and sexuality, but it also helps structure many other aspects of Chinese life, such as the way political power is exercised and contested and the way that the lines between Han and non-Han ethnic categories are drawn. It is the polymorphous, plural nature of gender constructs—which take on varied contours over time, among different social groups, and when put to divergent purposes—that generates the femininities and masculinities of our title. We have chosen these words for their vagueness. What exactly is femininity or masculinity—what anatomical details, behaviors, discussions, and ideas make a woman into a woman and a man into a man? The answer differs from setting to setting. Thus, we do not seek a universal definition, because we believe that in China, as in all other places, the most interesting and significant thing is the fact that unique judgments about femininity and masculinity are made by specific people in particular contexts.

One goal in producing this book is to help readers frame answers to the questions we have posed above, but we also want to give them skills and information that will aid them as they ponder similar queries of their own making. Our strategy has been to pull together an eclectic mixture of accessible and illuminating studies, most of them specially written for this volume, some reprinted here as a testament to their enduring value. Half of the chapters focus primarily on femininity, while half concentrate on masculinity; but all implicitly, and some of them explicitly, draw attention to the fact that we must view these categories as constructed in relationship to each other. In concert, the chapters of this book not only provide a wealth of interesting detail but also illustrate the plural nature of femininities and masculinities invoked by our title. The book also demonstrates, by alternating between looking at subjects traditionally associated with feminism (such as family life) and topics only rarely viewed through the prism of sexual difference (such as banditry), that gender studies are more than just a supplement to mainstream accounts. A serious appreciation of the forging and contesting of ideas about masculinity and femininity can help us better understand all aspects of the way both public and private lives have been, and continue to be, transformed in China.

We have tried to be as wide-ranging and inclusive as possible in constructing this volume, but we have placed most emphasis on certain periods, themes, and approaches. In terms of chronology, contributors focus primarily on the recent past. Aside from casual references to earlier epochs, our authors concentrate on the era of Qing dynasty rule (1644–1911), the Republican period (1912–1949), and the Communist era (1949–present).[1] In terms of themes, an interest in charting change over time, as well as in drawing attention to patterns of continuity, is central to many chapters. In terms of approach, we have looked mainly to authors whose works evoke a sense of how femininity and masculinity in China are constructed and performed as *lived experience*, as opposed to represented in artistic works or dealt with in formal government policies. In addition, most contributors are either historians (Theiss, Sommer, Mann, Glosser, Hershatter, Ownby, Honig, Furth, Evans, Wasserstrom) or anthropologists (Chen, Jankowiak, Schein, Litzinger, Brownell). The book contains only two chapters by specialists in literature (Liu, Larson) and a single one by a pair of political scientists (Perry and Dillon). Practitioners in other disciplines (such as sociology) have also made important contributions to what is now the flourishing interdisciplinary field of Chinese gender studies, but are not represented in the selections in this book. The breakdown by disciplines is in part a reflection of the backgrounds of the editors. But it is also in part a result of the emphasis, alluded to above, on how femininity and masculinity operate as experiential categories as opposed to objects of representation or factors that contribute to the formation of state policy.

The focus, topical variety, and disciplinary mix of our reader make it different in one or more ways from each of the various noteworthy collections of essays on gender and China that appeared in the 1990s. For example, both *Gender Politics in Modern China: Writing and Feminism* and *Body, Subject, and Power in China*—the first of which was edited by historian Tani Barlow and the second of which was coedited by her and Angela Zito, a specialist in Chinese religion—focus much more than we do here on issues of representation.[2] Meanwhile, what sets our volume apart from another collection— *Marriage and Inequality in China,* coedited by anthropologist Rubie Watson and historian Patricia Ebrey—is our attempt to look at the role of gender in aspects of life unrelated to familial concerns.[3] And our determination to pay equal attention to the experiences of men and women sets our reader apart from edited collections such as *Spaces of Their Own: Women's Public Sphere in Transnational China* and *Women and Chinese Patriarchy: Submission, Servitude, and Escape.*[4] The same thing also distinguishes this volume from what is perhaps the most wide-ranging and ambitiously constructed of recent collections, *Engendering China: Women, Culture, and the State,* the subtitle of which is revealing.[5] Each of the aforementioned books contains individual chapters that are quite similar to ones found in the present volume— indeed, one of our chapters (Hershatter's) first appeared in *Engendering China,* another (Mann's) in *Marriage and Inequality in China*—but when taken as a whole, this volume is quite different.

Moreover, our focus here on the interplay between ideas and practices associated with femininity and masculinity also makes the present reader different from the most important earlier contributions to Chinese gender studies, for those, too, tended to focus almost exclusively on male views toward women, or on the experiences of women only. This was the case with several pathbreaking single-author works and edited volumes published in the 1970s and 1980s. A short list of the most significant of these would have to include *Women in China* and *Women in Chinese Society,* each of which appeared in the mid-1970s and played a crucial role in laying the groundwork for the emergence of Chinese gender studies as an academic field.[6] And the major monographs and surveys on gender, as well as document collections pertaining to gender, that appeared prior to the 1990s tended as well to pay little attention to masculinity. This was true of major overviews such as *Feminism and Socialism in China* by anthropologist Elizabeth Croll and *Chinese Women in a Century of Revolution, 1850–1950,* by historian Ono Kazuko, as well as collections of documents such as Emily Honig and Gail Hershatter's *Personal Voices: Chinese Women in the 1980s.*[7] And even now, though other works have begun to appear that deal more extensively with issues associated with masculinity, still the most impressive individually authored works on gender tend to focus on women. This is true of such sophisticated and important recent additions to the literature as Harriet Evans's *Women and Sexuality in China: Female Sexuality and Gender since 1949* and Wang Zheng's *Women in the Chinese Enlightenment: Oral and Textual Histories.*[8]

The dissimilarities between the works mentioned above are enormous when it comes to issues such as the way sexual difference is approached. For example, in most early works, male and female are treated as unproblematic categories grounded in biology. By contrast, in Evans's and Wang's recent works, which draw upon the insights of deconstructivist feminist theorists such as Judith Butler, the complex links between bodies and ideas about bodies, as well as the defining and contesting of gender categories, comprise central subjects of exploration.[9] Nonetheless, the tendency to carry out old and new sorts of explorations of gender by focusing mostly on women and concepts of femininity has remained a constant in Chinese studies and is one that this volume seeks to reconsider.

Within the parameters we have set for ourselves, which are not unlike those that inform some very useful recent volumes dealing with gender dynamics in other parts of the world, readers will find a diverse array of authors and types of chapters.[10] This is a diversity that attests to the eclectic goal of our enterprise and the healthy state of the field a quarter of a century after its establishment. One sort of variety has to do with theoretical approach, for our contributors stand at different points on the spectrum running from positivist to postmodernist. In addition, they rely on varied kinds of sources—from legal records to informal interviews to popular magazines to medical texts. And although most of the contributors are known already for their scholarship on gender, there are a few whose contributions to this volume have taken them into new territory. In some cases this is because their previous work has not focused on gender (Perry, Ownby), in others because they have not typically written about masculinity (Larson, Chen).

Having provided this general sketch of the book and what differentiates it from many contributions to the field of Chinese gender studies we now turn to the goals of the remaining sections of this introduction. We begin by discussing the broad developments in feminist scholarship that form the background for this book, paying particular attention to the way they have affected historians of China. We then describe how analytical waves in gender studies that transformed the field during the 1970s and 1980s intersected with those that were simultaneously occurring within Chinese studies, focusing in this part on the other discipline we know best, anthropology. The third section positions this book relative to current trends in Chinese gender studies and describes in more detail the structure of the main body of the book. The final section explains our understanding and use of some key terms (such as *sexuality*) and explores some of the problems that arise when applying the language of Anglophone gender studies to China (such as the need to rethink some assumptions about categories). In this final section, we go on to outline the distinctive features in the recent history of Chinese gender, which will be illustrated in later chapters.

## FROM WOMEN'S STUDIES TO GENDER STUDIES

For several decades, there has been an ongoing tension within academic feminism between two basic approaches, which we represent here as over-simplified extremes. One approach begins with the problem of inequality and then proceeds to critique patriarchy. Adherents to this "inequality-patriarchy" approach take for granted the immutable existence of two biologically differentiated sexes and ask how power is divided between those on opposite sides of the divide. The other approach begins with the issue of difference and then proceeds to focus on constructions of gender. Practitioners of this approach do not take for granted an immutable male-female divide but rather see "man" and "woman" as socially and culturally created categories, the borders between which may be contested. They stress the possibility of "third genders," people who are typed as neither male nor female but as something that stands apart from or combines elements of the two. They also insist that gender-bending (or blurring) behaviors and identities of some sort can be found in virtually all cultures, and that these are worthy of scholarly attention.

The contrast between the two approaches can manifest itself in varied ways, leading scholars either to focus on different issues (cross-dressing, for example, is typically of more interest to those in the latter group than to those in the former) or to deal with the same problem in divergent ways.[11] One way to illustrate the kind of divergence that can occur where a common problem is identified is to think about the history and recent reemergence of female infanticide in the Chinese countryside. One obvious starting point for feminist discussions of China has long been the killing of daughters and the general preference in many villages for male as opposed to female children, which is rooted in patrilineal residence traditions and the endurance of lineage structures organized around fathers and sons. For those who take what we have called the inequality-patriarchy approach, the favoring of male offspring is a clear example of a case in which subtleties of gender categorization are irrelevant. This is a situation in which a biological criterion is being used to determine whether or not a person's life is valued, and in the process women are oppressed. Case closed.

However, those who begin with a concern for difference—while by no means excusing the practice of female infanticide—might not frame the issue quite the same way. They might call attention to comments in some of the literature that describe women within certain villages as being treated as less than "whole people" *(quanren)* until they bear sons. The scholars might then explore what we can learn about the politics of difference from this division of women into two different categories—those who have and have not produced sons—where a woman who has not produced a son is somehow denied the full status of her gender.[12]

In a nutshell, the inequality-patriarchy approach begins with four main points: (1) the fact that, throughout recorded history and across cultures, we find many cases in which men have monopolized positions of power or in other ways exercised domination over women; (2) the claim that systematic domination of females by males justifies the creation of a field, women's studies, devoted to examining critically this process of domination while honoring or simply bringing into the open the experiences of formerly or still voiceless members of the oppressed group; (3) the ethical claim that imbalances of power between the sexes are immoral; and (4) the assumption that scholars should try to elucidate the workings of, celebrate resistance to, and contribute to the destruction of patriarchal systems. *Patriarchy* originally referred to a system in which older men, as heads of households, possessed the ultimate authority over all members of their households. Often, though, it is invoked as a catchall word for all systems based on widespread inequalities between the sexes. This approach, if taken to the extreme, can be unsatisfying for several reasons. Adherents to it can fail to take into account cultural and historical differences in relationships between the sexes. They can fail to question the experiences of males, leaving men as universal subjects even as they try to question the negative stereotypes attached to women as the polar opposite of men. They can make it too easy for feminist positions to be marginalized by nonfeminists as works that need be taken seriously only by scholars working on women's roles. And they can make patriarchy seem static, as opposed to something continually undergoing change and being re-created in new ways.

Although it avoids most of these problems, the "gender studies" or "difference" approach also has its pitfalls if applied too simplistically. An interest in difference and gender systems can pull us away from focusing on the political dimensions of relations between the sexes, the unequal power relations that lead to the domination of women by men in so many cases. It can lead as well to just the sort of marginalization of feminist scholarship that it claims to be avoiding. Some critics also complain that, in the end, one can simply end up talking mostly about the experiences of men, and this is what is already done often enough by academics unaffected by or resistant to feminism. Various trends within gender studies are also seen as troubling. One is the tendency of practitioners to devote attention to subjects far removed from the experiences of ordinary women (such as the gendered dimensions of elegant poems written by male authors for male audiences).

Another is a tendency to focus on issues that have little to do with the political struggles that could bring about change (such as representations of sexual behavior in elite medical texts).

There are, it should be stressed, some very basic institutional, procedural, and conceptual implications attached to these two different starting points. For example, the two approaches can lead students of recent Chinese history in very different directions, and not just where the preference for sons in villages is concerned. The inequality-patriarchy approach can lead to focusing most of our attention on understanding why inequalities between men and women have seemed so stubbornly resistant to regime change, or to looking primarily at failed efforts to oppose the imposition of patriarchy by new ruling groups. It can also inspire work that is concerned above all simply with bringing into the historical record the experiences of powerless women. The gender studies approach, by contrast, can lead to asking whether, despite the appearance of continuity given by epoch upon epoch of male domination of women, visions of sexual difference have in fact changed more dramatically over time than was previously supposed. It can also lead to work that emphasizes the varied ways that women and men occupying different places in social hierarchies benefit from, resist, or otherwise experience various types of patriarchy. A brief survey of the ways that feminist historians approached the Communist Revolution from the early 1970s to the early 1980s, on the one hand, and from the mid-1980s through the 1990s, on the other, illustrates this point. We see here, in very general terms, a shift from a period when a fairly straightforward inequality-patriarchy approach held sway to one in which a concern with issues of difference became much more pronounced.

## WOMEN'S STUDIES AND GENDER STUDIES IN HISTORIES OF CHINESE WOMEN

Between the early 1970s and early 1980s, feminist social historians and historically minded social scientists in closely related fields produced a number of important books and articles that focused on the question of why, after taking power in 1949, the Communists failed to liberate women. This needed explanation, these scholars stressed, not just because it was something that the Chinese Communist Party (CCP) had promised to do but also because many of the men involved, including Mao Zedong, had written passionately in their youth about the injustices of patriarchy, as had radical young women of the day. How had young male participants in the New Culture Movement of the second and third decades of the twentieth century, for whom the subordination of women within "Confucian" family structures had seemed symptomatic of all that was wrong with the old order, ended up governing a patriarchal state? This was the kind of question asked by many talented and resourceful feminist scholars, including contributors to the major edited volumes of the time. Both *Women in China* and *Women in Chinese Society,* but especially the former—perhaps in part the result of the fact that so many of its chapters were by historians or historically minded sociologists—devoted chapters to the "woman question" and Communist attempts to solve or avoid solving it.[13]

The explanations for the CCP's failure to liberate women (or at least liberate them completely) offered by historians such as Delia Davin and Patricia Stranahan varied considerably.[14] And so did those of scholars in related disciplines who asked similar questions—such as sociologist Judith Stacey.[15] When trying to account for the continuing subordination of women under Communism, some authors favored social or cultural and others economic or strategic explanations. Some found the key turning point in a pre-1949 stage of the Communist movement, others in the era after the establishment of the People's Republic of China (PRC). Some were much more, others much less forgiving of the CCP for its failure. What bound all of these early works together was a tendency to treat "Chinese women" as belonging to a single basic category and to see continuities relating to the unequal distribution of power between men and women as the main thing to be analyzed.[16]

More recently, the situation has changed quite dramatically. Some of the same scholars mentioned above have been affected by novel trends and have published works that diverge from their earlier ones, and new generations of feminist historians have begun to make their mark by placing the Communist Revolution in different sorts of frameworks linked to gender. It is not just that interpretations of the CCP's approach to the "woman question" have changed, though some have, but also that varied ideas have been put forth concerning the kinds of issues that must be addressed. Wang Zheng, Christina Gilmartin, and some of the contributors to this volume (Glosser, Hershatter, Honig) have been among those who have reshaped the literature on this topic. They have done so in some cases by devoting more attention to describing the complex elements that constituted the patriarchal gender system that existed before the Revolution—the system against which New Culture Movement activists railed but which also shaped the outlooks of these young men and women. They have also explored the affiliations, such as class and regional ties and voluntary bonds created through sworn sisterhoods, that linked or divided particular groups of women. And some have looked as well at the issues that are the focus of this book: namely, the ways that ideas about femininity and masculinity were reconfigured as well as re-created in different phases of the Revolution.[17]

Some scholars, such as Tani Barlow and, again, contributors to this volume (especially Evans), have introduced a new element into the study of the "woman question" by tracking the linguistic dimensions of the moves between various types of patriarchal systems. They have argued that an important story to be told lies in the refashioning of terminologies and categories associated with gender, including that of "woman" itself.[18] This kind of scholarship fits in well with the direction taken by some historians of Chinese nationalism, such as Prasenjit Duara, who have expanded on ideas about the gendering of China (as a country) put forth by literary critics and anthropologists.[19] These historians have noted that, if we are to take gender categories as seriously as we should, we must ask how not only individuals but also larger communities are typed as feminine or masculine or seen as incorporating elements of both. Their work, like that of the historians referred to in the preceding paragraph, complements and builds on pioneering and justly influential studies of gender and history that focus on other parts of the world. The most notable of these, in many ways, remains Joan Scott's classic 1984 essay, "Gender: A Useful Category for Historical Analysis."[20]

Happily, what we have seen in historical works on Chinese women has not been a shift from one pole to another, a complete rejection of old approaches in favor of new ones. Instead, what has reshaped the field has been a series of moves toward giving increasing numbers of factors their proper due. There has not been a swing from focusing only on inequality to focusing only on difference, but rather, creative efforts have been made to incorporate a concern with both into our understanding of China's revolutions. At the same time (though moves here have been slower), scholars have begun to pay more attention to categories (such as that of the biological or sworn brother) and experiences (such as how it feels to be a father) associated with men and masculinity.[21] We have reached a point where most feminist historians have been sensitized to issues of both power and meaning and do not feel a need to choose between viewing a problem through the lens of inequality-patriarchy and that of difference-gender—and the same is true of feminist scholars in other disciplines. Most of them, including nearly all of those cited in the previous several paragraphs, would claim to fall between the poles. Certainly, many see themselves as using interpretive strategies associated with both camps.

This is definitely how the editors of this book see ourselves, and the structure of this volume is meant in part to reflect this. The contributors, almost without exception, see themselves, and would be seen by many, as occupying some sort of middle ground between the inequality-patriarchy and difference-gender approaches. For example, Hershatter's chapter on prostitution in early-twentieth-century Shanghai and Janet Theiss's on widow chastity in the Qing period present arguments that, although sensitive to difference, fit in well with some discussions that focus on patriarchy. This is in part simply because they deal with practices that could clearly be exploitative of women. Other chapters, such as Matthew Sommer's on male homosexuality and David Ownby's on Chinese bandits, complicate this picture and raise doubts about the "women's studies" paradigm in its extreme form. This is because they show how *men* can also be marginalized, victimized, and oppressed by hierarchical gender systems that legitimate power only in certain categories of men, excluding other men in a process that is both similar to and different from the ways in which women are excluded. Indeed, one of the significant themes that recurs in several chapters in this book is the pitiful plight of the marginal male. Unmarried, homosexual, or otherwise socially marginal men were in many cases dealt with more harshly by the law and regarded as more of a threat to legitimate, heterosexual male power than were any categories of women. An analysis that concentrated only on the power differences between men and women would gloss over or indeed completely miss this point.[22]

Having described some broad scholarly developments within feminism, as well as the way they have affected the study of one major topic linked to China, we turn to a more focused discussion of the discipline of anthropology. The purpose of including this discussion is to provide users of this book with a sense of the particular disciplinary histories that inform the work of the majority of contributors. Shifting from a focus on historical studies to a concentration on anthropological ones will also allow us to restate in a more nuanced way some of the points made above about changing scholarly fashions and the ebb and flow of interpretive tides.

## WOMEN'S STUDIES, GENDER STUDIES, CHINESE STUDIES, AND ANTHROPOLOGY

In the past several decades, there have been two main movements, relating to gender studies, in the discipline of anthropology: the first involved simply paying more attention to women's experiences; the second involved problematizing gender. These, we should stress, overlapped as well as followed one another. And, curiously, China specialists have sometimes been ahead of and sometimes behind the disciplinary tide.

In this volume, when discussing anthropological developments we look mostly, in the interests of convenience, at those that took place within, or that directly affected, the Anglo-American academic world in which the contributors were trained. Within the discipline as a whole, gender studies got their start in the early 1970s, when the women's movement began to make its presence felt within the academy. The first important text, *Woman, Culture, and Society,* arose out of an undergraduate lecture course organized by a collective of female graduate students at Stanford in 1971. Challenged by the lack of materials and theories for the course, Michelle Rosaldo and Louise Lamphere brought together a collection of chapters that explicitly focused on women; it was published in 1974. One year later, the second foundational text was published, *Toward an Anthropology of Women,* edited by Rayna Reiter. This first phase has been labeled the "anthropology of women" phase because its main accomplishment was to write women into the ethnographic record.[23]

The anthropology of China has always existed somewhat separately from the discipline as a whole because of its close links with the interdisciplinary mongrel of sinology. Until (perhaps) recently, sinologists have shared an interest in concrete information about Chinese history, language, culture, and society but not necessarily an interest in the latest theories or developmental trends emerging out of the separate disciplines. The effect on the anthropology of China has been that developments in sinology, more than developments in anthropology as a whole, have shaped it. With some exceptions, anthropological theory has contributed little to China studies, and China anthropologists have contributed even less to general anthropological theory.

Consistent with this trend, the anthropology of Chinese gender has followed a trajectory somewhat different from that of the anthropology of gender as a whole. Surprisingly enough, however, it might be argued that an interest in the lives of women was established in the anthropology of China (with the 1968 publication of Margery Wolf's *The House of Lim*) around six years before women got full-fledged attention in the discipline as a whole (with the 1974 publication of *Woman, Culture, and Society*). Since it is unusual for China anthropologists to *lead* a trend in the field as a whole, rather than lagging behind it, we might wonder what caused this anomaly. One of the more important factors, interestingly, is best described as a fluke of sorts, in the sense that it resulted largely from the interests, career path, and talents of a particular gifted individual, Margery Wolf.

The significance of her publications in the development of Chinese anthropological writings on gender is difficult to overstate: they began appearing at a time when very little was being done on the subject and, through their combination of skillful analysis and accessible style, proved enormously influential. Wolf's first book, *The House of Lim: A Study of a Chinese Farm Family,* was a novelistic account of the dramas of everyday life in the Lim family, a fairly well-off Taiwanese farm family on the verge of household division when Margery and her then-husband, Arthur, lived with them, from 1959 to 1961. Still popular today, it is often assigned in courses on China and on the anthropology of gender because of the evocative way in which it illustrates the joys, disappointments, and complexities of women's lives. Four years after that volume appeared, Wolf published *Women and the Family in Rural Taiwan,* which was written in a style halfway between the novelistic style of *The House of Lim* and the academic style common in the discipline at the time (for example, the entire book cites only ten references).[24]

Wolf thus disregarded two academic paradigms at the same time—the first being the focus on the lives of men, the second being the natural-scientific writing style. She was able to do this because she was not herself pursuing an academic career. She had no advanced degree, and she had lived in the field as the wife of an anthropologist engaged in more "scholarly" labor. Unlike career-oriented scholars, she was able to write about the things that moved her without worrying about convincing her dissertation committee and her colleagues that it was a worthy topic. Still, she began *The House of Lim* by almost apologetically stating, "I am not an anthropologist."[25] Her modesty seems to have turned into defiance by the time of *Woman, Culture, and Society,* a work to which she contributed a chapter.[26] In the notes on contributors, we read, "Margery Wolf has no academic degree and is a candidate for none."

We find a curious parallel between this development in anthropology and another in history. Here, too, an early work by an idiosyncratic and thoughtful scholar who happened to be an exceptional prose stylist played an important role in drawing attention to issues of gender. The significance and popularity of Jonathan Spence's *The Death of Woman Wang* (1978) is similar in some ways to that of Margery Wolf's *The House of Lim.*[27] In both cases the books in question were presented as works of nonfiction even though they contained very speculative sections (the novelistic aspects of his re-creation of the worldview of an obscure Chinese woman would earn Spence both devoted fans and some harsh detractors), and in both cases the works quickly found their way onto many a course syllabus. In contrast to Wolf, however, Spence did not follow up this study with a series of increasingly sophisticated analyses of gender. Instead, he simply moved on in other directions. Moreover, Spence's work did not become a takeoff point for further work on gender by historians. Although many scholars working on gender (including Theiss in this volume) have followed Spence's lead in using legal cases, folktales, and accounts of exemplary lives in gazetteers as windows through which to look at male-female power relations, the book is more often used as a tool for *teaching* about Chinese gender (or perhaps really just about the plight of Chinese women) than as a building block for scholarly analyses. A final point worth making about Spence's book is that although it appeared early enough that it had little competition as a work a teacher could assign students to give them a feel for ordinary female life experiences in imperial China, it did come out a full decade after Wolf's first book. One reason this matters is that, between the late 1960s and the late 1970s, several important collections of essays devoted to the subject of Chinese women were published.

One of the most influential of these, called simply *Women in China,* was described by its editor, historian Marilyn Young, as having a very basic aim. The volume's goal, she wrote, was to "draw together some recent essays on women so that students may have, in a convenient form, a sense of the range of problems, answers, and questions" being asked by scholars, influenced by feminism, who "share neither a common ideology nor methodology, but only the central query: what *about* women?"[28] Several of the contributors to this collection employed ethnographic interpretive approaches, but only one contributor, Norma Diamond, was actually based in an anthropology department at the time. Most of the authors, as already noted above, came from fields such as history and sociology.

A second ground-breaking and oft-cited collection to appear at almost the same time, *Women in Chinese Society,* was decidedly more anthropological in focus, though historians and literary specialists contributed to it. Co-edited by Margery Wolf and Roxane Witke (a historian who wrote two chapters for the Young collection), it contained chapters by four other anthropologists besides the author of *The House of Lim.*[29] The interdisciplinary format of these two early volumes has, as we have stressed, characterized all subsequent edited collections on Chinese women.[30]

The strength of the personalities of several individual North American scholars (including Wolf, Young, and Witke), as well as of their counterparts in other parts of the world (such as Delia Davin in Britain)—along with the growth of the women's movement at that time in countries such as the United States and the United Kingdom—was undoubtedly key to the early emergence of Chinese gender studies.[31] There were, however, other contributing causes as well. One, which was flagged early on by some contributors to the volumes just cited, was the considerable attention that many Chinese revolutionaries (male and female alike) had at some point in their careers paid to the "woman question" in their writings.[32] Another factor worth noting, one that has special relevance for anthropology, is the long-standing tendency of scholars in China itself as well as the West to assume that family and marriage served as central mechanisms of Chinese society. Decades before gender studies or women's studies had made places for themselves within the academy, social scientists had taken it for granted that it was impossible to understand China without understanding lineage structures. They had logically assumed that it was impossible to understand these structures if the sharp contrast between male and female roles was not analyzed carefully.

The impact of this orientation within anthropology was considerable, and acknowledging it helps us place Margery Wolf's work in a more comprehensive framework. For example, it is worth noting that, comparatively early on, male anthropologists who were themselves Chinese had begun writing about the lives of women with more sensitivity and detail than was common to either male Euro-American anthropologists writing about China or to anthropologists in general writing about other societies. Fei Xiaotong, for example, was trained by one of the early key figures in British anthropology, Bronislaw Malinowski, whose extensive publications on the Trobriand Islanders are today noteworthy in part for their almost total inattention to the lives of women. Yet Fei's *Peasant Life in China* (1939) contained insights into the lives of women, which, although brief, evoked a powerful sense of female subjective experiences, particularly surrounding marriage. Another example is Martin C. Yang's ethnographic and semiautobiographical account, *A Chinese Village* (1945), which provided a great deal of detail about women's lives and their relationships with other members of the extended family, both male and female.[33]

Of course, if Fei and Yang paid more attention to women's affairs than did contemporary Euro-American male scholars, it may have been simply because growing up in the societies that they wrote about allowed them more access to women's lives. They could not help but realize that women played active and important roles in at least some aspects of village life. It is perhaps not unimportant that Fei located his dissertation research in the village to which his sister had been sent to help run a silk cooperative. And it is worth noting that his first stay there was during a period of recuperation after a serious accident in which he was injured and his new wife killed.[34] These connections might have heightened his awareness of women's lives, particularly the lives of young wives.

What exactly did Wolf and these early anthropologists of China contribute to our understanding of women's lives and the social structures that shaped these lives? One thing that Fei, Yang, and Wolf all emphasized was the way that patrilineal exogamy served to isolate women once they moved into their husbands' families as virtual outsiders. Their new position was not secure until they had given birth to a son—an act whose symbolic importance has already been noted above. Afterward, their dependence on their sons was great, something that was reflected in the attempts women often made to secure the affections of male offspring in order to have some kind of power base within the family. Wolf coined a term useful for appreciating the competing systems of affection within which women made sense of and tried to gain control over their lives. A woman and her children formed an informal "uterine family," which was separate from, and at times competed with, the formal patrilineal extended family and lineage. Wolf also discussed the importance of the informal gossip networks that women formed with other women—the "women's community," which functioned, as it still does today, as a control on men's behavior.

As important as these analytical contributions were, they fell short of illuminating the meanings of manhood or womanhood; hence, they are better thought of as belonging to the "anthropology of women" than to the "anthropology of gender" phase of the discipline. The next step was to understand the symbols, ideologies, metaphors, and so on that not only make a man into a man and a woman into a woman but also construct these categories in opposition to each other. In the discipline of anthropology as a whole, the germinal text of this "anthropology of gender" approach was arguably Sherry Ortner's "Is Female to Male as Nature Is to Culture?" This piece appeared, in some senses well before its time, in *Woman, Culture, and Society*. In it, Ortner utilized, "with all due respect to Lévi-Strauss," a structuralist approach to "try to expose the underlying logic of cultural thinking that assumes the inferiority of women."[35]

More specifically, she proposed that women's universal second-class status was due to their association with nature; men, on the other hand, gained power from being associated with culture.[36] Over the years, this article provoked much discussion and response. In particular, it was argued that not all belief systems oppose nature to culture, and so the relation of women to this dualism cannot be taken for granted. Nevertheless, the strengths of Ortner's approach—her emphasis on "cultural logic" as a way of moving beyond naturalistic assumptions about biological sex, on female and male as categories culturally constructed in opposition to each other, and on detailed analysis of the local symbols and meanings attached to these categories—are evident in the fact that it remains vital today, albeit with some modifications.[37]

A further fruitful development of Ortner's theorizing emerged with the publication of *Sexual Meanings: The Cultural Construction of Gender and Sexuality* (1981), which she coedited with Harriet Whitehead. Several of the chapters in this book examined gendered roles that complicated the simple female/male binary by introducing a third category. In particular, Whitehead's chapter on "institutionalized homosexuality" among Native Americans was influential in proposing the *berdache* (typically, a man who dressed as a woman and performed women's tasks) as a third gender.[38] This brought to the attention of anthropologists the importance of considering all categories of gender and sexuality, rather than assuming that a simple heterosexual female/male division dominates all cultural constructions of gender. This shift from an anthropology of women to an anthropology of gender was mirrored, to a certain extent, within history since—as noted above— works by scholars such as Joan Scott also argued that the discussion should pay greater attention to how notions of difference are defined and contested. And, as also noted above, the impact of such works on studies of the gendered dimensions of the Communist Revolution was significant.[39] Initially, however, the shift in anthropology from women to gender, and from structure to meaning, was not echoed in the anthropology of China. Throughout most of the 1980s, then, work by anthropologists concerned with gender that focused on China tended to be behind rather than ahead of disciplinary curves.

Two early articles on China by anthropologists that were notable because they *did* focus on the symbolic meanings of gender are Emily Martin Ahern's "The Power and Pollution of Chinese Women" in *Women in Chinese Society* and Gary Seaman's response to it, "Blood Bowls and Black Dogs: The Sexual Politics of Karmic Retribution in a Chinese Hell" (1981).[40] Ahern's article looked at ideas, held by members of a Taiwanese village, about the polluting powers of menstrual blood and postpartum discharge. Linking these potent symbols to Wolf's work, she suggested that they might be perceived as dangerous because they are associated with childbirth, an event that threatens the boundaries of the (patriarchal) family. She suggested that women do not consciously use their power of pollution against men, and asked whether men might use it against women, concluding that they do not. Seaman disagreed, arguing that men encourage negative beliefs about women's sexuality in order to rationalize women's lower social status and control the threat that women pose to male-centered groups. Interestingly, Ahern's article was reprinted in Arthur Wolf's *Studies in Chinese Society* (1978) and is more widely read and cited than Seaman's. And so, even when a pair of corresponding articles existed, the article that focused on women received greater attention.[41]

Emily Martin Ahern (now Emily Martin) went on to do other work that took a symbolic approach, but in general the anthropological studies of Chinese gender tended to concentrate on social structural issues rather than on symbolic meanings. Also, within China studies generally, there has been no systematic interest in gender-crossing until recently. From the symbolic perspective, eunuchs should have been an obvious category that contributed to an understanding of sexual meanings by complicating the female/male distinction. However, eunuchs have not been studied as much as one might expect. The published works have almost all been politically oriented: their central problem has been to outline the role of eunuchs in imperial court politics.

Charlotte Furth's research on accounts of sexual anomalies in the late Ming also dealt with these questions—and her attempts to wrestle with the third-gender possibility remain the most important produced within Chinese studies to date.[42] Accounts of men who changed sex and turned into women were regarded as suspect, she claimed, but those of women who changed into men were not. She noted that once a person was socially defined as male, he had a good deal of latitude in the sexual roles he might play. He could not, however, be taken as a concubine, whereas a eunuch could. This would seem to be evidence that a eunuch was not regarded as a true male in every sense. Furth argued that social gender overshadows sexuality in the definition of male and female but not completely. Further, she felt that there was no room for an intermediate sex or gender in the late Ming gender system.

In the late 1980s, an interest in the ethnographic representation of emotions emerged in anthropology.[43] As William Jankowiak noted in a recent review essay, however, representations of emotions are rare in writings about Chinese gender, which tend to strip such accounts of a feeling for subjective experience.[44] Ironically, Margery Wolf's early work contained evocative descriptions of emotion: she portrayed outbursts of domestic rage in *The House of Lim;* and her article "Women and Suicide in China," although documented with graphs and statistics, still managed to convey the sources of despair that at different stages lead Taiwanese men and women to take their own lives.[45] In this as in other ways, she pursued an individual path that presaged later developments in anthropology. The kind of descriptions of gendered emotions in the discussions of romance, love, and parental affection that Jankowiak included in his first book and a later essay are also comparatively rare in the anthropological literature.[46] His chapter in the present volume as well is characterized by his interest in the dilemmas surrounding the emotions of romantic and parental love in changing times.

We have gone from the late 1960s to the late 1980s and have also come full circle in terms of China anthropologists and disciplinary curves. Whereas Wolf was in many ways precocious in relation to anthropology as a whole in the questions she asked about women in early works such as *The House of Lim,* two decades later China anthropologists were playing catch-up to trends in ethnographic treatments of gender that had passed them by. Whereas discussions of the possibilities of third genders had become commonplace in the anthropological literature in some other settings, it was not an anthropologist but a historian, Furth, who was doing the most interesting work on the subject in Chinese studies. Moreover, Furth was by no means an anomaly, as by the late 1980s many of the scholars doing work on gender in line with anthropological trends were in disciplines such as history and literature. One thing this indicates is that one can go only so far in structuring the story of Chinese gender studies—as we have done thus far— around a tale of two disciplines. To make sense of the 1990s and prepare readers for trends that are shaping the field as the twenty-first century proceeds, it seems best to abandon this framework and step back to assess what the field as a whole looks like at present.

## GENDER STUDIES AND CHINESE STUDIES: INTERDISCIPLINARITY IN THE 1990S AND BEYOND

It has never been easy to cleanly separate trends within disciplines where Chinese gender studies are concerned, in part because interdisciplinary collections of essays have always played such an important role in shaping the debates. In fact, if anything, it is even harder to do so today than it was in the early 1970s and the decades that immediately followed. One reason for this is the recent influence of cultural studies in general, and feminist theories in particular, within a host of social scientific and humanistic disciplines—a phenomenon that has led to a virtual explosion of studies of Chinese gender. Not only have the edited collections continued to be interdisciplinary, but also the theoretical and conceptual frameworks used by scholars from different disciplines have begun to merge. It is increasingly hard to tell whether a contributor to such a volume *is* an anthropologist, a historian, a literary theorist, and so on.

This cross-fertilization has led to an unprecedented multiplicity of voices among China scholars. And this multiplicity of theoretical perspectives has brought increased attention to the ways that understandings of gender can change according to a person's life stage, ethnicity, social class, or sexual orientation. We are also paying more attention now than in the past to the ways in which the meanings attached to maleness and femaleness help to structure other identities, such as nationality, ethnicity, social class, and so forth. And finally, mindful of Edward Said's critique of "orientalist" distortions of the "East," we are paying more attention to the ways in which our own subject-positions—for example, the nations where we were born and educated, our own sex and sexual orientation—shape the ways in which we write. A number of important developments in China gender studies have emerged out of these new sensitivities. Here, we want to flag just a couple of significant recent developments.

### Gender and Nationalism

One recent development has been the appearance of works that place at the center the links between gendered symbols and visions of the nation. In this regard, texts by literary critics such as Rey Chow, Lydia Liu, and Chen Xiaomei stand out—texts that, as noted above, have in turn influenced historians of nationalism such as Duara. In her study *Woman and Chinese Modernity: The Politics of Reading between East and West,* for example, Chow explores among other things the extent to which "China" has been feminized in the Western imagination.[47] An oft-cited essay by Liu, meanwhile, to which Duara pays a good deal of attention in his influential *Rescuing History from the Nation: Questioning Narratives of Modern China,* looks at similar issues while focusing on the gendering of China as a country within literature produced in that land.[48] Chen's *Occidentalism* similarly engages with issues of gender via discourses of national pride that play upon distinctions between East and West.[49]

### Gender and Ethnicity Studies

Another of the new developments in gender studies has been the work on gender and ethnicity by Dru Gladney, Esther Yau, and others—including two contributors to this volume, Schein and Litzinger. It has been only since the early 1980s that a critical mass of research on China's ethnic minorities, which focuses on ethnicity as a problem, has developed. Before this period, ethnographies of village life often presented the villagers as "Chinese," glossing over the fact that they were also members of a minority. Francis Hsu's 1948 classic, *Under the Ancestors' Shadow,* for example, had the subtitle *Chinese Culture and Personality* and presented life in "West Town" as representatively "Chinese," even though the West Towners were ethnic Bai, not Han.[50] In the 1980s, as the winds of change swept over academia as a whole, a greater consciousness of diversity appeared in sinology as well. *Diversity* has referred primarily to ethnic and gender diversity (and, to a lesser extent, sexuality). Surprisingly enough, however, many of the recent ethnicity studies do not devote a great deal of attention to gender, although a few argue that gender is absolutely central to ethnic identity.

An important addition to Qing history is Pamela Crossley's *Orphan Warriors,* which is the first book to treat the ruling Qing dynasty as the Manchu ethnic minority that they were, rather than taking the "Sinicization" of the Manchu over time as an unquestioned fact. Observations on women are found throughout the book, but it does not place gender in the foreground as if it were central in conceptions of Manchu-Han difference. Angela Zito's more recent book, *Of Body and Brush,* argues that the imperial ritual of the mid- to late-Qing presented the emperor as the perfect embodiment of yang masculinity according to the Han Confucian ideals of filiality and literacy. Read as a pair, the two books provide interesting insight into the intersection of masculinity and ethnicity in the mid-to-late Qing; read separately, each gives short shrift to one half of this equation.[51] Robert Van Gulik, for example, suggests that in the process of distinguishing between Manchu and Han, the Han rejected the Manchu martial masculinity as vulgar and suited only to the "Qing barbarians," stressing instead the frail, scholarly type by contrast.[52] And of course the natural-footed Manchu women were considered less than ideally feminine as well. A closer examination of notions of femininity and masculinity in Manchu-Han relations might shed further light on the sources of the late Qing literatus ideal, which later became the quintessential image of the feminized Chinese man, impotent against foreign imperialist penetration.

The anthropology department at the University of Washington in Seattle has been one of the influential sites for the emergence of minority scholarship in that discipline. Two edited volumes have crystallized around research by graduate students under Steve Harrell's guidance there: Stevan Harrell's edited volume *Cultural Encounters on China's Ethnic Frontiers* and Melissa Brown's edited collection *Negotiating Ethnicities in China and Taiwan.*[53] Neither book makes a central problem out of gender, although in *Cultural Encounters* Harrell's introduction contains an excellent but brief section titled "The Sexual Metaphor: Peripheral Peoples as Women," Charles McKhann's chapter contains a brief discussion of the eroticization of minority women, and Norma Diamond's chapter describes the gendered images in "Miao albums." In Brown's edited volume, Emily Chao discusses gender in Naxi religious practices, and Almaz Khan discusses the Han attraction to the masculine image of the horseback-riding Mongol.

Dru Gladney and Ralph Litzinger also received their Ph.D.'s in the program at the University of Washington. Gladney carried out ethnographic fieldwork among China's Muslim, or Hui, people. His book *Muslim Chinese: Ethnic Nationalism in the People's Republic,* too, does not make gender its central problem, though several discussions of Hui nationalism turn on Hui anger at Han depictions of their women, and one section discusses endogamous marriage practices in a Hui village on the outskirts of Beijing.[54]

Gladney and Louisa Schein (a chapter by the latter appears in the present volume) were the first to discuss the intersection of ethnicity and gender in China. They both utilize Edward Said's notion of "orientalism."[55] For Said, orientalism was the West's way of coming to terms with the East (his primary interest was the Middle East) by defining the West as masculine, rational, and active, in contrast to the feminine, mystical, passive East. Gladney and Schein both observe that the Han-dominated Chinese state tended to portray its ethnic minorities as feminine, backward, superstitious, and in need of masculine Han guidance. Gladney labels this "oriental orientalism" and Schein calls it "internal orientalism." In an influential article that combines some of Said's insights with an analysis reminiscent of Ortner's structuralism, Gladney suggests that "minority is to the majority as female is to male, as 'Third' World is to 'First,' and as subjectivized is to objectivized identity."[56] In other words, the majority Han and the ethnic minorities in China are categorized and opposed to each other in a hierarchical manner that parallels gender and political hierarchies. This can be seen in the fact that Chinese popular media tend to use eroticized female images to convey images of minorities. Further, minorities are often depicted as backward in contrast to the modernized Han. Gladney's work tends to concentrate on the unilateral use of minority images by the Han-dominated state and Han producers of popular culture, while Schein points out that minorities themselves actively participate in performing the popular representations of themselves. Her ethnographic fieldwork was conducted among the Miao (also known outside China as the Hmong) in Guizhou province. Schein tends to concentrate on popular culture (popular media, staged performances, public exhibitions). The chapters in this volume by Schein and Litzinger take issue with Gladney's static structuralist analysis, describing how minorities like the Miao and Yao actively engage in producing images of themselves in popular culture, and demonstrating the fact that they are not simply passively used by Han producers of culture.

Litzinger's chapter in this volume focuses less on state policy and popular culture and more on village life among the Yao in Hunan and Guangxi provinces, where he carried out his fieldwork. He pays particular attention to the influence of native Yao intellectuals who are interested in documenting and recuperating their own traditions. He shows that they do this selectively according to which "traditions" seem authentic and appropriate. Through such practices, Yao intellectuals also contribute to the gendered nature of state and popular representations of the Yao. He is interested in how, in the reform era, minority intellectuals came to be privileged by the state to speak for their respective ethnic groups. Schein's and Litzinger's chapters are good examples of the ways in which current studies of Chinese gender are utilizing feminist and postcolonial perspectives but going beyond them in their attention to the complexity of gender as it is experienced and lived by real people.

### The History of Homosexuality

A third important development in China gender studies is the work inspired by Michel Foucault's influential *The History of Sexuality*. Taking a cue from his work but also questioning some of its claims, specialists in Chinese studies have begun to examine how the Western discourse of "sexuality" insinuated itself into China in the early twentieth century. One avenue for inquiry that has opened up is the examination of homosexuality, which in the case of China (as in Foucault's work) has tended to focus on men rather than women.[57] In Foucault's history of Western "sexuality," a clear marker of an "epistemic break" was the increasing stigmatization of homosexuality as perverse and deviant from the eighteenth century onward. Bret Hinsch argues that, in China, hostility toward homosexuality was learned from Christian missionaries and other Western moralists in the twentieth century.[58]

Frank Dikötter disagrees, however, arguing that homosexuality was never singled out as a particular category of deviant behavior, not even in the twentieth century. Rather, he claims, it was thrown together with all kinds of extramarital sex (prostitution, sodomy, rape, adultery), which were undesirable because they did not lead to legitimate procreation within marriage. This attitude was evident in the late-Qing legal code from the mid–eighteenth century on, hence was not a Western import.[59]

Matthew Sommer has added considerable detail to this picture, showing that, although male homosexuality might not have been marked as "perverse," it was clearly regarded, along with the other forms of extramarital sex, as a threat to patriarchal authority—while female homosexuality was not.[60] Sommer's meticulous research, which is apparent in his chapter in this book, is an important contribution to understanding how the history of Chinese sexuality is different from the history of western European sexuality.

The developments discussed above certainly do not exhaust the list of new ideas that have emerged from interdisciplinary approaches to gender in China. We highlight them here because they resonate with some of the particular concerns of this book and are represented in many of our chapters. Having done this, we turn our attention back to the structure of the volume and the questions that inform it.

## CHINESE FEMININITIES/CHINESE MASCULINITIES: A READER'S GUIDE

How do you problematize masculinity without minimizing the oppression of women, past and present? How do you put into scholarly practice the ideal of treating masculinity and femininity as mutually constructed phenomena that should not be treated in isolation from one another? How do you move from an emphasis on patriarchy to an appreciation of various types of patriarchies that are continually being challenged and reconfigured, especially, perhaps, in times of revolutionary change? How do you draw upon models and theories developed by scholars of particular Western settings without ending up forcing Chinese experiences into inappropriate preset molds?

When we set about organizing this book, we had in mind the tensions associated with these kinds of question. Its structure takes the form of a series of two-chapter parts, each of which begins with an essay that focuses on women and ends with one that focuses on men. These pairings are shaped by the knowledge that, whenever a shift occurs in understandings of femininity, understandings of masculinity are likely to be changed to some degree as well, albeit sometimes indirectly—that is, the two concepts are always constructed in relation to one another. An effective way to get at a sense of how either masculinity or femininity is understood in a particular time and place is to look at the same topic from a pair of perspectives, one of which focuses on maleness and one on femaleness.[61] Although we have organized this book in binary chapters, we have also encouraged the authors to illustrate the fact that the male-female binary is not, in reality, a fixed, unchanging opposition. We can draw upon the classical philosophy of yin and yang to make our point here: as the proverb goes, there is femaleness in maleness, there is maleness in femaleness, and the two are in constant motion relative to each other. Where representations, expectations, and experiences associated with manliness and womanliness are concerned, members of social groups are always making choices, forming and contesting conventions, and, through speech and action, first codifying and then later destabilizing visions of what it means to be a woman or a man.

Our part introductions to each set of paired chapters are oriented toward teachers and students who might use this book as a classroom textbook. There, we briefly summarize the main historical trends in gender in the periods under consideration and discuss the main points raised by the chapter authors. We also mention a few complementary books and videos that we have found effective in the classroom. Quite a few of these are by writers and filmmakers who were originally from China or are still working there.[62] Since they represent the voices of Chinese people reflecting on their own culture and experience, they complement the largely Anglophone voice found in the chapters themselves. As mentioned previously, this division of labor, which characterizes our book, is also characteristic of the academic disciplines themselves. Although excellent and influential scholarship by native Chinese has been produced in the areas of literary and film criticism, and insightful novels and films have been produced by Chinese artists, European and American voices still seem to predominate in social and cultural history and cultural anthropology.

In addition to giving the chapters a binary structure, we have arranged these pairs in a roughly chronological order, from mid-Qing to contemporary China. The book opens with Theiss and Sommer looking at late-imperial legal matters, for example, and ends with a pair of chapters by Schein and Litzinger that take us up to ethnic Miao, Yao, and Han notions of gender in the 1990s. These chapters make a good ending to the main part of the book because they bring us back, full circle, to the plural *femininities/masculinities* in our title. Thus, we have outlined the trajectory of changes that have occurred over time in notions of femininity and masculinity, often as the result of hard battles fought in various realms of life—battles that may have ambiguous results for women and men alike.

This rough chronological order is intended to illustrate breaks and discontinuities as well as steady developments and continuities, and thus it manifests the complex and often fragmented nature of gender constructs among various categories of people and in various realms of life in China. In this sense, the book utilizes the "archaeological method" described by Foucault. We wish to draw attention to enduring cultural categories that have been used to impose order on things in China, and we also wish to draw attention to the "epistemic" breaks that have occurred when these categories no longer have meaning in the order of things.[63]

Although this book does not explicitly compare Chinese with Western gender constructs, the fact that it is written in English for a mostly American and European audience means that many of its readers will bring their own Western gender constructs to their reading of the text. The variety of topics and periods covered should amply illustrate the richness and uniqueness of gender concepts in China, although some issues may resonate with Western experience. There is obviously no clear contrast to be drawn between distinctively "Chinese" and "Western" visions of the two categories, but at the same time there are certainly some differing threads running through Chinese as opposed to Western discourses about masculinity and femininity that can be teased out of these chapters.[64] These threads are outlined below.

We have tried to strike a balance, as noted above, between, on the one hand, zeroing in on issues (such as family life) that are routinely seen as "gendered" subjects and, on the other hand, focusing on topics (such as rebellion) not normally thought of in this way. We argue that the latter certainly have gender dimensions, as do all cultural phenomena, but we also recognize the fact that it is easier to bring to the surface the workings of gender categories in some areas than in others. Finally, when it comes to power relations, we try to suggest by including chapters from opposite sides of watershed years such as 1911 and 1949 that the upheavals that have transformed modern China may not have destroyed inequalities but they have produced considerable variations within patriarchal patterns.

This book was not conceived as a strictly feminist intervention in the narrow sense. However, we hope that it ends up being a feminist intervention in a broad sense. By looking at the broader picture of the power differences that shape the lives of women *and* men, we gain a more thorough understanding of *all* of the mechanisms that put people in their places and keep them there. By attention to issues of meaning and emotion as well as structure and power, we gain a more thorough understanding of how people can even find a certain pleasure and comfort in actively assuming the places that are available for them to take. For power is not just repressive, it is also constructive; it moves people to act in ways they perceive as self-motivated and self-interested, even though their actions may end up reproducing their low status in the social order.[65]

## KEY TERMS OF ANALYSIS: SEX, GENDER, AND SEXUALITY

It is crucial in a work such as this to provide some explanation of the meaning of these three terms as they have come to be used in the Anglo-American academic world. Unfortunately, we must bring up the words *sex, gender,* and *sexuality* only to argue that their current uses in Anglophone scholarship are grounded in a set of Western intellectual traditions that cannot be applied wholesale to the history of Chinese gender. We use them throughout the book, but we hope that the following comments will lead the reader to look critically at them each time they are put to use.

### The Problem with the Sex/Gender Distinction

The emergence of gender studies in Europe and the Americas in recent years has been made possible by a basic theoretical insight: namely, that sex and gender are two different things. It is now commonplace in the social sciences to find scholars using the word *sex* to refer to reproductive anatomy, which is typically either male or female and is perceived as fixed at birth. By contrast, *gender* is used to refer to the roles, behaviors, and symbols attached to anatomical sex in a particular culture; it is said to be learned and culturally variable. A phenomenon that reinforces this point is that, while the vast majority of human beings fall into one of two sex categories (that is, are anatomically male or female), many cultures have "third genders" of some sort (that is, people who are seen as, in social terms, neither unambiguously male nor unambiguously female).

This basic notion of sex and gender being different has had both pragmatic and theoretical implications. In practical terms, it suggests the need to interrogate closely the categories that individual cultures use to draw distinctions between men and women, and it underlines the value of asking whether gender categories exist that fall betwixt, between, or beyond these binaries. On the other hand, in more theoretical terms, it has encouraged feminist scholars to look for ways of linking sex distinctions to other kinds of systems of difference. One of the most influential moves in this latter direction, the structuralist one made by anthropologist Sherry Ortner, has already been discussed above. Sex, in her theory, makes gender, and then sex and gender combined codify a wide range of social differences.[66]

As valuable as attempts to distinguish clearly between sex and gender have been, the important study of the history of anatomical discourse in the West, *Making Sex: Body and Gender from the Greeks to Freud,* by the cultural historian Thomas Laqueur, demonstrates that the approach just outlined is too simple. According to Laqueur, the very distinction that many now take for granted is itself the product of a particular moment in the history of sex in the West. This occurred when, because of developments in medical science and changes in social structure, it became conceptually possible to separate sex from gender and to claim that sex was somehow more fixed than gender. Before the Enlightenment, he claims, gender arguably was viewed as the more salient, primary category because it was given by God in the cosmic order of things, while sex was something of an afterthought that arose out of the gender roles that people played in life. Beliefs about sex, Laqueur argues, are always formed through the lens of the gender system in which they are found: gender determines sex, not the other way around.[67]

We bring up Laqueur here because the way in which he turns the sex-gender distinction on its head in describing the pre-Enlightenment West has relevance for China. There, too, beginning in ancient times and persisting even today (though the influence of Western medical science has complicated the picture since the early 1900s), gender has tended to determine sex. This is part of the argument by Charlotte Furth alluded to above. She argues persuasively that, at that point in China, social gender overshadowed sexuality in the definition of the categories male and female: whether one acted in ways seen as masculine or feminine was often more important than one's anatomy. Recent works by Matthew Sommer and Tani Barlow reinforce this point. Li Xiaojiang, a prominent Chinese feminist, argues that "it would be redundant to introduce the notion of gender *(shehui xingbie)* [literally, social sex difference] to the Chinese language, since *nü* [woman/

female] and *nan* [man/male] are already understood as social, and not natural, beings."[68]

### The Primacy of Gender over Sex in Chinese Traditions

The Western tendency to take male/female as a fundamental, immutable opposition may lead scholars to assume that the female/male distinction is the central organizing principle in all symbolic systems, but this has not always been the case in China. In separate works, Ann Anagnost and Susan Brownell observe that, in Chinese gender symbolism, sex-linked symbols are often secondary to other, more fundamental principles of moral and social life.[69] This is because the structure of sex-linked symbolism mirrors the social structure, in which gender is situated within a broader network of social relations that take precedence over the dyadic sexual relation.

To take a concrete example, traditional Chinese cosmology is a symbolic system in which sex is constructed by gender, not the other way around. Westerners typically misunderstand the yin/yang dichotomy, assuming that yin "means" female and yang "means" male. In fact, yin and yang originally connoted shade and light but later had no fixed meanings. They were a way of describing relationships between things. In Taoist cosmology, for example, yin was identified with the natural and the female—principles that were more highly valued than were yang, culture, and maleness. By contrast, as they were used in Confucian orthodoxy yin and yang referred to hierarchical human relationships, and the power relationship between yin and yang qualities was reversed. A wife was seen as inferior to her husband, as yin was to yang. Interestingly, a subject or government minister, however, was also seen as yin in relation to the yang of a ruler, and this was true even if both people in this dyadic relationship were male. Yin and yang expressed complementary, hierarchical relationships that were not necessarily between males and females, even though yang was typically associated with masculine and yin with feminine principles. Rather than being an irreducible polarity in traditional Chinese cosmology, sex was one concept caught up in a network of other, perhaps more basic, concepts.[70] This was because sex was simply one principle among many (e.g., kinship, generation, age, and class) that determined a person's position in the family and in society.

Because the notion of the primacy of social role over anatomical sex may seem counterintuitive to many readers, it may be useful to illustrate it with the example of Chinese eunuchs, who were mentioned earlier but deserve closer attention. As something of a "third gender," which is hard to place cleanly on either side of an imagined immutable male-female divide, a discussion of eunuchs can provide insights into dominant gender constructs. Considering how useful the status of eunuchs is for understanding aspects of the pre–nineteenth-century gender system, it is disappointing that almost no studies of eunuchs have been done from a gender-studies perspective. Instead, extant studies tend to focus narrowly on eunuchs' role in court politics, in which, it has been observed, they made up a curious "third administrative hierarchy" that was separate from the main "civil" and "military" ones of imperial times.[71]

In one of the few analyses of the gender of eunuchs, Jennifer Jay concludes that they "underwent no gender shift but remained unquestionably male."[72] Jay notes that they were referred to as males in formal address and kinship terminology, wore male attire, married, adopted children, and ran their households. Their sexuality, she argues, remained heterosexual in orientation. Her argument is complicated, however, by evidence that eunuchs were socially ostracized and denied proper Confucian burials because their castration was seen as unfilial. Many eunuchs went to great lengths to keep their male organs so that their bodies—gifts from their parents that they had damaged in life—could be buried and their wholeness (and with it their filial piety) restored in death. In addition, as noted above, a eunuch could legally be taken as a concubine while a "true man" could not.

The efforts of eunuchs to define themselves as social males can be regarded as strategic manipulations of gender symbols, an attempt to claim power in a patriarchal world. Their behavior illustrates the main symbols of proper masculinity: marriage, children, and household headship; occupation of male categories in the kinship system; and male clothing. On the other hand, the fact that in some ways they were still not regarded as true males shows that masculinity was defined not just socially but also biologically: the possession of a male organ and the ability to produce one's own offspring with it were also important aspects of manhood. However, the point is that, unlike in the modern West, the possession of a penis was not *primarily* important because of male sexual pleasure, but rather because of what it represented. And it represented the patriarchal power that had been passed down the patriline from father to son according to the rules of Confucian filial piety. The castration of a eunuch was not *primarily* perceived as an injury to the manhood of the eunuch but rather as an injury to the father who had created him.

The theme of the importance of social gender over anatomical sex and sexuality in China also recurs in many chapters in this book. Charlotte Furth's and Nancy Chen's chapters, for example, illustrate how conceptions of sexual physiology were and still are quite different in China and the West. This is in part because, as they note, Chinese concepts of physiology draw on the classical Chinese medical and philosophical concepts of the body linked to the binaries of yin and yang, as opposed to the different notions of modern Western medical science.

Although Furth's essay on the symbolics of blood covers the seventeenth to nineteenth centuries, and Chen looks at *qigong* cults in contemporary

China, one is struck by the homology in the gendered symbolic order imposed upon the human body. *Qigong* is based in a syncretic form of folk religion that holds out hope for increasing one's physical strength and improving one's health through special breathing techniques. Furth notes first that within many Chinese medical discourses blood is treated as a distinctively female entity that, though it runs through the bodies of men and women alike, governs female bodies and health more than it does male. She argues that *qi* (a hard-to-translate term that stands for a vaguely defined vital energy that is maximized through breathing techniques and is the first half of the term *qigong*) was often envisioned as the masculine physiological counterpart. This is because, although it too is thought of as being possessed by members of both sexes, it is imagined to rule male bodies to a greater extent than it does female. Chen's chapter shows how *qi* is still, in many ways, gendered male in contemporary China.

### The Categories of Woman and Man in Recent Chinese History

The work of the historian Tani Barlow adds yet more facets to our understanding of the historical primacy of social gender over anatomical sex in China. She argues that in imperial China there was no generic category of Woman: there were daughters in the family *(nü),* wives *(fu),* and mothers *(mu).*[73] Two neologisms—ordinarily translated as "woman" *(funü, nüxing)*—were created when sex-identity politics first emerged in the May Fourth Movement (1919). *Nüxing* (woman) was a Western-inspired concept used by Republican-era reformers (1912–49) to name the newly discovered transcendent category of Woman. Essentially, "she" was discovered when the reformers started to see themselves through Western eyes and decided that a major reason for China's relative weakness and backwardness was that the female population was brutally oppressed and living in a condition of virtual slavery. Before this time, of course, the seclusion of women from public life and the binding of their feet had been regarded as symbols of purity and morality. In the Republican era, however, these previously admired women became symbols of backwardness and the targets of modernization efforts.

Although Barlow's work is a foundational one for understanding changes in Chinese gender over the last century, we still need a similar analysis of the categories of sons, husbands, and fathers. Kam Louie and Louise Edwards argue that, in Chinese history, concepts of manliness have often been structured around the intertwining of two ideals. The first is associated with *wen* attributes (cultured behavior, refinement, mastery of scholarly works), the other with *wu* qualities (martial prowess, strength, mastery of physical arts). They claim, in short, that scholar-officials and military-officials represented two opposed poles around which masculine identity could be constituted.[74] The strong association of literary talents with masculinity may be one reason why, in the Chinese case, a distinctively feminine literary tradition raises the sorts of complex problems discussed by Lydia Liu in her contribution to this volume. It may also help explain why the questioning of traditional male literary genres by iconoclastic scholars of the second and third decades of the twentieth century had such serious implications for images of elite masculinity—a phenomenon discussed by Wendy Larson in her chapter on men and connoisseurship in modern Chinese literature. She points out that, since the literati were the keepers of the elite cultural tradition, the reformist attacks on that tradition in the early part of this century were simultaneously attacks on a long-held ideal of elite masculinity.

In other words, the category of Woman did not appear and develop independently of the category of Man. On the contrary, concurrently with the emergence of *nüxing*-Woman, there were feelings among male intellectuals that the Chinese *nanxing*-Man was being emasculated and feminized by Western and Japanese imperialism. Clearly, the category of the backward Woman in need of modernizing emerged in tandem with the category of the modern Man who was going to lead her. But what kind of man would the new modern Man be? Who was it, exactly, who would help China shed its image as either the "Sick Man of East Asia" (an emasculated male symbol invoked in some political tracts of the time) or a degenerate prostitute (a sexualized female representation of the country found in many novels of the day)? Larson discusses the crisis in elite masculinity that occurred with the fall of the Qing and the attacks on the literati who had defined the image of the ideal male. If Chinese femininity was in crisis, then even more so was Chinese masculinity. Susan Glosser's chapter in this book describes the contradictory position taken by progressive young men who, on the one hand, vehemently attacked the patriarchal family system but, on the other hand, never challenged the assumption that marriage and family were central to the political and social order. This assumption was unchanged since the Qing, a fact that is clear from a comparison with the ideals described in Susan Mann's chapter on women's preparations for marriage in the mid-Qing. Glosser observes that the contradictory attitudes held by the young men led to a great deal of dissatisfaction with their wives, who were seldom as "progressive" as they felt they deserved. Young men searching for new masculine identities expected their wives to acquire new feminine identities, against which they could define themselves.

The strength of family structure in defining notions of normality is evident in the chapters by Gail Hershatter and David Ownby. Hershatter's analysis of six different approximations of the prostitute as a female type and Ownby's complementary study of male bandits show that one learns a great deal about images of masculinity and femininity by looking at social types who are represented as liminal or transgressive figures—that is, as people on the fringes or completely outside of mainstream society, constant

Figure 1. In this illustration from the lesson "Citizen" *(guomin)*, in a 1929 primer
for learning characters, men and women both hold up the nation, but men lead
women and carry more weight. The characters read "Republic of China." *Shimin
qian zi ke* [Lessons in a thousand characters for citizens], published by *Zhonghua
pingmin jiaoyu cujin hui zonghui* [General Committee of the Chinese Association
for the Encouragement of Education among the Common People], 1929.

reminders that orthodox male and female roles are not the only ones that actually exist. Hershatter traces images of the prostitute that derive from sources that run from the romanticization of the courtesan in the late Qing to criticism of streetwalkers as diseased markers of national backwardness in the early nineteenth century. She shows that, in each case, part of what was viewed with favor or disdain was the sex worker's detachment from conventional sexual and familial relationships. Ownby maps a parallel progression of images, moving from a vision of the bandit as a heroic defender of the powerless to that of a depraved malcontent operating on the fringes of civilization. He also stresses, even more explicitly than does Hershatter, the outsider status of flesh-and-blood bandits, perceived as frustrated bachelors not rooted in lineages and other family structures.

Lydia Liu's chapter shows that the category of "female literature" (*nüxing wenxue*) was invented by women literary critics in post-Mao China to describe a supposedly homogeneous tradition that in fact did not exist. Women writers from the May Fourth to the reform eras were quite heterogeneous, and by no means can they all be characterized as feminist. The post-Mao critics used this invented "Woman's voice" to contest the authority of the official All-China Women's Federation to represent all women. This chapter is yet another example of the politicization of gender categories in particular historical moments for particular purposes, some more obvious than others.

After the Communist takeover in 1949, *nüxing* was rejected as "bourgeois" and the category *funü* (female family members) was revived to label women as a social category. Perhaps because it contained the word for sex (*xing*), *nüxing* was considered inappropriate for the androgynous ideals of the Maoist period.[75] To Western eyes, the Cultural Revolution–era image of the masculinized female Red Guards, dressed like soldiers in army green with caps and thick leather belts, might seem rather bizarre. It is interesting to be reminded, then, that this image developed out of a process that was put into motion by the Western criticisms of Chinese gender at the turn of the century. These distinctive images illustrate that, although they were influenced by Western contact, Chinese gender concepts clearly followed their own course of development. In her chapter on violence among female Red Guards, Emily Honig shows that students at elite girls schools were influenced by popular images of the "Iron Girls" who could do everything men could do. She suggests that the ferocity of female Red Guards might be attributable in part to a rebellion against the restrictive gender norms they experienced. Elizabeth Perry and Nara Dillon also suggest that many of the leaders of Shanghai's worker rebels were marginal males who were, in part, dissenting against the masculine norms of the previous decade. These two chapters illustrate the ways in which historical traditions and then-current politics intertwined with gender relations to produce ideals of femininity and masculinity unique to specific times and places.

The point that we wish to make here is that the categories of Man and Woman contain no universal, absolute truths. Rather, they are cultural constructs that vary across cultures and across time. They have been constructed differently in Chinese and European history, and they have been constructed differently in China over the last century.

### The Problem with Sexuality

Some scholars have argued that maleness and femaleness were not closely linked to sexuality in China. Foucault's *The History of Sexuality* (which dealt primarily with Western civilization and western Europe) began to influence some China scholars in the 1980s. Foucault's insight was to demonstrate that sexuality has a history: it is not a fixed psychobiological drive that is the same for all humans according to their sex, but rather it is a cultural construct inseparable from gender constructs. After unmooring sexuality from biology, he anchored it in history, arguing that this thing we now call sexuality came into existence in the eighteenth-century West and did not exist previously in this form. "Sexuality" is an invention of the modern state, the industrial revolution, and capitalism. Taking this insight as a starting point, scholars have slowly been compiling the history of sexuality in China. The works by Tani Barlow, discussed above, were also foundational in this trend. Barlow observes that, in the West, heterosexuality is the primary site for the production of gender: a woman truly becomes a woman only in relation to a man's heterosexual desire.[76] By contrast, in China before the 1920s the *jia* (lineage unit, family) was the primary site for the production of gender: marriage and sexuality were to serve the lineage by producing the next generation of lineage members; personal love and pleasure were secondary to this goal. Barlow argues that this has two theoretical implications: (1) it is not possible to write a Chinese history of heterosexuality, sexuality as an institution, and sexual identities in the European metaphysical sense, and (2) it is not appropriate to ground discussions of Chinese gender processes in the sexed body so central in "Western" gender processes. Here she echoes Furth's argument that, before the early twentieth century, sex-identity grounded on anatomical difference did not hold a central place in Chinese constructions of gender.[77] And she echoes the point illustrated in detail in Sommer's chapter on male homosexuality in the Qing legal code: a man could engage in homosexual behavior without calling into question his manhood so long as his behavior did not threaten the patriarchal Confucian family structure.

The authors of the present volume understand sexuality in a sense that is partly inspired by intellectual trends since Foucault but is not strictly Foucaultian. They understand sexuality as a cultural construct intertwined with notions about gender, but they do not completely deny its biological basis, and they do not limit their use of the word *sexuality* to describe techniques of the modern states and industrialized capitalist societies as did Foucault. Most important, they show that *sexuality* does not mean the same thing in the Chinese context. And they understand that it must always be historicized as well as understood as varying between cultures, since it can rise and fall in importance as a factor in defining visions of gender. In the Chinese case, for example, a late-imperial period when sexuality was not central to notions of gender difference was succeeded by the New Culture era (1915–23), during which the situation was very different and sexuality often served as a key definer of femininity and masculinity. Then, in the first decades of the People's Republic, and especially during the Cultural Revolution, this role was once again muted. This picture is further complicated by the variations in sexuality across social groups. Keith McMahon, for example, suggests that, even among the Qing elite, masculine sexuality might have been differently regarded by men who subscribed to orthodox Confucian ideals as opposed to Buddhist and Taoist influences.[78]

The 1990s witnessed a dramatic revival in sexuality's prominence as a definer of Chinese gender categories, a phenomenon linked to the increasing presence of global culture and capitalism in the PRC. In her chapter, Harriet Evans describes the reemergence of sexuality, particularly female sexuality, as a contested issue in 1990s China. She attributes this in part to the state's interest in regulating sexual practice in times of market-oriented reforms. Yet even in the midst of apparent change, she argues, an undertone in these debates has remained fairly constant since 1949: women fully realize themselves as people only through wifehood and motherhood. In his chapter, William Jankowiak also observes that since the 1980s there has been a shift away from the androgynous revolutionary ideals, but he attributes this more to the reemergence of already existing beliefs and less to the actions of the state. He also points out that market reforms have created an atmosphere of anxiety for men, because men feel that they prove their masculinity by achieving "success" yet are no longer sure what the standards for success are. In these changing times, the debates about fatherhood and status are just as heated as they were in the transitional second and third decades of the twentieth century, as described by Glosser.

The final chapters, by Louisa Schein and Ralph Litzinger, provide something of a rude awakening, reminding us that the People's Republic of China is a multiethnic nation, and that when Western academics (and Han Chinese people as well) speak about "Chinese gender," we (and they) often really mean Han gender. These chapters also show how ethnicity often destabilizes gender categories. For example, in some settings, a Han Chinese may find Miao "traditional" femininity more erotically appealing than the femininity of an urban Han woman. A Yao Taoist priest, meanwhile, may sometimes be seen as representing a more legitimate kind of "traditional" masculine power than an urban Han male. Taken together, these chapters reveal the complexity behind femininities and masculinities in China: we must always be ready to ask, *Whose* femininity and masculinity are being produced and displayed, and *by whom?* and *Whose* purposes are served by this production and display?

In summary, scholarship on Chinese gender seems to indicate that, before the period of extended contact with the West, (1) gender concepts were anchored in beliefs about family structure and social roles more so than in beliefs about biological sex (and even beliefs that we might call "biological" were based in classical Chinese medicine, not Western science); (2) "men" and "women" were plural categories rather than unified categories opposed to each other; (3) "manhood" and "womanhood" were not directly linked to heterosexuality, and reproducing the lineage was a more important aspect of sexuality than individual pleasure. The assumption is that in all of these ways, Chinese gender differed from Western gender after the Enlightenment (before this period, there may have been greater similarities). An interesting historical question, then, is, To what degree has contact with the West and its notions of gender influenced Chinese gender in the last two centuries?[79] The existing scholarship seems to indicate that contact with the West brought about profound changes; nevertheless, Chinese gender maintained its own distinctive character—in particular, sexuality did not occupy the central role that it does in Western gender. Sexuality seems to have regained importance in the 1990s, but concepts of femininity and masculinity still seem to be primarily anchored in the roles of mother/father and wife/husband. The main change since the Qing is that femininity and masculinity are less anchored in the roles of daughter/son.

As we have tried to indicate, the current moment is a fascinating but also confusing one at which to figure out what a concern with China and gender can add to our picture of both a particular cultural history and a set of theoretical issues. The chapters that follow are not intended as a road map for arriving at a single conclusive destination but rather as something more like a travel guide for those interested in exploring this exciting terrain. The authors point out some of the main landmarks and provide provocative details for readers who want to ponder the significance of these sites.

## NOTES

Discussions with various colleagues, including several contributors to this volume, have played an important role in shaping the discussion here, and comments by Marilyn Young, Christina Gilmartin, Jennifer Robertson, Kenneth Pomeranz, and several anonymous readers have been helpful as well. Rubie and Woody Watson deserve special thanks, since the idea for the volume was originally as much theirs as ours, originating as it did out of conversations held at their house over the course of a three-day visit by Jeff Wasserstrom. Susan Brownell was invited to replace Rubie as coeditor when Rubie's duties at the Peabody Museum left her little time for the project. Susan is grateful for Rubie's support in this, as in other endeavors. If books can be said to have godparents, Rubie and Woody are this one's. We should note as well that this book is intended to showcase *varied* approaches to gender and China by bringing together a mixture of a small number of influential and provocative published essays and a larger number of insightful original ones. Hence, neither the contributors who wrote chapters at our request nor the scholars whose pieces we reprint here should be held responsible in any way for the views expressed in this section of the book. We have learned much from all of them, but we realize that many (perhaps all) would disagree with some parts of our discussion or at least wish we had put more emphasis on some issues and less on others.

1. Useful critical introductions to the literature on the gendered dimensions of earlier stages of Chinese history include Jinhua Emma Teng, "The Construction of the 'Traditional Chinese Woman' in the Western Academy: A Critical Review," *Signs: Journal of Women in Culture and Society* 22, no. 1 (1996): 115–51; and Patricia Ebrey's "Women, Marriage, and the Family in Chinese History," in *Heritage of China: Contemporary Perspectives on Chinese Civilization*, ed. Paul Ropp (Berkeley and Los Angeles: University of California Press, 1990), 197–223. See also the historiographic opening to Kathryn Bernhardt, "A Ming-Qing Transition in Chinese Women's History? The Perspective from Law," in *Remapping China: Fissures in Historical Terrain*, ed. Gail Hershatter et al. (Stanford: Stanford University Press, 1996), 42–58.

2. Tani Barlow, ed., *Gender Politics in Modern China: Writing and Feminism* (Durham: Duke University Press, 1993); and Angela Zito and Tani Barlow, eds., *Body, Subject, and Power in China* (Chicago: University of Chicago Press, 1994).

3. Rubie S. Watson and Patricia B. Ebrey, eds., *Marriage and Inequality in China* (Berkeley and Los Angeles: University of California Press, 1994).

4. Mayfair Mei-hui Yang, ed., *Spaces of Their Own: Women's Public Sphere in Transnational China* (Minneapolis: University of Minnesota Press, 1999); and Maria Jaschok and Suzanne Miers, eds., *Women and Chinese Patriarchy: Submission, Servitude, and Escape* (London: Zed, 1994).

5. Christina K. Gilmartin, Gail Hershatter, Lisa Rofel, and Tyrene White, eds., *Engendering China: Women, Culture, and the State* (Cambridge: Harvard University Press, 1994).

6. Marilyn B. Young, ed., *Women in China* (Ann Arbor: University of Michigan Center for Chinese Studies, 1973); Margery Wolf and Roxane Witke, eds., *Women in Chinese Society* (Stanford: Stanford University Press, 1975).

7. Elizabeth Croll, *Socialism and Feminism in China* (London: Routledge, 1978); Ono Kazuko, *Chinese Women in a Century of Revolution, 1850–1950*, ed. Joshua Fogel and trans. Fogel et al. (Stanford: Stanford University Press, 1989); Emily Honig and Gail Hershatter, eds., *Personal Voices: Chinese Women in the 1980s* (Stanford: Stanford University Press, 1988).

8. Harriet Evans, *Women and Sexuality in China: Female Sexuality and Gender since 1949* (New York: Continuum, 1997); Wang Zheng, *Women in the Chinese Enlightenment: Oral and Textual Histories* (Berkeley and Los Angeles: University of California Press, 1999).

9. In addition to the books by these two scholars cited above, see Harriet Evans, "Defining Difference: The 'Scientific' Construction of Female Sexuality and Gender in the People's Republic of China," *Signs: Journal of Women in Culture and Society* 20, no. 2 (1994–95): 357–96; and Wang Zheng, "'Nüxing yishi,' 'shehui xingbie yishi' bianyi" [An analysis of "female consciousness" and "gender consciousness"], *Funü yanjiu luncong* [Collection of Women's Studies], no. 1 (1997): 14–20.

10. Collections of essays on other parts of Asia that pay equal or almost equal attention to issues of femininity and of masculinity, but which in some instances focus more than we do on topics linked to representation, include Aihwa Ong and Michael G. Pertz, eds., *Bewitching Women, Pious Men: Gender and Body Politics in Southeast Asia* (Berkeley and Los Angeles: University of California Press, 1995); and Wazir Jahan Karim, ed., *"Male" and "Female" in Developing Southeast Asia* (Oxford: Berg Publishers, 1995). An impressive recent work in this vein that deals with North American history is Laura McCall and Donald Yacovone, eds., *A Shared Experience: Men, Women, and the History of Gender* (New York: New York University Press, 1998). Tanya M. Luhrmann's *The Good Parsi: The Fate of a Colonial Elite in a Postcolonial Society* (Cambridge: Harvard University Press, 1996) discusses the feelings of emasculation of Parsi men, who constituted an elite in Bombay during the colonial period but lost status in the postcolonial era. The fate of the Parsi is somewhat reminiscent of the fate of the Chinese literati, discussed by Glosser and Larson in the present volume.

11. A wide-ranging and interesting recent collection on cross-dressing and related transgressive acts is Sabrina Ramet, ed., *Gender Reversals and Gender Cultures: Anthropological and Historical Perspectives* (London: Routledge, 1996); in that volume see, on China, Sophie Volpp, "Gender, Power, and Spectacle in Late-Imperial Chinese Theatre," 138–47.

12. For further discussion of female infanticide and related issues, see Jeffrey N. Wasserstrom, "Resistance to the One-Child Family," *Modern China* 10, no. 3 (1984): 345–74. It should be noted that this piece was written from what might be called, following the argument presented above, a fairly straightforward "patriarchal" perspective. A reference to the *quanren* category can be found in the text, but as the author had not yet read widely in the feminist literature that focuses on "difference," the implications of that term remain unexamined.

13. Young, *Women in China;* and Wolf and Witke, *Women in Chinese Society.*

14. Delia Davin, *Woman-Work: Women and the Party in Revolutionary China* (Oxford: Oxford University Press, 1976); Patricia Stranahan, *Yan'an Women and the Communist Party* (Berkeley: Institute of East Asian Studies and Center for Chinese Studies, University of California, 1983); Ono, *Chinese Women in a Century of Revolution;* and Kay Ann Johnson, *Women, the Family, and Peasant Revolution in China* (Chicago: University of Chicago Press, 1983).

15. Judith Stacey, *Patriarchy and Socialist Revolution in China* (Berkeley and Los Angeles: University of California Press, 1983); Croll, *Feminism and Socialism in China;* and Phyllis Andors, *The Unfinished Liberation of Chinese Women* (Bloomington: Indiana University Press, 1983).

16. A thoughtful critical discussion of several key works from this period is Emily Honig, "Socialist Revolution and Women's Liberation in China—a Review Article," *Journal of Asian Studies* 44, no. 2 (1985): 329–36.

17. Wang, *Women in the Chinese Enlightenment;* Gail Hershatter, *Workers of Tianjin*

(Stanford: Stanford University Press, 1986); Emily Honig, *Sisters and Strangers* (Stanford: Stanford University Press, 1986); Christina Gilmartin, *Engendering the Chinese Revolution* (Berkeley and Los Angeles: University of California Press, 1995).

18. Tani Barlow, "Theorizing Woman: *Funü, Guojia, Jiating*" [Chinese women, Chinese state, Chinese family], *Genders* 10 (1991): 132–60 (see p. 147); Harriet Evans, "The Language of Liberation: Gender and Jiefang in Early Chinese Communist Party Discourse," *Intersections* (zine) (September 1998) http://www.sshe .murdoch.edu.au.hum.as.intersections/.

19. Prasenjit Duara, *Rescuing History from the Nation: Questioning Narratives of Modern China* (Chicago: University of Chicago Press, 1995); the literary critics and anthropologists whose works provide the basis for the gendered part of his analysis are discussed below.

20. Joan Scott, "Gender: A Useful Category of Historical Analysis," *American Historical Review* 91, no. 5 (December 1986); reprinted in Scott's own collection of essays, *Gender and the Politics of History* (New York: Columbia University Press, 1988), 28–50.

21. See, for example, the articles by Adrian Davis, "Fraternity and Fratricide in Late Imperial China," 1630–40; Lee McIsaac, "'Righteous Fraternities' and Honorable Men: Sworn Brotherhoods in Wartime Chongqing," 1641–55; and Norma Kutcher (on male friendships), "The Fifth Relationship: Dangerous Friendships in the Confucian Context," 1615–29, in the forum *The Male-Male Bond in Chinese History*, in *American Historical Review* 105, no. 5 (December 2000).

22. See James L. Watson's pathbreaking study of the implications of being a marginal male and strategies to deal with this status in "Self Defense Corps, Violence, and the Bachelor Sub-Culture in South China: Two Case Studies," in *Proceedings of the Second International Conference on Sinology*, ed. Liu Pin-hsiung, vol. 4 (Taipei: n.p., 1988).

23. See the discussion of gender studies in anthropology by Micaela di Leonardo, "Introduction: Gender, Culture, and Political Economy: Feminist Anthropology in Historical Perspective," in *Gender at the Crossroads of Knowledge: Feminist Anthropology in the Postmodern Era* (Berkeley and Los Angeles: University of California Press, 1991), 1–6; Michelle Zimbalist Rosaldo and Louise Lamphere, eds., *Woman, Culture, and Society* (Stanford: Stanford University Press, 1974); Rayna R. Reiter, ed., *Toward an Anthropology of Women* (New York: Monthly Review Press, 1975).

24. Margery Wolf, *Women and the Family in Rural Taiwan* (Stanford: Stanford University Press, 1972).

25. Margery Wolf, *The House of Lim: A Study of a Chinese Farm Family* (Englewood Cliffs, N.J.: Prentice-Hall, 1968), vi.

26. Margery Wolf, "Chinese Women: Old Skills in a New Context," in *Woman, Culture, and Society*, ed. Michelle Zimbalist Rosaldo and Louise Lamphere (Stanford: Stanford University Press, 1974), 157–72.

27. Jonathan Spence, *The Death of Woman Wang* (New York: Viking, 1978).

28. Young, *Women in China*, 2.

29. Wolf and Witke, *Women in Chinese Society*.

30. Another noteworthy collection from roughly the same period is Richard Guisso and Stanley Johanesen, eds., *Women in China: Current Directions in Historical Scholarship* (New York: Philo Press, 1981), in addition to the several cited in previous notes.

31. A few male scholars, it should be mentioned, contributed to this early stage of Anglo-American Chinese gender studies as well. Aside from Jonathan Spence, particularly noteworthy is Paul Ropp, author of works such as "The Seeds of Change: Reflections on the Condition of Women in the Early and Mid Ch'ing," *Signs: Journal of Women in Culture and Society* 2, no. 1 (1976): 5–23.

32. See, for example, the discussions of Mao Zedong's attitudes toward gender equality and the essay by Soong Qinglin in Young, *Women in China.*

33. Hsiao Tung Fei [Fei Xiaotong], *Peasant Life in China: A Field Study of Country Life in the Yangtze Valley* (London: G. Routledge, 1939); Martin C. Yang, *A Chinese Village: Taitou, Shantung Province* (New York: Columbia University Press, 1945).

34. The accident is mentioned in the chapter by Ralph Litzinger in this book. It occurred while he was doing research among the Yao, the ethnic group described by Litzinger.

35. Sherry B. Ortner, "Is Female to Male as Nature Is to Culture?" in *Woman, Culture, and Society,* ed. Michelle Zimbalist Rosaldo and Louise Lamphere (Stanford: Stanford University Press, 1974), esp. 68 and 71.

36. The tremendous cultural variations in these logics are examined in detail in the various chapters of Carol MacCormack and Marilyn Strathern, eds., *Nature, Culture, and Gender* (Cambridge: Cambridge University Press, 1980).

37. An interesting recent critical summary of Ortner's argument and an attempt to apply aspects of it to a Chinese issue can be found in Tamara Jacka, *Women's Work in Rural China: Change and Continuity in an Era of Reform* (Cambridge: Cambridge University Press, 1997).

38. Harriet Whitehead, "The Bow and the Burden Strap: A New Look at Institutionalized Homosexuality in Native North America," in *Sexual Meanings: The Cultural Construction of Gender and Sexuality,* ed. Sherry B. Ortner and Harriet Whitehead (Cambridge: Cambridge University Press, 1981), 80–115.

39. Especially influential, as noted above, was Scott, "Gender."

40. Emily Ahern, "The Power and Pollution of Chinese Women," in *Women in Chinese Society,* ed. Margery Wolf and Roxane Witke (Stanford: Stanford University Press, 1975), 193–214; and Gary Seaman, "Blood Bowls and Black Dogs: The Sexual Politics of Karmic Retribution in a Chinese Hell," in *The Anthropology of Chinese Society in Taiwan,* ed. E. Martin Ahern and Hill Gates Rosenow (Stanford: Stanford University Press, 1981), 381–96. See also Emily Martin, "Gender and Ideological Differences in Representations of Life and Death," in *Death Ritual in Late Imperial and Modern China,* ed. James L. Watson and Evelyn S. Rawski (Berkeley and Los Angeles: University of California Press, 1988), 164–79.

41. Arthur Wolf, ed., *Studies in Chinese Society* (Stanford: Stanford University Press, 1978).

42. Charlotte Furth, "Androgynous Males and Deficient Females: Biology and Gender Boundaries in Sixteenth- and Seventeenth-Century China," *Late Imperial China* 9, no. 2 (December 1988): 1–31.

43. A key text was Catherine A. Lutz and Lila Abu-Lughod, eds., *Language and the Politics of Emotion* (Cambridge: Cambridge University Press, 1990).

44. William Jankowiak, "Chinese Women, Gender, and Sexuality: A Critical Review of Recent Studies," in *Bulletin of Concerned Asian Scholars* 31, no. 1 (January-March 1999): 31–37. Sulamith Heins Potter's article "The Cultural Construction of

Emotion in Rural Chinese Social Life" links emotion to concepts of the (ungendered) person but does not link emotion to gender per se. In Potter and Jack M. Potter, *China's Peasants: The Anthropology of a Revolution* (Cambridge: Cambridge University Press, 1990), 180–95. For a critical look at the relatively small amount of attention *historians* concerned with gender and China have paid to emotion, see Dorothy Ko, "Thinking about Copulating: An Early-Qing Confucian Thinker's Problem with Emotion and Words," in *Remapping China: Fissures in Historical Terrain*, ed. Gail Hershatter et al. (Stanford: Stanford University Press, 1996), 59–76.

45. Margery Wolf, "Women and Suicide in China," in *Women in Chinese Society*, ed. Margery Wolf and Roxane Witke (Stanford: Stanford University Press, 1975), 111–42.

46. William Jankowiak, *Sex, Death, and Hierarchy in a Chinese City: An Anthropological Account* (New York: Columbia University Press, 1993), and "Romantic Passion in the People's Republic of China," in *Romantic Passion: A Universal Experience?* ed. William Jankowiak (New York: Columbia University Press, 1995), 166–83.

47. Rey Chow, *Woman and Chinese Modernity: The Politics of Reading between East and West* (Minneapolis: University of Minnesota, 1991).

48. Lydia Liu, "The Female Body and Nationalist Discourse: Manchuria in Xiao Hong's Field of Life and Death," in *Body, Subject, and Power in China*, ed. Angela Zito and Tani Barlow (Chicago: University of Chicago Press, 1994), 157–77; Duara, *Rescuing History from the Nation*.

49. Chen Xiaomei, *Occidentalism* (Oxford: Oxford University Press, 1995).

50. Francis Hsu, *Under the Ancestors' Shadow: Chinese Culture and Personality* (New York: Columbia University Press, 1948).

51. Marriage as a tool for forming alliances between the Manchu and Mongol against the Han is discussed in Evelyn S. Rawski, "Ch'ing Imperial Marriage and Problems of Rulership," in *Marriage and Inequality in Chinese Society*, ed. Rubie S. Watson and Patricia Buckley Ebrey (Berkeley and Los Angeles: University of California Press, 1991), 170–203. This chapter precedes the chapter by Susan Mann reprinted in this book, and in some senses may be regarded as a complement to it in presenting some of the ethnic issues involved in Qing elite marriage strategies. See also Pamela Kyle Crossley, *Orphan Warriors: Three Manchu Generations and the End of the Qing World* (Princeton: Princeton University Press, 1990); and Angela Zito, *Of Body and Brush: Grand Sacrifice as Text/Performance in Eighteenth-Century China* (Chicago: University of Chicago Press, 1997).

52. Robert Van Gulik, *Sexual Life in Ancient China: A Preliminary Survey of Chinese Sex and Society from ca. 1500 B.C. till 1644 A.D.* (Leiden, Netherlands: E. J. Brill, 1961), 296.

53. Stevan Harrell, ed., *Cultural Encounters on China's Ethnic Frontiers* (Seattle: University of Washington Press, 1995); Melissa J. Brown, ed., *Negotiating Ethnicities in China and Taiwan* (Berkeley: Institute of East Asian Studies, University of California, 1996).

54. Dru Gladney, *Muslim Chinese: Ethnic Nationalism in the People's Republic* (Cambridge: Harvard University Press, 1991).

55. Edward Said, *Orientalism* (New York: Random House, 1978).

56. Dru Gladney, "Representing Nationality in China: Refiguring Majority/Minority Identities," *Journal of Asian Studies* 53, no. 1 (February 1994): 92–123 (see

p. 93). See also Esther Yau, "Is China the End of Hermeneutics? Or, Political and Cultural Usage of Non-Han Women in Mainland Chinese Films," *Discourse* 11, no. 2 (spring-summer 1989): 115–36.

57. Michel Foucault, *The History of Sexuality*, vol. 1: *An Introduction* (1976; reprint, New York: Random House, 1978). A noteworthy exception to the focus on male homosexuality is Tze-lan Deborah Sang, "The Emerging Lesbian: Female Same-Sex Desire in Modern Chinese Literature and Culture" (Ph.D. diss., University of California at Berkeley, 1996).

58. Bret Hinsch, *Passions of the Cut Sleeve: The Male Homosexual Tradition in China* (Berkeley and Los Angeles: University of California Press, 1990).

59. Frank Dikötter, *Sex, Culture, and Modernity in China: Medical Science and the Construction of Sexual Identities in the Early Republican Period* (Honolulu: University of Hawaii Press, 1995).

60. Matthew Sommer, "The Penetrated Male in Late Imperial China," *Modern China* 23, no. 2 (April 1997): 140–80.

61. Other strategies for highlighting the interplay between masculinity and femininity could, of course, have been attempted. Most notably, some scholars have tried to give equal weight to the two sides of the issue in the same piece. See, for example, Everett Zhang, "Tiananmen Square: The Rhetorical Power of a Woman and a Man," *Anthropology and Humanism* 20, no. 1 (1995): 29–46; and Zhong Xueping, "Male Suffering and Male Desire: The Politics of Reading *Half of Man Is Woman* by Zhang Xianliang," in *Engendering China: Women, Culture, and the State,* ed. Christina K. Gilmartin, Gail Hershatter, Lisa Rofel, and Tyrene White (Cambridge: Harvard University Press, 1994), 175–91. Given the present underdeveloped state of work on Chinese masculinities, however, we thought the strategy of paired chapters a particularly appropriate one, both for scholarly and pedagogic purposes.

62. Copies of these Chinese videos, subtitled or dubbed in English, can be found in major video stores, Asian markets with video sections, and university film collections or acquired from specialized book and video distributors such as Cheng and Tsui.

63. See Michel Foucault, *The Order of Things: An Archaeology of the Human Sciences* (New York: Vintage Books, 1970).

64. There are also, of course, various gendered threads that are not addressed in this volume. One of these has to do with the way time is experienced. Elisabeth Croll, in *From Heaven to Earth: Images and Experiences of Development in China* (London: Routledge, 1994), makes the interesting argument that, in the Chinese countryside, notions of continuity tend to be associated with masculinity, and discontinuity with femininity, in part because of the differing roles of sons and daughters within lineages.

65. Michel Foucault, *Discipline and Punish* (New York: Vintage Books, 1979).

66. Ortner, "Is Female to Male as Nature Is to Culture?"

67. Here is how he puts the issue: "I want to propose . . . that in these pre-Enlightenment texts, and even in some later ones, *sex*, or the body, must be understood as the epiphenomenon, while *gender*, what we would take to be a cultural category, was primary or 'real.' Gender—man and woman—mattered a great deal and was part of the order of things; sex was conventional, though modern terminology makes such a reordering nonsensical. . . . [When ideas such as this are taken seri-

ously] the comfortable notion is shaken that man is man and woman is woman and that the historian's task is to find out what they did, what they thought, and what was thought about them." Thomas Laqueur, *Making Sex: Body and Gender from the Greeks to Freud* (Cambridge: Harvard University Press, 1990), 8 and 13.

68. Li Xiaojiang, "With What Discourse Do We Reflect on Chinese Women? Thoughts on Transnational Feminism in China," in *Spaces of Their Own: Women's Public Sphere in Transnational China*, ed. Mayfair Mei-hui Yang (Minneapolis: University of Minnesota Press, 1999), 261–77 (see p. 262).

69. Susan Brownell, *Training the Body for China: Sports in the Moral Order of the People's Republic* (Chicago: University of Chicago Press, 1995), 219–22; Ann Anagnost, "Transformations of Gender in Modern China," in *Gender and Anthropology: Critical Reviews for Research and Teaching*, ed. Sandra Morgen (Washington, D.C.: American Anthropological Association, 1989), 313–42 (see p. 321).

70. See Alison H. Black, "Gender and Cosmology in Chinese Correlative Thinking," in *Gender and Religion: On the Complexity of Symbols*, ed. Caroline Walker Bynum, Stevan Harrell, and Paula Richman (Boston: Beacon, 1986), 166–95.

71. Taisuke Mitamura does briefly state that eunuchs were considered "deficient men" who were neither masculine nor feminine, but he does not carry out a systematic examination of gender ideology. Taisuke Mitamura, *Chinese Eunuchs: The Structure of Intimate Politics* (Rutland, Vt.: Charles E. Tuttle, 1970). In Shih-san Henry Tsai, *The Eunuchs in the Ming Dynasty* (New York: State University of New York Press, 1996), the question of where eunuchs fit into China's gender systems also receives relatively little attention. The term "third administrative hierarchy" is taken from that work.

72. Jennifer W. Jay, "Another Side of Chinese Eunuch History: Castration, Marriage, Adoption, and Burial," *Canadian Journal of History* 28, no. 3 (December 1993): 460–78.

73. Ibid., 254.

74. Kam Louie and Louise Edwards, "Chinese Masculinity: Theorizing *Wen* and *Wu*," *East Asian History* 8 (1994): 135–48. Very few comparably ambitious attempts to map out the range of cultural expectations associated with masculinity in China have been made, though some important case studies of pieces of the puzzle have been done, such as Watson, "Self Defense Corps, Violence, and the Bachelor Sub-Culture in South China: Two Case Studies." See also the *American Historical Review* forum *The Male-Male Bond in Chinese History*, cited in n. 21.

75. Li Xiaojiang in Yang, *Spaces of Their Own*, 268.

76. Barlow, "Theorizing Woman."

77. Ibid., 147.

78. Keith McMahon, *Misers, Shrews, and Polygamists: Sexuality and Male-Female Relations in Eighteenth-Century Chinese Fiction* (Durham: Duke University Press, 1995), 150–75.

79. Of course, this is only one of many interesting questions that can be asked. Regional influences, especially from Japan, have also been significant. However, in Chinese debates about gender, "the West" has occupied a much more important position than Japan as the "Other" against which Chinese people defined themselves. Thus, the focus is on the West in this introduction and the following chapters.

PART ONE

# Gender and the Law

Social and cultural historians have long shown an interest in documents associated with crime and with acts deemed immoral or improper by those in power. Court records, legal statutes, and quasi-legal texts—such as officially authorized statements codifying orthodox and unorthodox behavior, or inquisitorial interrogations—often give us rare windows onto the actions and sometimes even thoughts of ordinary people who could not or typically did not write things that would end up in archives. Such documents, by defining the acts that the state considered a threat to social order, can give us a feel for the experiences of those whose lives left relatively few traces in the historical record.

Interestingly, studies based on such sources are often able to contribute to understandings of gender roles and ideas about sexuality. Emmanuel LeRoy Ladurie's classic village study, *Mountaillou: The Promised Land of Error* (1975), was based on the records of a fourteenth-century inquisitorial investigation. Its chapters include "Body Language and Sex" and "Marriage and Love," among others. And the insights provided into early modern French understandings of gender roles are one of the great strengths of *The Return of Martin Guerre* (1983) by Natalie Davis, another pathbreaking contribution to the genre, which was based on a famous court case. In China studies, the most widely read foray into this genre is undoubtedly Jonathan Spence's *The Death of Woman Wang*. Its eponymous heroine is a figure who is known to posterity only because of a series of actions that violated laws of the Qing dynasty (1644–1911). Some of these are actions she herself took, such as running away from an unhappy marriage to join a lover. Others are acts committed by her husband: most notably, his killing her after she returned to him.

Next to Spence's book, perhaps the best-known English works to use Chinese legal proceedings and investigations of crimes to shed light on historical phenomena, including ideas and practices linked to gender roles and sexuality, are a series of overtly fictional works. These are the "Judge Dee" mystery novels of R. H. van Gulik, which detail the exploits of a famous magistrate who lived more than a millennium ago but which are based largely on Chinese novels written during the Ming dynasty (1368–1644) and, hence, often reflect that era as much as any earlier one. Van Gulik makes no bones about the fact that they should be treated as works of historical fiction as opposed to scholarship. He does, however, do a good enough job at making the stories hew close to plausible historical reality to make the books effective texts for use in the classroom as supplementary texts. *Poets and Murder: A Judge Dee Mystery* concerns a Chinese poet accused of whipping her maidservant to death, bringing to life issues of gender and class and how they are dealt with by the legal system. Van Gulik was a Dutch sinologist who wrote a carefully researched and still valuable overview titled *Sexual Life in Ancient China: A Preliminary Survey of Chinese Sex and Society from ca. 1500 B.C. till 1644 A.D.* (1961) long before the study of this sort of topic was considered respectable within academic circles (indeed, in order to lend a more scholarly air to the book and to prevent its being read by nonintellectuals as pornography, he translated key phrases into Latin). Despite its title, it has a good deal to say about the Qing period as well as earlier ones, and it provides considerable historical background and detail on the gender ideals discussed in the next two chapters by the historians Janet Theiss and Matthew Sommer, respectively. However, Charlotte Furth, whose chapter appears in part 6 of this book, has criticized *Sexual Life in Ancient China* for its romanticized claim that ancient Chinese were sexually liberated.

The following chapters by Theiss and Sommer, then, follow a well-established tradition in their discipline in using legal materials to illuminate late imperial ideals of femininity and masculinity. Theiss notes that historians of mid–Qing China typically describe femininity with reference to the "cult of chastity"—the state system of awarding plaques and money for the construction of ceremonial arches and shrines for widows who refused remarriage or committed suicide upon the death of their husbands—and women who committed suicide to prevent a violation of their chastity. Lineages and communities promoted widow chastity as a marker of respectable status. By using criminal case records about marital homicides, adultery, sexual assault, and widow remarriage, Theiss penetrates the official and elite discourse in order to show how the chastity cult functioned in the context of actual social practice and among groups outside the literate elite. An apparently happy marriage is pushed toward tragedy when the husband murders his wife with her sewing scissors not only for teasing him about his "small stalk" but also, more importantly, for implying that he is unable to produce sons and—most importantly—for saying that after he died she would remarry. A young woman who likes to use makeup barely manages to convince the magistrate that an attempted rape was uninvited, by demonstrating her obedience to her mother-in-law. A widow who jealously guards her independence and carries on extramarital sexual affairs is socially ostracized and slandered. Theiss notes that a woman identified as a "shrew"—a woman who is verbally aggressive, sexually immoral, and physically strong—was considered a justified target of rape and homicide; therefore, in such cases the attacker and his defenders often attempted to demonstrate that the victim was a shrew, while the victim's side attempted to show that she was chaste and filial. The significant contribution of this chapter is to demonstrate that female chastity was indeed a powerful ideal, but that it was also much more than a rigid ideology; rather, it was a fluid ideal often used in creative ways in everyday power struggles between men and women and between family members and neighbors. Thus, notions about chastity were not only the concern of women; everyone—men, women, families, communities—had a vested interest in monitoring and manipulating them.

Both Spence and Theiss draw upon the stories of Pu Songling (1640–1715) for depictions of widows and shrews. Several translations of stories from his *Liaozhai zhi yi* (Strange Stories from a Chinese Studio) are available.

If the defense of female chastity is the pivotal issue in the legal treatment of women, then the defense of patriarchal authority is the pivotal issue for men. Sommer observes that under Qing law a man was permitted to have sexual intercourse only with his wife and concubines. Under the category of "illicit sexual intercourse," homosexual anal intercourse had been banned since at least the sixteenth century. The ultimate goal of the Qing regulation of sexuality, he argues, was to defend a Confucian, family-based social order against marginal, outsider men who were regarded as predators on the women and boys of the household. Sexual predators were members of a bigger category of "dangerous males" who loomed large in Qing law. Such men were characterized as "bare sticks" *(guang gun)*, or men without roots (family) and branches (children), whose erect "sticks" *(gun*, a slang word for penis) threatened the social order. Celibate Buddhist and Taoist monks, interestingly enough, fell into this category and were singled out for greater punishment for sexual offenses than nonclergy. Men prosecuted for both homosexual and heterosexual rape were typically low-status, unmarried males in their early thirties. Victims of homosexual rape were typically from poor but reputable families, unmarried, and teenaged; the crimes were typically reported by a father or senior relative. Any man who had been anally penetrated was no longer considered "pure" *(liang*, the word translated as "chaste" with respect to women), and to be a victim of rape one had to first be "pure." By contrast, a woman who had been penetrated by her legal husband was still considered pure, and an attack on her virtue could legally be defined as rape. In addition to contributing further information about native Chinese attitudes toward homosexuality before extensive Western contact (discussed in the introduction to this book), Sommer's chapter is important because it outlines the standard of "normative masculinity" that was reinforced by Qing law, and reveals the contempt, distrust, and harsh legal treatment suffered by men who did not conform to it. Taken together, Sommer's and Theiss's chapters show how both women *and* men can be oppressed by hierarchical gender systems that allow legitimate power only to certain categories of men. They show how a widow could use her social marginality to carve out a degree of independence and sexual freedom denied to wives and concubines, but they also seem to indicate that, compared to the married patriarch, the status of a marginal, unmarried male offered very few advantages.

## COMPLEMENTARY READINGS

Pu Songling [P'u Sung-ling]. *Strange Stories from a Chinese Studio.* Trans. Herbert A. Giles. London: T. W. Laurie, 1916.

———. *Chinese Ghost and Love Stories.* Trans. Rose Quong. New York: Pantheon, 1946.

———. "Marriage as Retribution." Trans. Wang Chi-chen. *Renditions* 17–18 (1982): 41–94.

Spence, Jonathan. *The Death of Woman Wang.* New York: Viking, 1978.

van Gulik, R. H. *Poets and Murder: A Judge Dee Mystery.* Chicago: University of Chicago Press, 1996.

CHAPTER ONE

# Femininity in Flux:
# Gendered Virtue and Social Conflict
# in the Mid-Qing Courtroom

*Janet M. Theiss*

Historians have long described notions of womanhood and the social conditions of women during the Qing dynasty (1644–1911) with reference to the so-called cult of female chastity. In its narrowest meaning, the term *chastity cult* refers to the state system of awarding honorific plaques and money for the construction of ceremonial arches and shrines for widows who refused remarriage or committed suicide upon the deaths of their husbands, and for women who committed suicide to prevent a violation of their chastity. Construed more broadly, the notion of the chastity cult in the late Ming and early Qing encompasses a society-wide movement to extol chaste women as cultural heroes and promote the norms of feminine behavior they symbolized by building shrines to them, publishing their biographies, and recording their names in the thousands in local gazetteers. Chastity discourse did not monopolize the construction of femininity in the Qing, but, as this chapter will demonstrate, chastity lay at the heart of the paradigm of virtue that informed notions of gender difference and norms of proper behavior in mid–Qing China.

The chastity cult had its origins in the Yuan dynasty (1279–1368), when the state issued new regulations specifying the age, social status, and length of widowhood required for official recognition of faithful widows, thus for the first time systematizing what had until then been a rather random and occasional process.[1] The practice of widow chastity spread dramatically during the Ming (1368–1644), but these Yuan regulations continued to provide the framework for the state's approach to chastity honors, though the state continually tinkered with social status criteria of eligibility.[2] Finding widow suicide and, not incidentally, foot binding abhorrent, the first three Manchu emperors of the Qing dynasty attempted unsuccessfully to ban these practices and discontinue state honors for widow martyrs. Not only did the popularity of these practices persist among the Han population, but the bans encountered concerted opposition from Han literati, many of whom in the late seventeenth and eighteenth centuries were avidly promoting a broader orthodox moral revival, within which female virtue was a critical element. So the Qing state established its own political stake in the chastity cult, settling for further control of the inherited Ming system of awards for chaste widows and chastity martyrs and instituting elaborate regulations for the verification of chaste status and the punishment of fraudulent claims.[3]

Over the eighteenth century, as the popularity of the cult grew and the state expanded the categories of eligibility for official canonization, female chastity became a powerful institution in which not only the state and local elites but also commoners in every strata of society had a stake. Social and economic developments in the mid-Qing also worked to enhance concerns about the virtue and propriety of women more generally. This was a time of confusing economic growth, when increasing commercialization and prosperity fueled unsettling geographic and social mobility. The phenomenon of sojourning figured prominently in social commentaries, as ever-larger numbers of merchants, laborers, and literati left wives and families at home for prolonged periods to pursue distant work opportunities. Gender roles and markers of status shifted and were increasingly uncertain as literacy expanded, competition for literati status in the examination system intensified, and distinctions blurred between literati and merchant, respectable and mean, feminine and masculine.[4] In this context, the virtue of women—including not only sexual chastity but also modesty, obedience to family superiors and propriety in manners, speech, and dress—became a touchstone of social quality, moral refinement, and cultural identity. As Susan Mann demonstrates in her chapter in this volume, moral reformers saw widow chastity as an important marker of respectable status and promoted it along with the purification of marriage rituals as a means to ensure proper distinction between women of different classes in the marriage market and quell anxieties about social mobility.[5] The normative significance of chastity thus came to be disproportionately amplified by the concrete social and political value of female virtue as an attribute of family, clan, and community reputation.

Perhaps because of the far-reaching relevance of female virtue as a form of symbolic capital, the preoccupations of the chastity cult tilted the debates over proper expressions of femininity, the nature of womanhood, and women's role in society toward concerns about propriety and impropriety, the definition of chastity, and the violation of chastity. During the eighteenth century, the heroines of the chastity cult represented only the most extreme ideals of a much broader ethos of chastity that permeated High

Qing society and inspired widespread concern with and controversy over female propriety and virtue in diverse areas of social life. In discussions carried on by scholars, fiction writers, crafters of lineage instructions, and bureaucrats, the requirements of chastity and the propriety of many of the activities common among women of the day—like pilgrimages, pleasure outings, and poetry writing—were thoroughly debated.[6] Indeed, although the High Qing era was arguably the heyday of the cult of female chastity, it was also, paradoxically, a period of unprecedented controversy over the parameters of "proper" female behavior, the requirements of virtue, and the scope of women's abilities and social roles. Yet on all sides of this so-called *querelles des femmes*, for moralists and social critics femininity was pervasively and profoundly entangled with notions of virtue.

Criminal case records involving violations of gender and ethical norms, like marital homicides, adultery, sexual assault, and widow remarriage, provide a unique perspective on shifting and contentious notions of proper femininity because they deal with the norms in the context of social practice and offer glimpses of the values of people outside the literate elite. Qing law recognized women as embodiments of virtue and fulfillers of the social roles of wife, mother, mother-in-law, daughter, and daughter-in-law: it protected female chastity as an aspect of husbandly sexual prerogative and upheld patriarchal family hierarchy by differentially punishing assaults against inferiors and superiors. Yet because courtrooms were arenas for the pursuit of conflicts arising out of local communities and families, they provided a forum within which popular values and beliefs were expressed and contested alongside those represented by judicial officials. The arguments of the *querelles des femmes* were played out in legal practice and social life as people negotiated the limits of propriety in women's behavior and dealt with the consequences of moral transgressions within families and communities. In social practice, the delineation of gender roles and the enforcement of ethical standards were not merely subjects of abstract social theorizing and propaganda but concrete problems that gave rise to the most bitter and lethal forms of conflict.

This chapter explores the significance of chastity-centered virtue in the definitions of femininity and, sometimes, masculinity by examining contentions over female virtue in social conflicts that resulted in criminal cases during the Qianlong reign (1736–95).[7] It traces the theme of female virtue through some of the many variations of femininity manifested in vignettes of social practice: as a component of self-identity, as the fulfillment of a familial role-type, and as an attribute of reputation and source of social leverage. Finally, the chapter examines interpretations of unfemininity, or shrewishness, as a form of resistance to dominant gender norms and as a useful stereotype in social and legal discourse.

## THE INTIMACY OF VIRTUE: CHASTITY AND GENDER IDENTITY

Marriage was the most intimate arena for contesting gender roles and divisions of power and labor between women and men. Marital homicide cases reveal wide areas of disagreement—between men and women, and between judicial officials and those they judged—over the nature of the marriage bond and proper wifely and husbandly behavior. Testimonies in these cases illustrate how internalized chastity norms structured notions of womanhood in ways that affected the texture of family life and social interactions. The profoundly private and often instinctive concerns about the denigration of inner moral integrity and outer moral reputation expressed by both women and men indicate that the cult of chastity cannot be fully explained as state and elite orthodoxy imposed upon the populace at large by means of incentives and punishments.

Consider, for example, the tragic case of Fan Zhaoer, aged twenty-three, the studious only child of a chaste widow and scion of a prosperous lower-gentry family from Hancheng county, Shaanxi, who brutally stabbed his nineteen-year-old wife, Gao Shi, to death in an argument that began with her teasing him about his sexual inadequacy.[8] The couple had been married a little over a year and had gotten along very well with no conflicts at all, Fan explained in his confession:

> Except that because my stalk is small, my wife often complained with a joke and a smile, which I took as a marital jest and not something heartfelt. Then [one day] . . . my wife and I were going to bed, and she said further that I was delaying her from having a son and thus ruining her life. I got a little angry and said, "This is also your fate! Drop it! It's useless to complain." [One day a couple of months later] . . . I went out and drank a few cups of wine. Returning toward evening, I went into the study for a while. After the first watch I went home [to living quarters in the house]. Mother was already asleep, and when my wife saw that I was home she also undressed to go to sleep. As I was undressing for bed, I joked with my wife, thinking we would have marital intimacies. My wife said, "Such a useless thing as yours! What sort of uproar could it stir up? Why bother to afflict people's daughters?" I held back my anger and said, "Whose stalk have you seen that's bigger?" To my surprise, my wife took offense and reproached me that what I said was not worth listening to. Then she started to curse and quarrel with me. She also said that after I died she would marry someone else. I cursed back at her and she spewed out more and more abuse and insults.

In a fit of irrational fury, he grabbed her sewing scissors and stabbed her repeatedly. Summing up his motives, Fan finally stated, "My wife did not know shame, repeatedly complaining that my stalk was small, and finally said that when I died she would remarry, the kind of words that cut off feeling and sever obligation."

This extraordinary confession offers a striking glimpse of how orthodox chastity norms could be internalized, reinterpreted, and mingled with feminine and masculine identity. Aspiring to elite literati status, yet only one or two generations away from their commoner background, lower-gentry families like the Fans and the Gaos, each of which had men who acquired their degrees through purchase rather than the more legitimate path of completing the examinations, were particularly sensitive to the implications of chastity norms for social reputation.[9] Public reputation is not at stake in this case, yet concern with a virtuous self-image is clearly an issue in this most private of conflicts. Gao Shi's willingness to speak frankly about sexual matters with an air of savvy and self-confidence runs counter to our expectations of young gentry brides such as Gao Shi, presumed by many social commentators to pass their days in sheltered diligence, engaging in tasks like sewing and needlework. Hints of Gao Shi's own day-to-day activities appear in the arrangement on her *kang* [heated platform for sleeping and working] of her sewing basket and scissors, which, ironically, became her irate husband's weapons in her murder. Her mother-in-law suggested her success in fulfilling the difficult role of the young daughter-in-law, commenting, "My daughter-in-law was always a good person and they were considered a harmonious couple."

Lacking any evidence of her literacy or social life, we are left to wonder at the possible sources of her awareness of sexual matters: erotic literature, bawdy drama, and female friends or relatives were all common sources of sexual knowledge among women in fiction and all were blamed by moralists for their corrupting influences on women.[10] More striking than her knowledge is her seemingly paradoxical combination of sexual sarcasm and sensitivity to issues of propriety. Fan portrayed her as having no qualms about teasing him about his small penis, but when he shot back with the query about who else's genitals she had seen for comparison, implying that she had been unchaste, she flew into a rage. This suggests that, although her image and identity as a chaste wife were so important to her that she was extremely sensitive about the slightest hint that she might be unvirtuous, she did not find sexual banter and teasing to be incompatible with chastity.

Fan, for his part, admitted he was willing to accept a certain amount of lighthearted teasing at his expense, initially understanding it to be a normal part of marital repartee. But when Gao Shi suggested that he was incapable of fathering children, he began to feel that her bedroom banter carried a serious undertone that was not at all funny in its doubt about his ability to fulfill his Confucian masculine duty as producer of sons. In the wake of her betrayal of the bonds of marital loyalty and his own brutal revenge, he reassessed the propriety of her sexually explicit teasing, ending his confession with the judgment that his wife "did not know shame." Narrating the sequence of events in their final encounter, Fan indicated that in his fateful response to her teasing he had been annoyed and had intended to be hurtful in questioning her chastity, knowing that this would be a touchy issue for her. But what finally pushed him over the edge into homicidal fury, he claimed, was her declaration that she would not remain chastely loyal to him after his death.

Oddly, the magistrate concluded that the final straw for Fan was that his wife refused to have sex with him, a quite common catalyst for domestic violence in many other cases, but clearly an oversimplification of the conflict in this case. Wifely chastity here was not simply a matter of patriarchal sexual prerogative: it was more profoundly implicated on an emotional level both in feminine moral integrity and in masculine pride. In her fury, Gao Shi appears to contradict herself, one minute taking offense at the very suggestion that she might be unchaste, then in the next vowing to violate her chastity deliberately to hurt her husband. Yet from her perspective, there was no contradiction: precisely because of the high value husband and wife placed on her chastity, she could indeed use chastity discourse self-consciously to, as Fan put it, "cut off feeling and sever obligation." The very fact that this discourse could have carried such enormous emotional weight—as the medium of the most intimate, most private of marital arguments—reveals powerfully the degree to which these norms were internalized by women and men. Ordinary people could and did express love and its loss in the language of female chastity.

## DISCERNING PROPRIETY: FEMININITY AND FAMILY AUTHORITY

If the stakes in the chastity cult were personal, so too were the interpretations of the parameters and requirements of female virtue. Criminal cases indicate widespread belief in the importance of female chastity for self-identity and social reputation, but they also reveal that there was no consensus about its meaning or its implications for women's demeanor and behavior. In their discussions of the importance of feminine virtue and methods for its promotion, eighteenth-century moralists, jurists, and writers of lineage instructions usually imagined the ideal woman of virtue secluded in the inner quarters of her home, sheltered from casual contacts with people—especially men—outside the family of her husband or her natal family if she were not yet married. A threat to her chastity could only result, then, from a violation of the sanctity of the inner quarters by an outside intruder, or from her own transgression of the parameters of proper feminine behavior. The first question posed in the adjudication of cases of adultery, sexual insult, assault, or rape was always that of how the woman came to be in a situation where contact with a man outside her immediate family was possible.

Criminal cases, however, depict a society within which very few women, aside from the leisured elite, lived and worked in circumstances conducive to adherence to this strictest model of virtue. Women's work and leisure activities frequently took them outside the inner quarters. Most of their activities appear in criminal cases to have been routine and uncontroversial, but some, like conversing with male neighbors, visiting natal relatives, and going to temples and operas, were subjects of great contention not only among social commentators but between spouses and among family members. Arguments about the propriety of these sorts of activities for women were the focus of a large proportion of domestic violence cases and of many misunderstandings between neighbors.

In the absence of normative consensus about so many aspects of women's behavior, problems of propriety were often treated as problems of authority. Sexual propriety, in particular, was closely linked with obedience in the moral interpretation of feminine behavior. In countless cases of marital discord over ambiguous and contested female behavior, it was not the activity itself but the context of authority that determined its acceptability. The element of disobedience often marked an activity thought by a wife to be harmless as improper in the eyes of her husband. In a case from 1780, one Sun Tan ended up stabbing his wife to death after a prolonged feud that started with her making an overnight trip to light incense at a temple fair. He had expressly forbidden her to go, saying that there would be no one to care for the children in her absence. When she disobeyed, he suspected she was having an affair, even after he confirmed that she had stayed with a female relative. His wife's disobedience, an affront to his husbandly authority, automatically conjured up worries of sexual impropriety.[11]

Just as a woman's disobedience to husband or parents-in-law could serve as "proof" of her impropriety, obedience could work in a woman's favor as "proof" of her uprightness in muddled situations where words or gestures were misinterpreted. One night in 1766, a man named Wang Junshi sneaked into the house of a farming family in Haozhou county, Anhui, intending to have sex with the young daughter-in-law of the household, Wei Wang Shi.[12] Unbeknownst to him, however, she had gone home to her natal family's house for a visit that day; so when Wang sneaked into the house in the dark, he instead caressed her sixty-year-old mother-in-law, Wei Guo Shi, who jumped out of bed and grabbed him.

The critical judicial question for the magistrate in this case, as in all cases of illicit sex, was whether this was an attempted rape or a bungled tryst to which Wei Wang Shi had consented. Although she herself was absent from the scene of the crime, her character and demeanor as a woman implicated in a crime of illicit sex were of central importance in assessing the nature of the crime. In this case the defendant had in fact had prior contact with the woman. Arriving in the village some four months previously to seek a living as a peddler of baubles, Wang had struck up a friendship with another young bachelor, Guo Shisong. One day a few months later, the two passed by the Wei house and stopped to drink from the well outside the gate. Guo entered the Wei's courtyard to borrow a jug and ran into Wei Wang Shi, who handed him a jug and responded politely to his queries about her family's health. After she returned to the house, Wang commented that the young woman, whom he had never seen before, was very attractive. Three days later, he asked Guo whether the village had any improper women with whom he might start an affair. Guo told him that there was only Wei Wang Shi, whom, he suspected, "was a bit improper." Although he had never really had much interaction with her, he noticed "she likes to make herself up and is always giggling and joking with people, so how could she be a proper woman? If I could seduce her gradually, I could start something up [with her]. It's just that she has a father- and mother-in-law and husband, and also because I see her father-in-law every day it has not been convenient to try anything."

Guo explicitly linked the woman's care for her personal appearance and her sociable demeanor with sexual impropriety despite her respectable status as a married woman and her maintenance of a properly cloistered lifestyle that had prevented these men from knowing anything concrete about her. For these men on a quest for a sexual partner, cultivated beauty and social charm signaled feminine allure and hinted of sexual openness. Tantalized, Wang asked him how they might get access to her, and the two of them hatched the plan that resulted in Wang's abortive seduction attempt.

Contrasting the assumptions of these two would-be paramours with those of the women reveals that the appearance of feminine virtue or its lack is very much in the eyes of the beholder: here men and women read the signs of femininity in divergent ways. According to the most orthodox standards, Wei Wang Shi had behaved improperly simply by engaging in conversation with a man who was not a member of her immediate family. Guo's testimony suggested, moreover, that she often conducted herself in such an open manner with outsiders. So prominent and so vulnerable was female propriety in common social discourse that, despite the fact that Wang had broken into her house and fondled her mother-in-law, it was Wei Wang Shi's chastity that was questioned and the burden of its proof rested with her and her family. They thus had a powerful incentive to present her in the most virtuous terms possible to convict the defendants of attempted rape and to avoid the social stigma that would accrue to the family from the slightest hint of impropriety.

Given these high stakes, it is intriguing that, in defending her character, Wei Wang Shi and her mother-in-law did not deny her fondness for dressing up nor her sociability. Rather, to prove her uprightness, both of them stressed her filiality as a daughter-in-law, a virtue seemingly irrelevant to the circumstances of the case. Wei Guo Shi vouched unequivocally for her daughter-in-law, claiming that she "has always listened to my admonishment and instruction, obeyed me, and been well-behaved. [She] has never done anything improper." This line of defense, echoed in Wei Wang Shi's own testimony, assumed, in stark contrast to the male defendants' reading of her behavior and demeanor, that a woman's sexual propriety was most appropriately assessed by examining not her personal style but her performance as a daughter-in-law, which lay at the heart of the wifely way. The Wei women suggested here that filiality and obedience were sufficient indicators of chastity and that there was, moreover, no contradiction between these three essential feminine virtues, on the one hand, and a lively and outgoing personality and fondness for makeup, on the other. Despite the conservative tone of this assertion of the importance of role-fulfillment as wife and daughter-in-law obedient to family authority, these women were attempting to draw a distinction between personal style and moral substance that ran counter both to common male "readings" of the outward signs of femininity and to most eighteenth-century moralists' constructions of the good woman.

When the magistrate questioned her about her involvement with the defendants, Wei Wang Shi explained, "The men of the house were not home that day, but since [Guo] was on good terms with my father-in-law and often came over to the house, and also because people in my village do not try to avoid each other, I was acquainted with him. So I handed him a jug." Her defensive tone indicates her awareness of a normative standard of female virtue and of the questionable nature of her own behavior when measured against it. In response to the suspicions of the magistrate, she tried to justify her behavior by invoking community customs of sociability that varied greatly and were often more flexible than orthodox norms set down in law or elite commentaries.

The attempts of mother and daughter-in-law to defend the latter's virtue on their own terms and to stake a claim for the legitimacy of variations in local customs and standards of propriety met with tempered success. The magistrate concluded finally that Wei Wang Shi was not exactly an ideal representative of female chastity, but that she had indeed not invited or consented to a tryst with Wang. So he convicted him of attempted rape and Guo of conspiring in the crime. But his summary of the case revealed his disapproval of the young woman's behavior, commenting that she "was a young beauty who liked to use makeup and did not make the least effort to avoid conversation." Like the defendants, he viewed her behavior as mildly provocative and therefore tinged with impropriety, although not egregious enough to warrant punishment.

This case illuminates some of the many fault lines along which disagreements and tensions over the interpretation of feminine behavior might erupt: between men and women, among people of varying family and community statuses, and between local villagers and judicial officials representing state orthodoxy. In the context of such lack of consensus about the content and form of female virtue, a woman's obedience to family authorities was often a sufficient, indeed sometimes the only, measure of her chastity documentable by witnesses. We also see here the importance of appearances, of constructing and maintaining a moral reputation. There was an unavoidable gap between moral ideals that distinguished inner and outer and the muddled realities of women's lives in which the boundaries of propriety were much more fluid and negotiable. This gap made the construction and destruction of reputation a constant source of anxiety for women and a critical arena for the negotiation of definitions of femininity, as the next section will show.

## THE USES OF VIRTUE: REPUTATION AND SOCIAL POWER

The distinction between personal demeanor and the substance of chastity, which was the key point of contention in the previous case, points to one of the most fundamental tensions in the discourse on feminine virtue: that between personal integrity and moral image. In social interactions and conflicts, people experienced and expressed concerns about virtue and its violation in terms of loss of face. Parties to crimes involving violations of chastity, including adulterers, victims of sex crimes, and their families, often weighed the value of justice and redress against the consequences of the loss of face that would accompany public revelation of their violation either through private vengeance or legal action. The standard line in countless testimonies in such cases, that "I was afraid that this disgraceful matter would become known outside," served to justify failure to report many a crime to the local magistrate. This distinction between inner moral integrity and outer moral reputation, and the possible disassociation of the two, structured the workings of female virtue in social practice as symbolic capital that could be used to enhance or destroy the status and reputation of individual women or their families.

A woman's reputation within her clan and community was always of utmost importance in the moral assessment of her behavior. By the same token, slander, meaning here the public revelation of immoral behavior for ulterior motives, could be an extremely powerful weapon in family or community conflict. When a woman's moral reputation was threatened by slander, and there was no context of obvious victimization through sexual assault or harassment, it could be extremely difficult for her to establish her status as a chaste woman in the eyes of those around her and of adjudicating officials. Yet savvy women could and did make use of chastity discourse to defend themselves and sometimes to disguise less orthodox motivations and lifestyle choices.

One very independent-minded widow, Liu Shi, from Hezhou, Shaanxi province, played quite self-consciously on the image of the chaste widow to gain autonomy, to defend herself against her uncle's slander intended to pressure her to remarry, and finally to convince the magistrate that she had

Figure 2. Mencius's mother is cited as a paragon of motherly virtue in the lesson "Motherly Education," in the 1929 primer *Shimin qian zi ke* [Lessons in a thousand characters for citizens], published by *Zhonghua pingmin jiaoyu cujin hui zonghui* [General Committee of the Chinese Association for the Encouragement of Education among the Common People], 1929.

not been involved in his murder.[13] Although chaste widowhood was one of the noblest expressions of virtuous femininity, a widow was particularly vulnerable to suspicion because of the absence of a husband's controlling authority in her life.[14] If chaste, she was legally entitled to control over her late husband's property, which could provide her with the economic means to maintain considerable autonomy. But if she violated her chastity through adultery or remarriage, she forfeited the right to choose to remain unmarried and lost the property to her in-laws—which provided a powerful incentive for them to force remarriage.

Not bothering to embellish her motivation with the standard chaste widow rhetoric, Liu Shi testified frankly that, after her husband died, the family head, Zhao Xiangzhi, "told me to remarry because he wanted to make a little profit out of it. But my son was grown and our family had a few *mou* of land that I could live off of, so I was not willing to remarry." She continued to employ Zhao Qinhai, an older relative hired by her husband to help out on the farm. One day in a drunken fit, Xiangzhi screamed at her, "I know that you don't want to remarry because you have enticed Zhao Qinhai into your house." Outraged by this accusation, which could threaten her independent status and property rights, she shoved him out into the courtyard and her son, under her supervision, broke his legs with a club. When Qinhai later heard the story, he too was outraged. He suggested that, since Xiangzhi was "extremely poor and good-for-nothing," he would surely sue them after his legs had healed, so it would be best to just kill him. Liu Shi allegedly refused to get involved in a murder, but later that night after they had all gone to sleep, Qinhai strangled Xiangzhi.

Liu Shi jealously fought for her independence, asserting herself verbally and through physical aggression in defense of her reputation. Although she invoked the privileged status of the chaste widow, chastity was, by her own admission, a strategy to maintain control of her life, not a moral conviction. The magistrate noted that Qinhai was so humiliated that he was moved to kill, so "did you, a woman, suffer this [humiliation] with no sense of shame?" His implication was that, if she were truly chaste, as a woman she should have been more outraged than a man and motivated to seek revenge or, better yet, commit suicide, the more appropriate and common reaction of women to insults to their chastity. This widow was not demonstrating the expected degree and form of feminine vulnerability and humiliation. Her response reflects her eminently practical instinct for self-preservation: "At first, I was extremely humiliated and I shoved him out the door. Then, I and my son broke his legs and my anger subsided. . . . He was the head of my family. Would I dare to kill him?" She stressed, "I did not remarry and could live on my own. Why would I want to kill him when I would face prosecution?" Self-reliant, self-defining, and possessing great self-control, Liu Shi was not in the least moved to make herself a suicidal victim for chastity, and neither did she want to throw away her independent life foolishly in a murderous revenge. Despite his initial suspicions about her involvement in illicit sex and murder, the magistrate accepted her story, describing her in his final summary of the case as a "chaste widow" and sentencing her only for beating a family superior.

In an era when chastity mattered deeply to most people, any crack in the fragile surface of her moral reputation put a woman in danger of slander, blackmail, and their dire social and economic consequences: shame, divorce, and dispossession. Yet as Liu Shi's case demonstrates, women could reshape the contours of virtuous femininity to suit their own needs for power and autonomy as long as they invoked the familiar models of virtue as the framework for their actions. Sometimes, however, the maintenance of female chastity itself forced a woman into the normally improper behavior of challenging the patriarchal authority within her family. Chaste widows who resisted the demands of their in-laws to remarry are the most familiar victims of this contradiction between the values of chastity and family hierarchy. The widow Liu Shi, despite the limits of her victory, successfully defined herself as a chaste woman without conforming to stereotypes associating virtue with passivity, obedience, and weakness. Through deft use of the rhetoric of the chaste woman outraged by an offense against her virtue, she masked her exercise of domestic power, forceful personality, sharp tongue, and assertive defense of her interests in confrontation with family authority. Had she not played the chastity card, all of these qualities could well have led witnesses and the magistrate to dismiss her as an immoral, and thus culpable, shrew.

## THE UNFEMININE WOMAN: SHREWISHNESS AS SOCIAL STRATEGY

Nothing illuminates more clearly the inseparability of femininity and virtue, or the limits of women's power to reinterpret them, than the experiences of women who flouted orthodox gender norms and tried to live outside the structures of patriarchal authority. Ignoring the salience of reputation, some women made use of unvirtuous behavior to garner a measure of social distance and control over their lives. As we will see, this involved a dangerous gamble. If chastity discourse could be used by women for leverage in conflicts, so too could stereotypes of shrewishness be deployed against them.

One widow, Li Shi, from Jimenzhou in Hubei, was able to capitalize on her reputation for shrewishness to carve out a space for a highly independent lifestyle for herself.[15] Shortly after her husband's death in 1728, she began an illicit relationship with her late husband's cousin, Li Huanbang, also a widower. For almost twelve years, they continued their affair undisturbed, even after he moved in with her when she sent her son away to make his own living. Fellow villagers Liu Dahan and Liu Qunyi testified that the couple avoided community censure even though they had been "having illicit sex for many years and all the local folks knew about it, because Li Shi had a personality like a spiteful scorpion, so nobody dared to provoke her."

In 1739, Li Shi's life began to unravel and the drawbacks of her autonomous yet solitary lifestyle became evident. After a long absence, her son moved back to her house with his wife, so Huanbang moved out. Discovering that his mother had mortgaged all of their land to a neighbor, Liu Qunyi, he decided to redeem it back but came to blows with him over the terms of repayment. A month later, Li Shi borrowed some grain husks from a distant relative of her late husband, Liu Qizhen, also a widower, and in lieu of paying him back, began to sleep with him as well. A couple of months after this, Qunyi's dog killed the Li's pig. When Li Shi confronted him, the feud between the two families intensified to the point that the Lis never spoke to the Lius, who claimed that after this they did not have the nerve to even walk past her gate since her temper was so bad. One night after getting drunk, the first lover, Huanbang, got into a fight with Qunyi and Dahan, in the course of which they brought up the disgraceful matter of his affair with Li Shi. Furious, she decided to cut off all relations with Huanbang because she was afraid that, given their feud, Qunyi would make trouble for her. She testified, "It's true I resented Qunyi and those people, so I feared that, if Li Huanbang continued to come to my house, they would bear a grudge and stir up trouble." Since Li Shi refused to take him back, Huanbang frequently went to her house to harass her, beating her, breaking her furniture and dishes, and finally burning her wheat. "I was cheated and oppressed by him to no end," she stated. "My son and daughter-in-law did not dare to interfere and I had no family to speak up for me. Only Liu Qizhen was intimate with me." She and Qizhen finally decided it would be best to kill Huanbang to avoid further trouble, and they devised a plan to do just that.

Clearly a woman who did not care about morality or reputation, Li Shi attempted to declare her independence from dominant gender and ethical norms and did in fact exercise a large degree of control over her own life. Her position as a widow with almost no relatives, but a small amount of land available for her use, gave her room for maneuvering. Yet her independence, particularly because she used it to carry on illicit sexual relationships, entailed the sacrifice of all social ties to her community.[16] The extent and consequences of her isolation emerged in the course of her feuds with neighbors and, finally, with her lover: she had no one to turn to for support or assistance in times of trouble. Although her son showed some interest in the family property, he and his wife had long been estranged from Li Shi. When they moved back into her house, they lived in separate quarters, completely ignoring her. Her daughter-in-law said, "My husband and I did not venture to protect Mother-in-Law's evil household." Having abdicated her role as mother, she could hardly command filial support from her son.

In spite of her disdain for moral norms and her social isolation, Li Shi was vulnerable to slander both because of her independence and her sexual impropriety. She herself admitted the limits of her nonconformity when she showed that she could be upset by fellow villagers airing her "disgraceful affairs" in public. Although her long relationship with Huanbang was well-known to the community, the neighbor Liu Qunyi, in voicing this hushed and ignored immorality, somehow crossed a line for Li Shi, causing her to worry for the first time about her reputation. It was not, however, that she was concerned with appearing unvirtuous. Not only was it far too late to salvage any shred of public image for herself, but she still seemed genuinely unconcerned about moral integrity. What did worry her was the way in which Qunyi raised the issue only in the context of his ongoing feud with her and her son about the mortgage deal and the loss of the pig, matters that had immediate relevance for her material well-being. The emergence of her illicit sex as a point of leverage for Qunyi exposed her weakness in this regard, and Shi feared trouble on account of it. Although "tolerated" for years because of her "shrewish" personality, her sexual immorality always represented the limits of her control over her life and the vulnerability of her independence. It was, in a sense, a moral time bomb for her, which could be set off at any time by anyone wishing to manipulate her for any reason, as soon as exposing her behavior became useful.

The description of Li Shi's shrewishness conforms to a paradigmatic portrait of the unvirtuous woman that appears repeatedly in testimonies and judicial commentary. Such women are described as having a "ferocious and wild temperament," and as "throwing irrational tantrums" in conflicts. In adultery cases, the tropes of characterization usually include lust and illicit sexual behavior, which complete a portrait of the shrew very closely resembling those in fiction of the period.[17] Reflecting yet another level of the linkage between virtue, obedience, and femininity, these tropes describe behavior and personality that are at once improper, disobedient, and unfeminine. In a society where the value of female virtue was so inflated, the shrew's lack of sexual virtue and flouting of family authority made her inherently unfeminine, while her unfemininity was seen, in turn, to be immoral.

## THE SHREW DEFENSE: STEREOTYPES
## OF UNFEMININITY IN THE COURTROOM

Within the courtroom, during a period when so many behaviors and social interactions were morally ambiguous, the depiction of a woman as a shrew could bring a messy conflict into moral focus. In the judicial context, only virtuous women could be authentic victims, while the unvirtuous were often saddled with moral responsibility for crimes, even those committed against them. This moral assessment did not necessarily correspond to the legal judgment about guilt, nor did it preclude a final verdict based strictly on the relevant statutes. As we saw in the case of the widow Liu Shi, a chaste woman might retain her moral status even though convicted of assaulting the head of her family. Yet, in other cases, a shrewish murder victim could be deemed morally responsible for the crime, despite her murderer's conviction.

Male defendants often tried to depict women as shrews to detract from their own responsibility for a crime. Projecting an image of passivity and weakness could be useful for a male murder defendant; furthermore, the unvirtuous, unfeminine woman could be seen as undermining his masculine identity and authority: if she were a shrew, her male opponents must be henpecked, cuckolded, or simply weak. In a 1740 case from Qizhou, Zhili, the unvirtuous woman served as both a useful foil for a male defendant and an emasculating threat: in this case a man murdered his cousin's former wife because he believed that she had humiliated his family by having an affair and then scheming to divorce her husband and marry her lover.[18] The defendant, Zhu Sanpu, tried to convince the magistrate that his victim was a lascivious woman whose improper behavior had brought on their conflict, in which he was the underdog defending himself against her aberrantly unfeminine attack. According to Zhu, his cousin, Ning Liuer, a poor wage laborer, sold his wife, Li Shi, to a neighbor, Jin Zhonghui, because she wasted his wages on drink and was frequently seen in the company of Jin, so that villagers had begun to gossip about there being an affair. When Li Shi and her father had started complaining that he could not support her, Ning had decided, "I could not control her, so I told her to go and find another husband." When Jin and Li Shi's father offered Ning three thousand cash, he, like many poor men eager to get rid of an unwanted wife, readily signed the contract to sell Li Shi to Jin and moved away to a neighboring county.

Far less complacent about the deal, Ning's cousin, Zhu Sanpu, felt Li Shi had disgraced his family by "conspiring" with her father and Jin to cuckold Ning. Some eight months after the wife-selling, he discovered that sorghum from his field was missing. Later that evening, he heard Li Shi also yelling in the street about someone stealing her sorghum and thought she implicated him. In a huff, he ducked into a wineshop and got drunk. When he emerged, she was still shouting in the street. He wanted to hit her to "let off steam," he testified, but "since Li Shi was ferocious, wild and very strong, I would be no match for her." So he went to fetch an ax and hacked at her head from behind, but the ax head fell off. At this point he wanted to escape, but "Li Shi turned and grabbed me, knocked me down and pinned me on the ground. I struggled, but could not get up. I also thought about how Li Shi was always such an improper person and got the idea to kill her." So he grabbed the ax again and hacked her to death.

In court, in order to imply his own weakness and lack of control, Zhu justified his actions by drawing on the stereotype of the unfeminine shrew emasculating the men around her. In his confession Li Shi appears as an aggressive, sexually immoral, and physically overpowering woman who plots to overturn male authority and destroy the patriarchal family. Just like the stereotypical "shrew shouting abuses without provocation," she cursed in vulgar fashion in the streets and had almost superhuman physical strength to match her foul tongue and evil behavior.

This portrayal of Li Shi as an unfeminine and immoral monster was contradicted by her father and Jin, who depicted her as the helpless wife of a good-for-nothing husband that had left her to go hungry and had finally told her to remarry because he could not support her. Jin claimed that the rumors of adultery were false and had emerged when Li Shi asked him to find her husband once when he was away: "She didn't know how to thank me so she made me a pair of shoes."[19] He married her because "I saw that Li Shi was always a diligent and prudent person."

Even without these hints of another side to Li Shi's personality, Zhu's description of conquering his enemy made her out to be so inhumanly tough that it seems like a tall tale. Seeing through the exaggeration, the magistrate noted the unevenness of the match between a woman, however strong, and a man wielding an ax. Commenting that surely, after being hit in the head with an ax, Li Shi would have lost consciousness, he queried, "How could she have pinned you to the ground?" Zhu stuck to his story, emphasizing his helplessness in the face of such a virago: "That Li Shi was abnormally ferocious and wild. She even had the ability to force her own husband to divorce her. How would she fear anyone? . . . Although Li Shi was a woman, she had the strength of a wolf. I couldn't handle her."

In the end, Zhu was sentenced to decapitation after the assizes for intentional homicide. But Li Shi herself was not vindicated. On the contrary, despite his initial doubts, the magistrate suspended his disbelief of Zhu's story and fully adopted Zhu's characterization of Li Shi as a shrew and his version of the feud. Although no proof of any illicit sex in the relationship between her and Jin ever emerged, the magistrate concluded that she did not "uphold the way of the wife and unscrupulously had contact with [him]." Because she was "fierce and shrewish," her husband could not control her. He even accepted the defendant's telling of their final struggle, concluding that since Li Shi was "fierce and powerful," the defendant worried he was no match for her, got his ax, and finally killed her because the thought of how unvirtuous she was caused the idea to "sprout" in his mind.

Although from a judicial standpoint, she was the victim of Zhu's homicidal fury, the magistrate did not give Li Shi the moral status of a victim. Her interaction with Jin and her initiative in getting her husband to sell her made her public fury ultimately improper and disqualified her from portrayal as a victim. Successfully depicted by the defendant as a shrew, she was unfeminine both because of her aggressive demeanor and her purposeful abandonment of her role as wife. In the end, the magistrate found her unfeminine, unvirtuous behavior to be the ultimate cause of the crime against her.

## CONCLUSION

The various cases presented here illustrate the vitality of chastity-centered virtue as a component of femininity in personal identity and family reputation and the consequent potency of contested aspects of proper femininity as a source of social conflict and leverage in everyday life and the courtroom. They also suggest the potency of female virtue or its lack as an integral, but contradictory, part of definitions of masculinity. While female virtue was an effective aspect of male pride, identity, reputation, and authority, female unvirtue signaled emasculation. Yet, although an orthodox paradigm of feminine virtue was widely internalized in some form by people in every sector of society, the concrete components of propriety, the requirements of chastity, and the consequences of transgression were very much in contention. The women whose lives and travails we have glimpsed here were active agents in the production and reproduction of notions of femininity, morality, and propriety. They expressed a diversity of responses to the challenges and conflicts they faced in the fluid world of eighteenth-century China, interpreting norms of femininity in accordance with their own personalities, personal values, and needs. But whether they accepted and pursued conformity with orthodox social and moral gender norms or not, they all had to wrestle with the unavoidable social and symbolic significance of chastity as they worked to define their own identities and construct and control their images. In a society where chastity was a defining component of the feminine, and where female virtue was widely valued as an attribute of reputation not only for women but also for men, families, and communities, the construction of women as virtuous or unvirtuous was an extremely useful and prevalent tool in social conflicts and one whose power women ignored at their peril.

## NOTES

I would like to express my sincere gratitude to the following friends and colleagues whose comments on various drafts of this article have been invaluable: Tobie Meyer-Fong, Patricia Moore, Susie Porter, and Megan Armstrong. Funding for the archival research in 1994–95 on which this article is based was provided by a Fulbright Doctoral Dissertation Research Abroad Fellowship.

1. On the development of state policies promoting widow chastity in the Yuan, see Bettine Birge, "Levirate Marriage and the Rise of Widow Chastity in Yuan China," *Asia Major* 8, no. 2 (1995): 107–46.

2. On the emergence of literati patronage of the chastity cult in the Ming, see Katherine Carlitz, "Shrines, Governing-Class Identity, and the Cult of Widow Fidelity in Mid-Ming Jiangnan," *Journal of Asian Studies* 56, no. 3 (1997): 612–40.

3. On the development of the chastity cult in Qing law, ritual regulation, and social policy, see, for example, Mark Elvin, "Female Virtue and the State in China," *Past and Present* 104 (1984): 111–52; M. J. Meijer, "The Price of a P'ai-lou," *T'oung Pao* 67 (1981): 288–304; and Vivien Ng, "Ideology and Sexuality: Rape Laws in Qing China," *Journal of Asian Studies* 46, no. 1 (1987): 57–70.

4. Social status distinctions were weakened not only by increased economic opportunities but also by state policies in the 1720s, emancipating people in certain hereditary occupational categories that officially had been defined as polluted and thus were forbidden to intermarry with so-called respectable commoners. See Susan Naquin and Evelyn Rawski, *Chinese Society in the Eighteenth Century* (New Haven: Yale University Press, 1987), 117–18. Dorothy Ko, *Teachers of the Inner Chambers: Women and Culture in Seventeenth-Century China* (Stanford: Stanford University Press, 1994), which focuses on the emergence of women poets in the seventeenth century, is the seminal work on the consequences of commercialization and social change for definitions of gender roles, especially proper feminine activities, in the late Ming and early Qing.

5. Susan Mann, "Grooming a Daughter for Marriage: Brides and Wives in the Mid-Ch'ing Period," in *Marriage and Inequality in Chinese Society*, ed. Rubie Watson and Patricia Buckley Ebrey (Berkeley and Los Angeles: University of California Press, 1991); and Mann, "Widows in the Kinship, Class, and Community Structures of Qing Dynasty China," *Journal of Asian Studies* 46, no. 1 (1987): 37–56. T'ien Ru-kang's work has also suggested that the advocacy of orthodox female virtue on the part of literati men was a response to the status anxiety produced by increased levels of competition for official postings. T'ien Ju-kang, *Male Anxiety and Female Chastity: A Comparative Study of Chinese Ethical Values in Ming-Ch'ing Times* (Leiden, Netherlands: E. J. Brill, 1988).

6. Various aspects of this *querelles des femmes* have received a lot of scholarly attention. See, for instance, Susan Mann, "The Education of Daughters in the Mid-Ch'ing Period," in *Education and Society in Late Imperial China, 1600–1900*, ed. Benjamin A. Elman and Alexander Woodside (Berkeley and Los Angeles: University of California Press, 1994); Charlotte Furth, "The Patriarch's Legacy: Household Instructions and the Transmission of Orthodox Values," in *Orthodoxy in Late Imperial China*, ed. Kwang-Ching Liu (Berkeley and Los Angeles: University of California Press, 1990); and Paul Ropp, *Dissent in Early Modern China: Ju-lin Wai-shih and Ch'ing Social Criticism* (Ann Arbor: University of Michigan Press, 1981).

7. This article is part of a larger study involving some seven hundred cases, which take the form of Board of Punishment routine memorials *(xingke tiben)* from the Qianlong reign (1736–95). They were collected during a year of research at the Number One Historical Archive in Beijing, from 1994–95.

8. *Xingke tiben* (Board of Punishments routine memorial), Qianlong 32.7.28, *juan* 209, case 6. Women in case files are usually referred to only by family name. Sometimes both the husband's family name and the woman's natal family name are given. The term *Shi* following a woman's family name indicates that the name is her natal family name. Thus, Gao Shi means "née Gao."

9. On the link between female chastity and male literati status, see Mann, "Grooming."

10. Shen Fu in his 1809 memoir of his marriage, *Six Records of a Floating Life* (New York: Penguin Books, 1983), offers one of the few nonfictional references to women reading erotic fiction in this period.

11. *Xingke tiben,* Qianlong 45.7.2, *juan* 152, case 5.

12. *Xingke tiben,* Qianlong 32.7.29, *juan* 226, case 8.

13. *Xingke tiben,* Qianlong 5.4.4, *juan* 153, case 1.

14. See Mann, "Widows," and Matthew Sommer, "Sex, Law, and Society in Late Imperial China" (Ph.D. diss., University of California at Los Angeles, 1995), 201–91.

15. *Xingke tiben,* Qianlong 5.2.15, *juan* 150, case 8.

16. Independent lifestyles and sexual impropriety did not carry the same consequences for her two lovers: neither of these footloose widowers seems to have been ostracized at all. On the night of the murder, both men were invited to a birthday party for the wife of Li Shi's next-door neighbor.

17. On the depiction of shrews in late imperial Chinese fiction, see Keith McMahon, *Misers, Shrews, and Polygamists: Sexuality and Male-Female Relations in Eighteenth-Century Chinese Fiction* (Durham: Duke University Press, 1995); and Yenna Wu, *The Chinese Virago: A Literary Theme* (Cambridge: Harvard University Press, 1995).

18. *Xingke tiben,* Qianlong 5 run 6.11, *juan* 165, case 3.

19. Women making shoes for men other than their husbands was a frequent source of conflict in many types of cases. The making of shoes obviously carried some connotation of sexual intimacy, yet often women seem to have done this as a favor for a neighbor or friend, sometimes at the request of their husbands, without anyone thinking it improper. Clearly, this was another controversial form of behavior on which no consensus existed in Qing society.

CHAPTER TWO

# Dangerous Males, Vulnerable Males, and Polluted Males: The Regulation of Masculinity in Qing Dynasty Law

*Matthew H. Sommer*

## THE PHALLOCENTRISM OF THE LAW

When jurists in the Qing dynasty (1644–1911) attempted to regulate sexual behavior, how did they conceptualize masculinity? In the relevant legal texts (including codified law and case records), we can discern three basic categories of problematic males: dangerous males, vulnerable males, and polluted males. The logic behind these categories was an absolute phallocentrism that identified the act of penetration with domination, possession, and pollution. The dangerousness, vulnerability, and pollution of males all derived from the threat of penetration out of place.

The dichotomy of sexual orientation familiar today (homosexual/heterosexual) bears no relevance here; to impose it on the Qing evidence would risk, at best, a confusing anachronism.[1] Instead, the hierarchy of roles in a stereotyped act of intercourse (penetrator/penetrated) constituted the definitive framework for conceptualizing gender and sexuality in late imperial China.

As Charlotte Furth has shown, medical discourse in the Ming (1368–1644) and Qing dynasties blurred the lines of sex and gender so that physical difference and change were appraised in terms of capacity to fulfill normative social roles. For example, the most authoritative contemporary medical literature defined "false males" and "false females" (those with "useless bodies") largely in terms of inability to penetrate and to be penetrated, respectively. In a fundamental way, one became socially male or female to the extent that one played a specific sexual role.[2] Such thinking is equally apparent in the juridical field. The focus of judicial anxiety, then, was not the *sex* of the object of a man's desire but rather who penetrated whom and in what context.[3]

Hence, the fundamental problem in regulating sexuality was to keep penises in place: to confine the act of penetration to a legitimate marital context. Fear of the penis *out of place* found its most extravagant expression in the imperial institution of eunuchhood: the surgery required for male palace attendants eliminated the means both to impregnate (the testes) and to penetrate (the penis). Ideally, the only penis in the palace was that of the emperor—enjoying sole access to countless female vessels, who were guarded by thousands of emasculated attendants (whom Mitamura Taisuke terms "the artificial third sex"). The walls, moats, and guards encircling the palace's inner quarters provided a security that was sexual as much as it was political, securing the hegemony of the imperial phallus.[4]

According to Qing law, sexual intercourse should take place only within marriage (i.e., between a man and his wife or legal concubine). This principle was extended with uniform rigidity from the Yongzheng reign on, when prostitution was completely banned and the sexual use of female domestics by their masters sharply curtailed.[5] Of course, Qing law forbade heterosexual rape and adultery, but the proscription of extramarital penetration did not stop there. Since the sixteenth century at the latest, homosexual anal intercourse had been banned; during the Qing, laws against sodomy were incorporated into the larger body of laws against heterosexual offenses (under the rubric "illicit sexual intercourse"—*jian*). This synthesis rationalized the regulation of sexuality according to the principle that phallic penetration should take place only within marriage. In all other contexts, the act was banned.

Behind this legislative program, we can discern a number of anxieties that I shall address in turn. But at root, the High Qing regulation of sexuality aimed to defend a Confucian vision of family-based order against the threat of men who were excluded from that order. To what extent this threat was real, and whether it was growing or not, are questions that lie beyond the scope of this article.[6] What we examine here is how Qing jurists *imagined* masculinity and male sexual behavior in the larger context of defending familial order.

## DANGEROUS MALES

### *Legislative Discourse of the "Rootless Rascal"*

The principal target of Qing efforts to regulate male sexual conduct was the marginal man who stood outside of (and presumably opposed to) the family-based social and moral order that underpinned the imperial state. Discussing the crime of "illicit sexual intercourse" (*jian*), which included both consensual and coercive acts outside marriage, a Qing jurist commented, "A man who engages in illicit sexual intercourse debauches the wife or daughter of another man; he ruins the inner female quarters of another man's household."[7] In other words, illicit sexual intercourse represented an assault on the patriarchal household. Specifically, that assault was envisioned as being made by an *outside male* on *another man's* household—a woman's social identity was defined here by her relationship with husband or father. That outside male was an aggressive penetrator in sexual and symbolic terms: he ruptured the boundaries of the household and threatened to violate the women (and young boys) within.

This sexual predator was a subset of a more general stereotype of the dangerous outside male that runs through Qing legal discourse. We find this dangerous male mentioned repeatedly in the Qing code; he appears in some of the earliest laws of the dynasty, but with increasing frequency and urgency in the new ones that accumulated over the eighteenth and early nineteenth centuries. Qing lawmakers used a number of terms in various combinations to characterize him. He was "violent" *(xiong)* and "wicked" *(e)* and was described as one who "habitually fights" *(hao dou);* he was a "worthless, wicked reprobate" *(bu xiao e tu),* a "depraved rogue" *(diao tu).* But most important, he was a *"guang gun":* literally, a "bare stick."

*Gun* means a "stick" or "club" and thus, by extension, a man who stands alone (without "roots" or "branches"). The word implies both a lack of socializing ties and the roguery that resulted, and can be translated as "rascal," "hooligan," or "thug." The prefix *guang* (bare, naked, alone, and so on) emphasizes poverty and lack of a wife. A *guang gun,* then, was a man with no wife, family, or property to discipline him and give him a stake in the social and moral order. (A translation less literal than "bare stick" would be "rootless rascal.")

The Qing code's chapter on "extortion" *(kongxia qu cai)* is the section most explicitly devoted to the rootless rascal.[8] The original Ming dynasty statute that heads that chapter simply extends the robbery statutes to cover extortion; it says nothing specific about *guang gun.* But the substatutes appended over the course of the Qing dynasty did not elaborate on the theme of extortion and instead sought to punish habitual troublemaking by incorrigible individuals or groups. Many of these later substatutes have no direct link to extortion; indeed, over time, as new laws accumulated, the emphasis of the chapter shifted away from that specific crime to dangerous, antisocial behavior in general and to different groups of marginal men thought to threaten the social order.

Running through the judicial discourse of the rootless rascal is a consistent conflation of certain kinds of crime (extortion, kidnapping, rape, seduction, sodomy, intimidation, robbery, banditry, heterodoxy, and so on) with certain kinds of men (Buddhist and Taoist clergy, local toughs, rootless migrants in frontier areas and cities, yamen clerks and runners, dislocated Miao tribesmen, eunuchs who had escaped palace supervision, and the like). One way or another, all of these men were seen as existing outside the mainstream pattern of settled households, the network of family and community relationships on which the Confucian order depended to enmesh and socialize individuals. Their victims were portrayed as "the good people" *(liang min)*—that is, law-abiding commoners: "humble peasants," chaste wives and daughters, and so on. These laws mandated harsh penalties of exile and death not to punish individual crimes so much as to remove incorrigible troublemakers from society altogether.

The most important measure added to the extortion chapter of the code was referred to by jurists simply as the "substatute on rootless rascals" *(guang gun li)*:

> Evil rascals *[e gun]* who scheme to extort from officials or commoners; or who put up placards or make false accusations at any government office; or who extort loans by threat or blackmail; or who, because of a fight, gather a gang to seize someone, falsely accuse him of owing money, and force him to write a promissory note for the alleged debt; or who, having failed in an attempt at extortion, dare to beat or kill someone—in all such cases, if the circumstances are serious and the rootless rascals *[guang gun]* are truly to blame, then regardless of whether money was obtained, the leader shall be immediately beheaded and followers shall be strangled after the assizes.

The earliest version of this law was promulgated in 1656; in 1673, jurists added the following clause in an effort to impose family discipline on disorderly individuals: "The head of the household of any such offender, as well as the offender's father and older brothers, shall each receive fifty blows of the light bamboo. . . . If the head of an offender's household, or an offender's father or older brother, reports the offender, then he who made the report shall be spared, but the offender himself shall still be punished according to this substatute."[9] When first drafted, the "substatute on rootless rascals" obviously related to the original chapter heading of "extortion." But by the beginning of the eighteenth century, jurists had begun citing this law by analogy to punish an increasingly wide range of other crimes, including sex offenses, and this analogy was codified in many new substatutes promulgated during the Yongzheng (1723–35) and Qianlong (1736–95) reigns.[10]

For example, the "illicit sex" *(jian)* section of the code cited this substatute to add extra penalties for certain scenarios of rape. The 1734 substatute against sodomy *(ji jian)* reads (in part) as follows:

> If evil characters *[e tu]* gather in a gang and abduct a young man of good character/commoner status *[liang ren zi di*—literally, "a son or younger brother of someone of good character/commoner status"] and forcibly sodomize him, then the ringleader shall be sentenced to immediate beheading, according to the "substatute on rootless rascals"; the followers, if they have also sodomized [the victim], shall all be sentenced to strangulation after

the assizes. . . . These sentences shall apply regardless of whether the offenders have committed homicide in the course of the rape.

Even if he has not gathered a gang, whoever murders a young man of good
character/commoner status for illicit sex, or lures away a young boy of ten *sui*
or under and forcibly sodomizes him, shall also be immediately beheaded as
a "ringleader" according to the "substatute on rootless rascals."[11]

Other laws cited the "substatute on rootless rascals" in order to punish the
heterosexual variants of these same crimes: gang rape of a woman, rape and
murder of a woman, rape of a young girl, and so on.[12]

Male clergy, both Buddhist and Daoist, were singled out for special scrutiny in the Qing code. By taking vows of celibacy, abstaining from marriage,
and living apart from their natal families, these men stood outside the
mainstream family order in the most basic ways. Late imperial officials were
chronically suspicious of such men, seeing in them the very personification
of the rootless rascal and all the dangers he represented; both Ming and
Qing dynasties made repeated efforts to subject clergy to social and political control by registering them at particular institutions, by making novices
the responsibility of their superiors, by banning the wandering of mendi-
cant clergy, and by prohibiting men from joining clerical orders without
registering and receiving permission from the local magistrate.[13]

The judiciary seems to have been particularly predisposed to suspect
clergy of sexual aggression. According to Yasuhiko Karasawa, "A standard
narrative found in [legal] cases involving Buddhist monks was that of the
monk who attempts or commits illicit sex *(jian)* with women."[14] This bias
was reflected in legislation as well. For example, a Ming law adopted by the
Qing code punished Buddhist or Daoist clergy at temples who seduced or
abducted women, or who "swindle[d] them out of money." Another statute
increased by two degrees the severity of penalties for any sexual offense committed by clergy. A further measure cited the "substatute on rootless rascals"
to impose the sentence of immediate beheading on "lamas, Buddhist monks,
and other clergy who commit[ed] [heterosexual or homosexual] rape and
cause[d] the rape victim's death."[15] Clergy who committed sex offenses
(and were spared execution) would be forced to return to secular life.

To sum up, then, the sexual predator portrayed in Qing legislation was a
subset of a more general archetype of the dangerous male: the "rootless rascal" outside the family order, who posed a multifarious threat to that order.
If we shift from legislative discourse to the actual prosecution of rape, we
find that the "rootless rascal" was more than just rhetoric—although, of
course, there may be an element of self-fulfilling prophecy in the way Qing
authorities targeted men for prosecution. Based on a sample of cases from
central courts, we can develop a rough profile of the typical man who was
prosecuted for rape during the Qing.[16] In fact, the profile is about the same
for both homosexual and heterosexual rape cases. He was single, probably

of disreputable or lowly occupation, and almost certainly poor; there was a good chance he was an outsider unknown to the community in which his victim lived; he was a young man (in his late twenties or early thirties) but old enough, perhaps, to be frustrated at his lack of prospects; and he might well have a record of other disorderly conduct (theft, criminal conviction, drunkenness, and so on). In short, he was a marginal man without property, status, wife, children, or prospects—and hence, with little obvious stake in the social or moral order.

### The Sexuality of the Dangerous Male

What can we say about the sexuality of this dangerous male? He was represented, above all, as an aggressive penetrator—a specifically phallic threat to social order. As mentioned above, the dichotomy that framed thinking about sexuality during the Qing (in law and in social practice) was not one of sexual orientation (homosexual/heterosexual) but rather of a hierarchy of roles in a stereotyped act of intercourse, in which the *penetrator* played the definitively masculine role, dominating and possessing a feminized, *penetrated* object. In other words, the role one played far outweighed in importance the biological sex of one's partner and effectively gendered the partners as male and female, respectively. The evidence in both Qing legal cases and Ming and Qing fiction indicates that a powerful stigma pertained to a male who was penetrated (and thereby feminized), but no corresponding stigma attached to the penetrator, who played the definitively masculine role.[17]

We should note here the phallic connotation of *guang gun*—"rootless rascal" or "bare stick." In vernacular fiction, *gun* (stick) served as a metaphor for an erect penis—as it does in, for example, the late Ming novel *Plum in the Golden Vase,* when the Daoist priest Jin Zongming (himself something of a rootless rascal) prepares to rape a novice: "He manipulated his penis until it was very hard, a stick *[gun]* standing straight up."[18] A study of Beijing idioms states that "'*gun*' ['stick'] means 'penis'; that is why '*guang gun*' ['bare stick/penis'] is slang for a man without a wife."[19] The repeated use of *gun* in legal texts (*guang gun, gun tu, e gun,* and so on) clearly reinforced the image of the rogue male as a specifically *phallic* threat to social order.

Many legal cases portrayed the dangerous male as bisexual in object choice: he pursued both male and female objects while consistently playing the role of aggressive penetrator.[20] But this bisexual targeting of lust in and of itself does not appear problematic; jurists employed no special vocabulary to describe it, nor did they single it out for special explanation or commentary. Rather, it was the dangerous male's utter lack of respect for *all* boundaries and rules that threatened social order.

A fairly typical example is a 1745 case from Suining county, Hunan, in which Long Xiuwen (twenty-two *sui*) attempted to rape and then strangled his neighbor's son, Hu Yanbao (thirteen *sui*). Long was a poor peasant, single and without prospects, who secretly engaged in sexual relations with a neighbor girl, Zhang Wanmei (eighteen *sui*); she was betrothed, but Long planned to elope with her before she could be taken in marriage. One day, however, Long saw Hu Yanbao working in a field and felt aroused by the boy's youth and by the way "he looked so white and clean" *(sheng de bai jing);* so he lured Yanbao to a remote place and tried to rape him. When the boy resisted, Long strangled him. He then mutilated the corpse beyond recognition, hoping that the boy would appear to have been killed and partly eaten by animals rather than murdered; he also hoped that his girlfriend's parents might mistake the boy's corpse for *her* and not think to pursue them. But after being caught with incriminating evidence, Long confessed under torture and was sentenced to immediate beheading (according to the "substatute on rootless rascals") for the rape and murder of "a son or younger brother of someone of good character/commoner status."

The memorial on this case stresses Long Xiuwen's repeated, perverse defiance of all convention. Fornication, elopement, rape, murder, and dismemberment: he seemed willing to violate every conceivable taboo in order to indulge his criminal impulses. But there is no particular emphasis on the fact that he happened to desire both sexes.[21] In the presentation of cases like this one, bisexual object choice seems almost taken for granted, and homoerotic desire is not singled out for any greater or lesser censure than heteroerotic desire.

In vernacular fiction from the Ming and Qing dynasties, we find a complementary image of the aggressive penetrator in the role of the libertine. In terms of object choice, the libertine is bisexual too, although his primary obsession is women. The danger that the libertine represents is his insatiable pursuit of sexual objects. Thus, when Ximen Qing (hero of *Plum in the Golden Vase*) penetrates his page boy, Shutong, the episode seems relatively trivial, but it serves to underscore the protagonist's indiscriminate self-indulgence; Ximen's more dangerous behavior consists of his promiscuous seduction of other men's wives, leaving a series of wrecked households in his wake. Again, when Vesperus (hero of the early Qing novel *The Carnal Prayer Mat,* by Li Yu) finds no female vessel at hand, he substitutes the "south gate" of one of his young male pages; but his energies are spent primarily in the pursuit of other men's wives. These novels present their heroes' transgressive overindulgence as harmful to their own physical health; but more important, it ruptures the boundaries that frame familial and social order.[22]

The fictional libertine differs from the rootless rascal found in legal records by being a member of the privileged elite who enjoys material and social resources and, therefore, rarely falls afoul of the law. But he shares with the rootless rascal the aggressive penetrant role and therefore represented a specifically phallic threat to social order.

## VULNERABLE MALES

### Legislative Discourse and Case Records

If the archetypal dangerous male was the rogue outside the family system who played an aggressive penetrant role, then what kind of male was vulnerable to his sexual predation? Specifically, how did Qing jurists conceptualize the credible male rape victim?

Qing laws against sodomy (homosexual anal intercourse—*ji jian*) dealt almost exclusively with rape (although consensual anal intercourse was banned as well); they consistently characterized the male rape victim as "a son or younger brother of someone of good character/commoner status" or "of commoner family" (*liang ren zi di*). Translation of this phrase is awkward, given the double meaning in legal discourse of *liang*—which literally means "good," with a connotation of honorable, virtuous, or respectable, but which also denotes free "commoner" legal status.

*Liang* conflated morality of conduct and occupation with "good" legal status: the "common people"—*liang min*—were simultaneously the "good people." Below them was a stratum of "mean people" (*jian min*) whose stigmatized occupations and presumably immoral conduct determined their debased legal status. "Mean" status had long been treated as fixed and hereditary, but by the mid-Qing the vast majority of people in China proper (peasants, commercial and artisan classes, and so on) would have been classified as *liang* before the law; still, the law continued to discriminate against certain stigmatized occupations (prostitutes, actors, professional entertainers, some categories of hired laborers, domestic slaves, and so on). The basis for continuing discrimination was no longer heredity but rather the principle that *liang* status depended on respectable occupation and conduct.

The stereotypical victim of homosexual rape came from a law-abiding family of commoner legal status; but specifically, he was a "son or younger brother" (*zi di*) of such a family. Here, we see a significant difference with the corresponding characterization of the female rape victim, who was a "wife or daughter of good character/commoner status" or "of commoner family" (*liang jia qi nü* or *liang ren fu nü*). Wives and daughters were subordinate members of the household primarily by reason of gender; sons and younger brothers were subordinate members of the household by reason of *youth*. (Sodomy legislation says nothing about a "husband" of a commoner family to correspond to the "wife" envisioned as a potential rape victim.) In other words, jurists imagined the male rape victim as a young, junior member of a respectable, commoner family.

The importance of youth is, if anything, even more explicit in the law that addressed "males who commit homicide while resisting rape" *(nanzi ju jian sha ren).*[23] Judges were extremely reluctant to accept such claims of self-defense; they assumed that no man would need to resort to deadly force (usually a knife or other edged weapon) in order to prevent rape. "Why didn't you just struggle free? Why was it necessary to use a weapon?" they would ask homicide defendants who made this claim. The law mandated that only boys of fifteen *sui* or under who had been attacked by a considerably older man, and who could meet an unusually strict standard of proof, might be released without punishment (after paying a nominal fine). In contrast, a female of *any* age who immediately killed a man attempting to rape her would be spared any penalty whatsoever. Women were assumed to be weak enough that they would likely need a lethal weapon to repel a rapist; only a young boy might be weak enough to share this feminine vulnerability to penetration.

This stereotype is borne out by my sample of actual homosexual rape cases pursued by central courts.[24] The youth of the victims (and relative maturity of the rapists) is perhaps the most consistent and striking aspect of the sample: *in every case,* the rapist was older than his victim, by an average of fifteen *sui* in the rape cases and twenty *sui* in the self-defense homicides. The average age of homosexual rapists was thirty-three *sui,* while that of victims (including killers in the homicide cases) was only sixteen *sui.* In cases that involved homicide (of either rapist or rape victim), the homicide itself became the main focus of judicial inquiry and guaranteed prosecution; so if we exclude all such cases, we come even closer to the judiciary's "stereotypical" homosexual rape, in which that crime alone was the focus of concern. In this smaller sample, the average age of victims falls to thirteen *sui*—only eleven or twelve years of age by Western reckoning—strongly reinforcing the stereotype of the credible male rape victim as a very young boy.

Another factor distinguished victims from rapists. Most victims were poor but came from intact family units, and most sexual assaults were reported to the authorities by the father or another senior relative of the victim. This finding should not surprise us, given that Qing sodomy legislation defined the plausible male rape victim as "a son or younger brother of *liang* family." Like heterosexual rape, then, homosexual rape was seen as threatening the integrity of the patriarchal family as much as the person of the individual victim.

### Eroticization of the Young Male

This judicial stereotype of the male rape victim also resonates with widespread evidence that the young male was eroticized as an object of possessive desire. In Qing legal cases as well as in Ming and Qing fiction, the young male was cast in the "female" role as a penetrated object, and the penetrator seems to have been attracted to certain kinds of feminine features regardless of the sex of the individual who possessed them.

Memorials on homosexual rape cases routinely reported that a rapist's lust was aroused when he saw that his victim was "young" (nian you) or "young and beautiful" (shao ai); the latter term carries a strong connotation of femininity and was frequently used in the same context in judicial reports of heterosexual rape. Homosexual rapists explained that (for example) their victims were "young and lovely" (nian shao mei hao), or "had a clean and attractive face" (mian mu sheng de gan jing), or "looked so white and clean" (sheng de bai jing).[25] Just as the bisexual-object choice of rapists warranted no particular analysis, this sort of testimony was transcribed in case reports without comment; clearly, then, the memorialists assumed that no special explanation was necessary to make it understandable to their superiors (ostensibly including the emperor) who would review their reports.[26]

The reason they could make this assumption is that the eroticization of the young male as a penetrated, feminized object was by no means peculiar to a subculture of marginalized males. In Plum in the Golden Vase, males who play the penetrated role are uniformly eroticized for their youth and feminine refinement. For example, an encounter between Ximen Qing and his adolescent page, Shutong, begins thus: "Shutong had been drinking wine, so his fair face was glowing; his lips were red and fragrant, and his teeth were as white as grains of glutinous rice—how could one not be enchanted? At once, Ximen Qing's lust was aroused." Elsewhere we find the following account of the Daoist priest Jin Zongming's attraction to the males he pursues: "Under his supervision he had two novices who were fresh, clean, and young [qing jie nian xiao] and who shared his bed; but this had gone on for some time, and he was getting bored with them. He saw that Jingji had white teeth and red lips, and his face was as white as if it had been powdered. . . . So the priest arranged for Jingji to stay in the same room with him." (The novel mentions in passing that Jin Zongming also patronizes female prostitutes.) [27] In The Carnal Prayer Mat, Li Yu explains the hero's sexual attraction to his pages ("Satchel" and "Sheath"—appropriate nicknames for the penetrated!) in similar terms: "Both boys were attractive; indeed, apart from their big feet, they were on a par with the most beautiful women." The hero prefers Satchel because he is the more "artful" and "coquettish" of the two and can manipulate his buttocks "like a woman." In his story "A Male Mencius's Mother," Li Yu describes the willow-waisted boy Ruiliang as "a woman of peerless attraction," possessing a feminine charm superior to that of a genuine woman.[28]

In all these texts, both legal and fictional, the male sex object appears attractive to the extent that he possesses a certain feminized standard of beauty. Youth, whiteness, cleanliness, clarity of complexion, red lips and white teeth, a willowy physique—all these features are conflated and eroticized.[29] (Ming-Qing pornography depicts both women and penetrated males with lighter skin than their masculine partners.)[30] The aggressive penetrator depicted in these sources seems attracted to the object of his desire more by these gendered features than by the object's biological sex.

This evidence helps us to understand not only the eroticization of young males as feminized objects but also the threat from which "sons and younger brothers of good family" had to be protected. The legal discourse of the vulnerable male is pervaded by anxiety over the ambiguous gender of the adolescent boy, whose adult masculinity has not yet been confirmed by the social and sexual roles taken up with marriage (i.e., the penetrant role of husband and father). Being penetrated feminized a person in a profound and important way: it gendered a biological female as a *woman* (as wife and mother), just as to penetrate gendered a biological male as a *man* (as husband and father). From the point of view of a society and legal regime that radically subordinated women to men, the penetration of a young male threatened to derail his delicate journey to adult masculinity, to degrade or invert his gender.

## POLLUTED MALES AND NONMALES

### The Double Meaning of Liang

In the late seventeenth and the eighteenth centuries, the Qing judiciary formally adapted many of the standards long used for prosecuting heterosexual rape to the analysis and punishment of homosexual rape. Most important, perhaps, was the adaptation of the legal concept *liang* (good) to evaluate the victim of homosexual rape. *Liang* carried a double connotation, of "commoner" legal status (which depended on good family and respectable occupation) but also of good morals. As we have seen, the victim of heterosexual or homosexual rape was stereotyped as a commoner. To distinguish commoner status, Qing law discriminated in various ways against the inferior stratum of "mean" status occupational groups (including actors, prostitutes, slaves, and some kinds of hired laborers); for example, if a person of mean status raped a commoner, then he would receive a penalty far more severe than would someone who raped a person of equal status. If the reverse situation occurred, a commoner rapist would receive a reduced penalty (if prosecuted at all). Presumably, the damage inflicted by rape approximated the stigma already attached to "mean" status, so the perpetrator was guilty of a lesser crime.

But *liang* also implied a judgment of the rape victim's morality, in a specifically sexual sense. In heterosexual rape cases, *liang* meant "chaste"; so, as a "wife or daughter of good character/commoner status" or "commoner family" *(liang ren fu nü* or *liang jia qi nü)*, a female rape victim was credible only if chaste and a commoner as well. Any record of sexual experience outside marriage disqualified her from full consideration as a rape victim (lack of chastity ostensibly mitigating the damage that rape might cause), so her rapist, if prosecuted at all, would receive a reduced penalty. In an important way, the full penalty of death for rape represented a testimonial to the victim's chastity as much as punishment for the rapist.[31]

In applying the concept of *liang* to homosexual rape prosecution, jurists preserved the nuance of sexual morality, but with an important modification. A female who had been penetrated by her husband was considered as chaste as an unmarried virgin; but *any* history of being penetrated anally would disqualify a male from being considered *liang.* Here, we see an essential difference in the way jurists imagined male and female gender: a woman was defined and gendered by her penetrability—but that had to be reserved for her legitimate husband and master. A man was not to be penetrated *at all,* but to penetrate: he was a subject, not an object, of action. From a judicial perspective, there existed no legitimate context for homosexual penetration that corresponded to heterosexual marriage.

A male prostitute was the opposite of *liang* in both senses of the word, since he suffered from debased status and had a history of anal penetration. As early as the Song dynasty (960–1279), sources reported the prosecution of cross-dressing male prostitutes for the offense of *bu nan*—literally, "being not male." As its name suggests, the essence of this crime was gender performance that radically conflicted with normative masculinity.[32] In the Qing dynasty, both cross-dressing and consenting to anal penetration continued to mark males as "not male" in ways that had important implications for rape law.

### Professional Female Impersonators

By Qing legal standards, male actors who played female *dan* roles in opera were doubly debased: in terms of legal status (mean) and gender (female). As entertainers, they could not be treated in the same way as normative, commoner males. Moreover, their identity as female impersonators (whose onstage gender performance often strongly influenced their offstage personae) compromised their masculinity in a fundamental way. Indeed, their debasement had a sexual dimension as well, since actors had long been associated with homosexual prostitution.[33]

A 1653 case from Mancheng county, Zhili (some 150 miles southwest of Beijing), illustrates the extent to which Qing authorities treated such actors differently from ordinary, commoner males. Manchu troops seized two Han

Chinese men who had failed to shave the fronts of their heads (the tonsure was a mandatory sign of submission to the new dynasty, and the archives of the early Qing are full of reports of "rebels" summarily beheaded for non-conformist hairstyle). The two men were accused of rebellion (pan ni); but they defended themselves by claiming to be opera singers who performed female dan roles (chang xi zuo dan)—they were aware of the tonsure requirement but had assumed that it did not apply to them (one of the two had initially shaved his head but later let his hair grow back). Soldiers went to their home village to investigate, and it turned out they were telling the truth—they were the dan performers in a fourteen-man troupe of players—so their lives were spared. It is unlikely that any other Han male without the tonsure would have survived if taken into custody.[34]

What if a female impersonator were raped? In a case adjudicated by the governor of Shaanxi in 1824, two actors who performed dan roles were waylaid on the road and raped. Neither victim had any record of prostitution or other consensual sodomy; nevertheless, the governor argued, given their profession "they cannot be considered 'sons or younger brothers of commoner status'" (liang ren zi di). Since Qing law defined homosexual rape as the violation of a young liang male, the rapists in this case could not be held liable for the full penalty for rape (death). On top of their debased status as entertainers, dan actors in particular already embodied an inversion of gender akin to that which phallic penetration supposedly threatened to effect. Regardless of sexual history, they could not possibly suffer the same degree of harm that a normative male would suffer if raped. Nevertheless, such a crime could not be allowed to go unpunished, especially since it had been committed in broad daylight, on a public road, and by more than one perpetrator. The solution was to reduce the penalty by one degree, so that each rapist was sentenced to a beating and exile, instead of death. This lower penalty balanced the principle of status hierarchy against that of punishment for rape.[35]

Actors and other mean occupational groups were generally tolerated but stigmatized by the law; their pollution and supposed lack of morality helped define, by contrast, all that was "good" (liang) about the "good people" (liang min)—commoners who supposedly adhered to valorized norms of marriage, family, and occupation. Rape law reflected these assumptions; elsewhere, the code made strenuous efforts to separate debased from commoner and to maintain the boundary between. A high priority was to prevent the recruitment of commoner youth into mean occupations, especially acting and prostitution; severe penalties were mandated for those who attempted recruitment, whether by purchase, adoption, marriage, or coercion. Preventing the debasement of commoner youth by such means corresponded to efforts to guard against their pollution by rape.[36]

## Men Who Consented to Being Penetrated

What about the other meaning of *liang*—that is, what if a victim of homosexual rape had a prior record of consensual penetration? As a matter of judicial practice, the results were the same as when a man of "mean" status (like an actor) was raped. For example, in a case of homosexual rape memorialized by the governor of Shanxi in 1815, the victim, Guo Zhengqi, had previously, in the governor's words, been "sexually polluted" *(jian wu)* by another man in a consensual relationship. Guo Zhengqi was a commoner. Nevertheless, the governor reasoned, given his sexual history "there is a difference between [Guo] and a man who is *liang*"; so the rapist's penalty was reduced from strangulation to a beating and exile. In addition, for having consented to penetration by his partner, Guo himself was sentenced to one hundred blows of the heavy bamboo and one month in the *cangue,* according to the provision against "consenting to be sodomized" *(he tong ji jian).*[37]

Hence, a record of "sexual pollution" corresponded exactly to "mean" legal status for purposes of homosexual rape law ( just as in heterosexual rape law): either factor disqualified a male from being considered *liang,* a fact reflected in the lighter sentences meted out if he were raped. Either kind of taint to some extent approximated—and hence, mitigated—the damage that anal penetration might inflict on a normative male. Since a male who was not *liang* could not possibly suffer the full damage of rape, it followed that his rapist should not receive the full penalty for that crime.

In the Manchu banner system, we find interesting confirmation of the pollution or stigma specific to the penetrated male. If a man were found guilty of consenting to be penetrated, not only would he receive the regular penalty mandated by the code (a beating and a term in the *cangue*), but also he would be expelled from his banner registry. Bannermen who played the penetrant role in sodomy offenses would receive civil punishment as well but would not be expelled. In other words, homosexual attraction in itself was not incompatible with bannerman status; but consenting to penetration, and the gender inversion that implied, disqualified one from service.[38]

To the judiciary, the difference between a vulnerable male and one kind of polluted male was consent. The prohibition of consensual sodomy (since at least the sixteenth century) betrays fear not just of the coercive aspect of sexual predation but also of the possibility that the putatively vulnerable male might learn to enjoy a sexual role that radically contradicted the gender order.

## The Cross-Dressing Predator

In addition to the actor who performed female roles, judicial discourse included another, very different manifestation of the cross-dressing male: the imposter who employed female dress as a disguise to facilitate the seduction or rape of otherwise inaccessible women. This sexual predator was a stock figure in Ming and Qing fiction, closely related to the "monster" or "human prodigy" *(renyao)*, who supposedly could switch anatomy from female to male for the same purpose.[39]

The Qing casebook *Conspectus of Penal Cases* (Xing an hui lan) cites three cases of men who were prosecuted for dressing as women *(nan ban nü zhuang)*; but only one seems to fit the stereotype of the cross-dressing sexual predator. Cross-dressing in and of itself apparently did not get a man in trouble with the law; after all, female-impersonating actors were an accepted, if stigmatized, professional group. In all three examples, the men who cross-dressed also played the penetrated role in sexual relations with other men (which was illegal). However, they were prosecuted not simply for violating normative masculinity but rather, in each case, because cross-dressing was seen as part of a larger pattern of dangerous and deceitful behavior.[40] Far from being viewed as passive feminized objects, these men were portrayed as a sinister threat to social order because of their own self-conscious actions. All three (together with accomplices who did not cross-dress) were punished according to the statute on "deceiving the people with heterodox doctrines" *(zuo dao huo zhong)*, a catch-all law cited to punish sorcerers, medical quacks, con artists, religious practitioners suspected of fomenting millenarian rebellion, and so on.[41]

The example in which the perpetrator most closely resembled the stereotypical predator is found in an 1818 case from Hubei involving one Peng Ziran, who "dressed in women's clothes, studied charms and spells, practiced [quack] medicine, and cheated people out of their money." Peng also used his female disguise to facilitate illicit sexual intercourse with two women, one of whom he later tried to abduct. But his true sex was finally discovered by another man, Wang Shixian, who apparently used this knowledge to pressure Peng into submitting to sodomy; the two men then became partners in crime, passing themselves off as husband (Wang) and wife (Peng) for some time, until finally arrested. Peng Ziran was sentenced to strangulation as a "ringleader," under the statute against "deceiving the people with heterodox doctrines"; the statute called for strangulation after the Autumn Assizes (an annual procedure at which most death penalty sentences were reviewed and commuted), but since Peng's crimes were so numerous, a special edict ordered immediate execution. Wang Shixian, as an "accomplice," was deported to Xinjiang to be a slave.[42]

In this case, a cross-dressing predator was found out by another man, who then forced him to submit to a sexual role (being penetrated) that conformed to his outward gender persona. In a sense, then, it appears that the imposter was put in his place and the gendered sexual order restored well before the two men were arrested.[43]

The other two cases of cross-dressing discussed in *Conspectus of Penal Cases* involved no violation of women or other sexual predation. In an 1819 case from Beijing, a young monk named Zeng Liang had played the penetrated role in consensual sodomy with two other monks; he quarreled with one of them, beating and injuring him severely; then Zeng dressed as a woman to try to evade the authorities and, when arrested, claimed falsely, it appears (to get the court's sympathy), to have been raped at age twelve *sui* by the monk he had beaten. Clearly, Zeng Liang had committed multiple offenses, but his cross-dressing had not been intended to facilitate sexual predation, black magic, or swindling. As the Board of Punishment commented, "In the past, when this Board has adjudicated cases of men dressing in women's clothes *[nan ban nü zhuang]*, in any case that has involved violation or seduction of women *[jian yin funü]*, or swindling the common people out of their money *[huo zhong lian qian]*, the offenders have always been sentenced to strangulation, according to the statute on 'deceiving the people with heterodox doctrines.'" But Zeng Liang did not fit this profile; therefore, he received a reduced penalty of beating and exile instead of death.[44]

The third example is an 1807 case from Beijing: one Xing Da had dressed as a woman and pretended to be a "fox spirit" capable of curing illnesses, telling fortunes, and so on in order to cheat people out of their money. He also had engaged in sodomy with an accomplice, and the two men apparently had alternated sexual roles *(hu xiang ji jian)*.[45] There was no evidence that Xing Da had used his female disguise in order to debauch women; nevertheless, the sorcery and swindling earned him the full penalty of strangulation. His accomplice was sent into exile.[46]

I suspect that the prosecution of cross-dressing was extremely rare, and that cross-dressing sexual predators were rarer still. (In fact, most of the cases recorded in *Conspectus of Penal Cases* are exceptional in one way or another because the purpose of such casebooks was to show jurists how to apply codified law to peculiar and complex fact situations.) Although I have searched in Chinese archives through hundreds of Qing criminal cases involving sex and gender, I have yet to see a single actual record of prosecution for cross-dressing in any context. It seems, then, that the image of the cross-dressing predator tells us more about official and elite anxieties than about the practical problems of the judiciary.

The paranoid fantasy about the cross-dresser as sexual predator attempts to make sense of a gender performance that radically conflicts with normative masculinity. An ulterior motive explains it: the *apparent* embrace of femininity is, in fact, a disguise for that definitive form of dangerous masculinity, the aggressive penetrator. Behind a veil of feminine artifice, we discover the all-too-easily comprehensible danger of heterosexual predation. Ultimately then, the cross-dressing predator reflects anxiety less about gender inversion per se than about the vulnerability of chaste daughters and wives.

So the cross-dresser is a nonmale who turns out to be all too male. In this sense, the stereotype recalls the judiciary's chronic suspicion of clergy. Male clergy, too, appeared to be nonmales, a sort of third gender; Qing law tried to reinforce clerical vows by prohibiting clergy from definitively masculine activity (taking wives or engaging in sexual intercourse) and by mandating penalties of extra severity for violations. Apparently, jurists suspected that the vow of celibacy might be no more than a disingenuous facade that masked real motive and intent; that is, they believed that this apparent nonmale, like the cross-dresser, might actually be a predator made all the more dangerous by his disguise.[47]

## CONCLUSION: THE NORMATIVE MALE

In conclusion, what can we say about the standard of *normative* masculinity implied in Qing legal discourse? The normative male was a married, adult householder with a stake in the familial order so valorized by the Confucian state. He was a commoner, a man of respectable family and occupation. He had survived unsullied the delicate journey to adult masculinity; his masculinity was based, like that of the dangerous male, on the sexual role of penetrator—but it was a fully socialized masculinity, harnessed to the roles of husband and father. His centrifugal, penetrative sexuality was disciplined by the filial duty to procreate and by a sober fear of community sanction and imperial authority.

To this normative male, the imperial state delegated considerable authority. For example, a husband could beat his wife, with the complete backing of the state, unless he broke a bone or inflicted worse injury. Even if he murdered her, he risked capital punishment far less than someone who killed an unrelated person—let alone a wife who murdered her husband. The same weighting of penalties reinforced a father's authority over his children and a head of household's authority over servants and long-term hired laborers.

In principle, only the emperor could take human life; even homicide in genuine self-defense was seldom excused. But under exceptional circumstances, even the power to take life might be delegated, so that a head of household could kill with complete impunity. For example, if a man caught his wife in the act of adultery, he could kill her and her lover without penalty, as long as he acted at once. Equally, if a man immediately killed someone who had entered his house at night, then he was spared prosecution. The point here is that a householder could kill to defend the basic integrity and security of his home and lineage against extraordinary threats.

In addition, Qing law mandated that any offspring of an illicit sexual union (be it coercive or consensual) should become the responsibility of their father, the male offender: as the polluted fruits of outside penetration, such children should be excluded from the lineage of the mother's husband. Similarly, if a wife committed adultery or ran away, her husband gained the right to expel her or sell her off in marriage, and she forfeited all claim to his property and children. Each of these measures aimed to safeguard the patrilineal integrity of descent and inheritance against the polluting threat of the outside male.

In the course of prosecution, if a rapist were found to be married, then his interrogators often focused on that fact: why on earth would he commit rape if he already had a wife? Jurists seem to have assumed the *rational* reason for a man to commit rape, either heterosexual or homosexual, to be that he lacked a wife (yet another reason to suspect male clergy). It seems they expected imbalance between the sexes to result naturally in rape.

To what extent this expectation matched social reality we cannot know. But the Qing dynasty's fear of marginal, rogue males should not be dismissed as idle paranoia. For example, as Elizabeth Perry has noted, in rural Huaibei by the nineteenth century, perhaps 20 percent of males went unmarried (given the shortage of marriageable women), and unemployment was a chronic problem. Surplus males constituted a large, fluid, mobile source of labor—and of trouble as well. Such men often left their native villages as beggars, soldiers, or hired laborers but also provided the manpower for smuggling, banditry, and rebellion. Indeed, Perry shows that collective violence in "predatory" and "protective" forms constituted a basic survival strategy; under the right circumstances, endemic low-level violence could grow in scale, and might even explode into rebellion against the imperial state. The ubiquitous, underemployed rootless rascal served as the main recruit for such activity.[48]

The judicial constructs of the Qing dynasty, and especially its attempts to regulate sexuality, must be understood against a social background in which men outnumbered women, so that patriarchal stability was perceived as under constant threat from a crowd of rogue males at the bottom of the socioeconomic scale. The household of the normative male, that microcosm of imperial order, was under siege; the purpose of law was to strengthen its defense.

## NOTES

1. Sexual orientation is certainly a valid category for understanding identity and experience today; but it would be a mistake to assume that a fundamental social identity based on the sex of a person's object of desire has always and everywhere been experienced in the same way. For more on this admittedly controversial topic, see David M. Halperin, "Is There a History of Sexuality?" in *Lesbian and Gay Studies Reader*, ed. H. Abelove et al. (New York: Routledge, 1993); and Edward Stein, ed., *Forms of Desire: Sexual Orientation and the Social Constructionist Controversy* (New York: Routledge, 1992).

2. Charlotte Furth, "Androgynous Males and Deficient Females: Biology and Gender Boundaries in Sixteenth- and Seventeenth-Century China," *Late Imperial China* 9, no. 2 (1988): 1–31.

3. I have covered much of this ground before: see Matthew H. Sommer, "The Penetrated Male in Late Imperial China: Judicial Constructions and Social Stigma," *Modern China* 23, no. 1 (1997): 140–80, and *Sex, Law, and Society in Late Imperial China* (Stanford: Stanford University Press, 2000), chap. 4. Here, I am concerned less with the law itself than with what it can tell us about the conceptualization of masculinity and male sexuality.

4. Mitamura Taisuke, *Chinese Eunuchs: The Structure of Intimate Politics*, trans. Charles A. Pomeroy (Rutland, Vt.: Charles E. Tuttle, 1970).

5. See Matthew H. Sommer, "Banki teisei Chûgoku hô ni okeru baishun—Jûhasseki ni okeru mibun pafômansu kara no ritatsu" [Prostitution in the law of late imperial China: The eighteenth-century shift away from status performance], *Chûgoku: Shakai to Bunka* 12 (1997): 294–328, and *Sex, Law, and Society in Late Imperial China*, chap. 2.

6. I address these questions at length in *Sex, Law, and Society in Late Imperial China*. Also see Philip Kuhn's discussion of how the imperial state during the High Qing perceived the large underclass of vagrant, single men as a grave security threat, in his *Soulstealers: The Chinese Sorcery Scare of 1768* (Cambridge: Harvard University Press, 1990).

7. Yao Run et al., eds., *Da Qing lüli zengxiu tongcuan jicheng* [Revised comprehensive compilation of the Qing code] (1878; edition in UCLA East Asian Library), chap. 33, p. 1b. All translations in this article are my own, except where noted.

8. Xue Yunsheng, *Du li cun yi* [Lingering doubts after reading the substatutes], ed. and punctuated by Huang Jingjia (Taipei: Chinese Materials and Research Aids Service Center), statute 273-00; *Qing huidian shili* [Collected statutes of the Qing, with substatutes based on precedent] (1899; reprint, Beijing: Zhonghua Shuju, 1991), chap. 794, pp. 692–703.

9. Xue Yunsheng, *Du li cun yi*, substatute 273-07; for a translation of the full text, see Sommer, *Sex, Law, and Society in Late Imperial China*, appendix 1.4.

10. In addition, a series of edicts from the Qianlong and Jiaqing (1796–1821) reigns imposed on local officials the duty of "prohibiting rootless rascals"—i.e., rounding up and punishing vagrant troublemakers and deporting them to their home districts; these measures were closely associated with rules about arresting escaped convicts, and prohibitions against gambling, heterodox religious sects, and the gathering of large crowds. See *Qing huidian shili*, chaps. 130–32.

11. Xue Yunsheng, *Du li cun yi*, substatute 366-03; see Sommer, *Sex, Law, and Society in Late Imperial China*, appendix 2.1, for a translation of the full text. An infant is one *sui* at birth; a person ages one *sui* at each new year thereafter. As a result, age reckoned in *sui* is one or two more than if reckoned in the Western "years old." Thus, a boy of ten *sui* would be eight or nine years old.

12. For example, substatutes 366-02 and 04 in Xue Yunsheng, *Du li cun yi*.

13. Eighteenth-century officials feared that the "clerical underclass" provided "a breeding ground for sedition and lawlessness," and that many supposed clergy actually were "rogues who took clerical garb to evade the law." Kuhn, *Soulstealers*, 44.

14. Yasuhiko Karasawa, "Between Fiction and Reality: The Textual Framework of Qing Legal Plaints," *Ritsumeikan gengo bunka kiyo* 9, no. 5 (1998): 346. Karasawa goes on to explore the stereotype of Buddhist clergy as sex offenders in Ming-Qing crime fiction.

15. Substatute 161–01, statute 372–00, and substatute 366–09, in Xue Yun-sheng, *Du li cun yi.*

16. Of course, such records do not give an accurate picture of all rapes that actually occurred, especially if one embraces a feminist definition of that crime (to cite the most obvious example, the concept of marital rape was utterly foreign to imperial law). Rather, the records reveal the specific scenarios that satisfied the expectations of the judiciary. The sample on which I base the following generalizations consists of thirty-nine cases of homosexual rape and forty-nine of heterosexual rape (some cases involve homicide in addition to rape); all are drawn from central court records, so they represent "by the book" adjudication. For a detailed discussion of this sample, see Sommer, *Sex, Law, and Society in Late Imperial China*, chaps. 3 and 4.

17. Sommer, "The Penetrated Male," and *Sex, Law, and Society in Late Imperial China.*

18. *Jin ping mei cihua* [Plum in the golden vase] (Hong Kong: Taiping Shuju, 1992 [Ming]), chap. 93, p. 10a.

19. Cited in Chen Baoliang, *Zhongguo liumang shi* [A history of Chinese hooligans] (Beijing: Zhongguo Shehui Kexue Chubanshe, 1993), 161.

20. By "bisexual" I refer only to the fact that the predators in question pursued members of both sexes; I mean to imply nothing about the sexual orientation of the individuals described in Qing sources.

21. *Neige xingke tiben* [Grand Secretariat memorials on criminal matters, held at the First Historical Archives in Beijing], category "marriage, sex offenses, and family disputes," bundle 119/Qianlong 10.12.3. For further elaboration see Sommer, *Sex, Law, and Society in Late Imperial China*, chap. 4, where I present this same case along with other, similar examples.

22. See Roy's analysis of "the causes of social disintegration" in his introduction to *The Plum in the Golden Vase (or Chin P'ing Mei)*, vol. 1: *The Gathering*, trans. David Tod Roy (Princeton: Princeton University Press, 1993), xxix–xxxi; and Hanan's discussion of the fictional libertine in his introduction to Li Yu, *The Carnal Prayer Mat*, trans. Patrick Hanan (Honolulu: University of Hawaii Press, 1996), vii–ix.

23. See Sommer, *Sex, Law, and Society in Late Imperial China*, appendix 2.2.

24. See note 16 for an explanation of this sample.

25. Examples are drawn from Chang We-jen [Zhang Weiren], ed., *Zhongyang Yanjiuyuan Lishi Yuyan Yanjiusuo xian cun Qing dai Neige Daku yuan cang Ming-Qing dang'an* (Ming-Qing documents from the Qing dynasty Grand Secretariat Archive in the possession of the History and Language Research Institute, Academia Sinica) (Taipei: Academia Sinica, 1986), document 41–7; and *Neige xingke tiben*, category "marriage, sex offenses, and family disputes," bundle 70/Qianlong 4.9.5 and bundle 119/Qianlong 10.12.3.

26. In the memorials reporting death penalty cases up for review, the memorialists would anticipate reviewers' puzzlement about anything unusual in the testimony by adding specific follow-up questions to clarify those points. I have never seen fol-

low-up questions that address either this aspect of testimony by homosexual rapists or the issue of bisexual object choice.

27. *Jin ping mei cihua*, chap. 34, pp. 11b-12a, and chap. 93, p. 10a.

28. Li Yu, *The Carnal Prayer Mat*, 120–22; Sophie Volpp, "The Discourse on Male Marriage: Li Yu's 'A Male Mencius's Mother,'" *positions* 2, no. 1 (1994). (Translations are by Hanan and Volpp, respectively.)

29. Why was cleanliness such a fetish? Perhaps because the faces of so many people, by the time they reached maturity, exhibited a record of childhood disease and skin problems, and people did not have the benefit of treating or concealing the results with modern cosmetics or dermatology. A fair, clear complexion and clean skin must have been rare indeed in eighteenth-century China, especially among peasants, who were typically burned very dark by the sun.

30. Bret Hinsch, *Passions of the Cut Sleeve: The Male Homosexual Tradition in China* (Berkeley and Los Angeles: University of California Press, 1990), 146.

31. Sommer, "The Penetrated Male," and *Sex, Law, and Society in Late Imperial China*, chap. 3; Vivien Ng, "Ideology and Sexuality: Rape Laws in Qing China," *Journal of Asian Studies* 46, no. 1 (1987).

32. Sommer, *Sex, Law, and Society in Late Imperial China*, chap. 4.

33. For the gender education and offstage personae of males who performed *dan* roles, see Isabelle Duchesne, "The Chinese Opera Star: Roles and Identity," in *Boundaries in China*, ed. John Hay (London: Reaktion Books, 1994); for the homoerotics of actors and acting, see Sophie Volpp, "The Male Queen: Boy Actors and Literati Libertines" (Ph.D. diss., Department of East Asian Languages and Civilizations, Harvard University, 1995); and Hinsch, *Passions of the Cut Sleeve*. Qing jurists strongly associated male actors with homosexual prostitution, as seen in a substatute of 1852 (substatute 375–04 in Xue Yunsheng, *Du li cun yi*), which calls for punishment of any "female or male who decides on her/his own to become a prostitute or an actor and sell illicit sex" *(wei chang wei you mai jian zhe)*, as well as anyone who "sleeps with prostitutes or actors" *(su chang xia you)*.

34. *Neige xingke tiben*, category "criminal law," microfilm number 00661/Shunzhi 10.12.13. It may well be that Qing authorities eventually required actors to conform to the tonsure, but I have been unable to confirm this.

35. *Xu zeng xing an hui lan* (Supplement to the conspectus of penal cases) (1840?; edition in UCLA East Asian Library), chap. 14, pp. 2a-b; I treat this same case in Sommer, "The Penetrated Male," and *Sex, Law, and Society in Late Imperial China*, chap. 4.

36. Until 1723, Qing law preserved the long-standing legal fiction of fixed and hereditary status differences, so prostitution was tolerated among debased status groups but prohibited to commoners; from 1723 on, however, a series of imperial edicts extended commoner standards of morality and criminal liability to previously debased groups, so that all prostitution became illegal. Prostitutes and other entertainers continued to be considered debased, but that status derived from occupation and conduct rather than hereditary stigma. Sommer, "Banki teisei Chūgoku hō ni okeru baishun," and *Sex, Law, and Society in Late Imperial China*, chaps. 6 and 7; Terada Takanobu, "Yōseitei no semmin kaihōrei ni tsuite" [The Yongzheng emperor's edicts which emancipated debased status groups], *Tōyōshi kenkyū* 18, no. 3 (1959).

37. *Xing an hui lan* (Conspectus of penal cases) (1834?; edition in UCLA East Asian Library), chap. 52, pp. 7b-8a; I treat this same case in "The Penetrated Male," 152–53, and in *Sex, Law, and Society in Late Imperial China*, chap. 4. The *cangue* was a heavy wooden collar fitted around the neck as punishment.

38. *Xing an hui lan*, chap. 52, pp. 8a-b.

39. Judith Zeitlin, *Historian of the Strange: Pu Songling and the Chinese Classical Tale* (Stanford: Stanford University Press, 1993), chap. 4; Furth, "Androgynous Males and Deficient Females," 22–23. For comparison, see Kathleen Brown's account of the anxieties provoked in a colonial Virginian community by an individual of ambiguous genitalia who alternated between male and female dress: "'Changed . . . into the Fashion of Man': The Politics of Sexual Difference in a Seventeenth-Century Anglo-American Settlement," *Journal of the History of Sexuality* 6, no. 2 (1995): 171–93.

40. Cf. Marinus Meijer, "Homosexual Offenses in Ch'ing Law," *T'oung Pao* 71 (1985): 115.

41. Xue Yunsheng, *Du li cun yi*, statute 162–00.

42. *Xing an hui lan*, chap. 10, p. 22b.

43. Peng Ziran's case bears a remarkable resemblance to a fictional tale, "The Human Prodigy" (Renyao), written approximately a century earlier by Pu Songling, based on a possibly apocryphal Ming dynasty legal case. See Zeitlin's translation and analysis of the tale in *Historian of the Strange*, chap. 4.

44. *Xing an hui lan*, chap. 10, p. 23a.

45. It is rare to find an admission of alternating sexual roles in a Qing sodomy case; so far I have seen only one or two examples in actual case records from the archives. In all other cases, there is at least the pretense of a clear, consistent division between penetrator and penetrated.

46. *Xing an hui lan*, chap. 10, p. 22b.

47. From high antiquity, a similar paranoia was inspired by eunuchs—namely, the fear that an uncastrated male might masquerade as a eunuch and thereby gain access to the palace women. The locus classicus is Sima Qian's account of how the famous minister Lü Buwei disguised an exceptionally well-endowed servant as a eunuch (by plucking his facial hair and bribing the official in charge of castration), so that he could perform sexual services for the queen dowager of the state of Qin. Sima Qian, *Records of the Grand Historian: Qin Dynasty*, trans. Burton Watson (Hong Kong: Renditions and Columbia University Press), 163–64.

48. Elizabeth J. Perry, *Rebels and Revolutionaries in North China, 1845–1945* (Stanford: Stanford University Press, 1980). A substatute of 1845 in the "extortion" chapter of the code (substatute 273–15 in Xue Yunsheng, *Du li cun yi*) specifically targets the Nian banditry in Huaibei discussed by Perry.

PART TWO

# Ideals of Marriage and Family

In the following chapter, Susan Mann argues that in the Confucian revival of the mid–Qing period, an important element was a new discourse on marriage and intensified state campaigns to promote a common family ideal in which women were to be chaste and obedient. Mann asserts that this focus on the family was shaped by larger social change: society was becoming more commercialized and social mobility was increasing. In the early eighteenth century, female entertainers lost their hereditary position in the Office of Musicians in the imperial palace, which formed a prelude to the declaration that the formerly hereditary "polluted" (*jian*) occupations were eligible for commoner status. This produced a general anxiety among the literati about the boundaries between "debased" and "respectable" social categories;[1] and this debate extended to a concern with the boundaries between polluted and pure women—or, to put it another way, women who were sold versus those who were married and provided with wealth (dowry) by their families. One result was that dowries became socially necessary and increased in size, as a proof of the respectable status of a woman and her family. Another result was the increased emphasis on women's moral education. The importance of Mann's chapter is to show that a family's honor was closely linked with the status of its women, with the result that, in a time of greater social openness, there were intensified attempts to circumscribe elite women within the domestic sphere. As in part 1, it is clear that gender ideals are inseparable from class structure.

Mann's article also outlines the immediate historical backdrop for the attacks on the Confucian family structure that began with the New Culture Movement (1915–1923). In her chapter, Susan Glosser describes how New Culture radicals argued that China's inability to turn back the imperialist powers was due to the dependency and passivity of its people, traits produced by the patriarchal extended family. Essays in the popular journal *Family Research* ( Jiating yanjiu) portrayed the family patriarch as the greatest obstacle to individual freedom and national reform. In addition to chafing against the authority of their fathers, the reform-minded, young male writers were often deeply unhappy with their own wives, many of whom had been selected for them by their parents. They believed that their ability to act as productive individuals, and thus contribute to the modernization of the nation, depended upon the quality of their wives. However, they did not discuss how the quality of a woman's husband might affect her ability to contribute to the nation. Many of the essays used the traditional Chinese woman as a symbol for all that ailed China. In two centuries, the chaste, domestic wife had been transformed from a symbol of a civilized, prosperous empire to a symbol of a backward and weak nation.

Together, these two chapters remind us that "the Confucian family" was not a fixed, unchanging entity but rather was an ideal always in flux, and was promoted or denounced by various groups involved in the social and political conflicts of their times. The New Culture radical attacks on the ideal in the early twentieth century were in part a result of the strengthening of the ideal as an integral part of elite identity in the previous centuries.

One useful source of primary materials is the first volume of Stuart Schram's edited collection, *Mao's Road to Power,* which compiles important original documents that provide insight into the ills of the old marriage system as perceived through the eyes of Mao Zedong during the period of the New Culture Movement. It also includes all of Mao's writings about the famous suicide case of Miss Zhao (Chao), who slit her own throat with a dagger as she was being raised aloft in the bridal chair to be taken to her groom's home in November 1919. She had only met her groom-to-be a few times, in ritual settings, but had taken a dislike to him, and her parents refused to call off the match.

Ba Jin's *Family* ( Jia) is a classic Chinese novel that works well in the classroom to illuminate the ways in which these larger social changes played out within elite families. Set around 1930, the novel describes the lives of members of the Gao family, a large gentry family in Chengdu. What is particularly striking about the novel is the frustration felt by the Western-educated young men toward the uneducated women in the family, whom the young men regard as irrational and superstitious, and whom they feel are hindering them from fully living the "modern" lives they envision for themselves.

Another well-known novelist, Mao Dun, also vividly depicts the anguish of forced betrothals circa the May Fourth Movement in *Rainbow,* which is well translated by Madeleine Zelin.

*Bound Feet and Western Dress,* by Pang-mei Natasha Chang, is the story of Chang Yuyi, who became well-known in China as the former wife in the first modern divorce case in the early 1920s. Her husband, the famous author

Xu Zhimo, who was American- and English-educated, left her because he considered her too traditional and Chinese for him, and "bound feet and Western dress do not go together." The great irony was that Xu Zhimo died in 1931, but Chang Yuyi, after running the Shanghai Women's Savings Bank in the 1930s, left China for Hong Kong in 1949 and New York in 1974. At the age of eighty-three, when she was no doubt more "modern" than Xu Zhimo could ever have imagined, she narrated this moving story of betrayal to her grandniece, Pang-mei Natasha Chang.

Ida Pruitt's oral history *A Daughter of Han: The Autobiography of a Chinese Working Woman* narrates the story of a poor woman in Beijing from the end of the Qing through the Japanese occupation in 1938. The story of "Old Mrs. Ning" and her daughter is interesting because it shows the degree to which a lower-class woman aspired to the dominant, elite family ideals, even though in so many ways her station in life prevented her from realizing them. Lao She (1899–1966) wrote the well-known novel *Camel Xiangzi*, the story of a rickshaw puller, which presents the life history of a lower-class man in a similar period in Beijing from a rather misogynist male point of view.

Two powerful films that depict the old marriage system with more or less historical accuracy are *Yellow Earth* and *Raise the Red Lantern*. Set in the 1930s in a poor mountain village on the Shaanbei plateau, *Yellow Earth* tells the story of a young woman sent to live with her betrothed husband's family at the age of twelve. She is finally inspired to escape her inevitable oppressive marriage by an Eighth Route Army soldier who visits the village to collect the folk songs that she is constantly singing to express her sorrow. Set in the 1920s, *Raise the Red Lantern* portrays the life of a young woman who becomes the fourth wife in a wealthy polygamous household at the age of nineteen. Like *Yellow Earth*, the film depicts the inescapability of the old family system; in this case, there are no People's Liberation Army soldiers to rescue her, and she ends up going mad. It utilizes the interesting cinematographic device of always placing the husband as a blurry figure in the background, so that only the women are in focus. Directed by the famous fifth-generation director Zhang Yimou, it has been criticized for exoticizing Chinese culture and for historical inaccuracies.[2]

## NOTES

1. *Jian* is translated as "debased" or "polluted" and is opposed to *liang*, which is variously translated as "respectable," "pure," or "chaste"—see the introduction to part 1.

2. Jane Ying Zha (Zha Jianying) summarizes the charges of orientalism in "Excerpts from 'Lore Segal, Red Lantern, and Exoticism,'" *Public Culture* 5, no. 2 (winter 1993): 329–32. In the same journal issue, Dai Qing points out historical inaccuracies in "Raised Eyebrows for *Raise the Red Lantern*," trans. Jeanne Tai, 333–37.

## COMPLEMENTARY READINGS AND VIDEOS

Ba Jin [Pa Chin]. *Family* [Jia]. Boston: Cheng and Tsui, 1989. (Several versions of this book are available, including the first version, published by Doubleday [1972].)

Lao She. *Camel Xiangzi* [Luotuo xiangzi]. Trans. Shi Xiaoqing. 1955. Reprint, Bloomington: Indiana University Press, 1981.

Mao Dun. *Rainbow* [Hong]. Trans. Madeleine Zelin. Berkeley and Los Angeles: University of California Press, 1992.

Pang-mei Natasha Chang. *Bound Feet and Western Dress*. New York: Doubleday, 1996.

Pruitt, Ida. *A Daughter of Han: The Autobiography of a Chinese Working Woman*. New Haven: Yale University Press, 1945; reprint, Stanford: Stanford University Press, 1967.

*Raise the Red Lantern* [Da hong denglong gao gao gua]. Directed by Zhang Yimou. Distributed by Orion Home Video, New York, 1992. Videocassette.

Schram, Stuart, ed. *Mao's Road to Power: Revolutionary Writings, 1912–1949*. Vol. 1: *The Pre-Marxist Period, 1912–1920*. New York: M. E. Sharpe, 1992.

*Yellow Earth* [Huang tudi]. Directed by Chen Kaige. Distributed by Fox Lorber Home Video, New York, 1993. Videocassette.

CHAPTER THREE

# Grooming a Daughter for Marriage: Brides and Wives in the Mid-Qing Period

*Susan Mann*

*The bride's dowry at eighteen means nothing;*
*The grandmother's funeral at eighty tells all.*
—NINGBO SAYING (HO CHU 1973:227)

Marriage was the ladder of success for women in late imperial China. Even the bride who began with a modest wedding ("three cups of weak tea and a bow at the family shrine") could end her life in bounty ("mouth full of sweetcakes, playing with grandsons"). A lavish dowry nonetheless meant something: it testified to the bride's family status (Harrell and Dickey 1985), and it was likely to complement generous betrothal gifts, one gauge of the groom's ability to provide for a daughter's long-term security (Parish and Whyte 1978, 180–83). In a society that frowned upon remarriage, an extravagant dowry marked a family's confidence that their daughter would marry only once. In addition, dowry provided an awesome public display, enabling the dowered bride to enter her new home with style and dignity. Perhaps most important of all, dowry that clearly matched or exceeded the likely betrothal gifts and wedding costs shouldered by the groom's family meant that the bride was not being sold. The pervasive traffic in women is described elsewhere by Rubie Watson (1991) and Gail Hershatter (1991). The dowered bride belonged to that select category of women who were "espoused by betrothal" *(pin ze wei qi)*, chosen for their virtue to become wives, distinguished forever from concubines or courtesans.[1]

During the mid–Qing period, dowry was the hallmark of a respectable wedding. Commoners went into debt and postponed marriages in order to dower their daughters in style. Whereas during the Song period, as discussed in Ebrey (1991), the dowry was above all an upper-class concern—families complained about expensive dowries because they dissipated corporate estates—in Qing times dowry givers quite clearly included families of more modest means. Such households might exhaust their resources to

93

marry off a daughter, a practice that also caused upper-class writers to complain, as we see in the following remarks written by Ch'en Hung-mou in the middle of the eighteenth century:

> When it comes to marriage, people care only about keeping up with the times. They spend extravagantly on material things. When they present betrothal gifts [pin] or make up a dowry [lianzeng], the embroidered silks and satins and the gold and pearls are matched one for one. Utensils and articles for the home and business are the finest and the most expensive, and they must be beautifully made as well. The decorated pavilion to welcome the bride and her elegant sedan chair, the banquet where the two families meet and exchange gifts, all require the most fantastic outlays of cash. One sees the worst of this among poorer people, who will borrow heavily to give the appearance of having property, all for the sake of a single public display, ignoring the needs of the "eight months" at home. Families with daughters are the most burdened; the families with sons can procrastinate and put off [marriage plans].

Ch'en thought it would be a good idea if everyone limited dowry processions to six chests, an unlikely proposition in an area where twenty chests was apparently de rigueur.[2]

Concern about dowry was only one aspect of the bitter competition for status that pervaded eighteenth-century life. This competition produced an unusual series of conversations about wives and brides in the writings of mid-Qing intellectuals. Their conversations, which appear in a variety of texts (didactic, political, and scholarly), are reminiscent of Victorian writings on the subject of women. Like the Victorians, mid-Qing writers valorized the woman's role as wife, manager, and guardian of the "inner apartments." In fixing the place of wives in the domestic sphere, they also sought to fix the fluidity of social change that threatened to erode the boundaries defining their own respectability. In questioning classical conventions governing women's behavior, they simultaneously reasserted those same conventions. In this essay I shall argue that their conversations about women and marriage were a metonymic comment on larger social issues of mobility and class during the eighteenth century.

The conversations—which I shall call a "new discourse on marriage"—were part of the Confucian revival of the mid–Qing period, a revival that reached down through the ranks of the commoner classes and focused on the family. Among the scholar-elite, "textual research" or "Han Learning" called attention to the original language of ancient canonical works, including marriage rituals and kinship terminology. Even commoners who could barely read were caught up in the revival because of state propaganda campaigns promoting a common ideal of domestic life that emphasized wifely fidelity and service. The state campaigns contributed in turn to a growing interest in compiling genealogies and family instruction books for upper-class households and those newly arrived at respectable status. As a result of these conditions—which affected scholarship, official duties, and personal writing—the elite men who presided over large families were led to ponder and comment anew on the ambiguous position of women in the Chinese family system.[3]

At the heart of the concern about family was the remarkable social mobility, both upward and downward, that marked the mid–Qing era. Evidence for mobility comes from the revival of commerce and the flourishing of trade guilds; from the growth of new literati occupations outside formal government office; from an apparent rise in literacy rates among women as well as men; and from complaints about affluence, conspicuous consumption, and "petty" competition in the literary arts (Ho 1962; Naquin and Rawski 1987, 58–59, 114–33). Surely the most striking development with respect to mobility in the mid–Qing era was the series of imperial edicts eradicating the final remaining hereditary class barrier in Chinese society. Beginning in 1723, members of certain occupational and regional groups listed in the household registers as *jian*, or "debased," were declared eligible for commoner status once they had "purified" their family lines by abstention from polluting work for three generations (Terada 1959). Though the edicts did not eliminate "debased" status groups, I believe the promised emancipation of the lowborn and the intense scrutiny of "pure" blood lines that attended their proposed assimilation into the commoner classes were crucial elements in the changing consciousness this essay examines.

In sum, anxiety about blurred boundaries of all kinds—including the boundaries between "respectable" (*liang*) and "polluted" (*jian*) women—informed the conversations we are about to explore and gave them special urgency. At stake was not only the purity of marriage markets but also the reproduction of status in a competitive society. Classical revival, moral rebirth, and the unprecedented mobility of women throughout the stratification system prompted enormous concern about how to keep women in their place. Yet these conversations were only partly about women's roles within the family. They were also about marriage and the market: about reaffirming the endogamous marriage markets of the scholar-elite to exclude interlopers and to distinguish educated women of the upper class from their cultivated sisters in the courtesans' salons. The literati writers of this era identified wives and daughters alike as women who carried forward the status of their families and the honor of their class in the face of threats from all sides.

## HAN LEARNING AND THE RECOVERY
## OF CLASSICAL MARRIAGE NORMS

The scholars of the Han Learning movement looked to pre-Song texts for guidance as they sought the "original" pure meaning of Confucian norms and language. Among their rediscoveries was abundant material on the meaning of marriage. The *Li chi*, the *I li*, and the *Po-hu t'ung*, all important Han texts widely cited and read by these scholars, emphasized marriage as a rite of adulthood and stressed the proper preparation and education of women for marriage. A review of these texts will indicate the scope of their appeal in the mid–Qing period.

Han texts describe marriage as a ritual that simultaneously marked the individual's entry into a world of adult responsibility and reconstituted the conjugal fulcrum of family life. As the next generation entered adulthood, moreover, the elder generation prepared to step aside. Even though mourning and burial were ranked higher in the ritual order, and even though a funeral usually cost more than a wedding, marriage was recognized as the "root," or foundation, of all ritual.[4] According to the *Li chi* (Book of Rites), marriage marked the second of the series of crucial ceremonies in the individual life cycle, following the ritual capping (for boys) and the ceremonial hair-pinning (for girls). The "Ch'ü li" (Summary of Rules of Propriety) chapter says: "When one is ten years old, we call him a boy; he goes [out] to school. When he is twenty, we call him a youth; he is capped. When he is thirty, we say, 'He is at his maturity'; he has a wife" (Legge 1967 1:65; *LC* 1:4b).[5] A later passage, in the "Nei tse" (Pattern of the Family) chapter, elaborates on the significance of this transition to "maturity" at marriage: "At thirty, he had a wife, and began to attend to the business proper to a man. He extended his learning without confining it to particular subjects. He was deferential to his friends, having regard to the aims (which they displayed)" (Legge 1967 1:478–79; *LC* 12:15b).

The early years of marriage, then, for men marked the expansion of social networks and broad programs of study that prepared them for an official post (the next transition, conventionally said to begin at age forty). Marriage for the elite male was a significant public step toward a career in the larger society. For the upper-class woman, by contrast, the path leading to marriage steadily contracted her sphere of activities, confining her ever more strictly to the domestic realm. At the age of ten, just as her brothers were leaving the home to attend school, a young girl was cut off from all access to the world outside the home: she "ceased to go out from the women's apartments" and began instructions with a governess who taught her

> pleasing speech and manners, to be docile and obedient, to handle the hempen fibres, to deal with the cocoons, to weave silks and shape waistbands, to learn woman's work in order to supply necessary clothing; to be present at the sacrifices, supplying the liquors and sauces, filling the various stands and dishes with pickles and brine, and assisting in setting out the appurtenances for the ceremonies. (Based on Legge 1967 1:479; *LC* 12:15b)

For the young lady, the counterpart of her brother's capping ceremony was the hair-pinning ritual, which took place at the age of fifteen, to be followed by marriage at the age of twenty to twenty-three years (Legge 1967 1:479; *LC* 12:16a). At that point, a portentous choice was made: she became a bride if she went through the rites of betrothal, a concubine if she did not (ibid.). Following the elaborate rituals signifying her transfer into the household of another family, the young woman centered her activities in the home of her husband's parents, concentrating her energies on the needs of that household.

We are accustomed to viewing this transition in a young woman's life as the nadir of her life cycle, the point at which she became least powerful, most vulnerable, most isolated, most alienated (Wolf 1972, 128–41). Like all aspects of Confucian thought, however, norms governing marriage embodied what Benjamin Schwartz (1959) has called "polarities," and mid-Qing writers were looking to dignify, not degrade, their women. They therefore focused on passages that both sanctioned wifely obedience and subservience and also stressed the dignity and authority of the wife in her new husband's family. A close reading of the Han ritual texts reveals that from the time of her entry into the home of her husband, the bride was ritually marked as his mother's successor. The *Po-hu t'ung* makes this clear in a poignant passage: "The wedding is not [a case] for congratulations; it is [a case of] generations succeeding each other" (Tjan [1952] 1973 1:249; *PHT* 4 *shang:* 255–56). In the *Po-hu t'ung*, as the groom goes out to meet the bride, his father reflects that the son is soon to replace him at the ancestral sacrifices: "Go and meet thy helpmeet, that [with her] thou mayst succeed me in the sacrifices to the ancestral temple. With diligence lead her, [but also] with respect, [for she is] the successor of thy mother after her death" (ibid.).[6]

Thus, although it is true that a young bride's sphere of activity remained confined to the "inner" domestic realm after her marriage, certain ritual texts nevertheless emphasize the power she acquired, barring misfortune, in her new sphere. It was these texts that caught the eye of status-conscious bride-givers in the mid–Qing era, particularly the chapter on marriage in the *Li chi.*

The *Li chi* stresses wifely deference and submission, remarking frequently on the importance of "obedience," "duty," and "service." At the same time, it offers a view of the marital relationship that emphasizes affection, partnership, and shared responsibility. Affirming the overwhelming importance of finding a suitable wife, the *Li chi* elaborates on the wife's central role in her marital family. Noting that "the ceremony of marriage provides for the propitious union between two [families of different] surnames" (*LC* 44:1a), the text explains that the purposes of the bond were, first, to ensure the continuation of sacrifices in the ancestral temple, and, second, to secure the continuity of the family line. The *Li chi* emphasizes the seriousness and profundity of the rituals surrounding the exchange of information and gifts leading up to the engagement and the ceremonies marking the wedding itself. Part of the ceremony included the ritual eating of the same animal and sipping from cups made from halves of the same melon; this showed, according to the text, "that they now formed one body, were of equal rank, and pledged to mutual affection" (Legge 1967 2:429–30; *LC* 44:1b).

On careful reading, then, the *Li chi* could be interpreted to emphasize *distinctions* and *difference* more than hierarchy, dominance, or submission. A proper marriage was arranged and celebrated to underscore gender differences and to emphasize the complementary and separate responsibilities of man and woman in the conjugal relationship. Marriage was the primary human social bond demonstrating the "righteousness," or "propriety" (*yi*), of each distinctive human role. Like all primary relationships, marriage required deference and submission (wives are to husbands as sons are to fathers and subjects to rulers). But the *Li chi* stressed that husband and wife interact to demonstrate harmony, and it implied that a filial son would learn how to establish a warm and responsible relationship with his father, not by observing his mother's deference, but by watching his parents' loving interaction. A father who abused his wife would invite only his son's resentment and rejection, and a resentful and rebellious son, as everyone knows, makes an unreliable subject. Thus the *Li chi* revealed how a wife mediates the critical filial bond tying father to son. She was the pivot around which loyal and compliant subjects were socialized (*LC* 44:1b).

The complementary responsibilities of husband and wife were also summarized in a concluding passage of the "Hun i" ("The Meaning of Marriage") chapter, which explains how, in ancient times, the Son of Heaven took charge of instructions pertaining to the "public and external government of the kingdom," while his wife instructed the palace women "in the domestic and private rule which should prevail throughout the kingdom" (Legge 1967 2:432–33; *LC* 44:3a). Thus, the regulation and harmony of families was the responsibility of women, just as the regulation and harmony of government was that of men.

The natural basis of this gender division of labor in the governance of public and private spheres was proved by its correlations with the natural world: when the public sphere was in disorder, an eclipse of the sun occurred; when the private realm was in disarray, the moon was eclipsed. The Son of Heaven, or the queen, as appropriate, had to respond to these portents with purification rituals. Parents of the people, the emperor and empress were like father and mother, each attending to his or her appropriate concerns (*LC* 44:3b).

In general, the language of classical texts masked hierarchy in this way, stressing not subordination but complementary spheres and "natural" sequential transformations. A discussion of the relationships among the five elements in the *Po-hu t'ung*, for example, offered a cosmological explanation for patrilocal marriage. Referring to the relationships among the five elements, the text says: "The son not leaving his parents models himself on what? He models himself on fire which does not depart from wood. The daughter leaving her parents models herself on what? She models herself on water which by flowing departs from metal" (Tjan [1952] 1973 2:442; *PHT* 2 *shang:* 95). The principle of complementarity between husband and wife was apparent in other sections of the classics. Both the *Li chi* and the *I li* describe a particular ritual to be performed on the day after the wedding, dramatizing the importance of the entering bride. The ceremony required the parents of the groom first to toast the new bride. She then toasted them in turn, after which the parents were to leave the room by a door facing west, while the bride departed from the east. Commentators explain that these directions signify that the bride will ultimately take her mother-in-law's place in the family, becoming the woman responsible for carrying on the family line.[7] As a ritual statement, this ceremony followed by one day the rites in which the new bride served her parents-in-law a dressed pig, signifying her obedience.

For the bride, then, rituals expressing obedience were coupled with those emphasizing responsibility and authority. Obedience was critical not only because it upheld the authority of elders but also because it was essential to the harmony of the household; one day the bride herself would have to command obedience from younger women. The text repeatedly notes that the perpetuation of the family line depends on domestic harmony, for which the women who presided over the household were responsible. It is worth noting here that all power consigned to wives in the domestic realm was constrained on every side by fine distinctions of age and status. Teaching women how to use this power became an obsession of mid-Qing scholars, who were drawn to these ritual texts, as we shall see, for reasons of their own.

Constrained or no, the idea of complementarity between spouses so evident in Han texts formed an important theme in mid-Qing scholarly writing on women and the family. It appears prominently in the writings of Yü Cheng-hsieh (1775–1840), well-known as a critic of foot binding, widow chastity, and the double standard (Ropp 1981, 144–46).[8] A skilled philologist, Yü researched the history of language, which clearly influenced his views on women. In a short note on the historical meaning of the word *qi* (wife), Yü examined in some detail the "egalitarian" interpretation of marriage in Han texts, explaining why the classics could not be invoked to support the subordination of women in marriage and the family (*KSTK* 4:105–6):

The *Discourses in the White Tiger Hall* [*PHT* 4 *shang:* 268] states that *qi* [wife] means *qi* [equal], that is to say, she is equal to her husband. The "Chiao t'e sheng" chapter of the *Book of Rites* says: "Your husband is the person with whom you stand as an equal *[qi]* on the platform [of marriage]; you are never to leave him as long as you live." It is from this phrase that the word [wife] derived its meaning.

Now the term *fu* [husband] means *fu* [to support, to steady, to prop up]. This term originally was a *yang* [masculine, strong, active] word. The word *qi* [wife] derived from the word *qi* [to perch, to settle, to rest for the night], which is most assuredly a *yin* [feminine, weak, passive] term.

The "Hun yi" chapter of the *Book of Rites* says: "In ancient times, the emperor had one empress, three consorts, nine concubines, twenty-seven mistresses, and eighty-one paramours." The "Qu li" chapter says: "The emperor has an empress, consorts, concubines, mistresses, paramours, and lovers."[9] It also states that the feudal lords have consorts, mistresses, paramours, and lovers. In this case, clearly, the term *qi* does not mean "equal."

Confucians have a saying that an imperial paramour is the same as an imperial lover, which they explain is because the term *qi* means "equal." And what are we to make of the "Qu li" passage that mentions paramours and lovers in the same breath?

The term *qi* must be understood in its specific context. It is used by everyone from the emperor to the common people.

In textual research, notes such as these offered no larger analytical or moral message. They nonetheless show us how scholars of the mid–Qing era attempted to recover the consciousness and the values of the past and gave them new life in their writing and thought.

Understanding language in historical context made it possible, for instance, to distinguish the past practices of the imperial household and the ancient aristocracy from the standards that guided the scholar class in the present. Yü's short research note titled "Appellations" (*KSTK* 4:125) analyzed the classical terms used for affines, notably ego's wife's brothers and ego's sisters' spouses and their sons. The note specifically compared past practice with present custom, indicating that regular social intercourse between intermarrying families, including the brothers of wives and the spouses of sisters, was an important feature of mid-Qing family life. We shall refer again to Yü Cheng-hsieh's textual research and to the complementarity of conjugal bonds when we examine the common interests of intermarrying families in the eighteenth century.

Probably the aspect of Yü Cheng-hsieh's thought that has received the most attention (where it pertains to the status of women) is his critique of the double standard implicit in the ban on widow remarriage—a prohibition that was widely observed among the upper classes of the Qing period (Elvin 1984; Mann 1987). Yü's point of departure for his argument, in the essay "On Chaste Widows," was his research on the notion of *qi* (equality, matching) between husband and wife at marriage. He quotes from the "Chiao t'e sheng" chapter in the *Li chi:* "A match once made should never be broken" (*LC* 11:13b). This means, he says, that when one's spouse dies, one does not remarry. He concedes that Pan Chao in the Han dynasty, so widely cited as the model for young widows of later times, did in fact write that "a husband has a duty *[yi]* to remarry; for a wife, there is no written prescription for entering a second marital relationship. Therefore, for a woman, her husband is like Heaven [and she can never replace him with someone else]." But confronting this passage, Yü comments:

> Although it is absolutely true that no written permission is given for women to remarry, there is at the same time an unwritten assumption that men should not take a second wife. The reason why the sages did not make this standard of conduct explicit in their teachings is the same as the reasoning that underlies the following passage: "The rites do not descend to the common people, nor do punishments reach up to gentlemen." When we make this statement, of course, we do not mean that commoners cannot follow the rites, or that gentlemen will never be punished. By the same token, men who wantonly seek wives just because the meaning of the *Book of Rites* was not explicitly spelled out are ignoring their true duty. According to the ancient rites, husband and wife were to be honored or despised together, as a single body. But a man sets his wife apart in a lower position when he invokes the ancient phrase "never be broken." He should realize that the "never" refers to both men and women alike. "Casting out a wife for the seven reasons" in fact describes seven ways to break a match; "if his wife dies, a man should remarry" is the eighth way. When the principles and duties of men are so broadly defined and unspecific, it is truly shameful to read so much into a few words and then use them to establish limits on wives alone. (*KSLK* 13:493)

Classical revival, then, in calling attention to the double standard, emphasized the privileged role of wives. The *Po-hu t'ung* took great pains to distinguish principal wives from concubines: "The rites forbid the betrothal of a woman as concubine. This means that she cannot be raised [to the position of principal wife]" (Tjan [1949] 1973 1:258; *PHT* 4 *shang:* 264).[10]

There were good practical, as well as moral, reasons why mid-Qing writers were concerned about widower remarriage, and these shall be examined below. The point here, however, is to stress again the impact of classical revival on the views of mid-Qing literati. At every turn, it appears, they were discovering ways to valorize the status of brides and wives in their class and to emphasize the differences that separated marriageable women from concubines and women of lower rank.

## FEMALE LITERACY AND WOMEN'S EDUCATION

The Han Learning movement coincided with a proliferation of guidebooks for educated women, including reprints of the *Instructions for Women* (Nü chieh) by Pan Chao, the illustrious female scholar *(nüshi)* of the Han period. (Yü Cheng-hsieh's essay criticizing widow chastity begins by quoting from this important text, underscoring its high visibility in the mid–Qing period.) Interest in women's education followed naturally from classical injunctions requiring special preparation and training for aristocratic young ladies, preferably in the ancestral hall of their descent groups. Women were educated for marriage, and the best education for marriage was training in the Four Attributes (*si de*) appropriate to wives: proper virtue, speech, carriage, and work (Legge 1967 2:431–32; *LC* 44:2b). The connection between moral education and marriage was made explicit by Pan Chao, who used the idea of the Four Attributes to organize her own instruction book. Her text, a training book for wifehood, invoked concepts of complementarity in marriage found in the *Li chi*. She understood the tao of conjugal relationships to be metaphorically like the "natural" relationships of yin and yang, Earth and Heaven. She valorized marriage by calling attention to the honor accorded it in the *Li chi* and by emphasizing that it is celebrated by the first ode in the *Shih ching* (Book of Odes). She also criticized views of marriage that stressed only husbands' control over their wives, noting that though all classical texts portrayed marriage as a reciprocal relationship that depended on the wife's ability to "serve" her husband as well as on his ability to "control" her, both service and control depended on the "worthiness" *(xian)* of each partner. Men, she noted, were educated so that they could understand the foundations of their authority and wield it effectively; women too required education if they were to serve properly in the domestic realm:

> Only to teach men and not to teach women—is that not ignoring the essential relation between them? According to the "Rites," it is the rule to begin to teach children to read at the age of eight years, and by the age of fifteen years they ought then to be ready for cultural training. Only why should it not be (that girls' education as well as boys' be) according to this principle? (Swann 1932:84–85; *NC shang:*4b-5a)

These views on women's education, and Pan Chao's own eminence as a scholar and intellectual, were taken seriously by scholars of Han Learning during the eighteenth century. Until that time, from the Six Dynasties period through most of the Ming, Pan Chao was probably best remembered as a celibate widow (Swann 1932, 51). In the late Ming period, however, interest in female instruction took a new turn. Lü K'un anticipated the concerns of some mid-Qing intellectuals: he was interested in the complementarity of the husband-wife relationship and concerned about educating women as future mothers and heads of the domestic realm (Handlin 1975, 36–38). Handlin, in her analysis of Lü K'un's own instruction book for women, the *Kuei fan* (Regulations for the Women's Quarters), emphasizes that he was addressing a "new audience" of commoners *(minjian funü)* who "suddenly have three or five volumes in their chests" (ibid., 17).

During the eighteenth century, accessible schooling and rising standards of living expanded the market for books. Commoners attuned to concerns about proper marriage and behavior were avid consumers of works on managing the household. Women were part of this consumer market: literate women were prominent in Buddhist sutra–reading societies and in poetry classes, studying with Yuan Mei and other leading scholars (Ch'en 1928, 257–74).[11]

Concern about female education was mounting, as evidenced by the market for women's instruction books.[12] A compact new edition of basic books, self-consciously styled *The Four Books for Women* (Nü ssu-shu), was bound and printed before the middle of the nineteenth century under the editorship of Wang Hsiang, who contributed one of the four works—a collection of his own mother's instructions, the *Nü-fan chieh-lu* (A Brief Outline of Rules for Women).[13] The other three books were Pan Chao's *Nü chieh;* a T'ang text titled *Nü Lun-yü* (Analects for Women), written by Sung Jo-hua; and the *Nei hsun* (Instructions for the Inner Apartments), composed early in the fifteenth century by the empress Hsu ( Jen Hsiao-wen).

Education for women was the subject of a much-reprinted collection of moral instructions by Ch'en Hung-mou. In the preface to his *Repository of Rules for Education of Women* (Chiao-nü i-kuei), Ch'en explained the significance of female education:

> The girl who begins as a daughter in your family marries out and becomes a wife; she bears a child and becomes a mother. A wise daughter *[xian nü]* will make a wise wife and mother. And wise mothers rear wise sons and grandsons. The process of kingly transformation [literally, *wanghua,* the transformative influence of the ruler on his subjects] therefore begins in the women's apartments, and a family's future advantage is tied to the purity and the education of its women. Hence education is of the utmost importance. (*CNIK* preface: 2a)

Clearly, education was for Ch'en the mark that set apart the women of his class—those given and those taken as brides—from everyone else. But what sort of education should women receive? In Qing times, upper-class women were trained in the arts of needlework, poetry, painting, calligraphy, and music making.[14] Mastery of these arts alone, however, did not mark status, for they were also claimed by professional female entertainers and courtesans. What set apart the marriageable women of Ch'en's class from the rest was moral instruction: education in the *da yi,* or "ultimate significance," of classical texts.

In an essay addressing this subject—significantly, the first of his works to command widespread attention—Chang Hsueh-ch'eng sketched the history of "women's learning," or "women's studies," since ancient times. The earliest women's studies, he argued, were in fact professional curricula that trained women for specific occupations. Thus, female historians studied one body of texts, female soothsayers another, female shamans still another—just as men would select one of the arts for specialized training for a particular office. Later, however, more general studies for women as a gender category developed, and a body of learning proper to females (as opposed to males) emerged. This "women's studies" literature emphasized womanly virtue, speech, appearance, and conduct and linked these to the example and scholarship of Pan Chao.[15]

In Chang's mind, moral education of the sort espoused by Pan Chao contrasted explicitly with training in the arts for professional female entertainers. Chang praised the Manchu government for taking a strong stand on this issue by banning female courtesans from the palace Office of Musicians (Jiao fang si) and distancing itself from the patronage and training of female entertainers. To teach women music and poetry without requiring prior rigorous training in the rites—especially the rites of family relationships—was to invite loose morals.

The removal of courtesans from the Office of Musicians, which Chang called "the most illustrious act of our august ruling dynasty" to date, loomed large in the minds of mid-Qing intellectuals for another reason: it was the prelude to the general emancipation of debased peoples. The Office of Musicians was originally staffed by a hereditary class of professional entertainers called "music makers" (yuehu), some of whose descendants were already living in isolated communities in North China after being expelled from the palace in a political dispute early in the fifteenth century. The yuehu were the first of the major pariah groups named in the emancipation edicts, and scholars specifically linked the abolition of the hereditary court musicians' offices to the end of pariah status for the yuehu. Writing more than fifty years later, Yü Cheng-hsieh took the history of the Office of Musicians as his own point of departure for a long essay on the emancipation proclamations (*KSLK* 12:474–87).[16]

The end of debased-status groups, especially hereditary groups of female entertainers, threatened the integrity of endogamous marriage markets, and with it the very foundation of hierarchy among women.[17] As bearers of the honor and status of their class, marriageable female commoners had to be kept separate from those who were bought and sold.[18] Thus, debates about women's education simultaneously explicated and clarified anew the critical class barriers in this mobile society. One result was the essay by Chang Hsueh-ch'eng that attempted to draw more firmly the lines around the cloistered women's domain by scorning the attempts of some women to join male-dominated poetry and writing groups. The ending of legal restrictions on debased groups must be seen in the context of a more commercialized society in which status barriers of all kinds were becoming less salient.

## RULES FOR FAMILY LIVING: WOMEN IN THE DOMESTIC GROUP

To serve the new market, in addition to books on women's instruction, guides to family living that addressed wifely roles were printed in affordable new editions or privately circulated among friends. The classic family instruction books composed by Yen Chih-t'ui in the Six Dynasties period (*Yen-shih chia-hsun*) and by Yuan Ts'ai in the Song (*Yuan-shih shih-fan*) were rescued from the rare book market and reprinted in the *Compendium from the Never-Enough-Knowledge Studio* (Chih-pu-tsu-chai ts'ung-shu), bringing their cost within the means of most scholarly families.[19] Reading and rereading these old texts, a few scholars were inspired to compile their own books for the education of their offspring and family members. (We shall examine one such contribution, by Wang Hui-tsu, below.) Interest in advice books went hand in hand with another new fashion: publishing "clan rules" to accompany the genealogies that were at the peak of their popularity during this period (Hui-chen Wang Liu 1959a, 71).

Even the so-called statecraft writers of the mid–Qing era tried their hand at essays on family matters. Wei Yuan's classic *Collected Writings on Statecraft of Our August Dynasty* (Huang-ch'ao ching-shih wen-pien), compiled in 1824–25, devoted an entire chapter (*chüan* 60) to essays on family instructions (*chia chiao*), including the excerpt from Chang Hsueh-ch'eng's "Women's Studies" (Fu hsueh) discussed above.[20] Essays in the section on ritual examine the position of women in the patrilineal family system, especially the problematic ritual place of concubines and successor wives.[21] Domestic relations, particularly the conjugal bond, were not irrelevant to statecraft, if we may judge by Wei Yuan's selections.[22] Finally, the chapter on marriage rites in Wei Yuan's collection begins with an essay on women's education: it was "the foundation of a proper family, the beginning of kingly transformation" (*HCCSWP* 61:1–2).

Wang Hui-tsu (1731–1807), himself a writer of the statecraft school who published a famous guidebook for administrative aides, wrote his own guide for the domestic realm: a set of family instructions dedicated to his children and titled *Simple Precepts from the Hall Enshrining a Pair of Chaste Widows* (Shuang-chieh-t'ang yung-hsun). (The title commemorates the two women who were most responsible for shaping his views on such matters: his late father's second wife and his own mother, who was a concubine.)[23] The work is addressed to his sons and grandsons:

> Once while I was home nursing an illness, I began reading the *Yen-shih chia-hsun* and the *Yuan-shih shih-fan* every day, and I would expound on these texts

to my assembled family, to provide them with models for "maintaining their integrity while remaining involved with worldly affairs" *[chishen sheshi]*. Sometimes I would expound upon the general principles; at other times I would give concrete examples as illustrations. Felicitous words, elegant deeds, and the foundations of day-to-day relationships between teachers and pupils—on each of these subjects, from time to time, I was pleased to offer formal teachings in the Way of proper conduct, which they in turn were to record by hand. Gradually my notes filled a satchel with jottings. I organized the notes that amplified the sentiments in the Yen and Yuan texts into six broad categories, encompassing 219 small items. These I arranged in six chapters.

The first is called "A Record of Those Who Went Before." It commemorates the wisdom of our ancestors, beginning with the events in the life of my late mother and her actual deeds, without repeating anything that has already been written down. The next chapter is called "Regulating the Self." This means, as Confucius once said, being able to follow your natural desires without transgressing what is right. The third chapter is called "Managing the Family." This chapter is limited to the discussion of a fundamental principle: continuing the ancestral line requires the guidance of mothers. Therefore the chapter deals in some detail with women's behavior. The fourth chapter, titled "Responding to the Times," shows how if one has few occasions for blame, and few for regret, one will be able to rejoice many times over. The fifth chapter is called "Plan for the Future." It shows how to provide security for future generations, and how to sow the seeds of great things to come. The final chapter is titled "Teachers and Friends," and includes a discussion of relationships in school. (*SCTYH* preface:1a-b)

Picking up a theme from both the *Yen-shih chia-hsun* and the *Yuan-shih shih-fan*, Wang Hui-tsu examined the intricacies of remarriage and widowhood in a large Chinese family.[24] He lavished special attention on the plight of the widower who must find another mother for his children, a situation well understood in his own household, as his father took a second wife after the first died, though his own mother, a concubine, was still living. What kinds of problems confronted the widower? How irreplaceable was his first wife? And what pitfalls awaited the man who took a second wife instead of contenting himself with a concubine lacking the ritually high status accorded a spouse?

The first answer to these questions appears in a section titled "Taking a second wife makes it hard to be a father":

Your first wife may not necessarily be wise, but the children she bears will not resent her on that account. In the unlucky event that she dies, however, you may have no choice but to take a successor wife. And if *she* happens to be unwise, and insists on making narrow distinctions [presumably between her children and others, or between her conjugal interests and those of the larger household], patching up the quarrels that result will be a source of grief for you.

If conditions are optimal and your new wife understands the larger moral principles of family relationships, she will always be unfailingly kind. But even in those circumstances the children of your first wife will look on her as an outsider. And so if you give them instructions or assign them tasks, they will blame all their failure to carry out your orders on their stepmother.

For you, the father, this means that reproof and admonitions to your children will always provoke resentment and jealousy from them; even if you do nothing, you will invite slander from them. Who can be blamed for this situation? (*SCTYH* 3:2a)

Clearly, the person to blame is the father, for making the mistake of remarrying. Elevating a second woman to the formal status of mother to all one's children is a step to be taken only at the risk of alienating offspring and losing one's authority over the coming generation.

Wang Hui-tsu commented further on the relationship between stepmothers and their stepchildren in a note titled "Serving a stepmother":

Even if a stepmother is hard to please, she must be attended to according to the rules of propriety. How much more true this is if your stepmother is easy to please! Even so, we often find that a mother who is easy to please gets a reputation for being hard to please, even to the point where she is being called "narrow-hearted" [*buyi*] and the father is being called "unkind." Now what kind of an attitude is that?

There are exceptions to this pattern. For instance, no one could have been wiser than my [step]mother Lady Wang. Thus, when I was thirteen years of age, she restrained me with orders that were strict and spartan. An agnatic kinsman of my father's generation said to me privately: "Your mother treats your younger sister far more kindly than she treats you." I denied this passionately, and thereafter I listened to her instructions more diligently than ever. Within four years, my kinsman's son was dead, and a little over ten years later, he himself died. Now his descendants are also dead, and this causes me to wonder whether his words may not still be having an effect today. (*SCTYH* 3:2a-b)

A stepmother, we see here, easily became the object of gossip and slander among kinsmen. Her commitment to her stepchildren was ambivalent, and that ambivalence could readily be turned against her by gossip that alienated her spouse's offspring. Few stepsons, we may imagine, were as loyal to their stepmothers as the young Wang Hui-tsu.[25]

If the hapless widower chose not to remarry to avoid these problems, he only faced new ones. The plight of one unfortunate soul, in a large household full of conjugal units devoted to serving their own needs, is outlined in a section titled "In serving a widowed father or mother, one must be even more attentive than ever":

A widowed mother has her sons' wives to rely on and daughters to wait on her—although the sons' wives will have their own children, and the daughters their husbands and in-laws as well, so a widow cannot depend exclusively on her own children; if she is ill, or in pain, or hungry, or thirsty, she may have no one to complain to.

But how truly desolate is the father who is old and living alone! Recently I visited an elderly kinsman who had lost his wife in middle age, and who had been sleeping and eating alone well past his eightieth year. He said to me: "My handkerchief has been ruined for a long time, and I've been trying to get another one, but I can't." And so saying, he began to weep. I was greatly distressed by this, and I went to report it to his sons. They paid no attention. Not long after, his sons too went the same route, poorer than he. The mirror of Heaven is close at hand—isn't it fearsome! (*SCTYH* 3:2b-3a)

Each of Wang's homilies makes clear the intractable complications stemming from the death of a first wife in households that observed Confucian family norms. The father who remarried to ensure care and companionship in his old age risked the rebellion or alienation of his children; fathers shielded their children from the wiles of a stepmother at the price of a solitary and lonely retirement. Clearly, however, in mid–Qing times this was the price they were expected to pay.

Further discussion of the problems involving first and successor wives, from a slightly different perspective, appeared in Ch'en Hung-mou's *Repository*. Though the classics taught women that "one's husband is one's Heaven," in reality a wife had to serve three heavens: her father-in-law, her mother-in-law, and her spouse (*CNIK hsia:* 22b). Her primary duty there was to encourage him to be completely filial to his parents: "The full realization of filiality begins with the wife." But remarriage complicated the relationship between mother-in-law and daughter-in-law. For example, remarriage posed the possibility that a daughter-in-law might "distinguish between the first and the second." A "successor wife," that is, a woman who took the ritual place of a deceased first wife, might not command the respect of her status-conscious daughter-in-law. On this account, successor wives were warned to take care to be "polite" to their stepsons' wives, and daughters-in-law were enjoined never to make any distinction between the "first" and the "second" by such nasty little signs as passing through doorways first. Families were cautioned to watch for telltale signs of insubordination and correct the wayward daughter-in-law's thinking immediately (ibid., 24a).

These "petty distinctions" among women (widely decried as the source of all discord in Confucian families) could be drawn still more finely in cases where the daughter-in-law, as a ritually sanctioned first wife *(shixi)*, served a mother-in-law who was herself a concubine *(shugu)*. In such cases, the advice to the daughter-in-law was clear: "You may not presume upon your status as first wife to slight a concubine" *(buke shi shi man shu)* (*CNIK hsia:* 24b).

Ch'en's *Repository* therefore recognized that status-conscious (i.e., well-educated) brides could not be counted on to abandon their class consciousness within the confines of the domestic sphere. And if they were hard on mothers-in-law, they were even worse when it came to servants. Wives took out their frustration, their boredom, and their jealousies on their servants because propriety forbade striking relatives or even children. In fact, physical abuse of servants was so common among women of the upper classes that one text in the *Repository* supplies detailed descriptions of types of abuse as a warning to readers. Servants, by their conduct and appearance, offered a living testimony to the faults of an abusive mistress: "One may enter her home, observe her servants, and know whether she is a good wife or not" (*CNIK hsia:* 1a-5a). The *Repository* admonished its female audience that servants were not "a different order of being, like dogs or horses," but human. It stressed that scholars and commoners could not own slaves, though slaves were still employed in government service. Instead, male servants in commoner households were called "adopted sons" (*yinan*) and female servants "adopted daughters" (*yixi,* or *yinü*), to signify that they were "just like family members." They were to be so treated: well clothed, well fed, never abused (ibid., 1a-5b).

If young women with servants could be abusive, they could also be lazy. Sloth was a blot on the character of any bride, an all-too-common sign that she had abandoned one of the four cardinal womanly attributes. Young ladies who grew up waited on hand and foot never learned how to manage properly their role as mistress of the family servants and keeper of the household account books. Unlike wives in poor families—"busy all day, reeling thread, cooking food, drawing water, pounding rice, minding the farm, serving their mothers-in-law, suckling babies, generally working to exhaustion" (*CNIK hsia:* 14b)—the women who circulated through the marriage markets of the rich were spoiled, above all, by servants. Nursemaids took care of their children; maids and concubines even did their needlework! "All they have to think about is making themselves beautiful. Everything is done for them, so they don't know that rice comes from a stalk and silk is unreeled from cocoons. They treat money like dirt, and living creatures like bits of straw" (ibid., 15a).

Problems with household servants could be mitigated through fictive kin ties and prolonged association. But relations with women of low status outside the household were always dangerous. Every instruction book contained warnings about the "hags" whose marginal occupations gave them access to the cloistered inner apartments—female physicians, religious adepts, go-betweens, peddlers, nuns.[26] Wives had to be taught to "maintain strictly the separation of the inner domain from the outside world," lest they become the victims of gossip and manipulation by threatening females from outside who would "turn their hearts astray" (*CNIK chung:* 4a).

Repeated admonitions about the "six hags" reveal anxiety about female mobility and about defining boundaries around women. Women's religious practice, and the corrupting influence of the religious—not only nuns but also monks and priests—worried Ch'en Hung-mou, who wrote about the need to cloister women in an essay reprinted in the *Collected Writings on Statecraft* (*HCCSWP* 68:5b):

> A woman's proper ritual place is sequestered in the inner apartments. When at rest, she should lower the screen [in front of her]; when abroad, she must cover her face in order to remove herself from any suspicion or doubt, and prevent herself from coming under observation.[27] But instead we find young women accustomed to wandering about, all made up, heads bare and faces exposed, and feeling no shame whatsoever! Some climb into their sedan chairs and go traveling in the mountains. . . . We even find them parading around visiting temples and monasteries, burning incense and holding services, kneeling to listen to the chanting of the sutras. In the temple courtyards and in the precincts of the monasteries, they chat and laugh freely. The worst times are in the last ten days of the third lunar month, when they form sisterhoods and spend the night in local temples; and on the sixth day of the sixth month, when they believe that if they turn over the pages of the sutras ten times, they will be transformed into men in the next life.

The text goes on to condemn the monks and priests who seduce these mobile women in much the same tone reserved for the nuns and other "hags" who serve as liaisons between cloistered females and the outside world.

Again, concerns about women traveling abroad to monasteries were not new in the eighteenth century. But in the larger context of a mobile society, where competition for status was being promoted on many levels by action of the state, an obsession with boundaries in the writings of mid-Qing scholars assumes a heightened significance. Concern about boundary crossing in the domestic realm, I would suggest, was a metaphor for concern about boundaries in the society as a whole. Within the scholar class, female literacy was breaking down the walls that separated the sexes and kept women pure from the contaminating influences of the outside world. In the society at large, mobility was eroding occupational and class barriers that had once served to segregate marriage markets. Though women were the focus of much of the anxiety that attended these changes, in the discourse we have examined, women became a vehicle for expressing concerns about status shared by all men of the scholar class.

## CONCLUSION

That wives and marriage were a focal point in a discourse about class and mobility is hardly surprising. As in Renaissance Venice, nineteenth-century France, and colonial Mexico, marriage in mid-Qing China was a contract that aimed above all at reproducing class structures.[28] State law, and the system of moral beliefs we call Confucianism, sanctioned norms governing marriage, and thereby protected the existing class hierarchy. However, those sanctions cut two ways: they could protect class-endogamous marriage markets, or they could undermine them. The discourse on marriage that emerged during the mid–Qing period points to the ways in which the boundaries around sacrosanct marriage markets were being challenged. As the state moved to loosen status distinctions, Confucian morality was invoked to shore them up. Writers of the period show us, in their extended conversations about women and class, how the combined effects of affluence, literacy, and mobility threatened to destroy the conventions that lent stability and order to social life. Their conversations also remind us that codes lodging the honor of class and family in pure women were not confined to the shores of the Mediterranean. During periods of rapid social change, in China as elsewhere, women were named the guardians of morality and stability, charged with protecting the sanctuary of the family.

At the same time, as we have seen, women themselves posed part of the challenge to social order. Their literacy, their religiosity, and their own strivings for comfort and security helped to provoke the mid-Qing discourse on marriage. What we know now about this discourse is based on what men said and wrote. But the time will come when we will be able to see beyond men's interests and show how women construed their own roles in the dramatic changes of the mid–Qing era.[29]

## NOTES

This chapter was previously published in *Marriage and Inequality in Chinese Society*, ed. Rubie S. Watson and Patricia B. Ebrey (Berkeley and Los Angeles: University of California Press). Copyright 1991 by the Regents of the University of California. Reprinted by permission of the University of California Press. Book titles, author names, chapter titles, and a few commonly used words have been left in the Wade-Giles spelling used in its original publication. Dynasty names, place-names, and terminology have been converted to pinyin spelling. The author gratefully acknowledges research support from the Academic Senate Faculty Research Committee at the University of California at Santa Cruz. Fu Poshek and Yue Zumou provided invaluable research assistance. For critical readings of early drafts, I wish to thank Stevan Harrell, Robert Moeller, G. William Skinner, and participants in the "Conference on Inequality in Chinese Society," especially Rubie Watson and Patricia Ebrey, and Diane Owen Hughes, Gail Hershatter, and Susan Naquin.

1. For a keen appraisal of these sentiments, see Kulp 1925:166–77, esp. 174–75.

2. Ch'en Hung-mou, "Feng-su t'iao-yueh" [Several short points on local customs], *HCCSWP* 68:4. Chen's comments on dowry reflect an apparent rise in women's status in marriage dating from about the tenth or eleventh century. Patricia Ebrey (1991) shows that between the Han and the Tang periods, dowry increasingly replaced betrothal gifts as the focus of concern of families seeking to marry off their

children. She has also argued that by the Song, China had shifted from a bride-price to a dowry system (1981). So concerns about expensive dowries were hardly new in the eighteenth century. What was new about them was the greater participation of commoner households in the dowry system. Larger patterns of social and economic change from Song to Qing times, especially the elimination of fixed status barriers discussed later in this chapter, help to explain the increase in size and universality of dowry in China. See Harrell and Dickey 1985.

3. On the Han Learning movement, see Liang 1955; Elman 1984; Yü 1975; and Jones and Kuhn 1978. On the Qing propaganda campaigns, see Mann 1985, 1986, 1987. On the blooming interest in genealogies, see H. Liu 1959a, 1959b.

4. All the ceremonies were to be performed with utmost care in order to underscore "the distinction to be observed between man and woman, and the righteousness to be maintained between husband and wife." That distinction and the ensuing righteousness produced in turn the "affection" that bound father and son; and the affection binding father and son supplied the foundation for the "rectitude" between a ruler and his minister: "Whence it is said, 'The ceremony of marriage is the root of the other ceremonial observances'" (Legge 1967, 2:430). Mourning and sacrifice, as rituals, ranked higher in importance than marriage, according to the *Li chi,* but marriage was the "root" of all ceremony.

5. Legge notes in a footnote to this passage that age thirty should not be taken literally as the prescribed age for men to marry (Confucius, after all, was wed at twenty). Rather, he says, the passage means that no young man should reach the age of thirty still unmarried. The proper timing of marriage ceremonies is the subject of a review of classical injunctions printed in the *Collected Writings on Statecraft;* see Ting Chieh's essay "Marriage" [Chia-ch'ü], *HCCSWP* 61:17–18.

6. For more on classical views of marriage, see Tjan [1952] 1973, 1:244–63.

7. See Steele [1917] 1966, 30–31, which explains that, after the parents-in-law have given a feast for the bride, at the conclusion of the toasts "the father- and mother-in-law then descend before the bride by the western steps to indicate their demission of their position in the house, and the bride thereafter descends by the eastern steps, assuming the position they have demitted."

8. Ropp (1981) and Ch'en (1928:246–57) single out Yü Cheng-hsieh and Li Ju-chen, author of the *Ching-hua yuan,* as the main dissenters in an era of repressive sexual norms for women. My analysis takes a different view, placing Yü firmly within the mid-Qing discourse on women and class. His critique of the chaste widow paradigm does not challenge the fundamental place of wives in the home; like the others, Yü celebrated women by valorizing the conjugal bond.

9. For a discussion of the evolution of this "empress-consort" system from classical ideals to the Northern Song period, see Chung 1981:18–19. I am indebted to her translations of most of these elusive terms.

10. In fact the text here is ambiguous because the discussion about remarriage follows references to the "twelve wives" of the Son of Heaven. Clearly, it was not precisely known how to ensure that the ruler would produce a sufficient number of legitimate heirs. The text is also slightly ambiguous when discussing a case in which a principal wife predeceases her husband, citing precedents for promoting a concubine to the position of principal wife, and precedents that required a concubine

simply to substitute for the deceased principal wife in the ancestral sacrifices. Motives for remaining faithful to a deceased spouse are suggested ("Why must he only marry once? It is to avoid debauchery and to prevent him casting away virtue and indulging in passion. Therefore he only marries once; the Lord of men has no right to marry twice" [Tjan [1949] 1973, 1:252; *PHT* 4 *shang:*258]), but again they do not seem convincing where taking a concubine remained an option.

It is possible that the idea of faithful husbandhood (the paradigm of the *yifu*, or faithful widower) was achieving new prestige in Qing times. Elvin (1984:126) has observed that the definition of *yifu* (righteous subject) was changed in the early Qing period to refer strictly to husbands who refused to take a second wife after the death of a spouse. Such individuals would have been eligible, under the Qing government's programs to enshrine local saints and worthies, for special recognition in shrines and on memorial arches in their home communities. However, a systematic search of local gazetteers has yielded no evidence that men were honored for being faithful husbands during the mid–Qing period. Communities honoring so-called *yifu* continued to celebrate the deeds of philanthropists and brave community defenders, following the historical meaning of the term.

11. A comprehensive survey of Qing literary collections has identified works by 3,557 female authors (Hu [1956] 1985). The affluent Lower Yangtze region, economic heartland of the realm, was especially famous as the home of educated women: more than two-thirds of the eighty-five female poets whose works appeared in Ts'ai Tien-ch'i's mid-nineteenth-century anthology of works by female writers listed Jiangsu, Zhejiang, Anhui, or Jiangxi as their native place (Rankin 1975:41n).

12. The eighteenth century was the apogee of instruction books for women, beginning with Lan Ting-yuan's *Nü hsueh* [Studies for women], prefaces dated 1712, 1717, and 1718, and continuing through works collected by Ch'en Hung-mou, discussed below. See Ch'en 1928:275–82.

13. The title aptly likens these texts to the Four Books studied by men preparing for the civil service examinations. The exact date of publication of the *Nü ssu shu* is unclear (Liu Chi-hua 1934:30). According to Morohashi (1957–60: vol. 3: 6036.353), the first Japanese edition of the work appeared during the Kaei reign period (1848–54). I have seen an edition published in Yangzhou in 1838, which is held at the East Asian Library, University of California at Berkeley. A widely available reprint (cited in the references under *NC*) is dated 1893–94.

14. Dance appears to have remained the exclusive domain of courtesans and other professional entertainers, though further research may prove me wrong.

15. The rediscovery of Pan Chao and the reappearance of the motif of the female instructress in late imperial times has not yet been fully explored. See for example two seventeenth-century works by Ch'en Hung-shou, reproduced in Cahill 1967:33–34. Other painters of the Ming-Qing period found educated women an appealing subject. See, for instance, a painting attributed to Tu Chin portraying the famous scene in which the aged scholar Fu Sheng recites the *Book of History* from memory to a scribe, assisted by his daughter. The daughter translates her father's words, spoken in an ancient dialect incomprehensible to courtiers, and thus becomes the critical intermediary in the transmission of the orthodox canon (Hyland 1987:31, citing unpublished papers by Stephen Little).

16. "Singing girls" in the Office of Musicians were permanently replaced by eunuchs as a result of an imperial decree issued in 1659 (Shun-chih 16), following a temporary reversal of a similar decree issued in 1651 (Shun-chih 8). In 1652 a separate edict forbade commoners from becoming prostitutes. These state policies were linked to a growing commercial market for female prostitutes and entertainers during the eighteenth century by Wang Shu-nu ([1933] 1988:261–84).

17. Under Qing law, no commoner female could legally marry a pariah male. Punishment for a violation of this law was one hundred strokes for both the would-be husband and the head of the family of the bride (if he had knowingly betrothed his daughter to a man of debased status). By contrast, a commoner "who married a prostitute or singing girl went unpunished, but an official who married such a woman was considered dishonorable and given sixty strokes. The marriage was annulled and the woman was sent back to her . . . [natal] family" (Ch'ü 1961:161). Thus the marriage market drew clear lines between those families who held or stood to hold official rank, and those who did not. Contamination by intermarriage with a pariah female was risked only by families who did not aspire to the examination degrees. Note also that women were the bearers of their class's honor; pariah females could move up, but commoner females could never move down, in this patriarchal family system.

18. Rules protecting class endogamy were part of China's earliest political culture. Bans on intermarriage (reinforced by bans on foot binding for pariah women) hark back to ancient class barriers (Ch'ü 1961:155–58). According to Ch'ü T'ung-tsu, the gap between the *shi* class (scholars) and the *shu* (commoners) in medieval times was so wide that the latter were regarded as "untouchables." Intermarriage between *shi* and *shu* was forbidden by law under some dynasties. In fact, according to Ch'ü, "class endogamy prevailed among the *shi* until the last days of the Five Dynasties (907–960)" (1961:158). This traditional endogamy within the *shi* class, lasting from the third century through the ninth, was paralleled by endogamy within the *shu*, or commoner, classes, which took great care in turn to distinguish themselves from both mean people and slaves.

19. The two works appear in volumes 11 and 14, respectively. On various Qing editions of Yuan Ts'ai's work, see Ebrey 1984:324–27. The *Compendium* itself, compiled by the bibliophile Pao T'ing-po (1728–1814), was named for Pao's library in Hang-chou, where he kept an especially outstanding collection of rare Song and Yuan books. He was one of the four most generous contributors to the Four Treasuries (Siku) imperial compilation project in 1773. The Ch'ien-lung emperor is said to have named one of his own studios after Pao's (Hummel 1943 2:612–13). On the *Never-Enough-Knowledge* compendium, see Elman 1984:151–52. Elman explains that the inflated price of rare books in the eighteenth century increased the demand for collectanea that made expensive classical literature available at an affordable price.

20. Nivison (1966:274) comments that this essay was the first of Chang's writings to find a wide audience, appearing in anthologies and collectanea well in advance of his major historical and philological works. The *HCCSWP* reprints only a portion of the complete essay, under the title "Fu hsueh san tse" [Three precepts for women's studies]. The point of the essay, which was in part a thinly veiled attack on

Yuan Mei, is that women's education should be grounded in classical works and moral instruction, not poetry, and that men and women each have their own proper body of learning:

> In ancient times, studies for women began with the rites, and through them [women] progressed to an understanding of poetry and the six arts; or women might achieve mastery of all these fields simultaneously. But later these studies for women were no longer transmitted, and those women who were accomplished and literate proclaimed themselves professional scholars alongside men and flaunted their achievements. They did not realize that women originally had their own studies, and that those studies always had their foundation in the rites. (*HCCSWP* 60:12a)

Ch'en Tung-yuan (1928:267) takes a conventionally uncritical view of Yuan Mei as patron of women's letters, and does not address Chang's critique.

21. See "A Concubine Who Is a Mother Is Not Sacrificed To for More Than One Generation" [Ch'ieh-mu pu shih chi shuo], by Shao Ch'ang-heng (*HCCSWP* 67:19a-b), and two other essays arguing about the ritual place of wives and concubines in the ancestral shrine (ibid., 16a-17a, 18a-b). These writers, too, cited the *Li chi*, particularly the chapter titled "Record of Smaller Matters in Mourning Dress" [Sang fu hsiao chi], where the placement of concubines' tablets is discussed. See *Li chi* 15 (Legge 1967, 2:450-59).

22. See, for example, the essay on domestic relations ("Nei lun") by T'ang Chen (*HCCSWP* 60:8a-9), and Liu Shao-pan's "Letter to My Younger Brother on the Subject 'Family Division Always Starts with Women'" (ibid., 10a-b).

23. Wang Hui-tsu's father, K'ai-mu, was first married to a woman surnamed Fang and later took a concubine née Hsu. After his first wife died, he took a second wife, née Wang. When K'ai-mu died, neither the second wife nor the concubine remarried; both were honored with imperial rescripts of merit and a memorial arch in recognition of their chastity. See *SCTYH* 1:3a.

24. Both of the early texts contain warnings about taking a successor wife, though the *Yuan-shih shih-fan* is more optimistic than the *Yen-shih chia-hsun:* Yuan Ts'ai was certain that a "wise woman" could be found to meet the challenges of the role. See *YSCH* 1:7b-9b and *YSSF* 1:23b (Ebrey 1984:219).

25. Wang Hui-tsu's relationship with the "pair of chaste widows" has provoked comment. Patricia Ebrey points out that his widowed stepmother had only one stepson and no sons of her own, which may account for his close ties to her. Diane Hughes observes that the most ardent advocates of ideal family types may be those who were deprived of the ideal in their own experience.

26. This warning was sounded by Yuan Ts'ai (*YSSF* 3:17b; Ebrey 1984:304) and elsewhere throughout the lexicon of Qing writings on the domestic realm (H. Liu 1959b:94). Wang Hui-tsu warned about the "three old women and the six hags," especially nuns (*SCTYH* 3:26a). The conventional list names Buddhist nuns, Taoist nuns, diviners, procuresses, go-betweens, instructresses, peddlers, herbalists, and midwives. Accepted translations of the Chinese terms vary widely. For the list, see Chao I 1957:832. One standard translation appears in Ayscough 1937:87.

27. The phrase *kuisi* here conventionally means to keep a household under surveillance with the intention of robbing it: to "case," in other words.

28. On marriage and the reproduction of class and status, see the following

representatives of an extensive literature: Chojnacki 1975; Bourdieu 1976; and Arrom 1985:145–51. Stolcke (1981:39–40) offers a stimulating theoretical statement of this relationship. Maintaining the honor and purity of women, expressing status through dowry giving, and invoking the protection of state or church in the pursuit of class endogamy are cross-cultural patterns that appear in all complex societies.

   29. See Dorothy Yin-yee Ko, "Toward a Social History of Women in Seventeenth-Century China" (Ph.D. diss., Stanford University, 1989).

## REFERENCES

### Primary Sources

Chao I. *Kai-yü ts'ung-k'ao.* [c. 1775]. Shanghai: Commercial Press, 1957.

*CNIK Ch'ung-k'an chiao-nü i-kuei.* Comp. Ch'en Hung-mou. 1895 edition.

*CPTC Chih-pu-tsu-chai ts'ung-shu.* 1823. Comp. Pao T'ing-po. Shanghai: Ku-shu liu-t'ung-ch'u, 1921.

*HCCSWP Huang-ch'ao ching-shih wen-pien.* [Preface dated 1826] 1963. Comp. Wei Yuan. Taipei: Kuo-feng ch'u-pan-she.

Ho Chu. 1973. "Yung-su sang-li so-chi." In *Ning-po hsi-su ts'ung-t'an,* ed. Chang Hsing-chou. Taipei: Min-chu ch'u-pan-she.

*IL I li.* Ssu-pu pei-yao edition.

*KSLK Kuei-ssu lei-kao,* by Yü Cheng-hsieh. 1833. Shanghai: Commercial Press, 1957.

*KSTK Kuei-ssu ts'un-kao,* by Yü Cheng-hsieh. 1833. Shanghai: Commercial Press, 1957.

*LC Li chi.* Ssu-pu pei-yao edition.

*NC Nü chieh,* by Pan Chao. Reprinted in *Nü ssu-shu.* Shanghai, 1893–94 edition.

*PHT Po-hu t'ung.* Ts'ung-shu chi-ch'eng edition. Vols. 238–39.

*SCTYH Shuang-chieh-t'ang yung-hsun,* by Wang Hui-tsu. Preface dated 1794. Taipei: Hua-wen shu-chü, 1970.

*YSCH Yen-shih chia-hsun.* N.d. Reprinted in *CPTC,* vol. 11.

*YSSF Yuan-shih shih-fan.* Preface dated 1788. Reprinted in *CPTC,* vol. 14.

### Secondary Sources

Arrom, Silvia Marina. 1985. *The Women of Mexico City, 1790–1857.* Stanford: Stanford University Press.

Ayscough, Florence. 1937. *Chinese Women: Yesterday and Today.* Boston: Houghton-Mifflin.

Bourdieu, Pierre. 1976. "Marriage Strategies as Strategies of Social Reproduction." In *Family and Society: Selections from the Annales, Economies, Sociétiés, Civilisations,* ed. Robert Forster and Orest Ranum. Baltimore: Johns Hopkins University Press.

Cahill, James. 1967. *Fantastics and Eccentrics in Chinese Painting.* New York: The Asia Society.

Ch'en Tung-yuan. 1928. *Chung-kuo fu-nü sheng-huo shih* [A history of the lives of Chinese women]. Shanghai: Commercial Press.

Chojnacki, Stanley. 1975. "Dowries and Kinsmen in Early Renaissance Venice." *Journal of Interdisciplinary History* 5, no. 4:571–600.

Ch'ü, T'ung-tsu. 1961. *Law and Society in Traditional China.* Paris: Mouton.

Chung, Priscilla Ching. 1981. *Palace Women in the Northern Sung, 960–1126.* Leiden, Netherlands: E. J. Brill.

Ebrey, Patricia. 1981. "Women in the Kinship System of the Southern Song Upper Class." In *Women in China,* ed. Richard Guisso and Stanley Johannesen. Youngstown, N.Y.: Philo Press.

———. 1984. *Family and Property in Sung China: Yüan Ts'ai's Precepts for Social Life.* Princeton: Princeton University Press.

———. 1986. "Concubines in Sung China." *Journal of Family History* 11, no. 1:1–24.

———. 1991. "Shifts in Marriage Finance from the Sixth to the Thirteenth Century." In *Marriage and Inequality in Chinese Society,* ed. Rubie S. Watson and Patricia Buckley Ebrey, 97–132. Berkeley and Los Angeles: University of California Press.

Elman, Benjamin. 1984. *From Philosophy to Philology: Intellectual and Social Aspects of Change in Later Imperial China.* Cambridge: Harvard University Press.

Elvin, Mark. 1984. "Female Virtue and the State in China." *Past and Present* 104: 111–52.

Handlin, Joanna F. 1975. "Lü K'un's New Audience: The Influence of Women's Literacy on Sixteenth-Century Thought." In *Women in Chinese Society,* ed. Margery Wolf and Roxane Witke. Stanford: Stanford University Press.

Harrell, Stevan, and Sara A. Dickey. 1985. "Dowry Systems in Complex Societies." *Ethnology* 24, no. 2:105–20.

Hershatter, Gail. 1991. "Prostitution and the Market in Women in Early Twentieth-Century Shanghai." In *Marriage and Inequality in Chinese Society,* ed. Rubie S. Watson and Patricia Buckley Ebrey, 256–85. Berkeley and Los Angeles: University of California Press.

Ho Ping-ti. 1962. *The Ladder of Success in Imperial China: Aspects of Social Mobility, 1368–1911.* New York: Columbia University Press.

Hu Wen-k'ai. 1956. *Li-tai fu-nü chu-tso k'ao* [A review of women's writings throughout history]. Rev. ed. Shanghai: Commercial Press, 1985.

Hummel, Arthur W., ed. 1943–44. *Eminent Chinese of the Ch'ing Period.* 2 vols. Washington, D.C.: U.S. Government Printing Office.

Hyland, Alice R. M. 1987. *Deities, Emperors, Ladies, and Literati: Figure Painting of the Ming and Qing Dynasties.* Birmingham, Ala.: Birmingham Museum of Art.

Jones, Susan Mann, and Philip A. Kuhn. 1978. "Dynastic Decline and the Roots of Rebellion." In *The Cambridge History of China: Late Ch'ing, 1800–1911,* ed. John K. Fairbank. Vol. 10, pt. 1. New York: Cambridge University Press.

Ko, Dorothy Yin-yee. 1989. "Toward a Social History of Women in Seventeenth-Century China." Ph.D. diss., Stanford University.

Kulp, Daniel Harrison. 1925. *Country Life in South China: The Sociology of Familism.* New York: Columbia University Teacher's College.

Legge, James, trans. 1967. *Li Chi: Book of Rites.* 2 vols. New Hyde Park, N.Y.: University Books.

Liang Ch'i-ch'ao. 1955. *Chung-kuo chin-san-pai-nien hsueh-shu-shih* [Intellectual history of China during the last 300 years]. Taipei: Chung-hua shu-chü.

Liu Chi-hua. 1934. "Chung-kuo chen-chieh kuan-nien ti li-shih yen-pien" [The historical transformation of the concept of chastity in China]. *She-hui hsueh-chieh* 8: 19–35.

Liu, Hui-chen Wang. 1959a. "An Analysis of Chinese Clan Rules: Confucian Theories in Action." In *Confucianism in Action,* ed. David S. Nivison and Arthur F. Wright. Stanford: Stanford University Press.

———. 1959b. *The Traditional Chinese Clan Rules.* Locust Valley, N.Y.: J. J. Augustin.

Mann, Susan (see also Jones, Susan Mann). 1985. "Historical Change in Female Biography from Song to Qing Times." *Transactions of the International Conference of Orientalists in Japan* 30:65–77.

———. 1986. "Shapers of a Common Culture: Moral Education under Qing Rule." Paper presented at the University of California at San Diego, October.

———. 1987. "Widows in the Kinship, Class, and Community Structures of Qing Dynasty China." *Journal of Asian Studies* 46, no. 1:37–56.

Morohashi Tetsuji. 1957–60. *Daikanwa jiten* [Great Chinese-Japanese dictionary]. 12 vols. Tokyo: Taishjkan shoten.

Naquin, Susan, and Evelyn S. Rawski. 1987. *Chinese Society in the Eighteenth Century.* New Haven: Yale University Press.

Nivison, David S. 1966. *The Life and Thought of Chang Hsüeh-ch'eng (1738–1801).* Stanford: Stanford University Press.

Parish, William L., and Martin King Whyte. 1978. *Village and Family in Contemporary China.* Chicago: University of Chicago Press.

Rankin, Mary Backus. 1975. "The Emergence of Women at the End of the Ch'ing: The Case of Ch'iu Chin." In *Women in Chinese Society,* ed. Margery Wolf and Roxane Witke. Stanford: Stanford University Press.

Ropp, Paul. 1981. *Dissent in Early Modern China: Ju-lin Wai-shih and Ch'ing Social Criticism.* Ann Arbor: University of Michigan Press.

Schneider, Jane. 1971. "Of Vigilance and Virgins: Honor, Shame, and Access to Resources in Mediterranean Society." *Ethnology* 10:1–23.

Schwartz, Benjamin. 1959. "Some Polarities in Confucian Thought." In *Confucianism in Action,* ed. David S. Nivison and Arthur F. Wright. Stanford: Stanford University Press.

Steele, John, trans. [1917] 1966. *The I-li, or Book of Etiquette and Ceremonial.* Taipei: Ch'eng-wen.

Stolcke, Verena. 1981. "Women's Labours: The Naturalisation of Social Inequality and Women's Subordination." In *Of Marriage and the Market,* ed. Kate Young, Carol Wolkowitz, and Roslyn McCullagh. London: CSE Books.

Swann, Nancy Lee. 1932. *Pan Chao: Foremost Woman Scholar of China.* New York: Century.

Terada Takanobu. 1959. "Yōseitei no semmin kaihōrei ni tsuite" [The emancipation of the debased people during the Yung-cheng reign period]. *Tōyōshi kenkyū* 18, no. 3:124–41.

Tjan, Tjoe Som. [1949, 1952] 1973. *Po Hu T'ung: The Comprehensive Discussions in the White Tiger Hall.* 2 vols. Westport, Conn.: Hyperion Press.

Wang Shu-nu. [1933] 1988. *Chung-kuo ch'ang-chi shih* [A history of prostitution in China]. Shanghai: Shang-hai san-lien shu-tien.

Watson, Rubie S. 1991. "Wives, Concubines, and Maids: Servitude and Kinship in the Hong Kong Region, 1900–1940." In *Marriage and Inequality in Chinese Society,* ed. Rubie S. Watson and Patricia Buckley Ebrey, 231–55. Berkeley and Los Angeles: University of California Press.

Wolf, Margery. 1972. *Women and the Family in Rural Taiwan.* Stanford: Stanford University Press.

Yü Ying-shih. 1975. "Some Preliminary Observations on the Rise of Confucian Intellectualism." *Tsing Hua Journal of Chinese Studies* 11:105–46.

CHAPTER FOUR

# "The Truths I Have Learned": Nationalism, Family Reform, and Male Identity in China's New Culture Movement, 1915–1923

*Susan L. Glosser*

Susan Mann's discussion of women's education and marriage illuminates the central role that these rites of passage played in fulfilling the Confucian family ideal. Parents chose a wife for their son to ensure the continuation of the lineage and to maintain or improve family status. The bride's parents also acted with the broader issues of status and interfamily ties in mind. For example, as Mann demonstrates, the bride's dowry and education were intended to impress her in-laws and their community with the virtue and wealth of her natal family. That marriages were arranged with the welfare of the joint family in mind was an assumption that went largely unquestioned until the early twentieth century. With the advent of the New Culture Movement (1915–23), however, many urban intellectuals began to question the Confucian principles that ordered family and society. In their attack on the Confucian family ideal, young men rejected the principles that made marriage a family concern.

New Culture radicals wrote copiously about their dissatisfaction with the traditional joint family system *(da jiating)*. In fact, they laid the blame for most of China's problems at the door of this patriarchal, hierarchical institution. Unlike Western historians who view the emergence of the companionate marriage and the conjugal family as a sign of the growing privatization of the family, Chinese intellectuals believed that it was, in fact, the joint family that prevented its members from becoming involved in society at large. In their eyes, the joint family encouraged selfishness and an apathetic approach to national and social affairs because the sense of family was so strong that it supplanted all other allegiances. Moreover, the logistics and politics of the joint family demanded so much time and energy that its members gave little thought to affairs beyond the family. They claimed that China lacked the military and economic power to resist imperialist encroachment because the joint family encouraged dependency and passivity. They believed that Chinese society lacked creativity and energy because the joint family "buried alive" countless numbers of young people and wasted their talents. New Culture radicals touted the Western conjugal family *(xiao jiating)* as the antidote to China's ills.[1]

Structurally, the *xiao jiating* consisted of the husband and wife and their children, who lived apart from the joint family and operated as an independent economic unit. Emotionally, the family focused inward. The husband and wife were joined in a companionate marriage made of their own free choice. Husband, wife, and children looked to each other for emotional fulfillment. Early proponents of the conjugal family believed it to be more responsive to society's needs and able to rectify the weaknesses that foreign aggression had exposed. Because the husband and wife of a conjugal family survived only by virtue of their own thrift and initiative, its members learned independence and self-sufficiency. Even more important, the emotional satisfaction and companionship of the conjugal family made its members happy. Their happiness made them more productive, and their increased productivity, in turn, made China stronger.

Historians of the New Culture Movement have typically focused on either the movement's nationalism or its romantic individualism and portrayed participants' interest in family reform as an outgrowth of one of these two elements. In fact, the impulses that drove family reform were more complex than either of these representations suggests. Although much of family reform rhetoric prominently featured the language of nationalism and individualism, New Culture family-reform literature reveals that the primary impetus of the family revolution was the search of young urban males for a new identity in a modernizing, industrializing society. Not nationalism nor individualism, in other words, but socioeconomic issues drove young men to challenge traditional family structure and authority. We cannot, in fact, understand the significance of the family-reform movement or even account for its emergence unless we examine its socioeconomic components. Attention to this neglected aspect of family reform rhetoric in the journal *Jiating yanjiu* (Family Research) exposes the confluence of political, ideological, and socioeconomic factors that shaped the family-reform debate. It also reveals a New Culture radical quite different from the one we thought we knew. No romantic dreamer, this young, educated, urban man was deeply concerned about his own economic future and passionately involved in redefining himself as a member of an industrializing economy and a modernizing state.

### FOUNDING *FAMILY RESEARCH*

As the epicenter of the New Culture Movement, the Beijing University campus hosted a variety of student organizations. China's first Marxist study society began there in 1920. The movement's founding journal, *Xin qingnian* (New Youth), claimed the university as its headquarters. The campus seethed with the energy of a newly born youth culture. Mary Ryan has shown how the appearance of peer associations in early-nineteenth-century Utica, New York, created new social space that facilitated a reworking of family roles.[2] With the advent of the New Culture Movement, a similar phenomenon occurred in many of China's cities. In fact, the rise of peer associations is one of the most important characteristics of the New Culture Movement. Only by organizing and orienting themselves to their peers were the movement's young participants able to formulate their radical proposals for cultural, social, and political changes.

Traditional social order in China, and to a lesser degree in the United States as well, organized itself through the web of connections within and between families. Blood and marriage ties defined group membership; individuals typically found themselves embedded in vertical relationships governed by the hierarchies of gender, age, and generation. In contrast, membership in peer associations was voluntary. People of similar ages formed single-sex organizations around a common interest. Ties within these groups tended to be horizontal and egalitarian. In China as in the United States, peer organizations offered an implicit challenge to the traditional logic of social organization.

In January 1920, one of these peer groups coalesced to confront traditional family organization directly. Two Beijing students, Luo Dunwei (1901–64) and Yi Jiayue (Yi Junzuo, 1899–1972), called together several "comrades" to discuss the "cruel circumstances" and "barbaric aggravation" that young people suffered in their families.[3] Later that month, the group, which had grown by fifteen, established the Family Research Society with the intention of providing a forum for discussing family reform and publishing a journal. Members decided to welcome additional members regardless of age or gender. (In fact, most members were men in their twenties.) Interest in the society spread quickly. On the first of February the society held a general meeting. Three people from Shanghai and nine from Changsha decided to establish branch societies.[4] Their journal, *Jiating yanjiu*, devoted itself to discussing issues that affected young men—especially their economic, educational, vocational, and conjugal independence. The first issue appeared in mid-August 1920, and the journal continued publication for over two years. Original imprints may have numbered only a thousand, but each issue was reprinted at least once.[5] The Family Research Society had struck a nerve. Another measure of elite interest in family issues was the decision by one of Shanghai's largest and most prestigious publishing companies, Shanghai Commercial Press, to publish a volume of Yi Jiayue's translations of essays on the family by foreign scholars.[6]

Ultimately, these young men yearned to control their own destinies and to shape the future of China. In this regard too, New Culture radicals developed a vision of themselves that had much in common with nineteenth-century American ideals of masculinity. The American historian Elaine May has tried to capture the essence of Victorian American manhood. She writes,

> Millions of young men knew the formula, expounded most widely by Horatio Alger, that luck, pluck, ambition, and self-control were the ingredients necessary to become self-made. They learned in church, at home, and in the popular literature what was expected of American manhood. The key element was moral autonomy: total control over one's instincts as well as independent pursuit of one's calling. Perhaps the core of this code was economic self-mastery. Ideally, a man would be his own boss, own his own property, and control his own means of production. The industrious man worked without need of external restraints. Using his freedom to compete in an open economy, he served his own best interests as well as those of his family, community, and nation. The essence of this entrepreneurial ethos was in tune with the republican spirit of individual liberty. A striving man was the perfect citizen, for his ambition furthered, rather than hindered, the goal of national progress.[7]

Several generations later, New Culture radicals began to define themselves in similar terms. Like their American counterparts, young Chinese insisted on complete control of their lives and fervently believed that individual autonomy would fuel production and speed national progress. In fact, this is a parallel that Chinese radicals recognized themselves. Early issues of *New Youth* (Xin qingnian), the periodical that began the New Culture Movement, featured essays by prominent Americans and, to a lesser degree, Europeans on the proper and profitable use of one's intellectual and material resources. These essays, published in English and accompanied by Chinese translation, promoted the values of thrift, tenacity, self-discipline, independence, self-respect, science, political freedom, and love of learning. They included, for example, selections from Ben Franklin's autobiography and Edmund Burke's "The Spirit of Liberty in the American Colonies," Henry Beecher's essay "Genius and Industry," and an essay by Samuel Smiles titled "Money—Its Use and Abuse."[8] New Culture radicals looked to these essays for models of behavior and a philosophy of life that both valorized the individual and maintained a commitment to the communal good.

The two leaders of the Family Research Society, Yi Jiayue and Luo Dunwei, were Hunan natives.[9] Both were part of an early-twentieth-century Chinese student culture in which young men of elite families often received an education abroad. After graduating from Beijing National Number Four High School in 1916, Yi studied government and economics at Waseda University in Japan. Two years later he returned to China. That summer he joined the Young China Association (Shaonian Zhongguo). In the fall he entered the second year of Beijing University's law and government major. The following year he joined the Socialism Study Society (Shehui zhuyi yanjiu hui) and the Marxism Study Society (Makesi zhuyi yanjiu hui). In 1920 he helped found the anarchist Struggle Society (Fendou she) as well as its magazine and the Family Research Society and its organ, *Jiating yanjiu.* In January of 1921 he joined the Literary Research Society (Wenxue yanjiu hui). Later that year he graduated from Beijing University and returned to Waseda University to continue his studies. He returned to China the following autumn and went with Yu Dafu to teach for a semester at Anhui College of Law and Administration (Anhui fazheng zhuanmen xuexiao). After graduating from Waseda in March of 1923, Yi went to Shanghai. There, he taught literature at Shanghai China Public School (Shanghai Zhongguo gongxue) and served as an editor at Taidong Press (Taidong shuju). Yi joined the Guomindang in 1924. Thereafter, he applied his editing skills to Nationalist Party organs while also continuing to teach.[10]

We know much less about Luo Dunwei. He may have received some education in London. He wrote a number of books on marriage and family issues in China and on socialism, economics, and the nation. Before the War of Resistance (1937–45) he taught at Beijing University, China University, and Chaoyang University. Some time before the beginning of the War of Resistance, Luo also served as secretary to the Guomindang's Department of Business (Shiye bu).[11]

Yi and Luo were by no means unique in their interests. Rather, they articulated the ideas and concerns that preoccupied many of their young, college-educated urban contemporaries. The two men probably knew many of the men who contributed to and edited the literary and reform publications in the last years of the New Culture Movement. As students on the Beijing University campus, they could not help but be familiar with *Xin qingnian* (New Youth) and the ideas it popularized—among them, Marxism, anarchism, and family reform. While publishing *Jiating yanjiu* in Shanghai, Luo and Yi lived and worked in the Taidong Press building, where their magazine was printed. The first floor housed the printing presses, while the second and third floors served as offices and dormitories for Taidong editors. There, in the spring of 1921 Yi and Luo rubbed shoulders with Guo Moruo, popular at that time for his contributions to *Shishi xinbao*'s literary supplement, *Xuedeng* (Study Lamp), and soon to become famous for *The Goddesses*, a set of poems he would publish in *Chuangzao she congshu* (Creation Society Collectanea).[12] They also counted among their acquaintances Cheng Fangwu, one of the founding members of the Creation Society.[13]

Yi introduced *Jiating yanjiu* with a justification that neatly summarized the rationale for family reform and its connection to the rest of the New

Culture Movement: "Since the beginning of the 'New Culture Movement,' those of us who want to be a 'person' *[ren]* have been called upon to marshal our 'creative instincts' *[chuangzao de bennen]* and 'natural inclination to improve' *[xiangshang de tianxing]* in order to liberate and reform irrational and unnatural institutions and customs. But 'the family problem' *[jiating wenti]*, which bears an important relation to this, has been put to the side and ignored."[14] Yi's call to arms resonated with key New Culture concerns. The issue of personhood had engaged New Culture radicals from the beginning; they proffered the individual as a challenge to a society that subordinated the interests of the individual to the group. Yi's readers would surely have understood his use of "creative instincts" and a "natural inclination to improve" to refer to social Darwinist interpretations of individual and social evolution. His exaggerated claim that family problems had been "ignored" justified the need for a journal devoted entirely to the issue of family reform.[15] At the same time, it also expressed the frustration that gripped many participants as they struggled to live out their new ideals.

*The Family—A Historical Artifact*

The young men who organized *Jiating yanjiu* claimed that family reform was a necessary first step in China's modernization: if they were to develop their full potential and contribute to the reform movements sweeping urban China, they had to be happy at home. This amalgam of political and individual necessity pervaded the journal's essays. In lieu of a formal opening-issue manifesto, Yi Jiayue wrote a detailed and forceful essay that linked personal dissatisfaction in the family with faults in the family system. Individual problems, he argued, were manifestations of systemic crisis.[16]

By attributing family problems to a systemic breakdown, Yi suggested that the traditional family was not a universal organizing principle but a social construction subject to change. He contended that contemporary forces had besieged the foundations of the traditional family—the subservience of women to husbands and parental control of children—and would soon destroy it. By making women aware of their own personhood, the women's movement inspired them to rebel against the "irrational control by men" and participate directly in social and world progress. As a result, "the marital relationship . . . had become problematic." The increasing distance between parents and children dealt the family system a second blow: "Since the implementation of the educational system, children's education, for the most part, has been taken out of parents' hands and placed in the government's. The same is true with work." As industrialization moved work out of the home and into the factory, it also eroded family solidarity. The extended or patriarchal family system developed over time, Yi reminded his readers, clearly implying that the present family system was neither necessary nor self-evident and that it, too, would need to respond to socioeconomic pressures.[17]

Yi's historicization of the Chinese family system suggests that membership in the Marxism Study Society gave him the basic tools of historical materialism with which to attack the patriarchal family system. Although his economic analysis is simplistic, it successfully removed the traditional Chinese family from the realm of the universal to the world of economic and historical change. Placing the family in a historical context stripped it of its claim to universality and upset the normative moral construct of family by suggesting that socioeconomic forces determined family form. In short, Yi reduced what most Chinese had supposed to be a universal form to a historical particularity.

Although historians have focused on the nationalist and individualistic elements of family reform, New Culture participants credited industrialization and economic change for its impetus. Luo Dunwei listed four trends, all socioeconomic, that would result in the "natural extermination" of the joint family:

> (1) As transportation becomes more convenient, people travel far and are unable to be home very often. (2) Industry is concentrated in the cities; work is concentrated in the factories; there is no housing capable of holding extended families. (3) Life grows more difficult; one cannot marry early—[but rather] must marry late. One cannot focus on having children early in order to see five generations; extended families naturally cannot be established. (4) Wages do not surpass daily need. If one cannot gather together considerable property, then naturally one does not have the financial resources to set up a joint family. For these reasons, the joint family, which is ill-fitted to the times, is "falling apart on its own"; it doesn't need us to blow it over.[18]

The theme of industrialization and the subsequent limitation of wages and living spaces concerned many contributors to *Jiating yanjiu.*[19] Yet these students did not hold factory jobs. In fact, when Luo wrote this article, Chinese manufacture had barely begun to industrialize. How then, do we explain the omnipresence of this theme?

The rapidly expanding Chinese publishing industry allowed these students to keep abreast of contemporary scholarship on industrialization and the family in the United States and Europe. This awareness, coupled with their interest in social Darwinism and Marxism, led them (as it did Western scholars) to construct a model of the development of family organization.[20] Most Western and Chinese authors presented the conjugal family as the most socially and culturally advanced form of family organization and the hallmark of a capitalist economy. Luo and his contemporaries were not describing a contemporary process that they could observe but rather were invoking a universal law of economically determined social development dictated by a Marxist interpretation of history. By calling down the powerful forces of industrialization, Luo claimed a place for young men and for China within the process of modernization and industrialization that had empowered the West and Japan.

This "economic theory of evolution" not only helped New Culture radicals to place the Chinese family in a historic context but also gave them a way in which they and China could participate in history.[21] Thus, Arif Dirlik's observation about Marxist historians in the 1930s applies equally to men like Yi and Luo in the early 1920s: "Their primary concern was to understand the past so as to carry out the task of revolution in the present."[22] David Roy has traced Guo Moruo's adherence to Marxism-Leninism to a similar impulse: "He felt that by becoming an adherent of this doctrine he could join forces with history and regain his sense of pride and responsibility as a participating member of an ancient culture with a badly bruised sense of self-esteem."[23]

Thus, Marxist historiography, which began as an analytical description of the past, became a prescription for shaping the future.[24] As Guo Moruo declared, "For this age in which we live Marxism provides the only solution."[25] Family reformers seized upon the Marxist description of a historical process—industrialization destroyed the traditional family—and reversed its causal direction: the family must be destroyed so that China could industrialize. To this end, they marshaled both historical evidence and concrete examples of how patriarchal control of education, vocation, mobility, money, and marriage stunted youths' potential and restricted their productivity.

In the United States and western Europe, industrialization provided viable alternatives to the family economy. But in Republican China, occupational opportunities were much more limited. Despite Yi's and Luo's claims to the contrary, industrialization in China was still in its infancy. Factory jobs were restricted to the larger port cities. Moreover, a strong class bias discouraged educated men from taking up jobs outside of literary or governmental sectors. Finally, many white-collar jobs—clerk positions in banks and shops, managerial positions—were either nonexistent or still dominated by an apprenticeship system. Elite men (and women) who chose to strike out on their own confronted limited opportunities. Many feared to act on their principles and oppose patriarchal authority because their fathers would punish their radical behavior by refusing them financial support.[26]

### The Patriarch Problem

The vehement attack on the family patriarch (*jiazhang*) that occupied New Culture youth arose from a complex mixture of desire for individual freedom and concern for China's place in the drama of world history. They sought a social and economic solution that would ultimately free them from family dominance and realize individual potential. The frustration that is so evident in these essays originated from their belief that, if they were part of a universal pattern of historical development, patriarchy should have been breaking down. But their everyday experience told them that it was alive and well. As a result, these young men suffered doubly because they not only lived under traditional restrictions but also felt that history threatened to leave them and their country behind.

The centerpiece of *Jiating yanjiu*'s attack on the patriarch was Yi's two-part, forty-page essay "A Superficial Discussion of the Patriarch Problem." The essay articulated the complaints and criticisms that appeared in many letters to the editor and in the numerous essays.[27] Yi identified the patriarch as the primary obstacle hindering China's progress: "Although many aspects of the family need reform, the very first that must be eliminated is that disgusting thing—the family head. Because no matter what aspect we are discussing, the family head always represents power, class, and an impediment to social progress."[28] New Culture radicals attacked the patriarch both for the power he wielded and the power he represented. Because Confucian ideology set up each patriarch as the moral leader of his family and insisted on the interconnectedness of family, society, and state, it was not surprising that young men blamed the patriarch for the breakdown of the Chinese world order. As Wen-hsin Yeh has shown, the Republican era's most radical activists were often those young men who had most fully internalized Confucian morality and its tenets of benevolence, duty, and responsibility.[29] Once betrayed by that moral order, they cast it aside, determined to create a new one. As the representative of Confucian authority in the microcosm of the family, the patriarch became the scapegoat for the failed promises of the Confucian order. Moreover, toppling the patriarch, although difficult, was at least conceivable. Impatient for change but unable to effect an immediate transformation of the Chinese economy or political structure, these young men attacked the patriarch both for his control over their lives and as a stand-in for the nebulous forces of "power" and "class" that strangled China.[30]

If, however, social and economic circumstances produced the family head's dominance, changes in those circumstances could destroy it: "The recent instability of the family is a kind of natural tendency." Yi believed that at best, the family head no longer served his function and at worst the patriarch exploited his position. Public education, a police force, and the court system made clan unity unnecessary. Agricultural societies needed the leadership of the most intelligent rather than the most physically powerful and experienced. Under these criteria, the eldest male was no longer necessarily the best suited for leadership but continued to cling to power out of a desire to use his sons' and grandsons' labor and to secure care for his old age. Yi allowed that some still practiced ancestor worship because they believed in immortality, but he claimed that many family heads took advantage of these superstitions to identify themselves with the ancestors and ancestral authority. Yi also argued that the present system of financial management corrupted the original function, making the family head an emperor in his home.[31]

Yi sketched a memento mori for the patriarch when he recounted the history of the Roman family system. The Roman patriarch, he claimed, had also wielded an absolute power supported by veneration of the ancestors. Because kinship ran through the male lineage, the production of male heirs became paramount there too. Like his Chinese counterpart, the Roman patriarch also controlled family property. But, Yi reminded his readers, even the Roman patriarch, whose authority at one time seemed unassailable, succumbed to social and economic changes. The worship of gods and the spirit of scientific inquiry destroyed ancestor worship. The destruction of the old government system placed family heads under the supervision of city mayors. The increased frequency of divorce, initiated by both husbands and wives, further undermined his authority. Having developed among nomadic herders, the patriarchal family became increasingly obsolete in the subsequent agricultural, commercial, and industrial economies.[32]

Yi also cited historic Greece and Germany and nineteenth- and twentieth-century Russia as examples of countries where strong patriarchal systems had begun to collapse: "In sum, European patriarchy . . . , if not already long destroyed, is gradually weakening even now. This proves that this thing, the family head, is inappropriate for the times, and this is a natural trend. Nowadays, anywhere in Europe or the United States, try asking if the patriarch system still survives! Even the small-family system without a family head is unstable. Why even speak of the patriarchal joint family system? Looking back, what are we East Asians like? Ah! The family patriarch possesses not a little power!"[33] Yi's readers easily absorbed the implicit message in his historical survey: China was falling behind the march of progress. Familiarity with family systems of other times and countries refuted the necessity of the traditional Chinese family form. Marxist theory and Western sociologists' work on the connection between economic development and family transformation allowed Chinese intellectuals to add the weight of historical inevitability to their attempts to dismantle the traditional family.

In his critique of the patriarchal family system, Yi blamed patriarchal authority for obstructing young men's effective participation in the new economy: "The aspect of economic life that we think most important lies in free choice of occupation and the mobility of the labor force. With these freedoms each person may pursue the occupation that he believes suits him best. Only in this way can humankind develop and society benefit from the increase in efficiency. But the patriarchal system is diametrically opposed to this. One person controlling the whole family and forcing all its members to live together, who impedes on all sides their moving away or living separately, adding senseless restrictions to their choice of work and mobility really is preposterous!"[34] Thus, it was the patriarchal family that stood between China and a modern economy. The political assumptions upon which the patriarchal family system rested were also obsolete. Yi likened the family head to the emperor: both wielded absolute power on the basis of birth rather than ability. The family head might be illiterate, inept, "stupid as a deer or pig," and immoral.[35]

In addition to criticizing the patriarchal family system from evolutionary, economic, and political vantage points, Yi also questioned the pragmatic value of expecting the family head to control the family.[36] He claimed that often the patriarch lacked self-control and failed to keep his wives and concubines from wrangling. Yi also insisted that new values had changed the nature of the parent-child relationship. The great "new tides" of women's liberation and youths' independence created different criteria for the valuation of fathers and husbands: "They [women and youths] feel that the value of the father or husband rests only in ties of blood or love. Aside from this, authority, dignity, and filiality are all little wings on a paper tiger. They are nothing to be afraid of!" Because of these changes, Yi maintained, "Even if we act magnanimously and do not abolish it, the patriarchal system will give up the ghost by itself. Not only will the absence of the patriarch not result in the barbarization of the home, but on the contrary it will have a very good influence on the home, nation, and society." He further noted that students were acquiring the skills of self-government in their student organizations, thus further reducing the need for dictatorial patriarchal rule.[37]

Such was the patriarch's power that, even when he violated the injunction to support his children, they had no real means to force him to fulfill this duty. The law required the patriarch to support junior members, but only to the extent that his resources allowed. Yi interpreted this to mean that in reality, the family head had no responsibility to support family members: "Why is this? Because the extent of the patriarch's financial resources are known only to himself and perhaps his mistress. According to popular knowledge, the court's investigations are unreliable. The patriarch may obviously have money but may not want his son or daughter to go to school. He can say to the court, 'It is not that I am against my children receiving an education, but rather my resources are insufficient.' And the law will certainly forgive him. I have a cousin whose situation is just this."[38] Yi and his readers portrayed the patriarch as a man who had betrayed all trust in his ability or desire to administer funds wisely and fairly. The vitriolic attacks on the patriarch and the joint family system that appeared in *Jiating yanjin* essays and letters to the editors suggest that doubt about economic security and the predictability of life produced in *Jiating yanjin*'s contributors an almost frantic desire to control their own lives. Yi resented the family heads' financial stranglehold, and, in outlining a solution, he did not simply ask them to loosen their purse strings but also pointed out that financial dependency itself was unprofitable, that in return for work one received only one's support, and that such dependency was shameful. Moreover, the lack of freedom to choose an occupation denied young men the opportunity to develop their own abilities, because work for the family was forced, passive, valueless. Yi insisted that children become economically independent as soon as possible. The family should not even supplement their income. Meanwhile, the father should be allowed to manage only his own money, not the entire family's and not his children's.[39]

*Jiating xingqi*'s editors and contributors longed to strike out on their own; their essays brim with frustration. Whatever the truth about their fathers' authority and the presence of an industrialized economy, these young men experienced patriarchal power as a serious obstacle to opportunity. In their efforts to circumvent the father's control, they constructed a new family— the *xiao jiating*, or conjugal family—which freed them from patriarchal power and fit into the historical trajectory dictated by Marxist theory. Although New Culture writers presented free marriage as just one of many freedoms from the patriarch, it was, in fact, the reform that most fundamentally undermined the patriarchy.

### "Marriage Is Mutual Help, Marriage Is Love"

*Jiating yanjiu* devoted many pages to critiquing traditional arranged marriage and promoting the *xiao jiating*. One contributor, Liao Shu'an, drew together the family ideals of the New Culture Movement into an essay modestly titled "An Opinion on the Marriage Problem." Liao observed that, although the New Culture Movement had transformed intellectuals' ideas about marriage, society at large still lacked a "thorough awakening and concrete methods." As a result, most people still lived under the tyranny of the family, and parents continued to arrange their children's marriages.[40] To remedy this situation, Liao offered eight rules for marriage reform.

1. Marriage of the two sexes must be completely free; no one, no matter whom, may interfere.
2. Only men over twenty-two or twenty-five years of age and women over twenty years of age who are economically self-sufficient can marry.
3. Marriage of the two sexes must be based on their spiritual union; then all the ugly customs of excessive ceremony and exchanging horoscopes and gifts *[wenli nacai]* will be eradicated.
4. After marriage [the couple] must remove themselves from relations with the joint family and establish a *xiao jiating*.
5. After marriage both sexes should live in the spirit of mutual cooperation, each pursuing his or her own economic independence, and neither relying on the other.

6. In any marriage previously forced by the family, and in free marriages, if both parties are dissatisfied with the marriage, they may divorce without legal sanctions.
7. Employ a monogamous system. Taking concubines, collecting slaves, and other such vile improprieties will be prohibited. Whoever violates this law may be taken to court and divorced.
8. The rearing and education of children must be shared.[41]

Liao's ideal family form articulated the ideals that appeared in most of *Jiating yanjiu*'s essays on marriage reform. He drew a picture of a monogamous, companionate marriage in which the couple lived independently from the joint family and shared economic and child-rearing responsibilities.

Yet Liao did not deny that marriage served certain social and economic functions. Indeed, he and most other New Culture intellectuals interested in family reform advocated the companionate marriage precisely because they believed it would contribute to economic productivity and social progress. He valorized individual satisfaction and, at the same time, acknowledged the social contribution of marriage: "Marriage is a kind of baby-making machine, but in addition to this, does it not contribute to enterprise and to the development of society? If, indeed, it is related to supporting enterprise and developing society, then can it accomplish these if there is no spirit of cooperation? This kind of marriage in which a man and woman who do not know each other are forced to live together is simply barbaric marriage, marriage as commerce, slave marriage."[42] Liao objected to a traditional economic rationalism as a criterion for marriage choice but, at the same time, justified the *xiao jiating* because it made a new kind of economic rationalism possible. Instead of accepting sacrifice of the individual to the family's socioeconomic interests, he placed individual fulfillment first. But even as he promoted the individual, he remained steadfastly communitarian. Ultimately, individual fulfillment served the nation's interests. Thus, Liao and other New Culture radicals denied the family's right to subordinate the individual's needs to the family, but they willingly offered the individual's energies and talents—the products of his fulfillment—to the nation.

Another essay, "The Evils of the Old Marriage System," also outlined the economic rationale of the conjugal family. The author, Guo Xun, acknowledged that many people thought it nonsensical to condemn the traditional family system. How, they would ask, had it lasted so long if it were harmful? But, Guo countered, negative results were not often immediately apparent; they developed slowly and arose from indirect causes: "Those who are victims of its indirect harm are like those who die in their dreams, passing away without knowing it."[43]

Like Liao, Guo began his justification of marriage reform with an insistence that marriage was an individual, not a family, matter. Given that fact, he reasoned parents and matchmakers had no right to interfere: "Is marriage for oneself, or for one's parents? Or for the matchmaker? Who will experience the joy or suffering that results? If it reaches the point of being unhappy, will the parents or matchmaker be able to get one out of it?" Guo dismissed the matchmaker as a busybody and accused parents of treating their children like gifts and toys and of manipulating their lives in order to feel important and to obtain grandchildren.[44]

Guo's argument is characterized by a persistent inconsistency between rhetoric and structure. He followed his emotional appeal for the rights of the individual with a list of seven indictments of the traditional marriage system. Each point began with an observation about the harmful effects of arranged marriages and then abruptly shifted to a commentary on how these marriages impeded economic productivity and national progress. Taken as a whole, Guo's indictment of arranged marriage reveals just how closely connected New Culture radicals believed individual happiness and social welfare to be.

Guo's first point declares that the traditional marriage system leads to adultery and concubinage. Because they are not free, arranged marriages are loveless and often full of hatred. *This affects the wealth of the family* because members are not motivated to work for family welfare. The husband wastes money on prostitutes and concubines. The wife just looks for entertainment. Being miserable, the two spouses look for ways to harm one another. The wife lets a lover into the house. At this point morality has already fallen to the extreme. *"This impedes social progress."*[45]

In his second point he states that the traditional marriage system weakens *the family economy.* If two people love one another, they will be of one heart, consulting with each other and working together. *As a result the family economy will immediately develop.* If they do not love one another and are always at odds, any enthusiasm will quickly be lost. Both sides will just look for entertainment, eating and never working. A person with much free time easily tends toward lasciviousness. Because prostitutes and concubines cost a lot of money, [such a man] will soon be standing on the street corner in torn clothes begging. "Money spent on this ghost heap almost never reaches society. As a result, *even the economy will be shaken by him because he interrupts the flow of currency in the market."*

Guo's third point claims that the traditional marriage system robs people of hope and the little pleasures of life. "Who enhances hope and the little pleasures of life? Do you mean to say it is not one's own beloved wife? If husband and wife are harmonious, they will correct their faults together and cultivate their virtues. They will offer each other comfort in hard times and jokes to help dispel frustration. . . . The reason we can brave hunger and cold, hard work, run around in rain and wind is because we want a happy home.

*If we lose happiness at home, who can stand the bitterness of work? If a person can-
not put up with the difficulties of work, this has a direct effect on society's occupational
output."*

In his fourth point Guo insists that the traditional marriage system destroys filiality. "If the parents ruin their son's marriage, this cannot but produce rebellion. . . . But because of the oppressive strength of the old family
system, sons cannot oppose their parents. This leads to a kind of passive rebellion. The son resorts to a dissolute lifestyle. His parents will wonder at how
they are repaid for their efforts to make their son happy. There will necessarily be yelling and cursing; perhaps he will leave home. Without [one's]
knowing it, the more one oppresses, the more a person's anger rises. As a result, filiality is destroyed. [A person] may even violate various principles of
human relations. As a result *he will injure customs and impede social progress.*"

In his fifth point he claims that the traditional marriage system causes
people to kill themselves. "It goes without saying that those who oppose an
arranged marriage must suffer their parents' banishment, but they must also
suffer the attack of the general polluted atmosphere, leaving them no place
at all in society. People are not made of wood and stone. Who can stand this
kind of atmosphere? [They think,] 'Why stay on this earth to be bullied
about something that was originally one's own business . . . but which others interfered with?'" This causes many young people to kill themselves in a
moment of anger.[46]

In his sixth point Guo blames the traditional marriage system for *imped-
ing reproduction and the development of posterity.* "After the two sexes are united,
pregnancy is certain. If husband and wife are incompatible, the two sexes are
not easily united. This is also the way things go. Well then, where will childbirth come from? Without childbirth, the ancestors' bloodlines will be cut
off. *We will not be able to bring forth good citizens.*" Even if children are born,
parents who do not love one another cannot produce whole, healthy children. Moreover, with husband and wife at odds, they will also often get angry with their children. "And so [they] *will not only not teach their children to be
good citizens* but, by whipping them, will also make their children into passive playthings or even produce immoral outcomes."

In his final point Guo concludes that the traditional marriage system ob-
structs social and national progress. The nation is created from the gathering together of the people. And in this process the husband and wife are the
most important. The country is created by gathering most families together
couple by couple. "*If husband and wife are harmonious, the man plants and the
woman weaves; only then will the economy develop and good citizens be produced.*" If
the people are well educated, then society and nation will progress without
obstacles. If it is the opposite, society and country will regress—that is,
people will just consume and not produce.

In the concluding paragraph, Guo abruptly reprised his initial emphasis on the primacy of the emotional bond and the private nature of marriage: "In sum, marriage is only the affair of the two people involved. Of course, no one at all can interfere. . . . Marriage is possible only after the love between two people is very deep. . . . Love mobilizes the spirit. . . . It is not a matter of form."[47] Yet even here, Liao moved easily from the individual bonds of love that formed the basis of marriage to the communitarian potential—the mobilization of the spirit—such marriages released.

Like many other New Culture radicals, Guo presented his argument as a defense of individual rights and linked the personal unhappiness caused by the traditional marriage system to adverse economic and social effects. They could not help but link self and nation. New Culture individualism, if we can call it that, was quite distinct from Western individualism. These young men identified themselves so closely with their nation that, even as they elevated the individual, they did not, and perhaps could not, treat the self as an entity separate from family or nation. New Culture attacks on the family and traditional marriage were more than an expression of individualism and romantic self-indulgence. In *Jiating yanjiu,* individual happiness made possible by the opportunity for romantic love was part of a constellation of values that linked individual happiness to economic productivity, social progress, and national vigor. As Guo's essay shows, these values did not always sit easily together. Reformers' emphasis oscillated between the poles created by the linking of self, family, and nation. New Culture radicals gave their primary loyalty to the self, but they could not ignore society and nation. They attempted to address both individual and nation by placing China on the universal road of development outlined by Marxist theories of history. This allowed them to carve out an area of independence for themselves, to claim a place for China in the modern world, and to justify the former by the latter. As the source of creativity and productivity, the individual became the key element in effecting change. Consequently, whatever made the individual more productive could be justified by the claim that personal happiness also contributed to social well-being. This step in the family reform equation profoundly affected women's roles in family, state, and society.

## CHANGING EXPECTATIONS ABOUT WOMEN

The emphasis on the individual's happiness and productivity changed men's expectations of their wives. This is not to say that young women did not share some of the same ideals of companionate marriage, with its emphasis on shared interests, compatibility, and mutual help. One of the few essays written by a woman that appeared in *Jiating yanjiu* also advocated economic independence for both men and women, an opportunity to develop one's individuality, comparable education, the importance of finding a compatible mate, and the right to a freely chosen marriage.[48] Nor is it to suggest

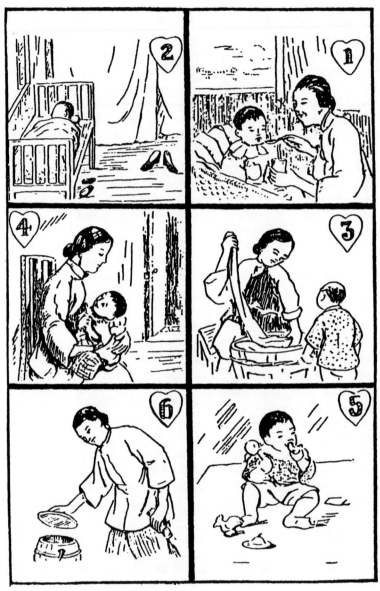

Figure 3. Child rearing is a woman's task, according to the lesson "Methods for Raising Children," in the 1929 primer *Shimin qian zi ke* [Lessons in a thousand characters for citizens], published by *Zhonghua pingmin jiaoyu cujin hui zonghui* [General Committee of the Chinese Association for the Encouragement of Education among the Common People], 1929.

that men cynically mouthed the language of women's rights. That differences in women's status and knowledge were the result of disparities in educational and economic opportunities was a common assumption. Essays insisted on women's value as individuals and their right to be free persons.[49]

Still, the vast majority of articles on family reform, both in *Jiating yanjiu* and elsewhere, were written by men and, not surprisingly, reflected their interests and biases. It was all very well to speak in an abstract fashion about the need for everyone to develop his or her individuality. But in the final analysis, these young men were deeply dissatisfied with their fiancées and wives. Moreover, this dissatisfaction worked its way into the linkages between individual happiness and economic, social, and political good discussed above. Although essays justified the importance of individuality and personhood for both men and women in terms of the greater social good, and in that sense did not make the individual intrinsically valuable in either gender, a man's happiness, and thus his ability to act as a productive individual, depended upon the quality of his wife.[50] A discussion of the reverse of this proposition, how the quality of a woman's husband might affect her ability to contribute to the nation, never appeared.

The editors sometimes printed letters from young men who had written to ask for advice about their marriage problems. The following letter not only articulates the young man's dissatisfaction with his arranged marriage but also reveals how he understands his unhappiness. The links this young man makes between personal satisfaction and the fate of the nation suggest that his personal misery has national implications.

> I am a person who has suffered very deeply from the tyrannical marriage system. I have searched for a solution for the longest time. Because of family oppression and a coercive environment, I have, in the end, failed.
>
> Today I will write down the painful experiences of the last ten or more years one by one for you gentlemen to read. I will be very grateful if you can come up with a happy solution so that I may escape this bitter sea. Ten years ago, my thought was such that I believed that a good society and human happiness all come from a happy marriage. I firmly believe in the purification of the race and eugenics. The very first sentence in Yan Fu's translation of *On Liberty* says, "To be a couple and at the same time teachers of one another, to [share] profound knowledge and lofty ideals of truth and essential principles: surely this arouses our aspirations." These words speak my mind. Who could know that she not only does not measure up to my ideals but to the contrary is not as good as an ordinary person.
>
> Before I married, I thought that even though this marriage, which was arranged when I was a child, was not as good as today's love marriages, if she were clever, I could teach her the truths that I had learned. We could often talk together and perhaps spend our days together after all. But when she arrived at my home, fat and naive, with ignorant behavior and muddled

speech, she really was just like a primitive. Using all of her intellect, she still cannot understand how to count to five. Everything else goes without saying.

To be told to live with this kind of wife . . . I am willing to teach her, but, pray tell, where should I start? Confucius said, "Rotten wood cannot be carved." She really is just like rotten wood. Ellen Key said, "Loveless marriages are immoral. . . ." This kind of immoral marriage is also the sacred and unassailable *shili* marriage that our old society took as a matter of course.[51]

If I had not received an education . . . I would also be able to acquiesce to this murderous *shili* marriage and willingly live in this spiritual hell. . . .

Unfortunately, I know that love is the foundation of the marital relationship. Who could have known the appropriate reason for a love marriage? Not only did no one help me, but my good friends all marshaled social customs to coerce me, leaving me to stand alone with no support. . . . My mother is very kind; she often sheds tears for me. My father is very hard; he often curses me. Relatives and old friends all criticize me with vile words. . . . Day and night I plan and ponder. Divorce is extremely difficult. Remarriage is against the law. I could stay single all my life, but I do not have the resolve for that. Or I could just carry on in this confused way, but that causes me great mental and spiritual pain.

Dear sirs, family reform is your objective; I am in this bitter sea! Do you have a way to save me? My friends who have suffered the same anguish, can you also think of a way for me to escape? I beg you all to give me a way, and I will soon leave this "living hell," ah!

*Jian Cheng*
1921.10.4[52]

This letter highlights several themes characteristic of young men's complaints about the women their parents chose for them. First, the author legitimizes his personal unhappiness by linking it to the social good. Moreover, he came to this realization very early, "ten years ago." His belief in eugenics charges his unhappiness with his marriage with a higher goal. He understands the importance of eugenics and would like to fulfill his social responsibility, but he has married a fat, ignorant, stupid "primitive." Given this raw material, even his noble intention to make the best of an arranged marriage by teaching her "the truths I have learned" has come to naught. Our would-be Pygmalion is not only thwarted but blameless because "rotten wood cannot be carved."

When Jian Cheng concedes that if he could only live in ignorance, he probably would not feel so cheated by his present marriage, he hits upon the crux of the matter. Men's expectations of themselves and their wives had changed. But the simple fact was that neither the educational nor the social system could produce the kind of wives they demanded fast enough. Some men took a much more sympathetic view of their fiancées but found themselves frustrated still. One man tried to convince his parents to send his fiancée to school before their marriage, but they refused. Another found it impossible to locate a school for his fiancée.[53]

The deep undercurrent of resentment stemmed not simply from misogyny—although that was sometimes present—but also from these young men's visions of themselves. Despite their iconoclastic aspirations, these men continued, like their fathers before them, to define themselves through their families and their marriages. Because it was so important to a man's identity as a modern, enlightened individual to make a freely chosen love-marriage, the quality of his marriage and his wife became absolutely essential to his self-image. Consequently, despite the rhetoric about women's rights to independence and full personhood, these men were most interested in creating women who met male demands for educated, enlightened companionship. And men complained bitterly when women failed to meet their husbands' expectations. One contributor expressed the frustration of many readers when he complained, "My wife is a good-for-nothing. Her talent is insufficient to meet her obligations, her virtue is insufficient to be of help to others, and her appearance is insufficient to satisfy my desires."[54]

Certainly, not all the contributors to *Family Research* took such a negative view of women. Editors and essayists sometimes reproved their readers for making women, rather than the family system, the target of their dissatisfaction. One writer chided his readers for attacking the marriage problem from the male point of view. Men's problems, he argued, were easier to solve. Because women struggled with greater educational, economic, and social restrictions, a critique of the marriage system from their point of view promised richer insights. He reminded readers that blaming women for their "deficiencies" unjustly held them responsible for being deprived of an education. Moreover, in marriage they suffered even more than men: not only were they married to men chosen by others, but they were also thrust into a family of strangers.[55] This sympathetic voice was all too rare. The clamoring for self-satisfaction and bitter complaints about old-fashioned wives frequently drowned out the voice of reason.

## CONCLUSION: A NEW MALE IDENTITY

The reshaping of the family was a first step in the process by which young men refashioned their economic, social, and political identities. At the same time, New Culture radicals' desire to participate in what they believed were universal economic trends—industrialization, the separation of home and work space, the need for a rational, independent workforce—inspired them to struggle against patriarchal authority. Faced with the prospects of establishing their own identity separate from that of their families and of spending more time with their wives in private nuclear households, young men became increasingly concerned about their ability to choose suitable wives. How these New Culture radicals reshaped prescriptive roles for women tells us a great deal about what young educated urban men envisioned for their own public and private lives.

Yet, although New Culture radicals set Confucian conceptions of filiality, family hierarchy, and marital relationships on their heads, their views of family and the socioeconomic conditions that shaped those views parallel in important ways the views of the elite young men Mann studied. These young men also found themselves engaged in "a bitter competition for status." Part of the anxiety they experienced over this competition resulted from the shift in how status was defined. In the new world that the New Culture radicals dreamed of, status would depend not on the wealth and connections of one's family nor on one's erudition in Confucian classics but instead on individual ability, ambition, and adaptability to a modern world. But at the same time, New Culture radicals still assumed that marriage and family were central to the social and political order. In the eyes of the New Culture radical, marriage was an individual, but by no means a private, affair. Mann's observation that "marriage for the elite males was a significant public step toward a career in the larger society" holds true for these men too. Like the Qing elite before them, Republican men believed that choosing the right wife was essential to their social position, a harmonious family, and worthy children. In fact, men wanted to reform the family system precisely because their marriages were still fundamental elements of their self-image and social standing.

Just as the debate about women's education in the Qing spread to a wide sector of society, so the family reform debate did not end with the New Culture Movement. The arena of family reform discourse soon widened to include middle-class liberals, reformers of various ideological inclinations, and entrepreneurs. Urban reformers soon accepted as truth the claim that social and national progress depended on some degree of family reform. But New Culture radicals did much more than introduce Chinese urbanites to the idea of family reform. They essentially defined the terms and set the scope of a debate that was to continue through the Republican era and well beyond 1949. In the decades to follow, the Nationalist government and entrepreneurs would manipulate the images and terms of the debate to their own purposes; but they would never fundamentally challenge the essential components nor the causal connections that linked them.

## NOTES

Many thanks to Carlton Benson, Alan Cole, Beth Haiken, Mark Halperin, Keith Knapp, Chris Reed, Robbie Roy, Tim Weston, Wen-hsin Yeh, and Marcia Yonemoto for numerous suggestions that improved this essay. Of course, all remaining errors of omission, fact, or interpretation are my own. Research for this project was funded by a fellowship from the Committee for Scholarly Communication with the People's Republic of China.

1. I use Goode's term *conjugal family* because it captures Republican reformers' emphasis on the companionate husband-wife relationship (William Goode, *World Revolution and Family Patterns* [London: Free Press, 1963], 7–10).

2. Mary Ryan, *Cradle of the Middle Class: The Family in Oneida County, New York, 1790–1865* (New York: Cambridge University Press, 1981).

3. "Faqi de jingguo" [The beginning], *Jiating yanjiu huikan* [Family research collection; hereafter JTYJHK] 1, no. 1 (August 1920): 68.

4. "Chengli de qingxing he xianzai de zhuangkaung" [The circumstance of founding (Jiating yanjiu she) and the present situation], JTYJHK 1, no. 1 (August 1920): 68.

5. A hardbound copy of the first volume was published in 1923. Letters to the editor indicate that the periodical drew readers from a broad geographical area— Beijing, Tianjin, Changsha, Changshu, Jiading, Suzhou, Wuxi, Shanghai, Canton, and other cities were represented. Those who became acquainted with the journal continued to correspond from as far away as Yunnan. Yi Jiayue, "Shewu ji bianji shi" [The society's and the editor's office], JTYJHK 1, no. 5 (December 1921): 121.

6. "Shewu jiyao" [Important society news], JTYJHK 1, no. 1 (August 1920): 69.

7. Elaine May, *Great Expectations: Marriage and Divorce in Post-Victorian America* (Chicago: University of Chicago, 1980), 17.

8. The fifteen-page excerpt from Franklin's biography appeared in vol. 1, no. 5 (January 1916); Beecher's essay was published in vol. 3, no. 1 (March 1917) and Smiles's essay in vol. 1, no. 3 (November 1915). The selection from Edmund Burke's essay appeared in vol. 1, no. 6 (February 1916) and ran to ten pages. In all, about two dozen different selections were published in *Xin qingnian*'s first three volumes. Some selections, like Oscar Wilde's "The Ideal Husband," appeared in installments. This practice of publishing exemplary biographies of Westerners and their exhortative essays continued in reform- and vocation-minded periodicals throughout the Republican era.

9. Yi was from Hanshou and Luo from Changsha (Chen Yutang, *Zhongguo jinxiandai renwu minghao dacidian* [The great dictionary of pseudonyms of historical figures in modern and contemporary history; hereafter JXDRWDCD] [Hangzhou: Zhejiang guji chuban she, 1993], 573, 585.)

10. Xu Youchun, *Minguo renwu dacidian* [The great dictionary of historical figures in the Republican era; hereafter MGRWDCD] (Shijiazhuang shi: Hebei renmin chuban she, 1991), 484; Chen Yutang, JXDRWDCD, 573, 585.

11. JXDRWDCD, 585.

12. David T. Roy, *Kuo Mo-jo: The Early Years* (Cambridge: Harvard University Press, 1971), 110, 116.

13. The information about Cheng Fangwu comes from "Zazhi fangmian" [About the journal], *Jiating yanjiu* [Family Research; hereafter JTYJ] 2, no. 1 (May 1922): 154; the other founding members of the Creation Society were Guo Moruo, Chang Ziping, and Yu Dafu (Roy, *Kuo Mo-jo*, 73).

14. "Faqi de jingguo" [The beginning], 68.

15. In fact, since the fall of 1915, when Chen Duxiu first touched off the New Culture Movement with his essay "Call to Youth," a great deal of discussion had centered on family reform.

16. Yi Jiayue, "Tao Lügong yu jiating wenti" [Tao Lügong and the family problem], JTYJ 1, no. 1 (August 1920): 1. Yi framed this essay as a response to a talk given by Tao Lügong, who, Yi claimed, had failed to recognize the systemic nature of the family crisis. Although I have been unable to find a record of Tao's talk, Yi's charge may have been exaggerated. In "Nüzi wenti" [The woman problem], an important contribution to the discussion of women's rights that appeared in *Xin qingnian* (4, no. 1 [1918]: 19), Tao placed women's issues within the global context of social change (Wang Zheng, *Women in the Chinese Enlightenment* [Berkeley and Los Angeles: University of California Press, 1999], 49–50).

17. Yi Jiayue, "Tao Lügong yu jiating wenti" [Tao Lügong and the family problem], 1–4. Yi believed that the economy was in a transitory phase of "cooperative labor." At present, women managed the home and men worked outside. Eventually this inherently unstable economic arrangement would disappear and all family economic relations would "dissolve."

18. Luo Dunwei, "Ni pei weichi xiaqu ma?" [Can you sustain your marriage?], JTYJ 1, no. 1 (September 1920): 67. Luo continued, "Nevertheless, I am not absolutely in favor of the 'xiao jiating.' But those gentlemen who would guard the cultural heritage, the president . . . , the Ministry of the Interior which assists the sacred way, you are only concerning yourselves with encouraging the traditional five-generation family. I am afraid that you will be unable to stop the reform of this social organization. Don't waste your energy."

19. Guo Moruo sometimes identified himself as a member of the proletariat (Roy, *Kuo Mo-jo*, 142–43, 150–52.)

20. The Chinese drew, for example, on the work of Edward Westermarck (1862–1939) (JTYJ 1, no. 5 [December 1920]: 123). Westermarck was a Swede Finn who impressed the academic world with *The History of Human Marriage* in 1921. Unlike most scholars of the family before and after, he discounted the theory that primitive societies were promiscuous. His explanation of the incest taboo was popular until the Freudian theory of family relations displaced it (Arthur Wolf, *Sexual Attraction and Childhood Association: A Chinese Brief for Edward Westermarck* [Stanford: Stanford University Press, 1995], 6–19).

Although some scholars debated the details, in broad terms they accepted the following evolutionary progression of family organization: promiscuous sexual relations or serial monogamy in the most primitive societies; matriarchy or female lineage in hunter-gatherer societies; the emergence of patriarchy in herding societies; the subsequent development of polygyny and monogamy in agricultural societies; and the ultimate appearance of conjugal families in industrializing societies. Although most of those who wrote on the topic agreed that not every society passed through every stage, they agreed that lifelong monogamy was the most evolved form of marriage.

21. Of course, the Chinese were participating in history. I am not exiling the Chinese to a Hegelian hell beyond history, time, and the divine. Nor do I think that

Levenson was correct in believing the Chinese had been cast adrift from history with only their "values" to buoy them ( Joseph Levenson, *Confucian China and Its Modern Fate: A Trilogy* [Berkeley and Los Angeles: University of California Press, 1968]). In this discussion, I am trying to understand history as these young men saw it. They wanted to participate in a particular process of growth and development that would allow China to compete with the industrialized and industrializing powers. The imperialist dominance of the "developed" countries led both imperialists and their would-be victims to identify industrialization with history itself.

22. Arif Dirlik, *Revolution and History: The Origins of Marxist Historiography in China, 1919–1937* (Berkeley and Los Angeles: University of California Press, 1978), 18.

23. Roy, *Kuo Mo-jo,* 5.

24. Dirlik, *Revolution and History,* 14.

25. Ibid., 166.

26. "Zhi wo siming de dongxi" [The thing that seals my fate], JTYJ 1, no. 3 ( January 1921): 104–6. This man wrote a passionate letter begging the editors of *Jiating yanjiu* for help. He desperately wanted to continue his studies, but his father forced him to work in the family business. To make matters worse, his family was also hurrying to find him a wife.

27. Yi Jiayue, "Jiazhang wenti qianshuo" [A superficial discussion of the patriarch problem], JTYJ 1, no. 5 (December 1921), and 2, no. 1 (May 1922). The text of part 1 is taken from JTYJHK, and the pagination given in the notes refers to that volume.

28. Yi Jiayue, "Jiazhang wenti qianshuo" [A superficial discussion of the patriarch problem], JTYJ 2, no. 1 (May 1922): 10. References to a future when the family could be eliminated altogether were not uncommon in the magazine, but they remained firmly in the realm of the theoretical. No one offered concrete details of how this might be accomplished. (For example, see also page 11 of the same article.)

29. Wen-hsin Yeh, *Provincial Passages* (Berkeley and Los Angeles: University of California Press, 1996), 4, 183–84.

30. The enormity of the effort to modernize China's economy is one that continues to overwhelm the government even today. In the Communist era, too, frustration with China's failure to industrialize has expressed itself in ideological campaigns.

31. Yi Jiayue, "Tao Lügong yu jiating wenti" [Tao Lügong and the family problem], JTYJ 1, no. 1 (August 1920): 9–14.

32. Ibid., 16–17.

33. Ibid., 21.

34. Yi, "Jiazhang wenti qianshuo" [A superficial discussion of the patriarch problem], JTYJ 2, no. 1 (May 1922): 2.

35. Ibid.

36. The Draft Civil Code accorded the family head the power to make all decisions related to marriage, inheritance, the division of the household, and place of residence (see lines 1323.2, 1338, 1373). Yi, "Jiazhang wenti qianshuo" [A superficial discussion of the patriarch problem], JTYJ 2, no. 1 (May 1922): 8.

37. Ibid., 10–11.

38. Ibid., 7.

39. Ibid., 3, 15, 16.

40. Liao Shu'an, "Hunyin wenti zhi yizhong zhuzhang" [An opinion on the marriage problem], JTYJ 1, no. 4 (August 1921): 46.

41. Ibid., 46, 48.

42. Ibid.

43. The author's metaphor is reminiscent of Lu Xun's iron house. Guo Xun, "Jiu jiating hunzhi de bihai" [The evils of the old family system], JTYJ 1, no. 4 (August 1921): 38.

44. Ibid., 39.

45. Italics added. The following seven points come from ibid., 40–44.

46. Whether suicide rates among the young actually climbed is unknown.

47. Guo Xun, "Jiu jiating hunzhi de bihai" [The evils of the old family system], 45.

48. Chen Zhishin, "Women Zhongguoren you jiating de kuaile ma?" [Do we Chinese have happy homes?], JTYJHK 1, no. 2 (n.d.): 53–54. Guo Xun, in "Jiu jiating hunzhi de bihai"[The evils of the old family system], also insisted on the necessity of compatibility in moral character, education, talent, and virtue.

49. See, for example, Lu Zongyi, "Gaizao jiating cong shenme difang zuoqi" [Where to start in family reform], JTYJ 1, no. 4 (August 1921): 24.

50. On the question of just how young men developed new expectations of their wives, see Wen-hsin Yeh's essay "Progressive Journalism and Shanghai's Petty Urbanites: Zou Taofen and the Shenghuo Weekly, 1926–1945" (in *Shanghai Sojourners*, ed. Wen-hsin Yeh and Frederic Wakeman Jr. [Berkeley: Institute of East Asian Studies, University of California, 1992], passim). Yeh suggests the possibility that newspaper literary supplements popularized new ideas about the qualities a wife should possess and, to some extent, commodified them.

51. Ellen Key (1849–1926), a Swedish writer and activist, glorified motherhood and urged feminists to focus their efforts on the elevation of women's "natural" function rather than on expanded political rights. She argued for recognition of women's right to live as sexual beings and bear children outside of marriage. She also believed that marriage without love was immoral and advocated divorce when love failed. Her views on love and marriage had been well-known and often cited in China since the New Culture Movement. *Shili* referred to the traditional marriage that met moral standards as expressed in Confucian classics such as the *Shijing* (The Book of Poetry) and the *Liji* (The Book of Rites).

52. Jian Cheng, letter to the editors, JTYJ 1, no. 5 (December 1921): 118–20.

53. Li Shuting, letter to the editors, JTYJ 1, no. 5 (December 1921): 120; Yan Lanqi, letter to Luo Dunwei, JTYJ 2, no. 1 (5 May 1922): 153–54. In 1922 only 656 women in all of China were attending university (Chen Dongyuan, *Zhongguo funu shenghuo shi* [A history of Chinese women's lives] [1926; reprint, Taipei: Shangwu yinshu guan, 1990], 389–92).

54. JTYJHK 1, no. 3 (15 January 1921): 75. Another expression, "De, yan, rong, gong haowu" (She is entirely without virtue, speech, beauty, or industry), appeared frequently in the journal's pages. JTYJHK 1, no. 3 (January 1921): 74, 76. Ironically, these were the four virtues that characterized the traditional ideal woman.

55. Chen Guyuan, "Luosu hunyin wenti yu jiushi jiehun" [Bertrand Russell's marriage problem and traditional marriage], JTYJ 1, no. 3 (January 1921): 1–21, passim.

PART THREE

# Gender in Literary Traditions

In many ways, literary and film criticism are the disciplines that have led the way in the analysis of gender as a system of representations in China. Postmodern theory has made a particularly useful contribution here in drawing attention to questions of "subjectivity" in literature and film (that is, the viewpoint from which the work is created, including gender, class, ethnic, national, and other identities, as well as the inequalities of power that structured the production of the work). In addition, there has probably been a greater degree of interchange of ideas between Chinese scholars publishing in Chinese in the mainland and diasporas; Anglophone scholars publishing in the West; and Chinese-born, Western-educated scholars publishing in English in the West than has occurred in anthropology, history, and other social sciences. While the reasons for this are varied, one factor is that literary criticism was a well-developed discipline in China long before the opening-up policies of the 1980s, and it was easier in literature than in the social sciences and history for scholars to find a common language on opposite sides of the Pacific. The social sciences and history suffered greatly under the intellectual repression of the Maoist period. And even in the 1980s and 1990s, social criticism continued to be much more politically dangerous than literary criticism. For this reason, as noted in the introduction to this book, historical and anthropological work on Chinese gender has tended to be dominated by Anglophone scholars and their theoretical approaches.

One of the important contributions of literary theorists working in different periods and genres has been to show that masculine Chinese identity has been established in literature and film through using Chinese femininity as its complementary but subordinate opposite. Another has been to examine the use of woman as a symbol in national identity, dissecting how the trope of the suffering, self-sacrificing Chinese woman is actually written from the subject-position of the Chinese man who feels impotent to save her. A third contribution has been the rethinking of the Cultural Revolution period as one of enforced masculinization of women rather than "socialist androgyny." These contributions and the scholars who made them are discussed more fully in the introduction and afterword.

The following section does not try to represent all of these developments but rather discusses the gendered nature of the literary tradition as a whole in China, considering the notion of a "literary tradition" itself as a construction manipulated within social and political struggles. To claim ownership of a literary tradition is to claim a certain kind of social and cultural power. For most of Chinese history, literary traditions were dominated by men. Literacy and literary traditions were arguably more closely tied to issues of masculinity and femininity in China than in the West because of the association of manliness with *wen* (literary arts).

Lydia Liu begins her chapter by recounting that, in the 1980s, "female literature" became a fashionable category in China. Having retrospectively invented a unified tradition of "women's writing," female critics could then reevaluate women's literature and argue for its importance to overall literary history. Liu analyzes the works of Ding Ling (May Fourth era), Zhang Jie (reform era), and Wang Anyi (reform era). In their works all three authors play with the relation between gender, authorship, and subjectivity. Men are made into sex objects; unusual narrative positions are chosen, such as Zhang Jie's device in which a daughter finds her mother's journal; and lead characters are fixated on issues of self and identity. All three authors challenge the prevailing ideals about womanhood with descriptions of female sexuality, adultery, narcissism, and attachments to other women.

But was there a female tradition in modern Chinese literature? Liu notes that the concept of the female tradition came into existence in the mid-1980s, *after* female literary critics began to find a voice in the previously male-dominated world of literary criticism and historiography. Liu's main point, then, is that the whole idea of the "female literary tradition" was invoked in the context of the women's movement of the 1980s, as Chinese feminists began to contest the monopoly on feminism held by the Women's Federation (Fulian).

Responding to Liu's question, Wendy Larson begins by asking whether there is a male tradition in modern Chinese literature. She notes that the concerns of women writers with gender, authorship, and subjectivity are not present or are not the same in male-authored texts. The Chinese literary tradition *is* male. But ownership of a tradition has its price. Utilizing the concept of connoisseurship, Larson argues that, before the May Fourth period, the literate, elite male ideal was one of elegant sensibility, sensitivity, and learning. This Confucian literatus is lampooned in the two stories by Lu

Xun discussed here, "Kong Yiji" and "Soap," in which the elite ideal is depicted as a kind of hypocritical adherence to empty forms with no real content. At least in Lu Xun's stories there are characters of non-elite social status who are not drawn in by the charade; but Su Tong's "Wives and Concubines," written in the 1960s, depicts all of Chinese culture as "an empty play of power and aesthetics." With the demise of the particular social class who were the arbiters of the literate tradition, there is no longer a specific target of attack, and the critique extends to Chinese culture as a whole. This position characterizes the other authors discussed by Larson as well: Mo Yan ("Divine Debauchery") and Feng Jicai (*The Three-Inch Golden Lotus*).

The connoisseur in his various forms may be criticized for the cultural traditions with which he is associated, but as the collector and arbiter of that culture he is still in a position of power. Larson's chapter suggests that the male claim to ownership of the literary tradition is still alive and well, although it is now expressed in more subtle forms.

An English-language collection that reflects the search to define a female tradition is *The Serenity of Whiteness: Stories by and about Women in Contemporary China,* translated and edited by Zhu Hong. The writers were born in the 1930s and 1940s, and they wrote these stories in the early and mid-1980s. In her preface, Catherine Vance Yeh argues that one can detect a shift during this period from an initial focus on women as human beings (a reaction against the dehumanizing effects of the Cultural Revolution) to a focus on questions of what it means to be a woman. In *I Myself Am a Woman: Selected Writings of Ding Ling,* Tani Barlow provides a good analysis of the works by Ding Ling, who is often recognized as the first important "modern" female writer.

### COMPLEMENTARY READINGS

Ding Ling. *I Myself Am a Woman: Selected Writings of Ding Ling.* Ed. Tani E. Barlow, with Gary J. Bjorge. Boston: Beacon Press, 1989.

Feng Jicai. *The Three-Inch Golden Lotus.* Trans. David Wakefield. Honolulu: University of Hawaii Press, 1994.

Lau, Joseph S. M., C. T. Hsia, and Leo Ou-Fan Lee, eds. *Modern Chinese Stories and Novellas, 1919–1949.* New York: Columbia University Press, 1981. (Contains the two stories by Lu Xun, trans. Yang Hsien-yi and Gladys Yang, which are mentioned in the introduction to this part.)

Lu Xun [Lu Hsun]. *Selected Stories of Lu Hsun.* Trans. Yang Hsien-yi and Gladys Yang. Peking: Foreign Languages Press, 1978.

Mo Yan. "Divine Debauchery." In *Running Wild: New Chinese Writers,* ed. David Derwei Wang, with Jeanne Tai, 1–12. New York: Columbia University Press, 1994.

Su Tong. "Raise the Red Lantern." In *Raise the Red Lantern: Three Novellas,* trans. Michael S. Duke, 11–100. New York: William Morrow, 1993. (In Chinese, the story's title is "Wives and Concubines." See the discussion of the film and bibliographic information in the introduction to part 2 of this volume.)

Zhang Jie. *Love Must Not Be Forgotten (Ai, shi buneng wangjide): Short Stories*. Trans. Gladys Yang. San Francisco: China Books and Periodicals, 1986. (Includes the short story of the title, as well as *The Ark*.)

Zhu Hong, ed. and trans. *The Serenity of Whiteness: Stories by and about Women in Contemporary China*. New York: Available Press, 1991.

# CHAPTER FIVE

# Invention and Intervention: The Making of a Female Tradition in Modern Chinese Literature

*Lydia H. Liu*

Is there a female tradition in modern Chinese literature?

By asking this question, I intend to bring to critical attention a number of interesting claims put forth by women critics in post-Mao China, particularly the generation that came to maturity in the latter half of the 1980s. To many of them, *nüxing wenxue* (female literature) is more or less a fait accompli, something that preexists the critical effort to name it as such.[1] The job of a critic is thus to establish the collective identity of women writers, pinpoint their difference from male writers, rescue them from the lacunae of historical memory, and restore them to a rightful place in literary history. The whole enterprise is undertaken with a view to bringing the female tradition to light. (Incidentally, the same has also taken place in the West.) For instance, the critic Zhao Mei claims that women writers as a group are the first to bring about a radical break with the previous literature. "In grappling with the mysteries of existence and the nature of life and desire through the mediation of self-consciousness," says she, "women writers successfully broke down the dominant convention of broad social and political themes in fiction."[2] Another critic, Li Ziyun, attributes a good deal of avant-garde experiments in modern literature to the initiative of women. Describing the most-recent developments in Chinese literature, she boldly asserts: "We are witnessing a second upsurge in the literary output of female writers in mainland China. This is marked not only by the extraordinary number and quality of women's works but by the vanguard role some of those works have played in Chinese literature. I am referring to their disregard for existing literary conventions, their exploration of new horizons in terms of theme and experience, and their experimentation with form."[3]

In the meantime, the women's studies series edited by Li Xiaojiang includes a number of major historical projects devoted to recognizing a female literature that has developed over time, enjoys a homogeneous textual and intertextual tradition, and is capable of legislating its own critical vocabulary. *Emerging from the Horizon of History,* a book coauthored by Meng Yue and Dai Jinhua, represents one of the most ambitious efforts.[4] On the basis of a rigorous analysis of women's literary texts, this book suggests that modern literature has produced not only a good number of professional women writers but a female literature and a female literary tradition as well. The authors regard the May Fourth generation as the harbinger of that tradition: "Having rejected the status quo, May Fourth women writers were able to initiate their own tradition in the cracks and fissures of their culture."[5]

What strikes me as important here is less the truth value of various claims for a female literary tradition (which women critics have no vested interest in calling into question) than the peculiar historical circumstances that seem to compel those critics to identify, legitimate, and, perhaps, invent a homogeneous tradition on behalf of women writers from the May Fourth period down to the present.[6] To the extent that the female tradition did not come into its own until *after* women scholars began to make significant interventions in literary criticism and historiography (a field heretofore dominated by men) in the second half of the 1980s, their endeavor deserves our unmitigated attention. Indeed, what is a literary tradition, be it major, minor, male, or female, but a product of the collaborative efforts of writers and critics engaged in the specific historical issues of their own time? In undertaking this study, I neither assume nor contest the raison d'être of the so-called female tradition, but try to understand it as an important historical project that involves the agency of both women writers and women critics in post-Mao China.

## OFFICIAL FEMINISM AND CHINESE WOMEN

The category of women, like that of class, has long been exploited by the hegemonic discourse of the state of China, one that posits the equality between men and women by depriving the latter of *their* difference (and not the other way around!). In the emancipatory discourse of the state, which always subsumes woman under the nationalist agenda, women's liberation means little more than equal opportunity to participate in public labor.[7] The image of the liberated daughter and the figure of the strong female Party leader celebrated in the literature of socialist realism are invented for the purpose of abolishing the patriarchal discriminatory construction of gender, but they end up denying difference to women.[8] During the Cultural Revolution, political correctness consisted largely in women wearing the same dark colors as men, keeping their hair short, and using no makeup. I am not suggesting that women ought to be feminine. The fact that the state did not require men to wear colorful clothes, grow long hair, or use makeup, which would have produced an equally iconoclastic effect, indicates that it was woman's symbolic difference that had been specifically targeted and suppressed on top of all other forms of political repression. Post-Mao Chinese women are therefore dealing with an order of reality vastly different from that which feminists in the West face within their own patriarchal society, where the female gender is exploited more on the grounds of her difference than the lack thereof. Being named as the "other" and marginalized, Western feminists can speak more or less from a politically enabling position against the centered capitalist ideology. By contrast, contemporary Chinese women find their political identity so completely inscribed within official discourse on gender and institutionalized by Fulian (the All-China Women's Federation) that they cannot even claim "feminism" for themselves. As Tani E. Barlow points out: "The importance of Fulian lay in its power to subordinate and dominate all inscriptions of womanhood in official discourse. It is not that Fulian actually represented the 'interests' of women, but rather that one could not until recently be 'represented' *as a woman* without the agency and mediation of Fulian."[9]

There are currently two translations of the word *feminism* in Chinese. The old *nüquan zhuyi* denotes militant demands for women's political rights reminiscent of the earlier women's suffrage movements in China and in the West. The new term *nüxing zhuyi*, emphasizing gender difference, has been in circulation for the past decade in Taiwan and only recently in China. The former is downright negative, and the latter sounds rather ambivalent. Contemporary women writers refuse to have their names associated with either term. When one scrutinizes their reluctance, one is furthermore struck by the fact that there is more at stake than the legitimacy of Western feminist discourse as applied to another culture. It appears that the very notion of *nü zuojia* (woman writer), a Chinese category, has been thrown into question by women writers such as Zhang Jie, Wang Anyi, and Zhang Kangkang. To them, once someone is designated (or stigmatized) as a woman writer, let alone as a feminist, she is trivialized by the mainstream (male) literature. Zhang Kangkang voices this fear in her article "We Need Two Worlds," using the analogy of the handicapped athlete to illustrate her point. In games held specially for the handicapped, people applaud the athletes because many of them think that "the handicapped cannot run in the first place." The same holds true for female writers, who are often classified as a category separate from mainstream male authors "as if it were a universally accepted truth that only men could be writers and as if they were born writers."[10] Women writers sharing the concerns of Zhang Kangkang feel that they must constantly fight against the condescension of their male colleagues and their own trivialization. The apparent contradiction between their objection to the term *woman writer* on the one hand and a strong female consciousness informing their works on the other must be understood in this light.[11]

Figure 4. The female is clearly wielding the pen in this cover drawing for *Film Criticism,* published during the most zealous period of the Cultural Revolution. *(Dianying pipan* [Film criticism], published by the August 18 Red Guard Film Criticism Editorial Group, Tianjin Medical Institute, Tianjin, 1967.)

To contemporary Chinese critics, it is not the term *woman writer* but *feminism* that must be kept at bay at all times. Most women scholars take care to stay away from the word even as they publish sophisticated views on the politics of gender, views that would probably be deemed "feminist" by some Western feminists. This is what critic Yu Qing does, for example, in her theorizing on the female tradition in Chinese literature. In her view, women's marginal position need not trivialize them:

> In coming to maturity, female consciousness does not seek to submerge its gender in order to arrive at some abstractly conceived and genderless human condition. It aims to enter the overall human conception of the objective world from the special angle of the female subject and to view and participate in universal human activities from the particular viewpoint of the female gender that is uniquely constructed as such . . . the female gender is formulated in societal terms. And as long as the social factors constitutive of the female gender remain, gendered consciousness and gendered literature will not go away. The so-called ultimate (transcendental) consciousness and ultimate literature, therefore, do not and will not exist.[12]

Like most other scholars in women's studies, Yu rejects the word *feminism* in her writing, although she has no scruples about quoting the works of Western feminists in support of what she calls her "female" position.[13] In order to grasp this complex situation, one must take into account Chinese women's relationships with the state, official feminism, and its representative, Fulian. As I mentioned earlier, the latter takes a strong position on all gender issues, claiming to represent women and protect their rights but functioning in reality very much like other hegemonic apparatuses used by the Party, even though it is the least important of all state apparatuses.[14] After all, the "ism" part of "feminism" seems to imply the same masculine area of power and knowledge as "Marxism" and "communism."[15] Women's rejection of "feminism" therefore expresses a strong desire to position themselves against state discourse on gender and its suppression of women's difference.[16] Consequently, terms such as *nüxing yishi* (female consciousness) and *nüxing wenxue* (female literature) are invented by critics who wish to conceptualize a female tradition that will recognize women as historical subjects rather than objects of male patronage. The new crop of journals in the eighties featuring women authors or female literature such as *Nü zuojia* (Female Writer) and *Nüzi wenxue* (Female Literature), the establishment of the first Women's Research Center in 1985 by Li Xiaojiang and her ambitious series on women's studies mentioned above, as well as the recent debates on female consciousness and female literature sponsored by critical journals such as *Wenyi pinglun* (Art and Literary Criticism), *Dangdai zuojia pinglun* (Studies on Contemporary Writers), *Dangdai wenyi sichao* (Current Trends in Art and Literature), and *Xiaoshuo pinglun* (Fiction Studies)[17]—all attest not only to a heightened awareness of women as historical agents but also to a significant breakaway from the totalizing discourse of official feminism.

Having invented the terms in which the debate on gender issues will be conducted, contemporary female critics proceed to reevaluate women's literature and identify a female tradition for which they claim nothing less than a vanguard role in modern Chinese literature. In so doing, they are actually reappropriating the historical category of women from state discourse for the purpose of empowering the female gender. When those critics talk about "female consciousness" and "the female literary tradition," they are not so much concerned with female identity as with female subject-position, or the question of who determines the meaning of female experience. The question "Who am I?" which is the title of a story by a contemporary writer named Zong Pu and which frequently appears in the works of Chinese women authors, indicates a desire to unfix the meanings that the state and traditional patriarchy have inscribed on the female body.[18]

The three women writers that I discuss here—Ding Ling, Zhang Jie, and Wang Anyi—figure prominently in contemporary literary criticism as architects of the female tradition. Ding Ling represents the legacy of the early twentieth century and is seen as prefiguring contemporary women's writing in a number of ways: the focus on female subjectivity; the critique of patriarchal ideology and institutions; and, most important, the problematization of writing and discourse through gender experience. When her "Diary of Miss Sophia" first appeared in the February issue of the *Short Story Magazine* in 1928, it was immediately perceived as a major event, as one critic recalled in 1930: "It was like a bomb exploding in the midst of a silent literary scene. Everyone was stunned by the author's extraordinary talent."[19] Other leading critics of the time, such as Qian Qianwu and Mao Dun, reviewed the story and called its author the first Chinese woman writer who "speaks out about the dilemmas of the liberated woman in China"[20] and whose understanding of the "modern girl" goes deeper than that of any of her contemporaries.[21] Some fifty years later, Zhang Jie's story "Love Must Not Be Forgotten" marked another turning point in Chinese literature following Mao's death, as is attested by the controversy it provoked. Chinese readers, accustomed as they were to socialist realism, were stunned by the subjective voice of the female narrator and the story's forbidden subject. A series of debates on love, gender, and the role of the writer began to appear in *Guangming Daily,* in the course of which a critic named Xiao Lin wrote: "As literary workers, shouldn't we be alert to and eradicate the corruptive influence of petty bourgeois ideas and sentiments? Shouldn't we stand in a higher position, command a broader vista, and think more deeply than the author of this story does?"[22] In rebuttal Dai Qing, a renowned writer and critic in the post-Mao period, defended Zhang Jie's story on the grounds of its moral complexity and bold exposé of social problems.[23] She argued for the legitimacy of the author's personal vision and welcomed her departure from the dominant literary orthodoxy.[24] Compared with Zhang Jie, the younger writer Wang Anyi is much less controversial. But her recent output has surprised readers with a wide range of experiments in eroticism, subjectivity, and socially transgressive themes. In the three stories known collectively as the "Three Themes on Love," she explores sexuality and female subjectivity as a means of testing the limits of reality and the boundaries of human consciousness.[25] "Brothers," a story published in March 1989, challenges the ideology of heterosexual love by pitting female bonding against the marital tie prescribed by the dominant culture. If Zhang Jie's novel *The Ark* centers on the sisterhood among divorced women, "Brothers" dramatizes the conflicting claims of marriage and the emotional attachment between women and, therefore, highlights the problematic of desire and choice. I hope that my reading of the three authors will help bring out the main features that most women critics in the eighties attribute to the female tradition.

## GENDER, WRITING, AND AUTHORSHIP

Ding Ling's "Diary of Miss Sophia" contains an interesting allegory of reading in which the narrator, Sophia, casts the young man Weidi in the role of a reader by showing him her diary. Weidi fails to grasp the import of those entries and, believing that another man, Ling Jishi, has successfully become Sophia's lover, he complains: "You love him! . . . I am not good enough for you!"[26] The diary cannot explain Sophia to Weidi, because he insists on reading his own gendered discourse into Sophia's diary and finds in it a stereotyped triangular situation in which his rival gets the better of him. His reaction to the diary is, therefore, highly predictable according to conventional male-centered readings. Weidi "mis"-reads it despite clear evidence that Sophia is more interested in herself than in either man. In this allegorical encounter between female discourse and its male counterpart, writing and reading come across as profoundly gendered practices.

The narrator's writing and her choice of a male reader in this story introduce gender difference into the production of text and write the female gender into the authorial position. In her involvement with Ling Jishi, the narrator takes up a similar position: writing herself as a subject rather than as an object of desire. The description of her first encounter with Ling Jishi shows a devastating reversal of male literary conventions: "I raised my eyes. I looked at his soft, red, moist, deeply inset lips, and let out my breath slightly. How could I admit to anyone that I gazed at those provocative lips like a small hungry child eyeing sweets? I know very well that in this society I'm forbidden to take what I need to gratify my desires and frustrations, even when it clearly wouldn't hurt anybody" (49). It is the narrator's female gaze that turns the man into a sex object, reversing male discourse about desire. Not only does the narrator objectify the man's "lips" as if they were pieces of candy, but she ignores the phallus and feminizes male sexuality by associating it with lips (labia). She is empowered by writing that gives full play to her subversive desires and constitutes her as a subject. If the first scene mentioned helps establish gender difference in discourse, the reversed subject/object relation pinpoints the power struggle implied in the rewriting of gender.

Zhang Jie's "Love Must Not Be Forgotten" also emphasizes the relation of writing, gender, and authorship. Unlike Ding Ling's story, however, this narrative takes place between the narrator, Shanshan, and her late mother, Zhong Yu, whose writing and ghostly memory she strives to decipher; that is to say, instead of writing a diary herself, the daughter tries to interpret the incoherent words contained in a diarylike notebook the mother has left behind. The self-reflexive technique of taking a phrase from the mother's notebook and using it for the title of the story calls attention to the textuality of her narrative, so that it comes across as a writing about writing, reading, and critical interpretation. Read in this light, the expression "love must not be forgotten" becomes ambiguous, for in the context of the notebook it sums up the extraordinary love the mother feels for another married man. But when the same appears in the title of the daughter's narrative, it sounds curiously like a warning that the tragic lesson must be remembered so that it will not be repeated by herself and others. Through writing, the daughter conducts a dialogue with the mother about desire and suffering:

> At first I had thought that it contained only notes for future writing, because it didn't read like a novel, or like reading notes. Nor did it seem like letters or a diary. Only when I read it through from beginning to end did her cryptic comments join with my own scattered memories to suggest the vague outlines of something. After a great deal of reflection, it finally dawned on me that what I held in my hands was not lifeless, antiseptic writing; it was the searing expression of a heart afflicted with grief and love.[27]

The mother's love affair that the narrator reconstructs from the notebook also has much to do with literature and writing. A novelist herself, the mother has a life-long fondness for Chekhov. "Is she in love with Chekhov?" The daughter recalls the mother's extraordinary obsession with Chekhov's stories. "If Chekhov had been alive, such a thing might actually have happened" (109). As the narrator infers, part of the obsession comes from the fact that one of the two sets of Chekhov that the mother owns is a gift from her lover, a gift that, shortly before her death, she asks to have cremated with her. But, judging from her mother's almost religious devotion to romantic love, the narrator is not far wrong in suggesting that the mother is infatuated with Chekhov, for romantic love is the legacy of the literary tradition that Chekhov represents, a tradition that idealizes love and emphasizes internal drama and moral conflict. As if to reinforce her point, the narrator also situates the love tragedy in the intertextuality of Shakespeare's *Romeo and Juliet:* "Juliet compared her love to riches when she said: 'I cannot sum up half of my sum of wealth.' I suppose Mother couldn't have summed up half of her wealth, either" (116).

The literariness of the mother's love finds embodiment in one of her own novels in which she casts herself as a romantic heroine and her lover as a hero. Interestingly enough, her lover is a devoted reader of her novels. Literature and criticism thus become the field across which they indirectly "talk love" *(tan lian'ai)* to each other. During one of their rare encounters to which the young narrator is a witness, the man says: "I've read your latest novel. Frankly, it's not quite right in some places. I don't think you should be so hard on the heroine . . . you see, loving someone is not wrong in itself, and she hasn't really hurt anyone else. The hero might also have been in love. But for the sake of another person's happiness, they find that they must give up their love" (112). Submitting to the lover's discourse on self-sacrifice, the mother can only use her notebook as his substitute and pour into it her yearning and unfulfilled desire until the moment of her death.

The story would not be so interesting if it were simply the love story some critics have suggested it is.[28] It turns out that the insistent presence of the first-person narrator blurs the transparency of its language and problematizes the discourse on romantic tragedy. After all, the mother's story is told because the daughter herself faces the dilemma of deciding whether or not she should marry her friend Qiao Lin, whom she finds handsome but intellectually inadequate. She recalls her mother's advice: "Shanshan, if you can't decide what you want in a man, I think staying single is much better than marrying foolishly" (105). Behind that advice, of course, lies the wreckage of the mother's life: her own marriage has been a failure, and she ends up in love with a man with whom she cannot even shake hands. The daughter refuses to repeat the mother's marriage, but that is not all. She goes further and questions the latter's romantic approach to love: "I weep every time I see that notebook with 'Love must not be forgotten' written across its front. I weep bitterly again and again, as if I were the one who had suffered through that tragic love. The whole thing was either a great tragedy or *a massive joke.* Beautiful or poignant as it may have been, I have no intention of reenacting it!" (121, italics mine). The daughter's final choice is that of rebellion—rebellion against the discourse of the literary tradition (Chekhov and *Romeo and Juliet*) to which her mother has subscribed as novelist, heroine, and woman. By reconstructing the mother's life in writing, the narrator is able to rewrite the story of a woman's destiny so that independence rather than romantic attachment to a man will become her priority. When she declares toward the end that "living alone is not such a terrible thing" (122), her writing goes beyond the mother's wisdom and overcomes the tragic/romantic discourse for which the latter has paid with her life. By asserting her difference and exercising independent authorship, the narrator achieves autonomy.

Insofar as the female subject is concerned, writing is always a matter of rewriting (the male text) and gaining authorial control. The same is true of Wang Anyi's story "Love in the Valley of Splendor," although, unlike the foregoing stories, it is told—playfully—in the third person. I say "playfully," because the narrator's subjectivity demands our attention, making us aware that she is making up a story about a young heroine whose life coincides exactly with hers in time and space. The story begins: "I want to tell a story, a story about a woman. The breeze of the early autumn feels so cool and clean, and the sunlight looks so transparent. All this fills my heart with tranquility; and in tranquility I imagine my story. As I think it over, it seems the story also takes place after an autumnal shower."[29] The narrator intervenes again and again to remind us of the fictionality of her work. For example, when the heroine stands in front of the office window looking out at a narrow lane, the narrator cuts in: "so I stand facing the narrow lane and continue to imagine my story" (7). The emphasis on fictionality might be interpreted as the author's reaction to the widely held view in China that fiction mirrors life itself. But this is not simply a case of modernistic subversion of realist conventions. The situation is greatly complicated by the narrator's gender. The recurrent imagery of the fallen leaves and the window, which provides the setting both for the fictional world and for the extradiegetic world of writing, pinpoints the female identity that the narrator shares with her heroine. Her closeness to the heroine in identity, gender and otherwise, is accentuated when she concludes the story thus: "She felt that nothing had really happened. It was true and absolutely true that nothing whatsoever had happened in actuality, except that the parasol outside the window had shed all of its leaves. And it's time that my story about a story that has never taken place came to a close" (43). In echoing the view that nothing has transpired in this story, the narrator more than coincides with the heroine. The truth is that the heroine exists as an extension of the narrator, who brings an alternative self into being through writing and imagination. Within the story proper, the heroine also tries to break out of the status quo by creating an alternative self during her trip to the Valley of Splendor in Lu Shan. This intricate relationship between the narrator, the heroine, and the latter's reconstructed self results in sophisticated writing about female subjectivity. If the narrator focalizes exclusively on the heroine's point of view, the fixed focalization does not mean the total effacement of the narrator behind the character as it normally does. The narrator does more here, for she claims that she knows more than the character: "I follow her on her way out . . . She felt tranquil in her heart at the moment. But something was going to happen to her. Yes, something was about to happen. I am the only one to know" (5). Of course, she is not an omniscient narrator in an ordinary sense, either. The authorial control derives solely from a sense of identification. The narrator knows what is going to happen to her heroine because the heroine is her written self. In short, she wills her story and her protagonist into being.

"Love in the Valley of Splendor" stands out from the rest of Wang Anyi's "Themes on Love," which focus on the human libido and its ubiquitous power. This story is not so much about indomitable sexual drives as about a woman's quest for self through the rewriting of the traditional story of adultery. The heroine yearns to break out of the old identity that her marriage has fixed upon her and to reconstruct a new self. When a total stranger, one who is about to become her lover, approaches her for the first time in Lu Shan, she takes him for granted: "He arrived as she had expected and she was not in the least surprised by it" (17). The language is highly reminiscent of the omniscient voice that the narrator used earlier, when she knew what was going to happen to her alternative self. The heroine anticipates her own story and takes authorial control over the situation. Her self-awareness and intelligence distinguish her from Flaubert's Emma Bovary and enable her to revise the old adultery plot: "She liked this new self, the self as presented to his [lover's] eyes. Her old self was so stale that she loathed it and wanted to cast it away. As a brand new, unfamiliar self, she was able to experience many brand new and unfamiliar feelings; or maybe the reverse was true: her brand new and unfamiliar feelings enabled her to discover and create a brand new, unfamiliar self. She was pleased to discover the boundless imaginative and creative powers this new self was capable of" (23). Echoing *Madame Bovary* (one of Wang's favorite novels) in an oblique way, the story rewrites the nineteenth-century French novel by situating the heroine in an authorial position. If Emma Bovary is a reader par excellence and deceives herself in terms of patriarchal discourse, our heroine and her creator, the narrator, reject the role of reader and engage in imaginatively reconstructing their female selfhood as "authors."

## CONSTRUCTING FEMALE SUBJECTIVITY

Female subjectivity has occupied the center stage of women's literature since Ding Ling, although the latter eventually decided to circumvent the issue when her interest shifted from gender to class and relegated the former to a secondary and contingent priority.[30] Her first published story, "Meng Ke," contains a scene in which the young heroine presents herself before a film director, hoping to be hired: "She had to submit herself to a most unpleasant request: she raised her hands in silence and held back the short hair that covered her forehead and the sides, exposing her rounded forehead and delicate ears to the scrutinizing eyes of the man. She felt horrible and nearly broke down in tears. But the man was apparently pleased with what he saw."[31]

The revolt against such objectivization of the female body leads to the author's next work: "The Diary of Miss Sophia," which focuses on female subjectivity with a vengeance. The first entry of the diary records an interesting mirror scene: "Glancing from one side you've got a face a foot long; tilt your head slightly to the side and suddenly it gets so flat you startle yourself . . . It all infuriates me."[32] Examining her own image in the mirror seems to indicate narcissism. If so, the reflexive act of diary writing can also be seen as a mirroring of the self, for Sophia is at once the writer, the subject, and the reader of her text. In this story both the mirror and the diary come to us as powerful metaphors for Sophia's discourse about female selfhood. Ironically, the mirror's distortion of her image, which irritates her so much, seems to foreshadow the inadequacy of narcissism just as the diary fails to resolve the enigma of selfhood. Sophia's attitude toward writing and self reflects the female dilemma of wanting to reject male-centered discourse about gender and yet finding no alternative fully satisfying within a largely male-centered language. The text, therefore, is filled with contradictory expressions of self-love and self-loathing.

To the narrator endeavoring to rewrite herself into a different text, a text that will no longer portray her as someone's daughter, sister, lover, or friend but as an autonomous subject, the task is a difficult one. She has no idea of what the so-called subject is, for the "I" as an autonomous female subject has hardly existed in traditional Chinese discourse. Sophia asks herself repeatedly: "Can I tell what I really want?" (51) and tries to understand what she calls her "pitiful, ludicrous self" (79). Self-interrogation, ambivalence, and uncertainty fill the pages of the diary as the narrator struggles to "evolve an intelligible and authentic image of the self."[33] But that comforting image is nowhere to be found in this much-convoluted writing of self by the self. What her writing does succeed in doing, however, is subverting the closure, the authoritative tone, and the complacency of male-dominated writing. Her love need not be consummated to complete a romantic story. Her pains, desires, narcissism, perversity, and self-criticism form part of a work that struggles with itself and gives no final resolutions.

It is hardly surprising that half a century later Zhang Jie's novel *The Ark* still faced the question of female subjectivity. As it happens, the story also contains a mirror scene in which Liang Qian examines herself in a way that reminds us of Sophia: "Liang Qian stood up from her chair and saw herself reflected on the surface of the glass insulation in the studio. She was pale and shrunken, her hair disheveled. Weak and tired as she was, her eyes and brows wore a fierce look as if she were determined to quarrel with somebody and fight with him to death . . . She had barely reached forty and yet she already had the look of an elderly woman."[34] Facing herself, Liang faces a confused desire that renders her nonidentical with herself. She envies the twenty-one-year-old violinist in her crew, who is youthful looking with beautiful hair and bright eyes (for she seldom cries) and a wrinkle-free forehead (for she seldom uses her brains). She is torn by the conflicting desires to be a woman and to be a professional. She feels inadequate as a mother and yet cannot imagine living without a career. Her dilemma and her insecurity are shared by the other two women in the same apartment, which is jokingly referred to by the narrator as "the Widows' Club." Unlike Sophia, who is younger, these women must face the consequences of their divorce and separation as well as problems brought on by age and illness. Liu Quan is harassed by her boss at work and stigmatized by her colleagues; Cao Jinghua suffers from a spinal affliction that will probably lead to paralysis, and at work she is persecuted for publishing her political views. Liang Qian, a film director, is the only one who is not legally divorced from her husband, Bai Fushan (on the pretext of protecting her name, he has agreed to a separation but continues to utilize the prestige of Liang's family). The latter exploits and harasses her and schemes to prevent the release of her movie.

Focusing on the common plight of the three women, the narrator projects female subjectivity as a form of collective female consciousness, a consciousness that the symbolism of the title suggests. The ark is inspired by both Chinese and Western cultural traditions, for the word *Fang zhou* (the Ark) comes originally from the *History of the Latter Han* and only acquires its later biblical meaning via translation.[35] As critics have suggested,[36] the biblical symbolism of the ark implies the regeneration of mankind and the vision of an alternative world that would eventually replace the world these women inhabit, one in which "you are particularly unfortunate because you were born a woman."[37] The allusion to the *History of the Latter Han,* on the other hand, emphasizes the dynamic spirit of the women who defy tradition and brave hardships in their voyage to freedom. In fact, the symbolism is already prefigured in Zhang Jie's earlier story "Zumu lü" (Emerald), in which the metaphor of the sailboat conveys the triumph and the cost of being a self-reliant woman and contrasts with the comfortable but unreliable steamboat that symbolizes married life. If the ark projects a hope, a new world evoked by its Western etymology, it also provides the means (in the Chinese context) through which the new world can be reached. In short, it is a collective female consciousness that looks toward the future but is determined to wage its struggle here and now.

In view of the women's desire to protect their dignity as female subjects, it is not difficult to see why the sense of privacy and the fear of invasion figure so strongly in their response to the outside world. The apartment in which the women live is an embodiment of the ark of female consciousness that shelters them from a hostile world, but even here they are frequently threatened by invasions from Bai Fushan and inquisitive neighbors. On one occasion, Bai pokes his head into Liu Quan's bedroom before she can grab a blanket to cover herself up. He visits without the slightest consideration for the women's privacy. The following describes one of his surprise visits: "On an early morning like this, Liu Quan and Jinghua had just woken up from their nightmares. But before they could recover from the effects of their bad dreams, Bai intruded on them in such a rude manner and destroyed their mood. His invasion completely ruined their plans for a peaceful Sunday" (9). Bai thinks that his wife is hiding somewhere and insists on entering, but meets with firm resistance from Jinghua, who shuts the door in his face. Shortly after his departure there comes another knock at the door. The visitor turns out to be the head of the neighborhood committee, Jia Zhuren, who takes it upon herself to spy on them, assuming that divorced women always try to attract men. Overhearing Bai's knocking in the early morning, she has come to check things out. Again Jinghua guards the door and refuses to let her in:

> "Has our cat by any chance gotten into your apartment?"
> "No," Jinghua said clearly and firmly, "what's your cat got to do in our apartment?"
> "Oh! Don't you know, Comrade Cao, that your tabby cat has turned on all six tomcats in our compound? Ha, Ha!" Jia giggled obscenely.
> Jinghua laughed aloud: "Ha, ha, ha! I'm proud of my cat. She is fortunate enough to have so many admirers." (17–18)

The animal allegory used by the chairwoman exhibits the insidious language in which people in this society relate to sex and think about single women; it reduces woman to no more than a signifier of sexuality. Although Jia is herself a woman, the fact that she is the head of the neighborhood committee, which holds itself accountable to the All-China Women's Federation and spies for the authorities, pinpoints her as an upholder of the patriarchal order. Her invasion of the private world of the women, therefore, is a political conspiracy designed to deprive them of their dignity. But the fact that neither she nor Bai succeeds in getting into the apartment that morning implies that it is possible for the women to guard their privacy and subjectivity, provided that they have a room of their own and the support of a collective female consciousness.

In "Emerald," an earlier story by Zhang Jie, the protagonist, Zeng Ling'er, becomes a female subject not through identifying with other women but through enduring intense isolation and overcoming her romantic love. As a young girl, she is ready to sacrifice everything for the love of a man named Zuo Wei. During the Cultural Revolution she saves him several times, even confessing to his political "crimes." She is banished to the countryside, where she gives birth to his illegitimate child and suffers humiliation and ostracism. In the meantime, Zuo Wei has married another woman. However, the years of hardship and bereavement Zeng has to endure—her son drowns in a river—do not defeat her. Instead, she is transformed from a romantic young girl into the independent, resilient, and strong-willed woman that the title of the story, her birthstone, symbolizes. Transferred back to the institute where her ex-lover works, she discovers that she is no longer in love with him: "At this moment Zeng Ling'er felt that she had scaled another peak in her life. Yes, she would cooperate with Zuo Wei in his work, but this time out of neither love nor hate, nor any sense of pity for him. She simply wanted to make her contribution to society."[38]

If self-reliance and collective female consciousness are the responses that "Emerald" and *The Ark* make to the problematic of the female subject as first posed in Ding Ling's story, Wang Anyi takes a different approach in "Love in the Valley of Splendor." Since the story also contains a mirror scene, it is interesting to compare it with those in the other stories:

> She got back to her hotel room and shut herself up in the bathroom for a long time. She didn't know how long it was that she stood in front of the looking-glass, gazing at her own image. The image in the mirror was like another self gazing back at her as if that self had a lot to tell her but had decided to say nothing, because they were able to understand each other quite well without words. She turned her face a little to one side and studied its angles unconsciously. But all of a sudden, she felt alienated from the self in the mirror as if it had become a total stranger. She wanted to recapture the self, reexamine it, and be in touch with it again. But the self remained a blurred image and became so unfamiliar, so remote and yet also strangely familiar.[39]

The mirror scenes in "The Diary of Miss Sophia" and *The Ark* express a strong discontent with the self, as the women struggle with conflicting ideas about womanhood and subjectivity. In the passage above, however, the female subject appears not so much contradictory as indeterminate and elusive—something the heroine tries hard to grasp.

Lu Shan, where the mirror scene occurs and which, moreover, alludes to the classical motif of revelation in Chinese poetry, serves here as a metaphoric locus for the heroine's pursuit of self. The mountain, its face shrouded in clouds, symbolizes the unfathomable depths of self, which dissolve, transform, and consolidate along with the mist, fog, and white clouds.[40] This is a world of imagination, dream, and fantasy in which the self becomes fluid and capable of change and reconstruction. The heroine delights in the miraculous transformation of herself into someone whom she no longer recognizes: "That image was beautiful, so beautiful that she felt it utterly unfamiliar. For her own sake and for his [the lover's], she resolved to cherish the new self dearly. To damage it was to disappoint herself, him, his gaze, and his feelings" (21). The heroine's sense of self is so positive that the male gaze is not perceived as a threat to her subjectivity as in Ding Ling's early stories. Instead, the gaze, which is mutual, reinforces her desire to bring about a new sense of self and to "regain the gender she has lost" in marriage (27). Like subjectivity, gender is presented as something to be acquired and constructed through constant negotiation with other beings rather than as a fixed category of identity. The protagonist's marriage, which has fixed a sexual identity on her, succeeds only in alienating her from a fluid sense of gender, whereas her relative autonomy at the present moment enables her to rediscover it in relation to another man. She is proud of being different from man and of being reminded of the fact by the male gaze, for that difference is central to her self-consciousness as a woman. What is more important, it turns out that her love affair is more fiction than reality, in which the true object of desire is the heroine herself: "Her love for the self that grew out of her intimate relation with him surpassed by far her love for the man himself, although she did not fully realize it at the moment. She thought that she was in love with him and felt sad at the thought of departure. Many years were to go past before the truth would gradually dawn on her" (31).

Like Ding Ling and Zhang Jie, Wang Anyi situates female subjectivity in a process that challenges the received idea of womanhood. But in subverting patriarchal discourse, she also tries to involve the male gender in the constructive process, a fact that opens up the writing of gender to a wide range of possibilities—to gender relations that are predicated not on the desires of either man or woman alone but on the reworking of the subjectivity of male and female each in its own terms and in terms of each other.

## LOVE, MARRIAGE, AND FEMALE BONDING

Love and marriage have been almost synonymous with the female character in literature, but the responses of twentieth-century women authors to those perennial themes have shown significant departures from previous literary traditions. Their works tend to focus on the conflict between marriage and self-fulfillment, and between love and independence. Romantic love and marriage are often rejected as a result of woman's quest for selfhood, which explains why the majority of female protagonists we discuss here are single or divorced or have troubled marriages.[41] In "The Diary of Miss Sophia," the narrator falls in love with the handsome Ling Jishi. But it is no ordinary case of romantic love. The equilibrium of the subject and object of desire proves fundamental in maintaining the relationship. In other words, the narrator's aggressive pursuit of Ling is also underscored by her secret fear that she will be reduced to becoming the object of his desire. So when Ling comes into her room to express his desire, Sophia recoils in fear and disgust: "The lust in his eyes scared me. I felt my self-respect revive finally as I listened to the disgusting pledges sworn out of the depths of Ling

Jishi's depravity."[42] She revolts at the idea of becoming the object of the male gaze. As a result, her own desire is doomed by the need to overcome her lover's desire. This is how she describes their kiss: "That disgusting creature Ling Jishi kissed me! I endured it in silence! But what did my heart feel when the lips so warm and tender brushed my face? I couldn't allow myself to be like other women who faint into their lovers' arms! I screwed open my eyes wide and looked straight in his face. 'I've won!' I thought, 'I've won!' Because when he kissed me, I finally knew the taste of the thing that had so bewitched me. At the same moment I despised myself" (80–81). This is a revelation of the power relationship in sexual intimacy as perceived by a woman who writes, directs, plays, and observes the dangerous drama of sexual liaison. The usurpation of power by the male at the climactic moment seems to deny the possibility of heterosexual love in the patriarchal order without power struggle. Sophia wins the battle but loses the lover.

Another important reason for Sophia's revolt against Ling is his language as he takes it upon himself to teach her how to be a woman while reserving the role of a male chauvinist for himself: "Our most recent conversations have taught me a lot more about his really stupid ideas. All he wants is money. Money. A young wife to entertain his business associates in the living room, and several fat, fair-skinned, well-dressed little sons. What does love mean to him? Nothing more than spending money in a brothel, squandering it on a moment of pleasure" (65). Ling's dream of marriage, family, financial success, and even extramarital love is perceived as a typically male-centered capitalist dream. Sophia's lucid perception of the link between the capitalist system and patriarchal culture shows the firm ideological grounding of her feminism.[43] She refuses to be written back into patriarchal discourse either as a wife or as an extramarital lover. (She later learns that Ling Jishi has a wife in Singapore.) She suffers from the thought that she has offered herself to him for his amusement like a prostitute (66). These traditional female roles alienate Sophia from the man she adores. The lovers' encounter becomes a contest between two radically different ideologies that ends in the estrangement of the lovers and in Sophia's despair.

By contrast, her emotional attachment to another woman, Yunjie, does not require such antagonism. Her memory of Yunjie is always pleasant. Recalling their final moments together, she writes:

> What a life I was living last year at this time! To trick Yunjie into babying me unreservedly, I'd pretend to be sick and refuse to get out of bed. I'd sit and whimper about the most trivial dissatisfactions to work on her tearful anxiety and get her to fondle me . . . It hurts even more to think about the nights I spent lying on the grass in French Park listening to Yunjie sing a song from *Peony Pavilion*. If she hadn't been tricked by God into loving that pale-faced man, she would never have died so fast and I wouldn't have wandered into Beijing alone, trying, sick as I was, to fend for myself, friendless and without family. (70)

The allusion to *Peony Pavilion* is important for undercutting fictions of romantic love.[44] In light of her death after her husband's abuse of her, Yunjie's singing of love seems particularly ironical. Sophia's account of her life inserts what a traditional male-oriented text would leave out, that is, what would happen *after* the "euphoric closure" of united lovers. By evoking *Peony Pavilion,* Sophia in effect accuses traditional literature of enticing young people into romantic relations. Ding Ling's treatment of women's emotional bonding in this and other stories such as "Summer Vacation" does not, however, envision female bonding as a positive alternative to romantic love and marriage. With the arrival of contemporary writers like Zhang Jie and Wang Anyi, female bonding becomes an ideological choice just as important as subjectivity itself.[45]

*The Ark* ends with Liang Qian proposing: "Let's drink a toast to women," at which the women pledge a female bond. Each of them is disappointed in her husband and lacks faith in a male-dominated society. Cao Jinghua has been divorced by her husband because she does not share his dreams of raising a family and, without his permission, she goes through an abortion. Liu Quan's stingy husband exploits her sexually as if he has paid for her in cash. She dreads each night, but he always attacks her in the same manner: "You call yourself my wife, don't you?"[46] Liang Qian's husband, Bai Fushan, who treats marriage as a business transaction, is keen on making deals. When Cao Jinghua and Liu Quan overhear him plotting against his wife, Cao comments: "Here is what you call a husband . . . To hell with husbands. We must rely on ourselves" (113). The three women therefore seek mutual support in their own community: "The single women would often spend the night sitting together in the deep shade cast by the lamp and no one in the grimness of her mood thought of clearing the dinner table piled high with plates. While one recounted the unfair treatment she had received during the day, the others would smoke and listen in silence. Or they would smoke in silence and listen to her pounding the arms of the chair with her fists in anger" (49).

If the divorced women in *The Ark* manage to create an ark of their own— an ark of female consciousness—in order to contend with a hostile, male-dominated society, the three women in Wang Anyi's story, "Brothers," are not so successful and eventually drift apart. The story goes beyond the male/female antagonism and raises questions about desire, choice, female bonding, and women's relation to men and family.

Like the self-reflexive title of "Love Must Not Be Forgotten," "Dixiong-men" (Brothers) alludes to an art exhibition that the female protagonists talk of organizing but fail to realize. It also refers to the relationship among the women themselves, which ends in frustration like the art show. The opening lines of the story place the subversive relationship of the women in perspective: "At college, they [the women] were three brothers: Laoda, Lao'er,

and Laosan. They called their husbands Laoda's, Lao'er's, and Laosan's, respectively. They were the only female students in the whole class and they
surpassed their male classmates in everything they did."[47] In choosing the
word *brothers* rather than *sisters*, the story calls attention to the lack of a conventional social and intellectual bond among women, particularly among
married women. In the light of the time-honored cult of male bonding, the
choice is highly symbolic. We are told that the "brothers," all art majors, are
sloppier in their dress and behavior than the male students. They are anything but feminine. Like the three roommates in *The Ark*, they open their
hearts to each other, describing their sexual involvements with men as self-
destruction and their own bonding as salvation. But when the time for graduation comes, each is faced with a different choice. Laosan decides to adopt
the traditional lifestyle in order to fulfill her obligations to her husband, and
she takes a job in her hometown. Lao'er becomes an art teacher at a high
school in Nanjing, and Laoda teaches at a normal school in Shanghai. After
their graduation, the initial bond formed at school develops into a close
emotional attachment between Laoda and Lao'er, who address each other
afterward as Lao Li and Lao Wang.

In sharp contrast to Bai Fushan and most other men in *The Ark*, the husbands of both Lao Li and Lao Wang in this story are model husbands. They
treat their wives with respect and understanding and perform the household duties with diligence. But Lao Wang is amazed at the way her husband
divides life neatly into two orderly parts, career and family, each serving as
the means and end of the other. When Lao Li visits her after many years of
separation, she finds her freedom suddenly restored to her. For once she
lives spontaneously: she need not get up, have meals, or go to sleep at the
usual hours. From then on, the two women write long letters every few days
and marvel at the fact that their attachment to each other is closer than to
their own husbands:

> They noted cheerfully that their correspondence gave them the illusion that
> they had returned to the time of their girlhood. At that time each girl had a
> bosom girlfriend, with whom she could talk about practically anything she
> wanted to. The girls knew each other intimately and spent days and nights to-
> gether, until the love affair of each drove a wedge between them. They began
> to betray each other, learning to tell lies, thinking about their boyfriends and
> guarding the secret from each other. The war of territory began. The women
> now felt that they had gone backward in time, that is, more than ten years ago
> before the discord of desire had invaded their female friendship. (20)

Lao Li and Lao Wang grow so attached to each other that, when the former gives birth to a son, the latter buys a longevity pendant for the child and
is moved to tears at the thought that they finally have a child of their own.
In her mind, the child has a mother and a godmother; the father is excluded
from the picture. She offers to take care of the mother during her confine-

ment. Lao Li's husband is grateful for her service but at the same time feels slightly resentful. Her presence seems to disrupt his normal relations with his wife and banish him from his own family. Lao Wang's husband is also puzzled by his wife's strange behavior. When the two families gather around the dinner table on the eve of the Spring Festival, he tries to understand what makes his wife so unlike her usual self when at home: "At first, he thought it was Lao Li's husband. But after a while he concluded it couldn't have been he, because underneath that man's politeness lay indifference to his wife. He then began to observe Lao Li. It was not long before he saw that it was Lao Li who indulged her whimsical behavior. Whenever his wife went to extremes, Lao Li would give her a loving, encouraging look" (26).

The climax of the relationship arrives with two juxtaposed events: the two women's attempt to articulate their love for each other and the accidental fall of Lao Li's child. They are taking a walk in the park when Lao Wang suddenly asks Lao Li: "What would happen if we both fell desperately in love with one man?" Lao Li says she would let Lao Wang have the man. But Lao Wang presses her further: "What if we were so much in love that neither could surrender him to the other." "Then I'd kill him" (27), upon which Lao Wang's eyes fill with tears of gratitude. The two women talk about their emotional attachment in a roundabout manner, and their narrative cannot but be completed at the male's expense. To articulate love for the same sex is almost an impossibility, so that they must invent a fictional plot about triangular love in order to arrive at it. What makes the story so interesting is that there is something more than male discourse that stands in the women's way. The event that follows the conversation puts their love to the test, a test that finally estranges them. As the women are talking, Lao Li's son falls out of his carriage and hits his forehead on the curb. The mother is suddenly transformed into a different person. She forbids Lao Wang to go near the injured child, as if she were to blame for the accident. Lao Li's husband begins to hate her and orders her to leave. Ironically, it is not until love is damaged beyond repair that Lao Li is able to express it. As the two take leave of each other at the station, Lao Li says: "I love you. I truly love you!" and the story ends on a pessimistic note: "They had never said the word 'love' between themselves, a word that had become so contaminated by male/female copulation. But she said it now. Tears gushed from Lao Wang's eyes as she wept: 'Too late. It's too late!'" (30).

Motherhood need not have stood in the way of their love, because before the accident they had both tended the child with motherly care. Lao Li's overreaction to the accident reveals a mind torn by ambivalent feelings toward desire and motherhood. Feeling guilty for indulging her illicit desire, she opposes motherhood to female bonding so that the crisis of the self can be resolved through self-sacrifice and self-punishment. The fragility and rupture of the female bond testify to the difficulty a woman encounters in sorting out her desires in a society that privileges heterosexuality.

To return to the earlier question I raised at the outset, do the works of these writers suggest a female tradition in modern Chinese literature? Most critics of women's fiction agree that female writers tend to grapple with the problem of subjectivity in connection with gender and explore the relationship of the female subject to power, meaning, and the dominant ideology in which her gender is inscribed. Inasmuch as gender does make a difference in reading, writing, and other literary practices, as my analysis of the three authors has demonstrated, it is not difficult to conceptualize women writers as a separate category. However, one might still wonder what enables contemporary critics to jump from the category of woman writer—heretofore a subcategory in mainstream criticism—to that of female literature and female literary tradition. In other words, what happens when a radically different conceptual approach and historical imagination are brought to bear on the study of women's works? In this regard, it might be of particular interest to recall that women critics in the eighties and nineties almost unanimously evoke the early Ding Ling, that is, the author of "The Diary of Miss Sophia," as a pioneer in the female tradition while rejecting the later Ding Ling for being a chief collaborator in socialist realism. This seems to indicate that the idea of the female tradition is no less a potent form of historical intervention than it is an invention. Linking women's writing of the post-Mao era with that of the May Fourth generation across several decades, the female tradition opens up the possibility for women critics to envision a departure from the practice of male-centered literary criticism in the past decades, which they see as patronizing women writers but refusing to grant them a subject-position. What we are witnessing here, it seems to me, is a form of engagement and a profound moment of history making, as women critics seek to institute a different narrative that will enable them to contest the claims of the state, Fulian, and official feminism as the sole representatives of Chinese women. In that sense, the female literary tradition is surely in the making and, with more and more writers and critics joining in, it will probably take on a life of its own in the future. Nevertheless, I should not be taken as prophesying a bright future for female literature. While my fascination with this new literary tradition remains strong, the foregoing discussion is also intended as a reminder of the historical contingencies of our own academic practice: To what extent are we all implicated in the making of particular histories even at moments when those histories seem most neutral and transparent? What does the making of a female literary tradition in post-Mao China tell us about the general practice of historiography and literary scholarship? Finally, in what ways does such an understanding transform one's own knowledge about the object of study?

## NOTES

Reprinted by permission of the publisher from *From May Fourth to June Fourth: Fiction and Film in Twentieth-Century China,* ed. Ellen Widmer and David Der-wei Wang (Cambridge: Harvard University Press). Copyright 1993 by the Presidents and Fellows of Harvard College. An earlier and different version of this essay appeared in *Genders* 12 (winter 1991) under the title "The Female Tradition in Modern Chinese Literature: Negotiating Feminisms across East/West Boundaries." The author wishes to thank *Genders* and the University of Texas Press for allowing this revision to be published.

1. As Wendy Larson points out in "The End of 'Funü Wenxue': Women's Literature from 1925 to 1935," *Modern Chinese Literature* 4, no. 1–2 (spring-fall 1988): 39–54, the term *nüxing wenxue* appeared as early as in May Fourth criticism and was interchangeable with *funü wenxue* (women's literature). In the 1980s, however, the latter more or less dropped out of women critics' vocabulary, whereas the former acquired a new historical dimension and became extremely popular. Most contemporary critics now regard *nüxing wenxue* as a literary tradition that has its origins in May Fourth criticism.

2. Zhao Mei, "Zhishi nüxing de kunhuo yu zhuiqiu: Nüxing wenxue zai xin shiqi shinian zhong" [The dilemma and quest of female intellectuals: Female literature in the decade of the new era], *Dangdai zuojia pinglun* [Studies in contemporary writers] 6 (1986): 30. Translation mine.

3. Li Ziyun, "Nüzuojia zai dangdai wenxue zhongde xianfeng zuoyong" [The vanguard role of women writers in contemporary literature], *Dangdai Zuojia pinglun* 6 (1987): 4. Translation mine.

4. Also see Li Xiaojiang, *Xiawa de tansuo* [Eve's pursuit] (Zhengzhou: Henan renmin chuban she, 1988), and her *Nüxing shenmei yishi tanwei* [A preliminary inquiry into the female aesthetic] (Zhengzhou: Henan renmin chuban she, 1989).

5. Meng Yue and Dai Jinhua, *Fuchu lishi dibiao* [Emerging from the horizon of history] (Zhengzhou: Henan renmin chuban she, 1989), 14.

6. For further reference, see Wu Daiying, "Nüxing shijie he nüxing wenxue" [The female world and female literature], *Wenyi pinglun* [Art and literary criticism] 1 (1986): 61–65; Jin Yanyu, "Lun nüzuojia qun: Xin shiqi zuojia qun kaocha zhi san" [On women writers as a group phenomenon: A study of contemporary writer groups], *Dangdai zuojia pinglun* 3 (1986): 25–31; Ma E'ru, "Dui 'liangge shijie' guanzhao zhong de xin shiqi nüxing wenxue: Jianlun zhongguo nü zuojia shijie de lishi bianhua" [Contemporary female literature and its conception of the "Two Worlds": A history of the changing perspective of Chinese women writers], *Dangdai wenyi sichao* [Current trends in art and literature] 5 (1987): 91–95; also see Ren Yiming, "Nüxing wenxue de xiandai xing yanjin" [The evolution of female literature in a modern age], *Xiaoshuo pinglun* [Fiction studies] 3 (1988): 17–22.

7. Mao's binary opposition of equality and difference on gender issues incapaci-

tated Chinese women more than it empowered them. It served the interest of the state through exploiting women's labor power. Whenever a labor shortage occurred, women's participation in productive activity was encouraged as a form of gender equality. See Hongjun Su's "Feminist Study on Mao Zedong's Theory of Women and the Policy of the Chinese Communist Party toward Women through a Study on the Party Organ *Hongqi*," *Chinese Historian* 3, no. 2 (July 1990): 21–35.

8. Meng Yue theorizes gender politics in the literature of socialist realism in "Nüxing biaoxiang yu minzu shenhua" [Female images and the myth of the nation], *Ershi yi shiji* [Twenty-first century] 4 (1991): 103–12. Briefly, she perceives three dominant female images that serve to eliminate female subjectivity and uphold the authority of the Party. They are represented respectively by the liberated rural woman Xi'er in *Baimao nü* (The White-Haired Girl); the intellectual woman Lin Daojing in *Qingchun zhige* (The Song of Youth), who becomes a bildungsroman heroine under the guidance of the Party; and the strong Party leader such as Jiangjie in *Hongyan* (Red Cliff) or Ke Xiang in *Dujuan Shan* (Mount Azalea).

9. Tani Barlow, "Theorizing Woman: *Funü, Guojia, Jiating*" *Genders* 10 (spring 1991): 146.

10. Zhang Kangkang, "Women xuyao liangge shijie" [We need two worlds], *Wenyi pinglun* [Art and literary criticism] 1 (1986): 57. The speech was given earlier at an international symposium on women authors in West Germany.

11. In a published interview by Wang Zheng ("Three interviews: Wang Anyi, Zhu Lin, Dai Qing," *Modern Chinese Literature* 4, no. 1–2 [spring-fall 1988: 99–119]), Wang Anyi speaks rather disparagingly of women and feminism. To gauge Wang's complex view on the issue, see, for example, Wang's 1986 essay "Nanren he nüren, nüren he chengshi" [Man and woman, woman and city], *Dangdai zuojia pinglun* 5 (1986): 66. Of course, a work of fiction always speaks for itself, and what it says does not necessarily coincide with the author's private opinion.

12. Yu Qing, "Kunan de shenghua: Lun nüxing wenxue nüxing yishi de lishi fazhan guiji" [The sublimation of suffering: Tracing the historical development of female literature and female consciousness], *Dangdai wenyi sichao* 6 (1987): 55. The English translation is mine.

13. Interestingly enough, Elaine Showalter's name is mentioned in her writing. In fact, the names of Virginia Woolf, Simone de Beauvoir, and other Western feminists are frequently brought up in the writings of Chinese women critics in the eighties who refuse to call themselves "feminists."

14. Li Xiaojiang, a university teacher who initiated women's studies programs in post-Mao China, did at first try to obtain support from the Fulian, but she did not get even a single response to the letters she sent out. In frustration, she decided to rely on herself and rally the support of her fellow female scholars. Their independent efforts have been very successful. Zhengzhou University, where Li teaches Chinese literature, became the first university to offer courses on women writers in China. See Li Xiaojiang, "Zouxiang nüren" [In search of woman], *Nüxing ren* [The female person], September 4, 1990, p. 260.

15. I am indebted to Wendy Larson for calling my attention to this problem when commenting on an earlier version of this essay.

16. The All-China Women's Federation is unpopular among Chinese men and

women for different reasons, which indicates the subtle ambivalence even in official feminism. The idea of getting women organized empowers women on a symbolic level, if not in the real sense of the word, and poses a threat to the traditional male strategy of isolating the female gender to render it powerless. To Chinese women, however, the organization never truly represents them. It obeys the Party just as much as do other mass organizations in China. For related studies in English, see Tani Barlow, "Theorizing Woman"; and Xiaolan Bao, "Integrating Women into Chinese History—Reflecting on Historical Scholarship on Women in China," *Chinese Historian* 3, no. 2 (July 1990): 3–20.

17. All four journals come from outlying cities rather than from Beijing or Shanghai (*Dangdai zuojia pinglun* from Shenyang, *Wenyi pinglun* from Harbin, *Dangdai wenyi sichao* from Lanzhou, and *Xiaoshuo pinglun* from Xi'an), which indicates the rise of the periphery against the centered ideology. This situation is compared to siege warfare by some, parodying Mao's famous saying: "Nongcun baowei chengshi" (Besiege the city from the countryside).

18. Zong Pu attracted a good deal of attention as early as 1956, when she had her "Hongdou" (Red Pea) published, for which she was persecuted. "Wo shi shui?" (Who Am I?) came out twenty-three years later; Li Ziyun calls it "the first psychological fiction after Mao."

19. Yi Zhen, "Ding Ling nüshi" [Miss Ding Ling], in *Ding Ling Yanjiu ziliao* [Research material on Ding Ling], ed. Yuan Liangjun (Tianjin, 1982), 223.

20. Mao Dun, "Nü zuojia Ding Ling" [Ding Ling the female writer], in *Ding Ling Yanjiu ziliao* [Research material on Ding Ling], ed. Yuan Liangjun (Tianjin, 1982), 253.

21. Qian Qianwu, "Ding Ling," in *Ding Ling Yanjiu ziliao* [Research material on Ding Ling], ed. Yuan Liangjun (Tianjin, 1982), 226.

22. Xiao Lin, "Shitan 'Ai shi bu neng wangji de' de gediao wenti" [On the moral legitimacy of "Love Must Not Be Forgotten"], *Guangming Daily*, May 14, 1980, p. 4. Note that the reviewer favors the authorial point of view in fiction as opposed to the first-person voice used in Zhang Jie's story.

23. Dai Qing, "Bu neng yong yizhong secai miaohui shenghuo: Yu Xiao Lin tongzhi shangque" [Life should not be portrayed in a single color: A response to Comrade Xiao Lin], *Guangming Daily*, May 28, 1980, p. 4.

24. Zhang Xinxin, whom I have not included in this study, deserves mention here. Like Zhang Jie, her debut in literature also caused a major controversy. Her novella "Zai tongyi dipingxian shang" [On the same horizon], *Shouhuo* [Harvest] 6 (1981): 172–233, published while she was a student of drama, shocked some critics, who later condemned her in the official press. For that reason she was unable to find employment after graduation. Accusing the author of "bourgeois individualism" and "social Darwinism," her critics ignored the fact that she was actually criticizing male egotism and exploring the identity of self and gender in its complexity. For a survey of Zhang Xinxin's career and works in English, see Carolyn Wakeman and Yue Daiyun, "Fiction's End: Zhang Xinxin's New Approaches to Creativity," in *Modern Chinese Women Writers: Critical Appraisals*, ed. Michael S. Duke (Armonk, N.Y.: M. E. Sharpe, 1989), 196–216.

25. The "Three Themes on Love" consist of "Huangshan zhi lian" [Love in a wild

mountain], *Shiyue* [October] 4 (1986); "Xiaocheng zhi lian" [Love in a small town], *Shanghai Wenxue* [Shanghai literature] 8 (1986); and "Jinxiugu zhi lian" [Love in the valley of splendor], *Zhongshan* [Bell Mountain] 1 (1987).

26. Ding Ling, "Shafei nüshi de riji" [The diary of Miss Sophia], in *Ding Ling duanpian xiaoshuo xuan* [Ding Ling's short stories] (Beijing, 1981), 73. The English version used is that translated by Tani E. Barlow, with minor modifications, in *I Myself Am a Woman: Selected Writings of Ding Ling*, ed. Tani E. Barlow and Gary J. Bjorge (Boston: Beacon Press, 1989). Further references to this work will be included in the text.

27. Zhang Jie, *Ai shi buneng wangji de* [Love must not be forgotten] (Guangzhou, 1980), 109. The English version used is as translated by William Crawford in *Roses and Thorns: The Second Blooming of the Hundred Flowers in Chinese Fiction, 1979–1980*, ed. Perry Link (Berkeley and Los Angeles: University of California Press, 1984), with minor modifications. Further references will be included in the text.

28. Most reviewers read this story as a romantic tragedy and overlook the important role that the narrator plays here. See Zeng Zhennan, Kou Shan, and Wang He's reviews in *Guangming Daily*, July 2, 1980, p. 4. Translation mine. Further references will be included in the text.

29. Wang Anyi, "Jinxiugu zhi lian" [Love in the valley of splendor], 4. Translation mine.

30. I am not interested in applying the Lacanian theory of subjectivity or any other psychoanalytical theory of the works under discussion. My immediate concern is to describe some of the specific tropes or textual strategies such as mirroring that literally allow the female subject to confront herself in the text.

31. Ding Ling, "Meng Ke," *Ding Ling duanpian xiaoshuo xuan* [Ding Ling's short stories] (Beijing, 1981), 37–38. Translation mine.

32. Ding Ling, "Shafei nüshi de riji" [The diary of Miss Sophia], 44.

33. Yi-tsi Mei Feuerwerker, *Ding Ling's Fiction* (Cambridge: Harvard University Press, 1982), 46.

34. Zhang Jie, *Fang zhou* [The ark] (Beijing, 1983), 23. Translation mine. Further references will be included in the text.

35. See the epigraph to *Fang zhou*, which quotes from *Hou han shu* [The history of the latter Han]: "Fang zhou bing wu, fu yang jile" (Two boats race along side by side, enjoying the full pleasure of diving and climbing).

36. See Alison Bailey, "Traveling Together: Narrative Technique in Zhang Jie's 'The Ark,'" in *Modern Chinese Women Writers: Critical Appraisals*, ed. Michael S. Duke (Armonk, N.Y.: M. E. Sharpe, 1989), 96–111.

37. Zhang Jie, *Fang zhou* [The ark], 1.

38. "Zumu Lü" [Emerald], *Huacheng* [Flower city] 3 (1984): 87. Translation mine.

39. Wang Anyi, "Jinxiugu zhi lian" [Love in the valley of splendor], 16.

40. Since the heroine's pursuit takes the form of a romantic adventure, the imagery of mists and clouds also retains its erotic connotations. The consummation of her love, for example, is depicted thus: "Finally, they stepped into the wall of clouds and, sure enough, before them lay another world" (p. 26).

41. Zhang Xinxin's novella "Zai tongyi dipingxian shang" [On the same horizon]

is another good example of a work in which female subjectivity is pitted directly against marriage and male egotism.

42. Ding Ling, "Shafei nüshi de riji" [The diary of Miss Sophia], 79.

43. When we recall the author's own life, it is not surprising that she eventually became a dedicated Communist. See Tani Barlow's introduction to *I Myself Am a Woman*.

44. The allusion to the "pale-faced man" is reminiscent of the stereotyped image of the romantic scholar-lover, or *xiaosheng*, popularized in traditional fiction and drama, such as *Peony Pavilion*.

45. The term *female bonding*, rather than *homosexuality*, is used here to describe the range of female relationships explored by the three authors. In choosing not to pin down the meaning of those relationships, I intend to emphasize the fact that identity politics, which seems to be the main thrust of the current debate on homosexuality in the United States, is not the way in which my Chinese authors deal with sexual relationships in their works, and that I see no reason why I should fix identities (gay, lesbian, bisexual, or straight) on their characters.

46. Zhang Jie, *Fang zhou* [The ark], 87.

47. "Dixiongmen" [Brothers], *Shouhuo* [Harvest] 3 (1989): 4. Translation mine. Further references will be included in the text.

# CHAPTER SIX

# The Self Loving the Self: Men and Connoisseurship in Modern Chinese Literature

*Wendy Larson*

Is there a male tradition in modern Chinese literature?

The question, constructed as a parallel to Lydia Liu's question in the preceding chapter, may appear ridiculous.[1] After all, doesn't almost all of modern Chinese literature—written by men for male readers—concern masculine problems that may be hiding under universalism and emerge out of a masculinist literary culture where women rarely gain fame? The questions Liu asks about the formation of a female tradition could hardly be asked in relation to a male tradition. For example, must male writers struggle to produce a collective identity? Need they differentiate themselves from a powerful female tradition, where women determine the topics, tone, and style? Do they have to gather together their resources to locate and publish lost works and claim their rightful place in Chinese literary history? Moreover, because these questions do not apply to male writers' work, the goals of their writing also must be different. Liu shows us how women writers have searched for their own subjective voice, looking for the female "I" in a tradition that does not recognize such a position. Investigating the relationship between gender and writing, women writers have had to rewrite male texts that privilege romantic attachment and motherhood for a woman but independence and creativity for a man. They have had to figure out the relationship between the female subject, on the one hand, and power, meaning, dominant ideologies, and state control, on the other hand. These objectives either do not apply to or are not the same in male writers' texts.

In other words, the Chinese literary tradition *is* male, and Liu quotes Zhang Kangkang's words to show that the contemporary Chinese literary field behaves "as if it were a universally accepted truth that only men could be writers and as if they were born writers."[2] Chinese literary culture, evolving out of a male-only educational and civil service examination system, has been so strongly identified with men that it puts them in a position entirely different from that of women, who are still fighting to be recognized as equals.

The claim to cultural ownership—at least at the elite levels—has its own costs, however. When China was attacked and defeated in the Opium War of the mid–nineteenth century and later repeatedly routed in battle, occupied by foreign powers, and confronted with Western culture and science, the Chinese literary tradition came under attack. Reformers pointed a finger at, among other things, the inherent and limiting sexism of the educational system, claiming that recent military and cultural disasters were all the fault of men and their narrowly gendered vision.[3] Schools for women were opened and, slowly, women started to enter all aspects of public life. Women's liberation was part of the modern Chinese antidynastic state, and exciting discussions on how women should function in society, including their roles as "woman writers" and in "women's literature," were carried on throughout the 1920s at universities and in newspapers and journals.[4] As Liu relates, a few women writers quickly gained popularity with some of the most shocking writing of the modern period, and although today many complain that the literary field is still largely composed of men, women writers have continued to write, publish, and gain prominence. Yet it was men who were held most responsible for what many felt to be the defects of Chinese culture.

The May Fourth period gained its name from a student movement on May 4, 1919, against the unequal Versailles Treaty, which ceded Chinese territory to Japan and other foreign powers. A time of unprecedented attack on traditional culture, the 1920s saw classical literary traditions criticized as useless, harmful, or sentimental elite entertainment. As the promoters and beneficiaries of literature and textual knowledge and the social power they bestowed, male writers found themselves in the difficult position of being forced to reevaluate and reconstruct a tradition many believed to be defunct.

In their approach to this problem, examples of which span the period from the 1920s to the present time, male writers problematized their relationship to the literary tradition in a way that directly questioned its gendered elitism and the limitations it produced. As I show in this chapter, one way they did this was by creating the fictional character of the connoisseur and investigating connoisseurship, particularly that which involved women. The connoisseurship envisioned by such writers included group activities such as contests, performances, and meetings; textual traditions and creations; eccentric and bizarre postures and behaviors; and the appreciation of aestheticized or fetishized items. Women were involved in various ways as objects of direct appreciation; as images or tropes of beauty, delicacy, or virtue; as sexualized prizes within ritualized practices; and as toys or pawns within social, psychological, or literary games. Because within connoisseur-

ship women were the focus of male admiration and a means of male pleasure, stories that feature connoisseurs can be subjected to a feminist critique
that will show not only that in these stories women became pleasure objects
but also that they were secondary and subservient to men in many ways. In
other words, the "action"—important and interesting issues—was often located in the minds of male characters, while female characters functioned
as fulcrums, catalysts, or tools.[5]

Connoisseurship, although practiced in many cultures, has a long tradition in China. Its qualities, including obsession, or *pi*, were outlined and
explicated by the scholar and poet Yuan Hongdao (1568–1610) in his
1599 treatise, *History of Flower Arranging* (Pingshi). Although there are many
early references in Chinese texts to obsession with objects or qualities, these
reached a height during the sixteenth and seventeenth centuries, during
which obsession was often a characteristic of the true connoisseur. Yuan
uses a variety of terms to refer to the connoisseur and connoisseurship, including "to love things" *(haoshi)*, "to enjoy" *(changhao)*, "elegant gentleman"
*(yashi)*, and "one who appreciates" *(shangzhe)*.[6] Representing an "ideal of
unswerving commitment and genuine integrity that is incompatible with
worldly success," Yuan's requirements for obsession included an association
with collecting and connoisseurship, excessive and single-minded qualities,
and an unconventional and eccentric attitude.[7] As early as the fifth century,
the idea that obsession should be useless and also that it could compensate
for worldly failure linked it with the romantic tradition of the recluse, a man
who does not work for success but regards fighting for power and wealth as
an inferior way of living. The sixteenth century saw an increased romanticization of obsession and the new idea that it was a means of self-expression
or, in Yuan Hongdao's terms, the "self loving the self."[8] Purity, aloofness,
studied self-cultivation, and the ability to recognize value in the ugly and
unadorned became qualities of the connoisseur. *Qing*—love, emotion, or
sentiment—came to embody Ming ideas of obsession, and cyclical stories of
desire-possession-loss of the loved object appear.[9]

The connoisseur was almost always male, and thus connoisseurship, a
broader category than obsession, is an important means through which to
evaluate masculinity in modern Chinese society. Connoisseurship was a
mark of elegant sensibility among the male elite, had a long tradition within
literati practices, and was often called upon by modern and contemporary
writers to represent either positive or negative qualities in well-educated
men and to symbolize large cultural issues. Although male Chinese writers
recognized male characteristics in the tough, physical, and adventuresome
man familiar to contemporary life in the United States, they elevated the
model of the sensitive, intelligent, and learned man. These two realms,
which can be represented by the concepts of *wen* (the literary or civilized)
and *wu* (the martial), delineate a sphere of masculinity open only to men.[10]

The connoisseur—who can be viewed as symbolic of, or as showing typical if excessive characteristics of, the *wen* sensibilities of the educated male elite—can indicate "a potentiality for ultimate power in a way that femininity does not."[11] Because it is a category open only to well-educated and generally powerful men, connoisseurship can function as a complex indicator of many things: traditional masculinity in the modern world, social power and the relationship between its "haves" and "have-nots," Chinese cultural models in the face of imperialism, and ritual forms and performances within high culture.

Marxist cultural theory, which developed in China after the founding of the Chinese Communist Party in 1921, demanded ideological clarity, and it took a dim view of the literary culture that sustained elite power. The old-fashioned literary connoisseur—immersed in books, writing poetry, drinking wine with courtesans, and spouting classical illusions—was an easy target for a critique that pushed for a new social engagement in writing. Such figures can be found in many stories and novels of the 1920s and throughout the Maoist period, when this satirical depiction was joined by more ambiguous representations.

I have chosen to write about four well-known authors, one from the 1920s and three from the post-Mao era, all of whom utilize the connoisseur to theorize and problematize Chinese cultural issues. Unlike female writers—who have their own significant cultural demands—male writers must both take issue with their relationship to a culture they created and forge a new link. This is slippery ground, a spot where any representation of the past contains an inherent danger. As the difficulty with attaching a clear and stable meaning to connoisseurship indicates, total repudiation destroys the ground on which male writers stand and opens them to another common complaint—that they have thrown the culture of China away. Wholesale denial simplifies the past, vilifies it, refuses to see the past in the present, and may exoticize traditions that are not necessarily exotic to those involved in them. Therefore, the problem of male power and how it has determined culture is an essential issue in the masculine tradition of modern Chinese literature. The stance any writer takes within that paradigm is open to interpretation. Moreover, that stance can challenge certain repressive aspects of society while merely reproducing others.

## LU XUN'S CONNOISSEUR OF CULTURE

Two famous stories by Lu Xun (1881–1936), "Kong Yiji" and "Soap" (Feizao), are profoundly parodic portrayals of the old-style literatus.[12] In these two examples of satirical critique, the connoisseur—a broad symbol of all literate men—represents the emptiness and hypocrisy of the literary tradition, along with its total inability to provide learning adequate to meet modern demands. The Confucian gentleman Siming in "Soap" is a stereotype of the hypocritical literatus, full of confusion, longing, and lust but cloaked by the moral expressions of writing and poetry. Symbolic of the May Fourth critique of the past, which portrayed the literatus as empty and useless, Siming is a ridiculous character who puffs himself up with old knowledge but cannot recognize the English word *fool* that young boys use to mock him. Siming's wife and children, both on the periphery of power because of gender or age, are far more cognizant than he is about the absurdity of his Confucian ideals.[13] Siming's obsession is the moral past and himself as its transmitter.

Central to the story is the eighteen- or nineteen-year-old beggar girl who hangs around town and tries to get food for her grandmother, ignoring her own hunger. She becomes the topic of discussion for Siming's literary society, and the group of men wishes to honor her in a published essay. Although the essay ostensibly will focus on the girl's filial piety, a central virtue of Confucianism, it quickly becomes clear that the girl is an erotic object for the cultured men. Siming is openly appalled by the comments of young men in the vicinity, who joke that, if she washed up with a bar of soap, she would be a fine piece of goods. He is even more disgusted that his literary friends take up the joke and laugh. At the same time, however, Siming transfers the loosely floating concepts of bodily cleanliness, morality, and sexual attractiveness to his wife, for whom he purchases a bar of foreign soap.

Under his wife's questioning, Siming admits that he failed to give the filial granddaughter money. Siming displaces the material poverty that underlies the girl's condition with two things: the first is his own investment in male power and pleasure, and the second is his desire to glorify poverty—especially young, vulnerable, and potentially attractive female poverty—by changing it into a moralizing literary form. One reason the girl cannot function well as a literary trope, however, is that she lacks poetic training: if she could write poetry herself, she would be better able to embody the cultured stance that Siming and his friends represent.

The main target of Lu Xun's critique is the Confucian literatus such as Siming, whose pompous hypocrisy is easy to ridicule. At another level, Lu Xun's satire of the Confucian connoisseur implies that the entirety of Chinese traditional culture is based on falseness. Siming and his friends have the power to deny material resources to the poor, a perspective that allows them to eroticize vulnerability, and the ability to transform suffering into a much-admired moral essay. They work entirely for self-benefit. In other words, the relationship among Siming, the beggar girl, and literary form is the same as the relationship among the literati, the populace at large, and traditional culture. Traditional culture is nothing but a kind of power play, an eroticized connoisseurship that turns the suffering of the weak into the aestheticized pleasure and moral posturing of the powerful.

In the story "Kong Yiji," Lu Xun takes a slightly different perspective on connoisseurship.[14] Focusing more clearly on the material conditions that differentiate the rich and the poor or the cultured and the uncultured, the story portrays an educated but inexplicably impoverished man, Kong Yiji, who admires literati convention and attempts to live by its dictates. Although Kong Yiji can read, write, and quote from the classics, because he does not have the wealth that allows the literate class to eat in separate quarters and wear impractical long robes he is not accepted as one of them. At the same time, however, workers also mock Kong for the pretensions to culture he maintains in the face of utter, relentless poverty.

Even though he is only a shell of the Confucian gentleman, Kong's relationship to culture is one of connoisseurship. Kong lectures the serving boy, from whose perspective the story is narrated, on the correct way to write characters. When he steals, it is to steal books, an act that he makes more virtuous by calling it *qie,* or purloining, rather than stealing. The words that come out of Kong's mouth are archaic phrases that nobody uses anymore. Although the culture he admires is no longer alive and is completely irrelevant to his own situation, Kong cannot rid himself of its pervasive and damaging influence. Kong's attempts to present himself as a cultural connoisseur are absurd, but like Siming, he appears unaware of the situation.

In both stories, Lu Xun parodies connoisseurship—of women, writing, the classics, and culture at large—in a scathing critique. Connoisseurship here implies the primacy of form over content, the essential meaninglessness of traditional culture, and the stance and network of masculine power and pleasure that underlie the Chinese cultural system. In the case of Kong Yiji, the glory of cultural convention is so overwhelming that it erases Kong's ability to perceive his own poverty as such. Siming is equally benighted, but the story's focus is not so much material impoverishment as the bankruptcy of cultural China. From Lu Xun's point of view, true vision, or the ability to see things as they really are, belongs only to those who have not been excessively corrupted by the obfuscating values and forms of traditional culture. Women and children, as well as poorer men, fall into this category, leaving to intellectual men and their imitators the responsibility for creating a useless culture of connoisseurship with themselves as its now absurd keepers. Working didactically, Lu Xun also places the modern intellectual reader into an enlightened spot, as one who is supposed to recognize the past as pathology and reject it in favor of a more equitable future.

## SU TONG: DEEPER INTO CULTURE

Whereas Lu Xun's stories are enigmatic enough that even today they sustain the interest of the more theoretically inclined, a great deal of fiction published during the 1950s, 1960s, and 1970s leaves less to the imagination. Writers could be banished from the Party, exiled to the countryside, or even executed for improper representation, so ideological clarity was a matter of life and death. After the death of Mao in 1976, writers turned back to the values of critical realism popular during the 1920s and began to write stories full of ambiguity, for which multiple interpretations were possible. Any kind of clear-cut stance came under suspicion, a form of cultural control that was, most writers felt, all too common under Mao. The typical Party hero disappeared, peasants were not always innocent and pure, and fiction was no longer so easy to interpret.

Yet the connoisseur remained, still functioning as a pivot of cultural critique even under the new conditions of representational complexity. Appearing in the avant-garde fiction of Su Tong, Mo Yan, and Feng Jicai, the connoisseur ceased to function as an object of satire and began to fill another role instead. For Su Tong (1963–), whose story "Wives and Concubines" (Qiqie chengqun) became the basis of the 1992 film *Raise the Red Lanterns* (Dahong denglong gaogao gua), directed by Zhang Yimou, connoisseurship embodies psychological and hierarchical elements of Chinese culture deeply embedded in the mind, social practice, and even architecture.[15] This deep cultural critique implies that, from top to bottom, Chinese culture is nothing but a corrupt artifice, a hierarchy sustained only by male lust. Within this narrative, women are victims used and abused to maintain male power, and a feminist reading would show that Su Tong blames men for containing, projecting, and continuing the worst aspects of Chinese culture.

What distinguishes Su Tong's approach from that of Lu Xun is that here, the connoisseur is not so much a part of the past to be satirized and disposed of as he is an integral aspect of contemporary consciousness. While Lu Xun creates self-deceiving connoisseurs as well as other less powerful characters who can see through the hypocrisy, Su Tong's construction of Chinese culture lays out a framework of relationships so profound that no character can escape its meaning. Implicit in this portrayal is the idea that at its most essential level, Chinese culture is an empty play of power and aesthetics. Many of Su Tong's stories are set in historical times, but his revision of connoisseurship has little to do with a critique of traditional ideas. Rather, it is aimed at the present day, and it illustrates Su Tong's belief that the values of connoisseurship, which may have developed within traditional culture, deeply inform contemporary practices.

Su Tong's story "Wives and Concubines" is in some ways similar to Lu Xun's "Soap." Like "Soap," "Wives and Concubines" depicts a man with power organizing a household according to his expectations. Although Chen Zuoqian is much wealthier than Siming, moves with more confidence in himself, and is violent with those who oppose him, in both stories, women and children are organized and arranged for the man's pleasure. Lu Xun's connoisseur is weak and ineffectual, implying that his cultural power is coming to an end;

Su Tong's, on the contrary, is powerful and strong, indicating that the cultural devastation he promotes and represents is pervasive.

"Wives and Concubines" begins with the entry of Lotus, an educated young woman who has been sold to Chen Zuoqian because of her father's death. In marrying Chen, Lotus joins his three other wives, all of whom live in the compound. Lotus quickly understands the games that structure their privileges, and she herself participates with increasing skill. She also takes charge of and abuses her maid, Swallow, eventually causing her death.

Chen Zuoqian is a connoisseur of women who arranges his household in highly aesthetic ways. The four wives who live in the courtyard are his playthings; he also fondles the maids at will. Meals are an opportunity for whomever is in favor to exercise power and order dishes she alone appreciates. The hierarchies of power set up by Chen's arrangement of women within buildings is mimicked by the wives, who seek out secrets to enhance their own power over each other, and by the maids, who use charms and gossip to establish their own position. Even children are dragged into the power network as they are manipulated into fighting and then telling on one another.

Although Su Tong portrays the entire household as functioning in the same structured way, he makes it clear that a man heads this organization and orders social life aesthetically for his own pleasure.[16] The moral casings that Siming and his friends employ are absent; in their place is a rigid and violently enforced code of male dominance. Although the middle-aged Chen Zuoqian is losing sexual vitality and must resort to new wives and increased stimulation, he reacts viciously against a wife who engages in an affair with the local doctor, ordering his servants to murder her by throwing her into a well. The well turns out to have been a final resting place for other rebellious women, and it stands as a symbol of the household.

Lu Xun's Siming rails against modern education, which trains women, teaches new knowledge, and recognizes authorities outside the Chinese classics. His own weakness indicates that the traditions he represents are defunct and virtually meaningless. By contrast, the few challenges to Chen Zuoqian's power are weak and easily crushed: minor acts of defiance by the wives are quickly suppressed, and major infractions result in death. Lotus, who comes in as an educated woman, is quickly absorbed into the system and eventually loses her mind. Chen's son Feipu stays out of the household as much as he can, handles the family business, travels with a male friend, and is afraid of women.

One interpretation of this novella is that it presents a general critique of Chinese culture at its most basic level. As part of the mid-1980s "roots" (*xungen*) generation of writers, Su Tong attempts not to dissect the flaws of the immediate past—Maoism and the Cultural Revolution—but to look beyond historical reasons and seek other explanations for social and cultural problems. The comprehensiveness of Su Tong's narrative structure suggests that Chen Zuoqian's ruthless connoisseurship infects the Chinese psyche. Lu Xun's version of connoisseurship—the primacy of form over content, the essential meaninglessness of traditional culture, and the stance and network of masculine power and pleasure that underlie the Chinese cultural system—is supplanted by another, one with a more reified and fundamental structure. For Su Tong, form and content are united in a cultural structure that may be corrupt but is omnipresent and thus meaningful at all levels. The network of male power and pleasure that appears ridiculous in the eyes of the young hecklers in "Soap" is, for Su Tong, a pattern that endlessly reproduces itself in the minds of those around him, in architectural monuments such as the well and the courtyards, and in all relationships.

## MO YAN AND THE ECCENTRIC

The kind of connoisseurship that Su Tong has identified as ubiquitous is nothing but the hierarchical organization of social and cultural life under generations of masculine power. By contrast, "Divine Debauchery" (Shenpiao) by Mo Yan (1956–) shows a playful, whimsical side to connoisseurship and implies that this purposeless arrangement of reality can stand as an alternative to the direction and control of the state.[17] In his narrative, connoisseurship has no element of self-benefit but rather incorporates a charming alienation from clear, pragmatic social goals. This alternative critique, also present in stories by other roots writers such as A Cheng (1949–), elevates the useless obsession above all forms of action and makes use of traditional aesthetic practices such as playing games and arranging flowers. Functioning as a challenge to Confucian and Maoist ideologies, the story sets in the place of logical, directed, clear-cut political goals the idea of floating, illogical, idiosyncratic actions and behaviors. In this radically alternative conception, Mo Yan dismantles a number of ideas common to Confucianism and Maoism.

The story's central character is Master Jifan, a wealthy but eccentric man whose odd behavior becomes legend within his village. Unlike Chen Zuoqian, Master Jifan appears to make no efforts to protect his property, increase his wealth, organize his household, or use others for his own benefit. When he goes out for a ride to enjoy the weather and is accosted by beggars, Master Jifan gives them his robe, his shoes, and eventually everything but his underpants. Although in the eyes of onlookers his near-naked, bony body astride a large horse cuts a hilarious figure, Master Jifan is oblivious, riding about and chanting poetry happily. When locust flowers bloom, Master Jifan goes into the groves and stays for days and nights, afterward existing in a trance he calls the "flower hangover."

Master Jifan's attitude toward his wife and six concubines is opposite that of Chen Zuoqian, to whom wives are nothing but property to use for his own pleasure. Although Master Jifan's concubines are all beautiful, he always sleeps alone in his room and ignores their affairs with farmhands and other men. That his only child is a mentally retarded boy, the son of the unattractive wife, shows his total disregard for the Confucian demand for healthy male descendents to carry on the family line. Even more eccentric is Master Jifan's version of lust. Inviting twenty-eight prostitutes to his house with the local literati, Master Jifan ends a night of drinking and game-playing by asking the prostitutes to lie down naked on a carpet, walking over their bodies, paying them each an exorbitant amount, and sending them home.

In many ways the picture of the enlightened, sagelike eccentric who refuses all structuring social forms, Master Jifan lacks the moral hypocrisy of Lu Xun's Siming and the malevolent organization of Su Tong's Chen Zuoqian. Purely a connoisseur, he has transcended common, grasping, and enslaving pleasures in favor of transcendent selflessness. Mo Yan's political message is directed at the entire Chinese past, right up to the present. Confucian ideas of self-improvement, proper relations between superiors and inferiors, and social decorum are nonexistent. Mo Yan pokes ironic fun at Maoist ideology, which includes the notion of communal work to benefit all, by showing how Master Jifan's system of useless pleasure redistributes wealth to beggars, poor farmworkers, and prostitutes—exactly what the socialist system failed to accomplish. Despite his lack of purposeful direction and organizational energy, in other words, Master Jifan can put into action the true principles of the socialist state.

In this critique, Mo Yan creates a worldview that sharply contrasts with the deliberate and clear goals of socialism. Master Jifan's actions achieve admirable ends, but not because they are meant to do so. Implicit in Mo Yan's portrayal is an attack on the overly organized and directed bureaucracy of the Maoist and Confucian systems, both of which, he suggests, leave little room for the kind of individual eccentricities that might produce better results. Contrasting the households of Chen Zuoqian and Master Jifan, we can see that acting according to the demands of filial piety results in rigidity and cruelty, but ignoring them produces a flourishing, carefree household. Master Jifan also has little regard for the class issues later problematized under Mao; nonetheless his behavior allows class lines to blur throughout his village: his lack of concern for the accumulations of wealth make the beggars of his village the most well-dressed of any around.

This alternative critique utilizes the extreme connoisseur, who exists as a legend from the past, to provide another, also extreme, view of how reality can be structured outside what the author believes to be the limiting demands of Confucianism or Maoism. Mo Yan is not suggesting that Chinese society be reorganized along the lines of Master Jifan's consciousness, but he provides the reader with an idealized model of undirected but beneficial thought, action, and behavior that can stand as a contrast to contemporary social organization.

## FENG JICAI'S NARRATED CONNOISSEUR

The controversial issue of foot binding is the focus of connoisseurship in Feng Jicai's novel, *The Three-Inch Golden Lotus*.[18] As Feng is well aware, late-nineteenth-century reformers fixed on foot binding as symbolic of national weakness; some even felt foreign intrusion into and domination over China was justified because of the inhumane tradition of foot binding. Societies were formed to fight foot binding, and well-known intellectuals took a stance, refusing to allow their daughters' feet to be bound. While paying his respects to the historical struggle against foot binding as an exceedingly painful and debilitating procedure performed on girls and women, Feng also shows us how the glory of the small foot was sustained by extensive connoisseurship expressed in intricate theories, unique regional traditions, special names, contests, familial power manipulations, and personal jockeying for position and control.[19] This narrative critique focuses on discursive meanings, or the way the foot is symbolized, represented, and incorporated into social life. Although women and men fight and eventually win the battle against the tradition of bound feet, both are implicated in its continuation as well. In showing women not solely as victims but as accomplices in a system of connoisseurship that grants them pride of place, Feng illustrates both the intricate power network that sustains any cultural system and the difficulty of change.

Foreigners have long been fascinated with China's tradition of foot binding, and contemporary criticism has located in this appeal the orientalizing tendencies of Western cultures as they attempt to fix and categorize others. According to critics, Westerners both eroticize and exoticize Chinese culture.[20] Their obsessive interest in the prurient aspects of China serves to set them apart as masters looking down on a vulnerable subject, as well as to situate Chinese culture as the object of their gaze and the cause of their pleasure. In other words, critics showed how foot binding feeds Westerners' appetite for the imperialization of other cultures and turns them into connoisseurs of the world.

Feng Jicai's novel constructs an ironic play on these various historical and contemporary meanings of foot binding. Written in the style of an old-fashioned Chinese novel, the story contains several subplots, digresses wildly, and utilizes nearly impossible coincidences to move the action along. Even more than the stories of Lu Xun, Su Tong, or Mo Yan, *Golden Lotus* brings the issue of connoisseurship to center stage. In this story, Tong Ren'an is a successful dealer in antiques, but he never sells any real antiques. Rather, he produces and markets nothing but forgeries in his shop. Even this deception is an act of connoisseurship, because he bases his excellent skills not only on his mechanical competence but also on his uncanny deftness in determining the spirit and tone of a piece.

Tong Ren'an's real obsession, however, is small feet. When he finds a young woman with "exquisite" feet, he immediately connives to bring her into his family. The story begins with the marriage of Fragrant Lotus to his son, a "half-wit" who is one of his four children. Although Fragrant Lotus comes from a poor family, because her tiny feet attract Tong's attention in his store she is able to marry into this wealthy and prestigious Tianjin family. The family's fame rests on its women's bound feet, the smallest in the entire city.

Tong Ren'an's compulsion with small feet structures the household. The size and shape of the bound foot determines who can marry into the family but also organizes daily life, consciousness, and social events such as games played by his literary friends and contests between feet that he puts on for the women in his home and outsiders. Although the family does not directly make money off bound feet, the aura of connoisseurship Tong's compulsion creates enhances his prestige as a dealer of antiques. Total engagement with small feet determines the sensibilities of everyone around Tong. He uses his tongue to poke holes in the paper windows of his son's bedroom so he can observe the fondling of feet, and sneaks in when his son is away and Fragrant Lotus is asleep so that he can delicately touch her feet, showing us that his enchantment is complete.

Although Tong's obsession centers on feet, his literary friends are connoisseurs of poetry, painting, and antiques as well. Straddling the line between appreciation and mockery, Feng Jicai both ridicules connoisseurship —which often sets its gaze on forgeries or fakes and turns into the business of selling artifacts a man can use to present himself to the world as a connoisseur—and admires it, showing how "true" connoisseurs transcend the ordinary and border on genius. Obsession, Feng suggests, is both false and real; or perhaps these binary categories do little to explain how obsession functions in the social world.

Feng does not shrink from showing readers the horrors of foot binding, where the child's bones are broken and skin torn as the toes are pressed under the sole. The fact that an entire aesthetic culture can be based on this horrific deed, however, implies that all acts are made meaningful only by their context. Foot binding is a form of erotic slavery, but it can cinch a woman's family position, and within the novel it is most actively supported by the women themselves.

Unlike Mo Yan, Feng Jicai does not completely romanticize the spirit of connoisseurship. Practical matters such as making money or appreciating ordinary female beauty, Mo Yan suggests, are too easily co-opted into the plebian search for power and wealth, and thus Master Jifan's connoisseurship functions only where it is the most useless. For Feng Jicai, connoisseurship serves both functions: it exists as a useless obsession that differs from conventional values, *and* as a corrupt and very ordinary social practice. It is only because Tong Ren'an recognizes and accepts the latter that he can make antique forgeries and become wealthy off the myths of art and aesthetics. Yet he is a true and extremely possessed connoisseur of the bound foot, a fact that sets him apart from those merely pursuing profit. Foot binding is a painful physical procedure that prepares a deformed foot to be transformed into an evocative icon of eroticism and connoisseurship. Because this operation replicates the making of antique forgeries, a process through which Tong creates the perception of value in useless goods, it is a perfect vehicle for the author's double-edged approach.

The power of the bound foot is maintained through an intricate, historically developed practice. The bare foot itself is never publicly displayed, and when political forces clash and reformist women wish to expose the fallacy of the foot for what it is, they demand the bared, twisted, naked foot to compare with their own large healthy feet. Without its adornments—first and foremost the shoe, which itself is embedded in various traditions of fabrics, styles, and regional variations, but also the social practices and stories that sustain it—the foot is simply a grotesque, misshapen appendage. As in the case of the painter Hua Lin, whose paintings have never been viewed, the ability to paint is not as important as the ability to construct a narrative that implies you can paint. What is important about the foot is not that it is broken and bound, but that it is enveloped within a signifying structure and thus transformed from a deformity into an infinitely evocative image, which then is incorporated into a series of life-determining acts.

Feng's humorous and engaging story indicates that the power of Chinese traditions rests not so much in deep beliefs or a distorted psyche, but in habit, which is expressed through stories repeated so often that they gain strength and power. The tradition of bound feet is sustained more by its stories than by anything else, and as Fragrant Lotus says, the foot contest has always been one of shoes, techniques, and tricks, more than one of the actual foot itself. Feng's narrative critique uses the connoisseur to contradictorily debunk and affirm the mysticism associated with obsession and to illustrate that powerful social practices are neither real nor false, but simply stories that more or less command belief.

The story's final challenge to the tradition of bound feet is undertaken by a reformist woman who turns out to be Pretty Flower, Fragrant Lotus's daughter who disappeared as a child. In a narrative twist, Feng Jicai tells us that it was Fragrant Lotus herself who sent the child away, so that she could avoid the pain of the bound foot. Pretty Flower speaks foreign words, smokes foreign cigarettes, and clearly has been the beneficiary of foreign learning.

As the proponent of an entirely different system of knowledge and being, she has the qualifications to put forth another powerful story that can dispel the romance of the bound foot.

Feng's critique of Chinese culture differs from that of the other writers. Whereas Lu Xun portrays literati culture as false, hypocritical, and anachronistic, Feng shows how ideology impels belief, and how a system of thought produces adherents in every group, from the elite connoisseurs to the women who bind their daughters' feet as they sob. Discriminatory traditions succeed and reproduce themselves precisely because, despite the relative power and positions that different constituents hold, no one is excluded from the overarching narrative that sustains and organizes daily life. Su Tong recognizes that each person is co-opted into the system of hierarchy and power, but still clearly differentiates masters and victims, an approach Feng rejects. For Su Tong, the power held by connoisseurs is evil and pervasive, able to infiltrate all social relations, and it works by forcing all to abide by its will. Feng portrays the system as far-reaching because it produces desires and values through relationships and daily transactions, not because it coerces through readily identifiable means. Mo Yan's story is specifically directed toward what he sees as the overly deterministic organization inherent in Confucian and Maoist social life: connoisseurship is a symbolic alternative to the clear-cut, goal-directed dictates of living that had been observed in the past. By contrast, Feng Jicai sees connoisseurship as itself another social form, one that is, like any other, capable of either allowing baser motives to emerge or producing a transcendent and mystical consciousness. Connoisseurship is a comprehensive story that works for those with bound feet as well as for those who are obsessed with bound feet, and only if the story can be changed will reality be transformed.

## CONNOISSEURSHIP AND THE GLOBAL LITERATI

The four writers I discuss in this article all are well-known twentieth-century male Chinese writers. Why have they used the character of the connoisseur as a trope of cultural critique? The question leads back to the issue of a masculine tradition in modern Chinese literature. Because the connoisseur traditionally was male, invoking his image in contemporary writing instantly brings to the fore the existence of past literati culture—the very culture in which these male writers, if they had lived before this century, would be working—in its recognition of the gendered construction of this culture. With its gendered edge, the writers' critique can harshly criticize men and their values, but through reproducing male cultural control it also can promote the same gender superiority. As those in charge of writing philosophical, historical, and literary texts; of mediating the relationship of elite women and commoner men and women to learning; and of educating elite boys to continue the traditions, the literati created Chinese elite culture. The connoisseur is only part of the literati tradition, but a part in which is concentrated the idea of aesthetic appreciation. Furthermore, the idea of the connoisseur contains within it a notion of excess, as if an abstracted meaning of culture can be distilled out of social life and considered on its own. The obsessiveness of the connoisseur can match the urgency of the contemporary male intellectual, who must criticize the past culture of his earlier counterparts as well as figure out his own present-day position. These three aspects—the gendering of cultural forms and control, the past and its relationship to the present, and the most essential and basic meanings of Chinese aesthetic life—make the connoisseur a potent symbol of the issues a modern masculine literary tradition must consider.

With the complexity and ambiguity characteristic of more contemporary depictions of the connoisseur comes another problem. Post-Mao avant-garde writers have been criticized as being misogynist, as being not interested in investigating gender issues and as promoting ways of thinking that are disadvantageous or even harmful to women.[21] For example, although Mo Yan's vision represents an anti-authoritarian stance set against the purposefulness of a totalitarian government, within this narrative women appear not as agents but as playthings. The new consciousness, much like the old literati elitism, is male, critics have claimed. To some extent, placing connoisseurship at the center allows for such an ambiguous stance. Because connoisseurship traditionally was a masculine social practice deeply tied to Chinese literary conventions, representing it as a multifaceted form that enervates its male practitioners means recognizing that it provides individual pleasure. Furthermore, connoisseurship locates not only men but also women within a system of aesthetic appreciation. Is Su Tong showing us familial relations that illustrate the system's eroticizing of women for male pleasure, or is he reproducing the system's eroticizing of women for the pleasure of contemporary men?[22] To show that women become as vindictive and cruel as men when inserted into the aesthetic and cultural systems of power, as Su Tong does in "Wives and Concubines," or that women are the rabid supporters of their own defacement, as Feng does in *The Three-Inch Golden Lotus,* also can be interpreted as a betrayal of women that solidifies the status quo of male power and violence.

The ambiguous image of the connoisseur has allowed for increasingly complex portrayals of cultural predicaments. From satire to the intricacies of stories, the connoisseur has come to indicate the problematic relationship of elite cultural producers to what they produce. This locally oriented investigation centers on the specifics of Chinese culture, such as values of Confucianism or Maoism, and also on the way in which elite culture works within historical and contemporary Chinese society. Yet the issues of connoisseurship are relevant in a more global sense as well, both to the representation of Chinese culture in the world and to those of us who study other cultures. Traditional sinology, which uses the methodology of philology or textual research, has been accused of assuming a connoisseur's position to engage in a rarified, aestheticized study of another culture's literary traditions. Within this critique, material culture, economic trends and realities, and the contemporary world in general are ignored in favor of the endless interpretations of classical texts. Chinese literature, critics claim, becomes an object of artistic appreciation within which foreign scholars can trace allusions, seek out obscure references, and play their own word games. Their knowledge of this arcane system then endows them with mystical power, which they use to establish themselves as experts within Western universities and at large.

However, traditional sinology is hardly practiced anymore, and only a few journals are devoted to publishing its research. A more cogent critique is aimed at the kind of ethnographic study that today takes place in anthropology, history, literature, and film studies.[23] Contemporary scholars here also have been accused of working from the connoisseur's position, as they isolate and study the foreign culture in question. Although these researchers often do not study elite culture but focus instead on popular forms, critics blame them for exoticizing the Other and promoting alienating theories of cultural difference, for emphasizing the odd or the bizarre, and for establishing themselves as the objective and universal neutral evaluators—the masters—and Others as the viewed or gazed upon. Under the aegis of Science and its categorization of knowledge, power is distributed: some study, others are studied; some view, others are viewed. According to this critique, almost any study of another culture is an act of connoisseurship that really is little more than an unequal power relationship.

Therefore it is appropriate that male writers, having produced Chinese literary culture and been blamed for its failings under imperialistic attack at the end of the nineteenth century, now choose the connoisseur as a symbol of its weakness and strength, a simultaneously global and local figure that addresses the global implications of any local culture. Constructed by and for elite men, literary and aesthetic culture is molded by distinct power relationships between elite men and the populace at large, and between elite men and all women. Gendered and marked by class, the connoisseur pivots on the aesthetic organization of reality that is the central core of a flourishing literary tradition. The connoisseur exists in Europe, China, and other places, but his manifestation is particular to each culture. In China, the small foot, flower arranging, poetry, and art were the connoisseur's objects. Yet because the connoisseur so readily speaks to power and its various forms of coercion, oppression, belief, and ideology, he also remains a potent image through which to approach the meaning of local culture within the contemporary global world.

## NOTES

1. Lydia Liu's article, reprinted in this volume, originally was published in *From May Fourth to June Fourth: Fiction and Film in Twentieth-Century China,* ed. Ellen Widmer and David Der-wei Wang (Cambridge: Harvard University Press, 1993), 194–220.

2. Ibid., 197.

3. Tan Sitong, a well-known reformer, writes that "to the extent that Westerners as well as Manchus and Mongols did not practice foot-binding, they were justified in establishing dominion over China." See Hao Chang, *Chinese Intellectuals in Crisis: Search for Order and Meaning (1890–1911)* (Berkeley and Los Angeles: University of California Press, 1987), 91.

4. See, for example, an article by Lu Xun's brother, Zhou Zuoren, "Nüzi yu wenxue" [Women and literature], *Funü zazhi* 8, no. 8 (August 1921); also Xie Wuliang, *Zhongguo funü wenxueshi* [The history of women's literature in China] (Shanghai: Zhongguo shuju, 1916).

5. For a discussion of how women are thus utilized in Zhang Yimou's films, see Wendy Larson, "Zhang Yimou: Inter/National Aesthetics and Erotics," in *Cultural Encounters,* ed. Soren Clausen and Anne Wedell-Wedellsborg (Aarhus, Denmark: University of Aarhus Press, 1995), 215–26.

6. For the discussion of obsession and connoisseurship in Yuan's work, I have relied on Judith T. Zeitlin's "The Petrified Heart: Obsession in Chinese Literature," *Late Imperial China* 12, no. 1 (June 1991): 1–26; quotes on pp. 3–4. The following quotes are taken from that article. For Yuan's original essay, see *Yuan Hongdao ji jianjiao* [The edited collection of Yuan Hongdao's work], ed. Qian Bocheng (Shanghai: Shanghai guji chubanshe, 1981). For the various references to different Chinese terms for the connoisseur or connoisseurship, see pp. 817, 823, 826, and 827.

7. Zeitlin, "The Petrified Heart," 4.

8. Ibid., 9.

9. For an informative discussion of the meaning of *qing* in Chinese literary culture, see Li Wai-yee, *Enchantment and Disenchantment: Love and Illusion in Chinese Literature* (Princeton: Princeton University Press, 1994).

10. For an analysis of masculinity and *wen/wu* ideology, see Kam Louie and Louise Edwards, "Chinese Masculinity: Theorizing *Wen* and *Wu*," *East Asian History* 8 (December 1994): 135–48.

11. Ibid., 141.

12. Lu Xun, whose original name was Zhou Shuren, is modern China's most famous writer. Although Lu Xun wrote voluminously (his work includes translations, histories, essays, and theories), his literary reputation rests on two volumes of short stories, *Nahan* (Outcry) and *Panghuang* (Wandering), published in 1923 and 1926. He became famous for his short satiric essay form called the *zawen,* in which he ironically and often humorously attacked his enemies and parodied their views. He wrote "Kong Yiji" and "Soap" in 1919 and 1923, respectively, and the two were translated by Yang Hsien-yi and Gladys Yang and published in *Modern Chinese Stories and*

*Novellas, 1919–1949,* ed. Joseph S. M. Lau, C. T. Hsia, and Leo Ou-Fan Lee (New York: Columbia University Press, 1981), 3–5, 33–38.

13. For a discussion of "Soap" that addresses some of its gendered meanings, see Carolyn Brown, "Woman as Trope: Gender and Power in Lu Xun's 'Soap,'" *Modern Chinese Literature* 4, nos. 1–2 (spring-fall 1988): 55–70.

14. Kong Yiji actually is the nickname that bar patrons give to Kong; it is based on the first three characters of a children's primer. Here Lu Xun emphasizes the fact that Kong does not even have a name, yet he worships the literary tradition.

15. Su Tong, from Suzhou, entered Beijing Normal University in 1980 and started publishing fiction in 1983. With Yu Hua, Can Xue, Sun Ganlu, Mo Yan, Ge Fei, and others, Su Tong is known as one of the avant-garde writers who, in the mid-1980s, moved decisively away from social and critical realism. "Wives and Concubines" was translated by Michael S. Duke and published as "Raise the Red Lantern" in *Raise the Red Lantern: Three Novellas* (New York: William Morrow and Company, 1993), 11–100.

16. For a critique of Su Tong's work, see Lu Tonglin, "Femininity and Masculinity in Su Tong's Trilogy," in *Misogyny, Cultural Nihilism, and Oppositional Politics: Contemporary Chinese Experimental Fiction* (Stanford: Stanford University Press, 1995), 129–180. Among other things, Lu criticizes Su Tong for allowing women to play only "purely instrumental roles in their relations to men" (154) and for refusing to portray female desire.

17. Mo Yan is a prolific writer who has published many short stories and several novels, including his well-known *Red Sorghum Clan* (Hong gaoliang jiazu), which was made into a film by the director Zhang Yimou. Mo Yan's versatile stylistics include avant-garde fiction, parodies, and sagas. "Divine Debauchery" was published in *Lianhe wenxue* in 1992 and was translated by Andrew F. Jones, with Jeanne Tai, and published in *Running Wild: New Chinese Writers,* ed. David Der-wei Wang, with Jeanne Tai (New York: Columbia University Press, 1994), 1–12.

18. Feng Jicai, from Tianjin, has been a painter, a basketball player, and a writer. *The Three-Inch Golden Lotus* originally was published in 1986 (by the Tianjin publisher Baihua chubanshe), following a number of Feng's historical novels. It was translated by David Wakefield and published as *The Three-Inch Golden Lotus* (Honolulu: University of Hawaii Press, 1994).

19. For an informative discussion of foot binding, see Fred C. Blake, "Footbinding in Neo-Confucian China and the Appropriation of Female Labor," *Signs: Journal of Women in Culture and Society* 19, no. 3 (spring 1992): 676–712.

20. See, for example, articles in the dialogue on third world culture in *Dianying yishu* (7, no. 216 [1990]: 30–58), by Yue Daiyun, Zhang Jinnuan, Liao Shiqi, Dai Jinhua, and Tang Xiguang. Articles by well-known contemporary critics such as Chen Xiaoming, Li Tuo, and Zhang Yiwu also indicate thorough knowledge of the orientalizing tendencies of Western culture made popular by Edward Said in his book *Orientalism* (New York: Pantheon Books, 1978).

21. See Tonglin Lu, *Misogyny, Cultural Nihilism, and Oppositional Politics: Contemporary Chinese Experimental Fiction* (Stanford: Stanford University Press, 1995). Lu argues that, after the death of Mao, the most well-known avant-garde male writers of post-Mao China—Mo Yan, Zhaxi Dawa, Su Tong, and Yu Hua—all needed to con-

struct a new "Other" against which they could establish their own subjectivities, subject positions, and critical intellectual stances. For the avant-garde writers, "woman" has been that Other, and their writing always is founded on an essential misogyny. For a brief but biting critique of Chinese male notions of feminism, see the male critic Yin Jinan, "Zhongguo nanxing de 'Nüxing zhuyi'" [The feminism of Chinese men] in *Dushu* 8 (1995): 136–38. Yin claims that Chinese male support for women's liberation is actually nothing but a self-indulgent interest in female sexuality: "I worry that Chinese male 'feminism' is still the old male goods of connoisseurship [*jianshang de*] of the new 'three-inch golden lotus'" (138).

22. As if to speak to this issue, three of Su Tong's stories, including "Wives and Concubines," have been collected together and published in China under the title *Funü leyuan,* which means "the pleasure garden of women" ( Jiangsu: Jiangsu wenyi chubanshe, 1991).

23. For a critique along these lines, see Rey Chow, *Primitive Passions: Visuality, Sexuality, Ethnography, and Contemporary Chinese Cinema* (New York: Columbia University Press, 1995), especially pt. 3: "Film as Ethnography; or, Translation between Cultures in the Postcolonial World."

PART FOUR

# Dangerous Women and Dangerous Men

Part 1 of this book outlines the official norms of masculinity and femininity in the late Qing as evidenced by the legal system, which clearly targeted some categories of people as threats to the social order. Part 2 further explores the dominant ideals of marriage and family in the Qing, which were attacked by reformers and radicals in the early twentieth century. Part 3 explores the ways in which notions of femininity and masculinity dominated literary traditions as well. This part of the book returns to the flip side of the coin by discussing two important categories of women and men that did not conform to the orthodox ideals: prostitutes and bandits. These chapters illustrate that one can gain greater understanding of dominant norms by looking at the people who violate them; they also remind us that dominant norms are never completely dominant, and that there are always substantial numbers of people who, for various reasons, cannot live their lives in conformity with them. How such liminal social types are dealt with can indicate larger social patterns. In the case of prostitutes and bandits, which have operated as quintessential transgressive female and male categories, respectively, it is possible to trace two very different trajectories.

In chapter 3, Mann notes that the social changes of the mid-Qing led to an increased effort to separate women who could be had for a price from respectable women, a move associated with the elimination of the hereditary position of female entertainers, which brought down the barriers to their entrance to orthodox society (as concubines, for example). In the following chapter, Gail Hershatter outlines a transformation of images of the prostitute. In the late nineteenth and early twentieth centuries, courtesans with an upper-class clientele had been viewed as sophisticated and urbane; in fact, guidebooks instructing their potential customers in proper self-presentation before such a woman became virtual "primers for the production of elite masculinity." However, with the rise of Western-inspired ideologies of nationalism and modernization in the 1920s and 1930s, prostitution was increasingly represented as dangerous and disorderly. Prostitution was considered to be one of the keys to China's national weakness, because a system that permitted the exploitation of women could not help but produce a weak nation. Prostitutes became diseased symbols of national backwardness. With the rise of nationalist ideology, then, the social status of these women shifted from ambiguous and potentially positive to generally negative. Hershatter's book *Dangerous Pleasures: Prostitution and Modernity in Twentieth-Century Shanghai* traces this history in much greater detail.

The relationship of bandit images with orthodox masculine ideals followed a somewhat different history. David Ownby defines bandits as rural outlaws, secret societies, urban gangs, religious groups identified by the state as "heterodox," some rebel bands, and even groups at feud. From imperial times to the present, the Chinese state has defined these men as uncivilized, violent rebels—an image clearly opposed to the official ideals of masculinity. However, the revolutionary nationalist movements at the turn of the century did not stigmatize these marginal men as they did prostitutes, but rather both Communists and Nationalists defined them as potential revolutionaries and drew upon bandit symbolism in their redefinition of orthodox masculinity. And so, in the realm of representation, images of marginal women suffered from the nationalist movements, while images of marginal men benefited. This forms the background to developments in later decades as well. As described by Elizabeth Perry and Nara Dillon in chapter 10, rebel groups in the Cultural Revolution period drew upon the bandit image in their self-definitions. In the 1980s, as Chinese men dealt with feelings of deficiency when compared to the Japanese and Western tough guys in films, they drew upon symbols of bandits to reinvigorate Chinese notions of masculinity, one example being the lusty and potentially violent protagonist in the influential film *Red Sorghum*.[1]

These two chapters, then, show how representations of the categories of marginal males and females have been differently utilized by groups seeking to define the orthodox society and claim control over it. The stereotypical egalitarian, nonsexual friendships between bandits offered an alternative model to the Confucian hierarchy that was threatening to the Confucianist Qing state, a model that could be incorporated into the utopian views of rebels attempting to overturn old social structures and create new ones. The sexual, hierarchical relationship between the prostitute and her male clients apparently did not offer the same kind of utopian possibilities.

The genre of the "courtesan novel" is discussed and selections are translated in Perry Link's edited volume *Mandarin Ducks and Butterflies: Popular Fiction in Early Twentieth-Century Chinese Cities* and in *Renditions*, vol. 17–18, which contains two chapters of Han Banqing's 1894 novel, *Flowers of Shanghai*, along with a discussion by Stephen Cheng.

The starting point for all representations of bandits is one of the best-known Chinese novels, first written down in the fourteenth century, *All Men Are Brothers*, also translated as *The Water Margin* or *Outlaws of the Marsh*, by Shi Nai'an and Luo Guanzhong. It is the story of a band of rebellious outlaws fighting for social justice in the Song dynasty.

The 1932 film *Shanghai Express*, starring Marlene Dietrich, was created from a Western point of view, but the representation of rebels and loose women as dangerous masculine and feminine characters is not dissimilar from the official Chinese point of view.

A book published by Victoria Cass after the following chapters were written presents a parallel discussion for the Ming period, and is coincidentally titled *Dangerous Women: Warriors, Grannies, and Geishas of the Ming* (1999).

## NOTES

1. Yeujin Wang, "Mixing Memory and Desire: *Red Sorghum*, a Chinese Version of Masculinity and Femininity," *Public Culture* 2, no. 1 (fall 1989): 31–53, esp. 44.

## COMPLEMENTARY READINGS AND VIDEOS

Cass, Victoria B. *Dangerous Women: Warriors, Grannies, and Geishas of the Ming* (Lanham, Md.: Rowman and Littlefield, 1999).

Han Bangqing, "Sing-Song Girls of Shanghai," first two chapters of *Haishang hualie zhuan* [Flowers of Shanghai]. Trans. Eileen Chang. *Renditions* 17–18 (1982): 95–110.

Hershatter, Gail. *Dangerous Pleasures: Prostitution and Modernity in Twentieth-Century Shanghai*. Berkeley and Los Angeles: University of California Press, 1997.

Link, E. Perry Jr. *Mandarin Ducks and Butterflies: Popular Fiction in Early Twentieth-Century Chinese Cities*. Berkeley and Los Angeles: University of California Press, 1981.

*Shanghai Express*. Directed by Josef von Sternberg. 1932. Distributed by MCA Universal Home Video, Universal City, Calif., 1993. Videocassette.

Shi Nai'an and Luo Guanzhong. *Outlaws of the Marsh (Shui hu zhuan): An Abridged Version*. Trans. Sidney Shapiro. Hong Kong: Commercial Press, 1986. (Other versions are available.)

CHAPTER SEVEN

# Modernizing Sex, Sexing Modernity: Prostitution in Early-Twentieth-Century Shanghai

*Gail Hershatter*

In early-twentieth-century Shanghai, prostitution was variously understood as a source of urbanized pleasures, a profession full of unscrupulous and greedy schemers, a site of moral danger and physical disease, and a marker of national decay. It was also discussed as a painful economic choice on the part of women and their families, since it was sometimes the best or only income-producing activity available to women seeking employment in Shanghai. The categories through which prostitution was understood were not fixed, and tracing them requires attention to questions of urban history, colonial and anticolonial state making, and the intersection of sexuality, particularly female sexuality, with an emerging nationalist discourse. Prostitution is always about the sale of sexual services, but much more can be learned from that transaction: about sexual meanings, about other social relations, about sex as a medium through which people talked about political power and cultural transformation, about nationhood and cultural identity. In some respects, China's modern debates about prostitution echoed those of Europe, where scholars such as Judith Walkowitz (England) and Alain Corbin (France) have traced the themes of medicalization and the desire to return prostitutes to an (imagined) safe family environment.[1] In China, prostitution was also invoked in urgent public discussions about what kind of sex and gender relations could help to constitute a modern nation in a threatening semicolonial situation. What it *meant* (to participants and observers) for a woman in Shanghai to sell sexual services to a man changed across the hierarchy and over time, as understandings of prostitution were shaped, contested, renegotiated, and appropriated by many participants: the prostitutes, their madams, their patrons, their lovers and husbands, their natal families, their in-laws, the police, the courts, doctors, the city government, missionaries, social reformers, students, and revolutionaries. Studying prostitution and its changes thus illuminates the thinking and social practices of many strata of Shanghai society. And since the debates about prostitution often took place in regional or national publications, such a study also suggests the contours of conflicts about gender and modernity in twentieth-century Chinese society.

From the mid–nineteenth to the mid–twentieth century, Shanghai was a treaty port—a place where Westerners governed part of the city, and where Western and Japanese businessmen, sailors, industrialists, and adventurers made their homes and sometimes their fortunes. Shanghai was also China's biggest industrial and commercial city, a magnet for merchants from around the country and for peasants of both sexes seeking work, and the birthplace of the Chinese Communist Party. Shanghai embraced populations from various nations, regions, and classes, and harbored political agitators ranging from Christian moral reformers to Marxist revolutionaries, all presided over by three different municipal governments (International Settlement, French Concession, and Chinese city).

Drawn mostly from the daughters and wives of the working poor and déclassé elites, prostitutes in Shanghai were near the bottom of both contemporary and retrospective hierarchies of class and gender. Yet their working and living situations, as well as their individual standing and visibility in Shanghai society, were strikingly diverse. Shanghai's hierarchy of prostitution was structured by the class background of the customers, the native place of both customers and prostitutes, and the appearance and age of the prostitutes. The hierarchy changed dramatically over the first half of the twentieth century, as courtesan houses and streetwalkers alike faced competition from "modern" institutions such as tour guide agencies, massage parlors, and dance halls. Any account of prostitution in this period must track a variety of working situations across classes and over time.

Prostitution was not only a changing site of work for women but also a metaphor, a medium of articulation in which the city's competing elites and emerging middle classes discussed their problems, fears, agendas, and visions. In the late nineteenth century, prostitutes appeared in elite discourse as the embodiment of sophisticated urbanity. By the 1940s, prostitutes served as a marker to distinguish respectable people, particularly the "petty urbanites," from a newly threatening urban disorder. Every social class and gender grouping used prostitution as a different kind of reference point, and depending on where they were situated, it meant something different to them. The shifting and multiple meanings assigned to the prostitute demand that we move beyond transhistorical references to "the world's oldest profession," or dynasty-by-dynasty catalogues of written references to courtesans,[2] and begin instead to historicize and localize sex work.

Across the century I am investigating here, the changing figure of the prostitute performed important ideological work in elite discussions, particularly as she was transformed into a victimized, disorderly, dangerous embodiment of social trouble. This transformation, and the regulatory regimes it generated, had multiple consequences for the daily lives, identities, and actions of Shanghai prostitutes (indeed, even helped to determine who was considered a prostitute). Changes in migration patterns and economic opportunities may have increased the number of prostitutes and the alarm over them. But changes in elite notions about the link between women's status and national strength helped create the language through which a rise in prostitution acquired meaning—even gave it the modern term for prostitute, *jinü* (prostitute female), which displaced the earlier *mingji* (famous prostitute). And the elite shaped the institutions which emerged to classify, reform, or regulate prostitution, all of which in turn became part of the material conditions of prostitutes' lives. Shanghai prostitution is a rich venue in which to explore the interlocking of material and ideological changes, since neither can be regarded alone as determinative in the last instance of the conditions of prostitutes' lives.[3]

Although the sources delineate an elaborate hierarchy of prostitution, two representations of sex workers dominate the written record: the courtesan and the streetwalker. Courtesans appeared in nostalgic memoirs, guidebooks, and gossipy newspapers known as the "mosquito press" as named individuals with specified family origins, brothel affiliations, famous patrons, and career trajectories. This was a literature of pleasure, devoted to the appreciation of beautiful courtesans and the depiction, often in titillating detail, of their romantic liaisons with the city's rich and powerful. This literature also contained warnings about the capacity of courtesans to engage in financial strategizing at the expense of the customer.

Side by side with this literature of appreciation, the local news page of the mainstream dailies and the foreign press carried accounts of the activities of lower-class streetwalkers, who were portrayed as victims of kidnapping, human trafficking, and abuse by madams, as well as disturbers of urban peace and spreaders of venereal disease. Streetwalkers were sometimes identified in the press by name, age, and native place, but they appeared only as transient violators of urban ordinances against soliciting. Initially, the two types of sex workers were seldom mentioned in a single context, although each embodied a set of dangers posed to and by women in an unstable urban environment. During the middle decades of the twentieth century, courtesans and streetwalkers came to share a wider variety of newly created discursive spaces: as shared objects of journalistic investigation, medical examination, reform, and regulation. In the process, the figure of the streetwalker loomed ever larger, supplanting the courtesan as the emblem of the sex trades.

This essay makes six approximations of Shanghai prostitution, drawn from guidebooks and the press in the first four decades of the twentieth century. "Approximations" is meant to suggest two things. First, each of these portraits is rough around the edges, with inconsistencies left in rather than smoothed out, because each is drawn from sources that are being read both with and against the grain. In addition, some of these portraits overlapped and coexisted in time, and it is not only impossible but also undesirable to try to reconcile them and produce a single seamless account of Shanghai prostitution. The dissonances between them are arguably where the most interesting mapping can be done.

### FIRST APPROXIMATION: THE URBANE COURTESAN

Among the richest sources on Shanghai prostitution are guidebooks, written by elite authors, devoted either wholly or in substantial part to descriptions of prostitution. The guidebooks have titles such as *Precious Mirror of Shanghai, A Sixty-Year History of the Shanghai Flower World, Pictures of the Hundred Beauties of Flowerland, A History of the Charm of the Gentle Village,* and, most colorful of all, *A Complete Look at Shanghai Philandering,* by an author who took the pseudonym "Half-Crazy One."[4] The guidebooks offer a wealth of information about the operations of brothels, simultaneously providing clues to the anxieties and aspirations of the authors. They include biographies of famous prostitutes; anecdotes about famous customers; exhaustive glossaries of the specific language of the trade; meticulous descriptions of brothel organization; instructions on the proper behavior required of customers when a prostitute made a formal call, helped host a banquet, or presided over a gambling party; lists of fees, billing procedures, and tips; explanations of festivals and the obligations of a regular customer at each season; accounts of taboos and religious observances; and warnings about various scams run by prostitutes to relieve customers of extra cash. The guidebooks can be read in conjunction with the mosquito press, tabloid newspapers that typically devoted a page or more to gossip about courtesans.

Most guidebooks are engaged in a literature of nostalgia. Guidebooks written in the 1920s locate the golden age of prostitution a quarter to a half century earlier. In fact, several of the main guidebook authors explicitly say in their prefaces that they are recording the definitive historical account of a world about to disappear because of reform movements to abolish prostitution. One author even compares himself to the famous Han dynasty historians Ban Gu and Sima Qian.[5] And, like classical historians of the Han and later, many of these authors reprint almost verbatim material from earlier guidebooks. Also like classical Chinese historians, many of these authors compare the current age unfavorably to the past. Just as historians frequently mourned the failure of contemporary rulers to measure up to the sagacious rulers of yore, guidebook authors deplored the decline in entertainment skill, refinement, and classical training of upper-class prostitutes.

This literature of nostalgia emerged in a time when urban China, and Shanghai in particular, was undergoing rapid and disquieting change. As many China historians from Joseph Levenson on have noted, the question "What is Chinese about China?" emerged as a serious and troubling one for members of the elite in the face of the Western assault in the nineteenth century.[6] Part of their answer was to glorify vanishing Chinese cultural practices (now coded as relative rather than universal). And a part of that glorification was to explicate meticulously the cultivated and refined social practices of courtesans. The production of this literature peaked in the years immediately after national civil service exams were abolished in 1905—in short, in years when definition of membership in the elite, and the understanding of China's place in the world, were both in flux. Seldom mentioned in this literature, the West is nonetheless a kind of unspoken standard against which these authors produce an account of the world they have lost.

Although nostalgia for times past was a prominent theme in the guidebooks, their authors were not insensitive to the possibilities available in contemporary courtesan houses. Both guidebooks and mosquito newspapers offered catalogues of the pleasure, explicit and implied, to be found in the high-class brothels. Most obvious were the pleasures of the gaze and the ear: looking at and listening to beautiful, cultivated women, showcased in exquisitely appointed settings, who could sing, compose poetry, and converse with wit. One famous prostitute, whose professional name was Lin Daiyu—taken from the name of the heroine of the classical Chinese novel *Dream of the Red Chamber*—was described in an 1892 guidebook as "just like a begonia after the fresh rain . . . she really is very delicate and attractive."[7] Descriptions of individual courtesans stressed their refinement and cultivation: a typical passage from one mosquito newspaper, the *Crystal*, read: "When guests leave, she burns a stick of incense, makes a cup of Longjing tea, and does watercolors."[8] Another woman was described thus: "She reads a lot and writes well, and knows foreign languages and Shakespeare."[9] Here the image of the courtesan looks both ways—to the literature of nostalgia and to the West. The courtesan is not only defined with reference to *Dream of the Red Chamber*, but also draws part of the repertoire of self-presentation—clothing, bodily stance, hobbies, markers of cultivation—from the West. Urgent conversations among Chinese elites about self-definition are refracted in representations of prostitution.

For the cultivated literati who patronized these houses, the pleasures of looking and listening were intimately related to the pleasures of skilled description and repartee among themselves. Many of the early guidebooks feature elegant poems written by customers in appreciation of courtesans.[10] Perhaps the most intricate ritual of describing and judging was a series of elections sponsored by the mosquito press, held irregularly from the 1880s to 1920. Local literati were invited to vote to enter the names of their favorite courtesans on the "flower roll," a list which paralleled that of the successful candidates on the imperial civil service examinations. The woman who received the most votes, like the man whose exam received the highest grade, was called the *zhuangyuan,* and other titles were awarded as well. After the fall of the dynasty in 1911, the nomenclature was modernized, and leading courtesans were awarded titles such as "president," "prime minister," and "general" instead. In the testimonials which accompanied their votes, patrons marshaled their powers of eloquence to extol the virtues of their chosen favorite, in the process exhibiting their authorial skill to their fellow literati. Courtesans were willing to participate in the elections because they brought prestige to them as individuals and business to their houses.[11]

Any discussion of guidebooks and pleasures should point out that the books themselves offered pleasure. In a study of courtesan novels, a related genre, Stephen Cheng argued that readership in the twentieth century shifted from "literati interested in sentimental love stories" to "shopkeepers, merchants, and clerks who either frequent or are surreptitiously interested in the pleasure quarters."[12] I suspect that guidebook readership underwent a similar transformation, and that for the new urban classes part of the pleasure was in vicarious access to the lives of the rich and famous, patrons and courtesans alike, in deliciously gossipy detail. Reading the guidebooks and mosquito press was part of being "in the know" about who and what was important in Shanghai. Reading about courtesans as the epitome of urbanity was an activity that itself conferred urbanity.

The sections that described summoning a prostitute out on a social call, going to the courtesan house for tea, hosting a banquet, and celebrating festivals can be read as a kind of etiquette guide to correct behavior for the uninitiated guest. Correct behavior included but was not limited to the formal fulfillment of the financial duties already mentioned. It also included the ineffable art of self-presentation. A successful customer enjoyed two benefits: he increased his likelihood of winning a courtesan's favor, and, equally important, he avoided ridicule by the group of courtesans who observed him at the brothel. Someone who failed to meet the requirements by not spending enough money or by spending too much money, by dressing inappropriately, by assuming intimacy too quickly—generally, by saying or doing the wrong thing—would be ridiculed, significantly, as a country bumpkin.[13] If the courtesan embodied urban sophistication, then, the new customer went to the brothel not only in search of the pleasures described earlier but also to create and exhibit his own urbanity. In the rapidly changing Shanghai environment, positioning oneself favorably in the urban hierarchy, and being validated by both courtesans and other customers, was not merely a matter of entertainment.

## SECOND APPROXIMATION: THE SCHEMING BUSINESSWOMAN

The guidebooks were also a repository for a vast and varied cautionary literature, in which the dangers enumerated ranged from the annoying to the deadly. Side by side with the loving and admiring descriptions of individual prostitutes were warnings that prostitutes had one purpose only: to relieve customers of their money. To this end, with and without the collusion of the brothel owner, they would perpetrate various scams. A woman might repeatedly claim to be a virgin in order to collect a defloration fee multiple times. Prostitutes of all ranks, customers were warned, were experts at what was called "the axe chop" *(kan futou)*, requesting clothing or jewelry from a frequent customer.[14] They were said to be as skillful in matching their requests to the customer's resources as a doctor writing a prescription of exactly the appropriate strength. The prescription was "flavored" with "rice soup" (a slang term for flattery), tears, "vinegar" (slang for jealousy), and sweet sugar syrup. One of the later guidebooks carries an illustration of a woman reclining under a quilt while a mustachioed man sits next to her on the bed. She is ticking off on her fingers items depicted in a cartoonlike balloon above her head: a fine house, a car, and a diamond ring.[15]

The hospitable and affectionate demeanor of such women, the guidebooks said, was only a cover for their calculating and deceptive nature, which was reflected in the terms by which they classified guests behind their backs. A "bean curd" guest, for instance, was one who would do the woman's bidding. A "walnut" guest needed one hard knock before he would "put out." A "soap" guest or a "stone" guest needed time and energy, but would eventually yield something. The worst were "flea" and "fly" guests, who buzzed around the brothels but vanished as soon as one "swatted" them for contributions.[16]

In efforts to increase her "take," the guidebooks said, a woman might practice the "bitter meat stratagem" *(kurou ji)* of pretending to be at odds with her madam. She would then beg the customer to buy her out and take her as a concubine.[17] In fact, the whole procedure of buying a beautiful courtesan as a concubine, which one might expect to find in the litany of pleasures, seems to fall almost completely in the "danger" category. The guidebooks and mosquito papers explain that many courtesans aspired to marriage to a powerful man—or more accurately to concubinage. Principal wives were usually acquired for a man by his family on the basis of matched backgrounds and with the aim of enhancing family assets and status, and a courtesan could not contribute much on any of these counts. Concubines, by contrast, were usually picked by the men themselves with an eye to sex, romantic attraction, and good conversation, as well as the production of male heirs. But, surprisingly, women who made such a match did not settle down into a relatively secure life, but often stayed in a relationship just long enough for the suitor-husband to clear their debts, pay them a "body price," and equip them with jewels and other valuables. The process of marrying under these circumstances was called "taking a bath," and one can find stories of famous courtesans, including Lin Daiyu, who "bathed" many times in the course of their long careers.[18] Many of the women, impatient with the confinement and emotional discomfort of being a concubine, left their husbands and used their newly acquired resources to open their own establishments. When they chose sexual partners for love rather than material advantage, they were said to prefer actors or their own drivers to well-heeled literati and merchants. "They please customers for money," wrote a 1917 guidebook, "but what they really like is actors."[19]

The exhaustive attention to scheming courtesans is perhaps best understood as a warning about the dangers of the urban environment, where some women were unconstrained by the financial and social controls of respectable marriage. Each of the schemes described in this literature centers on a moment when the prostitute slips beyond the control of the customer, taking his assets with her. Chinese writings did not always equate fidelity with marriage or disloyalty with prostitutes; novels and memoirs provide numerous accounts of both scheming wives and virtuous courtesans. But in the early twentieth century, the inability of a customer to secure the loyalty of a courtesan, even by becoming a regular patron or making her a concubine, signified an anxiety-provoking dissolution of conventional gender arrangements.

All of these stratagems, of course, can be read against the grain not as dangers but as possible points of negotiation or resistance on the part of the prostitutes, who tried to maximize both their income and their autonomy vis-à-vis madams as well as customers. "Axe-chop" income, for instance, went into the pocket of the courtesan, not the owner. When a courtesan became a concubine, the madam was usually paid a fee, but so was the woman herself, and she might use marriage as an interim measure to terminate an unsatisfactory relationship with the madam and accumulate financial resources. More broadly, the historian hears another message—although it is perhaps not exactly what the authors intended—that life in the demimonde, for a woman with an established clientele and acute business skills, allowed more space than marriage for a woman to arrange her own time and control her own income, and that women in the profession of prostitution recognized this, valued it, and acted accordingly.

### THIRD APPROXIMATION: THE DISEASED AND OPPRESSED STREETWALKER

If we track these same sources—guidebooks, mosquito papers, the newspapers of record—through the 1920s and 1930s, some voices grow louder, others become muted. Although the courtesan does not completely vanish (she appears in the literature of nostalgia and in classificatory lists through the 1940s), she is no longer the emblematic figure of the sex trades. She has been replaced by the disease-carrying, publicly visible, disorderly, and victimized "pheasant."

The deadliest danger to be found, according to the guidebooks, was venereal disease. Usually the warning about venereal disease was a code for class; very little disease was said to be found in courtesan houses, and guidebooks that dealt exclusively with high-class establishments sometimes did not mention it at all. But most guidebooks devoted space to a detailed discussion of the lower reaches of the hierarchy as well. Below the courtesan rank, these guidebooks admonished, venereal disease became distressingly common. "[The prostitute's] body today is wanted by Zhang, tomorrow is played with by Li, and this goes on every day, without a night off, so it is impossible to avoid disease," wrote a 1939 author. "If you want to visit prostitutes [piao], high-ranking courtesans [changsan] are somewhat more reliable."[20] If a customer insisted on frequenting houses below the courtesan rank, a 1932 guidebook advised him, he ought to take a number of precautions: when paying a call, he was told to squeeze the woman's hand and discreetly check whether it was inflamed; in bed, he should first inspect her elbow joint for lumps, and if he found one, he should "pull up short at the overhanging cliff." One of the most explicit passages elaborated, "When the front lines where the two armies connect are tense," the customer could press down on the stomach and lower regions of his opponent. If she cried out in pain, it meant that she had venereal disease, and he must "immediately throw down [his] spear, don't begrudge the funds for the payment of soldiers or continue to press forward with the attack."[21] Insofar as venereal disease warnings remained tied to the class of the prostitute, they could be read as indications that an elite man should seek out only courtesan houses, rather than as a generalized comment on the dangers of frequenting brothels or the wages of sin.

Prostitutes of lower-than-courtesan rank were typically portrayed as victims rather than perpetrators in this type of account—forced by their madams to have repeated sexual relations until and even after they became infected.[22] This note of victimization was amplified daily in the *Shenbao*, Shanghai's earliest Chinese newspaper. In the pages of the *Shenbao* appeared a group of poor, oppressed, exploited, often battered prostitutes. They were not courtesans but were usually the type of streetwalker colloquially known as "pheasants."[23] They were often barely out of childhood, although occasionally they were married women. Stories about them stressed their rural origins and the fact that they had either been kidnapped and sold into prostitution or else had been pawned by destitute parents. (No embodiments of urbanity they.) [24] In either case, the reports emphasized that they did not wish to be prostitutes, a sentiment reinforced for the reader by the repetition of a standard litany of oppression. Pheasants were most often seen in one of two situations: fleeing from a cruel madam and being sent by the municipal authorities to a relief organization; or being hauled in by the police for aggressively soliciting customers, fined five or ten yuan, and released, presumably to ply their trade again. Coverage of their activities lacked the loving detail lavished on courtesans. A typical article might read in its entirety: "Pheasant Dai Ayuan, from Changzhou, was arrested on Nanjing Road by Patrolman #318 from the Laozha police station and fined 5 yuan." [25] Occasionally, corroborating the guidebook accounts, an article might mention that a streetwalker had venereal disease and had been cruelly treated by her madam. [26] The victim status of these women, however, in no way modified their characterization as dangerous to city dwellers who recklessly sought them out.

Warnings about venereal disease were not confined to guidebooks or the daily press; they became a dominant theme in a growing medical literature that treated prostitution as a public health problem. [27] This theme appeared in documents written by foreigners in Shanghai as early as the 1870s, and was common in Western sources by 1920, as part of a general colonial concern with the "cultural hygiene" of governed peoples. [28] But by the 1930s and early 1940s it appears frequently in Chinese sources, usually with reference not to courtesans but rather to "pheasants" and other lower-class prostitutes. By 1941, in fact, a series of articles in the *Shenbao* stated that according to local experts, at least half of the Shanghai population was infected with venereal disease; that 90 percent of the disease was first spread by prostitutes; and that 90 percent of the lowest-class Chinese prostitutes and 80 percent of the foreign prostitutes had venereal disease. The new forms of disguised prostitution were said to be no safer: 80 percent of the guides in guide agencies were said to be infected, while masseuses were not only diseased but also clothed in filthy uniforms. Only in a handful of high-class brothels were the Chinese and foreign prostitutes said to "understand hygiene" or stop working if they became infected. [29] Many of the movements for regulation and reform of prostitution attempted by local governments were explicitly linked to the fear of venereal disease. Venereal disease in turn was linked to China's struggle for survival, which was figured in strictly Darwinian terms. As Lin Chongwu put it in 1936, "The harm of prostitution is none other than its being a site of the spread of disease, which has serious consequences for the strength or weakness of the race. The strength of the race depends on the abundance of good elements. According to the laws of heredity, weeds cannot be sprouts." [30] In the race for survival of the fittest, prostitution and venereal disease were seen to diminish the chances of success, and in themselves became markers of China's subaltern status.

Figure 5. This image serves as the cover of Sun Yusheng's *Jinü de shenghuo* [The life of prostitutes] (Shanghai: Chunming Shudian, 1939).

## FOURTH APPROXIMATION: PROSTITUTION
## AS A MARKER OF BACKWARDNESS

The idea that prostitution was a national disgrace and contributory factor in China's national weakness may first have gained currency among Chinese Christian elites. In a 1913 Chinese-language guide to Shanghai which bore the didactic English subtitle "What the Chinese in Shanghai Ought to Know," a Christian, Huang Renjing, commented on the propensity of Chinese men to conduct business and politics with one another in courtesan houses:

> Famous persons from all over the country go to brothels. They are the leaders of our people. When leaders are like this, one can imagine the situation among industrialists and businessmen . . . The development of the West is due to the skill of the craftsmen and the diligence of the merchants. They are not like the degenerates of our country, who make use of brothels to reach their goal [i.e., who entertain business associates and political cronies at parties in broth-els]. I hope that our people will learn from the Westerners, not go to broth-els, and forbid prostitution. It is possible to catch up with the Westerners. The reason they developed from barbarism to civilization at this speed is that most of them do not go to brothels. They have virtue; we Chinese should learn from them.[31]

Chinese Christians, like their secular May Fourth counterparts, linked pros-titution to China's political vulnerability in the international arena. "The amount of money wasted in Shanghai on prostitution in half a year," ob-served one Chinese Christian acerbically, "is enough to redeem the rail-roads which have been mortgaged to the Japanese."[32] Another commented that Japan's victory in the Russo-Japanese war, fought mostly on Chinese ter-ritory in Manchuria, was attributable to the fact that 80 to 90 percent of the Japanese soldiers had had no contact with prostitutes.[33] Here is a "nesting" of subaltern statuses, where sex work in China is taken as paradigmatic of a social decay which is then invoked to explain China's position vis-à-vis col-onizing powers.

Like the foreign missionaries whose categories they adopted, Chinese Christians located the ultimate cause of prostitution in individual moral weakness. Male and female sexual desire, economic need, and social custom were powerful but secondary factors. One Chinese Christian essayist argued that women became prostitutes not only because they were poor but because their parents, preferring money to virtue, were willing to sell them into pros-titution. Traffickers preyed on women who were not only economically vul-nerable but themselves morally deficient: "Anywhere there are weak, help-less, poor, stupid, or licentious women who might be caught, the agents of prostitution will be ready to go." Commercialized sex was facilitated by all those "local evil elements" who were willing to sacrifice their scruples for the sake of profits: traffickers and madams, certainly, but also "the landlords who ask a high price for the brothel's rent, the doctors who give prostitutes papers to prove that they are healthy, the lawyers who use clever arguments to defend the business, the pharmacy salesmen who sell forbidden drugs to prostitutes, the local officials and policemen who accept bribes, the tax collectors who have the right to reduce their tax, and some other institutions they deal with who are in charge of trade and transportation." In this analysis, men's patronage of brothels could not be explained by reference to ineluctable sexual desire; the essay cited French and American medical authorities who held that men could live perfectly well without sex. Therefore, prostitution could not be justified by arguing that it sacrificed a few women to protect womankind from uncontrollable male sexuality. In this rendering, prostitutes were both victims and morally deficient; customers went to the brothels because of their moral failings and ultimately became victims of both further moral decay and venereal disease.[34]

International practices shaped by the colonizing powers were not generally invoked as causes of prostitution. For missionaries and their Chinese converts, the continued existence of prostitution pointed to weaknesses in Chinese culture, weaknesses which might be ameliorated by preachers of the social gospel but could be cured only by Christian morality, which would improve the climate for individual moral choices. The necessity of Christianity, in turn, helped to make respectable the entire network of missionary presence supported by imperialist state power.

Like the Christian commentators, other Chinese critics often invoked prostitution as emblematic of weaknesses in Chinese culture, but in their case the solution was often linked to nationalism rather than Christianity. This was part of a larger argument in which gender relations were imbricated with national strength, since it was argued that a system which permitted the treatment of women as inferior human beings would inevitably be a weak nation. Chinese elites of the May Fourth generation argued that China, which mistreated "its women," thus figuring China as male, then was treated like a woman by stronger nations: subordinated, humiliated, with pieces of its territory occupied by force, rights to its use bought and sold with impunity. These critics set themselves in opposition to many elements of Chinese culture and politics, sometimes proposing an agenda for radical political transformation, at other times adopting the language of the social purity campaigns taking place in Britain and the United States.

Writing in the *Crystal*, one such Chinese author summarized three common explanations for prostitution. The first was that women lacked other employment opportunities, the second that prostitutes were victims of madams and male brothel keepers, and the third that prostitution was often a route up the social ladder, allowing a poor woman to become a wealthy concubine. Each of these explanations mandated a different solution: more jobs for women in the first case, abolition of madams in the second, and a lifelong ban on marriage for prostitutes in the third. Yet the author concluded that all three approaches shared a common theme: prostitution was a product of the social system, and any measure that tried to eliminate it without larger social change in the status of women was of necessity superficial.[35]

Many May Fourth commentators linked the elimination of prostitution to a complete program of social reform, in which a strengthened Chinese government and socially conscious members of the elite would both play crucial roles. The government was enjoined to revive industry and commerce so that poor people could support themselves without selling their daughters; to forbid gambling, opium smoking, and drinking so that males would not take up these habits and force their wives and daughters into prostitution; and to forbid trafficking. Other measures could conceivably have involved both state and private efforts: sponsoring public lectures about the dangers of prostitution, expanding charitable organizations, promoting vocational education for women. Still others seemed to rely on nonstate initiatives: promoting proper amusements, or perfecting the marriage system so that people did not seek prostitutes because of unhappy family situations.[36] Always implicit and sometimes explicit in such ambitious programs was the goal of a new culture that would support a strong state (and vice versa), with the elimination of prostitution helping to mark the move from backwardness to modernity.

Even when it was not cited as a direct cause of national weakness, prostitution was linked to it by analogy or simple proximity. A newspaper article titled "The Evil of Evil Madams" editorialized in 1920:

> In today's China, there are many who induce others to do evil, but each time avoid the consequences of their crime. Military officials induce the troops to harass people, while civil officials induce their underlings to harm the people. As soon as these activities are exposed, the troops and underlings are condemned, but the officials are calm and in fine shape . . . Furthermore, they shield their troops and underlings and cover up in order to avoid being implicated in the crimes themselves . . . To push the argument further, evil madams who induce prostitutes to solicit customers are in the same category. They force prostitutes to do evil, and also cause people to be harmed by their evil.[37]

To read this passage as a simple rhetorical flourish intended to dramatize the "evil of madams" is to miss an important and barely subtextual message. The practices associated with prostitution are here being invoked as part of a sickness in the culture, expressed in the exploitative and self-protective activities of anyone with power. In this rendering, prostitution was not so much causative as constitutive; prostitutes took their place alongside all those harassed by civil and military authorities, and madams became part of a pervasive and nested regime of power that was manifestly bad for "the people" and the nation.

## FIFTH APPROXIMATION: PROSTITUTION
## AS A MARKER OF MODERNITY

Throughout the 1920s and 1930s, municipal governments waged intermittent campaigns to ban unlicensed prostitution. Each of these campaigns, too complex to be taken up here, generated furious production of commentary by intellectuals, many of them associated with feminist causes, the communist movement, or both. Although I cannot yet attempt a detailed account of those commentaries, even a preliminary perusal of the 1930s literature turns up a striking shift in the way intellectuals positioned prostitution in China. While still treated as a serious social problem with specific local features, it had moved from a marker of China's cultural failings and national weakness to a sign of China's participation in universal human history.

A 1936 polemic by Mu Hua against licensed prostitution, for instance, began by invoking the standard May Fourth explanations for prostitution: economic difficulties, trafficking, the atrophy of moral values, the marriage system, and the low level of education. But it moved quickly to universalize the problem by juxtaposing Auguste Bebel's statistics on Parisian prostitutes with a survey of prostitutes who applied for licenses in Suzhou. Mu's conclusion to this section emphasized the primacy of economic causes regardless of venue: " 'In sum, [the cause is] just poverty!' The door of the brothel is open for the wives and daughters of the poor."[38] In this move, China is not positioned in a world economy or a colonial system—a positioning which might mark China as simultaneously wronged and backward.

This universalizing narrative was rooted in biology and culture as well as economics: "The male of the human species has a sexual desire which is not less extravagant [*wangsheng,* literally, "prosperous"] than that of the beasts, while the biological burden and the capability of the female in sexual intercourse are very different from that of the beasts."[39] Women's difference from beasts is not specified here, as the author races on, invoking Bebel and echoing Engels, to sketch out the establishment of private property, the rise in the status of men and the imposition of restrictions on wives, and the establishment of prostitutes as objects of enjoyment. With marriage and prostitution linked in a single system,[40] it remains for capitalism to create a situation where more and more men cannot afford marriage and turn to prostitutes. Here Mu Hua makes an unmarked move back to particular local Chinese conditions, arguing that

> because of the immaturity of industry and the desolation of commerce, with most households in economic distress, women in industry and commerce and maids in households make a meager income insufficient to carry the burden of supporting the household, and only by selling sex as a sideline can they supplement their insufficient wages. So the supply of prostitutes matches male sexual needs, leading to even greater inflation in the market in human flesh.[41]

What is striking about this passage, which echoes many standard depression-era descriptions of the Chinese economy, is precisely that it is left geographically unmarked and historically genericized. Coming as it does directly after Bebel and Engels on the universal evolution of marriage systems, it points away from anything that might be designated as specifically Chinese, even as it describes local problems. The insertion of China into a seamless world predicament is completed when Mu, after quoting the selling prices of women and children in various Chinese provinces, declares:

> In this capitalist era, prostitutes themselves are a commodity, and because of an oversupply of the commodity, the middlemen have to lower the price, and adopt the approach of selling more when the profit is meager. So flesh is cheap, and a transaction costs a few dimes, while on the other hand new selling techniques are developed . . . If we cannot use foodstuffs to fill their mouths, we cannot devise ways to have them not sell their lower bodies.[42]

Like the earlier May Fourth commentators, Mu Hua indicates that a comprehensive state initiative is needed to remedy this situation, and warns that if the state permits licensed prostitution, it will damage its own prestige.[43] Unlike the May Fourth precursors, however, Mu's narrative strategy puts across the message that Shanghai is just like Paris: both are mired in the problems of capitalism, with China as a full participant in capitalist ills. Prostitution and its attendant problems have become a badge of modernity.

Elite arguments against prostitution in the 1930s were not without cultural specificity. At one point in commentator Lin Chongwu's essay, after he has invoked the case of Solon and the authority of Parent-Duchatelet, Franz Hugel, Flexner, Rousseau, and Lincoln, his argument takes a sudden particularistic turn. He exhorts the state to promote traditional Confucian virtues for women, such as honesty, honor, propriety, and justice, so that women can resist the lure of Western ways:

> The European wind assails the East, leading to female vanity, beautiful clothes and makeup, powder and perfume, living in a fool's paradise and coveting pleasures, love of pleasure and fear of labor . . . If one can't be frugal, how can one be honest? . . . Abandoning a sense of chastity and shame . . . as this goes on, it leads to selling sex for a living. "If this is how it is in the higher reaches of society, how much more so in the lower reaches?" So promotion of virtue should start with the families of government officials—giving up pearls and jade, turning away from gold and diamonds, with coarse dress and simple adornment . . . This will promote the cultivation of female virtue.[44]

In spite of the Confucian overtones and undertones, however, Lin's discussion is firmly grounded both in the twentieth century—where China is one nation struggling among many—and in a universal moral discourse, where Rousseau and Lincoln are cited as sources of the belief that human trafficking cannot be permitted in a civilized society. When Confucian imperatives are set literally paragraph by paragraph next to Parent-Duchatelet, Charlemagne, Saint Augustine, and Max Rubner,[45] an invocation of unique cultural values becomes its opposite: an application to join a human march toward a civilized, moral society, in which both prostitution and the intent to eliminate it are credentials for membership.

## SIXTH APPROXIMATION: PROSTITUTE AS OBJECT OF STATE REGULATION

Prior to 1949, the police and the courts periodically undertook to regulate prostitution, at least at the margins where it involved the sale into prostitution of "women of good families," or street soliciting, which was seen as a threat to public order. Prostitution per se was not illegal in Republican China, but trafficking was.[46] Because of the structure of Republican laws about prostitution, women could obtain legal protection in exiting a brothel if they asserted that they had been removed from a respectable family and sold into prostitution. When leaving a brothel meant an improvement in a woman's material or emotional situation, then, she had to portray herself as a victim seeking reunification with her family in order to attain that goal. Thus, abduction and sale was a common story told by prostitutes who brought suits for their freedom, in spite of the considerable evidence suggesting that abductions accounted for a minority of trafficking cases, and that most involved the sale or pawning of a woman for the benefit of her family.[47]

Street soliciting was forbidden in Shanghai under municipal ordinances, and at certain points in the Republican period, brothels and prostitutes were required to obtain a license.[48] When prostitutes were brought before the courts or questioned by the police for violating these regulations, they commonly made one of two arguments on their own behalf. The first was that they were working as prostitutes against their will. For instance, in 1929 an eighteen-year-old named Tan Youxi was picked up in a sweep by Chinese plainclothesmen aimed at clearing the streets of prostitutes. Facing a court-imposed fine, she testified that she had been kidnapped in Suzhou two months before and sold into a pheasant brothel. Although the trafficker had long since disappeared, the brothel owner was charged with buying a good woman and forcing her to become a prostitute *(po liang wei chang)*. The owner was detained pending investigation in spite of his argument that Tan had willingly signed a contract and was entitled to half of what she earned.[49] Tan's assertion that she had not entered prostitution of her own free will, which may well have been accurate, was also strategic, serving to shift the court's attention from her to others.

The second argument made by streetwalkers was that they had reluctantly chosen prostitution in order to support dependent relatives. This type

of self-representation appears, for instance, in the transcripts of police interrogations of three prostitutes after their unlicensed brothel was raided in
1947. All three women cited dire economic necessity and the need to support dependents as their reason for taking up sex work. Tang Xiaolong, age
thirty-two, who came from Suzhou, told the police: "My mother recently
died, my father is old, and we have many debts. Forced by the situation, in
February of this year I came to Shanghai, and willingly placed myself [zitou]
at the above address, the home of Shen and Sun, as a prostitute . . . As soon
as I clear my father's debts, I plan to change occupation, either becoming a
servant or returning home. The above is the truth." Although Tang apparently had no husband, her co-worker, twenty-five-year-old Zhang Xiuying
from Yangzhou, found that marriage was no guarantee of financial security:

> I have an old mother at home and one son. My husband joined the army four
> years ago and has not returned. I had no means of livelihood, so on January 14
> of this year I left home and came to Shanghai, looking for a former compan-
> ion[,] Zhang Yuehua, and asked her for an introduction to a job. For a while
> I could find no regular work. The friend, with my agreement, introduced me
> into this brothel to be a prostitute in order to survive. Fees were split evenly
> with the madam, and room and board was provided by the brothel owner. I
> was definitely not tricked or forced into become a prostitute, but actually was
> driven to it by family poverty. The above is the truth. I ask for understanding
> in your judgment of this case and will feel very lucky.

Twenty-six-year-old Chen Abao, unlike the other two, had previously done
other work in Shanghai:

> I was formerly a wet nurse . . . After February I returned home, because my
> husband in the countryside was very ill. At the end of last year my husband
> passed away, leaving an old father at home, and a young son and daughter.
> Life was difficult in the countryside, so I recently came to Shanghai, borrowed
> a room at 7 Furun li, and entered into a system of dividing the profits with the
> madam [lao-banniang], becoming a prostitute in order to live. This is the truth.

Reviewing the testimony of the three women, the chief of the morals correc-
tion section of the police concluded: "The reason they became unlicensed
prostitutes was because all were forced by life circumstances. They were not
kidnapped or forced into it by others."[50]

These stories suggest that many women entered prostitution without en-
countering any traffickers, much less the kidnappers emphasized in so many
of the sources. Some were older than the archetypal kidnapping victims;
they had filial obligations to marital as well as natal families, and were often
the sole support of children or elderly dependents. The decision to take up
sex work was sometimes made by the prostitutes themselves, within the context of family as well as individual economic needs, and they often earmarked
income for the support of their families. Under arrest, they could have won

lenient treatment and constituted themselves as in need of state protection by arguing that they had been abducted. Instead, they situated themselves in a different nexus of respectability, one in which filial obligations required that they temporarily take up a distasteful occupation. The circumstances under which their confessions were made caution us against reading them as unproblematic statements of "fact." But their statements do complicate the portrait of women violently abducted and forced to sell sexual services. And the particular ways in which they formulated their statements suggest that they were not innocent of the craft of representation or its immediate practical uses in deflecting the expansive reach of the state. If they were participants in their own representation, then perhaps elites did not have a monopoly on the discursive construction of events, and we need not accept a single totalizing account as the only available material for "history."

Although the legal records indicate that prostitutes acted resourcefully on their own behalf and for their families, municipal regimes in Shanghai from the 1920s through the 1950s continued to see prostitutes as dangerously adrift from their proper social moorings, both agents and victims of a broader social disorder. Regulation of prostitution was always part of a broader project in which state authorities extended their reach into new realms in urban life. The Nationalist regime and its twentieth-century municipal governments sought to enlarge their domain of regulation to include the family, echoing both their Confucian antecedents and the modernizing regimes of Europe. In their view, encoded in regulations on trafficking and prostitution, women in families were indicative of a well-ordered society. The sundering of family networks through trafficking and sex work bespoke a larger crisis in the social order, one that would entail the reinsertion of women into families as part of its resolution.

This belief about the proper place of women was not challenged in 1949. In its early years the government of the People's Republic of China began a campaign to end prostitution, armed with organizing techniques that enabled it to succeed in extending the reach of the state into realms where earlier municipal governments had failed.[51] In Shanghai this campaign did not get under way until 1951, and continued with decreasing intensity until prostitution was declared eradicated in 1958. A major feature of the campaign was the detention of prostitutes in the Women's Labor Training Institute. Although they were not permitted to leave the institute at will, neither were they prisoners: the explicit strategy of the municipal government was to cure their venereal disease, equip them with job skills, reunite them with their families, and/or find them appropriate husbands. The key to the success of this entire project, in the view of government officials, was teaching the women to think—and to speak—as recently liberated subalterns. To that end they were organized into study sessions, the most important goal of which was to instill a sense of class consciousness. They had to be made to hate the old society and recognize their oppression in it, and they had to recognize that their own past actions were less than glorious, were now in fact illegal, and must not be repeated.[52] In short, their own understanding of their recent past had to be aligned with that of the state by encouraging them to speak that past—not in unison but in harmony with one another—in a language provided by the state. Their words were often published because they were considered to have didactic value for the larger urban population, most of which was engaged, to one degree or another, in a similar reinterpretation of the past.

In the post-Mao years, prostitutes have once again become visible in Shanghai. Although the organization of the contemporary trade bears little resemblance to the world of Republican-era brothels, regulatory discourse features many of the same themes that characterized earlier campaigns. Recent state policy toward prostitution centers on the task, in a rapidly changing reform economy, of returning women to stable work and family situations. In this way, the state argues, China can both modernize and resist the disruptions engendered by "bourgeois liberalization." In each of these cases modernity is seen as simultaneously displacing women (who are both victimized and set loose) and requiring that they be resituated (both protected and contained) with the help of strong state authority. At stake is the very control over what modernity looks like and means, as well as what "women" are and should be.


These different approximations of prostitution coexisted in treaty port Shanghai, and some aspects of them can be reconciled. One might, for example, point out that the mosquito press and the guidebooks both describe women at the top of the hierarchy of prostitution, whereas the *Shenbao* and other similar newspapers are describing women at the bottom. Both types of women sold sexual services, but there the similarity ended. Streetwalkers, unlike courtesans, worked in miserable and dirty conditions, under duress, for cash, in the process posing a danger both to social order (dealt with by the police) and to public health (as hinted at in the accounts of venereal disease). If we take these wildly differing accounts at face value, we have to question whether the single category "prostitute" assumes a similarity where one should not be assumed, whether in fact we should stop talking about "prostitution" as a unitary occupation and instead use subcategories such as "courtesan" or "streetwalker."

Ultimately, however, I would prefer to abandon attempts at reconciliation and look instead at the dissonance. Prostitution was an extraordinarily flexible signifier for many different kinds of Chinese engaged in many different conversations. The dissonant chorus they produced raises questions about both the contemporary meaning of the category "prostitution" and the concerns of the patrons and the wider urban population. Above all, we must approach with caution the notion that we can retrieve from history a single set of descriptive or explanatory "facts" about prostitutes.

The perpetual reconfiguration of the discourses on Shanghai prostitution certainly reflected the changing occupational structure of Shanghai, where commercial and industrial sectors grew in tandem with a deepening rural crisis, encouraging the migration, both voluntary and coerced, of peasant women and girls. These interlocked phenomena led to a swelling of the lower ranks of prostitution, changing the sexual service structure to one regarded as more disruptive of social order, and more dangerous to social and physical health.

Yet a research strategy that treats discursive construction as the unproblematic reflection of (prediscursive) social change misses something. One must also look at the eye of the beholder, considering the changing self-definition of urban elites, the effect of the May Fourth movement and the growing revolutionary movement, the development of reformist conversations on the position of women in general and prostitutes in particular, and the effect of language and categories drawn from Western missionary sources as well as Chinese radical politics. The discourse on prostitution should also be counterposed to parallel and intersecting struggles over the meaning of marriage, barely alluded to in this essay. It is interesting, for instance, that courtesans were initially regarded as social as well as sexual companions, and portrayed as offering a range of companionship and choice not to be found in arranged marriages. In the social ferment that followed the May Fourth movement, however, intellectuals began to articulate, if not to practice, a notion of marriage as a companionate partnership between equals. If marriage was companionate and desired as such, then courtesans were no longer important as educated women with refined skills, as a means to relieve the tedium of an arranged marriage, or as entertainers. All that was left for the world of the prostitute was sex. Simultaneously, prostitution was redefined as an exploitative transaction where the main connection—an oppressive one at that—was between the prostitute and her madam, not the prostitute and her customer. Because of these connections, prostitution must be looked at in conjunction with marriage and marriage customs.

Finally, the study of prostitution raises the problem of how we simultaneously retrieve and create a historical past. Because the sources on prostitution are so thoroughly embedded in discourses of pleasure, reform, and regulation, they cannot be used in any straightforward way to reconstruct the lived experiences of these women. The voices of a variety of men—the patron, the reformer, the lawyer, and the doctor—are far more audible than the voices of the prostitutes. In the writings of female reformers, representations of prostitution were shaped, if not by gender differences, then most assuredly by class. Their writings were rich in the rhetoric of social purity and pity for fallen sisters. Continually obscured in all of this are the voices of the prostitutes themselves—voices which, while they surely would not have been unified, given the variety of arrangements under which women sold sexual services, would certainly sound different from what we are able to hear at a safely historical distance today.

How can the sources, generated in circumstances of intense public argument about the "larger" meanings of prostitution, be read for clues to the lived (and mediated) experiences of prostitutes, a group that was subordinate and relatively silenced on almost any axis the historian can devise? The voices and actions of Shanghai prostitutes are not completely inaudible or invisible in the historical record. Their experience was bounded by legal, medical, moral, and political discourses that must have affected how they saw themselves, what alliances they sought inside and outside the brothel, what options they had. Prostitutes appear to have engaged in everyday practices which helped them negotiate the dominant discourses and improve their own living and working conditions—using concubinage and the courts, for instance, in ways that belied their portrayal as victims or as threats to the regulated social order.

In each of these representations of prostitutes, whether seen through the particular cautionary lens of the guidebooks or through their direct (though certainly mediated) speech to legal authorities, we discover instances of agency, even resistance. A courtesan who works to enlarge her tips and gifts from customers which are not paid to the brothel is challenging the authority of the madam over her income, and in a certain sense over her body. A courtesan who leaves the brothel with an attractive but impoverished young man who cannot pay the requisite fees—or a courtesan who chooses "actors and drivers" as her companions rather than the free-spending merchants the madam would prefer—is doing the same. A streetwalker who represents herself in court as the victim of traffickers resists being classified as a bad woman, a threat to social order, a spreader of disease.

Nevertheless, these are acts that can also be thought of as "working the system," and ultimately legitimating dominant norms. They not only leave unchallenged but actually reinscribe a larger ensemble of social arrangements in which prostitutes are multiply subordinated. In order to collect tips and private gifts, for instance, a courtesan must cultivate the patronage of customers in ways that can perpetuate her dependence on and vulnerability to them. When a prostitute wins release from a brothel on the grounds that she was illegally brought there, she helps to legitimize the court's authority to determine circumstances in which women may be legally placed in brothels, or more generally have claims on their sexual services transferred. Furthermore, in order to leave the brothels, many of these women averred a desire to be returned to patriarchal family authority, a desire they may well not have felt (given their family circumstances) but which represented their best chance of being seen by the courts as victims rather than offenders. It is important that we recognize these instances of women's agency, resist the desire to magnify or romanticize them, and admit, finally, that our readings of them are tentative and are limited by the many silences and irreducible ambiguities in the historical record.

By reading and listening in multiple registers, we can begin to understand the voices and actions of prostitutes *in relation to* those who were more visible and audible. In the process perhaps we can learn where the voices of prostitutes formed a chorus, where a counterpoint, where an important dissonant note in the changing discourses on prostitution. At the same time, we can trace the discursive uses others made of the prostitute. These are most apparent in arguments about the shifting meanings of urbanity, respectability, government, even nationhood, as elites and less exalted city dwellers sought to define for themselves what it meant to be an urban Chinese in the twentieth century.

## NOTES

Reprinted by permission of the publisher from *Engendering China*, ed. Christina K. Gilmartin et al. (Cambridge: Harvard University Press). Copyright 1994 by the Presidents and Fellows of Harvard College. Substantial portions of this essay appeared in Gail Hershatter, "Courtesans and Streetwalkers: The Changing Discourses on Shanghai Prostitution, 1890–1949," *Journal of the History of Sexuality* 3, no. 2 (1992): 245–69, © 1992 by the University of Chicago. All rights reserved. The author thanks Guo Xiaolin and Wang Xiangyun for invaluable research assistance. Critical readings and suggestions were provided by participants in the "Engendering China" conference, particularly Christina Gilmartin, Emily Honig, Lisa Rofel, Ann Waltner, and Marilyn Young, as well as by Wendy Brown, Judith Farquhar, Carla Freccero, Carma Hinton, and Angela Zito.

1. Judith R. Walkowitz, *Prostitution and Victorian Society: Women, Class, and the State* (Cambridge: Cambridge University Press, 1980); Alain Corbin, *Women for Hire: Prostitution and Sexuality in France after 1850*, trans. Alan Sheridan (Cambridge: Harvard University Press, 1990).

2. See, for example, the very useful but interpretively limited work by Wang Shunu, *Zhongguo changji shi* [History of prostitution in China] (1935; reprint, Shanghai: Sanlian shudian, 1988).

3. For an eloquent demand that historians attend to discursive constructions of gender and their historical effects, see Joan Wallach Scott, *Gender and the Politics of History* (New York: Columbia University Press, 1988).

4. Huang Renjing, *Huren baolan* [Precious mirror of Shanghai; English title: What the Chinese in Shanghai ought to know] (Shanghai: Huamei shuju [Methodist Publishing House], 1913); Wang Liaoweng, *Shanghai liushinian huajie shi* [A sixty-

year history of the Shanghai flower world] (Shanghai: Shixin shuju, 1922); Zhan Kai, *Rouxiang yunshi* [A history of the charm of the gentle village], 3d ed., 1st ed. 1914, author's preface dated 1907 (Shanghai: Wenyi xiaoqian suo, 1917), *juan* 3; Banchisheng [Half-crazy one], *Haishang yeyou beilan* [A complete look at Shanghai philandering] (1891), *juan* 4.

5. Qi Xia and Da Ru, eds., *Haishang hua yinglu* [A record in images of Shanghai flowers], rev. ed., vol. 1 (Shanghai: Zhongguo tushuguan, 1917), unpaginated.

6. Joseph Levenson, *Confucian China and Its Modern Fate* (Berkeley and Los Angeles: University of California Press, 1972).

7. Huayu xiaozhu zhuren [Master of the Flower Rain Villa], *Haishang qinglou tuji* [Records and drawings of Shanghai houses of prostitution] (N.p., 1892), *juan* 6, *juan* 1, p. 1.

8. *Jingbao* [The crystal], August 15, 1919, p. 3.

9. *Jingbao*, August 27, 1919, p. 3.

10. For examples of this kind of poetry, see Chi Zhizheng, "Huyou mengying" [Dream images of Shanghai travels], ed. Hu Zhusheng (March 1893), photocopy of edited version of unpublished manuscript *(chaoben)* in Wenzhou Museum, pp. 4–8; Li chuang wo dusheng [Student who lies on the goosefoot bed], ed., *Huitu Shanghai zaji* [Miscellaneous Shanghai notes, illustrated] (Shanghai: Shanghai wenbao shuju shi yingben, 1905), *juan* 6, p. 7, and *juan* 7, p. 7.

11. On the elections, see Chan Qingshi [Attendant who repents emotion], *Haishang chunfang pu* [An album of Shanghai ladies] (Shanghai: Shenbao guan, 1884), *juan* 4; Ping Jinya, "Jiu Shanghaide changji" [Prostitution in Old Shanghai], in *Jiu Shanghaide yanduchang* [Opium, gambling, and prostitution in Old Shanghai] (Shanghai: Baijia chubanshe, 1988), 166–67; Chen Rongguang [Chen Boxi], *Lao Shanghai* [Old Shanghai hand] (Shanghai: Taidong tushuju, 1924), 90–95; Huayu xiaozhu zhuren, *juan* 1, p. 2; Qi Xia and Da Ru, vol. 1, unpaginated, and vol. 2, unpaginated; Yu Muxia, *Shanghai linzhao* [Shanghai tidbits] (Shanghai: Shanghai Hubaoguan chubanbu, 1935), *ji*, pp. 37–38; Zhou Shoujuan, *Lao Shanghai sanshi nian jianwen lu* [A record of things seen by an Old Shanghai hand in the last thirty years] (Shanghai: Dadong shuju, 1928), 2:2–4, 38–51; Xu Ke, *Qingbai leichao* [Qing unofficial reference book] (Shanghai: Shangwu yinshuguan, 1928), 38:1–4.

12. Stephen H. L. Cheng, "*Flowers of Shanghai* and the Late Ch'ing Courtesan Novel" (Ph.D. diss., Harvard University, 1979), 252.

13. For examples of this kind of writing, see Sun Yusheng [Haishang juewusheng], *Jinüde shenghuo* [The life of prostitutes] (Shanghai: Chunming shudian, 1939), 8; and *Jingbao*, November 30, 1919, p. 3.

14. Wu Hanchi, ed., *Quanguo gejie qiekou da cidian* [National dictionary of secret language from all walks of life] (Shanghai: Donglu tushu gongsi, 1924), 9, 13; Wang Houzhe, *Shanghai baojian* [Precious mirror of Shanghai] (Shanghai: Shijie shuju, 1925), unpaginated; Ping Jinya, 160; Shuliu shanfang [pseud.], "Shanghai qinglou zhi jinxi guan" [A look at Shanghai brothels present and past], *Jingbao*, March 18, 1919, p. 3.

15. Wang Zhongxia, *Shanghai suyu tushuo* [An illustrated dictionary of Shanghai slang] (Shanghai: Shanghai shehui chubanshe, 1935; reprint, Hong Kong: Shenzhou tushu gongsi, n.d.), 42.

16. Wang Liaoweng, 135.

17. Sun Yusheng, 68–69; Wang Houzhe, unpaginated.

18. On her career and her frequent ablutions, and those of some of her fellow courtesans, see *Jingbao*, September 21, 1919, p. 3; Wang Liaoweng, 50–56; and Zhou Shoujuan, 1:172–77.

19. Qi Xia and Da Ru, n.p. For a list of forty-seven liaisons between prostitutes and actors, see Chen Rongguang, 123–28.

20. Sun Yusheng, 159.

21. Wang Dingjui, *Shanghai de menjing* [Key to Shanghai] (Shanghai: Zhongyang shudian, 1932), 25.

22. See, for example, Sun Yusheng, 170–71.

23. Various explanations for this term can be found in the guidebooks. One article notes both their gaudy dress and their habit of "go[ing] about from place to place like wild birds." "The Demi-Monde of Shanghai," *China Medical Journal* 37 (1923): 785–86.

24. This type of story about prostitutes is analyzed more fully in Gail Hershatter, "Sex Work and Social Order: Prostitutes, Their Families, and the State in Twentieth-Century Shanghai," in *Family Process and Political Process in Modern Chinese History*, ed. Zhongyang yanjiuyuan jindaishi yanjiusuo (Taipei: Zhongyang yanjiuyuan, 1992), 2:1083–1123.

25. *Shenbao*, November 12, 1919, p. 11.

26. See, for example, *Shenbao*, May 7, 1919, p. 11.

27. For a discussion of this literature, see Christian Henriot, "Medicine, V.D., and Prostitution in Pre-Revolutionary China," *Social History of Medicine* 5, no. 1 (April 1992): 95–120.

28. For a fuller discussion of these sources, see Gail Hershatter, "Regulating Sex in Shanghai: The Reform of Prostitution in 1920 and 1951," in *Shanghai Sojourners*, ed. Frederic Wakeman and Wen-hsin Yeh (Berkeley: Institute of East Asian Studies, 1992), 145–85.

29. *Shenbao*, October 31–November 3, 1941.

30. Lin Chongwu, "Changji wenti zhi yanjiu" [Research on the prostitution problem], *Minzhong jikan* 2, no. 2 (June 1936): 221. On the emergence of race as a prominent category of analysis during this period, see Frank Dikötter, *The Discourse of Race in Modern China* (Stanford: Stanford University Press, 1992).

31. Huang Renjing, 134–35.

32. *Chinese Recorder* (August 1920): 579–80.

33. Bu Minghui, M.D., of the Shanghai Moral Welfare League, writing in *Shenbao*, May 19, 1919, p. 11.

34. *Shenbao*, May 19, 1919, p. 11.

35. *Jingbao*, March 27, 1920, p. 2.

36. Hu Huaichen, "Feichang wenti" [The question of eliminating prostitution], *Funü zazhi* 6, no. 6 (1920): 9–10.

37. *Shenbao*, November 10, 1920, p. 11.

38. Mu Hua, "Gongchang zhidude bihai qiji lunjude huangmiu" [The harm of the licensed prostitution system and the absurdity of its grounds of argument], *Nüzi yuekan* 4, no. 4 (April 1936): 22.

39. Ibid.

40. Mu Hua uses Bebel to make this point, but other authors prefer Havelock El-lis, Ellen Key, Anton Gross-Hoffinger, Max Rubner, and Bertrand Russell. Whether the discourse cited is tied to political economy or sexology, the universalizing im-pulse is similar. See, for example, Guo Chongjie, "Lun suqing changji" [On ridding the country of prostitution], *Shehui banyue kan* 1, no. 6 (November 1936): 23–28; and Lin Chongwu, "Changji wenti zhi yanjiu," 215–223.

41. Mu Hua, 23.

42. Ibid.

43. Ibid., 25.

44. Lin Chongwu, 222.

45. Ibid., passim.

46. Individual cities sometimes undertook to ban prostitution, but their ordi-nances were effective only within city limits, usually with the result that prostitutes moved to neighboring cities. Article 288 of the 1923 Provisional Criminal Code of the Republic of China stipulated imprisonment and fines for "whoever for lucrative purposes induces any woman belonging to a respectable family to have illicit in-tercourse with any person for hire," with stiffer penalties for "whoever makes the commission of the offence under the last preceding section a profession." Ana-tol M. Kotenev, *Shanghai: Its Mixed Court and Council* (1925; reprint, Taipei: Ch'eng-wen Publishing, 1968), 413–14. The 1935 Criminal Code, while omitting a specific reference to respectable families, likewise made it a crime to remove "any person who has not completed the twentieth year of his or her age" from family or other "supervisory authority." The punishment was more severe if the person was re-moved without his or her consent or if the person was taken away "for the purpose of gain or for the purpose of causing the person who has been taken away to submit to carnal knowledge or to do a lascivious act." Shanghai Municipal Council Legal Department, trans., *The Chinese Criminal Code* (Shanghai: Commercial Press, 1935), 86–88.

47. For statements that kidnappings accounted for a minority of trafficking cases, see "The Prostitution Problem in Shanghai," *China Critic*, April 1, 1937, p. 7; *Shenbao*, November 1, 1941, p. 3. A 1951 survey of 501 prostitutes found that only forty-seven, or 9.4 percent, had been tricked or kidnapped. Yang Jiezeng and He Wannan, *Shanghai changji gaizao shihua* [A history of the reform of Shanghai Prosti-tutes] (Shanghai: Shanghai sanlian shudian, 1988), 61.

48. According to a 1937 *China Critic* report, the relevant laws in the Interna-tional Settlement were bylaw no. 36 and article 43 of Police Punishments for Viola-tion of Morals. In the French Concession, the relevant laws were consular ordinance no. 183 and the provisions of chapter 16 (221 and subsequent articles) and chap-ter 17 (237 and subsequent articles) of the Chinese Criminal Code, which was ap-plied by Chinese courts in the Concession. "The Prostitution Problem in Shanghai," *China Critic*, April 1, 1937, p. 7. After the Second World War, the Shanghai munici-pal government issued regulations prohibiting inducing others to become prosti-tutes in order to make a profit, or having sexual relations with people for profit. It is unclear how these regulations squared with the municipal government's elaborate schemes to license brothels and prostitutes. The relevant police regulations were

nos. 64 and 65. Shanghai shi dang'an guan [Shanghai Municipal Archives], *Qudi jiyuan an* [Cases of banning brothels], File 011–4–163, 1946–1948, case 4.

49. *Shibao*, July 15, 1929, p. 7.

50. Shanghai shi dang'an guan [Shanghai Municipal Archives], *Qudi jiyuan an* [Cases of banning brothels], File 011–4–163, 1946–1948, case 4, documents 2–6.

51. For details of this campaign, see Gail Hershatter, "Regulating Sex," 167–85.

52. This sentence is from ibid., 176.

# CHAPTER EIGHT

# Approximations of Chinese Bandits: Perverse Rebels, Romantic Heroes, or Frustrated Bachelors?

*David Ownby*

Rebels and bandits are hardly the masculine equivalent of prostitutes, but they occupy similar positions at the margins of mainstream Chinese society and sometimes also figure in comparable ways in elite and popular discourses about exciting or dangerous forms of behavior. Like prostitutes, rebels and bandits are threatening precisely because they are *liminal* rather than *excluded* groups, and because to some degree they speak to genuine needs frequently neglected by Confucian society. Certain categories of prostitutes, those more commonly known as courtesans, could and did marry, thus multiplying their spouse's chances of progeny (courtesans were rarely first wives) and perhaps of emotional fulfillment. "Successful" bandits could be co-opted by the state to serve as military officers in the emperor's army; a truly successful bandit could supplant the reigning dynasty and take the monarch's seat on the dragon throne. The possibility of social reintegration may have been soothing to those compelled to engage in prostitution or in banditry. At the same time, such possibilities troubled the collective conscience of orthodox society by suggesting that ordinary people were closer to such liminal groups than many liked to believe.

The liminal status of bandits and rebels inspires my discussion of "approximations" of banditry, which follows lines roughly parallel to those pursued by Gail Hershatter in her essay on prostitutes. One of my main arguments is that although Chinese authorities, from imperial times down to the present, have typically characterized bandit gangs as perverse, uncivilized savages; as heterodox and potentially violent rebels; or as greedy, scheming entrepreneurs, these negative approximations have always had to compete with the more romantic, Robin Hood–like images of bandits purveyed in popular fiction and drama. I also stress that, as the late imperial political and cultural order dissolved in the early twentieth century, Communists and Nationalists, competing parties in pursuit of national power, combined modern Western and traditional Chinese images of bandits to create a new approximation of the bandit-rebel as "potential revolutionary." After examining these approximations, all of which are grounded to some extent in actual political or socioeconomic considerations, I will contrast them all with a final, more explicitly gendered approximation: that of the "bandit as frustrated bachelor."

As my goal is to collect and examine depictions of bandits, I adopt a very broad definition of the term. In addition to rural outlaws, I also include for discussion secret societies, urban gangs, religious groups identified by the state as heterodox, some rebel bands, and even groups at feud.[1] Although there are undeniable differences among these categories, the groups they describe nonetheless share a number of common characteristics. First, they engaged in sporadic violence. Second, they maintained ambiguous relations with the orthodox world of lineages and Confucian literati. Third, they were on the wrong side of the law, either due to their own actions or to the decision of the Chinese state to label them as problems of social control. Finally, they tended to be composed of young, unattached men.[2] To search for commentary on these groups, I situated myself broadly, taking as fair game any bandit group from the late Ming on and, as already suggested, collecting approximations from elite and popular, traditional and modern sources. I make no claim to comprehensiveness.

## LATE-IMPERIAL ELITE APPROXIMATIONS

The Chinese imperial elite entertained several competing images of bandits and made little effort to sort out the contradictions among them. The most basic image of bandits and rebels, an image frequently reproduced, was that such miscreants were good subjects who had simply been led astray. A commentary by a censor at the turn of the nineteenth century is fairly typical: "According to my humble estimate, among the large number of bandits now existing, two in every ten are roused by their hatred toward local officials, three in every ten are driven to extremity by hunger and cold, and four . . . are either constrained to join after having been captured . . . or coerced to follow . . . after having been driven from their home villages. No more than one in ten . . . have willingly become bandits."[3] This elitist belief that the "untutored masses" were basically good but easily swayed was part Confucian homily (inculcated by a wide variety of texts, including ones that sought to impart basic literacy) and part calculus of control (given the limited span of control achieved by the Chinese state, prosecution of all those involved in banditry would have overloaded the Chinese penal system or — even worse — pushed originally apolitical predatory bandits toward rebellious confrontation with the state). This was a particularly apt consideration, since, as noted by our turn-of-the-century censor, a common factor pushing the "untutored masses" toward banditry was the occasional corruption and cruelty of individual Confucian officials. Such a belief thus justified the practice of harshly prosecuting the leaders of a bandit group while dealing much more leniently with the followers, a practice that permitted the Chinese state to maintain its stance of righteous benevolence toward the population at large.

This benevolent picture is different when we turn to the "one in ten" who, in our censor's estimation, willingly took up banditry. Here, the generous social determinism of the paternal state gave way to categorical condemnation: such men (and the vast majority were indeed men) were an evil to be extirpated. Interestingly, late imperial commentators rarely sought to *explain* how this small minority came to be beyond the pale and, when describing them, simply replaced their depiction of the "untutored" or "misled" followers with a condemnation of the "wicked" leaders or instigators.[4] Indeed, instead of analysis, we find *labels* that became stock phrases to justify police action against them, the three most common of these being: the uncivilized bandit, the heterodox bandit, and the greedy bandit.

Bandits were frequently depicted as uncivilized or, to use the more frequent Chinese expression, perverse *(diaohan)* brutes who had not learned the lessons that made men human. The Yongzheng emperor (r. 1723–35), in a Sacred Edict (a sort of imperial maxim) of 1736 makes this point quite directly: "The Mao, the Man, the Yao, and the Zhuang [ethnic minorities found in various parts of China], who are the most difficult to teach, have recently reformed and changed their ways in the hopes of becoming civilized. How then can the people of Zhangzhou and Quanzhou [prefectures in Fujian] not equal . . . [these non-Han peoples] in regretting their errors and moving toward the good, in discarding their heartlessness and following loyalty? How can they continue to throw themselves willingly into the net of the law?"[5]

What are the identifying features of "uncivilized perversion"? First, uncivilized people are "stupid," according to various elite texts, and, "being stupid[,] . . . are unable to calculate losses and benefits, and [they] make no long-range plans." They are likewise easy to anger and difficult to control once angry. Stupidity and anger manifest themselves frequently in violence and brutality, as well as in indifference to the social hierarchy of late imperial China. One commentator noted that "in many localities of Shensi, pugnacious, violent people abound, who rely on their strength to tyrannize . . . their neighbors, induce [innocent people] to join . . . or gather mobs to engage in highway robbery. They do not fear the imperial laws, nor do they submit to the discipline of their fathers or elder brothers."[6] Other adjectives employed by late imperial commentators include "haughty and unrepentant," "wild," and "shameless." In sum, bandits and their ilk are hardly better than animals: they "form bands and carry out despicable acts as if they were outside the pale of civilization." One literati commentator even suggested that his fellow officials adopt "the method of the hunter" to deal with perverse, feuding villagers.[7]

Another approximation frequently applied by late imperial commentators to a wide range of bandit activity was "heterodoxy." Heterodoxy is distinct from, if still related to, the "uncivilized" label just discussed. Although ignorance can be associated with heterodoxy as with perversity, to call someone heterodox suggests that he or she has made a conscious choice to forsake orthodox practices and beliefs for those that do not conform to the mainstream (as defined, of course, by the orthodox commentator). Thus if *perverse* suggests "uncivilized" or "unformed," *heterodox* suggests "deformed."

As in the West, the chief field of confrontation between orthodoxy and heterodoxy in imperial China was that of religion. In part, the Chinese state's brief against heterodoxy was built on a centuries-long history of what the state perceived to be religiously organized rebellions, beginning in the latter Han (206 B.C. – A.D. 220 ) and continuing sporadically throughout the dynastic period. Indeed, on more than one occasion, "religious bandits" succeeded in overthrowing the reigning dynasty. As one seventeenth-century commentator put it succinctly, "Heretical teachings start by [merely] inciting, deluding and gathering people, but end by planning rebellion."[8]

One should immediately add that China's imperial rulers justified their extraordinary power and privilege in theocratic terms. Enlightenment-period European philosophes who saw in China a rational, secular autocracy—as opposed to the arbitrary, divine rule of European kings—were uninformed polemicists rather than careful scholars.[9] In fact, the late imperial state took Neo-Confucian religious orthodoxy *very* seriously. For example, the Ministry of Rites (one of the six central ministries that constituted the core of the central bureaucracy) paid careful attention to the ritual comportment of the emperor and the court. The same ministry sought to absorb and thus sanitize popular religions that threatened to become too influential.[10] It is unclear if the Chinese elite genuinely feared the claims of paranormal and exorcistic powers that lay at the heart of much popular religion, or if the literati simply found these claims absurdly distasteful as well as dangerous in the hands of the ignorant masses. In any case, the laws treating the subject were harsh; beheading was the punishment specified for those found guilty of "employing spells and incantations, in order to agitate and influence the minds of the people."[11]

The definition of heterodoxy was broad enough to have justified its application to a wide range of activities. In practice, however, accusations of heterodoxy were largely confined to specific instances or to certain groups, such as the White Lotus, which Barend ter Haar argues was less a self-conscious, coherent tradition than a label created by the paranoid imperial state.[12]

"Conventional" bandits not directly affiliated with White Lotus sects, on the other hand, were more frequently condemned as criminally perverse or entrepreneurial, which is interesting since recent research has underlined the role of religion in the formation and practices of many bandit gangs. The clearest examples of this are the secret societies of the late imperial period. Traditionally believed to have been motivated by nationalistic political concerns because of their anti-Manchu slogans, secret societies were reinterpreted by scholars in the 1970s and 1980s as marginal, frequently criminal gangs, little different from "pure" bandits as we usually think of them.[13] More recently still, scholars have begun to emphasize the religious aspects of secret-society practices—without denying the violent, criminal, and indeed rebellious nature of many of their activities.[14]

In any case, the imperial state tended to employ most frequently the image of bandits as greedy, calculating entrepreneurs as opposed to heretics. This is hardly surprising, as many bandit gangs engaged in robbery, extortion, and other predatory criminal activities designed to enrich themselves at the expense of others; for every Robin Hood who stole from the rich and gave to the poor there must have been many who were less careful in selecting targets.

In many instances, approximations could overlap, and elite commentators often found examples of profit-seeking behavior that had their roots in perverse ignorance. One such example was the practice of naming "substitutes" in the context of the lineage feuds of Southeast China. Substitutes were impoverished lineage members who agreed to give themselves up to the authorities in the event of state intervention into the these deadly cycles of violence: they would offer themselves as guilty in order to satisfy state demands that a homicide be repaid with an execution.[15] There was of course much honor to be gained in sacrificing one's life for the collective cause, but there was material compensation as well, which went to the substitute's surviving family. It was this material aspect that caught the eye of elite commentators: "[Substitutes] ignore the personal consequences [of implicating themselves in feud violence]: for a few pieces of gold they fight to serve as substitutes. . . ."[16] "The people of Fujian rush toward profit as a duck toward water. Thus whatever can increase their profit excites them to put aside considerations of life and death."[17] Here, the desperate substitutes are brought to task for lacking the most basic judgment that life is more valuable than gold. Ignorance is at the root of both violence and greed.

More frequently, however, the depiction of the bandit as greedy entrepreneur is at odds with their being labeled "uncivilized" or "heterodox," as discussed above. As noted, in labeling bandits as perverse or heterodox, the

Chinese elite endorsed the image of bandits as either unformed or misled; bandits were in fact barely human. In emphasizing the entrepreneurial side of banditry, by contrast, the Chinese state broadcast the image of an intelligent—if evil—outlaw.

*Entrepreneurship* is a neutral, even laudatory term in modern Western vocabularies, and to employ it in discussions of late imperial Chinese images of bandits is somewhat misleading. Although merchants were a powerful social group in late imperial times, traditional Chinese moral discourse continued to depict commerce in opposition to morality, and those who sought profit instead of righteousness were often condemned as "small people." Such was the force of labeling bandits as entrepreneurs: the state hoped thereby to diminish the status that many bandit and religious leaders enjoyed in the eyes of their group members by pointing out that, in reality, they were only in it for the money and were no better than con men.

One kind of evidence Qing officials cited to support their characterization was the "fees" charged by secret society masters for the preparation of initiation ceremonies, fees that the masters themselves justified as necessary to defray the cost of the items used, or described as an investment in the written materials that would facilitate further recruitment.[18] Of course, there is no doubt that entrepreneurship *did* play a role in many secret societies (as it does in many religions), suggesting that the late imperial rhetoric was not completely false. The point of the approximation, however, was not to provide a neutral, accurate description of the activities involved but to condemn the society leaders and caution the potential followers not to be taken in.

## POPULAR IMAGES OF BANDITS AND REBELS

For all its power, the late imperial elite was unable to impose its approximations completely on the population at large. Indeed, competing—and largely favorable—images of bandits and rebels circulated widely in late imperial China in the forms of novels and popular theater, and less widely in rebel proclamations and in the depositions that arrested bandits and rebels made to state authorities. Some of the language of these approximations was taken up by ordinary commoners who had no personal connections to banditry, rebellion, or heterodoxy. At the base of these favorable images was the contention—which elite approximations also shared—that most bandits and rebels had been driven to perform these regrettable actions by extreme circumstances, often a conjuncture of natural disaster, human error, and official corruption or insensitivity. Of course, it is not surprising that, although beginning from the same presupposition, the popular approximation went on to develop a vocabulary and a set of powerful, positive images that are completely absent from the elite labels. Many readers will recognize here an affinity with "social banditry," as defined by the influential scholar E. J. Hobsbawm.[19]

Positive images of bandits were diffused widely in the late imperial period, but the most well-known sources of such images were undoubtedly novels such as *The Romance of the Three Kingdoms* and *The Water Margin*. *The Romance of the Three Kingdoms* is the fictionalized account of the struggle for nationwide political power—among the three kingdoms of Wei, Shu, and Wu—that followed the collapse of the Han dynasty toward the end of the second century of our era. The main characters are politicians and generals, and the main field of action military strategy; the novel has thus bequeathed to Chinese culture lasting images of Machiavellian plotting and treacherous betrayal. *The Water Margin*, by contrast, celebrates the exploits of a twelfth-century band of heroic bandits who, driven by corrupt officials and the appeal of brotherhood, take to the mountains. Here, the main characters are the bandits themselves, and the main sphere of action, fighting (supplemented by much drinking and general carousing; there is something rather Rabelaisian about parts of *The Water Margin*). Although as far as we know the two novels shared the same readership, *The Romance of the Three Kingdoms* depicts the (imagined) elite world of court intrigue, while *The Water Margin* paints a ribald tableau of the (imagined) popular world of those at the margins of commoner society.

The central value endorsed in popular treatments of bandits and rebels is that of *yiqi: yi*, borrowed from elite culture, means "righteousness" as defined by the Confucian canon; by extension, *yiqi* suggests the moral-intellectual quality of knowing right from wrong (whatever a "righteous" Confucian literati might say), together with the firmness of character necessary to act consistently on the basis of such knowledge. *Yiqi* is often connected as well to values of brotherhood, another central theme in the defense of the bandit and rebel. Brotherhood, often symbolized by the "meeting in the peach garden" in *The Romance of the Three Kingdoms*, where three main characters swear a blood oath to (nonbiological) fraternal fidelity, draws inspiration from the Confucian value of loyalty but implicitly rejects the conservative social hierarchy preached by the Confucian state (which is not to say that all rebel brotherhoods uniformly rejected all varieties of hierarchy). Those who succeeded in embodying *yiqi* or in honoring their vows of fraternity were known as *haohan*, rough-and-ready "good fellows," more straightforward versions of their counterparts in elite images, the wandering knights (*wuxia*). *Haohan* were often depicted as inhabiting the "greenwoods" (*lülin*), the Chinese equivalent of Robin Hood's Sherwood Forest, the woody refuge of unjustly maligned heroes (in real life, the Chinese "greenwood" was more likely to be a barren mountain on a provincial border, particularly as demographic pressure and poverty combined to destroy most of China's forests over the course of the nineteenth and twentieth centuries).[20]

The approximations purveyed in these novels and others much like them (best-sellers are frequently imitated in all cultures) circulated by means of a variety of vehicles. First, many people read the novels or listened to them being read aloud, since literacy in the late imperial period was higher than might be expected, professional storytellers were a common attraction at temple fairs and markets, and educated villagers would sometimes take on the role of storyteller in informal settings.[21] Interestingly, Westerners kidnapped by Chinese bandits in the early twentieth century reported that the bandits often whiled away their time by recounting the events of *The Romance of the Three Kingdoms*, presumably learned from a storyteller.[22]

Most of those familiar with these novels, however, probably never read the works or even heard them told but instead saw them enacted on stage. Popular drama was a central part of both religion and recreation across all social and cultural divides in late imperial China, and military drama *(wuxi)* —"concerned with brigands, battles, and affairs of state"—was one of the two categories into which most Chinese divided the huge corpus of popular theater.[23] One student of popular theater notes that a small village in Hong Kong (in the 1980s) put on "nine major performances of Cantonese opera and five dawn plays every year in connection with the so-called birthday of their tutelary divinity."[24] If we take this village as representative, a thirty-year-old Chinese who began remembering the operas he or she attended at age five (even infants were taken to the operas, outdoor events that represented a cross between tent revival and county fair) would have witnessed some 350 performances over the twenty-five-year period, each performance perhaps consisting of several dramatic pieces. We can assume that these performances—often the most spectacular events in an otherwise drab existence—made an impact.

Then as now, the impact of art on behavior is unclear: Does television violence stimulate viewers to engage in similar acts? Or are such programs merely a reflection of a popular culture already steeped in violence for other reasons? Chinese officials had no time for the niceties of such debates and would have preferred simply to ban the offensive material. Witness the remarks of Cheng Hanzhang, who served in Guangdong in the early nineteenth century (and who sounds for all the world like a twentieth-century American parent worried about Power Rangers or MTV):

> Local troupes present operas dealing with disloyal servants and rebellious [subjects]. They completely ignore ethics and principle and stress only strength, jumping and fighting throughout the performance. . . . This is teaching the people to be rebellious.
>
> Let the local officials prohibit this. Relay to the troupe heads that they are

only permitted to put on uplifting operas, not these lewd, heterodox, rebellious plays. . . . [And] let the local officials keep an eye on the book markets, where the publishers are coming out with lewd novels and tales of mountain rebels. These should all be burned.[25]

Although Cheng may exaggerate, there is no doubt that these images were rich in symbolic value. Many of the characters from these fictional works became gods of the popular pantheon. Guangong, the God of War drawn from *The Romance of the Three Kingdoms,* is considered by some commentators to be the most widely worshipped male deity in China. Xuantian Shangdi (the Lord of the Mystic Heavens, a Daoist deity also known as Zhenwu, the "true warrior"), hero of the late-Ming novel *Journey to the North,* was another widely worshiped martial deity. Virtually all of the gods from *The Enfeoffment of the Gods,* another popular novel of the late imperial period, are military figures as well.[26] There is no doubt that rebels and bandits drew on these images, in some cases even naming themselves after fictional characters. Indeed, the famous Boxers—who, although neither bandits nor rebels in the strict senses of the terms, attacked Chinese and foreign Christians in North China at the turn of the twentieth century—found much of their inspiration in the magical powers supposedly possessed by fictional characters as presented onstage.[27]

At this point, we might note a certain symmetry between elite and popular images of bandits. As already mentioned, elite and popular approximations share a core explanation of antisocial behavior: it is provoked by corrupt or evil officials who do not take their paternal obligations with the requisite seriousness. Of course, this too is an approximation; although there is no doubt that China knew its share of inadequate officials, we should note at the same time that this pretext allowed the emperor to maintain his pose of benevolence (by chastising the officials in question), and permitted the bandits or rebels to justify their otherwise immoral behavior. Be that as it may, there remains a logical flaw in the elite apology for banditry, for while the elites admitted the basic justice of the bandit cause, they went on to condemn—as perverse, heterodox, and greedy—the character of those who resorted to and, particularly, led the violence resulting from this same just cause.

It is significant that the images attached to the favorable, populist, "Robin Hood" approximation of bandits and rebels defend precisely against the elitist labels just mentioned. By the literary flourishes in their proclamations and by their insistence on the righteousness of their actions, bandits and rebels claimed that they were neither perverse nor heterodox. Instead, they summoned the symbolic authority of "the ancients" as they organized their activities and pledged to learn from one another's strengths while correcting one another's faults. Most important, the bandits and rebels held out as evidence of their righteousness their relationship with Heaven, which had authorized them to engage in violence that would cleanse their society. Indeed, some rebel gangs took pains to insist that they had no quarrel with the emperor (who, it must be recalled, claimed himself to be the Son of Heaven), only with his minions, of whose actions the emperor must have been ignorant.[28]

Moreover, in opposition to elite images of the bandit-rebel as a scheming con man, we find the popular image of the bandit-rebel as noble, generous, and unconcerned with material things. Indeed, some bandit groups in the late imperial period presented themselves as "levelers" of the social order. In the 1830s, for example, a literati commentator notes that "in the provinces of Chihli, Honan, and Shantung, *chiao-fei* [religious bandits] spread their creeds one to another. . . . Once famine occurs they, relying on their numerical strength, plunder collectively in broad daylight, calling their marauding activities 'equalizing the food.'"[29] Whether rebels and bandits were indeed "class enemies" of the traditional order is debatable; but to the extent that they sought to equalize wealth, they surely were not greedy entrepreneurs.

Some scholars have seen in this symmetry an "antitradition," a total rejection of elite Confucian values.[30] And there is no doubt that we are party to a contest of approximations here, a struggle for domination of the discourse: the antipodal images could of course serve as justification for violent rebellion against the state or for violent repression of bandit-rebel activities. At the same time, we can also see in this symmetry, if not a dialogue (which suggests discussion among equals), then perhaps the larger contours of a tradition that knitted together the "poles" of "elite" and "popular" in late imperial China. Indeed, it is not difficult to find within the approximations conveyed by each camp accommodations with, perhaps even admiration of, the other. For example, even as they condemned bandits and rebels, elites frequently acknowledged a grudging admiration of the values of bravery and loyalty often exhibited by bandit gangs. One eighteenth-century handbook written for officials destined to serve in Fujian province noted that "the border areas of Fujian lie between the mountain peaks and the sea, and most of the inhabitants are by nature perverse and evil. Fortunately, they also value loyalty and are eager for fame [i.e., recognition], so they are easily encouraged and brought to change their behavior."[31]

It is of course easier to find elite values and images in popular texts and approximations. As already noted, most bandits and rebels presented themselves as champions of righteousness who had been forced into their present straits by evil officials. Some modification of the definition of *righteousness* occurred with the bandit-rebel appropriation of the term, but the core values of respect for authority and moral conduct continued to be endorsed. This posture is perhaps clearest at points where bandits or rebels realized that the state was closing in on them and that their cause was, for the moment, lost. At such moments, as in the document drafted by pirates below, the rebel sought to reintegrate himself into society by stressing the common values that bound bandit and citizen, rebel and literati:

> Now we "ants" [the pirates' reference to themselves in humble terms] are living in a prosperous age. Originally we were good people, but we became pirates for a variety of reasons. Because some of use were not careful in making friends, we fell into a bad situation and became robbers. Others of us were unable to secure a livelihood or were captured while trading on the lakes and rivers and forced into piracy. Still others because of having committed some crime joined this watery empire to escape punishment[:] . . . as a result of the dearth of the last several years, people had nothing with which to maintain their living, and as time went on could not help but rob in order to live. If we had not resisted the government officials, our lives would have been in danger. Therefore, we violated the laws of the empire and destroyed the merchants. This was unavoidable. . . .
>
> The backgrounds of heroes are different. So are the hearts of the officials, for some are benevolent and others have patience. Therefore, the bandits of Liang-shan [in *The Water Margin*] were thrice pardoned for pillaging the city and became a pillar of the state. . . . Thus when the heroes of the world surrender, people from far and near are happy.[32]

If ever these pirates had seen themselves as thoroughgoing outcasts, it is clear that with such a proclamation they were seeking reinstatement within the orthodox body politic of late imperial China.

One final point regarding the interpenetration of elite and popular approximations: not all popular approximations of bandits and rebels were positive. Indeed, even if those bandits who took on the posture of "social bandits," to borrow a Hobsbawmian approximation, surely basked in the admiring glow of some locals, bandits of a less generous nature were surely detested—and feared.[33] For example, included in the scriptures of the Way of the Temple of the Heavenly Immortals (Tianxian miaodao hui) (a Henan religious tradition that, like the Red Spears, flourished in the Republican period and frequently rebelled against the state) are frequent admonitions against engaging in banditry: four of the "Ten Interdictions," for example, forbid resisting the army, forming bands, consorting with bandits, and disobeying the imperial law.[34] Even in popular literature, detective heroes tracked down and put in jail criminals who shared at least some characteristics with the bandit heroes of *The Water Margin* and other popular novels.[35] That the term *bandit* can still serve as a term of moral opprobrium in the popular vocabulary as well as in the elite one was illustrated in 1989: when the People's Liberation Army pushed aside popular resistance en route to Tian'anmen Square in early June, the people responded by hissing "Bandit" at the intruders.[36] Here the meaning was clearly not "thief" but "unvirtuous rascal."

## REVOLUTIONARY APPROXIMATIONS OF BANDITS AND REBELS

The collapse of the Chinese imperial state in 1911 created a vacuum that successive regimes have attempted (and are still attempting) to fill. The vacuum was comprehensive, calling into question traditional institutions as well as values—indeed the totality of China's traditional political culture. The almost immediate failure of the first Chinese Republic focused attention even more painfully on China's desperate plight. Part of the resulting May Fourth–New Culture Movement, in which iconoclastic Chinese intellectuals sought to overhaul the Chinese historical and cultural experience, prompted a reevaluation, indeed a valorization, of the role of commoners in the Chinese state, a reevaluation that came eventually to touch even images of bandits and rebels.

This intellectual engagement was prompted in part by political necessity. As had occurred during previous "dynastic transitions," bandits and rebels filled much of the vacuum created in the Chinese countryside by the fall of the imperial Chinese state. Contenders for political control at the local and national levels, whether warlords, Nationalists, or Communists, found that they had no choice but to cooperate with bandits in an attempt to co-opt them. In addition, both the Communist Party and, to a lesser degree, the Nationalist Party sought—at times only rhetorically, it is true—to mobilize the "people" in a manner that the traditional Chinese state had never done. In so doing, they developed approximations of bandits and rebels that combined new perspectives drawn from Western socialist ideas (and often trumpeted by certain May Fourth intellectuals) with the favorable images of bandits and rebels drawn from the Chinese popular tradition discussed above. Against such ostensibly far-reaching changes, we must note at the same time considerable continuity in relations between elite and mass: once a regime, be it warlord, Nationalist, or even Communist, seized power, part of the consolidation of that power was an attention to order and social control, in which bandits immediately changed from "fellow travelers" on the road to revolution, to "reactionary obstacles" to the consolidation of the "people's will."

In the context of the inversion of sociopolitical values connected to the Republican Revolution, and particularly to the iconoclastic New Culture Movement, it is hardly surprising that both Nationalist and Communist propagandists adopted the favorable images of bandits and rebels drawn from the Chinese popular tradition. In an article written in 1905, Song Jiaoren, one of Sun Yat-sen's most prominent advisors until his assassination in 1913, referred to the well-known Red Beard bandit communities of Manchuria as "Twentieth-Century Liangshanpo [the mountain refuge of the bandit gang in *The Water Margin*]" and two years later tried to enlist their support in a common cause against the Manchu rulers, emphasizing in his letter to this effect that bandits and revolutionaries would be equal partners in the struggle.[37] The Communists, given their greater embrace of the "people's" cause, adopted these images even more broadly. Mao Zedong, who—like millions of Chinese before and after him—had read and reread *The Water Margin* as a youth, once argued that the solution to China's problems was to "imitate the heroes of Liangshanpo!" And, later in life, Mao referred to himself as "both the last in the long line of peasant leaders and also a 'graduate of the university of the greenwoods.'"[38]

Furthermore, in their search for military allies, both Nationalists and Communists also found themselves compelled to don bandit garb when approaching potentially promising bands of outlaws. Nationalist operatives presented themselves as "homeless, wandering *haohan*" and learned the *heihua* (slang; literally, black language) of the bandit gangs and, on occasion, even participated in such "traditional" bandit activities as kidnapping local notables and holding them for ransom.[39] Similarly, Communists swore blood oaths and pretended to adopt bandit–secret society codes of brotherhood and loyalty—attempting, of course, to assimilate such values to Leninist discipline.[40]

Alongside this elite adoption of traditional popular images of bandits and rebels, we find new, Western images, growing out of the nineteenth-century European birth of socialism and anarchism. One of the earliest objects of European radical attention in China was the "Zheltuga Republic" (named for the Zheltuga River), established in the 1860s in northern Manchuria, largely by deserters from regional mines. This "state" of some twenty-five thousand people functioned according to two basic principles—"universal suffrage and a kind of absolute communism"—and endured until the early twentieth century, when Manchu-Russian cooperation facilitated its suppression. European observers who witnessed the "republic" in operation—some of whose writings Song Jiaoren and other Chinese radicals and revolutionaries may have read—were quick to find therein vindication of radical socialist theories, in which we find the seeds of new approximations of bandits and rebels.[41] Here, rather than the perverse bandit of late imperial sources, or the righteous bandit of traditional popular imagery, we are presented with an image of the self-consciously intelligent bandit capable of defining his own social order for himself. For example, as one commentator put it, "Because of the primitive living conditions of the outlaws of the Feltuga [*sic*], their experience bears little relation to the socialist theories of Europe. Yet at the very least it is heartening to observe a group of humanity's most wretched specimens creating a functioning society out of nothing."[42]

Such sentiments surely drew on the work of the great Russian anarchist Mikhail Bakunin (1814–76), who had argued more directly that the bandit was "the genuine and sole revolutionary—a revolutionary without fine phrases, without learned rhetoric, irreconcilable, indefatigable and indomitable, a popular and socialist revolutionary, non-political and independent of any estate."[43] Recent scholarship has emphasized the importance of anarchist thought in the early-twentieth-century history of radical ideas in China; indeed, as Arif Dirlik notes, "Most of the classics of anarchism were already available in Chinese translation by the early 1910s . . . and some made their way beyond radical periodicals to mainstream journals and newspapers."[44] Consequently, the "idealization of the bandit" that we find in anarchist thought may have been one of the sources that inspired Mao Zedong and other Communists.[45]

Nonetheless, the "inversion of values" that accompanied the attempt to forge a new political culture in China was only temporary—at least insofar as bandits and rebels are concerned. Actually, a certain cautious distrust characterized bandit-Party relations even during the period of "common cause." Even those former bandits who joined the revolution wholeheartedly appear to have been viewed as different from the "mainstream" Communists. When, for example, He Long, a former bandit and later Communist general, joined the Red Army, he kept his sedan chair and his personal cooks rather than submit to the (supposedly) egalitarian rigor of Communist life. Unsurprisingly, this was not appreciated by those on more meager rations.[46] Indeed, despite real and rhetorical attempts to transform bandits from renegades to revolutionaries, the traditional elite meaning of *bandit* continued to resonate, even for Communist officials. When the Central Committee censured Mao Zedong for adventurism in late 1927, they accused him of having behaved "like the bandit heroes of *Water Margin.*"[47] Another local organizer noted that, "despite their peasant origins, bandits change their political character the moment they undertake looting. Some even collaborate with local bullies to repress their fellow peasants. They are a reactionary social force."[48]

Indeed, in hindsight it is obvious that the alliance between revolutionary forces—be they Communist or Nationalist—and bandits was above all *tactical,* even if the expressed desire to pool their efforts must have been genuine in many cases. Those who have studied this relationship note that bandits were often used as little better than cannon fodder by the larger forces that sought to exploit them. One veteran of the 1911 revolution recalled, for example, that "in the revolutionary struggle, nearly all the dangerous and perilous tasks were carried out by members of the Elder Brothers Society,"[49] a secret society that engaged in banditry. A student of the Communist movement's relation to bandits states succinctly that "bandit policy was employed by the CCP solely as a quick means of building power when the party was weak. Once the party became strong, the Communists . . . allied with other local armed forces to eliminate the bandits, thus promoting a different image of themselves, that of protector of citizens."[50]

The clearest evidence of what now appears to be a continuity in elite attitudes toward bandits is the complete turnabout in these attitudes following the success of the Communist revolution in 1949. As the task of the Party shifted from popular mobilization to consolidation of power and regime-building, the bandits who had had "revolutionary potential" now became "counterrevolutionaries." Indeed, in the post-1949 Communist vocabulary, "the term 'bandit' *(tufei)* applied to all forms of armed resistance in a given area after it had been 'liberated,'" marking a return to a more general, pejorative image.[51]

During the period leading up to the revolution, bandits were linked to peasants and soldiers (as well as to prostitutes and robbers); the revolution accomplished, bandits took their places with landlords (the archetypal evil element under the new regime), criminals, and hoodlums. Indeed, from this perspective, efforts by Nationalists and Communists during the interregnum to forge alliances with bandits recall the thoroughly traditional practice of rewarding dangerous bandits with official posts as a means of rendering them less dangerous (whence the common folk saying "If you want to become an official, carry a big stick").[52] The fact that *bandit* has retained its traditional, pejorative connotation is underscored by the fact that the Chinese governments on both sides of the Taiwan straits refer to one another as "Communist bandits" or "Nationalist bandits."

## THE BANDIT AS FRUSTRATED BACHELOR

The approximations of bandits and rebels examined to this point—whether elite or popular, imperial or Communist—view bandits through the lens of their relationship to the state and the state's ideology, grounding these approximations in a moral-political discourse. Confronted by difficult socioeconomic circumstances, often made all the more bleak by inadequate government response, some individuals "choose" banditry, a "moral" choice that places them in opposition to the state. Elite approximations then go on to condemn those who exploit this conjuncture, while popular approximations defend the bandit response. This concluding section seeks to complement such perspectives by examining bandit-rebel behavior from the perspective of gender, suggesting that we can understand bandits as "frustrated bachelors" as well as "rational decision-makers," oriented toward the arena of political economy. Instead of individual morality and state politics, this gender perspective examines such factors as marriage markets, gender norms, and child-rearing practices.

At first glance, the mere idea of a marriage "market" clashes with dominant North American ideas of marriage as a product of romantic love and individual choice. Even in our society, however, relative scarcities of "appropriate" partners influence marital choices, and to say that someone "marries well" does not refer to the ceremony itself. In other times and places, the "economy" of courtship and marriage has been even more obvious.[53] In China, where romantic love as a determining factor in marital decisions is a recent import, the notion of a marriage market was readily understood by all concerned. Marriage in traditional (and to a considerable degree, modern) China was an affair between families rather than individuals, a social and economic exchange symbolized by the transfer of wealth and status in both directions (the groom's family paying a bride-price, and the bride arriving with a dowry).[54] The following quote, discussing early-nineteenth-century Fujian, succinctly summarizes the problem such exchanges posed, particularly for poor men: "It costs almost one hundred pieces of gold for a middle-class family in Zhaoan to finance a bride, and it costs a poorer family fifty to sixty pieces of gold, not counting the other gifts. The bride's dowry costs about as much, so marriage is difficult for both the groom's and the bride's families. Since marrying off women is hard, people raise few women. Since affording to marry is difficult, there are many bachelors."[55]

Why could poorer families not simply agree to forego the economic exchange that marked the marriages of the well-to-do, or set the price at a more affordable level? Here is where we learn the force of the idea of a marriage *market:* important scarcities of marriage-age women in many regions and periods maintained an upward pressure on the price of marriage, which consigned many young men to lifelong bachelorhood.

One important source of this scarcity was female infanticide: as the citation just above put it bluntly, "people raise few women." A widespread practice in many poor societies, female infanticide was very common in certain periods of Chinese history. Even now, sons are crucial to the well-being of aging parents in China's countryside (daughters "marry out" and serve primarily the family into which they marry), as the state's budget is insufficient to guarantee a decent retirement for China's 800 million rural residents. For this reason, reports of female infanticide in China are on the rise once again, as the state seeks to limit population growth without increasing pensions for the rural elderly.[56]

This current dilemma was created by China's rapid demographic growth over the course of the modern period, particularly from the eighteenth century forward. Analysis of genealogical records of the imperial Qing clan reveals, for example, that following the eighteenth-century dissemination of the smallpox vaccine, which dramatically reduced child mortality over the course of the eighteenth century, female infant mortality increased by a factor of six, so that "by the 1780s, as many as one-fifth of all daughters [of the Imperial Lineage] were victims of infanticide."[57] The obvious explanation for this is that families were not economically equipped to cope with the increase in family size occasioned by a revolutionary advance in medical practices. Such evidence from what was, after all, a relatively affluent slice of

the late imperial population lends support—if not actual confirmation—
to the very high estimates of female infanticide in the population at large in
the late imperial period, which approached even three hundred per thousand female births.[58]

The scarcity of women in the marriage market was influenced by other
factors as well. Chinese men were permitted multiple wives, concubinage
serving both as a status symbol and as insurance that sons would be born.
Some scholars have found that as many as 10 percent of all marriages fell
into this category, and in late imperial fiction, most men who could afford
concubines were depicted as having between one and five.[59] In addition,
high mortality rates across the age spectrum meant that many first spouses
died; wealthy men were more likely to have the resources to remarry than
were poor men. In short, in the apt words of one scholar, "high-status families were consuming more than an equitable share" of the available women.[60]
In terms of the bandits and rebels under discussion here, this "overconsumption" by the wealthy meant "underconsumption" by the less privileged.
Scholars estimate that poorer men had to delay their marriages by six years
in comparison with richer men, and that *20 to 25 percent of men were unable to
marry at all.*[61]

Even in twentieth-first-century North America, where "alternative lifestyles" are celebrated as part of our individualistic heritage, pressure to marry
remains strong. In traditional (and modern) China, marriage was and is a
virtual social imperative; it is the rare individual who "decides" not to marry.
In part, this imperative grows out of the near-religious obligation to continue the ancestral line. In the oft-cited words of Mencius: "There are three
ways of being a bad son. The most serious is to have no heir."[62] Although at
base religious, this imperative came to be attached to social roles and identities. In the eyes of most Chinese an unmarried man is not truly an adult,
not truly a man.[63] Indeed, even a married man who has not yet produced
(preferably male) offspring remains something less than an adult.[64] The social opprobrium such failures might engender came on top of the poverty
that accounted for the poor man's dilemma, and the loneliness and frustration that must have resulted therefrom.

There is evidence from other societies that inability to fulfill gender expectations can result in antisocial behavior such as machismo-driven violence. Following Freud, a literature on "protest masculinity" seeks to anchor
these conflicts in early childhood experience, arguing that such behavior often results when young boys identify, in infancy and early childhood, with a
domineering mother and then in later childhood and adolescence fail—
often for socioeconomic reasons—to transfer their identity to the masculine gender roles that accord with social expectations.[65] Such ambivalence
drives these young men toward hypermasculine displays in order to demonstrate to others, as well as themselves, that they are indeed "real" men.

On the surface, such an explanation might prove illuminating for Chinese society as well. The traditional Chinese father maintained a relationship with his son that was both "affectionate and informal" until the son reached the "age of reason"—six or seven.[66] At this point, however, the father withdrew into the formal remoteness that "builds the supports necessary to maintain the senior male's position of authority over his adult sons."[67] Whatever the effects of this sudden withdrawal on the psyche and gender formation of the young boy, the virtual emotional absence of the father left the field wide open for the mother.

It was to the mother's every advantage to exploit this opportunity to the fullest. As mentioned above, most Chinese women married "out," leaving their natal families and taking up residence in the homes of their husbands, where they knew no one and were expected to submit to the often capricious demands of senior members of the household. The status of the bride improved definitively only with the birth of a son, which represented her material contribution to the continuation of her husband's ancestral line. Thereafter, mothers lavished attention (if not always overt affection) on their sons, both for emotional solace as well as to nurture in their sons the sense of obligation that would assure the mothers a decent old age.[68]

Indeed, the pressure mothers could place on sons to fulfill social expectations—above all to succeed in the studies that would lead them to pass the Confucian examinations and become officials—surpasses by a considerable margin current North American notions of acceptability. One mother (that of Liang Ji, father of the "last Confucian," Liang Shuming)[69] had not only handwritten the first characters that her son learned, and hand copied and personally bound the texts he read, but every evening she also insisted on double-checking every piece of schoolwork he had completed during the day. These home tutoring hours, furthermore, were often followed by lengthy talks of the how-to-become-great-in-life sort. "In such moments," comments one scholar, "Liang's mother often asked him what he wanted to become when he grew up. 'I was then quite devoid of any ambitions' he later confessed, 'so what I came up with was often some menial thing that fell far short of her expectations.' In great distress and disappointment, his . . . mother often closed the books in front of him and wept."[70]

This anecdote obviously refers to the literati class, but we should not make the mistake of believing that such attitudes—and such pressures—were confined to the upper classes. In one of the "scriptures" of the Republican-period "heterodox" religion tradition, the Way of the Temple of the Heavenly Immortals, the wife of a Temple leader is depicted as delivering the following deathbed counsel to her son: "Quanfu, you are the eldest. You must work hard at your studies. . . . Recall the example of the [Han dynasty] scholar . . . who tied his hair to the rafters to prevent himself from falling asleep at his studies. . . . If you do not study when you're young . . . you will have no way of making your name. If you do not study, you will be no better than an animal, and you will bring shame on our house."[71] I should add that neither the wife nor her husband was educated.

If pressure to pass the examinations was this great, what are we to imagine about pressures on young men to marry, marriage being after all a more basic social obligation and certainly much more common than passing the imperial examinations? If little direct evidence is available, anthropologists have nonetheless found that there was a violent reaction on the part of young men unable to fulfill their gender expectations. James L. Watson has explored what he calls a "bachelor subculture" in the context of the twentieth-century New Territories (part of Hong Kong), finding that a "strategy that [unmarried] men use to enhance their male image is to make a regular practice of challenging the public face of other men. Face is essentially an attribute of married men who have families to protect and obligations to fulfill. Unmarried men . . . have little face to preserve because they do not command much respect in the community. . . . By definition . . . bachelors remain perpetual adolescents who cannot play a full role in society."[72] In this particular instance, community leaders made use of the potentially rambunctious bachelors, employing them to form a corps of guardsmen who protected the community from outside dangers (or enforced socioeconomic domination). The violence of the bachelor subculture was thus directed to the outside.

Of course, one man's guardian is another man's bandit. Those who found themselves the victims of the guardsmen's violence often referred to the guardsmen as "*ngok lo,* a Cantonese slur that literally means 'evil,' 'cruel,' or 'depraved men.' In colloquial usage the term also carries connotations of uncontrollable, animal-like behavior (*ngok* is often used to describe rabid dogs or enraged water buffaloes)."[73] This depiction of someone as not fully human calls to mind one of the elite definitions of the bandit explored above: uncivilized, "perverse" barbarian. Indeed, outside of the particular context explored by Watson, we find in other Chinese sources language and categories that conflate the two. The term *guang gun,* for example, which literally means "bare stick" (I hardly need point out the phallic connotations) refers both to violent, petty criminals and bachelors.[74] A nineteenth-century Western missionary described the "sublime ideal" of the "bare sticks" as "[making] it a sport and a matter of pride to defy the laws and the magistrates, and commit all kinds of crimes. To give and receive wounds with composure; to kill others with the most perfect coolness; and to have no fear of death for yourself."[75]

Furthermore, evidence suggests that many bandits were indeed bachelors. A study of banditry in Guangdong in the late eighteenth and early nineteenth centuries finds that some 55 percent of convicted bandits were unmarried.[76] Bandit gangs in Republican-period Henan primarily were made up of young, unmarried men in their teens and twenties.[77] These bandits decorated themselves with weapons and visible signs of wealth—both symbols of machismo—and, despite formal bans on rape in many bandit gangs, engaged in occasional "assaults on women from the privileged classes [that] were especially violent."[78]

Late imperial commentators were not unaware of the linkages between bachelorhood and violence, even if the notion of gender construction presumably did not figure prominently in their worldview. One official, for example, noted that it was the high price of marriage that prompted "homeless bandits" to "kidnap, steal, and feud."[79] The bachelors of eighteenth-century Taiwan serve as another example. The island of Taiwan was formally incorporated into the Chinese empire for the first time in the late seventeenth century, in response to Western imperialist incursions and efforts of Ming loyalist forces (termed "pirates" by the Chinese state) to use the island as a base against which to resist the imposition of Qing (Manchu) control. The purpose of incorporation being to ensure that the island not be used as a launching pad for further attacks against the mainland, the state sought to quarantine the island, reasoning that Chinese settlements would only attract pirates (whether Chinese or foreign). Consequently, family migration was banned for much of the eighteenth century, leaving eighteenth-century Taiwan populated predominantly by young, poor, unmarried men. These young men, in turn, proved to be uncooperative subjects, which some Chinese commentators explained by their bachelorhood: "If each [of the bachelors] had a wife, inner and outer would be distinguished and there would be no confusion and disorder. If each had to support a wife, drinking and gambling would diminish. If each had to protect a household, robberies would decrease."[80] Another commentator noted that such hooligans "have no land or property, no wife or children, . . . are not officials, farmers, artisans, or merchants, . . . [and] do not labor."[81] In other words, being unmarried, these men did not fit into the social matrix.

## CONCLUSION

This essay has been concerned with perceptions rather than causation. Each act of banditry is the product of individual and collective experiences and decisions, accidents of nature and history. General explanations of banditry possess only general validity; if it is true that poverty, or bachelorhood, was a precondition of banditry, it is equally true that hundreds of millions of poor Chinese bachelors over the centuries did *not* turn to banditry. Their "choices" would demand explanation as well, were we searching for ultimate causes.

That being said, approximations and perceptions are not irrelevant *academic* concepts. Products of experience and reflection on that experience, they are the images we carry in our minds to construct our maps of reality, to guide us in our decisions, and to justify the decisions we make. Approximations set the stage, provide the dialogue, and suggest how the audience of any social drama may respond. This essay has proven that alongside approximations drawn from the politico-moral discourse concerning banditry are found approximations that draw on the gender experience of Chinese men. At this stage of research, these images and their associations can only be suggestive; we would need a more fully articulated approximation of Chinese "masculinities" themselves before attempting more sophisticated analysis. Nonetheless, it seems plausible that when, for example, banditry turned violent, the culturally determined script that opened in a bandit's mind as adrenaline pushed him toward "fight or flight" may have directed him toward a performance of masculinity, which may have supplied the hard core of his politics as well.

## NOTES

In addition to the editors and anonymous readers of this volume, I would like to thank John Shepherd, Judith Zeitlin, and particularly Michael Szonyi for their assistance and comments.

1. For other definitions that focus more narrowly on the predatory dimensions of banditry, see R. G. Tiedemann, "The Persistence of Banditry: Incidents in Border Districts of the North China Plain," *Modern China* 8, no. 4 (October 1982): 396; and Hsiao Kung-ch'üan, *Rural China: Imperial Control in the Nineteenth Century* (Seattle: University of Washington Press, 1967), 453.

2. This is less true in the case of religious organizations, which often had a high percentage of female membership and even leadership. Susan Naquin, "The Transmission of White Lotus Sectarianism in Late Imperial China," in *Popular Culture in Late Imperial China,* ed. David Johnson, Andrew J. Nathan, and Evelyn S. Rawski (Berkeley and Los Angeles: University of California Press, 1985), 255–91.

3. Cited in Hsiao, *Rural China,* 464.

4. There were, of course, female bandits and pirates, groups that are discussed in, among other places, Elizabeth J. Perry, *Rebels and Revolutionaries in North China, 1845–1945* (Stanford: Stanford University Press, 1980), 67n; and Dian H. Murray, *Pirates on the South China Coast, 1790–1810* (Stanford: Stanford University Press, 1987), 152–53. The tendency in approximations, however, was to assume that the typical bandit and pirate was male.

5. *Daqing shichao shengxun, Shizongxian [Yongzheng]* [The Sacred Edicts of the ten emperors of the great Qing, Yongzheng] (Taipei: Wenhai chubanshe, 1965, original Guangxu edition), *zhuan* 26, *hou fengsu,* pp. 14a-15b. On Sacred Edicts see Victor H. Mair, "Language and Ideology in the Written Popularizations of the Sacred Edict," in *Popular Culture in Late Imperial China,* ed. David Johnson, Andrew J. Nathan, and Evelyn S. Rawski (Berkeley and Los Angeles: University of California Press, 1985), 325–59. For an additional example of the bandits-as-beasts imagery, see the

comments by a Fujian official in *Fujian shengli* [Statutes of the province of Fujian] (1768; reprint, Taipei: Taiwan wenxian congkan #199, 1964), 893–95.

6. Cited in Hsiao, *Rural China,* 458; see also Xie Jinluan, "Quan-Zhang zhifa lun" [On governing Quanzhou and Zhangzhou], in *Zhi Tai bigaolu,* comp. Ding Yuejian (1959; reprint, Taibei: Taiwan wenxian congkan #17), 97–113.

7. Examples of these kinds of pejorative expressions, which dehumanize bandits, can be found in many archival documents cited in David Ownby, *Brotherhoods and Secret Societies in Early and Mid-Qing China* (Stanford: Stanford University Press, 1996). See, for instance, Cheng Hanzhang, *Mulingshu jiyao* [Guidebook for magistrates], comp. Xu Zhizhu (n.p., 1848) *zhuan* 9, pp. 13a-16b; and Xie Jinluan, "Quan-Zhang zhifa lun," 105.

8. Cited in Barend J. ter Haar, *The White Lotus Teachings in Chinese Religious History* (Leiden, Netherlands: E. J. Brill, 1992), 237.

9. On this topic, see Donald F. Lach, *China in the Eyes of Europe* (Chicago: University of Chicago Press, 1968); and Virgile Pinot, *La Chine et la formation de l'esprit philosophique en France, 1640–1740* (1932; reprint, Geneve: Slatkine Reprints, 1971).

10. See Kwang-Ching Liu, ed., *Orthodoxy in Late Imperial China* (Berkeley and Los Angeles: University of California Press, 1990); and James L. Watson, "Standardizing the Gods: The Promotion of T'ien Hou ('Empress of Heaven') along the South China Coast, 960–1960," in *Popular Culture in Late Imperial China,* ed. David Johnson, Andrew J. Nathan, and Evelyn S. Rawski (Berkeley and Los Angeles: University of California Press, 1985), 292–324.

11. Sir George Thomas Staunton, *Ta Tsing Leu Lee* (1810; reprint, Taibei: Chengwen chubanshe, 1966), 273.

12. Ter Haar, *White Lotus Teachings.*

13. For an overview of the historiography of secret societies, see David Ownby, "Secret Societies Reconsidered," in *"Secret Societies" Reconsidered: Perspectives on the Social History of Early Modern South China and Southeast Asia,* ed. Ownby and Mary S. Heidhues (Armonk, N.Y.: M. E. Sharpe, 1993), 3–33.

14. See, for example, David Ownby, "The Heaven and Earth Society as Popular Religion," *Journal of Asian Studies* 54, no. 4 (November 1995): 1032–46.

15. See Harry J. Lamley, "Lineage Feuding in Southern Fujian and Eastern Guangdong under Qing Rule," in *Violence in China: Essays in Culture and Counterculture,* ed. Jonathan N. Lipman and Stevan Harrell (Albany: State University of New York Press, 1990), 45, 54.

16. Cheng Hanzhang, *Mulingshu jiyao,* 14a.

17. "Rambunctious Local Customs," in *Minzheng lingyao* [Essentials for the governance of Fujian] (1757 original; hand-copied edition from the Fujian Provincial Teacher's College in Fuzhan), ch. 18.

18. See, for example, Zhongguo renmin daxue Qingshi yanjiusuo and Zhongguo diyi lishi dang'anguan, eds., *Tiandihui* [The Heaven and Earth Society] (Beijing: Zhongguo renmin daxue chubanshe, 1980–88), 6:287 and 332.

19. See, for example, E. J. Hobsbawm, *Primitive Rebels: Studies in Archaic Forms of Social Movement in the 19th and 20th Centuries* (Manchester: University of Manchester Press, 1959). For critical views of Hobsbawm's work, see Richard W. Slatta, *Bandidos: The Varieties of Latin American Banditry* (New York: Greenwood Press, 1987); and

Robert J. Antony, "Peasants, Heroes, and Brigands: The Problems of Social Banditry in Early Nineteenth-Century South China," *Modern China* 15, no. 2 (April 1989): 123–49.

20. Robert Ruhlman, "Traditional Heroes in Chinese Popular Fiction," in *The Confucian Persuasion*, ed. Arthur F. Wright (Stanford: Stanford University Press, 1960), 166–76.

21. Evelyn Sakakida Rawski, *Education and Popular Literacy in Ch'ing China* (Ann Arbor: University of Michigan Press, 1979), 140; and James Hayes, "Specialists and Written Materials in the Village World," in *Popular Culture in Late Imperial China*, ed. David Johnson, Andrew J. Nathan, and Evelyn S. Rawski (Berkeley and Los Angeles: University of California Press, 1985), 75–111.

22. Phil Billingsley, *Bandits in Republican China* (Stanford: Stanford University Press, 1988), 129.

23. Barbara E. Ward "Regional Operas and Their Audiences: Evidence from Hong Kong," in *Popular Culture in Late Imperial China*, ed. David Johnson, Andrew J. Nathan, and Evelyn S. Rawski (Berkeley and Los Angeles: University of California Press, 1985), 183.

24. Ibid., 184.

25. Cheng Hanzhang, *Yuechuan weishigao* [The uncertain drafts of (Cheng) Yuechuan (Hanzhang's courtesy name)] (Cheng family woodcut edition, Daoguang period, *zhuan* 2, pp. 21a–36a, Yunnan, Jingdong).

26. Meir Shahar, "Vernacular Fiction and the Transmission of Gods' Cults," in *Unruly Gods: Divinity and Society in China*, ed. Shahar and Robert P. Weller (Honolulu: University of Hawaii Press, 1996), 199 and 200.

27. Joseph W. Esherick, *The Origins of the Boxer Uprising* (Berkeley and Los Angeles: University of California, 1987), esp. ch. 8.

28. Yuji Muramatsu, "Some Themes in Chinese Rebel Ideologies," in *The Confucian Persuasion*, ed. Arthur F. Wright (Stanford: Stanford University Press, 1960), 242.

29. Hsiao, *Rural China*, 447.

30. See, for example, Jean Chesneaux, "Secret Societies in China's Historical Evolution," in *Popular Movements and Secret Societies in China 1840–1950*, ed. Chesneaux (Stanford: Stanford University Press, 1972), 2.

31. "Rambunctious Local Customs," ch. 18.

32. Cited in Murray, *Pirates*, 172–73.

33. For this term, see Hobsbawm, *Primitive Rebels*.

34. Translated in David Ownby, "Scriptures of the Way of the Temple of the Heavenly Immortals," *Chinese Studies in History* 29, no. 3 (spring 1996): 40–41.

35. See Robert J. Antony, "Scourges on the People: Perceptions of Robbery, Snatching, and Theft in the Mid-Qing Period," *Late Imperial China* 16, no. 2 (December 1995): 98–132.

36. See Timothy Brook, *Quelling the People: The Military Suppression of the Beijing Democracy Movement* (New York: Oxford University Press, 1992), 122.

37. Billingsley, *Bandits in Republican China*, 239.

38. Ibid., 229.

39. Ibid., 238.

40. Ibid., 230.

41. Cited in Mark Mancall and Georges Jidkoff, "The Hung Hu-tzu of Northeast

China," in *Popular Movements and Secret Societies in China 1840–1950*, ed. Jean Chesneaux (Stanford: Stanford University Press, 1972), 129.

42. Cited in ibid., 132.

43. Cited in Billingsley, *Bandits in Republican China*, 228.

44. Arif Dirlik, *Anarchism and the Chinese Revolution* (Berkeley and Los Angeles: University of California Press, 1991), 27.

45. The quoted phrase is from Billingsley, *Bandits in Republican China*, 229.

46. Ibid., 234.

47. Ibid., 259.

48. Cited in ibid., 264.

49. Cited in ibid., 249.

50. Odoric Y. K. Wou, *Mobilizing the Masses: Building Revolution in Henan* (Stanford: Stanford University Press, 1994), 199.

51. Billingsley, *Bandits in Republican China*, 266.

52. Cited in Perry, *Rebels and Revolutionaries*, 72.

53. For two examples among many, see Lawrence Stone, *The Family, Sex, and Marriage in England, 1500–1800* (New York: Harper and Row, 1979); and Lawrence Stone, *Road to Divorce: England 1530–1987* (Oxford: Oxford University Press, 1990).

54. For a detailed discussion, see Patricia Buckley Ebrey, introduction to *Marriage and Inequality in Chinese Society*, ed. Rubie S. Watson and Ebrey (Berkeley and Los Angeles: University of California Press, 1991), 1–24. See also George W. Barclay, *Colonial Development and Population in Taiwan* (Princeton: Princeton University Press, 1954). For information on the marriage market in contemporary China, see Han Min and J. S. Eades, "Brides, Bachelors, and Brokers: The Marriage Market in Rural Anhui in an Era of Economic Reform," *Modern Asian Studies* 29, no. 4 (1994): 841–69.

55. Chen Shengshao, *Wensulu* [Inquiry into customs] (1827; reprint, Beijing: Shumu wenxian chubanshe, 1983), 85.

56. See, for example, Delia Davin, "Gender and Population in the People's Republic of China," in *Women, State, and Ideology: Studies from Africa and Asia*, ed. Haleh Afshar (London: Macmillan, 1987), 117.

57. James Lee, Wang Feng, and Cameron Campbell, "Infant and Child Mortality among the Qing Nobility: Implications for Two Types of Positive Check," *Population Studies* 48 (1994): 400.

58. See, for example, Mildred Dickeman, "Demographic Consequences of Infanticide in Man," *Annual Review of Ecology and Systematics* 6 (1975): 107–37; Dickeman arrived at the figure of three hundred per thousand.

59. Keith McMahon, *Misers, Shrews, and Polygamists: Sexuality and Male-Female Relations in Eighteenth-Century Chinese Fiction* (Durham: Duke University Press, 1996), 22.

60. Ted A. Telford, "Covariates of Men's Age at First Marriage: The Historical Demography of Chinese Lineages," *Population Studies* 46 (March 1992): 33.

61. Ibid., 24; Billingsley, *Bandits in Republican China*, 78.

62. D. C. Lao, trans., *Mencius* (Hong Kong: Chinese University Press 1979), 1:155.

63. See Rubie S. Watson, "The Named and the Nameless: Gender and Person in Chinese Society," *American Ethnologist* 13 (1986): 619–31.

64. See Charlotte Furth, "From Birth to Birth: The Growing Body in Chinese

Medicine," in *Chinese Views of Childhood*, ed. Anne Behnke Kinney (Honolulu: University of Hawaii Press, 1995), 182.

65. See, for example, Gwen J. Broude, "Protest Masculinity: A Further Look at the Concept," *Ethos* 18, no. 1 (January 1990): 103–22; and David D. Gilmore and Sarah C. Uhl, "Further Notes on Andalusian Machismo," *Journal of Psychoanalytic Anthropology* 10, no. 4 (fall 1987): 341–60. For a critical perspective, see Seymour Parker and Hilda Parker, "Male Gender Identity in the Israeli Kibbutz: Reflections on 'Protest Masculinity,'" *Ethos* 20, no. 3 (September 1992): 340–57.

66. Margery Wolf, "Child Training and the Chinese Family," in *Family and Kinship in Chinese Society*, ed. Maurice Freedman (Stanford: Stanford University Press, 1970), 40. Wolf notes that "although fathers do not play games with their children, they are apt to play with them in the manner that an American adult plays with a kitten."

67. Ibid., 41.

68. See ibid., 32–41; and Richard M. Wilson, "Conformity and Deviance Regarding Moral Rules in Chinese Society: A Socialization Perspective," in *Normal and Abnormal Behavior in Chinese Culture*, ed. Arthur Kleinman and Tsung-yi Lin (Boston: Reidel, 1981), 233–51.

69. On both Liang Shuming and his father, see Guy Alitto, *The Last Confucian: Liang Shu-ming and the Chinese Dilemma of Modernity* (Berkeley and Los Angeles: University of California Press, 1986).

70. Hsiung Ping-chen, "Constructed Emotions: The Bond between Mothers and Sons in Late Imperial China," *Late Imperial China* 15, no. 1 (June 1994): 99.

71. Translated in Ownby, "Scriptures," 83.

72. James L. Watson, "Self Defense Corps, Violence, and the Bachelor Sub-Culture in South China: Two Case Studies," in *Proceedings of the Second International Conference on Sinology* (Nankang: Academia Sinica, 1988), 216.

73. Ibid.

74. *Mathews' Chinese-English Dictionary*, rev. American ed., s.v. "*guanggun*," defines *guanggun* as "a bare stick—swindler, rogue, pettifogger; a bachelor." Hsiao, *Rural China*, 455, identifies *guanggun* with the "village bully."

75. Cited in Hsiao, *Rural China*, 457.

76. See Antony, "Peasants, Heroes, and Brigands," 133. Antony's calculations are based on "convicted bandits" and might possibly overrepresent bandit leaders. These leaders, who might have had greater wealth or status than their followers, could have used such wealth and status to procure wives.

77. Billingsley, *Bandits in Republican China*, 75; Cai Shaoqing, *Minquo shiqi de tufei* [Bandits of the republican period] (Beijing: Zhongguo renmin daxue chubanshe, 1993), 51 ff.

78. Billingsley, *Bandits in Republican China*, 142.

79. Chen Shengshao, *Wensulu*, 83.

80. John Robert Shepherd, *Statecraft and Political Economy on the Taiwan Frontier, 1600–1800* (Stanford: Stanford University Press, 1993), 149.

81. Chen Shengshao, *Wensulu*, 122.

PART FIVE

# The Gender of Rebels

In Marxist theory, social class was the ultimate source of exploitation, and the oppression of women was defined as a problem of social class. With the success of the Communist revolution and the founding of the People's Republic of China in 1949, leaders assumed that the end of class oppression had also liberated women. Because the focus in this period was on class struggle, many urban Chinese now say that the Maoist period, and particularly the Cultural Revolution period (1966–76), was characterized by "gender erasure." This period has also been described as a time of "socialist androgyny," when both men and women wore short hair and "Mao suits." Women who tried to look "feminine" were criticized for their improper attitude. However, feminist scholars in the Mainland and elsewhere have started to point out that this was not actually a time of "androgyny." Rather, it is more accurately characterized as "masculinization," because women were pressured to dress and act like men, but not vice versa. In her chapter on violence among female Red Guards during the Cultural Revolution, Emily Honig notes that the girls invariably dressed like male soldiers. Both of the following chapters show that gender norms had not been overturned at all—in fact, far from it. Both chapters posit that restrictive gender norms go a long way toward explaining some of the successes and excesses of efforts to reshape Chinese society during the Cultural Revolution. In her analysis of the ruthless violence by students of elite girls middle schools, Honig suggests that reaction against repressive gender norms might have played a role. In their analysis of the leaders of the Shanghai worker rebels, Elizabeth Perry and Nara Dillon point out that most of the leaders were socially marginal males who used the imagery of the marginal band of outlaws to symbolize their solidarity and commitment to creating a classless society.

In analyses of the Cultural Revolution period, a commonly asked question is, "What explains the seemingly senseless violence that occurred?" These chapters are innovative in suggesting that gender is part of the explanation.

There are many fascinating memoirs of the Cultural Revolution, and gender and sexuality play prominent roles in many of them. This prominence in itself should alert scholars to the fact that gender must be taken into account when analyzing this period. Gao Yuan's *Born Red: A Chronicle of the Cultural Revolution* describes, from the point of view of one male student, the violence at an elite middle school in Hebei province that was home to fifty boarding students, twenty-five boys and twenty-five girls. This book strikes the reader for the ways in which the students seem like typical adolescents while, at the same time, they are capable of brutal violence against fellow students and teachers. Anchee Min's *Red Azalea* describes the love affair between a seventeen-year-old girl sentenced to work at a labor collective and her female team leader. They seem impelled toward each other by internal desires that they cannot understand and by outside repression that is nearly unbearable. In different kinds of incidents throughout the book, Min manages to communicate the distorted sexualities that emerged in an atmosphere where the expression of femininity and sexual desire could result in ostracization, beating, rape, and worse. Rae Yang's *Spider Eaters: A Memoir* contains a chapter titled "Red Guards Had No Sex," which shows how adolescent sexuality could be channeled into violence.

Zhang Xianliang's *Half of Man Is Woman* (first published in China in 1985) stimulated heated debate about the sexuality it depicted.[1] The story follows the sexual history of Zhang Yonglin, a writer imprisoned during the anti-rightist campaign and again at the beginning of the Cultural Revolution. The plot leads from his frustrated erotic desires to his marriage to another labor camp inmate. After his years of frustration, he discovers on his wedding night that he is impotent. He recovers his potency after a heroic deed, but only to divorce his wife and leave her. This novel has been criticized from a feminist perspective because the woman essentially exists in order for the man to prove his manhood. Historically, it is important because it was one of the important early works of fiction in the reassessment of the Cultural Revolution through "Scar Literature" in the 1980s.

The movie *Hibiscus Town* (and the book upon which it was based) depicts forbidden love during the Cultural Revolution between a young widow classified as a rich peasant and a man classified as a rightist. Sentenced to sweep the streets every day, they fall in love and conduct a private marriage ceremony to sanction what the village and the Party refuse to recognize (even while the female Party secretary is carrying on her own illicit affair).

## NOTES

1. This book is discussed by Zhong Xueping, "Male Suffering and Male Desire: The Politics of Reading *Half of Man Is Woman* by Zhang Xianliang," in *Engendering China: Women, Culture, and the State,* ed. Christina K. Gilmartin, Gail Hershatter, Lisa Rofel, and Tyrene White (Cambridge: Harvard University Press, 1994), 175–91.

## COMPLEMENTARY READINGS AND VIDEOS

Gao Yuan. *Born Red: A Chronicle of the Cultural Revolution.* Stanford: Stanford University Press, 1987.

*Hibiscus Town* [Furong zhen]. Directed by Xie Jin. Distributed by China Film Imp. and Exp., Los Angeles, Calif., 1985. Videocassette.

Anchee Min. *Red Azalea.* New York: Pantheon Books, 1994.

Rae Yang. *Spider Eaters: A Memoir.* Berkeley and Los Angeles: University of California Press, 1997.

Zhang Xianliang. *Half of Man Is Woman* [Nanrende yiban shi nüren]. Trans. Martha Avery. New York: W. W. Norton, 1988.

CHAPTER NINE

# Maoist Mappings of Gender: Reassessing the Red Guards

*Emily Honig*

The Cultural Revolution (1966–76), most Western and Chinese observers agree, represented a period when both feminism and femininity were rejected. Feminism, or any discussion of women's specific problems, was declared bourgeois; femininity, or any assertion of a specifically female identity, was denounced. Instead, Mao's slogan "The times have changed, men and women are the same" was propagated and the Iron Girls—strong, robust, muscular women who boldly performed physically demanding jobs traditionally done by men—were celebrated in newspapers, pamphlets, and posters. Jiang Qing, Mao Zedong's wife, who rose to political prominence during the Cultural Revolution, appeared in military attire, symbolizing to her audiences a presumably gender-neutral style that was emulated by teenage girl Red Guards who cut their hair short (or more daringly, shaved their heads), donned army clothes, and marched barefoot through city streets. Almost all the art, literature, films, operas, and ballets produced during the Cultural Revolution featured women in leadership roles or as militant combatants in the revolutionary struggle before 1949.

Closer scrutiny, as well as historical materials about the Cultural Revolution, reveals that notions of femininity and discussions of gender were far more complex than state propaganda and Maoist slogans suggest. While the media valorized the examples of women who joined oil-drilling teams, assumed jobs as tractor, truck, and diesel locomotive drivers, or learned to repair high-voltage electric wires, managers of textile factories at least sometimes explained their continued preference for women workers by emphasizing their manual dexterity and patience. While the media glorified women's public roles as proletarian fighters, their domestic roles and responsibilities were left unexamined. Although foreign observers applauded the plain-colored loose-fitting clothes worn by men and women

alike for preventing the sexual objectification of women that they so ab-
horred in their own countries, countless young women sent to live in the
Chinese countryside were the objects of sexual abuse by local male officials,
and adolescent girls who remained in the cities were often the objects of
sexual exploits by young male neighborhood gangs. Finally, even though
Jiang Qing may have been most frequently associated with a rejection of
feminine attire, she also, in the early 1970s, designed and promoted a new
"national dress" for women that combined noblewomen's and maidens'
dress styles from the Tang, Song, Yuan, and Ming dynasties (her own dress
at that time included a full-pleated skirt embroidered with plum blos-
soms).[1] The Cultural Revolution, in other words, represented far more than
a simple rejection of femininity. Gender as a category of analysis may have
been denounced by the state, but gender identity and gender relationships
were being continually contested and reformulated.

This essay looks at some of the complexities of the articulation of gender
identity during the Cultural Revolution by focusing on one particular issue:
women's participation in the widespread violence that accompanied the
Red Guard movement when the Cultural Revolution began in 1966. On the
surface, Red Guard violence was gender blind: there was nothing gendered
about either its perpetrators or victims, whose class identity and political
affiliation were far more salient. Beneath the surface, however, personal accounts and memoirs of the Cultural Revolution reveal that its violence was
in fact deeply gendered, sexualized, and enmeshed in contested notions of
masculinity and femininity. This does not mean that violence was *about* gender, but rather that its practice and representations had clearly gendered
dimensions. Women may have acted like men and engaged in the same
forms of violence as men, but the meanings and implications of their experiences were profoundly different. The point of this essay, then, is not simply to "add" women to the historical record of Red Guard activities but
rather to explore the meanings people ascribed to female violence, and the
role of that violence in the remapping of male and female identities in the
Cultural Revolution.

## PRIMITIVE PASSIONS

Although the violent behavior of young girls is not the focus of any Red
Guard memoirs, almost every one relates incidents of female violence.
Some of these accounts are entirely matter-of-fact, implying that there was
nothing unusual or surprising about women's behavior at this time. It is
merely coincidental, if not obvious, that some violence was committed by
women. Zi-ping Luo, for example, in her account of the early Red Guard
movement in Shanghai, chronicles the attacks on her family by Red Guards.

The first group of Red Guards to arrive at their house was led by a girl, Luo reports, who "slapped the table with her broad leather belt" and commanded her to produce a report of her "anti-revolutionary crimes." Several days later, when Red Guards came to search her house, "two strong men yanked Father from the bed and dragged him from the house while two female Red Guards kicked my brothers and me from behind."[2]

If there is anything at all noteworthy about women's participation in Red Guard violence in these accounts, it is that women invariably dressed as men, or more precisely, as male army combatants. A female middle-school student in Beijing, for instance, remembered her enthusiasm for "continuing the revolution" after the appearance of Nie Yuanzi's poster at Beijing University. "We were all wearing army uniforms," she recalls, "because it was considered very glorious then to wear army uniforms. All the girls put on caps, like the boys, and we tucked our hair up under our caps so we looked like boys. We rolled up our sleeves. And we took off our belts and wore them around our waists, on the outside of the uniform. The belts were our weapons. When we wanted to beat someone, all we had to do was to take off our belts."[3] Even when these accounts *describe* the quasi-male attire donned by young girl Red Guards, they do not represent it as unusual, curious, or even significant. Moreover, for some participants, wearing pants with leather belts, as well as cutting their hair short, seemed to be as much about rejecting a bourgeois lifestyle as about blurring gender distinctions. As a young woman, a student at a Beijing middle school in 1966, recalls, "I had been criticized by the 'advanced elements' in my school for dressing in a weird bourgeois way—wearing a frock. Next day, I wore trousers and joined a Red Guard organization—the first one in the school."[4] Likewise, Rae Yang, in a recently written account of growing up in Beijing, emphasizes the class dimensions of Red Guard fashion: "When we went out, however, we always put on the complete outfit of a Red Guard: army uniforms with long sleeves and long pants, caps on our heads, belts around our waists, armbands, army sneakers, canvas bags, and little red books. . . . We would not wear skirts, blouses, and sandals. Anything that would make girls look like girls was bourgeois. We covered up our bodies so completely that I almost forgot I was a girl. I was a Red Guard. Others were Red Guards too. And that was it."[5]

Even as these accounts represent women's dress as a statement about class rather than gender, and even as Rae Yang asserts the existence of an ungendered "Red Guard fashion," the standard attire was not at all gender neutral but clearly marked male. Rejecting a bourgeois lifestyle *and* engaging in aggressive, violent attacks both mandated that girls dress like boys, cut their hair like boys, and borrow their fathers' (not their mothers') leather belts; in short, both required masculinity. Perhaps inadvertently, too, women's Red Guard fashion recalled the dress of revolutionary heroines from the Nationalist and Communist movement of the first half of the twentieth century—women such as Qiu Jin and Xie Bingying, famed for donning Western male suits when not dressed in military uniform.

Although the above accounts of women's dress imply a partial explanation of their violence during the Cultural Revolution (they became like men), they do not explicitly question women's Red Guard behavior. A far more prominent theme in memoirs of the Cultural Revolution is an interrogation of women's behavior: the portrayal of female violence as a radical departure from women's conventional deportment, as something strange and demanding of explanation. Ken Ling was initially surprised and dismayed by this apparent change in female behavior. "Many of the girls," he reports at the beginning of the Red Guard movement, "were becoming barbarous. . . . They were hot-tempered and merciless; they banged on the table and glared at people with round eyes. Once I overheard the kind of language they were using in interrogating the black gang: 'son of a bitch,' 'you stinking whore' and much more obscene words. Later they learned to pinch and slap faces. Others even wanted to 'compete' with the boys, calling this 'equality of the sexes' and the 'emancipation of women.'"[6] A number of women were themselves startled by the extent of female participation in violence. Zhai Zhenhua, an enthusiastic Beijing Red Guard during the early part of the Cultural Revolution (before she became its victim), recounts her participation in house raids and beatings of "class enemies." Describing herself as a previously timid person who was initially alarmed at the sight of fierce young girl Red Guards, she says, "When I first saw a Red Guard remove her canvas belt to beat her victim and saw his clothes tear and blood appear on his skin, I was afraid. I was not the most bloodthirsty person in the world; I was even afraid to watch wars or fighting in movies."[7] However, she became sufficiently accustomed to the new codes of behavior to instigate the beating of a "class enemy." Fifteen years old herself, she led a group of teenage girls to invade the home of a former landlord, where they beat to death the landlord's wife.[8]

If there is one instance of violence by female Red Guards that has been singled out by observers, it is the beating of teachers and the principal at the prestigious Beijing Normal University's Affiliated Middle School for Girls (Beijing shifan daxue fushu nüzi zhongxue). That the attack is perplexing is perhaps due to the concentration of high-ranking officials' daughters (including the daughters of Liu Shaoqi and Deng Xiaoping) among the ranks of students, or perhaps due simply to the fact that many former students (particularly those who had had the opportunity to live abroad) were proportionately better able than their peers to later produce memoirs of their adolescent experiences. Even if the school was unusual in a number of ways, reports on and retrospective analyses of the violent behavior of its students comprise one of the few instances in which any attempt has been made to reflect on the specific nature of female violence.

The most notorious episode at the Middle School for Girls was the beating to death of its vice-principal, Bian Zhongyun, in August 1966. She had already been attacked in late June: at a criticism meeting held by the school's work team, she was forced to wear a dunce cap and bow her head down. "They beat me with fists, kicked me, tied my hands behind my back, hit me with a wooden rifle used for militia training, filled my mouth with dirt, and spat on my face," she reported in a letter to government authorities, an act for which she was further punished.[9] Then, on August 5 she was one of five teachers and administrators beaten by first-year students in the upper-middle school. Accounts vary as to precisely what took place. According to Wang Youqin, herself a student at that school, "The students splashed ink on the clothes of the administrators, forced them to wear 'high hats,' hung boards from their necks on which their names were crossed out with a red X, forced them to kneel on the ground, hit them with nail-spiked clubs, burned them with boiling water, etc. After three hours of torture, the first vice-principal Bian Zhongyun lost consciousness and was put on a garbage cart. Two hours later she was sent to the hospital across the street. There she was found to have been dead for some time."[10] According to Yue Daiyun, who had a relative teaching at the school, the students, "filled with passion for the new movement and eager to conduct the struggle against their own enemies[,] . . . had forced the president of their school, famous as one of the first Chinese women to be educated, to climb through a narrow underground cement drainage pipe. When she finally emerged, they had brutally beaten her to death."[11] Though many rumors have circulated, to this day the identities of the girls responsible for the violence have never been established.)

Two weeks after these aggressive attacks, an unrelated event reinforced the school's reputation as a site of Cultural Revolution militancy. One of its students, Song Binbin, was among the many Red Guards who met Mao at a mass rally. When she appeared beside him on the rostrum at Tiananmen Square, she adorned him with a Red Guard armband. After learning her given name—"Binbin," meaning "refined," or "urbane"—he reportedly declared that it was suitable for a high-class lady, not a young revolutionary. "Is that the 'pin' [bin] in 'wen chih pin pin' (soft and gentle)?" she recalled Mao asking. "I said 'Yes.' Then he told me kindly: 'You want to be militant.'" He then conferred on her the now more fashionable name "Yaowu," or "seeking violence."[12] She subsequently led a group of her classmates to shave their heads and march barefoot through the main streets of Beijing.[13] And in the immediate aftermath of Song Binbin's moment of glory, the Middle School for Girls became the Red Seeking-Violence Middle School for Girls (Hingse yaowu zhongzue).[14]

In the broader context of Red Guard violence, the beatings at this middle school were not particularly remarkable or extraordinary. Nor was this the only instance of female students physically abusing their teachers and administrators. Indeed, Wang Youqin has chronicled numerous such episodes: at the Shanghai Number Three Girls' Middle School, students attacked the principal by using thumbtacks to attach a character poster on her back and then forcing her to eat excrement while cleaning the bathrooms; at the Beijing Number Eight Girls' Middle School, female Red Guards used hammers to strike teachers' heads; at the Beijing Number Five Girls' Middle School, students bound the principal with a rope, hung her from a tree, then let her fall to the ground. Wang's list of schools where students attacked teachers (which is not meant to be complete) includes an additional seven girls' middle schools in Beijing as well as two girls' middle schools in Shanghai, and she makes it clear that girls at coed schools were among the ranks of Red Guards who attacked teachers.[15]

Yet it is the violence of the adolescent girls at the Beijing Normal University's Affiliated Middle School for Girls that observers felt required special explanation. "In those years, the school I attended was a girls' school," writes Wang Youqin in an essay titled "Female Savagery": "The students who beat and killed teachers were not petty hoodlums. Instead, they were girls who were fourteen to nineteen years old. . . . How can one explain the fact that it was in our famous girls' middle school that the first acts of violence in the Cultural Revolution in Beijing took place?"[16] Ye Weili, also a student at the Middle School for Girls in 1966, highlights the girls' violent beating of the vice-principal as one of three episodes in the early Cultural Revolution that have perplexed her ever since.[17] And the author of several articles about female sent-down youth, Jin Yihong, remains deeply disturbed and perplexed by the violence of her classmates and is continually absorbed by the question "Why was it that the girls at our *girls'* school could have been so violent?"[18]

## FORMULATING FEMININITIES

The compulsion to explain the violence of such privileged girls is almost invariably linked to an assumption that it represented a dramatic deviation from their "ordinary" (pre–Cultural Revolution) behavior. Wang Youqin, for example, suggests that women are ordinarily gentle, implying that only under "special conditions [will] primitive savagery overwhelm women's gentleness."[19] "These teenage girls, ordinarily shy, mild, and gentle," Yue Daiyun remarks about the beating of Bian Zhongyun, "had somehow become capable of unimaginable cruelty."[20] "All of a sudden she was far from gentle, shy, or lovely," Jung Chang, the author of the popular memoir *Wild Swans*, writes of the female Red Guard who had once been the object of her brother's affections. "She was all hysterical ugliness."[21] The Cultural Revolution, then, presumably represented a corruption of women's innately timid, gentle nature.

For some women, learning to swear was the first step away from these conventions. Jin Yihong, for example, describes being shocked, at the beginning of the Cultural Revolution, to hear her female classmates swear, and very vividly recalls the first time she herself swore. She surmises that if, with practice, women could adjust to cursing, so, too, could acts of violence become "natural." An almost identical emphasis on cursing as emblematic of a new type of behavior for young women appears in the memoir of a young middle-school student in Beijing. "It was early in the summer of that year [1966]," she recalls, "that I first learned to swear. . . . The first time I heard one of my girlfriends swear, I was astonished, it was so unlike her. The first time I swore, I felt a little faint, then I thought my friend must have felt that way too, although she didn't show it."[22] For this woman, learning to swear seems to have represented a far more significant departure from convention than violence did, as she proceeds to describe in a rather casual manner how her Red Guard group, consisting entirely of girls, ransacked houses, and captured members of street gangs, whom they beat until "they begged us 'Red Guard ladies' for mercy."[23]

However, even if it had been previously unimaginable for women to curse (at least, young, highly educated urban women), it is not entirely clear that the students at the Middle School for Girls had always been so stereotypically mild and gentle as the above accounts imply. In reflecting on her pre–Cultural Revolution years at the school (and *not* in the context of establishing a pre– and post–Cultural Revolution comparison), Jin Yihong emphasizes how unconventional she and her classmates had been. They refused to wear feminine clothing and declared total disinterest in their physical appearance by refusing to own mirrors. "Girls at our school dressed like boys *before* the Cultural Revolution," she recalls. "We were extremely self-confident and believed we could do anything. We never felt limited because we were girls, and insisted that we could do everything boys could do. We were wild [ye]." Moreover, in the context of analyzing homoerotic relationships among girls at the school, she describes the explicitly masculine or feminine roles each member of a couple would assume.[24] If this portrait of the student body is at all true, then the notion of demure feminine girls who suddenly turned bold and violent is far too simplistic.

In spite of these characterizations, Jin Yihong herself has joined other former students in the quest for an explanation of female violence. At a recent informal gathering of both women and men who attended elite middle schools in Beijing when the Cultural Revolution began, several theories emerged. First, the attendees of the gathering concluded, women's violence could be attributed to the particularly severe forms of "sexual repression" to which young girls had been subjected. Whether sexual repression referred to control of women's sexuality per se, or to a more general social control of female behavior, remains unclear. The latter is not dissimilar to Marilyn Young's analysis of female violence. "Perhaps one way to understand the reports of the quite stunning ferocity of female middle-school students," she suggests, "against figures of authority (up to and including beating people to death) is as a rebellion against the weight of prior social repression, as well as a means to extirpate old stereotypes of feminine behavior."[25] A second theory was that "women were more susceptible than men to external pressures." Young girls were therefore more likely to respond to admonitions by Chinese leadership to attack "class enemies." Mao's famed statement that "a revolution is not a dinner party," for instance, is presumed to have had a particular influence on women. Implicit in this theory, however, is the conviction that female students were *more* violent than men—a conviction that says more about popular belief (or at least some segment of popular belief) than actual experience.[26]

Another category of explanation, not considered in these former students' discussions, might be relevant, and that concerns popular culture, particularly in the early- and mid-1960s. In several different contexts, it seems, female militancy (meant literally), if not ferocity, was valorized. First, young schoolgirls, like their male counterparts, participated in militia training. This was part of the broader militarization of civilian life noted by Lynn White in his study of the origins of violence during the Cultural Revolution. He describes the military camps established in 1964, where in one summer more than fifty thousand middle-school students and ten thousand university students in Shanghai were drilled in the use of military weapons.[27] In the countryside, young peasant women, organized into "red women's shock brigades," received basic military training: practicing for combat, they marched through fields carrying crude rifles (or sometimes hoes, as a substitute) on their shoulders.[28] Even in nursery schools, young children were trained for armed battle in defense of their motherland: instead of simply being taught "body movement" during physical education, they were issued wood sticks to use as rifles and taught games such as "little people's militia," "small air force pilots," and "learning to be the People's Liberation Army."[29]

The state-sponsored emphasis on military training that reached its height in 1964 was reflected in, and further propagated by, the popular women's magazine *Zhongguo funü* (Women of China). In the early 1960s its cover design had usually featured colorful images such as two "minority" women wearing festive dress and weaving, a young rosy-cheeked girl playing with a puppet, or two women happily browsing through a photo album. In mid-1964, however, cover designs began to honor the achievements of women combatants. One, featuring a drawing of a young woman holding a rifle at her side, included on its inside flap the lyrics and musical score for Mao's already famous 1961 poem "Militia Women," one he had initially inscribed on a photograph of himself standing with a group of women army combatants, each holding a rifle:

> Early rays of sun illumine the parade grounds
> and these handsome girls heroic in the wind,
> with rifles five feet long.
> Daughters of China with a marvelous will,
> you prefer hardy uniforms to colorful silk.[30]

Articles in subsequent issues reported on the accomplishments of women sharpshooters and crack shots, particularly those whose passion for the militia had replaced their previous interest in pretty clothes, and those who had overcome their initial "girlish" fear of gunshots.[31]

One can only speculate about the impact of this training on young women. Gao Xiaoxian, a student at an all-girl middle school in X'ian in the early 1960s, vividly recalls how she and her classmates routinely "practiced" for an anticipated war with the Soviet Union. Wearing plain blue shirts and pants and black cloth shoes, they learned to march in formation, to use rifles with live bullets, and to aim hand grenades. Among the songs they sang during their weekly military practice was the one based on Mao's poem "Militia Women." For Gao, the valorization of female ferocity expressed by Mao in 1966 when he changed Song Binbin's name to Song Yaowu, did not represent something new but rather had its precedents in the popularization of his poem throughout the early 1960s. (Furthermore, she believes that the preference for young girls to wear clothes made of plain-colored cloth rather than colorful, flowery prints first emerged in response to this poem in the early 1960s.)[32]

The emphasis on female military vigilance articulated in this song, as well as in actual militia training, may have been reinforced by other forms of popular culture. Although the famed eight model operas did not yet dominate the performing arts in the years prior to the Cultural Revolution, some were already circulating widely. Most relevant here is the *Red Detachment of Women*, which made its film debut in the early 1960s and then premiered as an opera in 1964. Based on real historical events, the *Red Detachment* takes place on Hainandao and centers on the heroic efforts of a young slave girl, Wu Qinghua, to resist a wicked and evil landlord. She does break free, "wreaking violence upon male guards along her escape route." Eventually, she joins the Chinese Communist Party's Women's Detachment, a group of heroic female guerrillas that successfully destroys the power of the local landlords. The story concludes with Wu's vow to abide by Mao's motto "Political power grows out of the barrel of a gun."[33]

Although the *Red Detachment of Women* was primarily a tale that glorified female militancy, its performance sometimes revealed more ambivalence about women's combat roles. Historical records show that in the actual events on Hainandao in the 1920s, women taught themselves to use rifles and were organized by a particularly militant female commissar. In the ballet version, however, women are taught by men to use rifles, they are led by a dashing male commissar, and when they are not fighting, they busy themselves mending soldiers' uniforms. When an American visitor to China in 1972 asked about the change, "the ballet troupe explained that the commissar was changed to a male for 'artistic reasons,' because there weren't enough male leads."[34] It is not entirely clear whether the change was made during the Cultural Revolution or during the versions produced in the pre–Cultural Revolution years. Nevertheless, this shift in male/female roles in the story that was so grating to a foreign feminist was probably unnoticed by Chinese audiences, for whom the *Red Detachment* remained a story that celebrated female militancy. Indeed, at least one woman's account of her success in the militia prior to the Cultural Revolution cites the influence of stories such as the *Red Detachment of Women*.[35]

The point is not that this particular story was a direct cause or explanation of female violence during the Cultural Revolution. After all, a celebration of the ferocity, confidence, and bold determination of women fighting Japanese, Guomindang, or landlord "enemies" is not equivalent to licensing the beating and whipping of teachers. But it may have represented and extolled a model of female militancy to which young girls aspired, so that it was this *style* (rather than content) of fierce militant behavior that women sought to emulate.[36] In the context of the popularization of stories such as the *Red Detachment of Women*, and the militia training of young women during the years preceding the Cultural Revolution, the appearance in 1966 of female Red Guards clothed in armylike attire, wearing (and wielding as weapons) broad leather belts, and displaying a capacity for attacks on figures of authority no longer seems so unprecedented, inexplicable, or deviant from prevailing codes of femininity.

Even if these forms of popular culture may have contributed to the authorization of female violence in a very general way, they do not explain its specific content. Indeed, any further exploration of the violence of female Red Guards would require more specific data about the women themselves. Aside from being female, what else might be said about them? Even if the prestigious Beijing Normal University's Affiliated Middle School for Girls has been singled out in many retrospective accounts, it was not a unique source of female violence. Some Chinese observers believe that students at all-girl schools were more prone to engaging in house searches and beatings during the early Red Guard Movement than students at coed schools, presumably because at coed schools they were more likely to defer to their

Figure 6. The caption of this Cultural Revolution–era poster commemorating the centennial of the Paris Commune reads, "Long Live the Dictatorship of the Proletariat!" Beijing, 1971. Poster F1 in the University of Westminster Chinese poster collection, London.

male classmates. (And one critic of gender roles in contemporary China, reflecting on her Cultural Revolution experience, complained that, once students from all-girl schools joined coed Red Guard units, they suddenly—almost automatically—assumed roles subservient to the male leaders.) They add that the girls most likely to be violent were daughters of high-ranking officials and, furthermore, ones who had not enjoyed academic success at school.[37] It is impossible to determine the veracity of these observations, but they do suggest the importance of probing beyond the simple fact of a female identity to analyze female violence. Finally, it is important to establish the actual extent of violence perpetrated by female Red Guards. Although many contemporary and retrospective accounts convey a picture of massive numbers of young women engaging in reckless attacks on authorities and class enemies, it is not entirely clear that such a large number of women or young girls were involved. Gao Xiaoxian, for example, stresses that of the roughly fifty students in her class at a middle school for girls in Xi'an, no more than five engaged in house searches and beatings.

Even if women Red Guards who engaged in early violence represented a small minority (both of women students and of Red Guards), an analysis of who they were, their activities, and the portrayals of those activities is crucial for understanding the gendered dimensions of violence during the early Cultural Revolution. Even if their superficial behavior was identical to that of their male counterparts, it had different meanings and implications. In other words, although young women and men alike donned leather belts that they used to whip "class enemies," popular interpretations of those actions invoked beliefs about appropriate gender behavior.

Gender was not an explicit issue in early violence by the Red Guard. The violence, even when women were its perpetrators, was not necessarily about "gender trouble," disorder, or discontent. Indeed, the seemingly obvious point that female violence reflected, at least in part, a rebellion against conventions of female behavior assumes that such conventions prevailed as a kind of static entity prior to the Cultural Revolution. Women themselves may have understood and described female violence as a radical departure from the past, but closer scrutiny may well reveal that the very articulation of those conventions—during and after the Cultural Revolution—was a means of explaining seemingly inexplicable behavior. Particularly in the context of memoirs crafted in the aftermath of the Cultural Revolution (when most were produced), it must have seemed more comforting to describe female violence as a radical aberration from the recent past rather than as continuous with the pre–Cultural Revolution socialist era.

Feminist critics of the Cultural Revolution have often pointed out that the Maoist slogan "The times have changed, men and women are the same," was not the plea for gender neutrality that it seems, at first glance, to be. Instead, it required women to behave like men, or at least implied that they would be measured by a male standard of success. (Men, it is often pointed out, were not encouraged to behave like women or to take on traditionally female roles and responsibilities.) To be revolutionary, critics suggest, one had to act like a man; to behave as a woman risked being labeled a "backward element."

Looking at one specific aspect of women's Cultural Revolution experience—violence by female Red Guards—reveals how much more complex an analysis is necessary. The ways in which that violence has been represented and analyzed by Chinese participants is embedded in beliefs about masculinity and femininity, beliefs that were themselves constantly being challenged and renegotiated. The very categories female and male, although invoked as if they had clearly fixed meanings, were far from static. Even while official policy declared gender, as a category of analysis, irrelevant, the Cultural Revolution involved a profound contestation and reconfiguration of gender identities.

## NOTES

1. For a more detailed account of Jiang Qing's "national dress" design, see Yen Chia-chi and Kao Kao, *The Ten-Year History of the Chinese Cultural Revolution* (Taipei: Institute of Current Chinese Studies, 1988), 460–62.

2. Zi-ping Luo, *A Generation Lost: China under the Cultural Revolution* (New York: Avon Books, 1990), 47, 51.

3. Anne F. Thurston, *Enemies of the People* (New York: Alfred Knopf, 1987), 160.

4. Zhang Xinxin and Sang Ye, *Chinese Lives: An Oral History of Contemporary China* (New York: Pantheon Books), 56.

5. Rae Yang, *Spider Eaters* (Berkeley and Los Angeles: University of California Press, 1997), 135.

6. Ken Ling, *The Revenge of Heaven: Journal of a Young Chinese* (New York: G. P. Putnam's Sons, 1972), 28.

7. Zhai Zhenhua, *Red Flower of China* (New York: Soho Press, 1992), 96.

8. Ibid., 97.

9. Wang Youqin, "1966: Xuesheng da laoshi de geming" [The revolution of students beating teachers], *Ershiyi shiji* (August 1995): 36.

10. Ibid., 34.

11. Yue Daiyun and Carolyn Wakeman, *To the Storm: The Odyssey of a Revolutionary Chinese Woman* (Berkeley and Los Angeles: University of California Press, 1985), 183.

12. For accounts of this incident, see Wang Youqin, "1966: Xuesheng da laoshi de geming," 42; Tai Xiaoying and Ma Li, "Mengyu hong bayue" [August of a dream], in *Hongweibing milu*, ed. Yu Hui (Beijing: Tuanjie chubanshe, 1993), 93; Yue Daiyun and Wakeman, *To the Storm*, 183 (in this account, it was Jiang Qing who changed Song's name). Also see Sung Yao-wu, "I Put a Red Arm Band on Chairman Mao," *Chinese Literature* 11 (1966): 23–26.

13. Tai Xiaoying and Ma Li, "Mengyu hong bayue," 93.

14. Ye Weili, "Sange changmian he yipian wenzhang: Guanyu wengede yidian sisuo" (essay manuscript, 1996).

15. Wang Youqin, "Xuesheng da laoshi," 35, 40, 45.

16. Wang Youqin, "Nüxingde yeman," in *Xiaoyuan suibi*, ed. Wang Youqin, (Beijing; n.p., 1988), 31, 39.

17. Ye Weili, "Sange changmian he yipian wenzhang: guanyu wengede yidian sitan."

18. Jin Yihong, interview by author, Santa Cruz, Calif., May 1996. Jin is currently head of the Philosophy Research Institute of the Jiangsu Academy of Social Sciences.

19. Wang Youqin, "Nüxingde yeman," 40.

20. Yue Daiyun and Wakeman, *To the Storm*, 183.

21. Jung Chang, *Wild Swans: Three Daughters of China* (New York: Doubleday, 1991), 309.

22. Zhang Xinxin and Sang Ye, *Chinese Lives*, 56.

23. Ibid.

24. Jin Yihong, interview by author.

25. Marilyn B. Young, "Chicken Little in China: Women after the Cultural Revolution," in *Promissory Notes: Women in the Transition to Socialism*, ed. Sonia

Kruks, Rayna Rapp, and Marilyn B. Young (New York: Monthly Review Press, 1989), 237.

26. There is some indication that popular belief held women accountable for the worst forms of violence. See, for example, Ken Ling, *The Revenge of Heaven*, 80, 91; Wang Youqin, "Xuesheng da laoshi," 40. The depiction of women as especially brutal in post–Cultural Revolution accounts of the Cultural Revolution is noted by Marilyn Young, who cites as examples the "antiheroine" of Liu Binyan's piece of reportage fiction, "People or Monsters," as well as a play popular in Beijing in 1985 that featured a "truly loathsome girl Red Guard leader who seemed to be the only Red Guard in her neighborhood." See Young, "Chicken Little in China," 240.

27. Lynn T. White III, *The Policies of Chaos: The Organizational Causes of Violence in China's Cultural Revolution* (Princeton: Princeton University Press, 1989), 205–8, 213–16.

28. James and Ann Tyson, *Chinese Awakenings: Life Stories from the Unofficial China*, (Boulder, Colo.: Westview Press, 1995), 193.

29. Beijingshi qi yi you'eryuan daban jiaoyan zu, "Zai ticao zuoyezhong zuzhi you'er zuo junshi youxi" [A demonstration of organizing children to engage in military affairs during exercise period], *Zhongguo funü* 5 (May 1966): 22–23.

30. See *Zhongguo funü* 3 (March 1964). The translation of the poem is from Willis Barnstone, trans., *The Poems of Mao Tse-tung* (New York: Harper and Row, 1972), 98–99.

31. See, for example, *Zhongguo funü* 8 (August 1964): 6–8, 11; 5 (May 1965): 6–8.

32. Gao Xiaoxian, interview by author, Santa Cruz, Calif., May 1996. Gao is head of the research office of the Women's Federation in Xi'an and the author of several articles about contemporary rural women.

33. Roxane Witke, *Comrade Chiang Ch'ing* (Boston: Little, Brown, and Company, 1977), 426–29.

34. Jane Barrett, "Women Hold Up Half the Sky," in Marilyn B. Young, ed., *Women in China: Studies in Social Change and Feminism* (Ann Arbor: University of Michigan Center for Chinese Studies, 1973), 188–89.

35. Guo Jianzhang, Dong Daojian, and Jiao Kelao, "Jinwo liang gun qiang" [Firmly grasping two rifles], *Zhongguo funü* 8 (August 1965): 10–11.

36. The celebration of female militancy was more explicitly propagated in early 1967, when the Chinese media publicized the historical experience of the Red Lanterns—the female counterparts of the Boxers, who dressed entirely in red, armed themselves with red-tasseled spears, and carried red scarves and red lanterns in their hands. This is discussed in Paul Cohen, *History in Three Keys: The Boxers as Event, Experience, and Myth* (Berkeley and Los Angeles: University of California Press, 1997).

37. Gao Xiaoxian and Jin Yihong, interview by author, Santa Cruz, Calif., May 1996. Gao Xiaoxian believes that it was not only all-girl schools that produced disproportionate violence but all-female work units as well. In Xi'an, at least, the Women's Federation apparently was reputed to be the site of unusual violence.

# CHAPTER TEN

# "Little Brothers" in the Cultural Revolution: The Worker Rebels of Shanghai

*Elizabeth J. Perry and Nara Dillon*

The Cultural Revolution (1966–76) was a period of extraordinary social turmoil, the full dimensions of which are only just coming into focus. When Chairman Mao called upon the masses to "bombard the headquarters," they often did so with a remarkable vengeance. Murders of teachers by their students at some of the most prestigious girls' schools in the country (see the preceding chapter by Emily Honig), tragic suicides by many of China's most gifted intellectuals, and even cannibalism figured among the atrocities of the day. But alongside (and often interconnected with) these terrifying personal events went serious efforts at political change.

Dubbed a Great Proletarian Cultural Revolution, Mao's campaign to continue the revolution under socialism pinned high hopes on the participation of the working class. More than a few workers—spurred by the promise that their country was ostensibly a "dictatorship of the proletariat"—took advantage of the Cultural Revolution to press for greater political authority. Nowhere was this effort to empower workers more sustained, or more successful, than in the industrial capital of Shanghai. There, a "rebel" organization called the Workers' General Headquarters (WGH) prevailed over "conservative" rivals to seize power from the Municipal Party Committee in the January Revolution of 1967 and gain effective control of the city government.[1]

The Cultural Revolution was officially a "class struggle," and gender issues never figured centrally in its agenda.[2] As Marilyn Young has noted, "In launching . . . the Cultural Revolution, the state put into high relief the inherently contradictory position of women. . . . Yet, finally, since class was the primary analytic category for understanding all social problems, the ideological attack on inequality left structural issues untouched."[3] Attuned to the official discourse of the day, neither "rebel" workers (who attacked factory leaders) nor "conservatives" (who defended their supervisors) articulated explicit concerns about gender inequity.

Moreover, both wings of the workers' movement were overwhelmingly dominated by men. (This was in stark contrast to the student Red Guards, where, as Honig shows, female activism was pronounced.) At the time of the January Revolution, men accounted for nearly 90 percent of Shanghai's worker-rebel leadership at all levels (1,586 out of 1,784), although they made up only about two-thirds of the city's permanent workforce.[4] Male dominance hardly comes as a surprise, but we think something can be gained by interrogating the expected. Asking how and why men came to dominate leadership roles during a time of crisis and institutional flux may provide further insight into the dynamics of gender relations in Communist China.[5]

The worker rebels in Shanghai, known colloquially as "little brothers" (xiao xiongdi), were a motley crew. Their leaders, as we will see, came from disparate backgrounds and were motivated by divergent concerns. Despite (or perhaps because of) such diversity, however, they turned to masculine metaphors of brotherhood to construct their new rebel community. The adoption of such metaphors reflected the dominant paradigm for rebel organization to be found in popular Chinese culture.

For centuries, the trope of brotherhood had been a building block of rebel gangs in China, popularized in vernacular novels such as Shui Hu Zhuan (Pearl Buck's English translation of which is titled All Men Are Brothers) and kept alive through stories, movies, and model operas about the Communists' own revolutionary struggle. Mao Zedong himself had celebrated the tales of ancient rebels, revealing in his interview with the American journalist Edgar Snow that as a schoolboy he had shunned the Confucian classics in favor of "the romances of Old China, and especially stories of rebellion."[6] Snow shows how Mao's fascination with rebel gangs—in particular the Elder Brother Society (gelao hui)—exerted an important influence on the evolution of the Communist movement.[7] In his famous appeal to the Elder Brothers, written in the summer of 1936, Mao called upon members of the secret society "to unite under the slogan of resisting Japan and saving the country, and constitute a close and intimate alliance of brothers!"[8]

Although the Elder Brother Society had been centered in Sichuan, Hunan, and other parts of central China, the city of Shanghai was not without its own traditions of fraternal organization. Shanghai's notorious Green Gang, which by some accounts was an offshoot of the Elder Brother Society, also relied on male fictive kinship nomenclature to consolidate its disparate constituency.[9] These clandestine organizations were banned during the Campaign to Suppress Counterrevolutionaries, launched shortly after the Communists' ascension to power, but they were not thereby obliterated from the popular imagination. We find evidence of the lingering influence of such rebel traditions in the urban youth gangs that predated—and prefigured—the activities of worker rebels during the Cultural Revolution.

## THE BACKGROUNDS OF WORKER-REBEL LEADERS

For the most part, the leaders of Shanghai's worker rebels were young men on the lookout for excitement and self-esteem in the heady new environment created by the Cultural Revolution. As we might expect from recent scholarship emphasizing the numerous possibilities inherent in constructions of masculinity, these young men traveled very different roads in their common quest for identity.[10] Rebel leaders of rival factions came to embrace a shared fraternal identity once the umbrella organization of the Workers' General Headquarters was established in November 1966, but their earlier paths to rebellion were as complex and variegated as the meanings of masculinity in contemporary China. Although we tend to think of the 1950s as a time of general social conformity in China, the biographies of the worker-rebel leaders suggest that the initial years of the People's Republic of China also afforded considerable space for diversity and even dissidence.

Take the case of Chen Ada, a rebel leader from the Shanghai Valve Factory who assumed the directorship of the municipal Bureau of Industry for much of the Cultural Revolution decade. Known in Shanghai dialect as *awu* (a good-for-nothing), Chen was widely regarded as a petty gangster, prone to profanity and coarse behavior. A common saying during the Cultural Revolution went, "Wherever there's an armed battle, you'll find Chen Ada." As a youth, Chen had lived with his father and younger brother in the "poor folks' district" *(pinmin qu)* in the western part of Shanghai. During the day, Chen's father and the dozen or so other peddlers who shared their room ventured forth to sell their wares. At night, once the vendors had gathered up their stands, they had nothing but time on their hands. Their chief recreation was to play cards for money and tell crude jokes. Growing up in this rough-and-ready all-male society, Chen Ada himself began to follow the older boys in the neighborhood to local disreputable places of recreation (dance halls, ice-skating rinks, and the like), where he learned to speak with bravado and harass girls.

In 1958, as part of the Great Leap Forward, an urban commune was briefly established in Shanghai. To rid the city of its unproductive residents, petty gangsters were rounded up and packed off to Chongming Island for labor reform. Most of Chen Ada's friends were seized in this initiative, but in view of his youth Chen himself was released after a warning. A few years later, Chen enlisted in the army. His experiences in the military seem only to have exacerbated his earlier wayward tendencies, however. After his discharge and assignment to the Shanghai Valve Factory, Chen spent much of his time gambling—an activity that was strictly prohibited.[11]

Chen demonstrated his belligerent style shortly after the onset of the Cultural Revolution, when a neighbor exposed the fact that Chen's father had been hiding a cache of gold on behalf of a former capitalist. Chen Ada's younger brother, Chen Aer, delivered a sound thrashing to the accuser, for which Aer was packed off to the police station. Chen Ada himself then gathered a crowd of boisterous followers that surrounded the police station until the frightened authorities agreed to release his brother and post a special notice exonerating his father.[12] By his own account, Chen's motives for joining the Cultural Revolution did not evidence much political sophistication: "As for the bunch of jerks in the factory, I wanted to settle accounts with all of them."[13] The "jerks" (chilao in Shanghai dialect) were the factory cadres.

Chen Ada maintained his feisty demeanor to the end. Even after the arrest of his radical patrons—the so-called "Gang of Four"—in October 1976, Chen advocated a militant response. At a meeting of rebel leaders in Shanghai to discuss military action, Chen exploded: "If Party Central goes revisionist, never fear. We'll counter it. I didn't die during the Cultural Revolution. Now I'm ready to die, but I'm not afraid. . . . Give me revolution or give me death! Everyone should swear an oath. Who wants to be a traitor, damn it?! Even in death, I'd take three bites out of such a person!"[14] Before he could take action, however, Chen was arrested and sentenced to a sixteen-year prison term.

Chen Ada's youthful exploits on the margins of orthodox Maoist society were not atypical of workers who became rebel leaders during the Cultural Revolution. Previous affiliation with all-male youth gangs seems to have been a formative experience for a number of activists. Shortly before the onset of the Cultural Revolution, for example, an alleged "KO counterrevolutionary clique" was uncovered at the Shanghai Diesel Engine Factory when some workshop cadres noticed that many of the younger workers had scratched the English initials "KO" onto their leather belts. Some of these same young men had posted inflammatory slogans on the factory walls, designed to incense their elders: "We can't but feel ashamed that half a month's wage is barely enough to buy a pair of leather shoes!" "Our spring has already lost its radiance!" "Let's hold dance parties at once!" "Long live women!"[15]

Most of the young male workers at the diesel engine plant lived in the factory dormitory or in the workers' residential district adjoining the factory. Far removed from the city center, they had few recreational options to fill their leisure time. Moreover, the economy had barely recovered from the disastrous period of 1959–62, and material pleasures were in short supply. The "KO" adherents were undoubtedly searching for some means of self-expression in the highly constrained environment of Maoist China. But after openly airing their frustrations, these young people were branded as dangerous elements. Although the selection of the "KO" insignia had been intended playfully (perhaps as a pun on the English word "okay," perhaps as an abbreviation for "knockout"), it was misconstrued as the secret password of some clandestine organization. Thus a "KO counterrevolutionary clique" was conjured up, which some thirty to forty workers were accused of joining. During the Cultural Revolution, the young men who had been charged with participation in the "KO clique" became backbone elements in one of the rebellious factions at the diesel engine plant.[16]

If young male workers were casting about for meaningful identities in the stifling atmosphere of the day, their methods of doing so were certainly not all of a piece. While some, like Chen Ada, seemed drawn to a kind of gangster machismo, others sought fulfillment in more aesthetic pursuits. This duality matches that which Kam Louie and Louise Edwards have highlighted within earlier periods of Chinese history. Although there was, they note, certainly a macho tradition in China, it was counterbalanced by "a softer, cerebral male tradition that is not found to the same degree in the secular West."[17] Although the ideal Chinese male was supposed to embody both attributes, aesthetic accomplishments (or *wen*) were often more highly prized than martial abilities (or *wu*).

The most famous worker-rebel leaders did indeed evidence both *wen* and *wu* qualities. Wang Hongwen, commander of the Workers' General Headquarters, had served in the army during the Korean War—but as a horn player rather than a soldier.[18] Pan Guoping, second in the leadership lineup during the early months of the Workers' General Headquarters, also combined military experience with more aesthetic inclinations. Pan Guoping's accomplishments were wide-ranging. In middle school he had been active in athletics. While a soldier, he had received second prize in an art contest. As a worker, he directed choral and theatrical troupes at the Workers' Cultural Palace. Pan's artistic flair left him dissatisfied with mundane factory labor, and he asked his superiors at the factory for permission to take the entrance exam for drama school. When the authorities refused to issue the letter of introduction that would have allowed him to sit for the examination, Pan developed a smoldering grudge—one that would burst into flames during the Cultural Revolution.

Pan Guoping's extraordinary gift for oratory (enhanced by a clear Mandarin accent cultivated for his thespian aspirations) propelled him to the forefront of the early rebel movement.[19] Despite his glib tongue, however, Pan came to be known as an unreliable loafer. He was widely referred to as a *xiao doulou*, Shanghai dialect for "hoodlum." Before long, Pan was expelled from the policy-making center of the Workers' General Headquarters, his title of vice-commander remaining only an empty appellation.[20]

Another important figure in the Workers' General Headquarters, Huang Jinhai, was known colloquially as a "dandy" *(afei fenzi)* because of his penchant for fancy attire. Huang's attraction to fashionable clothing rendered him a conspicuous figure in the drab atmosphere of Maoist China, where simplicity of dress was the near-universal norm.

As in the case of so many of the rebel leaders, Huang's childhood had been less than idyllic. Within a month after his birth, Huang's mother died of illness. His father was an opium addict who put his children up for adoption. When his foster mother could no longer afford to keep him, Huang was packed off to Shanghai to rejoin his natural father. Living with his still addicted and abusive father, he completed his elementary school education.[21]

In October 1950, at age sixteen, Huang Jinhai entered a private clothing shop as an apprentice. When the Three Antis and Five Antis campaign was launched two years later, Huang reported—to the "tiger-beating team" investigating capitalist abuses—that his boss had been withholding taxes. The shop was fined, and in May of that year it was closed down altogether. After an eight-month stint at an unemployed workers' training program, Huang attained a middle school certificate and was assigned to a cotton mill.[22]

At the mill, Huang Jinhai was known to be a diligent worker and energetic in extrawork pursuits. In spite of his dedication on the job, however, his opium-addicted father continued to present a problem. To support his drug dependence, Huang's father embezzled public funds—a crime for which he was sentenced to five years in prison. Huang Jinhai recalled, "When I heard this news I was devastated; I felt that I would never be able to cast off this terrible burden."[23]

Indeed, his father's impropriety became Huang Jinhai's Achilles's heel in the years ahead, blocking the recognition he felt he deserved:

> I knew that my application to enter the Youth League had been in limbo for many years, and now the prospects looked even dimmer. So I became depressed and no longer participated in extracurricular activities.
>
> The more I shouldered my political burden, the more despondent I became. For a time I grew a beard and spent most of my nonworking hours playing cards in the club. On Sundays, I went to the suburbs to fish instead of engaging in proper duties. I even bought a necktie and then went to a shop that sold exotica to buy a used Western suit. Sometimes I ventured to the city center in coat and tie. When I saw people wearing leather jackets, I spent more than forty yuan to buy one. I was totally preoccupied with my playboy lifestyle. My frivolous habits gave the older workers a very bad impression. I organized dances and the like, which the older workers didn't appreciate.[24]

Although we now know that Chairman Mao himself was enjoying dance parties—and more—within the protective walls of Zhongnanhai at this very time, such frivolity was not sanctioned for the populace at large.[25] As the political scientist Wang Shaoguang points out, the bleak economic situation following the Great Leap Forward had generated a strong ascetic tendency: "Now one might be considered backward if any aspect of one's life-style was out of the ordinary, such as wearing brightly colored clothes, applying hair oil, going to a restaurant, cultivating flowers, raising goldfish or playing chess."[26] Personal hobbies and eccentricities became grounds for designation as a "backward element" *(luohou fenzi),* even if one worked assiduously at one's job. Huang Jinhai, having been saddled with the label of "backward element" by his factory superiors, plunged into the Cultural Revolution with gusto.

The routes by which these leaders of the Workers' General Headquarters reached the point of rebellion were various, yet they shared in common the experience in their adolescence of having trodden paths that lay outside the officially approved channels for upward mobility in Communist China. The one notable exception to this pattern was Wang Xiuzhen—the lone woman among the nine top worker-rebel leaders. After 1967, Wang Xiuzhen ranked second in importance only to Commander Wang Hongwen. Thanks to Wang Hongwen's growing confidence in her, Wang Xiuzhen enjoyed a meteoric rise—becoming vice-chair of the Shanghai Revolutionary Committee, deputy-secretary of the Shanghai Party Committee, and vice-chair of the Shanghai Federation of Trade Unions. Wang Hongwen's favoritism toward Wang Xiuzhen probably stemmed in part from their shared native-place origins in Manchuria; it may also (as was widely rumored at the time) have grown out of a love affair between the two. In any case, it is clear that, whereas Wang Hongwen was suspicious of the motives of his fellow male rebels (who challenged his leadership on more than one occasion), he put full trust in the loyalty of Wang Xiuzhen. When Wang Hongwen "helicoptered" up to Beijing to become vice-chair of the Communist Party in 1973, it was Wang Xiuzhen whom he left in charge of the Shanghai scene.

In contrast to the male leaders of the Workers' General Headquarters, Wang Xiuzhen had enjoyed a relatively smooth work history. She had entered factory life in 1950, at the age of fifteen, as a weaver at the Liaoyang textile mill. Just at this time her father died of high blood pressure. Saddled with the entire financial burden of her struggling family, Wang labored diligently at her job. After two years, she entered the Communist Youth League and at the age of eighteen joined the Communist Party. Selected as an activist in her workshop, Wang was later celebrated as an "advanced producer" and a "labor model" at city, provincial, and northeast district levels. These were high honors, indeed the highest to which an industrious worker might normally aspire, and Wang had achieved them when she was only twenty years of age. But her accomplishments did not end there. Soon Wang Xiuzhen was named a people's representative to the city of Liaoyang and then to Liaoning province.

In August 1956, Wang Xiuzhen was sent to the Shanghai Textile Institute to develop her talents further. A few years later she was assigned to the number thirty cotton mill as a technician. Soon Wang was promoted to supervisor of the weaving workshop. This promising career was threatened, however, after the birth of her two children, when Wang was publicly criticized by the factory director for a deterioration in her work. Humiliated by this setback, she requested a transfer. Although temporarily loaned to the Textile Bureau to handle personnel dossiers, Wang was returned to her factory shortly before the Cultural Revolution began. After her reinstatement at the number thirty cotton mill, she managed dossiers in the factory director's office.[27]

Wang Xiuzhen had always been an activist, a target of cultivation by the Party. This made her unusual among the rebel leaders. At the start of the Cultural Revolution, thirty-two-year-old Wang Xiuzhen was even chosen as director of her factory's Cultural Revolution committee. Most workers with this sort of background became conservatives, but Wang was a notable exception. In explaining this anomaly, her fellow workers later pointed to Wang's ambition and avarice, charging that she had been afflicted with the "three clamors" (sanchao)—for wages, housing, and position.[28]

Wang Xiuzhen herself always insisted that her rebellion was a response to the call of Chairman Mao. However, she also emphasized that it was Wang Hongwen who had given her the personal courage to rebel. She later recalled, "Wang Hongwen told me how they had gone to Beijing to file a complaint against the work team at the number seventeen cotton mill and how the Cultural Revolution Small Group [composed of Chairman Mao's wife, Jiang Qing, and other radicals] had really supported them and asked them to return to wage battle against the capitalist line of the work team and the Shanghai Party Committee. . . . I felt emboldened and I went back and wrote a big-character-poster against the work team."[29]

The close relationship between the two Wangs was key both to Wang Xiuzhen's participation on the rebel side and to her rapid ascent up the leadership ladder of the Workers' General Headquarters. Unlike many of the other early rebel leaders, Wang Xiuzhen never questioned the supremacy of Wang Hongwen. As repayment for this allegiance, in early 1967 she was personally assigned by Wang Hongwen to the leadership of the Workers' General Headquarters to direct its propaganda and organization departments. From this point on, she became Wang Hongwen's most capable and most trusted lieutenant—second only to Wang Hongwen himself in the lineup of influential leaders of the Shanghai worker-rebel movement.

Wang Xiuzhen's enlistment under the rebel banner may have stemmed in part from embitterment over her reprimand following the birth of her two children. Forced into the double burden of child care and factory work, the lone woman among the top worker rebels was put at a disadvantage vis-à-vis her male coworkers. Even so, Wang does not seem to have translated her personal experience as a mother into a wider sympathy for the plight of women workers. There is no evidence to suggest that she used her substantial influence during the Cultural Revolution to articulate the special concerns of women workers.

Rather than serving as a champion for women's rights, Wang Xiuzhen focused her energies on ensuring that the "little brothers" remained obedient to Wang Hongwen's commands. Not having traversed the countercultural paths taken by so many of the male rebel leaders, she showed little patience for their sometimes freewheeling tendencies. It was not feisty independence, but rather her strict adherence to Wang Hongwen's orders, that secured Wang Xiuzhen's place in the leadership hierarchy.

## THE BAND OF BROTHERS

The emphasis on fraternal bonds helped to harmonize the divergent, and potentially discordant, strains with the rebel ranks. The resulting organizational synthesis drew upon both ancient and contemporary sources of inspiration.

In the tradition of the legendary bandit heroes of *All Men Are Brothers,* the worker rebels understood their rebellion as an act of loyalty to their king (Chairman Mao), whose will was being subverted by corrupt officials. Worker-rebel leader Dai Liqing later explained in his confession to the Public Security Bureau, "My constant thought was: 'People must follow the king's law like the grass must move with the wind.' . . . I had one desire: to obey Chairman Mao."[30] The ambition of the worker rebels, as with the heroes of Liangshanpo (home base of the bandits in *All Men Are Brothers*), was to wrest power from venal ("capitalist-roader") bureaucrats and assume such positions themselves. As Wang Hongwen stated in order to encourage his fellow rebels at the outset of the movement, "The Cultural Revolution is a great upheaval; upheavals give birth to heroes. As the saying goes, 'Victors become kings while the vanquished become outlaws.' Right now the situation is very favorable. Rebellion at the municipal level can gain us the mayorship; at the department level, directorships; and at lower levels, factory headships."[31] Or, as Dai Liqing confided to his roommates in the factory dormitory, "Last night I had a big dream. I was the emperor's son-in-law, a big official. Ha, ha! If I can be a big official, you can all become officials."[32]

At times, the similarities between the activities of the worker rebels and those of rebels of yore were quite striking. Once they had decided to form their new Workers' General Headquarters, for example, the founders agreed that they must immediately issue distinctive armbands. Like peasant rebels of imperial days, the worker rebels now faced the daunting task of procuring enough fabric to produce their identifying cloth badges.[33] Wang

Hongwen, having just been named "commander" of the WGH, announced that he would assume personal responsibility for securing the requisite red cloth to make armbands for his followers. Accordingly, he gathered a dozen or so fellow workers and Red Guards for a midnight raid on a fabric store. When the store clerk demanded that the rebels pay for their bolts of cloth, Wang retorted, "Tell old man Cao [i.e., Shanghai's mayor, Cao Diqiu] to foot the bill!"[34] The first "rebel action" of the newly constituted Workers' General Headquarters was thus a plundering expedition.

As had been true of secret societies in the past, the worker rebels turned to religious terminology—drawn especially from the Buddhist tradition—to empower their community. For example, Wang Hongwen referred to his top lieutenants as the "eight guardian gods" (bada jingang) in a boastful allusion to the four guardian gods (sida jingang) stationed at the entrance way to Buddhist temples. Other terms of Buddhist derivation were adapted by the worker rebels to symbolize their own virility. The phrase "horns on the head and thorns on the body"—originally a derogatory idiom referring to the denizens of Buddhist hell—was embraced by the worker rebels as expressive of their own fighting spirit. When Zhang Chunqiao advocated replacing toppled cadres with worker rebels, he alluded to the devilish imagery espoused by the workers themselves: "Those with long horns on their heads and long thorns on their bodies [toushang changjiao shenshang changci] should be sent to the center to raise a ruckus."[35]

Similarly, terms that had once connoted impudence (such as pola) were now used to characterize a proper revolutionary style. In recommending "little brothers" for admission to the Party or for promotion to cadre positions, the designation "impudent work style" (zuofeng pola) in their dossiers served as a ringing endorsement of a bold and vigorous manner. Ye Changming, the worker rebel who headed the Shanghai Federation of Trade Unions, described his method for choosing union cadres: "I considered whether or not they had been rebels, whether or not they had rebel spirit and fighting spirit as well as guts and impudence [dadan pola]—a willingness to speak out and make suggestions. I then considered whether or not they had feelings for the 'Gang of Four'; whether they would stick by us was a most important question. . . . After using these 'gang' [bang] criteria to make the initial cut, direct meetings and discussions were held to choose the people we needed."[36] Through means such as these, Wang Hongwen's faithful followers were rewarded first with union positions and then with Party and government offices. Worker rebels in the trade union convened regular brainstorming sessions that were, in effect, planning meetings to increase their leverage over Party and government affairs. Wang Xiuzhen noted that "after a brainstorming session, the 'little brothers' took the contents of the session to all departments of the Shanghai Revolutionary Committee and concerned bureaus."[37] Thanks to such stratagems, the rebels gained an impressive foothold in city politics. As Ye Changming recalled, "The 'little brothers' formed a 'gang' *[bang]* in both the municipal party committee and the municipal revolutionary committee."[38]

Reliance on a fraternal-gang model of organization had important implications for the collective identity of the worker rebels. As Elisabeth Clemens argues in her study of American labor, "Strategic choices between organizational models reveal themselves to be also choices between goals and collective identities."[39] The turn-of-the-century U.S. labor movement, Clemens shows, drew alternatively upon a fraternal model provided by the Masons (whose similarities to the Chinese Triads have often been noted) and a military model (borrowed from the American Civil War experience).[40] Although Clemens does not explore the gendered dimensions of these traditionally all-male institutional prototypes, it seems clear that they emphasized somewhat different dimensions of masculinity. Whereas Masonic lodges valued sentimental bonds of brotherly obligation, the army stressed impersonal obedience to higher orders.

Shanghai's worker rebels, like other Cultural Revolution activists, were influenced to some extent by military models of organization. The attraction of military exemplars was heightened by Mao's famous slogan, raised on the eve of the Cultural Revolution campaign, "Let the whole nation learn from the People's Liberation Army." Four of the top leaders of the Workers' General Headquarters—Wang Hongwen, Geng Jinzhang, Pan Guoping, and Chen Ada—had served in the People's Liberation Army (PLA) before the start of the Cultural Revolution. Not surprisingly, the groups they founded were given martial names: "Warriors Sworn to the Death to Carry Through with the Cultural Revolution to the End," "Mao Zedong Thought Warriors," "First Regiment," "Frontline Command Post to Grasp Revolution and Promote Production," and so forth. Military terminology was also drawn from China's prerevolutionary history: Wang Hongwen referred to five of his top advisors as his "five tiger generals" *(wu hujiang),* for example.[41]

Although the military was not insignificant as a source of inspiration for the worker rebels, the outlaw gang seems to have provided a much more compelling organizational paradigm. (The two were not entirely separate, of course, inasmuch as many bandit outfits and secret societies had also imitated certain military arrangements.)[42] As was true of gangs, the worker rebels were structured by personalistic patron-client bonds rather than by impersonal ranks. For example, the induction of new members into Shanghai's Green Gang, which required swearing fealty to a gang master, had been known colloquially as "honoring an old man" *(bai laotouzi).* During the Cultural Revolution, Zhang Chunqiao often boasted that the worker rebels in Shanghai "all regard me as their 'old man' *[ba wo dang laotouzi].*"[43]

Pledging brotherhood was another secret-society practice resuscitated by the worker rebels. Though "revolutionary comrade" was the politically correct address of the day, the worker rebels preferred the fraternal nomenclature of the gangs of old. The phenomenon was not unique to Shanghai. A participant in the Cultural Revolution in Wuhan recalls, "I once attended a meeting of the worker rebels. They referred to one another as 'brothers,' patted each other on the shoulder, clasped hands, uttered gangster language, went shoeless and with unbuttoned shirts—the spitting image of the old-style Green and Red Gangs."[44] The designation "brother" implied intimate obligations of mutual aid and loyalty that superseded officially sanctioned relationships. Among the worker rebels of Shanghai, the phrase *youshu*, meaning "it's under control," served as a kind of watchword—taking precedence over Party directives or national regulations. A rebel who found himself in trouble with the law (e.g., Dai Liqing killed a peasant while driving without a license, Chen Ada habitually harassed women sexually, and so forth) could be spared a jail sentence by a simple *youshu* from his "little brothers."[45]

What this camaraderie suggests about the sexuality of the rebel leaders is impossible to say with confidence. We do know that, when the WGH Standing Committee ordered an investigation into the behavior of several hundred of its top leaders, illicit sexual relations—both homosexual and heterosexual—figured prominently among the alleged transgressions.[46] Of course, homosexuality was not unknown in the Chinese secret-society tradition, particularly among pirate gangs.[47]

As David Ownby has shown, brotherhood associations in China since the late imperial period were "created by marginalized men seeking mutual protection and mutual aid in a dangerous and competitive society."[48] The chief function of the brotherhood was to provide security and assistance in times of trouble. Like their imperial forebears, the worker rebels of the Cultural Revolution were, for the most part, marginal young men in search of solace and safety. And although members of the Workers' General Headquarters did not swear a formal blood oath of fictive kinship, they took their mutual obligations seriously.[49]

At first glance, it may seem curious that a woman—Wang Xiuzhen—ruled over the band of brothers after Wang Hongwen left for higher political office in Beijing. Though the rank-and-file worker rebels derisively dubbed her the "housekeeping mother-in-law" (*guanjiapo*) behind her back, Wang wielded enormous power in Shanghai during the Cultural Revolution. Interestingly, the practice of female leadership, too, has precedents among the outlaw gangs of old. Women bandit chiefs were well-known figures in the late imperial and Republican periods.[50]

Sworn brotherhood was thus not an insuperable barrier to female leadership. Within the Triad secret-society tradition in particular, it was not uncommon for women—especially widows or paramours of powerful male chieftains—to assume leadership roles.[51] The famous woman pirate Zheng Yi Sao fit squarely within this mode.[52] Wang Xiuzhen's close relationship to Wang Hongwen was reminiscent of this familiar pattern. While a single, powerful female leader—deriving her legitimacy from intimate association with a slain or absent male commander—may have long been a part of the gang model of organization, broader participation by women was less easily accommodated within this fraternal framework. Women might serve as domineering stepmothers or mothers-in-law, but not as ordinary sisters.

The prevalence of brotherly imagery in rebel and revolutionary movements is, of course, hardly unique to China. Lynn Hunt notes in her provocative study of the French Revolution that "in their own self-image, then, the French revolutionaries remained brothers. They were romantic heroes . . . prepared to become martyrs to their cause, either on the battlefield or in the line of official duties. They expected the gratitude of the nation, but their chief reward was their sense of solidarity with their brothers."[53] Hunt is describing a situation in which the political father (Louis XVI) had been executed and a quest for a new political family was under way. By contrast, in Cultural Revolution China the political father (Chairman Mao) remained very much alive. As a consequence, the initiatives of the worker rebels—important as they were in placing workers in political posts and in raising the status of the proletariat in Chinese society—remained dependent upon the approval of higher authority. Thus, although the worker rebels had harbored ambitions of implementing a new Shanghai People's Commune, modeled on the Paris Commune of 1871, Chairman Mao quickly called a halt to the experiment.[54] The band of brothers was in the end subservient to the imperial will of Beijing—more in the tradition of the Liangshanpo outlaws than of the Paris revolutionaries.

Whereas the French fraternalism described by Hunt implied egalitarian relations among men (albeit not women), the Chinese vision of brotherhood was inherently hierarchical. The very term for "brothers" in Chinese *(xiongdi)* combines the unequal duo of "elder brother" *(xiong)* and "younger brother" *(di)*. According to Confucian norms, elder brothers were expected to offer moral guidance, while younger brothers were enjoined to display proper deference. Ruling these unequal siblings (or fictive brethren in the case of secret-society gangs) were stern fathers (or gang masters). In China, the principal distinction between fraternal and military models was thus not one of egalitarianism versus hierarchy but rather one of personal, family-style obligations versus impersonal, rank-based obedience.

## CONCLUSION

That the worker rebels were so influenced by secret-society precedents may help to shed light on several anomalous features of their movement, especially when compared to the student movement—whose chief inspiration (as Emily Honig explains) derived from military models. Whereas the workers were content to adopt the fraternal appellation of "little brother," the Red Guards proudly referred to themselves as "little generals." This fundamental difference in identity—bandit brother versus military commander—was reflected in the distinctive organization and activities of the two mass movements during the Cultural Revolution.

Although the student Red Guards seem to have preferred sexually segregated outfits, reflecting the situation in the Chinese army (as well as in some elite schools), the worker rebels operated in a somewhat more integrated fashion. Despite the overwhelmingly male composition of their leadership ranks, the workers did permit women to take charge of male subordinates. By contrast, the student Red Guards—mimicking PLA practices—seem to have tolerated female leadership only in all-female units. Moreover, unlike the women workers (who continued to wear their regular work clothes), female Red Guards donned male military uniforms. The latter practice evoked the legend of Hua Mulan, the mythical woman warrior who—disguised as a man—served for years in the army in her father's stead.

The all-female Red Guard units, as Honig notes, were often prone to extraordinary brutality. Rebel workers, on the other hand, proved far less violent than their student counterparts. In testimony, one worker rebel expressed shock at the cruel tactics of the students: "Red Guards came to our factory and captured sixteen of our rebels, using leather whips to torture them. They also made us kneel on little stools for as long as four hours. They shaved the heads of these sixteen comrades and wrote the characters "ox-devils and snake-spirits" on their bodies. Fourteen workers were injured and all sixteen were tortured in a torture chamber that the Red Guards set up. More than forty struggle sessions were convened, and some of our comrades were locked up for one to two weeks."[55]

Shanghai's worker rebels were certainly involved in several major bloody confrontations, most notably the Kangping Road incident of December 1966 (in which 91 conservative workers were wounded so seriously that they required hospitalization) and the assault on the Shanghai Diesel Engine Factory in August 1967 (in which 121 workers were permanently disabled from their injuries). However, even these large-scale armed struggles did not result in fatalities among the combatants.[56] Again the contrast with the Red Guards is telling: in the single month of September 1966 Shanghai suffered 704 suicides and 354 murders linked to student-instigated violence.[57]

Although it is impossible to determine exactly how much of the difference between student and worker initiatives was attributable to their distinctive organizational paradigms, it seems clear that the personal leadership of "gang masters" Zhang Chunqiao and Wang Hongwen was a critical factor in moderating the struggles of the worker rebels. In the tradition of gang chieftains, Zhang and Wang wielded enormous authority over the "little brothers" of the Workers' General Headquarters. Their decision to confiscate factory weaponry and to welcome erstwhile conservatives and renegade rebels to the ranks of the WGH helped to prevent an unrestrained reign of terror of the sort that Red Guards were then visiting upon much of the country.[58]

The most notable aspect of Shanghai's worker-rebel activism was not their violence—which pales in comparison to that of the students—but their pursuit of political power. After the January Revolution of 1967, worker rebels at the instigation of Zhang Chunqiao and Wang Hongwen augmented their political influence through a variety of programs: worker representatives, workers' Mao Zedong thought-propaganda teams, workers' theory troops, workers' new cadres, worker ambassadors, and the like. When the Shanghai Federation of Trade Unions was reestablished in 1973 as a metamorphosed Workers' General Headquarters, it was a remarkably powerful organization that often usurped Party prerogatives—especially in the area of personnel matters.[59] Although worker initiatives were limited by the ultimate authority of Chairman Mao, the "band of brothers" did make serious efforts to enhance the status of the proletariat in Chinese political life. Having operated on the fringes of orthodox society for many years, Shanghai's worker rebels—in the venerable tradition of Chinese rebel movements—seized the opportunity presented by the Cultural Revolution to forge a new brotherhood based on a common quest for political inclusion.

## NOTES

1. A fuller discussion of the Workers' General Headquarters can be found in Elizabeth J. Perry and Li Xun, *Proletarian Power: Shanghai in the Cultural Revolution* (Boulder, Colo.: Westview Press, 1997).

2. Kay Ann Johnson, *Women, the Family, and Peasant Revolution in China* (Chicago: University of Chicago Press, 1983). During the Criticize Lin Biao—Criticize Confucius Campaign of the mid-1970s, condemnation of "patriarchy" was officially encouraged. This occurred well after the demobilization of the mass movement, however.

3. Marilyn B. Young, "Chicken Little in China: Women after the Cultural Revolution," in *Promissory Notes: Women in the Transition to Socialism*, ed. Sonia Kruks, Rayna Rapp, and Marilyn B. Young (New York: Monthly Review Press, 1989), 234–35.

4. Workers' General Headquarters, ed., *Shanghai gongren geming zaofan zongsilingbu zaofandui zuzhi qingkuang tongji biao* [Statistical tables on the rebel organizations of the Shanghai Workers' Revolutionary Rebels General Headquarters], manuscript, November 1967, Shanghai Municipal Archives.

5. Judith M. Bennett, "Feminism and History," *Gender and History* 1, no. 3 (autumn 1989): 263–64 points out the usefulness of examining gender relations in times of crisis. See also Joan Wallach Scott, *Gender and the Politics of History* (New York: Columbia University Press, 1988), 40–41, on the need to historicize "the terms of sexual difference."

6. Edgar Snow, *Red Star over China* (New York: Grove Press, 1968), 133.

7. Ibid., 78–79, 135, 210, 221, 332.

8. Stuart R. Schram, ed., *The Political Thought of Mao Tse-tung* (New York: Praeger, 1969), 260–61.

9. For a discussion of the activities of Shanghai's most powerful twentieth-century gang, see Brian G. Martin, *The Shanghai Green Gang: Politics and Organization, 1919–1937* (Berkeley and Los Angeles: University of California Press, 1996). Shanghai also had traditions of sisterhood, especially among factory workers. See Emily Honig, *Sisters and Strangers: Women in the Shanghai Cotton Mills, 1919–1949* (Stanford: Stanford University Press, 1986).

10. See, for example, Harry Brod and Michael Kaufman, eds., *Theorizing Masculinities* (Thousand Oaks, Calif.: Sage Publications, 1994); Jeff Hearn and David Morgan, eds., *Men, Masculinities, and Social Theory* (London: Unwin Hyman, 1990); and *Theory and Society* 22, no. 5 (October 1993).

11. Chen Ada, August 10, 1977, testimony in the Shanghai Municipal Archives.

12. Shanghai Party Committee Cultural Revolution Materials Small Group, ed., *Shanghai "wenhua dageming" shihua* [Historical narrative of the "Great Cultural Revolution" in Shanghai], manuscript, p. 135, 1992, Shanghai Municipal Archives.

13. *Jiefang ribao* [Liberation daily], November 20, 1977.

14. Ibid., 164–66.

15. Chen Xianfa, *Minzu lei* [National tears] (Shanghai: Tongji University Press, 1988).

16. For more on the factional struggle at the Shanghai Diesel Engine Factory, see Perry and Li, *Proletarian Power*, 132–41.

17. Kam Louie and Louise Edwards, "Chinese Masculinity: Theorizing *Wen* and *Wu*," *East Asian History* 8 (1994): 138.

18. Shanghai Party Committee Small Group to Investigate the Gang of Four Case, ed., *Fandang fenzi Wang Hongwen zuixing nianbiao* [Chronology of criminal activities of antiparty element Wang Hongwen], manuscript, March 1977, Shanghai Municipal Archives.

19. Pan Guoping, interview by author, Berkeley, Calif., January 14, 1997.

20. Liu Guande, interview by Li Xun, Shanghai, 1987. Liu was a writer who also undertook a lengthy interview with Pan Guoping after the latter's release from prison in 1987. See also Pan Guoping, April 24 and 29, 1977, testimony in the Shanghai Municipal Archives.

21. Huang Jinhai, April 5, 1977, testimony in the Shanghai Municipal Archives.

22. Ibid.

23. Ibid.

24. Ibid.

25. Li Zhisui, *The Private Life of Chairman Mao* (New York: Random House, 1994), 93–94, 280, 345–46, 356, 479.

26. Wang Shaoguang, *Failure of Charisma: The Cultural Revolution in Wuhan* (New York: Oxford University Press, 1995), 34.

27. Wang Xiuzhen, 1980, testimony in the Shanghai Municipal Archives; Shanghai Party Committee Cultural Revolution Materials Small Group, ed., *Shanghai "wenhua dageming" shihua.*

28. Shanghai Party Committee Cultural Revolution Materials Small Group, ed., *Shanghai "wenhua dageming" shihua.*

29. Wang Xiuzhen, 1980 testimony.

30. Dai Liqing, October 18, 1979, testimony in the Shanghai Municipal Archives.

31. Shanghai Party Committee Cultural Revolution Materials Small Group, ed., *Shanghai "wenhua dageming" shihua,* 172.

32. Ibid., 137.

33. On the expense involved in procuring cloth for turbans and sashes for a nineteenth-century rebellion, see Susan Naquin, *Millenarian Rebellion in China: The Eight Trigrams Uprising of 1813* (New Haven: Yale University Press, 1976), 151.

34. Shanghai Party Committee Cultural Revolution Materials Small Group, ed., *Shanghai "wenhua dageming" shihua,* 141.

35. *Guangming ribao,* November 30, 1976.

36. Ye Changming, June 14, 1977, testimony in the Shanghai Municipal Archives.

37. Wang Xiuzhen, June 15, 1978, testimony in the Shanghai Municipal Archives.

38. Ye Changming, April 5, 1977, testimony in the Shanghai Municipal Archives.

39. Elisabeth S. Clemens, "Organizational Form as Frame: Collective Identity and Political Strategy in the American Labor Movement, 1880–1920," in *Comparative Perspectives on Social Movements,* ed. Doug McAdam, John D. McCarthy, and Mayer N. Zald (Cambridge: Cambridge University Press, 1996), 212.

40. Clemens, "Organizational Form as Frame," 205–26.

41. Liu Guande, interview by Li Xun, Shanghai, 1987, 405.

42. Elizabeth J. Perry, *Rebels and Revolutionaries in North China, 1845–1945* (Stanford: Stanford University Press, 1980), 70, 197–205.

43. Liu Guande, interview by Li Xun, Shanghai, 1987, 404.

44. Xu Mingxu, "Shilun wenge wenhua" [A preliminary discussion of the culture of the Cultural Revolution] (paper delivered at the "Conference on the Cultural Revolution and Its Consequences," University of California at Berkeley, January 10–11, 1977), 11.

45. Liu Guande, interview by Li Xun, Shanghai, 1987, 405, 446.

46. Workers' General Headquarters, "Guanyu yuan gezu, xian, ju, lianluozhan yishang changwei bei juliu, daibu de qingkuang baogao" [Situation report on detentions and arrests of standing committees at district, county, bureau liaison posts and above], manuscript, April 19, 1969, Shanghai Municipal Archives.

47. See Dian H. Murray, *Pirates of the South China Coast, 1790–1810* (Stanford: Stanford University Press, 1987).

48. David Ownby, *Brotherhoods and Secret Societies in Early and Mid-Qing China* (Stanford: Stanford University Press, 1996), 2.

49. Pan Guoping, interview by author, January 14, 1997.

50. Perry, *Rebels and Revolutionaries in North China,* 67n.

51. The ranks of the nineteenth-century Taiping rebellion were swelled when two female Triad chiefs from Guangxi joined the movement, each bringing several thousand followers with her. Theodore Hamberg, *The Visions of Hung-siu-tshuen and Origin of the Kwang-si Insurrection* (New York: Praeger, 1969), 54–55.

52. Murray, *Pirates of the South China Coast,* 152–53.

53. Lynn Hunt, *The Family Romance of the French Revolution* (Berkeley and Los Angeles: University of California Press, 1992), 79–80.

54. Andrew G. Walder, *Chang Chu'un-ch'iao and Shanghai's January Revolution* (Ann Arbor: University of Michigan Center for Chinese Studies, 1978).

55. Jiang Zhoufa, November 9, 1966, testimony in the Shanghai Municipal Archives.

56. The official history of the Cultural Revolution in Shanghai, published by the Shanghai Party Committee, does list one death in conjunction with the attack on the diesel engine factory, but other sources do not mention any deaths.

57. Shanghai Party Committee Cultural Revolution Materials Small Group, ed., *Shanghai "wenhua dageming" shihua.*

58. Perry and Li, *Proletarian Power,* 141–44.

59. Ibid., chap. 6.

PART SIX

# Blood, *Qi*, and the Gendered Body

Both Charlotte Furth's and Nancy Chen's chapters illustrate that, in China, notions of manliness, womanliness, and sexuality could be quite different from the European and American versions grounded in Western biology and medical science. The classical Chinese medical tradition presents an alternative understanding of the sexed body—its reproductive physiology, sexuality, and associated gender traits. In this tradition, *qi* and "blood" were the two most important life substances, and health and illness were defined as problems of vitality or depletion. Although male and female bodies contained both substances, blood tended to have associations of femaleness and *qi* of maleness. Women's blood was considered to be constantly depleted by childbirth and menstruation; moreover, to be ruled by one's blood meant that one was controlled by one's emotions. Thus, physiology was used to justify women's submission to the superior vitality of men.

Furth's book, *A Flourishing Yin: Gender in China's Medical History, 960–1665*, traces in much greater detail the role of gender in the classical Chinese medical tradition in the seven centuries before the period described in her chapter here.

Two centuries after that period, Nancy Chen finds that physiology is associated with gender in subtle ways that seem to reinforce male superiority. *Qigong* masters are quintessential examples of people who possess powerful vitality and are able to tightly control it. Almost invariably these masters are men, and one of the few women masters aroused suspicion and was ultimately jailed. More than half of the followers of the masters, however, are women.

There are very few books that discuss both concepts of the body and gender in China. It is hard to identify a common theme in these works other than the fact that they illustrate that the body is the starting point for a vast array of cultural beliefs about life, love, and the universe—and that these beliefs can be very different from Western beliefs. Kristofer Schipper's *The Taoist Body* describes the bodily training regimen of Taoist priests in Taiwan in the 1960s and 1970s. All of the priests he describes are men, no doubt for reasons similar to those outlined by Furth and Chen, but since he does not analyze this or other gender issues in his book they remain in the background. Angela Zito and Tani Barlow's edited collection, *Body, Subject, and Power in China,* covers a diverse array of topics, including conceptions of wind and sickness, the absence of a tradition of nudes in Chinese art, the role of the kowtow in rural Shandong weddings, and so on. It also covers all of recorded Chinese history from the Shang dynasty to the 1990s. Susan Brownell's *Training the Body for China: Sports in the Moral Order of the People's Republic* describes the larger relationship between the body, gender, and the nation that formed the background for the experiences of state-supported elite athletes in the 1980s and 1990s. One of her arguments is that the body occupies a particularly prominent role in Chinese social relationships, and that bodily metaphors are central in many different aspects of Chinese culture (the "somatization" of Chinese culture).

This point is illustrated by Gang Yue's *The Mouth That Begs: Hunger, Cannibalism, and the Politics of Eating in Modern China,* a creative history of the relationship between eating and politics in China that surveys all the ways in which this basic bodily function has served as a central metaphor of social and political life—ways that Yue feels are unique to the Chinese culture of the time. Although gender is by no means central to the book, the book does contain numerous interesting observations on the relation of women to this key metaphor.

Mo Yan's novel *Red Sorghum,* which was the basis for Zhang Yimou's much-acclaimed film of the same name, is (like the film) replete with vivid descriptions of sexuality, rape, blood, skin, bones, and other bodily acts and parts.[1] The end result is two works that almost pull the reader's or viewer's own body into the story by means of sympathetic pains, producing something like an embodied experience of the events described, which take place during the Japanese occupation of the 1930s. The fact that the story is told through the eyes of a grandson recollecting the life of his grandmother and grandfather leads to interesting issues of gender and voice.

## NOTES

1. The gender images in this film are discussed by Yeujin Wang, "Mixing Memory and Desire: *Red Sorghum,* a Chinese Version of Masculinity and Femininity," *Public Culture* 2, no. 1 (fall 1989): 31–53.

## COMPLEMENTARY READINGS AND VIDEOS

Brownell, Susan. *Training the Body for China: Sports in the Moral Order of the People's Republic.* Chicago: University of Chicago Press, 1995.

Furth, Charlotte. *A Flourishing Yin: Gender in China's Medical History, 960–1665.* Berkeley and Los Angeles: University of California Press, 1999.

Mo Yan. *Red Sorghum.* Trans. Howard Goldblatt. 1988. Reprint, New York: Penguin Books, 1993.

*Red Sorghum* [Hong gaoliang]. Directed by Zhang Yimou. Distributed by China Film Import Export and New Yorker Films, New York, 1991. Videocassette.

Schipper, Kristofer. *The Taoist Body.* Trans. Karen C. Duval. 1982. Reprint, Berkeley and Los Angeles: University of California Press, 1993.

Yue Gang. *The Mouth That Begs: Hunger, Cannibalism, and the Politics of Eating in Modern China.* Durham: Duke University Press, 1999.

Zito, Angela, and Tani Barlow, eds. *Body, Subject, and Power in China.* Chicago: University of Chicago Press, 1994.

# CHAPTER ELEVEN

# Blood, Body, and Gender: Medical Images of the Female Condition in China, 1600–1850

*Charlotte Furth*

Menstruation, when it has been thought of as an acceptable subject for scholarly inquiry at all, has been studied mostly by anthropologists interested in women and ritual pollution. In many cultures, including China's, folk practice shows that female blood has been shunned as dangerous. Imagined as a source of contagion, liable to make crops wither and to offend the gods, it has been associated with female threats to forms of cosmic and social order managed and defended by men. Some anthropologists, such as Mary Douglas, have argued that menstrual blood, like other bodily discharges, is symbolically linked with dangers to social order because it is "matter out of place" that has left the normal confines of the body to mark the perilous transitions of birth and reproduction. In such a view, ritual avoidances and taboos symbolically restore cosmic and social boundaries, and they suggest control over the powers of life and death associated with conception and birth.[1] Other interpretations emphasize that pollution beliefs express male anxiety over female power and male unease at society's dependence upon women as childbearers.[2] In both views, a culture's beliefs about female pollution shape the way it defines gender—the social construction of sexual differences. Menstrual taboos represent women as sources of dirt and disorder yet mistresses of generation. These taboos create a symbolic system in which female pollution and female power are intertwined, warred on by male authority.

A difficulty with these anthropological accounts of gender has been that "the power of pollution" has never easily translated into social categories that reflect women's experiences rather than male myths and fantasies. No one has shown that pollution beliefs are strongest in cultures where male solidarity is in fact most threatened, or that women themselves are normally aware of their condition as "power." These omissions suggest that explanations of gender in China (and elsewhere) that are based on folk taboos surrounding female blood may be flawed or at least incomplete.

My strategy in this chapter is to look beyond popular attitudes to medical symbolizations of female blood in China. The presence of a premodern, literate, massively documented Chinese medical tradition enables us to see theories about female biology in complex historical development, and to trace alternative perceptions of social roles based on them. We can thus see how pollution beliefs were transformed in a classical system of thought that contributed to a more elaborate and diverse gender system. The tradition recorded in the medical literature was not merely an elite alternative to folk practice, but an eclectic system that constantly borrowed and adapted grassroots ritual and medical ideas, and then fed these back into the mainstream of popular culture, often in altered form.[3] The medical texts that I draw upon here date from the late sixteenth to the late nineteenth centuries. They range from imperially sponsored encyclopedias to popular household manuals. Without exception they reflect a mixture of scholastic, ritual, and empirical modes of reasoning, in the course of which female biology was redefined, not around symbolic poles of power, purity, and pollution but around those of vitality and loss. What emerges is positive model of female generativity, symbolized by the menstrual function but seen as a biological exchange economy that condemned women to bodily depletion and loss. In the course of elaborating this model, Chinese medical experts developed stereotypes of female sickliness and emotionality that contrast with the "power of pollution" of folk taboo. Their conceptions suggest a gender system that stressed female weakness and enslavement to reproductive necessity.

"In women, blood is the ruling aspect" *(nüzi . . . yi xue wei zhu)*, wrote Li Shih-chen in 1596.[4] On one level this was a worldwide medical cliché, generalized from women's reproductive functions. However, in classical Chinese thought this commonplace observation must be seen against the background of a theory of the human organism in which *xue* (blood) stands for life energy at several levels of generality, always paired with a male principle, *qi* (untranslatable but sometimes rendered as *pneuma* or *breath*).[5]

Most abstractly, "*qi* and blood" *(qi-xue)* referred to the vitality underlying all organic processes and essential to the survival of all the organ systems of the body, but not specific to certain bodily functions or structures. It was in part "prenatal" *(xiantian)*, or "received from Heaven," that is, an endowment that is bestowed at conception. When *qi* and blood are exhausted, the human being dies.

Other aspects of *qi* and blood are "dependent upon food and drink." Postnatal *(houtian)* vitality is produced in the functioning material body, which needs nutrients to survive and grow. This aspect of *qi* and blood is derived from, if not entirely reducible to, food and breath. In keeping with this, Chinese biology identified two reservoirs of vitality in the body—the "sea of blood" *(xue hai)*, a lower abdominal center that stored the energy of generation and assimilation, and the "sea of breath" *(qi hai)* in the chest area, which concentrated the energy of respiration. Thus paired, two forms of energy flow through the body's circulation tracts.[6]

All of these connotations of blood and *qi* keep to the symmetrical yin-yang dualism underlying Chinese cosmology.[7] Symbolically, they show blood sexualized as female both in the formal aspects of the dualism—according to the familiar complementary poles—and, more strikingly, by blood's internal dependency in any pairing. In terms of the basic cosmology outlined in the *Book of Changes* (I ching), blood is "receptive" *(kun)*. In thinking of body functions, the medical men put it this way: "Blood follows *qi.*"[8]

Even more specific female associations of blood begin to emerge in the paired term "essence and blood" ( *jing-xue,* literally, semen and blood). At times "essence and blood" refers to the concentrated form of life energy in the functioning organism. In this usage it is close to the second meaning of "*qi* and blood" above. The buried metaphor in "*qi* and blood" evokes the assimilation of food and the respiration of air, but that in "essence and blood" suggests reproduction. This is because of the literal meaning, which implies the male and female contributions to the conception of a child or, even more, the generative capacities of both sexes. Each sex draws on reservoirs of both "essence and blood." Thus women are said to have sexual fluids (essence), and male "essence" (semen) is made of blood.

Finally, there is "yin blood" *(yin xue)*, the aspect of blood identified with the woman's contribution to reproduction as a physical process. Yin blood is the unity underlying all manifest forms of reproductive fluid: it appears now as menses, now as breast milk, now as the blood that nourishes the fetus.

Within the yin-yang dualism, the symbolic depictions of blood in human biology, which are more explicitly feminized as functions, move from the supraphenomenal realm of creation, associated with *qi* and heaven; pass through a sphere of body growth and maintenance based on relatively complementary yin-yang functions; and reach the concretely material female sphere of sexual acts and reproductive processes. In both males and females, the sexual zones of the body are "yin," as in *yin zhong* for the center of generation below the navel, or *yin chu,* "private parts." Still, although its materiality identified the sexual realm with female aspects of the cosmic dualism, female generativity was never divorced from cosmic creation but allowed to share in it on a lower plane. Similarly, a woman's sexual function, like a man's, was seen as dependent upon the energy of "essence" *(jing)*, a yang energy symbolically associated with maleness.

Dozens of common folk beliefs and practices show the traditional Chinese fear of blood loss, a fear that gains strength from these symbolic associations. Even today, many older Chinese remain suspicious of hypodermic injections that draw blood. The association of blood with specifically female forms of vitality is especially clear in classical prescriptions for the use of human blood in medicine. Since the sixteenth century, the standard classic of pharmacy has been the *Pen ts'ao kang mu*, by Li Shih-chen (1518–93), a brilliant and encyclopedic rationalizer of two thousand years of pharmaceutical tradition.[9] Li classified medicinal "blood" in four forms: plain blood, menses, breast milk, and placenta. The interchangeability of the last three is clear from his remarks explaining the nature of breast milk: "It is made of transformed yin blood; it grows due to the action of the digestive systems and is maintained and supported by the action of the highway and conception channels [*chong ren mai*]. Before conception it appears as menses below; during pregnancy it provides nourishment for the fetus; after birth, red changing to white, it ascends as milk. The subtleties of these creative transformations are nature's marvels."[10] Moreover, while authorities on pharmacy labeled plain blood "toxic" *(du)*—that is, a powerful substance with dangerous side effects if incorrectly used—the other three were classified as benign *(wu du)*.

Table 1 outlines the commoner types of disorders that blood in its various forms could be used to cure.[11] As the table suggests, blood worked first of all to replace itself. It was prescribed as a remedy for traumatic blood loss, especially from wounds by weapons, bites, or mauling by wild animals. It served to counteract the effects of abnormal bloody discharges, such as nosebleeds, bloodshot eyes, hemorrhages or the exudates of certain ulcerations and sores. A second major group of disorders responsive to blood were sexual dysfunctions in males and wasting diseases identified with serious blood or *qi* depletion. In the form of placenta and breast milk, blood was highly recommended for males as "yang support" to preserve a youthful body and prolong life. Placenta was often prescribed for barren women and as a postpartum tonic. In sum, these various forms of female yin blood were prized for efficacy against most disorders treatable by plain blood, and for others as well, particularly where a deficiency of sexual vitality was implicated. Judging by the frequency of recommendation, these were treatments of choice.

Moreover, it is clear that Li Shih-chen, as a scholarly gentleman, excluded from his catalogue a large number of popular recipes that used menstrual blood to increase vitality and potency. Indeed, his commentary criticized the "practitioners of heterodox arts" *(xieshujia)* who concocted the menstrual "red lead" or peddled breast milk as "converted menses that makes mother's milk" *(fan jing wei ru)*.[12] He predicted that the men who took these doses would dissipate the sexual vitality they wished to hoard. Other sources indicate that such remedies enjoyed a lively underground reputation in late Ming elite circles.[13]

TABLE 1    Therapeutic Use of Substances Derived from Blood

| Disorders by Type | Drug |
| --- | --- |
| Traumatic wounds: from weapons, bites, etc. | 1, 2, 4 |
| Qi exhaustion in males | 2, 4 |
| Body sores, scarlet birthmarks | 1, 2, 4 |
| Shrinking penis, sores on penis (from sexual contact) | 2 |
| Fits from epilepsy or fright syndrome, delirium, etc. | 2,3 |
| Amenorrhea | 4 |
| Red, weeping, swollen eyes | 3, 4 |
| Vomiting, blood loss through hemorrhage, nosebleed, etc. | 1 |
| Poisoning | 3, 4 |
| Fatigue and debility disorders (emaciation, etc.) | 1, 3, 4 |
| Used to replenish qi and blood | 3, 4 |

NOTE:    1 = plain blood; 2 = menstrual blood; 3 = placenta; 4 = human milk.

Concerning placenta, Li was responding to an alchemical tradition that prized this "immortals' cloak" *(xianren)*, or "purple river carriage" *(zihe che)*, to convey adepts to immortality, and to old popular rituals in which women ate their own afterbirths, "like animals."[14] As ritual medicines, both menses and placenta threatened to cross the razor-thin divide between sources of creative vitality and dangerous power, provoking a familiar reaction of disgust. "Women's menses are rank and dirty," Li remarked, "and so the gentleman avoids them, considering them unclean and liable to injure his yang."[15] His ambivalence toward placenta was evident in his suggestion that such medicines be consumed dry in pills rather than cooked and eaten in a broth.[16] Li's aversion was as much an acknowledgement of medicinal potency as a warning of danger; reproductive substances remained staples of the classical medical repertory.

In sum, medical symbolizations of blood were permeated with connotations of femaleness. Even within the course of a single author's discussion, these ranged from images of the "prenatal" cosmic vitality of earth, to the constructive energy of the growing and reproducing body, to the dangerous efficacy of reproductive substances able to cure or kill. Female gender in the medical imagination implied sources of symbolic power. Nonetheless, the blood of life and generativity was also the substance whose disorders and depletions made women the sickly sex.

"It is easier to treat ten men than one woman." Medical authorities of the Qing period repeated this saying as a well-known distillation of conventional wisdom, bearing out their conviction that women were more prone to illness than men and harder to cure. Consider the image of a woman's life cycle in the following sketch of a medical history, laid out year by year in the eighteenth-century *New Book of Childbearing:*[17]

At the time of her first menses (12 to 13 years), a girl may experience pain or fever; her face may become red, or there may be a bitter taste in her mouth; she may suffer alternate hot and cold sensations or fainting spells as well. As a maiden she may suffer from blocked menses (amenorrhea), knots or lumps of congested *qi [jiekuai]* in her belly, melancholy, headaches, dizziness, nausea and "anxious sensations" *[fan men].*[18] She may be pale and unable to think of food. At the time of her menses a young married woman of 18 to 21 years may ache all over, feel numbness in her hands and feet; she may be now hot, now cold, dizzy and faint. Women in their midtwenties are liable to irregular periods and intermittent fevers and are vulnerable to the serious wasting disease "bone-steaming."[19] By 24 or 25, a woman's "sea of blood" is already in danger of depletion and attacks from cold. In addition to the usual symptoms of headache, dizziness, hot and cold sensations, and cramping, these women will often suffer from vaginal discharges, menstrual flooding or spotting, or protracted periods. By 28 or 29, childbearing has taken its toll. Her *"qi* has dispersed and her blood is depleted," and she suffers from "blood depletion with stomach heat, a condition of fatigue."[20] At 35 internal weakness has made her so vulnerable to noxious invasions from without that her best defense when menstruating is to take to her bed. By her early forties her menstrual cycle has ceased, leaving her with a chronic depletion of *qi* and blood. She is now subject to disorders caused when old, bad blood is not dispersed, but congests and stagnates within.

On the one hand, this sad chronology simply recognizes a typical pattern of gynecological disorder. Amenorrhea is common in adolescents, leukorrhea plagues sexually active married women, while older mothers are more likely to be heavy bleeders. In traditional societies repeated childbearing was a universal drain on women's health. The rapid aging of a married woman, seen here as declining in vigor by thirty and worn out by forty, also conforms to life patterns that were all too common. On the other hand, the account also outlines a socially acceptable pattern of female sickliness and some of the biological premises underlying it. Women were expected—in fact taught— to experience all sorts of diffuse bodily distress as part of their monthly reproductive cycles and to be permanently weakened by childbearing. Moreover, the holistic bias of Chinese medical theory pushed diagnosis toward the assumption that disorders of reproductive function played a key role in the underlying pattern of almost any disease in women. *Fuke,* properly translated, does not mean "obstetrics and gynecology" but "the women's department of medicine," that is, all internal female disorders, especially during the childbearing years.

This classic outline of a distinctive female pattern of disease, frequently quoted by Qing dynasty physicians, originates in *Prescriptions Worth a Thousand* (Pei chi ch'ien chin yao fang, ca. 650):

The reason that there are special prescriptions is that women become pregnant, give birth, and suffer from uterine damage. This is why women's disorders are ten times more difficult to cure than those of men. The Classic says of women that they are a gathering place for yin influences, always exposed to dampness. From the age of thirteen their yin *qi* is replete to the point of overflow, and all sorts of thoughts pass through their minds, damaging the organ systems within and ruining their beauty without. Their monthly courses stop and go, now early, now late, [leading to] congestion and coagulation of blood and blocking central pathways of circulation. The injuries that arise from this can't be fully enumerated. Cold and heat affect the organ systems, depletion *[xu]* and repletion *[shi]* conditions interact, noxious blood leaks within, and the circulation vessels become worn out. Sometimes undisciplined diet causes more than one kind of trouble. Sometimes before skin sores have healed, they [women] take part in "the union of yin and yang." Sometimes when they relieve themselves at open privies, wind enters below and brings on the twelve chronic diseases. For all these reasons, women have their separate prescriptions.[21]

In answer to the question "Why are women more sickly than men?" a late Ming standard treatise on women's health closely paraphrased this passage, adding an additional comment on the pathological consequences of female emotionality: "Women are gripped by compassion and love, aversion and envy, melancholy and grief. Since they are unable to control these feelings, their illnesses are deep-rooted and cure is difficult."[22] Of course women were not viewed medically as a separate species. External agents of disease were the same for both sexes, as were the basic principles of biological functioning and of diagnosis. Nonetheless, doctors agreed about female vulnerability and its systemic nature.

Female health evoked metaphors of easy circulation, reliable periodicity and free flow of blood. These images resonated with an organismic cosmology of harmonious parts, orderly in their movements and interpenetrating without hindrance. Despite these obvious associations, the rhetoric of female illness began with evocations of stoppage, congestion, stagnation—of blood diverted from its normal paths, chaotic and unpredictable in its movements. When stagnant *(yu)*, blood was responsible for pain; congealed *(jie)*, it presented itself as swellings, tumors, bruises, or contusions; static *(zhi)*, it impeded circulation, blocking bowels and impairing digestion; reversing course *(ni)*, it leaked out through sores, hemorrhages, or bloody discharges. Old blood needed to be dispersed and new blood created, a process dependent upon the regular rhythms of the specifically female "conception and highway" circulation tracts *(ren chong mai)*. This ambivalent model of a woman's pathology led naturally to a focus on menstruation, the bodily function that displayed blood ideally in its harmonious, reliable rhythms of health, or else revealed via incipient signs an underlying disorder.

This is how the Song medical classic *Good Prescriptions for Women* (Fu jen liang fang) put it:

Figure 7. Eighteenth-century Japanese visitors to China observed and depicted traditional obstetrical practices. Here, the new mother rests upright, supported by blankets, to aid postpartum discharge. From Nakagawa Tadahide, *Shinzoku kibun* [Observations of Qing dynasty customs] (N.p., n.d.).

The highway tract makes up the sea of blood; the conception tract rules the womb. When the kidney *qi* is full and flourishing, there is an easy flow in these two tracts; the menstrual fluid gradually increases to fill its reservoir and then descends at the proper time. So we may say that the menstrual period of one with healthy, harmonious *qi* appears regularly once every thirty days, a counterpart to the moon's waxing and waning. During the menses it is most advisable to protect one's health carefully. A woman who fails in this risks disorders like those following childbirth, ranging from minor night upsets to fatal illness. In general, fright will disorient blood and *qi*, stopping the tracts from circulating, reversing blood flow within the body to produce chronic wasting diseases. Hard labor and fatigue at this time will give rise to depletion and hot type disorders, leading further to intolerable pain. If a woman is angry, her flowing *qi* will reverse course, reversing the course of blood. If this affects the waist and legs, she will have severe pain there as long as the period lasts. If the reversal affects head, belly, heat, lungs, back, sides, hands or feet, the resulting syndromes will be the same. If her anger is great, the liver will be injured; she will feel dizzy, her sides will ache, she will vomit blood and suffer from tubercular lymphadenitis *[lei-li]*, abscesses, and sores. Further, if menstrual blood soaks into her body, it will drip out all her bodily openings. If during her menstrual period she is exposed to wind, she will fall ill of a wind disease; if she is exposed to cold, she will catch a cold disorder. If these are not cured quickly, she will experience innumerable pathological changes. Carelessness, although at the time it seems light as down, may give rise to illness that weighs heavy as a mountain peak! Is this not something to dread?[23]

This is not saying that menstrual irregularity caused other illnesses in women, so much as that it is a sign, either a precipitating factor or dependent response, of an underlying bodily imbalance. The linkage of menstrual patterns with other syndromes made diagnosis complicated and allowed for diverse pathology, ranging from fevers and wasting diseases to ulcerations, tumors and inflammations, and indigestion. Questions about menstrual function were thus imperative in any medical consultation involving an adult woman, and menstrual symptoms always implicated a total organic pattern. In the words of the authoritative medical encyclopedia *Golden Mirror of Medical Orthodoxy* (1742), "a woman whose courses are regular will be healthy. If her courses are irregular, then a hundred disorders will arise."[24] Or, as Ch'en Nien-tsu, a famous early-nineteenth-century physician and medical popularizer put it, "Medicine for women takes the monthly cycle as its fundamental topic."[25] Texts on *fuke* invariably began with a section entitled "menstrual regulation" *(tiao jing)*.

An enormous variety of symptoms entered the complex typology of menstrual dysfunction (see Table 2).[26] Timing of flow was basic, but the consistency and color of the discharge, the quality and timing of pain or cramps, and the presence or absence of feverish sensations also contributed to the pattern. Early, profuse periods were usually associated with yang excess and heating conditions, and their opposites with cold, stagnation of blood, and depletion. Pain carried connotations of blood congestion or invasion by external cold factors. Clots particularly were likely to indicate internal Fire (extreme and usually reactive yang manifestations) accompanying yin depletion,[27] while a pale and watery discharge suggested exhausted, dry blood.

TABLE 2    Classification of Menstrual Irregularity by Symptoms

| Irregularity | Sensation | Character | Color |
|---|---|---|---|
| Onset | | Early (heating) | Dark |
| | | | Pale |
| | | Late (depleting) | Dark |
| | | | Pale |
| | Heating (feverish) | Early | Dark |
| | | | Pale |
| | | Late | Dark |
| | | | Pale |
| Flow | Pain | Scanty (dry blood) | Dark |
| | | | Pale |
| | | Profuse | Dark |
| | | | Pale |
| | Heating | Scanty | Dark |
| | | | Pale |
| | | Profuse | Dark |
| | | | Pale |

Medical authorities warned that correct diagnosis was tricky because it was difficult to identify underlying as opposed to superficial patterns. Yang excess, for example, could mask an underlying yin deficiency. One common view was that all irregularity, whatever its surface type, involved underlying patterns of depletion.

Medical management of menstrual irregularity began only with the commonplace advice against exposure to cold, anger, stress, and overwork during the period. Chinese therapists expected women to avoid exposure to drafts, washing with cold water, doing laundry, and getting their feet wet.[28] They also recommended, as they did for other disorders, a complex drug therapy, minutely adjusted to individual patients and their symptoms. The *New Book of Childbearing* summarizes a simple, commonsense approach to prescription in easy-to-memorize form:

> Early menses is a sign of heat.
> Late menses is a sign of depletion.
> If blood is stagnant, break it up.
> If blood is dry, build it up.
> Regular flow with early pain means accumulation of blood.
> Late pain means blood is depleted.
> If she feels feverish throughout, she has blood depletion and stagnant accumulation;
> If she feels feverish afterward, she has blood depletion and a hot disorder.[29]

The remedies most often prescribed for menstrual disorders were drugs with warming properties, those that cleared up stagnation, and above all, those that counteracted depletion by building up and vivifying blood. Drug functions were grouped into "four *qi*," namely, heating, warming, cooling, and chilling; and "five 'flavors'" *(wu wei)*, namely, sweet, salty, sour, bitter, and aromatic. These were abstract classifications, the first identified two by two with the yin-yang dualism, and the second (which need not coincide with the taste of the drug) with the Five Phases, of traditional cosmology. In practice a neutral subclass was added to each. The combination of these two rubrics determined the locus and kind of action produced. Restoring a normal level of vitality was called "replenishing" *(bu)* when applied to *qi*, and "vivifying" *(huo)* when applied to blood. Other drugs were used to disperse *(san)* or break up *(po)* stagnation, or to clear *(qing)* heat or phlegm.

Holistic medical reasoning allowed for a wide variety of initial strategies, using many possible combinations of drugs. One might prescribe to replenish *qi*, because "blood follows *qi*." One might stimulate the spleen system, because some kinds of depletion and congestion attack digestive functions. Or one might warm the energy circulation tracts to defend against invasion by cold. Though menstrual disorders were divided into hot and cold types, physicians usually considered heat a symptom of depletion. Drugs classified as chilling or bitter were rarely recommended.[30]

The most important of the blood-building "replenishing and vivifying" medicines preeminent in menstrual therapy was Chinese angelica *(Angelica sinensis, tang gui)*. According to F. Porter Smith, it was among the most frequently prescribed simples in the whole materia medica for stagnations and depletions of blood. Angelica's special affinity for women was considered implicit in the name (literally, ought to return). Popular tradition explained the name by the root's ability to "return" a woman to her husband, presumably strengthened for her procreative functions.[31] Angelica was usually compounded with three other plant drugs—Sichuan lovage rhizome *(Ligusticum wallichii, chuan xiong)*, peony root *(Paeonia lactiflora, bai shao)*, and Chinese foxglove root *(Rehmannia glutinosa, di huang)*—in the popular Four-Ingredients Infusion *(si wu tang)*.[32] Angelica and lovage are noted for their warming and replenishing functions. Peony and foxglove are slightly cooler in nature, regulating excess heat (a by-product of yin depletion or liver Fire) and dispersing blood stagnations responsible for pain or blocked flow. This pharmacodynamic discourse evoked the vulnerability of a woman's body to monthly loss, and the chill of yin influences liable to inhibit an active flow. The dominant therapeutic metaphors were restoration and renewal; the dispersal of the old blood was less a purge than a quickening of blood-building constructive energy.

Following these broad principles, the composition of Four-Ingredients

Infusion could be modified minutely for individual symptoms, the season of the year, or the patient's bodily constitution. It could also be altered for serious reproductive crises such as amenorrhea, miscarriage, difficult labor, or postpartum depletion.[33] Other drugs with similar properties could be recommended instead. Chen Nien-tsu raised eyebrows among his disciples when his treatise on female disorders included "only" nineteen recipes for treatment of menstrual irregularity. The master's explanation was that the multiplicity of such formulas was a vulgar mercenary practice, particularly notorious among modern lineages of "family" (i.e., hereditary) practitioners.[34] The pharmacy section of a standard barefoot doctor's manual of the People's Republic of China is not so selective. It identifies sixty-one common plant substances as useful for menstrual disorders.[35] In Taiwan today, common patent medicines in pill or infusion form are recommended as daily doses for the entire intramenstrual phase of the monthly cycle. A Hong Kong scientist who recently surveyed the traditional materia medica found thirty-five botanical emmenagogues and forty-nine deemed good for amenorrhea. Interestingly, only twelve were listed primarily as remedies for menorrhagia, and only one specifically for dysmenorrhea (menstrual pain). This distribution seems to reflect the traditional preference for replenishing and vivifying yin blood over other therapeutic strategies.[36]

Nor did the therapeutic repertory end at the druggist's door. Many Chinese women today still avoid "chilling and raw" foods during their periods, and dose themselves with warming and clearing concoctions such as ginger tea and hot brown sugar solution. There is every reason to suppose that these domestic remedies have been known and available for centuries.[37]

As the medical preoccupation with amenorrhea suggests, menstrual regulation was important for fertility as well as general health, if indeed the two could be separated. The assumption that absence of menses means inability to conceive is medically plausible. It becomes obvious in a population under conditions of natural fertility, for frequent pregnancy and lactation would substantially reduce the portion of a woman's life during which monthly periods would signal that her body was prepared for conception.[38]

There is no way to tell whether amenorrhea was particularly widespread in the population these healers observed. They linked it to the disorders one would expect—serious wasting fevers, anemia, and anorexia. They also associated it with fatigue and anxiety. The special vulnerability of young girls, who suffer from "the first stirrings of human emotions" and even from "fright" at the sight of their own menstrual blood, is interestingly analogous to the maiden's "green sickness" of European medical tradition.[39] In any case, amenorrhea was only the most serious of the menstrual disorders likely to cause barrenness.

In thinking about conception, medical men recognized that fertility was a complicated matter that they did not understand. Observation bore out old accounts of anomalies, of women who menstruated quarterly *(ju jing)*, yearly *(bi nian)*, or not at all, without effect on their fertility.[40] Nonetheless, the experts offered menstrual regulation as the key to fertility: "If a woman's periods are regular and she has no other disease, she will inevitably conceive."[41] This was plausible, given the belief that menstrual blood in some sense makes the child in the womb, as the woman's contribution to the equal parts of blood and essence from which the fetus develops. Moreover, theories of conception stressed the lunar periodicity of female fertility: "Yang [the sun] ascends daily, so male *qi* arises every day; yin [the moon] has a monthly cycle, so woman's time is once a month."[42]

Accounts of a woman's fertile period differed slightly. One very old view, still repeated in the Qing dynasty, identified it as the moment "one day each month and at one time of that day" when a woman's "*qi* steams and she is dizzy with desire."[43] This theory, like others, assumed that the moment occurred as the menstrual period ended. According to one widespread formula, boys would be conceived on the first or second day after a period ended, and girls on the third or fourth day. The common rationale was that menstruation was the turning point when stagnant old blood was dispelled and vital new blood began to grow. Following this line of reasoning to one logical extreme, some medical authorities identified the critical fertile moment as two and one half days after the onset of the menses itself, or halfway through. A popular jingle, freely translated, went as follows:[44]

Count two and a half days—the hours are thirty;
At twenty-eight or -nine you'll know she's ready.

Ch'en Nien-tsu explained the jingle and its strategy for conception by four considerations:

Select the place, cultivate the seed, seize the moment, cast into the vacancy. "Place" refers to the mother's blood, "seed" to the father's essence. The "time" is the moment when blood and essence will commingle, and the "vacancy" is when the old has gone and the new is engendered. . . . Note the time when the menses come and count thirty [Chinese] hours [i.e., two and a half days]. This is the time of "vacancy," when the dirty *qi* is cleansed and the new blood has just begun to germinate.[45]

Once again yin blood is divided into the good and the bad, passing through cyclic phases of growth and decay, where the ideal pattern includes both cleansing and renewal. In the technique that Ch'en recommends to the husband, the association of menstrual blood with fecundity licenses sexual relations during the period itself.[46] This flawed rhythm strategy for conception has persisted. As recently as 1982 a health manual published in the People's Republic of China thought it useful to correct the notion that "it is easy to get pregnant" during a woman's menstrual period.[47]

To be ruled by blood is to be subject to the rule of one's emotions. Irregularity in monthly rhythms had its counterpart in unstable and excessive feelings, those extremes of "resentment, anger, jealousy, and envy" that medical men especially lamented in women.[48] Doctors connected good health with a steady temperament, free of emotional excess. They were also suspicious of erotic passion. Indulgence in the bedchamber was blamed for a variety of debilitating illnesses in both sexes. Emotions were always linked with physical manifestations. Sometimes psychic phenomena were discussed as if they caused morbid body changes. Sometimes the emotion would be treated as a symptom triggered by somatic pathology. Because doctors did not divide mind and body, their understanding was not psychosomatic but somatically physic. Bodily conditions were inseparable from emotions, and influence could act in either direction. There is the "hepatic Fire" *(gan huo)* of anger; on the other hand, melancholy engenders "static congestions" *(yujie).*

A contemporary psychiatrist and anthropologist has suggested that the traditional Chinese concept of disease included diverse "somatized" syndromes, in which psychic states are described in terms of bodily sensations.[49] This is a useful insight, provided we remember that the concept of distinct psychic and physical realms is our own culture-bound construction of experience. There is no objective way, free of all such assumptions, to decide whether in illness Chinese were experiencing negative or excessive emotions physically. We can only know that this way of interpreting behavior reveals the rich social meanings attached to illness and lets us elaborate gender-specific patterns of disorder. Though men indeed suffered from many of the same syndromes as women, such syndromes were considered gender-specific because women were especially susceptible and because their susceptibility was associated with a causal pattern implicating female blood.

Thus, according to the standard late Ming treatise *One Hundred Questions on Female Disorders,* a major cause of female sickliness was women's "inability to control their emotions." The resulting excesses of "compassion and love, aversion and envy, melancholy and grief" led to bodily imbalance.[50] But the causal chain ran both ways. Ch'en Hsiu-yuan warned that menstrual irregularity usually made women "become perverse in nature," and the *New Book of Childbearing* classified menstrual and fertility disorders according to a woman's psychophysical type. Thin and repressed women suffer from "static congestion"; hot-tempered and jealous types are afflicted with "liver Fire"; while lethargic and plump ones can be expected to suffer from "phlegmatic stagnation" and "fat blocking the womb."[51]

Stereotypes of dangerous female emotionality took both expressive and repressed forms. On the one hand, women were seen as particularly prone to anger, which could cause barrenness, trigger amenorrhea or miscarriage, or lead to a variety of functional blood disorders. Anger, as we have seen, was visualized as a kind of heat associated, when extreme, with the Fire of the Five Phases. It affected somatic functions such as those associated with the liver, producing through this interaction sensations of feverishness and dryness and fits of temper. On the other hand, women were particularly subject to "static congestion," a kind of melancholy syndrome of congealed blood associated with spleen system dysfunction. It was experienced as feelings of oppression and suffocation, pressure or tightness in the chest, languor and loss of appetite, all linked to pent-up resentments and repressed desires. Physicians knew that static congestion and liver Fire were related, just as psychologists today know that anger and depression often mask each other. "Static congestion" and "static anger" *(yu nu)* were often paired. Congestion, by blocking yin splenetic, hepatic, or cardiac functions, could produce reactive heat, as excess yang surged in the vacancy left by underlying yin depletion, leading to manifest "Wind and Fire ascending" and overconsumption of blood. Alternatively, such congestion was thought to produce circulation blockage and manifest itself in stagnant and coagulated blood. Static congestion was especially a woman's complaint because it could arise from social repression. As the *Golden Mirror of Medical Orthodoxy* explained it, "Women must follow others and do not command their own persons; therefore they suffer from worry, resentment, and static *qi.*" Further, this disorder particularly afflicted young and humble women whose circumstances did not allow them to "fulfill their desires": "Maids and concubines often suffer from stasis; their emotions are not outgoing and unimpeded."[52]

The sexual implication is clear. We can see how people also associated "static congestion" with sexual frustration. The famous late Ming novel *Golden Lotus* describes an illness of Vase Lady, a lovesick widow. Vase Lady loses her appetite and is listless. At night she dreams of her lover, and of fox spirits in human form that feed off her "essence and marrow." A doctor diagnoses her condition in a pastiche of medical jargon: "Yin and yang are at war; you are now hot, now cold, as if there was some static congestion within from unsatisfied desires. It seems like a malarial fever, but it isn't; it seems like an attack of chills, but it isn't. You feel languid and low-spirited all day, and at night your spirit is restless and you dream of intercourse with ghosts."[53] The anonymous novelist suggests a pathology in which spirit possession, psychological depression, and physical illness are all at work. Moreover, this doctor warns Vase Lady that she risks slipping into the serious wasting disease, "bone-steaming" *(gu zheng* or *zheng gu).*

The popular novel followed medical practice in associating static syndromes in women with the graver, potentially life-threatening "depletion and wasting disorders" *(xu lao).* "Bone-steaming" was often presented as a final, fatal transformation of such disorders. According to the *Outline of the Salvation of Yin,* "depletion and wasting" was a broad group of depletion disorders due to fatigue. Because "women are ruled by blood," this group takes a gender-specific form.[54] Medical experts identified several variants but generally agreed that the underlying pattern was one of depletion due to menstruation and childbearing, emotional excess, or immoderate living. Manifestations of these protean yin deficiency diseases included irregular menses, emaciation, and recurrent fevers and chills; dizziness and fainting spells, cold extremities, hot sensations in the "Five Hearts" (*wu xin*, the heart region, palms of the hands and soles of the feet); and serious respiratory symptoms such as chronic coughing, aching ribs, and spitting blood.[55]

To a modern student this disease pattern suggests nutritional deficiency disorders or tuberculosis. To Chinese medical experts it was the quintessential disorder of female blood, which, overconsumed and depleted, assumed chaotic form and motion, discharging above rather than below, producing heat now felt as flashes of fever, now as steam consuming the flesh itself.

Ultimately, the progress of this disease was associated with sexual exhaustion. In female sufferers, "dreams of intercourse with ghosts" were counterparts to the "spontaneous seminal emissions" expected in men who came down with depletion and wasting disorders.[56] The male or female victim's sexual essence was drained away and lost in the course of uncontrollable, pathological erotic excitation. The underlying Chinese biological exchange economy made such loss of yin essence always a dangerous sign. For males, ancient, persistent traditions of physical hygiene made conservation of vital essence, through continence or techniques for control of semen in intercourse, a key to longevity. However, women did not have the option of strength through abstinence. Sexual dreams, medical wisdom had it, were especially likely to trouble celibate women, such as widows, nuns, palace women, and those whose marriages were too long delayed. Sexual activity was imperative if a woman was to remain normal, but at long-range cost. Static congestion and depletion and wasting disorders, as gender-linked syndromes, were associated both with sexual frustration and with the results of sexual fulfillment. They began as disorders of melancholy virgins and were associated with menstrual irregularity and bodily lassitude, with the resentful frustrated emotions of the inner quarters, secluded from male influence. But depletion and wasting disorders were also endemic in worn-out mothers, who had expended their sexual vitality in childbearing.

Any system of beliefs about health and disease in an indigenous medical system raises questions about the actual medical profile of the population in question, and about the efficacy of the therapies available. One can only wonder whether tuberculosis and menstrual disorders like amenorrhea were particularly common among women patients of Ming-Qing dynasty physicians, or only particularly feared. The foregoing account of female disease could simply reflect the anxieties of a profoundly pronatalist society, or it could center female health on menstruation because the rhythm of the latter meshed with underlying cosmological beliefs. It is intriguing that, by encouraging anxiety about menstrual function, doctors might have contributed to the menstrual anomalies they warned their female patients about. On the other hand, we are ignorant about the physiological activity of even the most prevalent drugs used for such purposes. Many were used for a broad range of illnesses, some in men as well as women.

There are some interesting correspondences between certain stereotypical "female disorders" in Chinese medicine and in traditional Europe. "Green sickness," or chlorosis, a malady often diagnosed in Western girls, was characterized by listlessness, poor appetite, pallor, amenorrhea—symptoms associated with menstrual irregularity in Chinese maidens. Modern medical authorities consider chlorosis an obsolete form of iron-deficiency anemia usually due to bad diet. There is no conflict between this view and that of historians who see it as a culture-bound syndrome of traditional adolescence. Similarly, depletion and wasting disorders and bone-steaming sound suspiciously like variants on the "consumption" to which young adult women were thought particularly vulnerable in eighteenth- and nineteenth-century Europe. Consumption was also a broad category of wasting disorders encompassing pulmonary tuberculosis and other kinds of chronic debility. In parts of northern Europe it indeed struck women disproportionately, for reasons that are not well understood. Facts of this kind and related statistical evidence on maternal mortality have caused Edward Shorter to argue that, in early modern Europe, women were in truth "the sickly sex," though others disagree.[57] In fact, no historian has successfully balanced for any historical population the risks of childbirth, neglect, and poor nutrition against the presumably greater ability of female infants to survive and the greater life expectancy of older women.

Whether or not there were worldwide patterns of female disorder, medicine offered women a range of authoritative models for their experience of gender. Concepts of disease and disease behavior are not biological universals but culturally patterned and socially taught ways of understanding normality and abnormality. Chinese medical texts do not directly express the patient's experience, but they pay a great deal of attention to symptoms and describe in detail the patterns of psychological and somatic distress expected in ill people. These texts also cluster symptoms into syndromes and often suggest a biosocial context for their occurrence. Above all, they describe the ill and the healthy in evocative symbolic language that maps the psychic dimensions of bodily experience and links them to cultural assumptions about cosmos and value.

The classical medical model taught women that menstrual function was central to their overall pattern of health or disease, and encouraged minute attention to its variations. It suggested patterns of somatic distress that were likely to accompany monthly cycles. It portrayed women as prone to emotional instability that could be expected to trigger diffuse physical symptoms of disorder. It predicted that female susceptibility to disorders of blood and depletions of blood inclined them to sickliness in general, not only in reproductive functions. While warning against any excess of erotic appetite, in all these ways it taught that reproduction was the reason for woman's existence. It suggested that this vital function must be paid for in gradual physical decline and early exhaustion, against which medicine offered only a partial defense. Finally, the system encouraged them to be the pharmacists' best customers. Although the genesis of disease was manifold and often insidiously gradual, relief came straightforwardly and reliably in a bewildering array of drugs and tonics.

The medical model of sexual relations was not organized about the equal and complementary yin-yang poles of classical cosmology. Nor did it endorse the image of inexhaustible female vitality communicated by old Taoist bedchamber manuals, Ming pornography, and the rich folklore of male illness caused by sexual exhaustion.[58] Physicians repeatedly warned against the popular notion of the sexual act as combat, in which partners vied for each other's "essences," arguing instead for a mild creed of continence. Medically speaking, if males were worn out through dissipation, females exhausted themselves in childbearing. The destructive power of unrestrained female sexuality in the novel *Golden Lotus* is evidenced by Lotus, the barren heroine. Yet while males could find the way to longevity through sexual control, women had to menstruate and become mothers, to the detriment of their health.

Moreover, in considering the nature of yin blood, medical accounts stressed vitality and its loss over purity and pollution. Pollution of blood survived, reinterpreted as disease, coming into play mainly in connection with childbirth, not menstruation. It was postpartum discharge that physicians called "noxious" *(e lu)*. The polite phrase for menses was "monthly constancy" *(yuejing)*. The pollution of birth, medically speaking, had gravest consequences for the child, not the mother. It was held responsible for much infant mortality and early childhood illness.[59]

For male healers, then, beliefs about the "power of pollution" were repressed, either resurfacing as largely pediatric disease categories or undergoing a positive transformation. Biology had tamed the powers of pollution associated with the borders between life and death, replacing them with a set of naturalistic symptoms controlled within a system of healing. It thus became easier for males involved in the female business of reproduction, as doctors or fathers, to act as masters of the situation. Threatening symbols of female sexual power were replaced by benign symbols of female generativity and weakness that moderated pollution taboos and permitted an interpretation of gender based on paternalism, pity, and protection.

How did women themselves interpret the classical medical model? An analysis of cultural symbols cannot predict individual behavior. Such models suggest but do not dictate. These images of the female condition were not only medical, based on experience with people who were sick rather than well, but male, not derived directly from women's own experience. Nonetheless, they concerned not only disease but the nature of biological reproduction and the bodily processes universally associated with it. Given the social power of dominant ideologies, and the burdens of childbearing, it is unlikely that many women would be bold enough to reject physicians' assumptions as an alien projection.

A more likely response would be to adapt male images of the feminine to subversive, purely female uses. Sickliness could become a means of self-protection against male sexual demands or burdensome work, as well as a strategy for winning sympathy. Menstrual therapies stressed fertility and procreation, but if a woman wished to have no more children, such medication could disguise an attempt at abortion. Pharmacy texts considered dozens of drugs unsafe during pregnancy, and a number, including common labor-hastening drugs, were known as abortifacients.[60] The author of *Outline of the Salvation of Yin,* recognizing that some women, worn out with childbearing, wished to stop, warned of the debilitating consequences of drugs strong enough to sterilize.[61] The novel *Golden Lotus* portrays an informal network of female healers and midwives whom the ladies of this polygamous urban household preferred to the male specialists recommended by their husband. These healing women were always ready with nameless aphrodisiacs, fertility drugs, and abortifacients to serve female sexual strategies. If nothing else, this account suggests the existence of a masculine anxiety that reproduction was not theirs to control. "The six kinds of old women" of the conventional moralists' stereotype—those that conservative gentlemen kept away from their inner quarters—included two who provided medical services, namely, midwives *(wen po)* and drug peddlers *(yao po).*[62]

Further hints about female interpretations of these norms may be gleaned from field research among Chinese women today who continue to believe in traditional medical ideas. One sample of native Taiwanese women from Taichung included a few who accepted the generalization that women are inherently sickly, but considered themselves fortunate exceptions—individuals with naturally strong constitutions and a "lucky fate." Theirs was the resilience of healthy minds and bodies evading the cultural logic they did not reject. Old peasant women who took part in the same survey understood the privileges of dependency. They complained of having been too poor to take care of their health with monthly rest and expensive medicines.

Concerning the more subversive issue of contraceptive abortion, an anthropologist working with Hokkien-speaking Chinese women in rural Malaysia has found that they used herbal formulas to aid the menstrual flow when they were late and feared they might be pregnant. Here "menstrual regulation" thrived on ambiguity about the facts of a woman's internal bodily state. The desire for an abortion could remain inarticulate and so relatively blameless.[63]

If the classical medical system had to contend with informal female health networks and the manipulations of the segregated inner quarters, it could offer the gentry woman respectability. The lesson society taught was that Chinese women had a choice between the power to disrupt the agnatic kingroup, and positive esteem as procreators if they accepted the weakness that physicians told them was their fate. If this is true, to be one of the "sickly sex" was a way of defining one's place as a proper woman in the web of social relations.[64]

## NOTES

Book titles, author names, chapter titles, and a few commonly used words have been left in the Wade-Giles spelling used in the original publication. Dynasty names, placenames, and terminology have been converted to pinyin spelling. This article previously appeared in *Chinese Science* 7 (December 1986).

The following abbreviations are used in the endnotes:

| | | | |
|---|---|---|---|
| CPISCC | *Chen pen i-shu chi-cheng* | NKPW | *Nü k'o pai wen* |
| CYKM | *Chi yin kang mu* | PTKM | *Pen ts'ao kang mu* |
| ITCC | *I tsung chin chien* | TCHS | *T'ai ch'an hsin shu* |

1. Mary Douglas, *Purity and Danger: An Analysis of the Concepts of Pollution and Taboo* (London: Routledge and Kegan Paul, 1966).

2. Frank W. Young and Albert A. Bacdayan, "Menstrual Taboos and Social Rigidity," *Ethnology* 4, no. 2 (1965): 225–40. For folk beliefs surrounding menstruation in China, see Emily M. Ahern, "The Power and Pollution of Chinese Women," in *Women in Chinese Society*, ed. Margery Wolf and Roxane Witke (Stanford: Stanford University Press, 1975), 193–214.

3. For a discussion of the medical tradition, see Nathan Sivin, "Ailment and Cure in Traditional China" (manuscript).

4. Li Shih-chen, *Pen ts'ao kang mu* [Systematic materia medica; hereafter PTKM], (Jen-min wei-sheng ch'u-pan-she edition, 1596; reprint, Beijing, 1975). On the nature of blood, see vol. 4, pt. 52: 2952–66.

5. The word *energy* is used here in the original qualitative sense, not the special sense of modern physics or chemistry.

6. *Jingluo*, sometimes mistranslated "meridians."

7. See most recently A. C. Graham, *Yin-Yang and the Nature of Correlative Thinking*, Occasional Paper and Monograph Series, No. 6 (Singapore: Institute of East Asian Philosophies, 1986).

8. PTKM, 52:2955.

9. On Li see *Dictionary of Scientific Biography*, s.v.

10. PTKM, 52:2950.

11. Table 1 draws upon PTKM, 52. I have simplified the original by combining

similar syndromes under a single heading and by leaving out some miscellaneous entries. For example, breast milk is recommended for loss of voice and for removal of insects from the ear, therapies hard to explain by the natural symbolism used elsewhere. For a detailed analysis of the same text, category by category, see William C. Cooper and Nathan Sivin, "Man as a Medicine: Pharmacological and Ritual Aspects of Traditional Therapy Using Drugs Derived from the Human Body," in *Chinese Science: Explorations of an Ancient Tradition,* ed. Shigeru Nakayama and Sivin (Cambridge: MIT Press, 1973), 203–72. The authors conclude that "if the ingredients of the Chinese prescriptions had been chosen by the most stringent criteria of clinical pharmacology, fewer than one-quarter of the ailments treated could have been relieved strictly by known properties of the constituents or their combinations" (262).

12. PTKM, 52:2950.

13. Ibid., 2952–53.

14. Ibid., 2963.

15. Ibid., 2953.

16. Ibid., 2963–64.

17. *T'ai ch'an hsin shu* [New book of childbearing; hereafter TCHS] (Shanghai, 1793). This compilation of three titles, *Nü k'o mi yao, Nü k'o mi chih,* and *Nü k'o chih yao,* is one of many attributed to the monks of Bamboo Forest Temple (Chu-lin ssu) of Mt. Xiao, Zhejiang.

I have used the reprint in Ch'iu Chi-sheng, ed., *Chen pen i-shu chi-ch'eng* [Collected rare medical texts; hereafter CPISCC] (Shanghai, 1936). For the passage cited see *Nü k'o chih yao,* 1:175–82 (vol. 8).

18. Though *fan men* today means "anxiety," Chinese physicians associated the emotion with physical sensations: palpitations, faintness, constricted chest, etc.

19. Contemporary diagnosticians link "bone-steaming" with pulmonary tuberculosis, but its original scope was broader.

20. TCHS, *Nü k'o chih yao,* 180.

21. *Pei chi ch'ien chin yao fang* (Edo Igaku edition, 1849; reprint, Taipei, 1965), 2:1.

22. *Nü k'o pai wen* [One hundred questions on female disorders; hereafter NKPW], in CPISCC, 8:2. This book is attributed to Ch'i Chung-fu and dated ca. 1220, but it was not widely available until printed (or reprinted) in the late Ming.

23. Ch'en Tzu-ming (fl. 1237), *Fu-jen ta-chüan liang fang* [Complete good prescriptions for women] Ssu k'u chüan shu [Complete collection of the Four Treasuries], ser. 7, vol. 129 (Wenyuange edition; reprint, Taipei: Taiwan shangwu yinshuguan, 1983), 1:1a-2a.

24. Wu Ch'ien et al., ed., *I tsung chin chien* [Golden mirror of medical orthodoxy; hereafter ITCC] (the medical encyclopedia sponsored by the Ch'ien-lung emperor) (Ta Chung-kuo t'u-shu kung-ssu edition; reprint, Beijing, n.d.), III, 62.

25. Ch'en (who styled himself as "Hsiu-yuan"; 1753–1823) *Nü k'o yao chih* [Essentials of female disorders] (Peking, 1959), 1.

26. This table is based on the section on "menstrual regulation" *(tiao jing)* in Wu Chih-wang, *Chi yin kang mu* [Systematic aid for disorders of yin (i.e., of women); hereafter CYKM] (preface dated 1620, K'o-chi wei-sheng ch'u-pan she edition; reprint, Shanghai, 1958), 1–17.

27. Fire was one of the five phases (Fire, Metal, Wood, Water, Earth), a system for classifying patterns of change in the natural world.

28. For warnings about damp and drafts, see NKPW, 14; TCHS, 40.

29. TCHS, *Nü k'o mi yao*, 1 : 1.

30. Wang Meng-yin (*zi* Shih-hsiung), *Shen shih nü k'o chi yao* [Master Shen's collected essentials of female disorders] (preface dated 1850; reprint, Hong Kong, 1959), 4. The text is based on a family tradition of the Hangzhou region attributed to a Master Shen. Wang was a physician known for his critical acumen.

31. F. Porter Smith (rev. G. A. Stuart), *Chinese Materia Medica: Vegetable Kingdom* (Shanghai: American Presbyterian Mission Press, 1911), 133.

32. For these drugs and their pharmaceutical properties, see Chiang-su hsin i-hsueh yuan, ed., *Chung yao ta tz'u-tien* [Unabridged dictionary of Chinese materia medica] 3 vols. (Shanghai, 1977–1978), I, 220, 706, 805. The standard authority for English translations is Shiu-ying Hu, *An Enumeration of Chinese Materia Medica* (Hong Kong, 1981), s.v.

33. Hsieh Kuan, ed., *Chung kuo i-hsueh ta tzu-tien* [Unabridged dictionary of Chinese medicine] (1921; reprint, Shanghai, 1927), 724–29. This dictionary lists ninety-nine variants of *si wu tang*, of which fifty-one were prescribed for women's disorders. Most of the rest were for both sexes.

34. Ch'en, *Nü k'o yao chih*, 5.

35. *A Barefoot Doctor's Manual: The American Translation of the Official Chinese Paramedical Manual* (Bethesda, Md., 1974; reprint, Philadelphia, 1977), 570–942. Translation of *Ch'ih chiao i-sheng shou-ts'e* (Changsha, 1971).

36. Yun Cheung Kong et al., "Potential Anti-Fertility Plants from Chinese Medicine," *American Journal of Chinese Medicine* 4, no. 2 (1976): 105–28, esp. 122–24. This list, drawn up as a guide for future laboratory and clinical research, is based on the traditional medical literature.

37. From informants in China, 1981–82, and in Taiwan, 1985.

38. This point is made by Barbara Harrell in her cross-cultural study of lactation amenorrhea, "Lactation and Menstruation in Cultural Perspective," *American Anthropologist* 83 (1981): 796–823.

39. Wang Meng-yin, *Shen shih nü k'o chi yao*, 8, and NKPW, 14. "Fright" at the sight of menstrual blood was listed as one of the "three illnesses" in maidens. On fright syndrome see Marjorie Topley, "Chinese Traditional Ideas and the Treatment of Disease: Two Examples from Hong Kong," *Man*, n.s. 5, no. 3 (1970): 421–37, esp. 429–34. The analogy to green sickness is discussed below.

40. PTKM, 52 : 2953. NKPW, 54, notes that *ju jing* was sometimes used to suggest that a woman was three months pregnant.

41. Ch'en, *Nü k'o yao chih*, 12.

42. ITCC, 1 : 173.

43. CYKM, 182.

44. The jingle in Chinese reads "Sanshi shichen liangriban / Ershibajiu jun xu suan." It is also quoted in CYKM, 182, and in T'ang Ch'ien-ching, *Ta sheng yao chih* [Essentials of life] (preface dated 1762), 1 : 2a. One Chinese hour *(chen)* is two Western hours long.

45. Ch'en, *Nü k'o yao chih*, 14.

46. I have found two medical cautions about danger to health from sexual rela-

tions during the menses, in TCHS, *Nü k'o mi yao*. The author lists this as a cause of "fever with blood depletion" (3:28) and warns that young women risk irregular and pathological blood loss if lustful men use them at this time (4:43). ITCC, 4:150, warns that intercourse during the period can cause menstrual irregularity. All of these texts are concerned with female, not male, health. The paradoxes of medical reasoning converge in PTKM, 52:2954, where males suffering from penis sores due to sexual contact during the menstrual period are prescribed menstrual blood as a cure!

47. Shu Huai-yin and Pa Ching-yang, *Fu nü wei-sheng wen ta* [Questions and answers on female health] (Shengyang, 1982), 16.

48. "Women in general are stubborn in their feelings and too much inclined to resentment, anger, jealousy, and envy." TCHS, *Nü k'o mi yao*, 4:43.

49. Arthur Kleinman, *Patients and Healers in the Context of Culture: An Exploration of the Borderland between Anthropology, Medicine, and Psychiatry* (Berkeley, 1980), 138–45 and passim.

50. NKPW, 2.

51. Ch'en, *Nü k'o yao chih*, 2–3; TCHS, *Nü k'o mi yao*, 4:43–44.

52. ITCC, vol. 4, 44:150; CYKM, 208.

53. *Chin p'ing mei* [Gold, vase, plum] (Chung-yang shu-tien edition, 1610; reprint, Shanghai, n.d.), I, 175. For a medical version see CYKM, 3, 12, 126–27.

54. CYKM, 122–26.

55. In males the "depletion and wasting" syndrome was described in terms of *qi* exhaustion and associated in older men with "localized pain" disorders due to blood dysfunction (*xue bi*, often rheumatic) and in younger ones with semen loss.

56. ITCC, II, 187–88; CYKM, 126–27; NKPW, 9–10. Edward H. Schafer has studied medicinal substances recommended by *Pen-ts'ao kang mu* for incubus and succubus dreams in "Notes on T'ang Culture, II," *Monumenta Serica* 23 (1964): 138–39.

57. On chlorosis, a typical source is Maxwell M. Wintrobe et al., eds., *Harrison's Principles of Internal Medicine*, 7th ed. (New York, 1974), 1582a. On consumption, see Lester S. King, *Medical Thinking: A Historical Preface* (Princeton, 1982), 16–69; and Edward Shorter, *A History of Women's Bodies* (New York, 1982), 250–54.

58. R. H. Van Gulik, *Erotic Colour Prints of the Ming Period*, 3 vols. (Tokyo, 1951), and *Sexual Life in Ancient China* (Leiden, Netherlands: E. J. Brill, 1961), discuss both the cosmological and erotic views.

59. I discuss fetal pollution in "Concepts of Pregnancy, Childbirth, and Infancy in Ch'ing Dynasty China," *Journal of Asian Studies* 46, no. 1 (1987): 7–36.

60. See Yun Cheung Kong et al., "Potential Anti-Fertility Plants from Chinese Medicine," 122 ff, for a list of traditional abortifacients and drugs counterindicated during pregnancy.

61. CYKM, 208–9.

62. For a discussion of this cliché, see Chao, *Kai yü ts'ung kao* [The step-by-step collection of studies] (ca. 1775; reprint, Shanghai, 1957), 632.

63. Charlotte Furth and Ch'en Shu-yueh, "The Influence of Traditional Chinese Medicine on Beliefs and Practices Surrounding Menstruation" (manuscript, 1985) (a study of sixty respondents, conducted in Taichung); Chor-Swang Ngin, "Reproductive Decisions and Contraceptive Use in a Chinese New Village in Malaysia" (Ph.D. diss., Anthropology, University of California at Davis, 1985), 100–106.

64. Author's afterword: It is gratifying to see that this essay written fifteen years

ago still serves as a useful introduction to late-imperial medical representations of the female condition. However, readers of my recently published book, *A Flourishing Yin* (Berkeley and Los Angeles: University of California Press, 1999), may notice an interpretive shift in the latter work. In "Blood, Body, and Gender" blood itself serves as the material marker of female bodily gender, and I focus on comparing medical ideas of blood as generative vitality with ritual ones of it as magical and polluting. In the book my starting point is yin and yang, which in the medical classics are not attributes of sexed bodies but themselves the foundations of gendered meanings diffused both in bodies and in the cosmos at large. The most learned physicians in the orthodox tradition, therefore, constructed a medical body that I call "androgynous." In this interpretation, males might well suffer from the same syndromes of yin and yang *qi* imbalance as so often afflicted females, and the designation of women as "the sickly sex" would be more the result of social condition than bodily essence. However, "Blood, Body, and Gender" remains a credible reflection of the Qing period's popular traditions of *fuke,* and my colleagues in literary studies tell me that the trope of female sickliness carries great resonance in the belles lettres of that era.

CHAPTER TWELVE

# Embodying *Qi* and Masculinities in Post-Mao China

*Nancy N. Chen*

In the post-Mao reform years, *qi* has been the subject of numerous conversations and popular texts as well as traditional medical texts. It is viewed as a miraculous element that can vitalize people and the environment. As a bodily substance considered to be life energy with cosmological properties, *qi* is usually inseparable from blood, and it courses along channels and paths similar to those that blood travels. Although *qi* is not inherently marked or differentiated by gender, certain elements of *qi* and the practice of *qigong* have come to be associated with male masters and images of hypermasculinity. As Charlotte Furth's work in the previous chapter shows, blood has come to be associated with female bodies and emotions, which are ruled by change. Rather than addressing semen as the essence of male bodies, this chapter will consider the links between *qi* and masculinity both through physiological explanations in traditional Chinese medicine and through the social context of *qigong*, where the power of *qi* is amplified beyond the body.[1] Thinking about masculinities in the contemporary Chinese context requires careful analysis of how bodies are defined in medicine and in everyday somatic regimes.

In the mid-1980s and early 1990s *qigong*, the practice of breath work and healing through cultivating one's *qi*, became an immensely popular form of exercise and healing in urban China. Throughout major cities and towns one could always find practitioners at dawn in parks, on sidewalks, near public buildings, on campuses, and even in streets participating in daily regimens of *qigong* exercise. Even more noteworthy was the ubiquity of its presence not only in terms of everyday practice but also in terms of the social awareness and popular discourse of ordinary citizens and mainstream state newspapers. As a medical anthropologist studying the social phenomena of this practice and related medical disorders in the 1990s, I was struck by the fact that nearly each day I would encounter heated debates or impassioned testimonies about the healing powers of *qigong* masters or about their supernatural capabilities. Elsewhere, I have discussed the multiple forms of *qigong* that were prominent in the urban centers, such as exercise, meditation, and healing, and the specific associations that emerged in relation to these forms.[2]

Popular encounters with *qigong* often involved impromptu street performances by a master who gathered a crowd with his demonstrations of *qigong* abilities using *wai* (external) *qi*. In Southwest China, in my first encounter with a master performing on a street, a male master dressed in black baggy pants and an open vest began pounding and breaking open bricks with his forehead without any apparent wounds. He proceeded to demonstrate other superhuman abilities, such as walking barefoot on glass shards and touching hot iron rods taken from a nearby fire kettle. With each action the crowd murmured louder, until finally the master closed his act with an exuberant lecture about the powers of *qi* and how he was capable of demonstrating more once he was shown support from the crowd in the form of donations. As the crowd quickly dispersed, one onlooker commented, "This guy is just a little one, the great masters can do much more, like move an entire room full of people around, turn electric lightbulbs on with their hands, or heal you of any sickness."

Indeed, there were several arenas where *qigong* masters performed their powers of healing and raw energy. While street performances were quite theatrical and focused on the physical capabilities and external powers of a single master, the larger exhibitions in stadiums or mass *qigong* sessions in parks led by more prominent masters were impressive not only for the feats carried out but also for the social experience of being in the company of hundreds of skeptical onlookers and believers for several hours. Not since the Cultural Revolution had such spectators occupied these arenas to capacity with such emotional fervor. Although initially only dozens of individuals might have visible emotional responses to a master's lecture, eventually the whole arena would be filled with people openly sobbing and responding to the transmitted *qi* energy in the room. Individuals could be seen writhing on the ground, running up and down aisles making uncharacteristic body movements, or sitting alone in a trance moving slightly from side to side. Such scenes often reminded me of evangelical services and even rock concerts, where the energy of a charismatic performer moved onlookers and had visible effects on members of the audience.

My intent in this chapter is to focus on the charismatic leaders of this practice and illustrate the ways in which gender, specifically masculinity, becomes intertwined with power in the post-Mao context. *Qigong* practitioners come from all backgrounds, and there are an equal number of male and female practitioners. However, at the level of master, there are significantly fewer prominent women masters with large followings. Though I have met many female masters, I contend that *qigong* masters have come to represent a naturalized category of masculinity, and that forms of *qigong* practice are gendered in the social context. This chapter explores how the paths to being a master tend to be determined not only by physiological difference but also by gender ideologies that shape the practice of *qigong* and official discourses about it. Bodies do matter, both as corporeal and social historical entities.[3] The ways in which conceptions of bodies and their materiality are historically situated and experienced reveal how gender operates as an ordering principle. Sexual differences and dimorphism are often explained through the body, where the natural body becomes the generative device for gender.[4] Although acknowledging the importance of corporeal bodies in historical framings of sex and gender, my discussion of *qi* and masculinity also relies on the notion of gender as a politicized and social performance.

Multiple meanings of masculinity also need to be addressed. Recent literature, referred to as the new sociology of masculinities, reflects on masculinity and femininism as specific gender projects that are embedded in institutional and everyday practices of gender relations.[5] In the contemporary Chinese context, meanings of masculinities have shifted to reflect the growing engagement with a market economy and consumer culture. Colloquial terms such as *nanxingde,* translated as "male sexuality," and the more popular term *nanzihan* (manly) center upon characteristics that in the 1990s referred to having masculine looks, the ability to make money, and power.[6] Urban-based intellectuals are quick to point out that *nanzihan* in this era is much different from what it was a generation ago. *Nanzihan* during the Maoist era was a set of characteristics, such as revolutionary fervor and selfless work, that described male ability and power in a specific context. In this discussion I propose that, while popular images of masculinities seem to be based on social abilities and external physical features, properties of *qi* attributable to physiology that circulate in discourses of *qigong* further underscore Chinese notions of masculinity. Moreover, among both onlookers and practitioners, in the public display of *qigong* there is a heightened sense of hypermasculinity, where masters seem to have superhuman powers of invulnerability and longevity.

After addressing notions of the physiology of *qi* in traditional medical texts and in *qigong* manuals, I will turn to laypeople's notions about masculinity and how these are linked to the practice of *qigong.* Finally, in an examination of state responses to several prominent masters in the public realm, I will address the gendered meanings of power operating in the post-Mao state.

## BODY, SUBSTANCE, GENDER

*Qi* and blood are intimately linked substances that travel in similar, and sometimes the same, channels and are based on analogous principles of yin and yang. Loss of or shifts in these powerful and potentially dangerous substances can indicate health or illness. According to Furth, there is an understood hierarchy between blood and *qi* in premodern medicine in which "blood follows *qi.*" Such notions about the relations between *qi* and blood continued in traditional medical theory of the late twentieth century. Liu Yanchi's modern text, *The Essential Book of Traditional Chinese Medicine,* notes that, though "blood is the material basis for the generation of *qi,* at the same time, the formation and circulation of blood depends on *qi. Qi* plays the leading role in this process. The flow of blood follows the flow of *qi.*"[7] Stagnant or lagging levels of *qi* are usually viewed as life threatening, as the presence of *qi* is necessary for life itself. Most ailments and disorders are due to the depletion or excess of *qi,* indicating a lack of balance. In addition to problems caused by the deficiency, sinking, stagnation, or adverse flow of *qi,* there are also five specific disturbances that may occur when *qi* and blood interact. The following descriptions of the five disturbances, quoted from Liu's text, indicate the intricate relationship between *qi* and blood in pathogenesis.[8]

Stagnation of *qi* and blood stasis:
Blood circulation depends upon *qi.* A retardation of the flow of *qi* causes stasis, which leads to pain. Painful masses in the abdomen are characteristic of this condition.
Prostration of *qi* after great loss of blood:
Massive hemorrhaging is often accompanied by simultaneous or subsequent prostration of *qi.* The result is coma, due to deficiency of both blood and *qi* as well as a failure of yin and yang.
Failure of *qi* to control blood:
Weakness of spleen *qi,* in particular, can lead to abnormal bleeding. The characteristic symptoms are rectal bleeding, blood in the urine, uterine hemorrhaging, and rupturing of blood vessels beneath the skin. These symptoms are accompanied by those of weak spleen *qi* and insufficient spleen yang.
Abnormal flow of blood due to abnormal flow of *qi:*
This condition is traditionally known as the "upward rush of blood after *qi.*" It is characterized by hemorrhaging in the upper portion of the body due to an excessive ascending motion of liver *qi,* upward invasion of the lung by liver fire, or an abnormal upward flow of both lung and stomach *qi.* The symptoms can include hematemesis, spitting up blood, epitaxis, and coma.
Insufficient *qi* and blood to nourish the vessels:
Any derangement of *qi* and blood immediately hinders their ability to nourish the vessels and limbs, creating local deficiencies of *qi* and blood. The characteristic symptom of this condition is numbness of the limbs.

Although there is no discussion of blood transfusion in traditional Chinese medical texts, the flow of *qi* within one's body as well as from one living entity to another is considered crucial in restoring and maintaining health. The loss of blood, although viewed with horror, is not always entirely damaging, whereas the loss of *qi* can be disastrous. Flows of *qi* are crucial to well-being, hence most medical texts talk more prominently about the restoration of *qi* than about the restoration of blood in healing.

In many pre-1949 medical texts, *qi* as a substance tends not to be differentiated based on gender. Rather, in these books there are multiple manifestations of *qi*, and their qualities are distinguished according to the dual properties of yin and yang.[9] The systematic organization of these phenomena and of other entities with these dual properties can correspond to male and female qualities in the corporeal body. Although different forms of *qi* can correspond to such male or female categories, *qi* still does not necessarily have fixed masculine or feminine properties. Instead, it has multiple forms and functions and is an active entity as well as a material substance. In her extensive study of the epistemological roots of traditional Chinese medicine, Judith Farquhar points out that there has been a transition in the definition and uses of *qi* from early premodern discourses to contemporary texts.[10] For instance, in traditional Chinese medical texts such as the *Yellow Emperor's Canon of Internal Medicine* (Huangdi Neijing Suwen), *qi* was defined as a cosmic force as well as a bodily substance. It was an entity believed to be found both in the body and in the natural environment. The body was referred to as a microcosm of the universe. The notion of *qi* in post-1949 medical texts, however, tends to embrace solely physiological dimensions and emphasize *qi* primarily as a substance like blood and other bodily fluids. Such a transition is due in part to discourses of scientific Marxism, in which social, environmental, and phenomenological meanings of the body and its forms are reconfigured into more material categories with physical properties. The body becomes less an energetic entity than one that is more predictable and diagrammable.

In contrast to present-day medical discourses that identify *qi* as a mere bodily substance, many contemporary practitioners and popular *qigong* manuals have defined *qi* as a form of energy or a universal force present in the environment and atmosphere, as well as a bodily force like breath. *Qigong* is understood as the movement of that energy through the body, either by internal visualization and meditation or by external bodily practices. In *qigong* practice, masters and other practitioners do not view *qi* merely as a physical substance but also embrace the cosmological aspects of *qi* as vital energy. Such popular views of *qi* as a healing force seem to subscribe to earlier, more "traditional" notions of *qi*, in which individuals draw upon or embody the transformative powers of *qi* present in the environment and cosmos rather than those confined to the medicalized body.

Most *qigong* manuals, however, do reflect traditional medical texts in the discussion of yin and yang and how *qi* is manifest with these dual qualities. Experiencing *qi* is a central component of practice that all practitioners encounter and discuss on a daily basis. Yet there are multiple forms of *qi,* and the ways in which *qi* is invoked to describe the practice vary widely. Depending upon the source and context of its use, the concept of *qi* has several meanings in practice. Tracing the genealogy of *qigong* thus entails a closer examination of the concept of *qi.* In practice it is possible to find some gender-specific forms of exercise, breath work, or positions. When I asked one female master how she learned special techniques for women practitioners, she told me that some techniques are handed down from master to student, while other forms are devised in practice after trial and error. In many group-practice sessions, I have observed masters instructing female practitioners to hold their right hand over their left hand and male practitioners to do the opposite. Such distinctly gendered positions and even specific forms of breath work are believed to enhance the flow of *qi* in one's body.

After observing qigong practices in public parks in Beijing and Shanghai, I often asked, in discussions with masters and practitioners, how *qi* could be a universal component and whether it was diversely experienced in individual bodies. In all my discussions with masters and other practitioners across a wide range of ages and backgrounds, I was told that "everyone has different forms of *qi.*" One master took me aside and talked about how he could see what type of *qi* was contained within each body, especially the bodies of sick persons, whose *qi* was stagnant and no longer flowed. So, while all individuals may have elements of yin and yang as organizing principles in their bodies, the transformation of these entities at different times and through regular practice was the basis of difference between bodies, a difference further underscored by male or female physiology. As Furth and Emily Martin have shown, female bodies tend to be medicalized and diagnosed as having more ailments than male bodies.[11] Correspondingly, in the practice of *qigong* it is not unusual to find that more female practitioners and followers seek care or that *qigong* masters tend to be male. One explanation given by a male master who also practiced traditional Chinese medicine states that "women's bodies change too much and need constant alignment and balance, whereas a male body does not change on such a regular basis." Although *qi* is not readily engendered by physiological difference, as stated in early texts, in the context of daily practices certain forms of *qi* are increasingly aligned with male bodies in popular conception.

How then has *qigong* become affiliated with masculinity? In my research I found that the gendered hierarchy of healing ability—that is, the presence of more male masters—is the result of perceptions about physiological differences and of social discourses. All masters wield certain powers, and it is the performance of those powers, and their reception, that matters.

The reception by followers and audience members is an integral component of both the performance of a master's powers that are considered masculine powers and the performance of healing. Even though, in traditional Chinese medicine, gender and *qi* can be linked as part of systematic correspondence, I argue that it is not only discourses of the corporeal body that account for the overwhelming number of male masters but also the social context and performances of *qigong* during a specific period that have associated *qi* with male essence. In the 1990s particular individuals emerged as masters who embodied naturalized categories of masculinity. It is crucial to acknowledge the social relations of power in which the expression of *qigong* healing and power articulated a gendered cosmology of *qi* in addition to the "natural" cosmology.

Despite the multitude of styles and genealogies of practice, *qigong* can be differentiated into two types—external and internal. The external form, *yinggong* (sometimes referred to as hard *qigong*)—the form described earlier with the example of the street performer—tends to emphasize hard *qi* and hard bodies that can withstand much force and perform superhuman feats. This martial form tends to be practiced not so much in public parks but in arenas such as streets, sites of acrobatic displays, and even in military compounds. One well-known master told me that he was often invited to give special *qigong* training sessions for the public security forces and People's Liberation Army troops. The masters and practitioners are primarily men, and masculine displays of power are a factor in the performance of *qigong*. In contrast, there tends to be a greater number of female practitioners of the internal and meditative form *(neigong)*, and it would not be unusual to find practitioners of all backgrounds in parks practicing this form. However, internal forms of *qi* cultivation greatly appeal to male practitioners too, as such forms help to promote the circulation and transformation of *qi* and blood—crucial steps toward enhancing male potency and preventing pathologies such as sexual impotence, seminal emission (sometimes referred to as *shenkui*, a form of yang deficiency due to semen loss), or *suoyang* (another culture-bound syndrome, also known as *koro*, which refers to the near-fatal fear of genital retraction). Though an already extensive range of aphrodisiacs and a male potency–enhancing pharmacopoeia exists, *qigong* practice is by comparison more effective in the long term and a cheaper alternative. In sum, both forms of *qigong* address masculine desires for hard, impenetrable bodies and self-generating potency. In the following sections I explore how *qigong* masters emerged in the public realm.

## PERFORMING MASCULINITIES

In a 1990 Chinese political cartoon that questioned the capabilities of the aged leadership, a state leader was portrayed as unwittingly holding the tail of a tiger turning back to pounce on him. Unlike such leaders, however, *qigong* masters were said to embody the ultimate ability to "ride the tiger," a cultural metaphor that describes the ability to master difficult situations rather than be subsumed or defeated by them. This essay focuses on the intersection between gender and power, and on how discourses of bodies anchor these notions. Rather than defining masculinity on the fixity of sexual difference or from a psychoanalytic perspective, this essay draws from Judith Butler's idea that the performance of gender is "not a singular act but always a reiteration of a norm or a set of norms." Thus my questioning of how masculinity and *qigong* powers intersect is not fixed solely at the level of physiology.[12] My analysis also turns to the social and political contexts in which *qigong* powers and, ultimately, masculinity are performed. The norms of being in control and capable of maintaining rightful power were questioned especially in the post-1989-Tiananmen-demonstration period. In the period prior to the major economic transformations after 1992, masters were adept at maintaining professional personas that demonstrated immense powers of healing and discipline. In this vein, the public identity of *qigong* masters and their demonstrations of healing can be viewed as means of performing masculinity in post-Mao China. Masters thus were capable not only of riding the tiger but also of upstaging state leaders by being in control of both material wealth and symbolic capital. Not only were they able to harness tremendous power, thus garnering thousands of followers—including even state officials among them—they were also popularly viewed as having the ultimate powers that *qi* energy could bring: longevity, prosperity, and superhuman abilities. In sum, they were the embodiment of power in a period when capital, both material and symbolic, became increasingly more important to one's status and the social economy.

Healing in the post-Mao period, prior to the formations of a massive market economy later in the 1990s, emerged simultaneously as a private act for individuals and as a public performance for masters. In contrast to previous decades, in which socialized medicine attended to the masses, with a focus on public health, the emergence of *qigong* in the 1980s was linked to desires for self-care and individualized forms of healing and daily practice. Elderly people could attend to their complaints of rheumatism or arthritis, long-term sufferers of neurasthenia or chronic pain could seek relief, and even parents of children with congenital disorders could seek help when no other options could be found in either traditional Chinese medicine or biomedicine. *Qigong* promised release and hope. Whether one practiced in parks or in stadiums, it became accepted to cry openly or express fervent belief in something that was not state ideology. Particularly as some forms of *qigong* began to overlap with Daoist, Buddhist, and other spiritual practices, references to *qigong* as a religion or new age spiritualism also emerged.

Popular narratives about *qigong* emphasized the fantastic and super-human powers of *qigong* and its masters. In the initial period of accom-modation when *qigong* proliferated widely (1983–90), the official state discourse seemed to mirror the public view that *qigong* was miraculous, and the government even took steps to acknowledge it as a state treasure. Each week, broadcasts on radio and television, in addition to stories in print media ranging from state news organs to popular magazines, described people cured of terminal diseases and masters demonstrating their special skills. During this moment, many individuals stepped forward to show their skills in parks or, if they had greater capabilities, to perform publicly in larger arenas. Public hearsay and claims about *qigong* powers circulated quickly not only via media channels but also by word of mouth on buses, trains, and planes across the country. It was in this public, semiofficial space of popular discourse and imaginaries that masters came to embody ultimate power.

The 1990s was a period in which many masters could emerge into the public realm *(chu shanle)*. This term roughly translated means "emerging from the mountains" and refers to a Taoist tradition among masters to re-treat from the larger populace in order to practice self-cultivation and other abilities. To leave the mountain is to return to mundane daily life. In the nu-merous interviews that I had with masters and practitioners of various forms, I often asked how one became a master. From my observations in public parks, it seemed that this category was quite flexible, and that anyone could claim to be a master. However, not all masters had the same capabilities or number of followers. Especially since it was possible for practitioners to heal themselves, having "true" *qigong* capabilities *(gongneng)*—such as being able to exert *qi* and heal others—was frequently invoked as a primary charac-teristic of a master. In fact, it was not unusual in the early 1990s to see indi-viduals lined up in parks each morning to seek diagnosis and prompt heal-ing from a master reputed to have special powers.

Being a descendent of a practice lineage—a martial arts school or *qigong* line with generations of descendents—was also mentioned as a way to be-come a master. As with other forms of martial arts and Taoist or Buddhist practices, the world of *qigong* has multiple forms or styles of practice, and different masters embody particular schools or lineages of training. A com-mon term for the descendents of a particular master is *tudi*, which identifies a special disciple or apprentice who will eventually inherit the master's spe-cial knowledge and even lead the followers after the master's passing. As in the traditional forms of patrilineal descent, disciples tend to be male, unless a father wishes to pass on his skills to his daughters as well. But as one prac-titioner cautioned me, "Even if a master has several *tudi*, the master may never tell which one will be the ultimate inheritor of his special skills until the very end. Or they may never find out and will have to contest each other until the most powerful disciple wins out." Such a strategy ensures that a master will remain in power until his or her time is up. This structure of relations between disciples and master also means that each generation, even within the same school, can have quite different levels of skills and knowledge.

In addition to these two, more common pathways to power, another recent pathway to masterhood involves creating a network of clients that subscribe to the healing powers of the master. The more powerful and well connected the clients, the more prestige the master accumulates. Hence, status is more a reflection of secular power than of the relative powers of a master. Nonetheless, this strategy has become a prominent path to power. In many autobiographies by masters and in popular *qigong* manuals, photos of the master next to state leaders, intellectuals, or even movie stars are prominently displayed within the first pages. This form of display signifies that the masters have the tacit if not official recognition of state representatives.

In 1991 there were several great masters *(da shi)* who captured the public imagination and who were discussed both in official state discourse and the popular realm. I use the terms *popular* and *semipublic* to refer to social spaces, sometimes thought of as civil society, that emerged in the late 1980s, in which the state did not necessarily control all aspects of daily life. Examples of the popular realm include the expanded publishing industry that spawned the huge number of *qigong* manuals and other self-help guides. In this realm I also include popular discourses of *qigong* that occurred in public spaces such as buses, parks, stadiums, and the media. But even as public spaces became disengaged with official state discourses, many *qigong* practitioners felt the need to legitimate their practices with official recognition by, for example, registering with the state *qigong* administration bureau for a license to practice.

Individual practice and magical claims about *qigong* in contemporary China existed within the same space that was created for post-Mao economic reforms and Chinese modernization. In the late twentieth century, ideologies of Chinese socialist modernization relied heavily upon scientific rationality, which emphasized global economic dominance and orderly, productive, docile citizens. Yet local and private meanings of this process meant greater stress in everyday life—crowded urban centers, increased costs of living, and imposed order. *Qigong* was readily embraced in this context because it provided a chance to transcend the burdens of everyday life, both in the personal sphere of meaning and in public moments of shared meanings. Moreover, the practice of *qigong* as a bodily regimen offered the means of transforming one's body and self according to personal notions of order and discipline.

## ENGENDERING *QIGONG* IN THE BODY POLITIC

Although daily practice was the most common form of social interaction for practitioners of *qigong*, devotees also attended mass *qigong* sessions, where a master lectured and gave *qi* to the audience. Before martial law was declared in 1989, this was the way that charismatic masters could address hundreds, sometimes thousands, of followers (and skeptics). Such masters were considered to be among those who could ride the tiger, immerse themselves in chaos, and emerge with true power in health and wealth. Zhang Xiangyu was one such master. Formerly an actress with the Qinghai Performance Troupe, she was youthful and vivacious; she claimed to be endowed with special powers to heal others and speak in tongues, referred to as "universal language" *(yu zhou yu)*. Her visions of the universe as a new creation of humanity, along with other aspects of her spiritual journey and enlightenment, were documented in her autobiography, *Da Ziran de Hunpo* (The Soul of the Great Nature). She accumulated a large following of people, ranging from cadres and professionals to workers and chronically ill persons of all ages and backgrounds. In a former imperial temple, followers of her style would move in a *qigong*-induced trance around a big tree that was said to be infused with her *qi*. At the height of her popularity, several hundred people would go to this tree to practice collectively and speak in tongues.

During six months of martial law in Beijing following the Tiananmen Square demonstrations, large public gatherings were banned. Despite the ban, this *qigong* master managed to hold a series of *qigong* sessions in March 1990, using the coming Asian Games as the reason for a fund-raiser, which generated over a million yuan. Over several nights Zhang Xiangyu lectured to several thousand participants, who paid thirty-five yuan each to hear her speak and receive *qi (shou gong)*. Shortly after her performance, many individuals claimed to be able to speak in tongues and had visions of ancestral spirits or the master herself. Outpatient clinics at mental wards suddenly became deluged with concerned relatives who brought in patients with hallucinations and disruptive behavior associated with attending Master Zhang's session.

In the weeks following this performance, as part of a government campaign for the secularization of *qigong*, editorials in the *People's Daily* and *Health News Daily* began to question Master Zhang's motives and responsibility for bringing such large numbers of people to uncontrollable emotional outbursts and mass hysteria.[13] The language of witchcraft and superstition began to emerge. Terms such as "witch" *(wupuo)* and "swindler" *(pianzi)* were used to describe Zhang Xiangyu, who was accused of dabbling in superstition *(mixin)* and mysticism *(shenmi)* along with her own form of evil *(xie) qi*. It was clear that state officials found that her version of *qigong*, which included apocalyptic statements about the present regime, resembled too closely evangelical faith-healing meetings or heterodox cult groups. When several patients who sought her healing powers died shortly afterward, this was enough evidence for Beijing municipal authorities to call for her arrest and charge her with treating patients without a license. In addition, physicians and public health authorities demanded that the government regulate *qigong* in order to prevent devious charlatans from harming more patients. Soon it became clear to followers that if one were to continue to practice, either as a master or student, one would have to register and pay regular dues to an officially sanctioned school.

The action divided her followers and practitioners of other *qigong* groups. In the months following Zhang Xiangyu's arrest, many masters either aligned themselves along the official boundaries of *qigong*—by getting licenses to practice, paying dues to officially sanctioned schools, and practicing specifically sanctioned forms of *qigong*—or went underground. In the latter part of 1991, at the big tree to which master Zhang had reportedly imparted special powers, only a handful of the most devoted followers still continued to practice. Throughout parks one could see the red-and-yellow banners that indicated official forms of *qigong* practice *(zheng qigong)*. While the Chinese socialist state viewed the outcome of Zhang Xiangyu's performance as an incidence of mass hysteria and an issue of public health, individual practitioners were outraged and indignant. "How dare they lock her up!" a woman cadre in her late fifties vehemently responded when I asked her about Zhang Xiangyu. She continued, "The reason they locked her up was because she was a woman and she did not have powerful enough clients to back her up when she started to make a lot of money." Another follower, who worked in the mental hospital, burst into tears when I inquired about her master, saying, "She did no wrong. Have you heard anything about her?" These deeply felt sentiments were equally matched by impassioned arguments by bureaucrats and physicians that "Zhang Xiangyu is nothing but a modern-day witch."

It was possible for an observer in the mental wards to see the concerns of family members and physicians who were suddenly confronted with new diagnoses of *qigong* deviation, more formally known as the culture-bound syndrome of *qigong*-induced psychosis. Yet among *qigong* circles in the parks, the emerging conclusion was that state officials used Zhang Xiangyu as a convenient scapegoat in order to reassert authority in an arena that was quickly being dominated by unlicensed healers. It is important to point out the gendered nature of state-level accusation. While a national campaign denouncing the popular legitimacy of this female master was mobilized, other masters who operated with an equally large following managed to escape both the label "modern-day witch" and imprisonment. In the case of Zhang Xiangyu, a female master who managed to attract a popular following, her form of *qigong* was threatening to officials who found her claims as a woman unorthodox and unsettling to the political cosmology that had developed around *qi* and *qigong* healing. Following her imprisonment, more orthodox and uniform forms of "real" *(zheng) qigong* began to be constructed. The magic of healing by means of *qigong* became bound to the claims of the state, which quickly defined orthodox and secular *qigong* as opposed to "false" practices.

In 1990–91, official state discourses about *qigong* began to be situated apart from popular *qigong* debates. Although testimony about *qigong* healing continued, there were calls to differentiate between "real" *(zheng)* and "false" *(jia) qigong*. This was an attempt to separate those individuals who claimed to be masters but who healed for lucrative purposes from those with "true" abilities. Needless to say, the bureau appointed by the state to regulate *qigong* used science and scientific *qigong (kexue de qigong)* as a means to cleanse and discipline the ranks of "false" masters. The state and its representatives were crucial gatekeepers that countered popular images of *qigong* masters. As one example of the attempt to rein in masters who seemed to run with the tigers, the treatment of Zhang Xiangyu illustrates how notions of illegitimate power, or the pollution of the powers of *qi*, are constructed by administrators.

In recent years *qigong* masters continue to flourish outside of China, where there is little regulation. Most of the masters in the public eye tend to be male—further reinforcing images of *qigong* as the embodiment of male power. Yet, as in China, over half of the practitioners are female. For instance, Falun gong, a transnational organization that was denounced as a cult and that became the subject of an intensive government crackdown in 1999, was led by a middle-aged male master, Li Hongzhi, while most of the practitioners were older women. When I queried a group of Chinese feminist scholars about the continued phenomenon of gender hierarchy in such organizations, one responded, "It's analogous to churches where all the priests and ministers are men, but the followers are mainly women." In spite of possible similarities between gender hierarchies found in *qigong* and those in other social institutions, the prominent role that official discourses play in defining orthodox *qigong* practices and masters reveals the coextensive relations between the post-Mao state and masculine power.

## CONCLUSION

In his consideration of the historical emergence of two sexes from a single model of the body in European biomedicine, Laqueur reminds and cautions readers about "the fundamental incoherence of stable, fixed categories of sexual dimorphism" that lie beyond the boundaries of the body.[14] Similarly, in thinking about bodies and their meanings in gender systems, we must carefully consider how bodily substances, such as blood and *qi*, operate as organizing principles both within and beyond bodies. *Qi* is simultaneously embodied in and engendered through physiological explanations, as well as in the social context. Even as medical texts emphasize the plurality or multiple manifestations of *qi*, it is especially in the realm of everyday practice and in the social relations of *qigong* that masters gain prominence and ultimately embody gendered meanings of *qi*. The miraculous "nature" of *qigong* healing illustrates how *qi*, unlike blood, is viewed positively as a healing force rather than as one that pollutes.

Although analyses of gender have considered biological constructs of gender difference, in this chapter I have examined how, in contemporary China, social and phenomenological discourses about *qi* also anchor a political cosmology of power. The practices of *qigong* by specific masters have reconfigured meanings of masculinity to include the performance of both bodily and political prowess. Though certain female masters have challenged the continuities between official and popular meanings of *qi*, residual images of hypermasculinity remain closely associated with the practice of *qigong* and with the intervention of official media and state representatives. Masculinities in such contexts in post-Mao China remain linked to bodily substance as well as to official structures of power.

## NOTES

The author would like to thank the coeditors for their support and immensely helpful suggestions. Additional thanks go to Anthony S. Chen for sharing his research findings on Chinese-American masculinities and to Everett Zhang for earlier conversations about cultural categories of masculinities. This research was conducted with a fellowship from the Committee for Scholarly Communication with the People's Republic of China (1990–91). Additional support for follow-up research came from the Committee on Research Sciences at the University of California at Santa Cruz (1996).

1. In "Technologies of Everyday Life: The Economy of Impotence in Reform China," *Cultural Anthropology* 14, no. 2 (1999): 155–79, Judith Farquhar's insightful study of the new specialization in *nanke* (male medicine), she shows that recent Chinese medical texts have focused on *jing* (seminal essence) as the root of male impotence. While *jing* seems more specific to male bodies, she acknowledges Nathan Sivin's notion of *jing* as a type of "indeterminate" *qi* that is in transition from one form to another.

2. Nancy N. Chen, "Urban Spaces and Experiences of Qigong," in *Urban Spaces in Contemporary China*, ed. Deborah D. Davis, Richard Kraus, Barry Naughton, and Elizabeth Perry (New York: Woodrow Wilson; Cambridge: Cambridge University Press, 1995).

3. See R. W. Connell, *Masculinities* (Berkeley and Los Angeles: University of Cali-

fornia Press, 1995); and Judith Butler, *Bodies That Matter* (Berkeley and Los Angeles: University of California Press, 1995).

4. Thomas Laqueur, *Making Sex: Body and Gender from the Greeks to Freud* (Cambridge: Harvard University Press, 1990).

5. For an insightful analysis of this literature, see Anthony S. Chen, "Lives at the Center of the Periphery, Lives at the Periphery of the Center: Chinese American Masculinities and Bargaining with Hegemony," *Gender and Society* (October 1999). See also Connell, *Masculinities;* Jeff Hearn and David Morgan, eds., *Men, Masculinities, and Social Theory* (London: Unwin Hyman, 1990); and Michael Kimmel and Michael A. Messner, *Men's Lives,* 3d ed. (Boston: Allyn and Bacon, 1995).

6. Xueping Zhong, *Masculinity Besieged: Issues of Modernity and Male Subjectivity in Chinese Literature of the Late Twentieth Century* (Durham: Duke University Press, 2000), 5, 174–75.

7. Liu Yanchi, *The Essential Book of Traditional Chinese Medicine,* vol. 1: *Theory* (New York: Columbia University Press, 1988), 182.

8. Ibid., 185.

9. Manfred Porkert's discussion of these related entities provides useful information about the discrete characteristics of yin and yang. In his careful analysis of the terms and their context, yang can signify "something incipient, something inchoate," "something setting loose," "something setting in motion," "something transforming," "something developing, expanding," "something dissolving, dispersing," or "something indeterminate yet determining." Yin can signify "something completing," "something confirming," "something composing, quiescent," "something sustaining," "something condensing," or "something awaiting organization yet at the same time something determinate." *The Theoretical Foundations of Chinese Medicine: Systems of Correspondence* (Cambridge: MIT Press, 1978).

10. Judith Farquhar, *Knowing Practice: The Clinical Encounter of Chinese Medicine* (Boulder, Colo.: Westview Press, 1994).

11. Emily Martin, *The Woman in the Body* (Boston: Beacon, 1985).

12. Butler, *Bodies That Matter,* 12.

13. It is important to note that not all newspapers took the same view. More popular dailies, such as the *Guangming Daily* and *Beijing Daily,* were sympathetic to Zhang Xiang Yu and continued to publish articles about her abilities. The two papers mentioned above are state publications that directly voice official views.

14. Laqueur, *Making Sex,* 22.

PART SEVEN

# Shifting Contexts of
# Gender and Sexuality

The 1980s were a key transitional period between the Cultural Revolution–era constructions of gender and those that were to follow, but marked changes did not begin to appear until the late 1980s, picking up speed in the 1990s. Chinese people hailed the reemergence of gender difference in dress, hair style, and self-presentation as one of the newfound freedoms of personal expression. Women were said to have a natural and innate love of beauty that had been repressed in the previous era; thus, the "pursuit of beauty" was turned against the Party-state and its policies. Feminists both inside and outside China, however, were not so sure that the renewed expression of gender difference was equal to real freedom, and they observed that the market reforms were increasingly disadvantageous to women in the workforce. The female "pursuit of beauty" and the debates about changing gender norms in the 1980s are well documented and illustrated in Emily Honig and Gail Hershatter's *Personal Voices: Chinese Women in the 1980s,* which translates original articles from popular media and provides insightful commentary on them.

Harriet Evans's chapter summarizes some of the themes documented in much greater detail and historical depth in her book *Women and Sexuality in China: Female Sexuality and Gender since 1949.* One of Evans's significant contributions has been to point out and document the fact that there is more continuity between gender norms in the reform era and the previous decades than was often assumed; in fact, the enthusiasm for the break with the past was a rhetorical strategy in the critique of the Maoist period, particularly the period of the Cultural Revolution. During the previous decades there had been brief periods when the expression of gender difference was allowed and even praised; and even in magazine photos during the Cultural Revolution one could often note the collars of flowered blouses peeping from under military green "Mao suits." Further, the state's new attention to issues of sexuality appeared to be as much a strategy of control as a liberation of sexual behavior.

William Jankowiak agrees that there is more continuity to gender norms than is superficially apparent. Since his conclusions are based on his ethnographic interviews on gender stereotypes in the early to mid-1980s, rather than on the (often state-supervised) published sources that Evans uses, he emphasizes that people believed in differences between the sexes even when state ideology had erased them, and he downplays the role of the state in their reappearance. Jankowiak also reveals the pressures felt by men in these changing times, reminding us that changing gender ideals do not affect women in isolation from men. Jankowiak discusses his research in much greater detail in his book *Sex, Death, and Hierarchy in a Chinese City: An Anthropological Account.*

A classic film about changes in women's lives in rural China of the 1980s is Carma Hinton and Richard Gordon's *Small Happiness: Women of a Chinese Village.* In it, moving scenes depict the reminiscences of older women recalling bitter lives, and younger women struggling with the changing expectations in the reform era.

As the 1990s came to an end, a stronger feminist voice began to emerge inside China, independently of the state-sponsored Women's Federation (which had monopolized advocacy for women since the establishment of the People's Republic of China), and Chinese feminists began to form alliances with other feminists outside China. This newly emerging network, not being strictly limited by national boundaries, offered Chinese women the possibility of a more autonomous voice, which was crucial to help mitigate the negative effects of the economic transition on women. Mayfair Yang's edited collection, *Spaces of Their Own: Women's Public Sphere in Transnational China,* explores the possibilities of this new transnational public sphere. Yang has also produced a video, *Through Chinese Women's Eyes,* that reiterates some of the themes of her book.

## COMPLEMENTARY READINGS AND VIDEOS

Evans, Harriet. *Women and Sexuality in China: Female Sexuality and Gender since 1949.* New York: Continuum, 1997.

Honig, Emily, and Gail Hershatter, eds. *Personal Voices: Chinese Women in the 1980s.* Stanford: Stanford University Press, 1988.

Jankowiak, William. *Sex, Death, and Hierarchy in a Chinese City: An Anthropological Account.* New York: Columbia University Press, 1993.

*Small Happiness: Women of a Chinese Village.* Directed by Carma Hinton and Richard Gordon. Distributed by Long Bow Group, New York, 1987. Videocassette.

*Through Chinese Women's Eyes.* Produced and directed by Mayfair Mei-hui Yang. Distributed by Women Make Movies, New York, 1998. Videocassette.

Mayfair Mei-hui Yang, ed. *Spaces of Their Own: Women's Public Sphere in Transnational China.* Minneapolis: University of Minnesota Press, 1999.

CHAPTER THIRTEEN

# Past, Perfect or Imperfect:
# Changing Images of the Ideal Wife

*Harriet Evans*

Women steelworkers, farmers, parachutists, and political activists, robust and healthy, gaze into the distance, their eyes shining with revolutionary zeal. Young beauties, slender and languid, lounge on sumptuously uphol-stered sofas, appealing to the romantic longings of their audience. Wealthy urbanites, dressed in designer fashions and expensive accessories, display the material benefits that the consumer economy has brought them. These images of women from the revolutionary and reform periods are so striking in their contrasts that finding any similarity between them might seem to be out of the question. At the most obvious level of interpretation, the con-trasts correspond to radically different discourses of Party policy, framing radically different practices and expectations about the individual's rela-tionship with the group or collective and the state. In the former period, consistent with the ideological emphasis on collective endeavor, the possi-bilities of gender ascription had nothing to do with subjective or individual expression. The practices and relationships implied by representations of the ideal woman suggested principles of group stability and social order, with no explicit reference to the idea that hierarchical gender relations might be involved.[1] In the latter period, the refeminization of images of women cor-responds both with the attack on the "gender sameness" of the revolution-ary years and with the possibilities for individual expression and experi-mentation that the market economy has legitimized.

However, a reading of these sets of representations as aspects of a gender discourse produces a different interpretation. It suggests that common as-sumptions are embedded in the images of both periods, the most promi-nent of which is the view that gender is a naturally ordained set of charac-teristics and attributes corresponding to biological functions.[2] According to this view, female gender is defined by a series of innate and essential characteristics associated with certain responses, needs, and capacities that naturally make women wives and mothers. Wifehood, and its invariable expression in motherhood, is the relational and biological state in which women find their truest expression. Upheld by law since 1950 as the only legitimate relationship for sexual relations, marriage sexualizes women and enables them to reach their full maturity. A look at the discourses surrounding the ideal wife thus permits us to identify central meanings associated with being a woman.

Dominant discourses since 1949 have insisted that men are obliged to be monogamous, as women are. However, the consistent focus on women's behavior as exemplary of appropriate behavior in marriage indicates a clear attachment to female conduct as the principal standard and agent of marital harmony. Representations of wives between the 1950s and the 1970s suggested a tension between requirements of service to the husband, on the one hand, and to the state, on the other. One mode of resolving this—in discursive terms—was by minimizing the importance attached to the subjective and affective aspects of the marital relationship. Another was by indicating that a woman's duty to the state could be, and at times should be, mediated by her commitment to her husband and children. Since the early 1980s, the "privatization" of matters associated with love and marriage has been accompanied by widespread use of romantic and domestic imagery to contextualize descriptions of marital harmony. As part of this, the wife's self-sacrificing support of her husband has been reinforced as a gender-specific requirement of the ideal of happy conjugality. Despite prevalence in the media of positive constructions of women as achievers in the world of public, male-oriented interests and as potential initiators of sexual activity, these constructions have not seriously destabilized the hierarchized representation of women's attributes and duties as wives—as sexualized women. An essentialist underpinning to what are defined as gender characteristics has served to constrain and limit the ways—in the dominant public media at least—in which women are thought about as persons.

Confronted with the gendered effects of the expansion of the market economy in China—including the abduction and sale of women into marriage and prostitution, increasing levels of domestic and sexual violence against women, the rising divorce rate, and most recently the enforced "return home" of women laid off by their employers—women have begun to raise a whole series of questions about their responsibilities and needs as women and, therefore, as wives. Although it is still too soon to assess how significant these challenges are in altering the range of gender-subject positions available in public discourses, they are clearly contributing to the destabilization of the essentialist approaches to gender.

## THE REVOLUTIONARY WIFE

The new style marital relationship is influenced neither by class nor money, nor does it consist of simple physical attraction. Rather, it is based on unanimity of political consciousness and harmonious sympathy of ideas and emotions. Husband and wife are tender toward each other; they also honor each other and respect each other's rights and domestic position. . . . The new-style marital relationship is also reflected in mutual responsibility to each other and to society. . . . Since husband and wife have joined their lives together, they have the responsibility to help each other and cooperate in ideological matters, studies, and daily life. They should share responsibility for domestic affairs and childcare.[3]

Ideals of wifehood publicized between the 1950s and the 1970s were set within the framework of socialist conjugality upheld by the 1950 Marriage Law of the People's Republic of China. This projected a relationship of equality and companionship without regard to gender. Husbands were urged to discard the idea that, because a wife's "level" *(shuiping)* was lower than their own, she was not worth discussing political issues with.[4] Suggestions that a wife should be slightly less educated than her husband were condemned as sexist ideology *(nanzun nübei)*.[5] Ideally, a "revolutionary couple" were "social activists," and a revolutionary husband had no right to demand that his wife stay at home all day looking after his own comforts, any more than a woman should desire to spend her time servicing her husband.[6] A husband's desire for a "virtuous wife and good mother" *(xianqi liangmu)* who was "gentle, considerate, playful and who took care of everything" *(wenrou, titie, huiwan, shenghuo zhaoguo zhoudao)* was criticized as an expression of "selfish" *(liji)* desires that were, by definition, incompatible with commitment to the collective's needs.[7]

For their part, women who claimed to find happiness after marriage in the "narrow" interests of the home were told that their priorities were wrong. They were not only denying themselves a "future" by thinking that life simply consisted of their own "little world" *(xiao tiandi)*, but they were also failing to provide the revolutionary example on which their children's healthy development depended.[8] Expanding one's interests beyond the domestic domain was an essential ingredient of the new-style marriage, for without it a wife might become "narrowminded" and develop an "exaggerated view" of the importance of marital love. Wives who described feeling neglected by husbands who spent all day at work were criticized "for their inadequate understanding of the meaning of revolutionary work."[9] A wife's love for her husband should include comradely affection and love for others, and should be a "powerful stimulus to doing even more for the revolution."[10]

The pressure on women to shift their loyalties away from exclusive focus on the domestic sphere clearly challenged traditional gender associations of marriage, which bound a women to serve her in-laws, husband, and children without any consideration for public-oriented concerns. In this respect, the main features of representations of "model wives" were consistent with the principles of the Party's "woman's work," which were intended to revise the gender positions with which women were encouraged to identify. Descriptions of the ideal wife might suggest that a wife's commitment to the public good could be a source of inspiration to her husband, as in the case of a young peasant wife whose symbolic gesture of public commitment in decorating the household cow with her red wedding ribbon convinced her husband to contribute the cow to the cooperative.[11] Others conveyed the message that a wife's political and educational development would make her a better companion to her husband and earn her his respect. For example, a man who used to beat his wife was described as having become her "respectful companion" once she began to study and show an interest in political affairs.[12] Another man, who left his unsophisticated young rural wife to attend the university, described how she gained a place in his affections once she began to study.[13]

These descriptions can easily be read as examples of the "gender sameness" of the revolutionary period, according to which women's "liberation" lay in approximating standards established by masculine example. At the same time, they indicate a gender asymmetry in notions of the "ideal woman." Aspiring to public participation and attainment in terms already well established for her husband did not obviate the duty of a wife to be responsive to her husband's needs. Just as the wife was required to show an appropriate response to her husband's sexual demands, so her sensitivity was also required when her husband's work demanded it. Whether describing the model peasant "dependent" (*jiashu*) who, after seven years without her husband, was commended for her loyalty to him in encouraging him to continue fighting in Korea, or describing the wife whose gratification lay in caring for her husband so that he could become a member of the Party, images of marital harmony invariably included that of the woman serving her husband in the name of the public good. The ideal wife should strike a balance between sacrificing to support her husband and acquiring "masculine" skills associated with entry into the world of public affairs. Too enthusiastic an approach to attaining educational and professional skills could signify a dereliction of domestic duty. Having a university education, for example, might cause a young woman to betray her husband and her class background in pursuit of urban attractions.[14] In ideological terms, such representations of the possible limits of women's identification with new skills and opportunities could be interpreted as putting the interests of the group— refracted through her relationship to husband, fiancé, and family—before her own. On one obvious level, these representations conformed to the redefinition of the relationship between private and public commitments that ideally applied to everyone, men as well as women. However, their gendered aspects signified more than a reiteration of the familiar requirement that the individual first direct her loyalties to the group. At no point should a wife's attachment to symbols and practices of public engagement allow her to threaten male authority. By contrast, representations of men's responsibilities to their wives during the same period contained no such message. Women thus found themselves in the impossible situation of being asked to identify with a set of subject positions that signified a rejection of conventional gender constructs and, at the same time, to renegotiate them in order to achieve domestic balance. The relative absence of men as active agents in discussions about marital and domestic responsibilities meant that women appeared as the guardians of marital harmony. Women had the chief responsibility of patrolling their own public and marital conduct to preserve marital stability.

A more obvious aspect of gender asymmetry in discussions about wives' attributes lay in views about women's appropriate domestic role in marriage. Despite the apparently "genderless" images of the ideal couple, women were commonly represented as possessing biologically based characteristics that made them naturally responsive to particular responsibilities in marriage. The same biological structure that made women "born to be mothers" made it natural for women to continue to take on the lion's share of domestic tasks, regardless of what other responsibilities and needs they might have. Official advice to women about how to "resolve the contradiction between domestic chores and work" was premised on the assumption that it was natural for women to "have chief responsibility for the home" until the state could take over their role.[15] Women who expressed concern that having children would interfere with their work, or who "refused to see their husband" for fear of becoming pregnant, were told that such approaches were inappropriate; on the contrary, they would create marital conflict and "provoke their husband's estrangement."[16]

The essentialist assumptions of these approaches to women's domestic role were immediately evident at the level of central policy in the mid-1950s, when to relieve the pressure of unemployment in the urban areas, women were encouraged to "go back home." The pages of the women's magazine *Zhongguo funü* were full of articles extolling the virtue of the "socialist housewife," and references to Lenin's stigmatization of housework as the "drudgery of the most squalid, backbreaking, and stultifying" kind were replaced by a new attention to women's work for the family and home, now hailed as a contribution to "working for the country" that was as "glorious" *(guangrong)* as any other.[17] Despite its declared commitment to full female participation in social production as the key to women's emancipation, the official discourse fundamentally did not question the gender assumptions underlying the equation between women and the domestic sphere. The re-assertion of gender hierarchy during the mid-1950s was simply justified in terms of economic exigency. Despite the potentially progressive implications of disassociating women from the domestic or private sphere, naturalized assumptions about who women were could easily resurface when official policy regarding the greater good so required.

## THE FEMININE IDEAL

Representations of wives in the public discourses of the post-Mao period have depicted women with a very different range of subject positions. Against the collective-spirited, selfless, and androgynous images of the earlier discourse, the 1980s gave new meanings to the notion of wifehood. The wife could now be variously represented as the busy professional mother, the financially comfortable domestic manager, the pretty and endlessly available companion to a busy husband, or the diligent educator of a growing child. She could now withdraw from employment to identify entirely with domestic concerns, or she could be the "female strong woman" *(nü qiangren)* who managed to combine mothering with success in public life. The growth of the market, private entrepreneurship, and increased consumer capacity seemed to find full expression in a new range of diverse possible identities for women.

At the same time, considerable evidence indicated that a new homogenous ideal had replaced that of the former discourse. Numerous articles in both the popular press and academic publications indicated that a woman who was "obedient" *(tinghua)* to her husband, considerate of his needs, and "gentle and soft" *(wenrou)* in her approach was the ideal of the new era.[18] Surveys about the criteria men use in selecting a wife, and advice about how a wife should behave in order to avoid marital conflict and liven up a dull marriage, time and again suggested that men wanted a wife who would put her interests after their own.[19] Discussions in popular magazines held to solicit readers' views on the attributes of the "good wife" foregrounded the image of the supportive, caring, and servicing wife.[20] Even *Nüxing yanjiu,* the women's studies journal published by the research branch of the Beijing Women's Federation, used the argument that men "really do have more responsibilities than women" to legitimize expectations of wifely service and support for her husband.[21] Echoed in comments about the "gentle" nature of successful national sportswomen, or in the "Chinese characteristics" of the *hanxu* (reserved and shy) female image, the significance of "soft and gentle" also became a symbol of national difference and dignity, as well as of gender affirmation of masculine authority.[22]

The appeal of the gentle and caring wife was widely apparent in the popular reception given *Yearning* (Kewang), a soap shown on national television in 1991 and frequently referred to in magazine debates and articles for some time after.[23] The story centered on Liu Huifang, a factory worker and modern "virtuous wife and good mother" *(xianqi liangmu)*. Liu Huifang had married a university student called Wang Husheng, but her marriage fell apart as it became apparent that Wang was a selfish and weak coward and completely insensitive to her needs. After she failed her university entrance exam, other disasters befell Liu. Her marriage broke up, she had a car accident, and in the end, the abandoned child she had struggled to bring up walked away from her. Public response to the film not only indicated sympathy for the plight of Liu Huifang but also suggested that the image of the self-effacing, gentle, and unassertive wife was incredibly popular among both the young and the middle-aged. For the younger group, Liu Huifang represented the gentle femininity then associated with the ideal wife, whereas for the older group she represented the selfless commitment and hard work reminiscent of the model woman of the 1950s.

Dominant visual representations of women since the 1980s correspond with many, though not all, of these narrative descriptions. Public spaces and popular magazines such as *Hunyin yu jiating* and *Aiqing, hunyin, jiating* display image after image of beautiful and sexually appealing young women. Elegant, slender, gentle, young, urban women have replaced the images of the collective-spirited cotton picker and the sturdy militia-woman of the previous decades. Dressed in a variety of fashionable clothes, from Chinese haute couture to the designer labels of Europe's big fashion houses, the women of these images are surrounded by the symbols of consumer wealth and satisfaction—fine clothes, jewelry, a successful entrepreneurial husband, domestic consumer durables, and luxurious furniture. The symbolic and representational values of the ephemera that contextualize women in such images clearly position them within particular social and economic categories in the reform era. And as do the equivalent images of Western women's magazines, they beckon to the absent spectator and suggest a dependence on his or her arrival for complete satisfaction. Indeed, the romantic and sexual appeal they promise the spectator appears to be a trophy of "reformist" success. Hence, the contented girlfriend or young wife emerges as a sign not of women's self-realization but of the absent male's in being able to "complete" her as the feminine ideal.

The inscription of an essential and dependent femininity in these images is a ubiquitous aspect of current public representations of gender and sexuality in China. Though the inside pages of women's magazines may feature photographs of unfashionable, middle-aged professionals or of elderly revolutionaries unconcerned with physical appearance, both are visually and spatially subordinated to the image of the sexy urbanite. The speed with which these feminine images have spread across urban spaces in the past fifteen years makes it almost impossible to imagine their absence less than two decades ago. Various factors associated with recent ideological and economic developments offer partial explanations. Some have argued that the appeal of the erotic feminine image was a reaction to the gender uniformity of the Mao period.[24] It is also a notable effect of the commercial appropriation of women's bodies and interests in a market economy increasingly influenced by the cultural signs of global capitalism. Such interpretations do not in themselves, however, explain the particular images used to define the "modern woman." What makes the particular form of contemporary femininity possible—even to the extent of seeming natural—are founding assumptions about gender distinctions. It could also be argued that the global omnipresence of such forms of femininity have reinforced the essentialist approaches already well established in dominant Chinese approaches to gender and sexuality. Although Meng Yue argues that the essentialist vindication of female gender had a progressive function during the early 1980s, it also had the function of reasserting gender hierarchies in ways that were much more apparent—because of the expansion of channels carrying public discourses—than in the former period. An analysis of representations of the wife's sexual relationship with her husband will make this even clearer.

## SEXUAL DIFFERENCE AND SEXUAL HARMONY

Views about the sexual component of marriage as set out in dominant discourses of gender and sexuality since 1949 have consistently been premised on two core principles. Whether offered in official publications, women's journals, or advice booklets to newlyweds, explanations of the sexual response and responsibilities of the married couple have first of all assumed that legally recognized monogamous marriage is the only legitimate framework for sexual relations. Advice about what are considered appropriate sexual attributes, needs, and responses in women is framed by the assumption that a woman's relationship is with her husband, her exclusive and lifelong sexual partner. Legitimate female sexual conduct continues to be defined with reference to the legally recognized heterosexual relationship. Such a conflation of sexual relations and marriage is reinforced by a naturalized view of marriage as the inevitable culmination of the developmental processes of adolescence and early adulthood. As a recent commentator put it in a discussion about "the family" (*jia*), "Women—all women, not just ordinary women but media stars as well—always naturally look toward marriage."[25] This is not far removed from the terms used by an earlier commentator: "Marriage is an individual's natural biological need; not to marry is abnormal [*bu zhengchang*] and does not have any physical benefit."[26]

The second principle of dominant public discussions about sex is a conceptualization of sexuality as a bounded harmony of binary opposites governed by fixed physiological differences.[27] Male (yang) sexuality is "strong

and active" and is associated with sudden *(chongdong)* and excite
urges; it is described as a naturally spontaneous force, a kind of ins,
urge that is "easily aroused and satisfied" and demands immediate g\
cation. By contrast, female desire is "relatively weak" *(xiangdui jiao ruo);* it
"gradual and slow" and has to be patiently encouraged within a context of
intimacy and tenderness.[28] Female sexuality is essentially contingent and
dependent on the autonomous power of the male urge; it is constructed in
response to the powerful male urge and depends for full expression on the
consideration, care, and sensitivity of the male. Conversely, it is also vulnerable to destruction by the overactive and demanding male. Inadequacies in
a husband's sexual approaches—whether in being "too hasty and rough on
the night of the honeymoon" or in "suffering from premature ejaculation
and impotence"—are identified as causes of a woman's lack of sexual enjoyment.[29] From this perspective, the projection of mutual orgasm as the highest expression of sexual harmony indicates little more than the man's success in controlling his own and encouraging his wife's sexual pleasure. By
the same token, expressions of female sexuality outside the proper boundaries of monogamous marriage—in other words, those that challenge the
supremacy of male desire—commonly appear as expressions of some physical or mental abnormality. The figure of the woman who chooses not to
marry, for example, may be discussed from time to time in the pages of popular women's magazines, but her very naming invariably appears as a means
of denying her recognition as a full woman.[30]

This basic approach to defining sexual difference has consistently informed views about the importance of a "good sex life" in marriage. Although between the 1950s and the 1970s the dominant collectivist ideology
gave little opportunity for public discussion about the affective and sexual
aspects of marriage, "harmonious sexual relations" nevertheless did feature
as a necessary component of a good marriage.[31] Sex, however, was given low
priority in view of the other, weightier factors considered indispensable to
a solid marriage. The representation of sex as a measure contributing to
physical and mental health did not focus on its place as subjective experience, but on its function as a means of enabling the individual person to
contribute more to the family and society. The notion of "sexual harmony"
*(xing hexie)* did not overtly contradict the collective emphasis of the discourse, since it was invoked in the service of conjugal and family happiness—in other words, in the service of the group. A "good sex life" was more
a bonus to a marital relationship founded on mutual interests in work and
political outlook than an essential component validating the marriage tie.

The desirability of a "good sex life" to "deepen the love between a couple"
has been a standard component of representations of marriage and marital
ideals in the past fifteen years or so. Alongside the positive gloss put on romantic aspirations in selecting a spouse, health magazines contain numer-

ous articles with titles like "The Ten Great Benefits of a Good Sex Life." As a commentator put it not so long ago, "Recently, sex has suddenly become a topic everyone talks about with great interest again . . . as if it has again become an important thing in marriage."[32] While the editorials of many journals still take pains to tell their readers not to attach more importance to sex than to other aspects of the marital relationship, the prominent attention paid to "sexual harmony" in marriage signifies an evident departure from former approaches, consistent with the discursive restoration of the realm of "private" experience.

In recent years, views about sexual difference have begun to focus on the influence of culture and society. Although the idea that women's sexual "passivity" is physiologically determined continues to enjoy wide currency, more people are challenging it. "Modern sexological research," one writer argues, "that shows that women have no spontaneous sexual excitement has no scientific basis."[33] Empirical evidence demonstrating generally low levels of sexual satisfaction among women should be interpreted not as an aspect of female sexuality per se but rather by reference to mistaken, yet dominant, ideas about female passivity, shaped by historical and cultural biases.[34] The same writers have also suggested that the differences between men and women in expressing sexual pleasure are no greater than the similarities, and that the naturalized value given the traditional asymmetry between female and male has been largely responsible for denying and hiding women's potential enjoyment.

A significant feature of the concern with the sexual aspect of marriage has been an explicit and unprecedented interest in women's needs and desires as sexual partners. Positive references to women's satisfaction and the publication of articles that encourage women to take the initiative in expressing sexual desire suggest an approach to sexuality that is no longer associated with the simple binary model of the active male and passive-responsive female. Warnings to women about the negative consequences of treating sex as a conjugal obligation are accompanied by other, no less important suggestions that they begin to view their own bodies and their sexual relationships with their husbands as a source of pleasure. Sex education materials not uncommonly contain references to the bodily and sensual locations of women's sexual pleasure: descriptions of the clitoris and the G spot make explicit references to the sources of female orgasm, signifying a recognition of the autonomous possibility of female pleasure that was with few exceptions absent from the former discourse. Materials for newlyweds— often assumed to be relatively ignorant about the different characteristics of men's and women's sexual needs and behavior—also draw attention to the need for women to assert their desires and dislikes in sexual relationships. Popular newspaper articles urge women to be critical of culturally determined feelings of shame and embarrassment and not to "hide their orgasm."[35]

Evidence linking women's sexual disinterest with the increasing rate of divorce offers one explanation for this apparently newfound interest in women's sexual desire. According to a random sample of divorce cases brought before the court in a particular district of Shanghai, "sexual incompatibility" was mentioned by one or both partners in 1955 in only 3.5 percent of the cases, while in 1985 this had risen to 20.9 percent. Another survey of one hundred divorce cases in the same court in 1985 revealed that of the 48.4 percent of partners who noted sexual incompatibility, the majority were women.[36] Sociological surveys, presented as scientific evidence of changing sexual practices, reinforce the gender implications of these figures. For example, the nationwide survey of sexual attitudes and practices carried out under the supervision of the Shanghai sociologist Liu Dalin found that large numbers of women of different ages, but particularly of the middle-aged and older cohorts, are totally disinterested in sex.[37] Sociologists offer various explanations for this. In her *Zhongguo ren de xing'ai yu hunyin*, Li Yinhe described divorcées' sexual experiences as a series of negative responses, from "initial lack of interest to total antipathy."[38] Other analyses link women's low expectations about romantic and sexual gratification to the reportedly "rough and selfish" sexual behavior of their husbands (a view reinforced by the increasing publicity given to domestic violence against women in recent years.) Indeed, according to Xu Anqi, women often attribute the failure of contraceptive methods to their husbands' "excessive desire and lack of reason."[39] However, Xu Anqi also points out that the greatest barriers to women's sexual enjoyment are the common assumptions that "a virtuous woman has no sexual desire" *(nüzi wu xing bian shi de)* and that "the only purpose of sex is reproduction" *(wei shengzhi mudi lun)*. Standard publications about love, marriage, and the family frequently assume that the wife's sexual desire has to be gently coaxed out of a natural state of reticence and passivity: "Women have to be educated out of treating sex as a burdensome marital duty."[40] All such representations convey a double message: that women should learn to assert themselves and reject unwanted advances, and men should think of sex as an expression of mutual desire rather than as an act driven by unilateral need.

Factors that derive from the implementation of birth control policy may also help explain women's sexual disinterest. Despite the legal requirements on both male and female partners to use contraceptive means to control fertility, evidence demonstrates that the responsibility for doing so invariably falls on women. The very high rates of sterilization of women at "high tide" periods of implementation of the birth control policy, and the frequent use of abortion as a follow-up to contraceptive method failure, im-

plicate women's bodies and psychological responses in explaining their resistance to sex in ways that are often associated with pain, brutality, and coercion.[41] The fear of becoming pregnant in itself may be enough to discourage many women from showing much interest in sex.[42] That women are
still, in practice, the target of the fertility control program may, for many
women, destroy altogether the possibility of heeding the experts' encouragement to think positively about sexual desire.

Attention to women's sexual behavior may be interpreted as an aspect of
the increasingly prevalent emphasis on sexual compatibility as an essential
component of a satisfactory marriage. By implication, sexual incompatibility is constructed as a potential source of marital conflict in ways that, given
the relative lack of importance attached to sex by comparison with other aspects of married life, were inapplicable in previous decades. However it is
approached, the current interest in women's sexual enjoyment thus concerns the durability of the official model of monogamous marriage, an institution vital to the process and results of economic and social reorganiza-
tion.[43] Improvements in levels of women's satisfaction are described as a
contribution to protecting marital stability, particularly in social contexts in
which women potentially enjoy much greater freedom of social, cultural,
and sexual activity due to the reduction of their childbearing and child care
responsibilities. In this light, contemporary discourses construct women's
sexual satisfaction as a requirement of and a contribution to demographic
and economic policy, with little direct reference to women themselves.

The unprecedented attention given to the sexual component of marriage in the last decade or so, and the similarly unprecedented emphasis on
the desirability of a "good sex life," has created new spaces and possibilities
for the invocation of sexual difficulties in the dominant discourse. Surveys
analyzing the various aspects of the married couple's sexual relationship put
as great a store on the difficulties and disparities as on the "good" sexual behavior constitutive of "harmony." Notions of a "good sex life" are constructed
with reference to inverse examples of incompatibility just as much as via affirmative description. Texts analyzing the reasons for sexual difficulties—
which frequently identify disinterest on the part of the wife and excessive
demands by the husband—and their place in cases of marital conflict have
made a significant contribution to the message that "sexual harmony" is the
normative objective. Though the immediate concern in such an approach
is to identify the sources of sexual incompatibility that reportedly are fuel-
ing the rising divorce rate, it simultaneously reinforces the view that marital
harmony depends on, among other things, sexual satisfaction.

However, the foregrounding of women's sexual experience within marriage has not substantially interfered with the hierarchical representation of
the sexual relationship within marriage. Even Li Wenhai and Liu Shuyu's
condemnation of the "myth" of female passivity did not question the fun-

damentally biological, noncontingent nature of the dominating male urge. Li and Liu's defense of women's right to sexual enjoyment does not, in itself, challenge the hierarchical order established by dominant views of sexual difference; the emphasis on women's sexual enjoyment has not disturbed the assumption that a wife's sexual awakening depends on the assistance and encouragement of her husband. The ideal of mutual orgasm as the ultimate goal of sexual activity—the undisputed aim to be aspired to by all sexually active couples—is thus contained within a paradigm of sexual activity in which the husband is the guide and mentor. Despite specific encouragement for women to discover different aspects of their own sexuality, the relational context for such advice suggests that experimentation should be oriented first and foremost to consolidating the marital relationship. From this perspective, female sexuality continues to be represented as a means of contributing to familial, and thereby to group and social, stability.

## THE NATURAL MOTHER

The Marriage Laws of 1950 and 1980 shared a conceptualization of women's role as wives and mothers that centered on a redefinition of the husband-wife relationship. According to this redefinition, the key relationship holding the household network together was, ideally, the monogamous marriage. Indeed, a major interest in the new government's commitment to strengthening the conjugal relationship was to secure a stable source of labor to contribute to the official program of socioeconomic transformation. This emphasis meant a shift in focus from the traditional axis of intergenerational, vertically structured relationships, according to which family authority depended on gender and generation, to one that constructed women and men as equal partners. The legal stipulations concerning the rights and duties of husband and wife represented the wife as the equal partner of her husband, enjoying "equal status in the home," subject to the same requirements of love, respect, and assistance, and with the same "freedom to engage in production, to work, to study and to participate in social activities."[44] The reassessment of the values accorded women as wives and as mothers created the possibility for a new conceptualization of the dominant attributes defining "woman." The official discourse no longer identified motherhood as the major subject position with which women should identify. Motherhood was modified by the new construction of wifehood, a social as well as sexual and gender category, which repositioned women as the equals of their husbands. Women's principal value was no longer to derive from producing male children, and no longer were women obliged to define their gender responsibilities with exclusive reference to husbands, sons, and mothers-in-law.

Such privileging of wifehood did not, of course, exclude motherhood.

Since 1949, official discourses have created wifehood not as a substitute for motherhood but as a position of responsibilities, expectations, and new possibilities that granted new meaning to the category of woman; wifehood has not replaced motherhood but has been given a new status in the hierarchy of roles and positions mediating women's experience. Thus, although the emphasis in discourses about women's natural attributes shifted to include subject positions associated with the new image of the working wife—subject positions not formerly available to women—they remained, and continue to remain, attached to a notion of motherhood as a desirable state for all women. From this perspective, motherhood emerges as an inalienable aspect of wifehood. The gender attributes and characteristics associated with women in the conjugal relationship emphasize women's role as mothers as much as their role as wives.

The step from constructing wifehood and motherhood as two sides of a coin to naturalizing motherhood as a universal aspect of being a woman is a small one. For a start, it closely corresponds with practice. The vast majority of women in China marry, as noted above, and more than 90 percent of these have their first child within their first year of marriage.[45] The almost universal practice of marriage and motherhood in China, and the common assumption of a biologically grounded correspondence between marriage, sexual intercourse, and reproduction, reinforces the image of the "natural mother." That women are "born to be mothers" is variously conveyed in Chinese discourses, from references to women's reproductive functions and physiological structure to the emotional and behavioral responses a young girl develops. In the 1950s, reproduction of the next generation was projected as woman's "natural duty" *(tianran yiwu),* and failure to fulfill it was considered irresponsible.[46] More recent representations of womanhood have focused on the psychological loss experienced by childless women. Remaining single, and thereby "foregoing the joys of motherhood," makes women feel "incomplete and unfulfilled."[47] It may also be the expression of sexual needs and desires not condoned by the exclusively heterosexual bias of the dominant discourse. Only in exceptional cases of "mental or contagious disease" is it considered legitimate—indeed given the full backing of a eugenics law—for women "to defer marriage" and not to have children.[48] Notwithstanding the disruption of the link between sexuality and reproduction signified by the prevalent use of contraceptive methods, as well as the frustrations of having to obtain bureaucratic permission from the work unit and street committee in order to conceive, the common assumption is that marriage means children, and that as soon as people marry they begin trying to have a child. Indeed, those who delay having children are frequently subject to gossip and ridicule; women who show no signs of pregnancy within a year or so of marriage may be rumored to be sick or too old, or their husbands "too weak," or as in the 1950s, reneging on their duty.[49]

The natural positioning of women as mothers in dominant discourses since 1949 has also clearly emerged in advice and information about contraception. Coinciding with the formation of a rudimentary birth control policy in the mid-1950s, much of the early discussion about contraception set out to persuade a cautious audience of the benefits of the different methods available. Details of contraceptive techniques that made use of Chinese medicine as well as more standard Western methods were explained to allay popular worries that, for example, the use of condoms would impair male potency or would cause tuberculosis in women—a disease commonly associated with female sexuality in the 1950s—by preventing the "yin and yang from joining together."[50] Through the 1970s, as the "later, more spaced, fewer" birth control policy gathered steam, discussion about contraception emphasized its more general benefits to "the health of mothers and the next generation" by reducing the average number of babies women gave birth to.[51] Since then, discussion about contraception has been situated firmly within the context of the single-child family policy and has also assumed a much greater familiarity on the part of its audience. Official statistics from the State Statistics Bureau in 1991 indicated that the national use of contraceptive methods among married women rose from 13.47 percent in 1970 to 73.24 percent in 1988.[52] Even though the contraceptive methods were still less popular in the rural areas than in the towns and cities—by 1988, 64.45 percent of rural married women were using contraceptives—these figures clearly demonstrated that persuading a reluctant constituency of potential users was no longer the major problem.[53] However, detailed information about and access to contraception remains firmly controlled by the family planning agencies and is not generally available to unmarried couples. Although contraceptives are easily obtainable over the counter in pharmacies and sex shops in towns and cities, and unmarried couples often obtain them through married friends, sex education courses, even at the university level, do not formally include information about contraceptive methods. To include such would be inconsistent with the administrative attempts to prohibit students from sexual activity and marriage, which include obliging visitors to register their name and work unit, or not permitting friends to stay overnight in the same room. Although, as earlier chapters have shown, sex education is considered vital to the health and happiness of the married couple, and premarital pregnancies are often attributed to sexual ignorance, contraception is still formally excluded from discussion in materials for young people on the grounds that its inclusion would be an invitation to premarital promiscuity. Public discussion about contraception is bound by the assumption that sex can legitimately be referred to only within the context of marriage.

Advice about the benefits of contraception draws a direct link between fertility control and the quality of a couple's sex life. Ever since it appeared as an item on the official agenda, the use of contraception has been represented as an aid to "marital feeling" and to "resolving the difficulties of early marriage" imposed by the burdens of childcare.[54] The equation of womanhood and motherhood, or wifehood and motherhood, is no longer automatic. Accounts of women who choose to remain single and forgo childbirth do not necessarily condemn them as abnormal or irresponsible. Occasionally, articles put a positive gloss on representations of the single woman and suggested that rejection of marriage did not necessarily lead to solitude and despair.[55] However, the use of contraception continues to be represented as an aid to a couple's sex life because it limits the number of children, not because it challenges the requirement to reproduce. Although in theoretical terms contraception severs the link between sexuality and reproduction, in the terms of the dominant discourse it is treated as a means of controlling that link, not of breaking it. The representation of reproduction as a natural biological need and a social duty denies women this alternative. In this light, contraception grants women no more than the possibility of determining the length and timing of their childbearing careers. Though the government's desire to control the birthrate would logically be served by encouraging women not to have children—by positively constructing childless women as an aid to social and economic development—the dominant discourse offers women no real alternative to their naturalized role as mother.

Despite the legal requirements on both partners to use contraceptive methods, texts about contraception commonly—though not exclusively—assume that birth control is principally a woman's responsibility.[56] Evidence from surveys indicates that the intrauterine device (IUD) and tubal ligation are the preferred methods of contraception, with the pill, condom, and cervical cap ranking some way behind.[57] Female responsibility for practicing birth control, however, does not simply refer to women's instrumentality in deciding what form of contraception to use and when to use it. Policy and official discourse construct women as the responsible agents of birth control: their bodies are targeted as the means of restricting the number of pregnancies at any particular time, whether through the use of the IUD or abortion. A survey carried out in 1991 and 1992 among women of the thirty- to thirty-nine-year-old age group in two counties in Sichuan and Jiangsu provinces showed that, between 1980 and 1990, most abortions were performed to terminate pregnancies after the first birth, and that in all cases these pregnancies had occurred without official permission.[58] Moreover, as if women's "responsibility" for implementing the fertility limitation program were not enough, the eugenic concerns of the state's family planning personnel, expressed in the 1995 Law on Maternal and Infantile Health Care, also construct women as the key agents guaranteeing the wholesome birth, physical health, intelligence, and psychological development of the next generation. Contemporary discourses on sexuality thus concur with empirical evidence in showing that women bear the major responsibility for supporting the state's demographic policy. Although theoretically removed from reproductive considerations—a notable effect of the single-child family policy has been to extend women's nonreproductive sexually active life— female sexuality continues to be underpinned by a series of expectations, naturalized assumptions, responsibilities, and burdens inextricably identified with women's reproductive functions.[59]

In the foregoing sections I have argued that the contrasts between revolutionary and reformist images of the ideal wife have obscured certain assumptions about the meanings associated with being a woman. Contrary to appearances, these assumptions have enjoyed an enduring influence in dominant discourses on women and gender in China since 1949. This is not, of course, to deny the radical new possibilities that the current diversity of images offers. However, the range of positions covered by this diversity is contained within parameters determined by the changing character of the market within a global commercial system. China's domestic market itself is a thriving site of gender hierarchies—in employment, unemployment, income, and consumer capacity. The gender representations that dominate globalized visual culture serve to reinforce these hierarchies and the naturalist gender assumptions inscribed in them. For decades, wifehood has thus been represented as a kind of erasure of difference, any challenge to which has been vilified as a physical abnormality, sickness, or moral and ideological degeneracy. The erasure of difference has thus not simply indicated a denial of gender as a field of different subjectivities but a particular mode of women's subordination within the hierarchies of power to convey dominant, or hegemonic, views of appropriate and inappropriate conduct. The conclusion of a recent popular article on the changing ideals of femininity suggests the same message. "From Liu Huifang to Tian Manfang; How Far Have You Women Gone?" paints a picture of a successful deputy manager of the biggest joint-venture company in her town.[60] Born into a poor family, Tian Manfang struggled against social and economic pressures to acquire a higher education. She became, in effect, an example of the perfect "strong woman" of the mid-1990s. But despite the obvious contrasts with Liu Huifang, in "inner, psychological terms" she had not necessarily moved on much at all, or so the article's author suggests.

## CHALLENGES

In recent years increasing publicity has shed light on aspects of women's lives—many of which entail gross violations of women's human rights—

that make a mockery of the image of the ideal wife. Information about the rising divorce rate as an expression of women's changing aspirations, domestic and sexual violence against women, and the abduction and sale of women into marriage and prostitution all suggest the enormity of the divide between the ideal and hard reality.[61] Resistance to images that objectify women's bodies for sexual and commercial gratification is apparent in a number of debates about sexuality and gender. Women conducting research on marriage and divorce refer to possibilities of female sexual pleasure in ways that indicate a radical departure from the values of the former discourses. Surveys that demonstrate a significantly increased incidence of premarital and extramarital sex in China's cities demonstrate that, whether in lived sexual experience or in media representations, monogamous marriage is not necessarily identified with lifelong sexual exclusivity. Increasing numbers of young married couples, notably professionals and intellectuals, are choosing not to have children. Some professional women are rejecting marriage altogether, not in the name of celibacy but in order to enjoy the possibility of social and sexual independence outside the perceived limitations of marriage. Lesbians are forging a space within which their voices can be heard in activists' groups and on Web sites.

Alongside these departures, adultery has emerged as a specific topic of debate in which conventional representations of women in sexual contexts are being contested. As in the 1950s, women who transgress the normative boundaries of sexual propriety are commonly represented as evildoers, the creators of misery for themselves and others. Stories about adultery widely focus on the immorality of the female "third party," constructing her as responsible for leading the weak-willed man astray. A 1986 report noted that 86.1 percent of the respondents of an investigation conducted in Shanghai felt that the intruding female "third party" should be punished according to the law.[62] An article of 1991 further suggested that among the 60 percent of divorce cases brought to court on the grounds of adultery, the female "third party" was invariably to blame for "being prepared to construct her own happiness on the basis of someone else's misery."[63] Although many accounts criticize both parties involved in adulterous affairs, the assumption that "triangular relationships" are created by the intervention of a calculating "third party" was still, according to a 1992 report, widely shared by men and women alike.[64] The implication that women are responsible for the increase in extramarital affairs is inescapable. However, some evidence—albeit limited—indicates that women may be beginning to publicly question the assumption of female guilt. A woman who, after twelve years of an arranged marriage and two children, fell in love with a younger man received a not unsympathetic response when her story was published in a magazine debate about the "third party."[65] Proposals to legally punish the "third party" in divorce cases have recently been robustly criticized by feminists in China, who argue that such punishment is neither feasible nor desirable, and that it simply does not address the fundamental issues of women's vulnerability in divorce settlements.[66] Such sympathy may be uncommon, but it nevertheless signifies an attack on the conventional double standard of sexual morality, according to which women are censured for activities for which men bear just as much responsibility. It also challenges the familiar representation of female conduct as the fulcrum of sexual morality, responsible for sustaining marital stability by supporting and servicing her husband.

One very recent theme relevant to discussions about wives suggests not only a disavowal of the ideal but also a significant disturbance of the assumptions embedded in it. As state enterprises throughout the country continue to lay off female workers, and as academics continue to insist that economic efficiency is incompatible with sexual equality in employment, large numbers of articles point to the conflicts that arise when women are obliged to "return home." The national press and mainline women's journals such as *Zhongguo funü* have featured numerous stories about women whose professional and economic interests have been sacrificed to the government's attempts to alleviate financial burdens on urban enterprises. In Tianjin, for example, by the first half of 1996, 260,000 workers in state enterprises had been laid off, 70 percent of whom were middle-aged women. A factory in Kaifeng laid off 70 percent of its female workforce—altogether 7,000 women—in the same period.[67] Another article featured nine workers, half of them women, who took their former factory employers to court to protest their unlawful dismissal. Evidence also shows that many women are unwilling to accept the explanations given to them, that women's biological needs explain the "imperfections of the economic system."[68] Autobiographical descriptions by women who have been laid off indicate they are far from happy to return to their "natural" context, even when their income is no longer necessary to support the family. A Women's Federation survey assessing the difficulties faced by laid-off women workers showed that, for 70 percent of the 700 women interviewed, family conflicts followed their return home. The women reported depression, low self-esteem, and a loss of social status and recognition. Women also wrote that the "move back home" required them to confront the realities of men's backwardness as well as of the lack of sexual equality. Even more stridently, one woman argued that the main problem had little to do with women's biological characteristics but everything to do with "masculinity" *(nanxing)* and patriarchy *(fuquan).*[69]

That women challenge the idea that they must sacrifice themselves for the sake of the market economy is also an act of contesting the feminine ideal as represented in the dominant media. Their unwillingness to return to a domestic context that, at least for some, requires submission to the husband implies rejection of the gender assumptions about service and support that, since 1949, the image of the "ideal wife" has consistently emphasized.

## CONCLUSIONS

The state's continuing interest in regulating sexual practice at a time of market-oriented economic reform has contributed to the emergence of sexuality, particularly female sexuality, and gender as a contested terrain. On the one hand, woman is constructed as the key agent of sexual and marital order, enjoined to patrol her own sexual conduct for the sake of marital and familial harmony. On the other hand, she is represented as an object for men's sexual gratification, waiting to be made whole, even given life, by the active and dominant male. However, woman is also beginning to be the guardian of her own body and fate against male attempts—whether by husband, state, or market—to appropriate them. Not only are an increasing number of voices suggesting that the biological underpinnings of sexuality do not stand up to scientific scrutiny, but new spaces for articulation of individual experiences are empowering women, arguably for the first time in the history of the People's Republic of China, to examine their own gender and sexual identities in ways not automatically mediated by male or state interests. These aspects constitute a marginal aspect of public representations of the woman as wife—indeed, too marginal for us to assess how they may contribute to the creation of new subject positions for women. Messages to women to uphold the sanctity of monogamous marriage and to protect standards of sexual behavior by patrolling their own sexual conduct still figure prominently in public discussions about marriage. But indications from the divorce courts as well as from women who have been forced to "return home" suggest that the ideal image of the gentle wife is becoming a key site where women's self-identification is in flux and where the essentialist assumptions embedded in the ideal are no longer fixed. The insistence of the reform strategy on invoking women's essential femininity has produced— by default—the possibility for contesting it.

## NOTES

1. During the first three decades after 1949, there were only two significant moments when women's domestic and marital positions were explained in terms of gender rather than class. During the 1950–53 period, when extensive efforts were made to publicize the radical potential for women of the Marriage Law of the People's Republic of China, domestic discrimination against women was repeatedly condemned, albeit as an aspect of continuing feudal practices. Again, during a brief period of the Criticize Confucius, Criticize Lin Biao campaign (1971–73) women were encour-

aged to examine the domestic aspects of their subordinate position in society. Apart from these two moments, gender inequality within the domestic and marriage contexts was invariably explained as the consequence of socioeconomic (class) issues and ideological failings. For a fuller discussion of this, see my *Women and Sexuality in China* (London: Hurst; New York: Continuum, 1997), chap. 1.

2. For a fuller treatment of this argument, with reference to other constructions of "woman," see ibid. Frank Dikötter traces the modern development of these assumptions in twentieth-century approaches to sex in China in his *Sex, Modernity, and Culture in China* (London: Hurst, 1995).

3. Sun Ming, "Tantan fuqi guanxi" [Talking about marital relationships], (Shanghai: Shanghai Renmin chubanshe, 1958), 17–19.

4. Ibid., 19.

5. Gan Zhongqing, "Qizi bi zhangfu nengli qiang jiu shi 'bu xiangchen de hunyin' ma?" [When a wife is more able than her husband, are they a poorly matched pair?], *Zhongguo funü* [Women of China] 7 (1959): 28.

6. Sun Ming, "Tantan fuqi guanxi," 21.

7. "Kefu jiating shenghuo zhong de lijizhuyi sixiang" [Overcome selfish thinking in family life], *Zhongguo funü* 6 (1956): 14–16.

8. Li Zhen, *Zhenzhen de aiqing* [True love] (Beijing: Zhongguo qingnian chubanshe, 1956), 12–14.

9. Zhang Fan, ed., *Lian'ai, hunyin yu fufu shenghuo* [Love, marriage, and married life] (Shanghai: Zhanwang zhoukanshe, 1952), 68.

10. Xia Gengfen, "Lian'ai wenti bu yinggai yingxiang wo canjia junshi ganbu xuexiao" [The love question should not affect my participation in the military cadres' school], *Zhongguo qingnian* [Chinese youth] 55 (1955): 13.

11. Hu Xian, "Xin xifu" [The new daughter-in-law], *Zhongguo qingnian* 1 (1954): 10–14.

12. Liu Dezhen, "Wo liang you xinxin jianli yige xin jiating" [We two have the confidence to set up a new home], *Zhongguo funü* 1 (1952): 31.

13. Pang Hui, "Wo yinggai ai ta" [I should love her], *Zhongguo funü* 23 (1959): 18–20.

14. Zheng Hao, "Cengjing zouguo de wan lu" [The twisted path I once went along], *Zhongguo qingnian* 2 (1957): 33–34.

15. Cai Chang, "Gao hao jiawu laodong, zhiyuan guojia jianshe" [Do domestic work well and support state construction], *Zhongguo funü* 9 (1957): 2–5. At the time, Cai Chang was chair of the All China Women's Federation.

16. These comments were made in response to readers' letters in *Zhongguo funü* (1957): 14–15.

17. Zhang Yibai, "Zhengque de duidai ziji de gongzuo wenti" [Treat correctly your work problems], *Zhongguo funü* 4 (1957): 1–2.

18. Jiang Wenyu, "Xingxing sese ze'ou xinli" [The diverse psychology of mate selection], *Nü qingnian* [Young women] 3 (1986): 7.

19. Li Jiangtao, "Yige bei hushile de wenti" [A problem that has been overlooked], *Zhongguo funü* 2 (1986): 6–7.

20. "Ni xiang zuo ge hao qizi ma?" [Do you want to be a good wife?], in *Funü zhiyou* [Women's friend], *Funü baike daquan (xia)* [Women's encyclopedia, vol. 2],

ed. *Funü zhiyou* [Women's friend] (Beijing: Beifang funü ertong chubanshe, 1991), 12–19.

21. Shu Huaimeng, "Nüren bu lao dao cheng ma?" [Would it be OK if women didn't gossip?], *Nüxing yanjiu* [Women's studies] 5 (1993): 61. This journal had a radical "facelift" when it appeared under the new title of *Nüxing yuekan* [Women's monthly]. Glossier, sexier, and more fashionable, it now contains many more ads, many more articles to appeal to a popular audience, and correspondingly far fewer articles on the serious issues indicated by its former title.

22. For a discussion about successful national sportswomen, see Susan Brownell, "The Body and the Beautiful in Chinese Nationalism: Sportswomen and Fashion Models in the Reform Era," *China Information* 8, nos. 2–3 (autumn-winter 1998–99): 36–58; for a discussion of the *hanxu* female image, see San Wanqun, "Chongsu nüxing mei de kanke zhi lu" [The rough road to remolding female beauty], *Zhongguo funü* 2 (1992).

23. In the course of many discussions I had between March and April 1993 with academics and Beijing Women's Federation representatives about women, marriage, and the family, repeated reference was made to this soap as evidence of the popularity of the image of the gentle supportive wife. Lisa Rofel argues that far from being simply a popular form of entertainment devoid of politics, *Yearning* represented a "hegemonic" cultural form that contained significant political meanings. Lisa Rofel, "'Kewang': Funü he tongsu wenha" ["Yearning": Women and popular culture], in *Xingbie yu Zhongguo* [Gender and China], ed. Li Xiaojiang, Zhu Hong, and Dong Xiuyu (Beijing: Sanlian chubanshe, 1994), 292–302.

24. Meng Yue expresses this view with reference to the need to rebuild female subjectivity and desire on the basis of foundations laid in the May Fourth period and in response to the socialist revolution's substitution of masculinist desire for female sexuality. Meng Yue, "Female Images and National Myth," in *Gender Politics in Modern China*, ed. Tani Barlow (Durham: Duke University Press, 1993), 118–36. Wendy Larson refers to contemporary narrative configurations of a similar view in the work of contemporary writers and filmmakers in "Women and the Discourse of Desire in Postrevolutionary China," *boundary* 2, 24, no. 3 (1997): 201–23.

25. *Zhongguo funü* 8 (1996): 30–31.

26. Zhang Xijun, "Cong shenglixue jiaodu tan hunling wenti" [Talking about the age of marriage from a physiological angle], *Zhongguo qingnian* 6 (1957): 34. As many writers have pointed out, marriage is almost universal in China. According to 1990 census figures, the figures for unmarried women and men were 41.21 percent and 62.52 percent, respectively, for the 20–24-year-old age group in 1990, 4.3 percent and 16.71 percent for the 25–29-year-old age group, and 0.65 percent and 7.18 percent for the 30–34-year-old age group. By comparison with 1982 figures, these figures signified an increase in the number of women who married while under the legal age of 20, and a drop of 15 percent in the number of unmarried women under the age of 30 (Zheng Xiaoying, ed., *Zhongguo nüxing renkou wenti yu fazhan* [Problems and development of China's female population] [Beijing: Beijing daxe chubanshe, 1995], 135).

27. Frank Dikötter analyses the modern development of "scientific" approaches to human sexuality in his *Sex, Culture, and Modernity in China*. He suggests that the paradigm upheld by modern biomedical science in China combined Western sexo-

logical theories of individuals such as Havelock Ellis with indigenous views of sexuality as a series of complementary forces.

28. *Xinhun weisheng bi du* editorial group, *Xinhun weisheng bi du* [Necessary reading for newlyweds] (Beijing: Renmin weisheng chubanshe, 1982), 28–30; Li Wenhai and Liu Shuyu, *Chengren xing jiaoyu zhimi—xing de wujie he duice* [A guide to adult sex education—misunderstandings and ways to deal with sex] (Changsha: Hunan kexue jishu chubanshe, 1992), 47–50.

29. Liu Changqing, "Nüxing xing gaochao zhang'ai xunyin" [Seeking to explain the barriers to female orgasm], *Dazhong jiankang* [Popular health] 6 (1995): 28; Xu Zhong, "Xing kuaigan quefa zenmo ban?" [What should be done when sex is not pleasurable?], *Nüxing yanjiu* 1 (1994): 53.

30. Evans, *Women and Sexuality in China*, chap. 7.

31. The only substantial exception was during the brief period of "liberalization" in early 1957, after publication of the famous booklet by Wang Wenbin et al., *Xing de zhishi* [Knowledge about sex] (Beijing: Renmin weisheng chubanshe, 1956), and related articles such as "Guanyu xing zhishi de jige wenti," *Zhongguo qingnian* 13 (1956): 27–28.

32. Zhang Biao, *Fuqi qingmi* [Conjugal secrets] (Beijing: Zhongguo huaqiao chubanshe, 1991), 30.

33. Fang Fang, *Nüxing shengli yu xinli* [Female physiology and psychology] (Chengdu: Sichuan renmin chubanshe, 1987), 80–81.

34. Li Wenhai and Liu Shuyu, *Chengren*, 61–62.

35. *Jiankang wenzhai bao*, 14 April 1993.

36. Xu Anqi, "Beidongxing, juezu quan he di manyi" [Passivity, the right to choose, and low satisfaction], *Shehuixue yanjiu* (Sociological Research) 3 (1990): 106–7.

37. Liu Dalin, ed., *Zhongguo dangdai xing wenhua* [Sexual behavior in contemporary China] (Shanghai: Sanlian shudian, 1992), 410–25.

38. Li Yinhe, *Zhongguo ren de xing'ai yu hunyin* [Sexual love and marriage among Chinese people] (Zhengzhou: Henan renmin chubanshe, 1991), 186.

39. Xu Anqi, "Beidongxing," 104–7.

40. Gao Fang and Zeng Rong, eds., *Jiushi niandai nüxing baishi zhinan* [A comprehensive guide for women in the nineties] (Beijing: Nongcun duwu chubanshe, 1991), 35–37.

41. In their study of family planning policy and practice in four counties, Joan Kaufman, Zhang Zhirong, Qiao Xinjian, and Zhang Yang found that sterilizations and intrauterine device insertions peaked in 1979–80 and 1983, when the single-child policy was most stringently implemented, lending support to the argument that coercive methods were being used to achieve birth control objectives ("Family Planning Policy and Practice in China: A Study of Four Rural Counties," *Population and Development Review* 15, no. 4 [1989]: 707–29, see esp. 722).

42. Xu Anqi, "Beidongxing," 104. The effects of the fertility control program on women's sexuality is a topic that cannot be adequately treated in this chapter. It is worth pointing out, however, that it is one of the many issues concerning women's lives and experiences that has been ignored in the massive amounts of material published about the population control policy.

43. The idealized model of lifelong monogamy has been increasingly threat-

ened by the rising incidence of divorce, particularly in the larger cities. Although the number of divorces in 1994 was only 1.2 percent higher than in 1990, and divorces are still uncommon by Western standards, the fact that 12.38 million people ended their marriages in 1994 attracted widespread public and official concern in China (*People's Daily* [Overseas Edition], *China News Digest,* 23 March 1995). Whatever the reasons explaining this increase, the considerable incidence of adultery in divorce cases heard before the courts clearly indicates that marriage is far from being the exclusive domain for sexual relations, even though this may still be the ideal propagated in educational and popular materials. However, representations of extramarital sexual activity (images, narratives, cautionary tales, and so on) commonly suggest a range of negative sanctions that call attention to the dire consequences— to body, mind, family, and society—of nonconformity to the dominant model. The clear contrast between the positive representation of sexual relations within marriage and the harm derived from sexual activity outside marriage constitutes a means of reinforcing the unique legitimacy of sex within marriage.

44. Article 11, 1980 Marriage Law of the People's Republic of China.

45. Zeng Yi, *Family Dynamics in China: A Life Table Analysis* (Madison: University of Wisconsin Press, 1992), 6, noted that births by women aged twenty to twenty-nine accounted for 80 percent of all births in China at the time of writing.

46. See, for example, Wei Junyi, "Yang haizi shi fou fang'ai jinbu?" [Does bringing up children impede progress?], *Zhongguo qingnian* 21 (1953): 13–14.

47. Yu Yan, "Nüren: Danshen de kungan" [Women: The miseries of being single], *Nüxing yanjiu* 5 (1993): 48).

48. The Law on Maternal and Infantile Health Care, previously named the Draft Eugenics Law, went into effect on June 1, 1995. For more detailed and polemical discussion about this, see Frank Dikötter, *Imperfect Conceptions: Medical Knowledge, Birth Defects, and Eugenics in China* (London: Hurst and Company, 1998), chap. 4.

49. Emily Honig and Gail Hershatter, *Personal Voices: Chinese Women in the 1980s* (Stanford: Stanford University Press, 1988), 188.

50. Tan Zhen, "Biyun yingxiang jiankang ma?" [Does contraception affect health?], *Zhongguo funü* 7 (1956): 26. Tuberculosis was commonly associated with women's sexuality in the 1950s, according to Liang Zhao, "Jihua shengyu bing bu nan" [Birth control is not at all difficult], *Zhongguo funü* 4 (1957): 26.

51. For example, Shanghai diyi yixueyuan fushu Zhongshan yiyuan fuchanke [Department of Gynecology and Obstetrics of the Zhongshan Hospital, affiliated to the Shanghai Number 1 Hospital], *Funü baojian zhishi* [Knowledge about women's health] (Shanghai: Shanghai renmin chubanshe, 1974), 10.

52. Zheng, ed., *Zhongguo nüxing renkou wenti yu fazhan* [Problems and development of China's female population], 247.

53. A 1987 survey of four counties in Fujian and Heilongjiang revealed a contraceptive prevalence rate for 1986 of 91 to 98 percent. See Kaufman et al., "Family Planning Policy and Practice in China," 707–29. The researchers attributed the differential between these and the official figures to the possibility that the "ineligible" women ("newly married and waiting for the first birth, breastfeeding, pregnant or infertile") were omitted from the lists they (Kaufman et al.) used to select their sample, or that some women may not have answered honestly (716).

54. For example, "Buyao guozao jiehun" [Don't marry too early], *Zhongguo qing-nian* 4 (1957): 9.

55. Shang Zisong, "Nanren yan zhong dedanshen nüren" [Single women in men's eyes], *Nüxing yanjiu* 2 (1992): 35–36.

56. Marriage Law of the People's Republic of China, Chapter III, Article 12, states that "husband and wife are in duty bound to practice family planning."

57. Although men used condoms in three of the four counties Joan Kaufman and colleagues surveyed, it was the least-favored method. Male sterilization was also uncommon and was not used at all in the two Heilongjiang counties of the sample (716).

58. Mu Aiping, "Rural Women's Economic Activities and Fertility Behaviour in Selected Areas of China during 1979–1990" (Ph.D. diss., University of Glamorgan, Wales, 1994), 179. According to Mu Aiping's findings, the average number of abortions for the decade in question was .46 per woman (179), in contrast with Susan Greenhalgh's finding of .14 percent, cited in her *The Changing Value of Children in the Transition from Socialism: The View from Three Villages*, Research Division Working Paper No. 43 (New York: The Population Council, 1992). Mu Aiping explains this discrepancy with reference to Greenhalgh's sample, which covered all women married between 1971 and 1987, while her own focused on women who were between thirty and thirty-nine years old in 1990.

59. Persistent references to the harmful effects on fertility and fetal development specific to having sex at particular moments of the female cycle indicate that reproduction remains a key organizing principle of the discourse about female sexuality. Expert opinion of the 1950s was consistent in its warnings against sexual intercourse during menstruation and during the first three and last three months of pregnancy, on the grounds that the introduction of bacteria into the uterus would cause uterine inflammation, potentially impairing fertility. Texts of the 1970s reiterated the same message in almost identical terms. See, for example, Xie Bozhang, *Qingchunqi weisheng* [Adolescent hygiene] (Beijing: Beijing renmin chubanshe, 1975), 81; Shanghai diyi yixueyuan fushu Zhongshan yiyuan fuchanke [Department of Gynecology and Obstetrics of the Zhongshan Hospital, affiliated to the Shanghai Number 1 Hospital], *Funü baojian zhishi* [Knowledge about women's health], 4. In the reform period, sex during pregnancy is still regarded as a possible cause of miscarriage and premature labor. See, for example, Guangdong sheng funü lianhe hui [Canton Women's Federation], *Xin shenghuo zhidao* [A guide to life for newlyweds], ed. Guangdong sheng jiating jiaoyu yanjiu hui [Canton Research Association for Domestic Education] (Guangzhou: Xin shiji chubanshe, 1986), 26. And whether the advice is in booklets distributed to newlyweds or in more general texts about female physiology and psychology, sex during menstruation is widely seen as a potential danger to the female reproductive capacity because of the vagina's vulnerability to bacterial infection and because of sex's effects on prolonging the menstrual period (*Xinhun weisheng bi du* editorial group, *Xinhun weisheng bi du*, 24; Fang Fang, *Nüxing shengli yu xinli*, 117). Even though women's desire for sex sometimes increases around the menstrual period, both women and men are urged to exercise self-restraint in order to prevent any reproductive complications.

60. Guan Ting, *Zhongguo funü* 6 (1996): 48–49.

61. One of the discriminatory dichotomies embedded in this same divide is the

familiar urban-rural one, according to which the rural effectively becomes a feminized metaphor for all that is backward, uncivilized, and undesirable. The idea that the "rural" might signify a legitimate site of experience, and that affirmative publicity about it might empower women rather than remind them of the impossibility of the ideal, has been ignored by the homogenizing urban emphasis of standard images of the ideal.

62. *Minzhu yu fazhi* (January 1986): 27–28.

63. *Funü baike daquan* (May 1991): 44–45.

64. *Jiating yisheng* (April 1992): 22.

65. *Funü zhi you (xia)* (May 1991): 42–43.

66. For a critical article about these proposals, see Li Yinhe, "Pei ou quan: Hunwai xing guanxi yu falü" [Partners' rights: Extramarital sexual relations and law], *Du shu* 1 (1999): 3–18. In this article, Li Yinhe analyzes the historical and contemporary factors contributing to women's vulnerability in divorce cases and argues that, in the current period, "both in economic terms and in access to jobs and facilities, women are in a position of relative disadvantage, and [because of this] their economic dependence on men may perforce increase" (18). She also writes that "in a significant category of divorce cases, particularly those in which the intervention of a 'third party' is involved, invariably the party that seeks divorce (the majority of whom are middle-aged men) is wealthy, successful and has a certain social status" (14). In her view, therefore, the new proposals do nothing to address the material problems faced by the divorcée. Added to the continuing disdain frequently shown to female "third parties" as well as divorcées, her argument further implies that any attempt to punish the "third party" would reinforce women's vulnerability and victimization rather than seriously address its causes. Li Yinhe is a feminist sociologist working in the Institute of Sociology, Chinese Academy of Social Sciences. Her recent publications on homosexuality, female sexuality, and sadomasochism have provoked widespread critical comment in the Chinese media.

67. *Zhongguo funü* 8 (1996): 14, 46–48.

68. Ibid., 10 (1996): 17.

69. Ibid., 18, 20.

# CHAPTER FOURTEEN

# Proper Men and Proper Women:
# Parental Affection in the Chinese Family

*William Jankowiak*

The study of Chinese gender, especially over the last twenty years, has been oriented predominantly toward exploring how structural forces have shaped the formation of public institutions ranging from the nation-state to the family. Whatever the focus, the emphasis is the same: gender studies examine the relationship between external structures and the formation of patterns of association. In the case of studies of Chinese gender, focusing on the structural dimension has contributed to a disregard of the intimate domain, especially as it pertains to the emotional sphere of pleasure, sentimentality, loyalty, compassion, ardent love, and passionate self-sacrifice. Researchers of Chinese gender have been more interested in understanding the interplay between factors that produce structural inequality than in understanding the interplay between those that produce harmony, cooperation, or unity. For most, the study of gender is intertwined with the study of social marginalization, discrimination, domination, and resistance. The intimate domain is seldom explored, not so much the result of a lack of interest but of the absence of a conceptual framework within which to interpret it. This is especially so when action within that domain stands in sharp contrast to behavior found in the corporate sphere.

This bias in the study of gender relations in Chinese society was not evident in the work of the previous generation of ethnographers, many of them husband-wife research teams (e.g., Bernard and Rita Gallin, James and Rubie Watson, and Arthur and Margery Wolf), who wrote inclusive ethnographic accounts of rural Chinese society. Their work stands in sharp contrast to the structural approach favored by the British social anthropologists of their day or the political economists of the 1990s. It is ironic that the anthropological trend of the 1990s, which has focused on "emotionality," has, with the exception of the work of Sulamith Potter, Yunxiang Yan, and myself, completely bypassed the anthropology of China.[1] In this way the previous generation of "China scholars were ahead of their time, and China anthropology has yet to catch up or build on their work."[2]

In this chapter I discuss how structural and emotional issues are intertwined in the lives of men and women in Huhhot, capital of the Inner Mongolian Autonomous Region of the People's Republic of China. Huhhot is a city with a population of over five hundred thousand, of which 80 percent are Han and the remaining 20 percent are either Chinese Moslem (Hui) or Mongolian. The material that forms much of this research was collected between 1981 and 1983 and again in 1987, over a total period of two and a half years. My description of family dynamics comes from my regular visits to seventy households during these periods. My knowledge of intimate matters of the heart comes from the many hours I spent in conversation with people, often over drinks; I discovered that I had to be willing to share part of myself as an offering in genuine communication across the borders that define culture. My research on women's emotions was aided by a female assistant.[3] These research methods allow me to explore in this chapter how gender ideals are displayed in playful and earnest conversation among men and women in unisex groups, as well as between men and women in the domains of marriage, emotional intimacy, and parenting. By focusing on the relationship between the subjective and the structural, I hope to contribute some insight into the emotional dilemmas Chinese men experience in striving to find a place in society as well as in the family, at a period when both are undergoing rapid change.

## CONTEMPORARY CHINA: AN OVERVIEW

In 1949, the Communist Party came to power promising to curb governmental complacency, corruption, and economic individualism and thereby rescue Chinese society from impending economic and moral bankruptcy. Under the Party's guidance, a "socialist ethos" was promoted that stressed public virtue over individual gain, the importance of self-denial and social obligations, and an overall egalitarian lifestyle. This ethos, the Party felt, would improve the moral climate necessary to create its utopian vision—the egalitarian society.

Besides diminishing considerations of social class, the Party also wanted to eliminate sex discrimination by providing jobs and education and creating a less hostile environment in which women could participate as full citizens in the new public culture. By the 1980s, however, this idea was rejected by most Chinese, who focused on their own interests within and outside the nuclear family. That the Party encouraged consumption as the primary means for stimulating economic growth of the nation was well received by most people, who had long desired to accumulate things and experiences in contemporary China. The new consumer culture provided a more open and tolerant public context, in which men and women felt comfortable displaying cherished cultural assumptions about the "naturalness" of men and women, and of maleness and femaleness, within a variety of different social settings.

The elimination of most family property had forced the urban populace to rely on bureaucratic agencies for housing and other critical resources, thereby weakening the traditional patrilineal and patrilocal forms in favor of a more flexible system organized around the principles of neolocal residence and bilateral descent. In the process, the politics of kinship had been transformed. Urban women, unlike their rural counterparts, earned a salary that was of paramount importance to the family budget as well as to management of family finances, and they had equal access to educational opportunities—so they had a greater opportunity to achieve parity with men in the family decision-making process. Hence, they were able to more readily achieve independence and security within the domestic sphere. Margery Wolf found that, as a consequence, urban women were less concerned than rural women with protecting their personal interests against the interests of a hostile mother-in-law and an indifferent or threatening husband.[4] These new realities have enabled urban women to achieve a sphere of power and domestic independence faster than had been the case in their mothers' generation, when women achieved their greatest domestic power late in life. In addition, love, marriage, and spousal intimacy are widely regarded as important and worthwhile aspirations.[5]

## HIERARCHY, PERSONHOOD, AND GENDER IRRELEVANCE

The rise of the market economy has resulted in a new value system, whereby the former heroes of the collective era have given way to new heroes—the sports athlete, the rock star, and the wealthy businessman. These "new men" embody excellence and success and, as such, stand in direct opposition to the previous ideologies, which had held the high-government official and the college professor in greater esteem. The reversal of fortunes has resulted in the businessman being perceived, much like the scholar of previous eras, as the repository of talent, ability, and intelligence.

The shift in China's economic and social order has not, however, resulted in the formation of completely new notions of maleness or femaleness. For the Chinese, as elsewhere, manhood depends upon achieving some level of mastery within a specific field of action. In this way manhood is a process and not a state of being.[6] Throughout Chinese history there have been two competing emblems of maleness: the warrior or military man, who emphasized physical toughness; and the gentleman, who represented gentility and who disdained physical exercise in favor of the arts and other forms of cultural refinement.

To possess authentic womanhood rarely requires proofs of action or confrontations with dangerous situations.[7] This is especially so in contemporary Chinese society, in which womanhood is organized around images of physical attractiveness and reproduction, whereas manhood remains based in achievement. Throughout Chinese history, the underlying appeal of that representation of maleness has remained constant: it is focused on nonbiological achievement. This is a common cross-cultural finding about "masculinity" and "femininity": manhood is deemed to be something achieved through acts of competition with other men, whether physical or mental, whereas womanhood is linked to considerations of erotic attractiveness, reproductive success, and other related domestic achievements.

Women who challenge or reject the conventional sexual division of labor are faced with a dilemma. If they want to excel in traditional male activities, they must adopt the prevailing standards used to measure excellence and success. Since these activities and roles have been associated with men's pursuits, the criteria for assessing competence has been similar to that used to measure manhood. These criteria are not gender irrelevant or neutral but rather coterminous with male attributes, complicating the issue for those women who veer out of traditional social roles.

Honig observes that, at the height of the radical egalitarianism of the Cultural Revolution, there was very little mixing or blending of sex roles.[8] Rather, she points out, the blending flowed one way: women dressed and acted like men, while men did not get involved with childcare or housework. She concludes her discussion by noting that one of the unintended consequences of women's striving to be perceived as competent revolutionaries was their "masculinization." It is not clear, however, if they really saw themselves as "desexed" beings who passed for male or as women playing the necessary game. Honig acknowledges that none of the women she interviewed felt de-sexed, at the time. Only in the context of a new age, in which they have rethought and rephrased their version of the events against the 1990s perspective, has a new version of the past emerged. It would appear that their original intention was simply to be competent in what happened to be a male-dominated field. Since their credibility depended upon achieving a standard, they often "acted like men" simply as a consequence of the "job description" but did not necessarily identify with maleness as a gender category. From this perspective, Chinese women's behavior resembled that of men only in role execution, not in psychic identification.

## URBAN CHINA: GENDER IDEALS AND GENDER RELEVANCE

In Huhhot, I found that the Cultural Revolution–era militant egalitarianism had no lingering impact on how urbanites discussed underlying sex differences. Most of my informants saw men's and women's personalities and behaviors as by-products of different biologically based essences. This belief is not a new one. An analysis of magazine cover photos from 1949 to 1987 shows a noticeable shift in the way men and women were represented in photos. In contrast to the period in which photos depicted men and women posed as earnest, albeit content, hard workers—photos designed to instill respect for the collective good—during the periods of low political fervor photos depicted men and women engaged in personal activities that ranged from the pursuit of private hobbies to flirting. It was during these brief political lulls (1953 and 1960–62) that conventional gender stereotypes were most vividly and convincingly demonstrated. Since these eras predate the reform period, it is incorrect to infer that gender stereotypes found throughout the 1980s and 1990s are recent artifacts of the "opening" of Chinese society. The present-day gender images have a much longer history.

Huhhotians readily acknowledged that there are distinct differences in men's and women's personalities. Urban Mongol and Han women, when asked to list the attributes of men, described them as rough, absentminded, self-confident, serious, emotionally tight-lipped, dominant, secure, adventurous, clever, easygoing, quiet, aggressive, strong, ambitious (for promotions), and inclined to talk about work; they also noted that men use crude language and hide emotion. On the other hand, urban Mongol and Han men perceived women to be pretty, not very strong, gossipy, timid, gentle, anxious, sentimental, tenderhearted, and inclined to make a fuss out of nothing; they also noted that women speak in a soft voice, dress well, use polite language, prefer a slim figure, and are unable to do hard work. These opinions cut across every social class and were expressed in a variety of social situations. It is understood by these men and women, however, that, depending upon a person's social class as well as the context, men and women will assert, modify, or reject different aspects of the gender configuration.

Generally speaking, although men's and women's conversational topics are often similar, there are a number of differences in the choice of topics broached in unisexual settings. The differences are most clearly manifested in the content and style of conversations and aesthetic delight with which specific topics are discussed. Men's conversational topics tend to focus on work, adventure, moral opprobrium, social success, and, especially in the case of workers and actors, sexual banter. Women's conversational topics dwell on child behavior and health issues, work-related personality conflicts, and, on occasion, boisterous put-downs of the male sex. The sex dif-

Figure 8. Four *gemer* (brothers, buddies) engage in banter while taking a break from harvesting rice in Yuanming Yuan, Beijing. Photo by Susan Brownell, 1985.

ference in conversational style is most explicitly manifested in a variety of discourses about the opposite sex that range from angry sarcasm to playful amusement. It is not unusual, therefore, for women and men in unisexual groups, whenever the conversation turns to the subject of the opposite sex, to engage in marked hyperbole. In this setting, gender slurs are not uncommon.

The motivation for invoking gender slurs comes from aesthetic bravado, gender solidarity, gender anxiety, or the assertion or denial of rank within a patriarchal ideal, or perhaps it draws a little on each. Men and women in unisex group social settings engage in gender slurs often for no other reason than just for the fun of it. In Huhhot, uneducated women, for example, especially in unisex group settings, refer to their husbands or males in general as "stupid," "cocky like a blind rooster," or possessing all the attributes of a "mother's cunt." Because of concerns with class distinction, college-educated women seldom invoke sexual imagery to put down the opposite sex; they do not hesitate, however, to refer to men as "ignorant" or "stubborn fools." For men, sexual banter often serves as a means to convey, however momentary, a sense of "brotherhood" or male bonding. Uneducated men, for their part, in unisexual groups are quick to note that women are "loud," "demanding," "stupid," and "too silly to be real." Concurring, college-educated men are more restrained in voicing their irritation at what many considered to be the unfortunate habits of the opposite sex.

Within unisexual settings, men and women readily acknowledge those qualities desirable in a good spouse. For women, it is someone who is tall, healthy, kind, strong, intelligent, brave, handsome, and well-mannered, who has a good position and could provide for a family. Men's image of an ideal wife, regardless of class, is more extensive. Like women, men prefer someone who is tall, healthy, and kind. Ideally, she should also be beautiful, soft, well-mannered, loyal, virtuous, and skilled in domestic arts (e.g., sewing, cooking, and, most important, child care). Of course, both sexes typically compromise between their fantasy ideal, personal preference, and the realities of the marriage market.

It is also within unisexual group settings that men tend to become more demonstrative in expressing their sexual desires and anxieties. For example, an enjoyable activity for young Chinese men is to rank a woman's relative physical beauty. Unlike American men, who typically use a ten-point scale, Huhhotian men use a scale based on a hundred points, with one hundred representing the greatest attractiveness and ten the least. The activity is often engaged in openly. I noted that, whenever educated and uneducated young men gathered in small groups, it was not uncommon for many of them to playfully apply this point scale to any young woman who passed in front of them. If the woman overheard their comments, she either hurried away or turned and cursed their bad manners. This behavior was especially evident when city youth encountered foreign female tourists, whom they thought could not understand their language. In these instances the youth, thinking they were free from reprisals, more openly commented on the physical attributes of the opposite sex. Married men, even in the company of their wives, reported that they often enjoyed viewing and silently assessing other women's relative "good looks."

Even bathroom graffiti seems to differ by sex. My female assistant and I surveyed all the bathrooms in three university campus dormitories and in one library and found sexually explicit drawings on the door frames of the men's bathrooms but not the women's. The drawings were exclusively of male and female genitalia; unlike in the case of American drawings of this kind, images of female breasts were nonexistent among the drawings. Despite stringent antipornography laws in China, men often buy underground pornography or, sometimes, make their own. It is also not uncommon for men to see "porno films" smuggled into Huhhot via Hong Kong, which are shown on either private or work-unit VCRs. In 1987, over one-half of my male informants between the ages of twenty-three and twenty-eight indicated that they had seen a "porno movie," whereas only five women out of twenty-one interviewed indicated the same.

Cases of sexual harassment of women are common in China, and such harassment is informally classified as follows: speaking crudely to a woman, acting obscenely or touching a woman, and forcing a woman into bed. In every social class, these behaviors are considered improper.

The corporate arena is another setting where folk assumptions about innate male and female essence shape hiring, promotional, and retiring policies. These folk assumptions can result in women being urged to quit their jobs upon marriage, pregnancy, or reaching forty-five years of age. There is evidence, however, that some of these folk assumptions are giving way to other realities. William Parish reports that "younger women were better represented in higher status professional, technical, and clerical occupations."[9]

Within the home, assumptions about sex differences continue to structure the sexual division of labor. Men are responsible for heavier tasks, such as buying and transporting coal and bottle gas and carrying the family bicycle upstairs, whereas women do most of the shopping, cooking, sweeping, clothes washing, and child care. However, a person is more than the sum of the cultural assumptions that structure the sexual division of labor. Men and women, especially in interactions with siblings, parents, classmates, spouses, and the public at large, are more prone to assert androgynous or non-gender-relevant traits. In these contexts, gender ideals of appropriateness, in and of themselves, are not representative of how individuals actually interact with the opposite sex. Women do not, nor are they expected to, act timid, passive, mild, or coy; likewise, men are not expected to always appear confident, ambitious, and goal oriented.

### URBAN KINSHIP: SIBLING TIES

Unlike their rural counterparts, whose siblings often live in the same village, urban individuals and their siblings and other kin tend to live scattered throughout the city. Neolocal (new) residences are more common than patrilocal (father's) residences. Because there is a shortage of available housing, any apartment is better than no apartment. This pragmatic concern contributed to the Chinese rejection of the traditional patrilocal resident rule in favor of the more flexible neolocal norm.

The urban Chinese family is organized into two different forms: nuclear and stem families. Although the nuclear family is the preferred form of family arrangement, most Chinese at one time or another enter into some form of stem-family arrangement (i.e., a family with a married couple, children, and another relative, usually a parent of one member of the couple). Within the nuclear family, relations are ideally warm and supportive, and in truth, this ideal is more often honored than breached. Still, there are examples of animosity among family members. Margery Wolf found that sibling rivalry, particularly among brothers, pervaded rural Taiwanese domestic family life.[10] I found this to be true in Huhhot as well. Brothers, like their counterparts around the globe, privately admitted feeling resentful and not particularly close to the brother to whom they were closest in age.[11] Older brothers revealed that they harbored deep resentment toward younger brothers during their childhood years. However, this sentiment was not symmetrical. Younger brothers tended to be bewildered by their elder brothers' periodic bursts of anger and hostility. However, when there was a significant age difference, of eight years or more, there was little demonstrable animosity. In these cases, the eldest brother consistently acted more protective and supportive than competitive. Although I did not conduct any research on relationships between sisters, I did find that cooperation between brothers and sisters was strong, with the closer ties being between older sister and younger brother. In these cases it appeared that a wide age gap was conducive to promoting a type of mentor-apprentice relationship that continued to thrive well into the individuals' later years.

Although the range of Chinese kinship bonds is shrinking, the value attributed to marriage and family life has never waned. People continue to think of the family as the dominant metaphor by which to assist and evaluate another's progress through life. Marriage and the establishment of a family remain critical, yet truncated, markers that the urban Chinese use to sort one another into relative degrees of social maturity, adulthood, and psychological stability. In this and many other ways, Chinese kinship sentiments and obligations remain strong.

### MARRIAGE: MEN'S AND WOMEN'S PERCEPTION

Many of the domestic changes in the contemporary urban Chinese family's organization are typical of a worldwide pattern that tends toward the formation of a nuclear family, a decline in fertility, and the decreasing power of the senior generation. These changes were already under way prior to the 1949 Communist revolution.[12]

The meaning of marriage in urban China has shifted, so that marriage is no longer based on a complementary sexual division of labor but instead idealizes the love match. In arranged marriages or marriages of convenience, if a couple respects one another they repeatedly strive to maintain mutual consideration. In these kinds of marriages, which can be found among all social classes, individuals make simple adjustments to the love ideal: they continue to either independently visit their friends, or they go together and then separate into unisexual groups to "discuss things."

The emerging trend among the twenty-something urban generation is to strive for something much more—a love marriage—which means, in the words of one woman, "a bond between equals who do not keep secrets and who prefer to do everything together." For the most part, men, regardless of class or educational background, shared similar expectations of marriage. For example, a forty-two-year-old man told me that, after "marriage, you should eat together, go to the movies together, and always strive to be an ideal couple." He added, "It's okay to visit your best friend together. The people you don't know very well, you should introduce to your wife, but this can be boring, so you might want to go yourself." Another man told me that he enjoyed playing cards with his worker friends but had stopped because his wife had become upset and missed him. Though not every man interviewed responded with similar sensitivity, a wife's wishes greatly influence how a husband spends his free time. Sacrifice and compromise are not constitutionally foreign to either spouse. Nor are consideration and mutual respect. In effect, these concerns are gender irrelevant or androgynous.

Still, there are class differences. Working-class men are more defensive than college-educated men, who, being more comfortable with open discussions, find it easier to compromise. Working-class men, especially those under forty years of age, tend to be more resistant. For them, compromise implies the inability to achieve mastery of the social role. In the face of their wives' obvious disappointment, it was not uncommon for some men to insist that "they did other things for their wives," and that it was inconvenient of their wives to demand they cease "having fun."

Huhhotian men and women are highly cognizant of the fact that domestic relations are radically different from those found in the countryside and on the grasslands. They are aware that Mongolian herding-family organization places a tremendous burden on women while providing a great deal of leisure time for men. They believe this indicates that, in other times and in different social contexts, men had more power and control within the family. It is an idealization, however, that was far from true even in imperial China.

Chinese men, particularly the uneducated, believe that female domestic power is both authentic and onerous, and that they have little power to effect change. Although no one in my sample believed it is proper or correct for a wife to be dominant within the family, everyone agreed that typically the wife dominates. One man remarked, "In the past the mother-in-law was fearsome; now the wife is fearsome."

Men are keenly aware, for example, that women's style of self-presentation shifts according to social context. For example, whereas a woman prefers to speak softly on a date, once married she is just as likely to shout commands at both her child and husband. A male worker of mild temperament, accustomed to listening to his wife issue pronouncements, turned to me one day and matter-of-factly said, "Women shout a lot. It's their way. We just have to accept it." Women are not sympathetic to this disappointment. It is not that uncommon for an angry wife to yell at her husband when he leaves the house, thereby communicating to her neighbors her preeminence and authority within the family. Margery Wolf notes a similar occurrence in rural China.[13] It is also a recurrent theme in contemporary Chinese literature.[14] The frequency with which men talk about it in daily conversation further suggests that men feel more ambivalent and less secure about their position within the family and society than in former times. In this way, jokes about "henpecked" husbands manifest a deeper underlying, but unspoken, uneasiness men have about their position and duties in the domestic sphere.

Evidence of men's insecurity can be found in unisexual settings, where men tend to joke about the advantages of being a woman. They note that everyone "cares for" and "helps" women. In addition, men believe that, regardless of the rhetoric, it is more their responsibility and not that of their wives to achieve a promotion, increase household income, and expand personal connections. It is a responsibility, an expectation, that they find demanding and take seriously. Failure to perform satisfactorily often results in a wife's complaint that her husband "let the family down." It is a complaint that a man does not want to hear, because such remarks undermine his image of himself as a man.

Although most Huhhotian wives *do not* habitually lament and describe their husbands' overall shortcomings, they do note and comment on their husband's underachievements. Typically, Chinese women expect men to demonstrate clear competence in their work and to provide evidence of worldly ambition and the likelihood of future success. In this way women continuously assess men's and, in particular, their husbands', performance, achievement, and relative social standing vis-à-vis other men in the prevailing social hierarchy.

In turn, men feel compelled to maintain the pretense that they are on their way to becoming something that most will never actually be: an important and influential person. Not surprisingly, the striving for "success," with its accompanying emphasis on symbolically indicating that success is within one's grasp, can promote an uncertainty that is sometimes acute. Ambitious women, in particular, expect and demand more from their husbands and often become extremely disappointed with their failure to deliver. Both men and women are equally demanding of their mates and, even though the two desire different things from one another, both often become disinterested, critical, or unresponsive when their demands are not at least partially met.

## MARITAL SATISFACTION: EMOTIONAL AND SEXUAL INTIMACY

Individual marriages in China, as in America, go through cycles of adjustment in expectations and pressures: unsatisfactory marriages often become more satisfying over time and even develop into relationships of deep love and attachment.[15] Those couples who enjoy one another's company and accommodate, if not actually enjoy, their spouse's personality style and individual quirks seem to have the more satisfactory marriages.

In Huhhot, a common means of communicating anxiety, especially fears about losing the other's love, is for one spouse to ask the other to interpret his or her dreams, a request that is treated very seriously. The request is an invitation to subjective intimacy. Typically, discussion of the dream leads to a lengthy dialogue of possible interpretation and meaning, often laced with reassurances that the dream means the opposite of what it appeared to be saying. Some spouses admitted to me that they were never certain if their spouse actually had had the dream described or had made it up to elicit the detailed discussion.

Sexuality is another means by which affection is expressed or withheld and intimacy given or denied. It is clear that women generally control the frequency of intercourse in marriage. If a wife feels the marriage is good, she more than amicably acquiesces to her husband's advances; if not, she rejects these advances directly or with "various excuses." This is especially true if a woman does not like her husband. Rather than focus on him, she focuses on their child and seeks companionship outside the marriage with friends. In this way the parent-child sleeping arrangement—which may entail the wife sleeping with the child in order to avoid the husband—is a tacit index for the intensity of a couple's emotional intimacy.

For example, a man who had just become a father observed that, "after the child comes, the wife plays with it and not with the husband." Another man admitted that after a child arrives men associate with male friends, adding that "the lovers are no longer deeply committed to one another; they are committed only to the child." On the other hand, if a woman loves her husband, she will strive to maintain his interest and involvement. A thirty-one-year-old woman, for example, confided to me that, "after I had given birth, I no longer cared for him [her husband] as I had before. The only reason I continue to have sex with him is because he is a good man and I like giving him nice things." The ability of women to control sexual frequency is vividly revealed in the comment of a thirty-seven-year-old man who asserted that it is common to hear wives teasing and even, at times, threatening "to withhold sex if their husband failed to perform some household task." When women do not like their husbands, they commonly reduce the frequency of sexual intercourse or discontinue it altogether. A forty-three-year-old man admitted, for example, that "my wife did not like sex before we had a child. Afterward, she did not like me, so we stopped having sex."

There is a folk belief which holds that too much sexual activity is unhealthy. For example, in 1983 one twenty-five-year-old intellectual told me,

"On your wedding night you can have sex a lot. But afterward, you should have sex only once a week. Otherwise, you will lose your strength." In 1987 I met him again and found that he had since been divorced and was actively seducing many women, without constraint. He no longer agreed with the traditional folk belief. Nonetheless, many people, especially those living in the countryside, continue to believe in the folk ideal. It is common in the Chinese countryside for peasants to admiringly tease those who admit they are tired. It is assumed that their tiredness is due to sexual intercourse the previous night. In one case, when a peasant admitted to having sex four times a week, his friends, visiting urban workers, responded that that was "too much," as it would tire him. Another worker countered that he "was never tired, only refreshed," by sex. The point is that, although the folk theory that posits a relationship between physical exhaustion and sexual frequency is still accepted, it is not clear whether that belief is responsible for a reduction in the frequency of sexual intercourse. A thirty-four-year-old intellectual offered another reason for voluntarily reducing the frequency of sexual intercourse: "Too much sex is bad [that is, ethically bad] because you will start to enjoy it, and then that will be all you want to do. You will not be able to concentrate on your work." He added, "How then will you be able to accomplish anything?"

Chinese culture of the 1980s did not sanction the pursuit of sexual variety. Although some men fantasized about having love affairs, some kept an active correspondence with women living in different cities, and a few daring married men had "lovers," everyone conducted these "relationships" with the utmost discretion. The cultural mores simply did not sanction this kind of behavior. Sexual promiscuity is not equated with male identity in socialist China, unlike in the Thai and Latin American cultures and in pre-Communist China. Male identity is, however, equated with sexual performance. If a husband is impotent, a Chinese woman is within her rights to request and immediately receive a divorce.

Chinese males' sexual techniques vary by social class. For the most part, educated men are aware that women's sexual arousal differs from their own, and they stress the importance of foreplay as the primary means for stimulating their wives to orgasm. Independent interviews with their wives found, however, that husbands are not generally successful in satisfying their wives. College-educated and non-college-educated women told my female research assistant and, on a separate occasion, repeated to me that their husbands were sexually too demanding and, thus, they did not really enjoy sex. Although my sample size is small, it is consistent with a Shanghai sex survey's finding that Chinese women regard sexual relations as a "duty" from which they receive little pleasure.[16]

A popular Chinese proverb from the Republican era asserts that women's sexual appetite increases with age: "Women in their thirties are tigers and in their forties are wolves."[17] If this proverb is an accurate representation of behavior, then one explanation for contemporary women's disinterest in sexual intercourse may lie in the negative impact of the Communist revolutionary ideology that de-emphasized the body as a site of sensual enjoyment. As a consequence, many men and women were raised to regard sexual intercourse as a necessary, albeit perfunctory, activity. Moreover, the one-child family policy put tremendous pressure on couples, especially wives, to avoid pregnancy. It may be that the return to a consumer economy will stimulate a renewed appetite for physical pleasure and erotic experimentation.

Evidence for this trend can be found among China's educated class, which tends to believe that marriage should be based on emotional and spiritual compatibility. Within this class, it is not unusual for men to become upset if their wives never experience an orgasm. This concern was vividly revealed to me when one informant lamented that "nothing he did" aroused his wife and, hence, he felt personally responsible for his wife's inability to reach an orgasm. In exasperation, he did the unexpected: he turned to his friends for advice. They told him to kiss her breasts and to talk to her; some suggested that he show her some pornographic pictures (easily obtainable in the city's underground market). Unfortunately, their suggestions did not lead to any noticeable changes.

Unlike workers, peasants, and herders, some members of the city's educated population are concerned with a new notion of eroticism, one that assumes women should also enjoy the sex act in and of itself. For them, this is a truly new idea. In imperial China, the primary motive behind an educated man's interest in stimulating his lover was the belief that an aroused and satisfied woman could transfer *yin*, the female essence, to her male lover. In Huhhot, not one informant believed this. The growing concern of some educated men with their wives' sexual satisfaction is consistent with other studies on human sexuality, which found that the scope and intensity of a person's erotic experimentation is associated with his or her level of education.[18] For example, among Huhhot's educated class, almost half of my sample of educated men admitted that their wives or lovers performed fellatio on them; however, among the city's working class, no one reported engaging in oral sex.

## MOTHER–CHILD BOND

In the past, one of the primary means whereby rural Chinese women attempted to secure and protect themselves from hostile mothers-in-law and often unsympathetic husbands was to foster an intense emotional dependency with their children so that, once grown, the children would take care of them.[19] In Margery Wolf's study of contemporary urban life in the People's Republic of China, she observes that recent socialist changes make it no longer necessary for urban women to foster this type of parent–child dependency. She adds, "The uterine family has disappeared because the need for it has disappeared. Urban women do not express the same degree of anxiety about their old age that they used to. Young women work and expect pensions, older women who do not have pensions are assured by the government that they are cared for."[20] I found in Huhhot that parent–child dependency has not disappeared. It persists, however, for a different reason than in the past: the continuing preference for, and habit of cultivating, bonds of intense emotional dependency. Mothers continue to exercise tremendous psychological control over their offspring. In fact, the mother–child relationship is the most admired parent–child dyad. For example, in fifty-eight cases that I collected that involved parental intervention in an offspring's mate selection, it was inevitably the mother who was the deciding force. Middle-aged men and women frequently confided to me that their emotional involvement with their mothers remained remarkably strong after their marriage and throughout their adult lives.

The intensity of the emotional adoration was expressed to me by several college students in their twenties, who permitted me to read sections of their diaries. A nineteen-year-old student who was suffering from a cold acknowledged, "I think of my dear mother. If she were here, she could cook delicious food for me and comfort me. But here, five thousand miles away from home, who could be as dear as my mother?" A twenty-one-year-old male student recorded rather bleakly in his diary: "Another Sunday of loneliness and restlessness. I'd rather be a bird; then I could fly back home and see my mother."

Adoration is probably not too strong a word to describe the emotional connections between mother and child. The extent to which Chinese symbolically extend this connection was vividly and dramatically revealed to me when I asked twenty-nine people to respond to the following hypothetical situation. I asked each to imagine walking across a bridge with his or her mother and father. Suddenly the bridge collapses and everyone is thrown into the water. If they could save only one person, who would it be? Of the twenty-nine informants (nineteen males and ten females), twenty selected their mother for saving, while the remaining nine refused to answer.

For reasons other than simple fear of a vengeful mother-in-law or hostile spouse, the emotional bond a woman forms with her child during its infancy and the early childhood years is maintained. The bond is sustained in large part through a Chinese tradition that legitimizes and promotes an intense lifelong emotional bond between mother and child.[21] It is a bond idealized in literature and in conversation as a celebration of harmony, remembrance, and enduring love.[22] Moreover, the intensity of its expression signifies to every Huhhotian the continued importance, influence, and power of the Chinese woman.

## THE TRADITIONAL FATHER–CHILD BOND

Throughout Chinese history, men, as fathers, believed that their role, as a counterpoint to the role of women as mothers, was to *not* encourage or tolerate emotional indulgence to promote that dependency. They assumed instead the role of the stern disciplinarian.[23] Chinese fathers were not, however, without compassion or love for their children. Most Chinese fathers, in fact, felt a warm, deep sentiment toward their children, though articulation of that sentiment was restrained by their traditional parenting role and its expectations.[24] In some cases, a father supplied strict discipline as a complement to the mother's overindulgence, or at least a balance was to reached between a mother's understanding and a father's demands. A cultural tradition emerged that justified different parenting postures: the father facilitated a child's entry into the outside world, whereas the mother provided a secure and loving environment within the home. It was assumed that these roles were inevitable and unchangeable. Moreover, it was assumed this sexual division in parenting roles contributed to producing a more responsible and ethical person overall.

The sex-linked roles were sustained, if not developed, because men and women occupied different positions within the social structure. In addition, by controlling the distribution of the family inheritance a father could effect a special, if not psychological, dependency on the part of the child. On the other hand, a mother's parenting style was seen as being as much a result of her being considered an "outsider" as it was of a "natural" attachment fostered through childbirth and early child care.[25] Given her reduced importance and status in her husband's family, the mother needed a friend, an ally, and what better one than her own child?[26] In this way, the different access to and use of economic and psychological "resources" contributed to the establishment and elaboration of the two complementary parenting styles: the father as a disciplinary provider, the mother as a intimate nurturer.

## THE EMERGENT URBAN FATHER–CHILD RELATIONSHIP

In China, the emergence of a new urban infrastructure has fostered a supportive environment for the expression of warmer sentiments and closer interaction between father and child. This expression is a result of a new attitude readily found in casual conversation and reflective comments, and it stresses the importance of intimate father–child interaction. As such it challenges the traditional father-child role, a role and style of interaction that was, in fact, seen by the previous generations' fathers as no longer satisfying or necessary.

Unlike their fellow Han, who are limited to one child per couple, urban Mongol couples are allowed by state policy to have two children.[27] However, my survey of Mongol marriages formed after 1976 found that only three out of fifty-seven families had more than one child. This extremely low ratio is a response less to state policy than to the internalization of a new posture toward urban life, which is no longer organized around children but rather affection and consumption.

There are three factors that contribute to the increasing intimacy of father-child interaction in both public and private settings. First, over 80 percent of women between twenty-six and forty-six years of age work—a fact that compels even the most reluctant father to become more involved in caretaking activities. Second, the economy of domestic space, or the typically small one-room apartment, places the father in constant and close proximity to his child, thereby enabling more intimate parent-child interaction. Third, a new folk notion promoting fatherly involvement has emerged within many households.

The socialist transformation of cultural meanings has had a corresponding impact on men's conception of themselves as husbands and fathers. Young fathers continue to assume a firm and somewhat formal posture toward their sons while paradoxically insisting they do not want to be as formal and reserved as their fathers were with them. In Huhhot, I often heard a man insist (much as in traditional China) that, while he "loved his father, he did not like him." Younger male Huhhotians feel strongly that it is improper for a child to grow up and not like his or her father. Although contemporary Huhhotian fathers wish to become close friends with their children, as opposed to assuming the more traditional stance of the stern moral authority ever ready to criticize shortcomings, they are uncertain and confused as to how to express this wish. Warmth and immediacy of affection are more easily achieved with a daughter than with a son. Fathers are more ambivalent than mothers in balancing their obligations as both spouse and parent. This ambivalence was profoundly articulated by many college-educated fathers who voiced concern to me that their children loved their mothers more than them. Men's desire to become more emotionally involved is frequently expressed in intimate conversation among close friends. As such, it has enormous implications for the quality of future parent–child relations and the development of the next generation.

## CONCLUSION

My research in Huhhot suggests that, in contemporary China, men and women easily distinguish what they perceive to be fundamental differences between the sexes. The manipulation of gender imagery finds its most salient manifestation in unisexual group settings, as well as within the sexual encounter (i.e., the context in which one strives consciously or unconsciously to present an image that the opposite sex finds most attractive). Both contexts serve as settings in which to invoke, albeit often in exaggerated form, cultural ideals of male and female propriety. Outside of these contexts, men and women are more willing to engage in other types of behavior that may or may not be deemed sexually significant or even gender relevant. There are, however, recurrent sex-linked patterns of behavior: men and women differ in their approach to pursing erotic pleasure, their criteria in mate selection, and the style in which they care for their children.

The transformation of China's economy—away from collectivism and toward a more open market economy—has heightened men's anxiety and confusion. For intellectuals, the emergence of a fully developed market economy fosters, at least, in some sectors of society, the perception that intellectuals are talentless people who, like the low-ranking government cadre, are not able to achieve mastery over anything of social worth. The shift in public perception that success in the marketplace, and not government position or educational achievement, is the better index for assessing a person's social worth is a recent occurrence. It has not, however, resulted in the rejection of achievement or competence as the primary index for evaluating manhood. Given China's ever-oscillating nature, there will continue to be competing value systems, and thus hierarchies of distinction, that will further problematize life, thereby making it stressful for men to know what accomplishments and competencies matter in contemporary Chinese society.

## NOTES

Partial funding for research for this essay was provided by a University of California General Research Grant, Sigma Xi, and National Academy of Sciences. I am grateful to the following scholars for their advice, encouragement, and thoughtful suggestions: Jim Bell, Susan Brownell, Tish Diskan, Ellen Oxfeld, Tom Paladino, Tom Shaw, Jeffery Wasserstrom, and Libby Whitt.

1. Sulamith Heins Potter and Jack Potter, *China's Peasants: The Anthropology of a Revolution* (Cambridge: Cambridge University Press, 1990); Yan Yuxiang, *The Flow of Gifts* (Stanford: Stanford University Press, 1996); William Jankowiak, *Sex, Death, and Hierarchy in a Chinese City* (New York: Columbia University Press, 1993); Jankowiak, ed., *Romantic Passion* (New York: Columbia University Press, 1996).

2. Susan Brownell, conversation with the author, April 1999.

3. For a more detailed description of my research methods, see Jankowiak, *Sex, Death, and Hierarchy in a Chinese City*, Appendix A: Methodology.

4. Margery Wolf, *Revolution Postponed* (Stanford: Stanford University Press, 1985).

5. J. Cao, "Single Women and Men over 30 in China," in *New Trends in Chinese Marriage and the Family* (Beijing: China International Book Trading, 1987); E. Honig and G. Hershatter, *Personal Voices: Chinese Women in the 1980s* (Stanford: Stanford University Press, 1988); M. Whyte and W. Parish, *Urban Life in Contemporary China* (Chicago: University of Chicago Press, 1984).

6. F. Gilmore, *Manhood in the Making* (New Haven: Yale University Press, 1986).

7. Gilmore, *Manhood*, 12.

8. See chapter 9 in this volume. Chinese women's behavior during the Cultural Revolution was not unlike that of American working-class women who, during World War II, wore men's clothes, de-emphasized physical attractiveness (on the job), and talked tough (on the job). These American women never considered that they were passing for men as much as doing a job that men used do. The issue for American women, like the Chinese women, was job performance and not maintaining a stereotypical gender-salient role posture within every social encounter.

9. Wenfang Tang and William Parish, *Chinese Urban Life under Reform: The Changing Social Contract* (Cambridge: Cambridge University Press, 2000), 209–31.

10. Margery Wolf, "Child Training and the Chinese Family," in *Family and Kinship in Chinese Society*, ed. Maurice Freeman (Stanford: Stanford University Press, 1970).

11. F. Sulloway, *Born to Rebel* (New York: Crown, 1996).

12. Whyte and Parish, *Urban Life*, 191–92.

13. Wolf, *Revolution Postponed*.

14. Tonglin Lu, ed. *Gender and Sexuality* (Albany: State University of New York, 1993).

15. W. Goode, *World Revolution and Family Patterns* (New York: Free Press, 1963).

16. Dalin Liu, Man Lun Ng, Li Ping Zhou, and Erwin Haeberle, *Sexual Behavior in Modern China* (New York: Continuum Publishing Company, 1997).

17. F. Dikötter, *Sex, Culture, and Modernity in China* (London: Hurst and Company, 1995), 60.

18. A. C. Kinsey, W. B. Pomeroy, and C. E. Martin, *Sexual Behavior in the Human Female* (Philadelphia: W. B. Saunders, 1953).

19. Margery Wolf, "Uterine families," in *Women and the Family in Rural Taiwan*, ed. Margery Wolf (Stanford: Stanford University Press, 1972).

20. Wolf, *Revolution Postponed*, 207.

21. L. Pye, *Asian Power and Politics* (Cambridge: Harvard University Press, 1985); R. Solomon, *Mao's Revolution and the Chinese Political Culture* (Berkeley and Los Angeles: University of California Press, 1971).

22. P. Link, *Mandarin Ducks and Butterflies* (Berkeley and Los Angeles: University of California Press, 1981).

23. X. Fei, *Peasant Life in Rural China* (Shanghai: Shanghai Press, 1935); D. Ho, "Fatherhood in Chinese Society," in *The Father's Role: Cross-Cultural Perspective*, ed. M. E. Lamb (Hillsdale, N.J.: Erlbaum, 1987).

24. Solomon, *Mao's Revolution.*

25. J. Bowlby, *Maternal Care and Mental Health* (Geneva: WHO, 1951); M. Daly and M. Wilson, *Homicide* (Hawthorne, N.Y.: Aldine De Gruyter, 1987).

26. Wolf, "Uterine Families."

27. China has a two-tier birth-control policy that allows minorities to have more than one child. Until 1985, Mongols were not restricted by the state's one-child policy and could have as many children as they chose. In 1986, the state limited urban (but not herding) Mongols to two children, the same number allowed to the region's Chinese Moslems (or Hui).

# PART EIGHT

# Gender, Sexuality, and Ethnicity

According to China's official classification system, the Chinese population consists of fifty-five ethnic minorities (in official parlance, "minority nationalities" or *shaoshu minzu*) in addition to the Han majority, which makes up 92 percent of the total population. Dru Gladney's slim textbook, *Ethnic Identity in China: The Making of a Muslim Minority*, summarizes the politics of ethnicity in China, discusses marriage practices in a Hui (Muslim) village outside of Beijing, and touches upon gender issues elsewhere.

Gladney and Louisa Schein, whose chapter follows, have both discussed the fact that, in official and popular portrayals of minorities (such as the colorful coffee-table albums published by state presses and the paintings of minorities by Han artists), the minorities tend to be depicted as backward, female, and erotic, in contrast to the modern, male, sexually inhibited Han. They have argued that this serves to reinforce Han economic and political superiority as well as male privilege. Schein's chapter here represents themes developed in more depth in her book, *Minority Rules: The Miao and the Feminine in China's Cultural Politics*. Her ethnographic fieldwork was carried out among the Miao (also known outside China as the Hmong) in Guizhou province.

Litzinger carried out ethnographic fieldwork among the Yao ethnic minority in Hunan and Guangxi provinces. In his chapter, he adds that, since the late 1980s, native Yao ethnologists have been recuperating traditions discontinued during the Cultural Revolution. In so doing, they emphasize some practices as being truly Yao but scoff at others (and discourage Western anthropologists from studying them). And so some traditions, such as the drinking games that are an important symbol of Han masculinity, are dismissed, while others, such as the practices of Taoist male priests, are emphasized. In this way an alternative Yao masculinity is created that is different from the Han masculine stereotypes—but at the same time, this may be perceived as feminization by the Han, and perhaps even by young Yao drinkers themselves. Litzinger develops these themes more fully in his book, *Other Chinas: The Yao and the Politics of National Belonging.*

There are several films and videos that vividly illustrate the images of minorities discussed in these works and elsewhere. It is important not to take them at face value, however, but to approach them with the critical viewpoint outlined here. *Sacrificed Youth,* by the fourth-generation filmmaker Zhang Nuanxin, is about a young Han woman sent down to a Dai village during the Cultural Revolution, where she learns from the "uninhibited" minority girls to express her femininity.[1] The video *Amazing Marriage Customs* is a government-sponsored survey of marriage customs throughout China, in which practices are structured along an evolutionary line from "matrilineal" to "patrilineal," concluding with monogamy.[2]

*The Horse Thief,* a film by the fifth-generation director Tian Zhuangzhuang, departs from this pattern and as such may represent a new development in depictions of minorities. Set in Tibet in 1923, not only does the film portray more stereotypically masculine equestrian nomads, but in it the Han state is notably absent.[3]

### NOTES

1. Teachers who wish to use these films in the classroom might consult the critiques that have been written. *Sacrificed Youth* is discussed in Dru Gladney, "Representing Nationality in China: Refiguring Majority/Minority Identities," *Journal of Asian Studies* 53, no. 1 (February 1994): 92–123; and in Esther Yau, "Is China the End of Hermeneutics? Or, Political and Cultural Usage of Non-Han Women in Mainland Chinese Films," *Discourse* 11, no. 2 (spring-summer 1989): 115–36.

2. This video is discussed by Gladney in "Representing Nationality."

3. This film is discussed by Dru C. Gladney in "Tian Zhuangzhuang, the Fifth Generation, and Minorities Film in China," *Public Culture* 8, no. 1 (1995): 161–75.

### COMPLEMENTARY READINGS AND VIDEOS

*Amazing Marriage Customs* [Jingu hunsu qiguan]. Directed by Suen Wan and Guo Wuji. Distributed by Nanhai Film Company, Milbrae, Calif., 1992. Videocassette.

Gladney, Dru C. *Ethnic Identity in China: The Making of a Muslim Minority.* Case Studies in Social Anthropology. New York: Harcourt Brace, 1998.

*The Horse Thief* [Dao ma zei]. Directed by Tian Zhuangzhuang. Distributed by Nanhai Film Company, Milbrae, Calif., 1987. Videocassette.

Litzinger, Ralph. *Other Chinas: The Yao and the Politics of National Belonging.* Durham: Duke University Press, 2000.

*Sacrificed Youth* [Qingchun ji]. Directed by Zhang Nuanxin. Beijing Film College, Youth Film Studio Production Company, 1984. Videocassette.

Schein, Louisa. *Minority Rules: The Miao and the Feminine in China's Cultural Politics.* Durham: Duke University Press, 2000.

CHAPTER FIFTEEN

# Gender and Internal Orientalism in China

*Louisa Schein*

On a visit to the nearest city—Kaili—during my 1988 field year in southeast Guizhou, I encountered an unexpected ritual.[1] Or was it really so unexpected?

In 1986, a new six-story building had been constructed to supplement the mildewed older structure that used to house the city's No. 1 Guest House. Kaili was, after all, the capital of the Miao and Dong Autonomous Prefecture of Southeast Guizhou province in China's southwest, and its mountainous and scenic but barely arable terrain inhabited by several minority groups meant that its best hope for economic development was the promotion of tourism.[2] The new hotel complex was dubbed the Nationalities Guest House.[3] Teenaged girls were recruited from the countryside to work as receptionists, waitresses, and chambermaids—and to stage culture. A representative sampling of different minorities, subgroups, and costume styles had been chosen and each employee was to wear her distinctive headdress at all times. Regular duties included not only the usual hotel drudgery but also an occasional pose in full costume for foreign travelers' cameras, and performances of song and dance for visiting tour groups.

The ritual I witnessed on this particular day, however, was another variant of packaged ethnic performance. Kaili has also been promoted as a site for domestic meetings, and that day it was delegates to a regional conference of mayors that convened at the hotel. This group of largely male, urban conferees assembled in the open parking area to be greeted with a special form of local welcome. A glamorous set of exotic maidens, adorned in colorful garb, serenaded them with ethnic song. In an enactment of a local custom used to welcome guests from afar at the entrance to a village, delegates went through a line in which the young women popped local delicacies straight into their mouths and insisted they drink ritual welcome spirits out of the horns of bulls.[4]

At first glance this ritual seemed anomalous because it was neither a local village practice nor propelled by the simple commodification logic of international tourism.[5] Yet it was part of a widespread phenomenon in the 1980s involving voracious domestic consumption of minority cultures. I challenge here the common assumption that China's packaging and production of representations of minority ethnicity in recent years was solely a consequence of the state's attempts to generate foreign currency by actively complying with Western (and other foreign) orientalist desires for the experience of a more plural and colorful China.[6] Instead, coincident with this trend was also the rise of what I will call "internal orientalism." This is a set of practices that occurs *within* China, and that, in this case, refers to the fascination of more cosmopolitan Chinese with "exotic" minority cultures in an array of polychromatic and titillating forms.[7] As was the case with the Kaili mayors' conference, these encounters were most commonly structured by a class-gender asymmetry in which minorities were represented chiefly by rural women, while Han observers appeared characteristically as male urban sophisticates. This article explores the ramifications of such uneven configurations as a means of gaining insight into China's post-Mao social order.

## THE CRISIS OF IDENTITY AND THE RISE OF INTERNAL ORIENTALISM

The decades after 1949 saw dramatic upheavals in both minority and Han Chinese identities. Han perspectives on non-Han peoples were paradoxically both oppositional and incorporative as the latter came to be partially constitutive of what was seen as the Chinese people. During the 1950s the state actively organized ethnicity by designating groups eligible for central and regional representation in government and for regional autonomy. Official recognition was given to fifty-five "minority nationalities," including Tibetans and Mongolians, several Islamic groups, and a number of highland and lowland peoples scattered primarily across the southwestern provinces. My own research has focused on the Miao nationality, a highland agriculturalist group with a dense concentration in southeast Guizhou province.[8]

Altogether the so-called minority nationalities number 91.2 million persons, or only 8.1 percent of China's total population of 1.13 billion (as of the 1990 census), but they are spread over 50 to 60 percent of China's land area (Fei 1981, 25).[9] While Han Chinese tend to be concentrated in the fertile plains and trading ports of central and coastal China, minorities occupy the strategic, resource-rich periphery to the north, south, and west. Yet despite their relatively small numbers and their spatial marginality, minorities have figured prominently in the areas of cultural policy and Chinese consciousness of self.

During the 1950s era of ethnic classification, minority cultures were meticulously researched and publicly celebrated as part of a policy of diversity within unity.[10] This period was often recalled to me as a heyday of cultural pluralism, when a range of cultural difference was tolerated, even valued, on its own terms. However, from the Anti-Rightist Campaign (1957–58) through the Cultural Revolution (1966–76), this policy of protecting heterogeneity was dramatically reversed with a call instead for cultural homogenization and the smashing of old ways *(po sijiu)*. For both minorities and the Han, a more uniform socialist culture was gradually to supersede the local differences that had constituted China's multifarious "traditions." The legacy of this latter policy persisted throughout the 1980s, leaving many Chinese with a powerful yearning to recuperate what was lost during the ten "turbulent years." This concern for preservation seems to have been enhanced, especially for urbanites, by the reform-era drive for "modernization" and opening to the West. Highly ambivalent, they at once hungered for the novelties, riches, and "freedoms" that they perceived as flowing through the open door and feared the permanent loss of what was seen as their essentially Chinese identity.[11]

The suppressions of the Cultural Revolution, then, combined with the perceived emptiness of imported culture from abroad, seem to have left a void at the core of Chinese ethnonationalism, leading individual and state culture producers to turn to minority cultures as reservoirs of still-extant authenticity.[12] In what Ivy (1995) has described as "elegiac" style, this undertaking romanticized the primitive and the traditional, the distinctive and the colorful, at the same time that it essentialized and crystallized those features of the Other held to be intrinsic and tied to the past.

As Edward Said (1978) has pointed out, orientalism is productive, and what is produced are ideas and statements that constitute a hegemonic description of the object. Those represented are rendered mute while the culture of the producers of such ideas "gains in strength and identity" by contrasting with the Other as a "sort of surrogate and underground self" (3). Said's discussion pertained, of course, to Western representations of the East, particularly to the Muslim "orient" with which his study was primarily concerned. This totalizing bifurcation of the globe into the categories of representer-represented obscures, as critics have begun to argue, the historical multiplicity of axes of domination, many of which, despite being non-European, were decidedly colonial and others of which were more broadly imperializing. Furthermore, it excludes the "West" as a potential object of essentialist representation, as Carrier (1992) has noted, stopping short at the conclusion that the "East" is mute and is therefore inherently incapable of othering. Approaches such as these, as Robertson has put it, "both further privilege Euro-American intellectual and theoretical trends as universal and obfuscate and neutralize the histories and legacies of non-Western imperialisms and associated 'othering' practices" (1995, 973).

The alternative pursued in this chapter is to investigate practices of othering internal to the "East," an approach akin to Robertson's treatment of Japanese colonialism within Asia (1995) and to Harrell's treatment of "civilizing projects" within China (1995a). This approach is distinct from another class of revamped "orientalisms," such as Heng and Devan (1992) on "internalized orientalism," Ong (1993) on "petty orientalism," Tang Xiaobing (1993) on "self-orientalization," and Chen Xiaomei (1995) on "occidentalism." These formulations stress the adoption of Western orientalist logics and premises for self-representation in the course of Asian processes of identity production—processes that are complicit, in their mimetic quality, with universalist modernizing ideologies (see Tang Xiaobing 1993). To retain the critical force of Said's original formulation, and to reference the global stage on which othering practices have been elaborated, I adopt the phrase *"internal orientalism"* to describe a relation between imaging and cultural-political domination that takes place interethnically within China.[13] In this process, the "orientalist" agent of dominant representation is transposed to that sector of the Chinese elite that engages in domestic othering. In other work (Schein 1994, 1996a), my analysis also includes a vision of China as representer of the West.

For twentieth-century China, then, an internal Other (or Others), in the form of the non-Han peoples positioned at the geographic-cognitive periphery of the Chinese state, came to represent the hope for recovery of a self weakened and threatened at the center by the vicissitudes of the forgoing decades of radical change. In what appears to be a contradiction, minorities were represented by way of contrast at the same time that their customs were (selectively) appropriated and valorized as elements of Chinese culture. Fei Xiaotong, a well-known Han anthropologist, for instance, introduced a 1982 collection of minority poetry by suggesting, "Only when contrasted to the vigor and vitality of minority peoples, can one be shamed into a sense of self-realization of one's own dull and feeble character" (Fei quoted in Alley 1982, ii). This kind of statement epitomizes the sense of oppositional and yet complementary identities that Said described, but it appears to lack the kind of implicit derogation of attributes of the Other that so insidiously characterizes orientalist discourse. I argue that closer examination of the *gendered* content of representations of minorities reveals subtler messages underlying the purported praise of cultural difference that came to characterize the 1980s.

The remainder of this article pursues two trajectories. One traces the prevalence and specific features of gendered images of minorities in terms of their ideological impact within Chinese mass culture.[14] The other examines some of the particular *sites of the production* of such images and the social-interactional dimensions of gender and ethnic relations that emerged in these contexts. This ethnographic approach constitutes my second modification of classical Saidian analysis. Rather than being limited to discourse and images, an anthropological method can also offer firsthand accounts of what happens at the actual sites of othering encounters—sites where difference is actively manufactured through interpersonal engagement. These instances not only result in discursive products that achieve wide circulation but also have palpable effects for the persons involved. Both of these phenomena, then—the currency of images of minorities in popular culture and the practices involved in the production of such representations—are assessed in light of their consequences for minorities, particularly minority women. My data are drawn primarily from my research on the Miao people. I concern myself mainly with the 1980s, that moment of acute flux in which the decisive close of the culturally flattening and xenophobic Cultural Revolution collided with the dramatic flinging open of the door to the outside effected by the policies of economic and cultural liberalization.

## MINORITY WOMEN AND THE PRODUCTION OF DIFFERENCE

Predictably, the figure of the ethnic Other in post-Mao China was for the most part represented by a female. This was part of a recurrent constellation of features that merged femaleness with rural backwardness with relative youth (in the sense of lack of seniority) with non-Han cultures. This conflation invoked a resilient set of status relationships that, taken together, were unambiguous in their hierarchical ordering of Chinese society. As I have suggested, reading representations as texts tells us a great deal about the producers of such representations and little about those represented. Images of minority women in the 1980s appeared as contrapuntal to urban elite culture, their difference signifying both a longing for modernity and the nostalgia that that kind of "progress" so often inspires.[15] An interpretation of these images reveals ways in which their creators positioned themselves not only in relation to minority cultures but also within Chinese society as a whole.

Not surprisingly, the oppositions of modern-backward, civilized-wild were tellingly revealed in the predictable association of the minority woman with nature.[16] In mass media images, she frequently appeared communing with animals or nestled among trees and flowers. Around her, luscious fruits abounded for the picking.[17] Waterfalls and streams framed carefree, laughing teenagers. Youth was stressed not only by the age of the women represented but also by their identity with the innocence of the natural.[18]

Figure 9. Outside Xijiang, a Han urban photographer cajoles a young Miao woman into posing for him. Photo by Louisa Schein, 1988.

A series of cards and bookmarks issued by the Nationalities Publishing House in Beijing emphasized the kinship between the female, the young, and the nonhuman. In each, a minority female was pictured, bedecked in a decorative costume that identified her nationality. In several of the images she was accompanied by such companions as birds, lambs, or butterflies. Although the elaborateness of her dress was unmistakably that of an adult, she was often presented with the physical features of a child. And this girl-woman occasionally appeared to be in direct communication with the animals who inhabited her environs.

The effect was of infantilizing and trivializing. Yet these representations were also imbued with a kind of warmth—albeit patronizing—and an intense fascination. This can be highlighted by examining the dynamism by which producers of such representations were also themselves consumers of minority cultures. The mountain community of Xijiang in southeast Guizhou, my field site for the year 1988, was a popular destination for artists, photographers, journalists, ethnographers, and officials, who came in search of images or information for their urban pursuits and for a first-hand experience of rural otherness.[19] I witnessed over and over again the quest for and the creation of the quintessential and the typical out of the partiality and disarray that characterized village life.

One team that visited Xijiang was making a video documentary on atmospheric conditions and other natural phenomena in the region for a meteorology institute in another province. The "remote mountains and ancient forests" *(shenshan laolin)* of Xijiang and the surrounding area have long held interest for tourists and "scientists" alike. Not content, however, with nature per se, this team decided that a bevy of local maidens would be the perfect companionship for their work and the perfect ornamentation for their meteorology video. Networking the young Miao fellow who manned the Xijiang culture station, they hired four local teenaged girls to accompany them on an arduous climb to a mountain pass twelve hundred meters above the village and to be filmed along the way. The ostensible terms of employment were that the young women were to be filmic objects adorning the video product. The models were coached to look good—both attractive and ethnic. Although it was a dank, chilly day, and the mountain peaks were enveloped in thick mist, the models donned their best hair decorations and braved the steep muddy path in feminine plastic shoes with heels rather than the rubber-soled canvas shoes that peasants find most practical on slippery slopes. Intermittently along the climb, the filmmakers stopped at strategically chosen scenic spots and arranged the models with precision. The latter were then coached to perform such activities as washing in a stream or singing a Miao song as if they were unaware of the camera. The effect was to be of naturalness, the local women skillfully embedded in their wilderness environment.

Participant observation revealed another more subtle facet to the job description of these young women. Joking and giggling characterized the mood of the climb, as the filmmakers took a somewhat transgressive pleasure in their ingenue escorts. When they reached the top of the pass, the girls rested with their employers in the thick mist on an expansive level area before beginning their long descent home. The filmmakers were to continue on to a more distant cluster of villages nestled in the next valley. There, for a moment, an easy camaraderie seemed to dispel the asymmetry in their relationship. Then one of the filmmakers held out a handful of candy—a seldom-eaten luxury for peasants in this region—in what the girls took to be a gesture of gratitude and parting. But when they reached out to accept it, he snatched his hand back, demanding that they sing him one more Miao song.

In this example, minority women experienced a double objectification. On the one hand, they were arrayed among the massive trees and trickling brooks as part of the intriguing wildness that drew urban visitors. On the other, they were treated as ethnic automatons, expected to produce folk culture at a moment's notice for the reward of a mouthful of candy. This latter dynamic is of course ubiquitous in ethnic tourism worldwide. What I am examining here is in effect a pretourism moment in which peasants were being socialized to commodify their culture, to regard it as a discrete medium of exchange. What happened in this case, however, was that the young women subtly resisted. They stalled, claiming embarrassment and eventually persuaded the filmmaker to give them the candy without a song. Acts such as these may be seen as strategies by which local people foiled attempts at dominant appropriation, insisting on themselves defining the contexts in which particular cultural practices were appropriate.

## THE EROTICIZED OTHER: DANGER AND ALLURE

Although Chinese internal orientalism commonly represented minority women as colorful flowers among the natural flora and fauna, it just as often represented them as very human objects of erotic fascination. In many images their bodies appeared voluptuous, more extensively revealed than would be proper for a Han woman, and their expressions were unabashedly inviting. Accounts that bespoke their imagined availability abounded. In whispered lore as well as in bluntly scientistic ethnographic reports, tales circulated about minority courtship practices, freedom of choice in marriage partners, and even sexual promiscuity.

Thus, the imaginings that surrounded minority women constituted a powerful attraction. Yet they were also attended by a kind of repressive fear and repulsion toward the implied baseness and breaches of morality that made these women so Other. It was not uncommon, upon mentioning to a Chinese urbanite one's interest in minorities, to be told in scandalized tones of confidentiality and admonition that, for example, the women "there" wear no tops, or that the unmarried young people are said to have socially sanctioned orgies. Routinely, tones of disapproval mixed with titillation characterized these whispered accounts.

In an insightful analysis, Norma Diamond (1988) has addressed the problem of the danger surrounding minority sexuality and marriage practices through an examination of allegations by the Han of Miao women's use of magic poisoning. Diamond suggests that the power attributed to Miao women to cause illness and even death through sorcery was a kind of projection of the fear held by Han Chinese of the perceived strength and relative freedom in Miao women's gender roles. This was profoundly threatening to the Confucian moral order and was compounded by the fact that, during the Ming and Qing dynasties, large numbers of male migrants and demobilized soldiers who had been sent to suppress Miao rebellions were dependent upon the Miao for marriage partners. The stories of poison potency constructed by the Han in this context continued into the 1980s. They epitomize the kind of mythmaking that may be generated by attempts to resolve a highly contradictory relationship in which the "Other" woman's attractiveness and sexual availability also constitute her danger.[20]

The 1980s, with its ostensible emphasis on diversity and tolerance, was a period filled with the excitement of breaking the taboos that had distanced the mysterious minority woman. She was brought in from the country to the city, domesticated, and made into an object of household consumption. She also became prime material for movies, television, and other forms of entertainment (Gladney 1994, 1995). One Han man, a Hunan native working as a musical director for the Guizhou Culture Bureau, conceived a "new" form of exhibition: a traveling display of words, photographs, and artifacts portraying Guizhou folk festivals accompanied by staged demonstrations—a kind of living museum. He traveled around the Guizhou countryside to recruit young people with particular talent. Once he had chosen some, he instructed them to bring with them not only their best local festival attire but also a song or dance that was typical of their locality. He then synthesized these "raw" materials into an artfully choreographed performance representing the songs, dances, and instruments of Guizhou folk life. Surrounded by tastefully mounted artifacts, the young people would do several acts a day, thrilling both foreign and domestic museum-tourists who were accustomed to seeing only ancient culture frozen in objects. The exhibition traveled to major cities such as Beijing, Xi'an, Tianjin, and Shenzhen.

Although traveling minority performing troupes have been commonplace in China for decades, what was seen as novel in this one was that the performers were minimally trained peasants from the countryside, holding out the promise of authenticity and a kind of immediacy of (first) contact whose resonances with the lure of virginity were less than subtle. The director was the constructor and mediator of these desires. Among the recruits were two teenaged girls from Xijiang. The director had traveled to Xijiang and fallen head over heels into the embrace of Miao "hospitality." At a meal prepared in his honor, the girls had proffered spirits to him with two hands and welcomed him with song. As he and the girls recounted it to me with great pleasure and affection, this treatment sent him into such reveries that he was inspired, that night in Xijiang, to compose two original songs. Their lyrics epitomize the conflation of the pastoral fantasy with romantic-sexual intimations. The first song was dense with evocative natural imagery:

I am a cloud in the sky; you are a spring in the mountain
I am mist in the forest; you are a lotus in the water
Xijiang, ah, Xijiang, would that I was a spring rain sprinkling upon your
    fertile fields
Xijiang, ah, Xijiang, would that I could become the morning dew to kiss
    your smiling face.

The second song went even further in linking nature imagery with that of romantic desire. It was a veritable catalog of the symbols most commonly used to characterize Miao culture. Delivered as a courtship dialogue between a young man and a young woman, it bespoke a fascination with the kind of unrepressed passion that is seen by the Han as propelling legitimate Miao courtship practices. Through his virtually ecstatic lyrical creation, the director vicariously accessed the romance of companionate courtship so long tabooed among the Han.

My evocation of this sexual tension is, however, in no way meant to imply that the Xijiang girls were actual sexual playthings of their director or of other men they came into contact with in their work as traveling performers. On the contrary, they described their director as a fiercely protective father figure who cited their country naïveté as his reason for forbidding them to go out in the cities without "adult" accompaniment, and sheltered them from seeing many of the things they might otherwise have seen. He also maintained that they would be uncomfortable enduring the stares that their appearance, and particularly their hairstyles, would elicit from passersby on the street. On his part, this protectiveness points to another aspect of the relationship, one in which he became the critical consciousness subsuming and conserving their difference and containing their allure. On their part, it reveals a powerful dilemma faced by minority women with cosmopolitan aspirations: their ability to reproduce their exotic difference was their ticket out of the village, but once in the metropolis they found with great frustration that it was this difference that was the basis for their continued, enforced segregation.

The experiences of both the young women in the traveling show and those who sang and danced as part of their hotel employment reveal deep contradictions. State and dominant discourses constructed their cultural practices as what Kligman calls "cultural artifacts . . . [to which are] attributed only a historical referentiality" (1988, 259). Their valorization as constitutive of "national heritage" was also their derogation as backward and tied to the past. There are two problems with confining such cultural "traditions" to the category of living artifacts. First, doing so denies their present embeddedness in the lives of practitioners, who still see them as linked to social relations and imbued with local meanings. For minority peasants, rituals and customary dress are matters of everyday practice with their own significations, not simply vestiges of the past. Second, to cast such practitioners as "living guardians of a creative . . . cultural heritage" (260) is to freeze them in time, denying them the longings for modernity that have gripped the rest of the country.[21] The prestige associated with symbols of modernity was no less significant in rural areas than it was in the cities, but rural and especially minority areas bore the double burden of questing to modernize while being suspended in time by the representations and implicit injunctions of urban culture.

## MIAO WOMEN, AMBIVALENCE, AND
## THE REPRODUCTION OF DIFFERENCE

Miao women, especially when they traveled to urban centers dominated by ethnic Han and characterized by a kind of monocultural metropolitan homogeneity, experienced a strong ambivalence about the marking of their difference. Women told me of traveling to visit relatives now working in Guangzhou or Tianjin, and of the conflicts they underwent in deciding whether to put their hair up in characteristically Miao style. In each case, just out of habit, they twisted it atop their heads at first, but after enduring the curious and objectifying stares of urbanites on the street, they decided to take it down and braid it when they went out. The young women working in the Nationalities Guest House in Kaili told me that they would prefer to wear their hair down, living as they were in the city, but that they were required at work to comb it up as emblematic of their cultural distinctiveness. By contrast, when they were seen on the street after hours, they often groomed themselves to be indistinguishable from the Han urban residents in more Western clothing and hairstyles.

Depending on their situations, these dilemmas provoked two types of internal conflict among Miao women. For rural women traveling to cities for a short time, ambivalence derived from the feeling that dressing like the Han was like putting on a disguise, a kind of betrayal of self. For women working in cities, such as those in the hotels or the traveling performers, the ambivalence arose from their work that brought them to the cities and accustomed them to its ways but also required of them to maintain their otherness as the basis for them having this work in the first place. Confronted with a larger society that lauded their difference even as it stigmatized it, the practices of Miao women in cities revealed a complex dialectic between collusion in and resistance to their representations as Others.

Urban public culture evoked in Miao women what Aihwa Ong (1988, 89) has characterized as "deep divisions, confusion, and unresolved tensions between tradition and modernity." More recently, Virginia Cornue (1996) has documented this "confusion" as a central feature of women's experience in post-Mao China. For minority women, the dilemmas are especially acute, for these women must negotiate not only fluid definitions of propriety in gender roles, morality, and sexuality but also the dissonances between urban Han and ethnic discourses scripting their identities.

Turning to rural sites, in what ways, then, did Miao women in the countryside come to terms with their imaging as quintessentially ethnic? The vast majority of these young women were peasant daughters living in rural settings perhaps more remote than those of most of the Han peasantry. Their interactions with Han Chinese were rare: Xijiang's population was 99.5 percent Miao and the population of the entire county was 82 percent Miao, with the Han and other minorities clustered mostly in the county seat and in a handful of spatially distinct villages. Many of the outlying villages were without electricity and, consequently, without television. Mail was delivered over the mountains on foot, and the rare newspaper or magazine that arrived was scarcely glanced at by young women because of their widespread illiteracy. Their choices to adorn their hair or wear ethnic clothing were governed by local norms that as a rule called for everyday dress of simple Miao style but did not necessarily disdain more Western-style clothing. Decisions about other practices were also influenced by local pressures to conform and were unconcerned with image management vis-à-vis the larger society. Thus, unlike in urban points of "contact," in the countryside, Miao peasant women did not experience their actions as "minority" practices that defined them in relation to the Han.

It was only in the larger, more central villages, the sites of periodic markets or of important bus routes, that the heavier volume of traffic by Han and more cosmopolitan Miao brought a kind of self-consciousness to Miao young women. In Xijiang, a popular destination for domestic tourism, this kind of awareness was particularly intense. Young women knew that a handful of them would be chosen to pose for journalists' cameras or to sing for folklorists' tape recorders. Gossip circulated regarding who was picked and for what reasons. There was a range of responses to this display element of their lives. Many young women, professing shyness, eschewed cameras and other forms of scrutiny under all circumstances. Some confided indignation at being at the receiving end of such an exploitative gaze. Others reluctantly complied and were occasionally even persuaded to change into "better" clothes for photographs. A handful, however—those discussed above—routinely accepted remuneration in exchange for more formal labors in the creation of "authentic" images.

Some rural women had become so accustomed to this commodification of their bodies that they had altercations with visiting photographers. For example, three young male journalists from high-profile newspapers had requested their cooperation for group poses, in ethnic dress, that were laboriously staged. Background settings were calculatedly varied to portray, for instance, the characteristic open balcony of regional Miao architecture and alternately the cascading rice terraces of Miao mountain farms. The photographers called for frequent changes of positioning, for smiles, and for simulations of cheery interaction. When the models demanded pay before completing this trying photo shoot, the photographers balked, claiming that what they were producing was good publicity *(xuanchuan)* for Xijiang. This, they argued, would have a larger effect, resulting in social and material benefits for the community. The models, impervious to arguments about the wider consequences of their cooperation, insisted, through their advocate in the culture station, on direct compensation. Ultimately, they prevailed.

The young women's demands for payment revealed their resistance to the utilization of their bodies, their smiles, and their time in the service of an amorphous community principle. Likewise, they withheld themselves from the urban gaze until they were sure of remuneration. Although the end result was still the reproduction of orientalist representations, their insistence on payment may be seen as a counterorientalist practice in that it attempted to supplant a kind of colonialist cultural plundering with a more clear-cut market transaction.

Tacit forms of sabotage likewise revealed the subtlety of the relationship between reproduction and resistance. Young women hired for photo shoots would sometimes fail to show up at the appointed time, or simply not show up at all, thereby underscoring the value of their service. They dragged their feet in assuming required poses and refused to keep still, thus requiring photographers to use greater quantities of film to obtain the "perfect shot." When posing, or particularly when asked to sing, they would burst into giggles midverse, holding their hands to their mouths and, piercing through the solemnity of the constructed moment, expose the artificiality of the context. Although by no means readable as resolutely volitional, these practices permit multiple, overlapping readings of their effects and their implicit meanings. They may be understood as attempts to personalize cultural production and to refuse to become interchangeable "ethnic automatons." They may also constitute an implicit critique of the decontextualization of cultural forms that, to the young practitioners, were far more than fossilized artifacts. And, they had the potential to subvert an imposed labor discipline that might otherwise have effectively contained the excesses of their cultural otherness.

Lest these young women be viewed simply as cultural conservators, however, it should be stressed again that they also had an acute longing for "modernity" and attached considerable prestige to its trappings. This was clearly seen in their marriage strategies. Although subject to certain strictures of exogamy and to parental interventions, Miao young people had a considerable degree of latitude in choosing their partners. Since village exogamy was the norm, market days and annual festivals—when young people traveled out from their home villages—were the most common times for getting acquainted with potential partners. Miao young women participated actively in courtship practices such as improvised antiphonal singing between groups of boys and groups of girls at festivals, and in the more routine promenading with flashlights on Xijiang's main road after nightfall.

But although market and festival might have appeared to provide for the unstructured mixing of all comers, young people from all over the region shared a finely honed understanding of a system that gauged different vil-

lages according to their desirability as places to live. Prized features included large size; proximity to a road and to long-distance bus routes; presence of a periodic market; availability of goods, electricity, and television;
and so forth. All these features contributed to the relative ranking of villages
as *da difang* (big—i.e., cosmopolitan—places) and *xiao difang* (small—i.e.,
stifling—places). Long-standing practices of patrilocality determined that
young women would be the ones most concerned with these distinctions because it was they who would have to uproot themselves and become accustomed to living in a new place. Xijiang young women, for instance, usually
said that they would never marry into an outlying village that was far from a
road, but that they would consider marrying into a smaller village as long as
it was along the bus route and closer than their natal village. Young women
from small villages, on the other hand, wanted very much to find a partner
who resided in an economic and social center like Xijiang. Moreover, even
minority women in the remotest parts of China were not outside the nationwide system of valuation that attached superior status to urbanites and
state-salaried workers (Potter 1983). Thus, as I have argued, status distinctions penetrated far into the rural hinterland and affected the hierarchical
ranking even of remote villages.

## MINORITY MEN AND SELF-OBJECTIFICATION

Rural Miao women, then, were at least as concerned with striving toward the
social and economic "modernity," so idealized in contemporary China, as
they were with manufacturing their cultural distinctiveness. Where they engaged in the latter, it was often with specific instrumental intentions. But
the marking of minority otherness, discussed above, was not only the consequence of the collusion between members of the dominant culture and
the minority women whose images were consumed. Minority men also
figured as key producers *and* consumers of difference. Their complicity in
commodifying and objectifying "their" women as ethnic reminds us of the
importance of recognizing the heterogeneity that always characterizes minority communities (Lowe 1991). The Miao and other groups are not uniform entities defined by a common identity; rather, they are internally
crosscut by significant class, status, regional, and gender distinctions.

As mentioned before, the local culture station in Xijiang was staffed by a
local Miao man, as was its parent organization in the county seat. These culture brokers were pivotal actors in the construction and presentation of local color for outsiders. When visitors to Xijiang wanted to organize a formal
photo shoot or stage an ethnic event, it was usually to the local culture station that they directed their requests. In the course of these transactions the
young culture worker in Xijiang, who had little education but some world-
liness from having served in the People's Liberation Army for four years,

had been gradually socialized into the expectations of the dominant culture. When asked what skills his work entailed, he replied that he was good at finding the girls with looks *(maoxiang)* and figures *(shencai)*. It was he who explained to visitors that if they wanted to photograph ethnic subjects, they ought to pay them to get dressed up. And it was he who collected the money and distributed it to the models when they were hired. The function of the culture station, as an organ of the state, was in effect to monetize relations of cultural exchange between villagers and outsiders. The agent of this commodification was, more often than not, in Xijiang and elsewhere, a minority man.

The participation of local people in cultural production about themselves should be understood, as Linda Layne (1989) has argued, as a "dialogic process." She employs Bakhtin (1981) to examine the ways in which representations in dominant discourse are filled with local content, yielding a "more nuanced view of . . . simultaneous compliance and resistance" (Layne 1989, 34). It must be stressed that Miao elites not only facilitated *Han* consumption of their culture as embodied by their women but also engaged in a kind of ritualized objectification in which they themselves partook of reified representations of their own "traditions." This was especially common among those who had left the countryside and—living among the majority, separated in space from their home villages—had begun to cultivate a kind of romantic nostalgia for essentialized versions of their forgotten culture. The chief symbol of this still-recoverable past was the richly adorned Miao girl, usually depicted in song.[22] Their celebration of her as symbol has special significance because, in making her a symbol, they were claiming her as their own, as contrastive with the dominant culture rather than simply constitutive of it. The phenomenon confounds the uncritical application of Said's orientalism paradigm in the Chinese-minority context, because it shows that (at least some) Miao were not mute objects of representation but rather were active subjects engaged in the molding of their own representation.

In 1988, members of the Miao intelligentsia in Guizhou convened the first annual meeting of the newly founded Miao Studies Association. The conference was characterized by a combination of intellectual production and cultural consumption. Election of officers, formal speeches, and presentation of academic papers took place alongside such events as a visit to a Miao festival in a nearby village, attendance at an ethnic performance in the evening, and banquets in which feasting, toasting, and Miao drinking songs were standard fare. Of relevance here, however, was the first event of the conference. When participants piled off buses or out of cars at the conference headquarters, they were greeted by elaborately garbed Miao young women who presented them with ritual spirits out of the horns of bulls—a ritual identical to that described for the *non-Miao* mayors at the beginning of this essay, and one that had, significantly, become canonized via glossy tourist brochures promoting the region.

Minority intellectual practices such as these that effectively entrench status distinctions even as they purport to celebrate difference reproduce the hegemonic order that defines non-Han groups by their difference at the same time that it subsumes and appropriates such difference. Interpreted along the gender axis, the cultural politics become even more apparent, for if tradition is feminized, it is also automatically, but subtextually, devalued, since the feminine is recognized as an unequivocal signifier of subordinate status.

## THE POWERS AND PERILS OF MODERNITY

My emphasis on the consumption of women in the above examples may seem overdrawn. In fact, minority men also regularly appeared in performances and images as objects of dominant consumption. However, minority women, as emblematic of the natural, the traditional, and the exotically titillating, were foregrounded in such representations, with men simply serving as a foil to highlight the women's distinctiveness and allure. This is particularly apparent in the plethora of images and accounts that dealt with minority courtship practices. In these representations the girl regularly appeared coy but sassy and inviting. The boy, often pictured gazing at her, functioned as a vehicle for the desire she provoked. In this way, minority men, in their intimate proximity to the desired object, focused and redirected the consumer's gaze from the indeterminate panorama of colorful culture to the body of the minority woman. However, what is important is not minority women as objects per se, but what they signified in the context of a profoundly ambivalent Chinese consciousness torn between the appeal of modernity and its threat of corruption. Following Lata Mani, I suggest that these women became the "site[s] on which tradition was debated and re-formulated" (1987, 153)—and in this case domesticated.

The presence of the minority woman as a colorful element in Chinese national culture was reassuring to cosmopolitan Chinese in two apparently contradictory senses. On the one hand, she was evidence of the uninterrupted existence of a well-preserved "traditional" culture in changing China.[23] On the other hand, her intractable otherness, as Enloe (1989, 42) has pointed out for other contexts and Harrell (1995a) has detailed for the Chinese case, emphasizes the need for the civilizing practices of the "superior" Han. In everyday consciousness, these two ideologies may not be irreconcilable. One of the groups of art students that visited Xijiang achieved an apparent synthesis. During the day they searched out Miao authenticity to be captured in their representations; they painted, photographed, interviewed, and otherwise documented "the past." But in the evening, they organized a party at the culture station to share a little of their imported Western culture with local youth. Cassettes of Chinese and Western pop music were rounded up, a dance floor was cleared in the one-room culture station, and the (mostly female) local guests were urged into coed dancing and entertained with performances of such novelties as Western break dancing. The urban visitors experienced no contradiction between their daytime and evening practices. On the contrary, the opportunity to act as envoys of (imported) "modern" culture further confirmed for them that they had come to a remote and backward place of difference where "archaic" cultural forms were dominant.

Practices such as these open a window onto a wide sea of cultural struggles that permeated Chinese public culture and resonated with larger global processes. The valorization of "modernity," thick with its connotations of First World prestige and an infinitude of material abundance, was not solely an elite project but rather an ideological complex that saturated Chinese society as it has the transnational arena. My charting of the representations of difference it incites departs from other analyses of the Chinese context (cf. Anagnost 1994; Gladney 1994) that portray the chief cultural struggle to be between discourses attached to the (usually post-Mao) state and local articulations or enactments of difference. Even those treatments that complicate the picture by detailing local deployments of modernizing and retrospective discourses still overprivilege the state through such formulations as "hegemony" (Chao 1996), "immanence" (Cheung 1996), or "interpellation" (Litzinger 1995). I am arguing instead for a vision of a dominant representational regime that crosses national boundaries and captures popular fancy with both the promises of the "modern" and the soothing comforts of reinvented tradition.[24] The Chinese Party-state, as will be shown below, presented its own specific variant of this bifurcated imagery.

## THE STATE AND THE SOCIAL ORDER

Turning, finally, to official state imagings, one finds both echoes of and divergences from what was being produced in the more popular domain. At the core, the state situated itself as a locus of the civilizing mission and of a kind of paternalistic authority. Official policy stresses a horizontal relationship among the nationalities, each of which is formally recognized as having equal status in the Chinese polity. Representations of this type of "multiculturalism" constitute what Leong (1989, 76) calls "national image-management," which despite being primarily directed abroad also serves to indoctrinate local citizens into a consciousness of the prescribed social order. To be sure, images of horizontal fraternity abounded in official culture, recalling the trope of classless solidarity purveyed during the Cultural Revolution, but significantly supplanting it (see Litzinger n.d.). Many publicly circulated images, however, upon close reading betrayed a more vertical vision of China's social order. A 1986 billboard promoting development in southeast Guizhou showed two minority women in full festival regalia standing on either side of a Han male, taller and clearly older, in urban worker's clothing. The conflation of minority with such categories as female, rural, and backward stressed the vanguard role of the Han urbanite on the road to "progress." A further interpretation is suggested by Ann Anagnost, who observes that the state, constituting itself as center, manipulates such contrasts in order to represent itself as a "modern, activist state opposed to all that is irrational, traditional and local" (Anagnost 1994, 229).

A society's self-representation as modern is often an assertion of what Laura Nader (1989) after Said (1978) refers to as "positional superiority" over those constructed as less modern. Such discourses are commonly premised on the assumption of an improved position of women in the society that is making claims to being more "advanced." In China, contemporary problems and reversals in the status of women may be glossed over by focusing attention on "Other" women putatively less civilized than the urban Han. As Nader puts it, "If progress is incremental then the place of women continuously improves, and evidence to the contrary is either minimized, or denied, or dealt with by turning the lens to the image of women in other cultures" (1989, 19). Ironically, the image of sexual promiscuity and fluidity of gender roles that was commonly used to characterize minorities was misrecognized as a mark of backwardness in an evolutionist Chinese framework that continued, despite itself, to assess "civilization" according to the fixity of Confucian gender and status hierarchies. As Anagnost points out, in the official regime of representation, that which was excluded from state-defined modernity (i.e., local tradition) was not "disappeared" but rather rendered hypervisible in order to highlight, by contrast, the civilized character of the state: "Out of these practices is constructed an 'otherness' against which the Party can exercise its legitimating activism" (1994, 231).

A 1984 poster introduced a generational element to emphasize this paternalistic role of the Party. Literally infantilized minority children, again in full festival regalia, some holding toys and some holding musical instruments, along with one or two Han, were shown playing gleefully with, holding the hands of, or even embracing a fatherly Mao Zedong, Zhou Enlai, Liu Shaoqi, and Zhu De. Both this image and the development billboard mentioned above invoked a Confucian vision of authority—the first employing the elder sibling–younger sibling relationship, the second conflating the father-child relation with that of the emperor-subject—to emphasize the ascendancy of the Han state. The spectacle—from rosy-cheeked cherubs to ethnologically accurate costumery—was itself what enabled the Party to emerge in high relief, triumphant and progressive.

A final example illustrates the ubiquity of these messages. In 1980, new images began to be printed on the face of Chinese paper currency *(renminbi)*. Industrial and agricultural scenes were replaced with two elaborately adorned heads of minority women (or occasionally men) on each of the small denominations. Passed daily from hand to hand, these diversely headdressed, cheery tokens served to remind all Chinese of the multiethnic makeup of the Chinese polity. The new one-hundred-yuan bill, however, told a superseding story. It pictured the solemn profiles—again—of Mao Zedong, Zhou Enlai, Liu Shaoqi, and Zhu De. The flurry of bills barraged the cash-user with a "cross-section" of China's peoples, but the progression from small to large denominations left no doubt as to the ultimate relations of authority.

## CONCLUSION

In the representations of 1980s China, minority women were fraught with contradictions. They were both othered and incorporated, sources of contrast as well as identity. In popular consciousness they were objects of desire, but an ambivalent desire that was saturated with other meanings, particularly those concerning the tension between tradition and modernity. Their imaging betrayed the ascendancy of the Party-as-patriarch over more egalitarian, horizontal visions of the Chinese social order. It was within this complex and highly charged ideological context that minority women and men colluded in reproducing their difference.

The data presented here suggest that, especially in the post-Mao period, it is possible, and indeed necessary, to talk about spheres of cultural production that may be characterized as nonstate, popular, or emerging in civil society. Although the state is, of course, a key agent in the manufacture of representations of minorities, it may be thought of as one sphere of production among others; the latter include the dominant Han intelligentsia, the minority elite, and local cultural practitioners. The interplay between these latter spheres and the extent to which their practices may be considered autonomous from or oppositional to state discourses remain to be clarified.

A second point, a corollary of the first, is that a dichotomy that would characterize the Han as representers and minorities as the represented is inaccurate. Although this relationship prevails in many of the encounters described here, minorities do also have a voice, however marginalized. In that domain of dominant cultural production that was engaged in the creation of images of the non-Han (only one of many sectors that comprise the Chinese culture industry), many minority elites were operating, both reproducing their otherness and potentially contesting its essentialized quality. At the grass roots, as I have described elsewhere (Schein 1989, 1991), local individuals also strove to revive Miao culture and to control its presentation to outsiders. Minority self-representation, despite its frequent subsumption or appropriation by the mainstream, and despite its appearance of complicity, still constitutes a distinguishable voice and must be considered in its own right. Here, the analysis departs from Said's orientalism paradigm, in which the Other is silenced by a singular dominant discourse.

A third point—the resemblance of Chinese internal orientalism to that of Western colonialism—leaves unanswered the question of whether internal orientalist practices arose independently or were themselves imports, modes of representation that entered China as stowaways in the periods of more or less wholesale emulation of Western ways that have recurred since the late nineteenth century. Arguably, China has an indigenous history of othering "barbarian" or less "civilized" peoples that dates back many centuries (see Diamond 1988, 1995; and Dikötter 1992, for specific instances). Likewise, Western practices for marking alterity must be seen as historically specific (see de Certeau 1988, 209–43).[25] But it is also likely that cultural intercourse between China and the West—including Chinese urbanites' avid consumption of Western arts, literature, and consumer goods, along with the advent of large-scale international tourism to China in the 1980s— has had a profound effect on Chinese styles of othering. Some of the influence may be a consequence of straightforward imitation, as in the case of artists inspired by the modernist primitivism of Gauguin (Lufkin 1990, 33), and some may be the result of calculated attempts to create tourist products expressly suited to the consumer tastes of Western visitors. At any rate, the effect has been the emergence of a specifically Chinese approach to othering that is at the same time highly resonant with that of the West.

The production of difference may be informed by a logic not unique to Western orientalism. In China, the ostensibly celebratory spotlighting of minority women in all their fascinating particularity was also insidiously orientalist. The chain of signification that linked ethnic to female to rural to backward served, in effect, to encourage a derogated, subordinate positioning of minorities, women, and peasants in Chinese society. Moving into the early 1990s, harsh consequences in the form of economic marginalization began to suggest themselves (see Schein 1994, 1996a). Whether such orientalist representations constitute ratifications of new postcolonial forms of domination demands continual reexamination.

## NOTES

This chapter was originally published in *Modern China* 23, no. 1 (January 1997): 69–98. Copyright 1997 by Sage Publications. Reprinted by permission of Sage Publications. Author's Note: A version of this article was first presented at the Annual Meetings of the American Anthropological Association, New Orleans, December 2, 1990. Portions have appeared since then in my article "Multiple Alterities: The Contouring of Gender in Miao and Chinese Nationalisms," in *Women Out of Place: The Gender of Agency and the Race of Nationality,* ed. Brackette F. Williams (New York: Routledge, 1996). I wish to express appreciation to the following people for providing references and comments on earlier drafts: Ann Anagnost, Tani Barlow, Susan Brownell, Kate Campbell, Stevan Harrell, Gail Kligman, Felicity Lufkin, Aihwa Ong, Ara Wilson, and an anonymous reviewer for *Modern China.* The views expressed and any errors remain my responsibility.

1. Research was conducted in Xijiang zhen, Leishan county, Guizhou province, from January through December 1988, under the auspices of the Committee on Scholarly Communication with the People's Republic of China, the Fulbright-Hays Doctoral Dissertation Research Abroad program, the Chinese State Education Commission, and the Guizhou Nationalities Institute. Shorter research trips in 1982, 1985, and 1986—under the joint sponsorship of the Central Nationalities Institute as well as the Yunnan, Guizhou, and Southwest Nationalities Institutes—were supported by a Samuel T. Arnold Fellowship, Brown University; a Humanities Institute Graduate Research Grant; a Department of Anthropology Robert H. Lowie Grant; and an Institute of East Asian Studies Travel Grant, University of California at Berkeley. I am grateful to all these organizations as well as to many local people, scholars, and levels of government within China for their support of my research.

2. Qiandongnan, or southeast Guizhou, was established as an autonomous prefecture in 1956 based on its dense population of minorities. As of 1986, Miao were the most populous ethnic group, constituting 37 percent of the prefecture population and 60 percent of Kaili's population. The Han comprised 32.5 percent of the prefecture population and the Dong followed, at 24 percent. The remaining 6 percent included Buyi, Shui, Zhuang, Yao, Yi, and several other nationalities (Qiandongnan 1986, 1). For reasons of numbers as well as history, the region has come to be regarded as a locus of Miao identity and determinative of what is considered Miao culture, despite a great deal of variation among subgroups both within the region and scattered over the rest of China (cf. Diamond 1995; Cheung 1996). Thus, Qiandongnan is where people look to find the "typical" *(dianxing)* Miao.

3. The term *nationalities (minzu)* has several senses when used as an adjective in proper names. When used for such work units as "nationalities institutes" *(minzu xueyuan)* or "nationalities song and dance troupes" *(minzu gewutuan),* it denotes actual participation by members of various nationalities, including the Han. By popular connotation, however, it operates as a shorthand for the term *shaoshu minzu* (minority nationalities) and designates ethnicities other than the Han. In this case, it may have referred specifically to the fact that the guest house is in a minority area and may have been intended to play on tourists' presumed interest in this facet of

the exotic. It also may have indicated that the construction of the building was at least partially funded by the Nationalities Affairs Commission (Minzu shiwu weiyuanhui) as an extension of policy designed to develop minority areas. See Harrell (1996) for a discussion of the term *minzu.*

4. On the hierarchical gendering of drinking/hospitality rituals, see Schein (1996b, 93–96).

5. On tourism development in southwest China, see for instance Oakes (1995), Swain (1990), Cheung (1996, 253–80), and Chao (1996, 226–28). For a somewhat anecdotal comparison of domestic and foreign tourism styles, see Harrell (1995b).

6. I encountered this assumption not so much in print but in interactions with scholars and other observers of China who routinely associated the commodification of ethnic culture with the influx of international capital and the designs its advent inspired.

7. For a thorough and provocative exploration of the "semantic dimensions and political implications" of the exotic, see Foster (1982).

8. My use of the term *Miao* is not intended to reproduce the reification of the official category used by the state. The people who comprise the current officially defined Miao are internally diverse and are scattered across seven provinces within China as well as several Southeast Asian countries. A strong case for the consideration of such regional and "subgroup" heterogeneity has recently been made by Stevan Harrell (1990) in his study of three Yi communities in Sichuan. See also Cheung (1996) for an extended discussion of the identity politics and struggles engendered by the imposition of the state category.

9. In the 1982 census, minority nationalities represented 6.7 percent of China's population (*Renmin ribao,* 31 October 1990). The staggering increase in less than a decade, and the change in ratio vis-à-vis the Han, arises in part from the widespread voluntary reclassification by former Han who now wish, for various reasons too complex to explore here, to have official minority designations.

10. On this process, see Cheung (1996, 182–281), Diamond (1995), and Schein (1993, 20–100) on the Miao, and Gladney (1991), Harrell (1995a), and McKhann (1995) on other groups. For a treatment of official cultural production during this period and a comparison with the contemporary era, see Yau's 1989 discussion of the political and cultural uses of minority women in Chinese cinema since the 1950s.

11. For an analysis of "culture fever" *(wenhua re)* and the rise in studies of Chinese culture in the decade after the Cultural Revolution, see Wang He (1986). For an overview of the Chinese search for "national character" since the turn of the century, see Wakeman (1991).

12. Karnoouh (1982) has described a related dilemma for the elites of the Central European states created upon the dismantling of the Ottoman and Austro-Hungarian empires. He suggests that they faced a crisis of national identity as they confronted their own tenuous grounding, first in imported Western institutions and nation-state ideologies and then in imported international Communism. They turned to the folklore of the peasantry as a basis for unification of these awkwardly multiethnic states that were hoping "to rediscover at the heart of the rural world the essence of [their] difference and the ultimate recourse elaborating national unity"

(100). Thus peasant creation was channeled to become a source of legitimacy for regimes caught in the contradictions of imported modernity. See also Ivy (1995) on Japanese notions of loss and the "nostalgic appeal to premodernity."

13. Gladney (1994, 113–14) employs the term "oriental orientalism" to describe similar othering processes.

14. While what I am describing here is unquestionably a recent cultural *trend,* I am grateful to Bao Jiemin for pointing out that awareness of such things as minority cultures, preservation, and the tensions over identity should not be characterized as a widespread element of *everyday* popular consciousness in China. Rather, these concerns deeply informed certain domains of contemporary cultural production — both popular and official — and were arguably inseparable from the feverish cravings for modernity that were more dominant in everyday consciousness.

15. Rey Chow found a similar othering in the Chinese literature of the early twentieth century. She suggests that backwardness was projected onto more oppressed members of Chinese society — women, children, servants, and rural people — as a consequence of the impotence felt by Chinese literati vis-à-vis the modern West (1989, 153–54).

16. The use of the singular "minority woman" is in no way intended to obscure the unquestionable heterogeneity in and between minority populations. To be sure, there is no such thing as "the minority woman." Rather, the term is meant to highlight the ways in which the representational modes that I am discussing deftly gloss over such internal variation in their construction of a homogenized Other defined solely by contrast to the Han subject.

17. See Pollock (1987, 46) for a discussion of the association of fruit with women's breasts and genitals in Western commodity culture. This raises the question of whether these modes of representation were imports of or influenced by Western styles, or whether similar modes occurred independently within China.

18. For a fuller discussion of the infantilization of minorities in China, see Harrell (1995a, 13–15) and Lufkin (1990).

19. The community of Xijiang, whose residents made it home for me for a year, was unusual for several reasons. Nestled in the remote mountains and commonly dubbed the "Thousand-Household Miao Village" (Qianjia Miao zhai), it has a population of over five thousand persons, 94 percent of whom are agriculturalists. In 1988 it was the administrative seat of Xijiang *qu,* which exercised jurisdiction over almost seventy natural villages and consequently had a middle school, a government building, a small courthouse, and other state offices; it also was the site of a periodic market and the end of the line for the long-distance bus from the county seat. All this, combined with the high concentration of Miao in one locality, made Xijiang a popular destination for urban travelers. The more it was trafficked by tourists, the more its reputation as a locus of Miao cultural identity was assumed. Ironically, this led to Xijiang regularly being represented as a typical *(dianxing)* Miao village, despite its exceptional features. Beyond simple tourism, this "learning from the experience of real life" *(tiyan shenghuo),* a common practice at least since Mao's Yan'an talks on art and literature in 1942 (Mao 1967, 84), and recently celebrated in the 1984 film *Yellow Earth* (Huang tudi), has in the post–Cultural Revolution era taken up even more than before the minority subject. This practice, under different names, may in

fact be similar to movements that occurred as early as the beginning of this century. Chang-tai Hung (1985) has documented the romanticism and "going to the people" *(dao minjian qu)* movements among Chinese intellectuals occurred late in the second decade of the twentieth century and the 1920s. According to Hung, these movements, too, were characterized by the valorization of "rural innocence and primitivism," an interest in folklore, and a link with Chinese nationalism.

20. On the dangerous and transgressive eroticism of the Other woman, see also Schein (1996a).

21. See Adams (1996) for a provocative discussion of this dynamic in Tibet.

22. Chao found a similar move among Naxi intellectuals in Yunnan who strove to situate pristine culture in the mountains and among illiterate women "so that men and town-dwelling and lowland Naxi could be *comparatively* associated with civilization" (1996, 234).

23. In an extremely sophisticated reading of the 1987 cinematic event *Red Sorghum,* Yuejin Wang suggests that the film "and many other culturally specific texts do *not* reflect the *appearances* of a culture; they mirror what the actual cultural landscape *lacks.* They reflect fantasies and imagined memories—that which society expels" (1989, 53). Wang's conclusions are highly resonant with those I propose here for Chinese cultural production on minority women.

24. For a more global treatment of modernity in specific relation to the development of ethnic tourism in Guizhou, see Oakes (1995).

25. I am indebted to Judith Farquhar for this reference and for stressing this point.

## REFERENCES

Adams, V. 1996. "Karaoke as Modern Lhasa, Tibet: Western Encounters with Cultural Politics." *Cultural Anthropology* 11, no. 4:510–46.

Alley, Rewi. 1982. *Folk Poems from China's Minorities.* Beijing: New World Press.

Anagnost, A. 1994. "The Politics of Ritual Displacement." In *Asian Visions of Authority: Religion and the Modern States of East and Southeast Asia,* ed. Laurel Kendall, Charles Keyes, and Helen Hardacre, 221–54. Honolulu: University of Hawaii Press.

Bakhtin, M. M. 1981. *The Dialogic Imagination: Four Essays by M. M. Bakhtin.* Ed. Michael Holquist. Austin: University of Texas Press.

Carrier, J. 1992. "Occidentalism: The World Turned Upside-Down." *American Ethnologist* 19, no. 2:195–212.

Chao, E. 1996. "Hegemony, Agency, and Re-presenting the Past: The Invention of Dongba Culture." In *Negotiating Ethnicities in China and Taiwan,* ed. Melissa J. Brown, 208–39. Berkeley: Institute of East Asian Studies, University of California.

Chen Xiaomei. 1995. *Occidentalism: A Theory of Counter-Discourse in Post-Mao China.* Oxford: Oxford University Press.

Cheung Siu-Woo. 1996. "Subject and Representation: Identity Politics in Southeast Guizhou." Ph.D. diss., University of Washington.

Chow, R. 1989. "'It's You, and Not Me': Domination and 'Othering' in Theorizing the Third World." In *Coming to Terms: Feminism, Theory, Politics,* ed. Elizabeth Weed, 152–61. London: Routledge.

Cornue, Virginia. 1996. "Love, Sex, and New Social Forms: Producing Identity and Organizations in Contemporary Beijing." Paper presented at the Association for Asian Studies Annual Meeting, Honolulu, 11–14 April.

de Certeau, Michel. 1988. *The Writing of History.* New York: Columbia University Press.

Diamond, N. 1988. "The Miao and Poison: Interactions on China's Southwest Frontier." *Ethnology* 27, no. 1:1–25.

———. 1995. "Defining the Miao: Ming, Qing, and Contemporary Views." In *Cultural Encounters on China's Ethnic Frontiers,* ed. Stevan Harrell, 92–116. Seattle: University of Washington Press.

Dikötter, Frank. 1992. *The Discourse of Race in Modern China.* Stanford: Stanford University Press.

Enloe, Cynthia. 1989. *Bananas, Beaches, and Bases: Making Feminist Sense of International Politics.* Berkeley and Los Angeles: University of California Press.

Fei Xiaotong. 1981. *Toward a People's Anthropology.* Beijing: New World Press.

Foster, S. 1982. "The Exotic as a Symbolic System." *Dialectical Anthropology* 7:21–30.

Gladney, Dru C. 1991. *Muslim Chinese: Ethnic Nationalism in the People's Republic.* Cambridge: Harvard University Council on East Asian Studies.

———. 1994. "Representing Nationality in China: Refiguring Majority/Minority Identities." *Journal of Asian Studies* 53, no. 1:92–123.

———. 1995. "Tian Zhuangzhuang, the Fifth Generation, and Minorities Film in China." *Public Culture* 8, no. 1:161–75.

Harrell, Stevan. 1990. "Ethnicity, Local Interests, and the State: Yi Communities in Southwest China." *Comparative Studies in Society and History* 32, no. 3:515–48.

———. 1995a. "Introduction: Civilizing Projects and the Reaction to Them." In *Cultural Encounters on China's Ethnic Frontiers,* ed. Stevan Harrell, 3–36. Seattle: University of Washington Press.

———. 1995b. "Jeeping against Maoism." *Positions* 3, no. 3:728–58.

———. 1996. Introduction to *Negotiating Ethnicities in China and Taiwan,* ed. Melissa J. Brown, 208–39. Berkeley: Institute of East Asian Studies, University of California.

Heng, G., and J. Devan. 1992. "State Fatherhood: The Politics of Nationalism, Sexuality, and Race in Singapore." In *Nationalisms and Sexualities,* ed. Andrew Parker, Mary Russo, Doris Summer, and Patricia Yaeger, 343–64. New York: Routledge, Chapman, and Hall.

Hung, Chang-Tai. 1985. *Going to the People: Chinese Intellectuals and Folk Literature, 1918–1937.* Cambridge: Harvard University Press.

Ivy, Marilyn. 1995. *Discourses of the Vanishing: Modernity, Phantasm, Japan.* Chicago: University of Chicago Press.

Karnoouh, C. 1982. "National Unity in Central Europe: The State, Peasant Folklore, and Mono-Ethnism." *Telos* 53:95–105.

Kligman, Gail. 1988. *The Wedding of the Dead: Ritual, Poetics, and Popular Culture in Transylvania.* Berkeley and Los Angeles: University of California Press.

Layne, L. 1989. "The Dialogics of Tribal Self-Representation in Jordan." *American Ethnologist* 16, no. 1:24–39.

Leong, Wai-Teng. 1989. "The Culture of the State: National Tourism and the State Manufacture of Cultures." In *Communication for and against Democracy,* ed. Marc Raboy and Peter A. Bruck, 75–93. Montreal: Black Rose Books.

Litzinger, Ralph A. 1995. "The Politics of the Margin: Constructions of State Power in Post-Mao China." Paper presented at the Third Workshop in Culture and the Production of Insecurity, Minneapolis, 27–29 October.

———. n.d. "Memory Work: Reconstituting the Ethnic in Post-Mao China." Manuscript.

Lowe, L. 1991. "Hegemony and Ethnic Immigrant Heterogeneities: Marking Asian American Differences." *Diaspora* 1, no. 1:24–43.

Lufkin, Felicity. 1990. "Images of Minorities in the Art of the People's Republic of China." M.A. thesis, University of California at Berkeley.

Mani, L. 1987. "Contentious Traditions: The Debate on Sati in Colonial India." *Cultural Critique* 7:119–56.

Mao Zedong [Mao Tse-tung]. 1967. "Talks at the Yenan Forum on Literature and Art." In *Selected Works of Mao Tse-tung.* Vol. 3. Beijing: Foreign Languages Press.

McKhann, C. 1995. "The Naxi and the Nationalities Question." In *Cultural Encounters on China's Ethnic Frontiers,* ed. Stevan Harrell, 39–62. Seattle: University of Washington Press.

Nader, L. 1989. "Orientalism, Occidentalism, and the Control of Women." *Cultural Dynamics* 11, no. 3:323–55.

Oakes, Timothy. 1995. "Tourism in Guizhou: Place and the Paradox of Modernity." Ph.D. diss., University of Washington.

Ong, Aihwa. 1988. "Colonialism and Modernity: Feminist Re-presentations of Women in Non-Western Societies." *Inscriptions* 3–4:79–93.

———. 1993. "On the Edge of Empires: Flexible Citizenship among Chinese in Diaspora." *Positions* 1, no. 3:745–78.

Pollock, G. 1987. "What's Wrong with Images of Women?" In *Looking On: Images of Femininity in the Visual Arts and Media,* ed. Rosemary Betterton, 40–48. New York: Pandora.

Potter, S. 1983. "The Position of Peasants in Modern China's Social Order." *Modern China* 9, no. 4 (October): 465–99.

Qiandongnan Miaozu Dongzu zizhizhou gaikuang Editing Group. 1986. *Qiandongnan Miaozu Dongzu zizhizhou gaikuang* [A general survey of the Southeast Guizhou Miao and Dong Autonomous Prefecture]. Guiyang: Guizhou People's Publishing House.

Robertson, J. 1995. "Mon Japon: The Revue Theater as a Technology of Japanese Imperialism." *American Ethnologist* 22, no. 4:970–96.

Said, Edward. 1978. *Orientalism.* New York: Vintage Books.

Schein, Louisa. 1989. "The Dynamics of Cultural Revival among the Miao in Guizhou." In *Ethnicity and Ethnic Groups in China,* ed. Chien Chiao and Nicholas Tapp, 199–212. Hong Kong: New Asia College Academic Bulletin VIII, Chinese University of Hong Kong.

———. 1991. "Nostalgia and Cultural Production: Miao Canonization of Self." Paper presented at the Center for Chinese Studies Fall Regional Seminar, University of California at Berkeley, 5 October.

————. 1993. "Popular Culture and the Production of Difference: The Miao and China." Ph.D. diss., University of California at Berkeley.

————. 1994. "The Consumption of Color and the Politics of White Skin in Post-Mao China." *Social Text* 41:141–64.

————. 1996a. "The Other Goes to Market: The State, the Nation, and Unruliness in Contemporary China." *Identities* 2, no. 3:197–222.

————. 1996b. "Multiple Alterities: The Contouring of Gender in Miao and Chinese Nationalisms." In *Women Out of Place: The Gender of Agency and the Race of Nationality,* ed. Brackette Williams, 79–102. New York: Routledge.

Swain, M. 1990. "Commoditizing Ethnicity in Southwest China." *Cultural Survival* 14, no. 1:26–32.

Tang Xiaobing. 1993. "Orientalism and the Question of Universality: The Language of Contemporary Chinese Literary Theory." *Positions* 1, no. 2:389–413.

Wakeman, Frederic Jr. 1991. *In Search of National Character.* Pre-Prints, No. 1. Berkeley: Center for Chinese Studies, University of California.

Wang He. 1986. "Traditional Culture and Modernization: A Review of the General Situation of Cultural Studies in China in Recent Years." *Social Sciences in China* 7, no. 4:9–30.

Wang, Yuejin. 1989. "Mixing Memory and Desire: *Red Sorghum,* a Chinese Version of Masculinity and Femininity." *Public Culture* 2, no. 1:31–53.

Yau, E. 1989. "Is China the End of Hermeneutics? Or, Political and Cultural Usage of Non-Han Women in Mainland Chinese Films." *Discourse* 11, no. 2:115–36.

# CHAPTER SIXTEEN

# Tradition and the Gender of Civility

*Ralph Litzinger*

This essay explores the dangers and pleasures of identity—and especially gendered identity—among the Yao. One of China's fifty-five officially recognized minority nationalities, the Yao are found predominantly in the mountains of Guangdong, Guangxi, Hunan, and Yunnan provinces. In China they are known for their adherence to an esoteric form of Taoism and for their participation in some of the final battles against the Guomindang; and they have been made popular in large part through the writings of the internationally acclaimed anthropologist and sociologist Fei Xiaotong.[1] In 1987 I began to work at the Central Nationalities Institute in Beijing with some of the leading scholars of the Yao. A small coterie of middle-aged Yao men and women, these scholars had been recruited in their home villages in the 1950s to come to Beijing to study Marxism-Leninism and nationality theory and policy. They were assigned by authorities to teach me about the culture and history of the Yao, but our discussions often focused on the twists and turns of their careers as minority intellectuals, and especially on their training in ethnology.[2] Since its institutional inception during the May Fourth period, ethnology in China had taken the non-Han Other as its object of analysis.[3] After the founding of the People's Republic in 1949, many ethnologists were called upon to assist in a massive state-sponsored ethnic identification *(minzu shibie)* project, and they were called upon to assist in the socialist development of minority regions. Ethnological research fell into disrepute during the anti-rightist campaign of 1957. A decade later, during the Cultural Revolution, ethnology was labeled as a capitalist bourgeois practice and criticized for its fascination with outmoded remnants of backward and primitive cultures, an intellectual pastime that did little to serve the continuing Maoist revolution. As happened to intellectuals across China, many leading ethnologists were sent to the country-side to learn from the peasants and to temper their revolutionary sensibilities and commitments.

The reforms would remake this history of marginalization. In the late 1970s, ethnology and other social sciences were officially rehabilitated. Deng Xiaoping implored minority scholars to discard the ideology of class struggle and to "seek truth from facts." A new, reform-era elite was required, one that would bring new discourses of nation building and new practices of development to minority populations, many of whom, such as the Yao, were still seen to be lagging behind the rest of the nation. The Yao scholars I worked with in Beijing were, like many of the Han intellectuals, critical of the class politics of the Maoist era and, at the same time, fascinated with the "cultural traditions" of their people. This dual focus on the excesses of Maoist socialism and the location and status of ethnic culture reminds us that debates about how to define the post-Mao nation extended well beyond the think tanks and research institutes dominated by the Han cultural elite in Beijing and other urban centers.[4] Elaborately planned and staged international conferences, television documentaries, personal videotapes, photographic pictorials, museums, exhibits, and films had all found something desirable in the image and, indeed, in the body of the ethnic minority subject. And yet despite this fascination, troubling questions persisted. How, after the nightmare of the Cultural Revolution, were minorities to belong to the Chinese nation? How was minority culture to be promoted by the reform regime? What forms of behavior, consciousness, and ideology were to be encouraged as the reform regime sought to bring socialist modernization to remote ethnic regions?

In recent years a plethora of writers have examined the question of tradition in nationalist discourse.[5] Some of the best work on this subject, such as Marilyn Ivy's study of Japan's modernist phantasms, has shown how desires for "traditional" culture are inflected by critical assessments of modernity and its effects on social worlds.[6] Tradition is never simply modernity's Other, nor is it an ontologically given social category that lies outside regimes of power and everyday social practice. Tradition is always interior to the modern; it always in some way marks the margins of the nation or the ruins of history.[7] As the quintessential marker of the nation's heritage, the material signs of tradition merge with the commodity form; at festivals, at cultural exhibitions, and in museums, the past is put on display and made universally available to a consuming public.[8] Jean and John Comaroff remind us that tradition and modernity have become the late twentieth century's most pliable signs. Even though academic discourse has thoroughly deconstructed and discarded these terms, they nonetheless continue to circulate in a wide array of local, national, and global contexts. They exhibit a plurality of meanings and are increasingly used in the stories "people tell themselves about themselves."[9]

The stories people tell themselves about their past, present, and future often contain traces of the discursive orderings of dominant regimes of power, whether these be colonial, nationalist, or postsocialist.[10] How then to read the continued use of these terms, and what do they tell us about social science theories of power and its subversion? Some scholars have shied away from what David Sutton has called the "trivial utopianisms" of resistance theory.[11] Others, especially those interested in the politics of indigenous representation, tell a somewhat different story. Appeals to tradition can also work to empower marginalized groups, to give voice to that which has been forbidden or pushed to the margins of dominant social orderings and classificatory schemes.[12] This is especially the case when a people's traditions have been treated as an obstacle to nation building, when their claims to identity are said to retard projects of development, or when they are asked to mark themselves as subalterns worthy of recognition and inspection.[13] The politics of culture and identity are never too far removed from the question of how peoples on the periphery of dominant regimes mobilize the resources available to them in any given historical or social context. Stuart Hall reminds us, "The issue of cultural identity as a political quest now constitutes one of the most serious global problems as we go into the twenty-first century. The emergence of questions of ethnicity, of nationalism—the obduracy, the dangers and pleasures of the rediscovery of identity in the modern world, inside and outside of Europe—places the question of cultural identity at the very center of the contemporary political agenda."[14]

My essay takes up these questions by exploring the relationship between post-Mao discourses of civility and gender difference. As many observers of post-Mao ethnic politics have argued (including Louisa Schein in the previous chapter), often public images of ethnic difference have centered on an eroticized female subject.[15] This has especially been the case in arenas of Chinese national and global tourism, where images of a feminized ethnic Other have been appropriated to represent the ethnic diversity of the nation. In the films of China's fifth-generation filmmakers, to point to yet another example, the feminized ethnic Other appears sexy and flirtatious, uninhibited by the constrictive sexual and gender mores that are said to predominate among the Han. She is sometimes seen gazing upon the contours of her own body, or she is depicted as an alluring object just out of reach of a Han male subject who wishes to rediscover his own sexuality, a sexuality lost to the gender politics of radical Maoism.[16] Minority elite have also been involved in the staging of a desirable feminized Other, a process highlighted by Schein in her ethnography of Miao cultural politics.[17] This is typically accomplished by garbing the female subject in the colorful costumes of her particular subgroup, or by having her play the gracious wine-distributing hostess at international conferences and ethnic festivals. These various eroticized displays of gender difference strongly suggest that it is the female body that is most often appropriated in displays of tradition and modernity. The female body becomes the ground upon which nationalist imaginings are enacted and performed and upon which the meanings of tradition and gender are both inscribed and contested.[18]

This essay builds upon these critiques. Unlike other studies, however, this essay focuses on the politics of masculinity. Drawing upon research conducted in Jinxiu Yao Autonomous County in Guangxi, I argue that the politics of tradition, ethnicity, and gender difference has also centered on debates about masculinity and its meanings in a modernizing and globalizing China. This is especially the case in situations in which minority elite and local officials debate the meanings of post-Mao conceptions of civility, or *wenming*, and discuss how young men are to behave in a reform period that has seen the unleashing of new economic energies.

## MASCULINITY AND THE ETHNIC SUBJECT

As I indicated above, scholars of reform-era Chinese nationalism have had much to say about the relationship between ethnic representation and gender. We have learned that the reimagining of the Chinese nation after Maoism has been not only about the manipulation of symbols to maintain national or social cohesion or about the articulation of national icons such as the Yellow River or the Great Wall or the Forbidden Palace, it is also been a feminizing and eroticizing process that has relied on phantasmagoric displays of gender difference. Gender especially has been a crucial social domain in the reforms and the cultural politics of post-Mao nationalism. Yet few scholars have inquired into the politics of masculinity. As with the question of gender and feminization, I argue that masculinity should also be approached both as a cultural construct that becomes naturalized through dominant social practices and as a domain of social struggle.[19]

I argue additionally that many studies exploring processes of feminization in representations of ethnic minority difference have assumed a masculine subject that gazes at the "titillating" ethnic female subject. It is not my intention to deny the objectifying and denigrating power of this male gaze. I insist nonetheless that there is a certain danger in this assumption, for it suggests that the female subject is present in post-Mao China only for the purpose of serving the needs and desires of the male figure, whether this figure is the Han Chinese male, the male foreign tourist, or the Chinese Party-state apparatus. This formulation arguably denies agency to women, in that it fails to come to theoretical terms with the many observable ways in which both women and men have been active agents in the making of gendered representations of ethnic minorities. Moreover, it fails to address the fact that the binary between the masculine and the feminine—or, more specifically, how the masculine and the feminine are often conceived only in terms of sexual difference—has itself become a contested notion in the social sciences.[20]

In an influential article on majority/minority identities in China, Dru Gladney has argued that the objectified portrayal of minorities has been largely about the construction of a Han Chinese majority, a majority evidently ridden with anxieties about its own practices of gender and sexuality. "The representation of minorities in such colorful, romanticized fashion," Gladney writes, "has more to do with constructing a majority discourse, than it does with the minorities themselves."[21] If this is the case, then how am I to make sense of situations and encounters in my own fieldwork in which minority elite were trafficking in "exotic" and "erotic" representations of themselves? How are we to think about the staging of ethnic minority women by women, in which young women were unambiguously marked as the carriers of tradition? How are we to understand situations in which older Yao women silenced male Yao scholars, as they instructed them on the proper way to organize a domestic ritual? How might we read the actions of a Yao female scholar who expressed a wish to work with a European photographer who had come to China to document the physical beauties of Yao women? The same woman who argued that images of young Yao men drinking, smoking, and gambling were inappropriate representations of Yao youth?

The situations from which these questions emerge point to the complicated and sometimes unpredictable ways in which understandings and images of the "masculine" and the "feminine" were used when Yao represented "traditional cultural" to a range of interlocutors. In her introduction to the influential volume *Gender Politics in Modern China*, Tani Barlow argues that around the mid–nineteenth century two new social subjects, woman *(nüxing)* and man *(nanxing)*, emerged as elemental categories of colonial modernity in China.[22] How, she asks, did these new formulae for masculinity and femininity get encoded in semicolonial China, in socialist China, and in post-Mao China? My aim in this essay is a more modest one. I am concerned less with tracing genealogies of gender in modern China and more with pointing out certain tensions and contradictions over gendered representations and behaviors in the reform period. I want to explore how desires for certain representations of male ethnic subjects reveal anxieties about the relationships between the reforms and masculinity. I will argue that the body of the ethnic male is also caught up in reform-era debates over the place of "tradition" in a socialist-modernizing present. In pushing for an approach that attends to the politics of who represents masculinized, as well as feminized, ethnic subjects, I seek to make sense of ethnic minority participation in modes of representation that many outside observers have taken to be "derogatory, colonial, and useful to the state."[23]

Focusing on the desire for and representation of a certain kind of male subject, I want to show that the making of the post-Mao "traditional" male involves modes of representation that idealize certain forms of behavior while refusing others. The tension over the desirable and the undesirable is played out here by means of a contrast between public performances, festivities, and representations and what we might call "unofficial" modes of behavior and thinking.[24] I begin the next section by describing the representation of the traditional Yao male at an international research conference in south China and then move on to an interpretation of an incident that occurred in the course of my fieldwork among Yao in Guangxi. The public performances I describe might be productively approached by regarding them as what Charles Tilley has recently termed "travelscapes," referring to domains of tourist display and consumption.[25] Analyzing a number of staged rituals at the Wala Island Tourist Resort in Vanuatu, Tilley writes that the "global travelscapes of tourism are entirely dependent for their success on the production or finding of authentic cultural difference."[26] These are thus practices of production and consumption in which the local, the national, and the global become fused, and in which producers and consumers of the authentic traditional or ethnic culture actually confront each other in person. I want to extend Tilley's work by arguing that these travelscapes also traffic in the representation of masculine and feminine subjects, in that they entail the visual objectification or the conversion of cultural and gender difference into spectacle.[27] In these travelscapes, ethnic minorities—both men and women, as we shall see—were put on display, photographed and videotaped, and studied and contemplated, as evidence of China's cultural and ethnic diversity.

My initial point here—to return to the discussion with which I began this essay—is that the practice of Yao ethnology in the late-1980s and early-1990s was influenced by serious academic debates on the status of the Chinese nation and its "peripheral" or "frontier" minorities.[28] But the ethnological study of minority culture was also characterized by practices of ethnic display in which traveling scholars, tourists, and officials were singled out as the main consumers. By examining these processes and practices of display and objectification, and contrasting them to other debates over proper forms of gender representation, we will see that representations of masculine and feminine ethnic subjects are characterized by shifting meanings, unstable power relations, and inherent contradictions.[29] In this way, post-Mao Chinese nationalism, and its imaginings across the bodies of ethnic minorities, emerges less as a case of uncontested domination than a space of cultural struggle. National identity is continuously crosscut and recreated by discourses of gender, class, and ethnic difference.[30]

## ETHNIC TRAVELSCAPES

I first encountered practices of ethnic display when, in November of 1988, I was invited to attend a conference in the town of Chenzhou, Hunan. Nestled in the foothills of the southern reaches of Hunan province, Chenzhou is surrounded by mountains, where Yao and other ethnic minorities are said to have lived for centuries after migrating from the region around Hunan's northern Dongting Lake.[31] I was traveling with a Yao ethnologist who had grown up in the mountains around Guilin City and who had been educated in Beijing. He had never before been to the Yao villages in the south of Hunan, though the state's ethnic discourse assured him he was about to visit his Yao "brothers and sisters." The conference itself was pitched as one of the first major academic gatherings in China to specifically address the "relationship between Yao traditional culture and socialist modernization." Chenzhou was chosen because of its location on the main railway line between Beijing and Guangzhou (Canton), but also because the Public Security Bureau had promised to provide safe and efficient transportation for a one-day investigation of Yao villages. As the brochure for the conference announced, here, in the hills beyond the modern buildings, wide avenues, and flourishing markets and restaurants of Chenzhou, a contingent of Chinese, Yao, and foreign scholars would visit Yao villagers, who would graciously feed us and later perform ritual dances that had been passed down from generation to generation.

I was soon to discover that these conferences did not merely signify the reform regime's openness to exchanges with foreign academics. Rather, these conferences were ideologically overdetermined venues where Yao traditional culture could be presented in a more authentic *(zhenshi)* way, no longer interpreted through the theories of the ultraleftists that predominated during Mao's reign of power. They can be approached as highly performative state-sponsored rituals in which the Chinese Communist Party presents itself as the main agent for the return and promotion of ethnic minority culture in a socialist modernizing China.[32] For example, after several days of workshops and the guided trip to the Yao mountain village, the conference ended with a festival sponsored by the provincial government commemorating the original ancestor of the Yao, a mythical dog turned human named Pan Hu, or King Pan. Held in the large central park of Chenzhou, the festival was an attempt on the part of provincial and local authorities to demonstrate publicly the Communist Party's new thinking on both the "problem of ethnicity" and the "problem of religion." In the wake of a week-long media blitz, hundreds of residents of Chenzhou observed the proceedings; the festival was videotaped and broadcast on local television; and a slew of city, county, and provincial journalists were given the opportunity to be photographed with Yao women in their early twenties dressed in various costumes and with older men outfitted in the robes and hats of the Yao Taoist priesthood (many of whom were brought down from the southern Hunan hills in Public Security Bureau vans). This public celebration was also an attempt to make an ideological statement to the fifteen or so foreign guests in attendance. The Yao were not only being recuperated as important subjects in the socialist modernization of China, they were also being marketed as desirable objects of knowledge in the new internationalization of Yao studies in the late 1980s.

The festival began with the welcoming of invited dignitaries, followed by a series of speeches by local- and provincial-level leaders. Banners and other gifts were then formally exchanged, symbolically linking the guests from other regions of China to guests from around the world in the mutual honoring of the Yao. The speeches, read aloud in *putonghua* (also known as Mandarin Chinese—the national, "northern" language taught in most schools and used on national television), stated that King Pan had once again returned to the homes of the common Yao person (the Yao *laobaixing*), a clear reference to the fact that Pan Wang activities had been forbidden during the Cultural Revolution. The agent of this return, this recovery of King Pan, was repeatedly marked as the reform state: religious activities had returned to social life because of the enlightened reform policy on how to treat ethnic minorities. The mistakes of the past would not again be made. The discourse was explicit on this point: the official commemoration of religious activities fully demonstrated that the central branch of the Communist Party has a profound interest and concern for the welfare of the country's minority nationalities. The Party and the ethnic minority were once again to become mutual partners in the rebuilding of China.

The articulation of a new relationship between the ethnic minority subject and the Communist Party is embedded in a larger discourse on the need for productive ethnic citizens. The Yao ethnologist with whom I traveled made clear to me that these were manufactured ritual performances, but he also argued that these state-sanctioned displays of tradition served a function. Public celebrations of ethnic traditional culture (especially when documented by journalists and broadcast on local and sometimes national television) would serve to strengthen the unity of all peoples within the country; they would promote connections on all fronts of social life and develop productive relations in the mutual quest for socialist modernization. This language is easily recognizable as the ritualized propaganda of the reform regime in the mid- and late 1980s. What is perhaps less apparent is how such public performances, stripped of the once-dominant political language of class struggle, are themselves calls for ideological mobilization: these public performances are believed to arouse the spirit of productivity, a spirit said to be rendered dormant during the height of Maoist class struggle. This Pan Wang festival in particular was heralded as an important event in the modernization of the Yao hills: it would inspire the Yao to return to the mountains and undertake China's nationalist venture. In public proceedings of state domesticated rituals such as this one, in which a spirit of productivity is said to be aroused through the popularization of practical and realistic activities such as dancing, singing, and the telling of traditional tales, the term worship *(chongbai* or *baibai)* is rarely employed, nor does one encounter the burning of incense or the offering of food to various deities. When I queried my Yao ethnologist colleague on this discrepancy, he assured me that worship was largely a private, household affair, one that the Party allowed yet continued to closely monitor.[33]

It is clear that in these reform-era festivities, domestic and village ritual events have been transported into economies of meaning that celebrate the aspiring modernity of the nation.[34] That is to say, after decades of suppression, these ritual activities are not simply being celebrated as part of the grand repertoire of the Yao traditional world but are also being reinterpreted as signs of cultural and ethnic diversity as China attempts to refashion its image in the outside world, the world of foreign anthropologists, investors, government and nongovernment officials, and tourists (Chinese, Yao, and foreign). Thus, they arguably have less to do with the Yao than with how the Chinese nation, and the Community Party in particular, projects an image of itself to the population for whom it claims to speak.[35]

In addition to these discourses of ethnic diversity and the need for productive minority citizens, the marking of gender difference is also a salient feature of these conferences and staged performances. These festivities use gendered representations of Yao men and women, in which men and women of different ages are decked out in traditional costume and are asked to perform activities that mark the particular cultural attributes of the Yao. That is, these gendered representations are made across the bodies of both men and women, in that men as well as women are asked to stand in, mark themselves, and speak for and on behalf of the Yao "traditional" world. For example, during the public performances of the Pan Wang Festival in Chenzhou, young Yao men were brought onstage dressed in the robes of the Taoist religious specialist to enact various rituals. As I learned later in the day, some of these young men had yet to be initiated into the Taoist priesthood and, in fact, only recently had been trained in how to do the moves and ritualized steps associated with the practice of Taoism. One young man professed to me that he actually had very little understanding of the complex ritual meanings associated with Yao Taoism. He told me that he had been taught to do the dances so that the performance itself could demonstrate that young Yao men were still engaged in learning the trade. While such performances are meant to suggest that Yao ritual is flourishing in the remote mountains of south China, they reveal a certain anxiety over the fact that many young Yao men eschew these religious practices (as many young Yao men professed to me). What seems to be important at these state-sponsored public festivities is the creation of an image that young men are still part of, still involved in the reproduction of Yao ritual practice. They suggest that there is still a place for young Yao men in the post-Mao recuperation and public depiction of the Yao religious tradition.

To be sure, in the public performances of Yao tradition, men are never asked, as Yao women often are, to pander to guests by serving wine in suggestive ways, nor do men find themselves the center of attention in the ubiquitous photo session. They are thus rarely, if at all, treated as eroticized subjects.[36] Nonetheless, as we have seen in the training of young men to perform the dances of Yao Taoism, male subjects are often employed to represent Yao ritual and other aspects of the tradition. What is elided in these public festivities is the fact that there are other forms of post-Mao masculinity that many Yao cadre, scholars, and elders find distasteful. These are forms of masculinity that many people claim have nothing to do with the Yao tradition and that they associate with behaviors and modes of thinking unleashed by the reforms. These forms of masculinity are kept on the margins of public depictions of Yao cultural difference. They give rise to debates over the proper role of the male subject in disciplinary projects of bringing civility *(wenming)* and modernization *(xiandaihua)* to young urban and rural Yao youth, and they create discourses about desirable and undesirable forms of gendered behavior. Put somewhat differently, as certain images of Yao masculinity are recuperated in the imagining of the Yao tradition, others become equated with a kind of unleashed modernity and thus are pushed to the side, ultimately denied representational space in the images of the traditional. In the process, both the modern and the traditional become reified categories. Each is treated as a enclosed space with associated behaviors and modes of thinking.

## THE UNDESIRABLE MASCULINE SUBJECT

In 1990—after the Tiananmen Square incident of 1989—I returned to China and the Central Nationalities Institute in Beijing. Subsequently, I traveled south and began research in the town of Jinxiu in an area known as the Great Yao Mountains (the Dayaoshan) in Guangxi. During my stay in both places, I spent a good deal of time with young Yao men. Some of this time was spent engaged in informal language training, but often we simply hung out listening to music; debating the differences between American,

Yao, and Han Chinese culture; commenting on national and local politics; and ruminating on the Yao men's attempts to find suitable marriage partners. In Jinxiu especially, I was often in the company of Yao men in their mid- to late twenties, and we spent evenings wandering the county seat of Jinxiu, eating, drinking, and visiting friends. I want to now describe one particular incident that resulted from my desire to record visual images of these rituals of male sociality.

One evening in the winter of 1991, just after the Chinese New Year, I was invited to have dinner at the home of a young Yao couple in the village of Xidi. Abutting the administrative seat of Jinxiu county, Xidi was populated entirely by members of the Chashan, or "tea mountain," Yao. The village had been transformed into a production brigade in the 1950s, and, in large part because of its close proximity to the county seat, it was enjoying renewed prosperity under the reforms. Many of the residents were remodeling their homes, for example, or were building new cement structures, which were considered to be an improvement over the older style homes. This dinner was to be a special meal, since the husband had just returned from market with a dog. Many of my young male friends had been enthusiastically encouraging me to join them for a meal of dog meat since I arrived in Jinxiu some months earlier. In part this was because they thought foreigners who visited the mountains rarely had the opportunity to indulge in this local delicacy. It was also because in Jinxiu county eating dog meat was somewhat of a transgression. Many of the Yao groups (in particular the Pan, or Mien-speaking Yao) never ate dog, for they traced the original progenitor of their subgroup to the mythological mottled dog-turned-human named Pan Hu. I was in fact living among a valley-dwelling Yao group—the Chashan Yao—who were linguistically and culturally related to the Zhuang nationality and who frequently ate dog. On this particular evening we shared a delicious dog soup and great amounts of local wine. Our eating and drinking festivity went late into the night, and we soon turned to the game of finger gambling, in which two people try to outwit each other through a complex game of addition and subtraction, with the loser quickly downing a glass, sometimes a small bowl, of wine.

Toward the end of the evening, we all became increasingly loud in our drunken state. Before long, a member of the village Party committee stopped by the house to investigate the nature of the ruckus. Part of this person's charge was to see that members of the village honored the tenets of the Civilized Village Campaign. One of the local tenets concerned gambling, which was often associated with excessive drinking. When this elderly village woman entered the house, I asked her to photograph me with my young friends. She quickly denied my request, asserting that such episodes were not worthy of photographic documentation. She reminded me additionally that I was in China to learn about Yao tradition. My male friends gently responded to her scolding, arguing that my request simply reflected my desire to have a photograph of this momentous evening. She would not budge, asserting this time that we would all do well to drink less and be less "uncivil" *(bu wenming).* Clearly, our boisterous behavior had transgressed some limit of what was deemed, at least by this elderly cadre, as appropriate "civil" behavior.

Several days later, I brought up this event while talking to the family with whom I was then living. They had already heard the story of the scolding in some detail. They too proceeded to remind me that a young scholar such as myself should probably spend less time hanging out with these *shao huozi,* these young men who seemed to be, they argued, distracting me from my work. I attempted to offer a counterexplanation. I suggested these evenings of boisterous drinking were actually quite productive, that they provided me with knowledge of youth culture that many Euro-American anthropologists had ignored and that many Chinese ethnologists had never written about. But these drinking games, they countered, were in no way a part of Yao traditional culture; they had been borrowed from the Han Chinese and they had become, they regretted, increasingly popular in recent years. I suggested that this was because all of these young men were now contracting their labor clearing the forests in the nearby mountains, that they had disposable income to spend, and that this in itself was something any anthropologists should pay attention to. Nonetheless, an older cousin shot back, all of this was not part of "traditional culture." This, after all, was what I had come to China to study.

This incident reveals something about the dilemma of doing fieldwork among and with ethnic minority cadre in post-Mao China. In my case, these cadre were explicitly assigned by the local governmental apparatus to keep tabs on my whereabouts, wanderings, and queries. The creative and sometimes stifling modes of control associated with one's official *peitong* (research guide) is something that many anthropologists have commented on but few have theorized.[37] At issue here is the disciplinary nature of ethnological research under the reforms, where certain cultural practices and histories are marked as belonging to the space of ethnic traditions— the proper object of ethnological research in China, at least in the late 1980s and early 1990s. But more than this, these modes of fieldwork control and disciplinary classification have everything to do with gender or, more specifically, with gendered behaviors that are deemed appropriate to the study of tradition. I had come to China and specifically to Jinxiu to learn something of Yao Taoism. Along the way, I had grown increasingly interested in the labor practices of young men, what they did with their money, and how they, to use an American idiom, "partied" in their free time. For the cadres who watched my movements, the late-night leisure time of these young men was not within the scope of my proper anthropological work.

Put differently, how they passed their time in the not-so-quiet-and-ordered realm of the everyday was simply not "traditional." It was not something I should write about. It was certainly not something I should photograph.

What then was I to record? What in fact was worthy of the photographic image? And what does this tell us about what kinds of masculine subjects are permitted within the frame of the ethnological and the traditional? One clue to this is provided in a glossy photographic album published by the People's Press in Beijing in 1990. Simply titled *The Yao Nationality*, this spectacular book was presented to me as a gift during the course of my fieldwork and can be purchased at ethnic minority museums and some bookstores throughout China. As with other books that visually document the customs and traditions of the ethnic minority subject, *The Yao Nationality* was compiled and edited by the leading Yao scholars in China, such nationally and internationally known Yao as Huang Yu, Pan Chaoyue, and Zhang Youjun.[38] All three of these Yao are prolific writers on Yao society, history, and culture and are associated with the Guangxi Nationalities Institute in Nanning. They have been instrumental in the organization of international Yao studies conferences (such as the Chenzhou conference) in both China and abroad. I first met Huang Yu's son, Huang Fangping (also an important scholar in the field of Yao studies) at a Yao studies conference in Richmond, California, in 1987. Several years later, in Nanning, I asked him (a question I would pose to many of my research associates) why these photography books had become so important in ethnic minority publishing circles in China. He responded that they were one way in which the Yao could show that their customs and traditions had survived the "ten bad years," a common reference to the Cultural Revolution. When I asked about the written commentary in the book, he said it was informed by the new turn in Yao ethnology and history. This new turn was a reference to Deng Xiaoping's socialist modernization campaign, but it also referred to an interpretive practice whereby reform-era minority scholars were working to expunge the system of class analysis that had been used with destructive fervor by the ultraleftists. This new turn was also informed by an ideologically selective gendered imaginary, one that would make space for both images and representations of masculinized and feminized subjects, but only subjects of a certain kind.

Paging through the resplendent images of *The Yao Nationality*, the viewer gazes upon men in indigo trousers and top shirts and women in embroidered turbans—that is, subjects who evidently still pass their days dressed in the traditional clothing of their particular subgroup. Juxtaposing portraits of particular individuals with documentary photography of ritual practices, and with an occasional panoramic view of an unnamed mountain dwarfing a Yao village, one is taken on a tour, in effect, of the landscape of Yao traditional life. The photo album is organized into chapters of ethnological interest. One looks upon scenes of local conditions, the diversity of Yao customs, instances of material culture, and the many natural resources found in the place in which the Yao reside. The final chapter is a closing refrain celebrating the new "socialist modernization" chapter in the history of the Yao. All of the chapters give a sense of the functional interrelatedness of the Yao cultural and social totality. The once-dominant narrative of class struggle is entirely erased, aside from the occasional reference to "backward" practices the Yao have "thrown off." One photograph, for example, depicts a stele erected in the 1980s commemorating the Yao resolve to do away with "ancient" stipulations against intermarriage with other ethnic groups.[39] Gathered around the stele are young men and women dressed in traditional costume, together reading the stele's inscription: "A reminder to our descendants" *(qiu liu hou ji)*. This depiction of a milestone in the "Yao ideological revolution" is one of the few situating the Yao in a specific historical moment, the mid-1980s. Yet the sense of functional interrelatedness is never abandoned. For even with certain ideological adjustments in family, economy, and social structure, Yao culture today remains a fully ordered totality. This is a cultural totality that has evidently endured into the reform present despite decades of political campaigns and developmental projects aimed at nothing less than the complete transformation of that which is now rendered visible in all its splendid diversity.

The book also contains images of the division of labor. Women are shown engaged in household duties or tasks: washing vegetables by a roaring stream; sewing baskets on a verandah, with the expanse of the mountains in the background; or embroidering detailed and multicolored skirts and headdresses, the quintessential marker of China's upland ethnic groups. The men appear as hunters, almost always dressed in indigo clothing, as they embark for the hills with old rifles or crossbows strung over their backs, or they appear as performers preparing for a major ritual event. Scenes of the everyday also predominate. Men are shown loading a tobacco pipe or sharing a smoke; women sit around domestic spaces seemingly engaged in gossip. These divisions of traditional labor and idle time are also crosscut by yet another division within the social body, as many images depict the Yao in the company of Party cadre, almost always male, dressed in the green and blue overcoats and trousers of socialist uniformity. It is here that the state exerts a visible presence, but always in the most benign fashion and usually in the form of smiling spectators at some everyday "traditional" activity. In another image we encounter a political slogan etched into a rock face, reminding the viewer that certain stretches of the Yao mountains belong to the memory of the Long March: "The Red Army will protect the Yao."

The presence of smiling Party cadre at traditional festivities and of other signs of Party history in the remote mountains is meant to show that the Yao and the Chinese state have finally reconciled past tensions and antagonisms. Additionally, Yao traditional culture, while still subject to the gaze of the state, nonetheless has something to contribute to the reimagining of the Chinese nation in the aftermath of the ideological excesses of Maoism. There is also a space for gender differences in this social totality. However, these differences have been contained—domesticated, one might say— within an image repertoire of a naturalized world of male and female forms of productive labor, ritual involvement, leisure time, and bodily adornment. In addition, these forms of social activity are treated relativistically, as though each has an equal role to play in how the Yao contribute to the making of a socialist modern future. The relationship between Yao gender difference and Yao cultural specificity is accomplished through a discourse of social harmony and solidarity. The ensemble of photographic images and sparse textual commentary that constitutes *The Yao Nationality* is completely devoid of any hint of disruption in the contemporary reform moment, as though social order has now been achieved, with men and women happily engaged in the everyday tasks of Yao social life.

In short, then, one can say that a place has been found for the masculine ethnic subject in the post-Mao nation. This subject does not compete with representations of feminized ethnic subjects. I argue, in fact, that both subjects are part of the same technology of power, one that is invested in the making of a nation-space predicated on ethnic diversity and cultural plenitude. Part of my aim in this brief discussion has been to show that discourses of proper gender difference inform the imagining of a new Yao social totality. This is a totality that recuperates the traditional as a space occupied by both men and women. Certain images of gendered tasks and behavior are allowed into this enclosed space of the traditional, while others— such as drinking and gambling among Yao youth—are omitted, effectively denied presence. It would be a mistake to assume, however, that this solves the problem of the post-Mao ethnic minority as an always already exotic and eroticized feminized space. The inclusion of a discourse of masculinity in the politics of post-Mao ethnicity does not necessarily get us beyond "the issue of power as symbolized in the subject-object relationship between he who represents and she who is represented."[40] That is, it is not enough to say that the male body and discourses of masculinity also inform debates over the place of tradition in post-Mao China. Let me attempt to explicate this point by way of conclusion.

## CONCLUSION: GENDER AND THE QUESTION OF OBJECTIFICATION

In this essay I have approached three separate spaces—the Chenzhou conference, the celebratory photographic text, and an incident revolving around forms of male sociality—as each belonging to the "field" of my anthropological research. I have argued that each speaks to questions of gender representation in Yao cultural discourse. How are we to read this "field" (however multisited) in terms of China's post-Mao gender politics? How are we to theorize the multiple sites in which questions of gender and ethnic difference are revealed? Do these sites suggest a singular or universal post-Mao gender politics, one that can be generalized across the complex and varied terrain of contemporary China? And how, finally, have different social actors in China—men and women, Han and minority, elite and commoner—understood the relationship between ethnic revival and gender representation? Recent scholarship on the practice of anthropology has strongly suggested that "the field" is not simply the space from which anthropological knowledge emerges.[41] It is also a kind of fantasy site, a space that anthropologists and others invest with a multitude of meanings, though these meanings are often highly gendered and eroticized. As Andrew Killick has written, "We can no longer hide from ourselves the sexual symbolism by which the ethnographic Other, the erotic-exotic, is imagined as inhabiting an enclosed space, the field: stronghold of cultural secrets, breeding ground of experience, virgin territory to be penetrated by the ethnographer's interpretive thrust."[42]

As I noted at the outset of this essay, scholars of Chinese nationalism attentive to questions of gender have shown that minorities are often represented as feminized Others. The Chinese nation occupies the center of power and knowledge. This center is often assumed to be male and to be empowering itself by gazing upon the Other and transforming it into its own image. As Gladney has persuasively argued, objectified portrayals of ethnic minorities as exoticized and eroticized Others reveal little about the subjectivities of minorities themselves and more about the construction of the Han Chinese majority.[43] There are three important dimensions to this form of critique that I would like to highlight. First, Gladney demonstrates that post-Mao discourses about tradition and modernity, progress and backwardness, civility and vulgarity, have been made by referencing a discursively constructed Other. The nation is inscribed not just through the imagining of a new kind of community, an argument found in, for example, the work of Benedict Anderson and others. The project of reimagining the nation feeds upon the appropriation and display of internal Others, be they minorities in remote regions, costume-clad women, the uneducated peasant, or, as is often the case with the Yao, the ubiquitously displayed male Taoist priest. Second, Gladney's attention to the politics of appropriation calls into question the mimetic claims of modernist representation. Representations of smiling, seemingly happy ethnic women and men embracing the Chinese motherland do not accord with any singular reality, even while they purport to represent a total reality—in this case, a unified yet plural national body. Realism, in short, is put into the service of nationalist power. And third, Gladney's critique draws attention to questions of power and knowledge. What is reported in the ethnographic text is no longer the culture of minority X. Rather, we encounter complicated processes of struggle over the meanings of culture and the nation, identity and gender.

Gladney argues that these mimetic representations of the nation's diversity admit only one vision—the constitutive gaze of the male Han subject. The subject of representation is the Han state, absolutely centered, unitary, and masculine. Commodified and objectified, the ethnic minority finds subjectivity only through its own feminization. As I argue above, Gladney tells us that dominant representations of ethnic peoples in China (those associated, for example, with the cinema of the so-called fifth-generation filmmakers or the Yunnan school of painting in the 1980s) have little to do with the minorities themselves. Appropriation is thus understood as a politics of erasure. Gladney's reading thus works to return agency to China's ethnic minorities. He convincingly shows that the homogeneity of the majority is made at the expense of the minority, and he implicitly suggests that a distinct cultural space for the ethnic minority can never fully be captured in the phantasmagoric and gendered imaginings of the Chinese nation.

One concern I have with this argument—and this problem is regnant in criticisms of dominant colonial and nationalist representations—is that it runs the risk of imputing an authentic subject position to the Other. The identity of the Other can never be captured, never brought to representation in the desires, musings, and cultural productions of the dominant Han regime. Who, then, is left to recover the identity of the Other? Is it the anthropologist, gazing out upon the terrain of the Chinese ethnic and nationalist discourse, who alone possesses the power to rescue the ethnic back from the Chinese nation-state? I argue that our attention should be shifted away from the politics of misrepresentation and the recovery of authentic subjects and toward the politics of what I call participation and national belonging. The question then becomes of one of theorizing how different actors participate in the making of images that anthropologists and other critical interlocutors find essentializing, degrading, and disempowering. Take the following example. When discussing the minority song-and-dance routines shown on the CCTV Central Broadcasting System's New Year's Day show in 1991, Gladney asserts in a footnote that the Hui tend to eschew the iconographic depiction of the song-and-dance routine. Yet they are nonetheless there, singing and dancing like any other minority, marking their own alterity by reciting the traditional Arabic greeting over and over again.[44] In this critical moment in his discussion, the Hui subject is at once capable of standing outside this system of representation and central to it, an active participant in its making. The Other may be aware of the denigrating or trivializing aspects of this mode of performance. But she may also embrace it, or find pleasure in it. At the very least, we might want to understand this participation—to return to the Stuart Hall quote in the first section of this essay—in terms of how different actors mobilize the resources available to them in different historical and social contexts.

To reiterate, then, the crucial issue is not the politics of appropriation and misappropriation, an issue that will invariably lead us down the slippery slope of authenticity. It is how one theorizes different modes of participation in different regimes of power. Such a methodological shift is evident in Lisa Rofel's reading of the popular Chinese television drama *Yearning*, which first aired in China in 1991. Although Rofel aims to bring popular media into the purview of anthropological research, she is also interested in a broader theoretical agenda. This concerns the question of how to understand the agency of people who become intensely involved with the fictionalized characters of a popular media event. She writes, "Accounting for the interpretive agency of people with conflicting views requires moving beyond a celebration of spectators' autonomy or resistance that relies on positivist assumptions about 'choosing' meanings. . . . The popularity—as well as the controversy—of *Yearning* signals an emergent process, a contested moment in the making of Chinese national political culture. It reflects a similarly contested historical moment regarding how the future of the citizens of the nation-state is being fantasized."[45]

This passage show us that a people's passionate and often critical involvement in the images they see of their nation, country, and history is not necessarily about the search for authentic selves and subjects, but may be about contests over how the nation and its citizens should be imagined. As different people become involved in these media productions, they do not mindlessly reproduce their forms in their own fantasies and desires, or in the stories they tell themselves about themselves. Rofel does not see their passionate and critical involvement as an oppositional force, as if a critical engagement or reflection with a cultural form or production automatically undermines the state and its narratives of history and progress. Rofel also refuses to see various actors' participation in this national media event as mechanically reflecting a shared cultural system. Rather, she shows how spectators, as well as the fictional characters they embrace and reject, belong to complex national, class, and gender positionings. These positionings are constantly thrown open to question as people respond to historical events. This is a model of agency without an origin in a fixed cultural identity, but also without a future already mechanically determined by a dominant narrative.

I initially thought that telling a story about the place of masculinity in the recuperation of Yao "traditional" culture would complicate our understandings of how gender and ethnicity have been central to post-Mao national imaginings. Perhaps this has been the case. I want to end with a caveat, however. The desire to write the masculine into our narratives of Chinese nationalism can come perilously close to recuperating masculinity as a counterform of gender power, one that can be easily contrasted to, perhaps even serve as a foil for, processes of ethnic feminization. This has not been my aim. I have, rather, sought to situate the imagining of the feminine and the masculine within processes of contested representation. I have shown how specific kinds of masculine and feminine subjects are deemed desirable when civility, or *wenming*, becomes the quintessential marker of progress and national belonging. To be sure, I desired to celebrate the wine-drinking and dog-eating escapades of my Yao male friends as oppositional moments, especially given the fact that they drew the attention of Party officials and other elite who found these acts vulgar and disgusting, unbecoming of a national minority that best serves the Chinese nation by acting *wenming*. These modes of behavior are associated with the unruly dimensions of the reforms. They are contested behaviors and, thus, have become one of the new objects of ideological struggle in gendered discourses of civility and post-Mao socialist modernity.

## NOTES

1. For discussions of Yao Taoism, see Jacques Lemoine, "Yao Culture and Some Other Related Problems," in *The Yao of South China: Recent International Studies*, ed. Lemoine and Chao Chien (Paris: Pangu, Editions de l'A.F.E.Y, 1991), 591–612; and Zhang Youjun, *Yaozu zongjino lunji* [Collected essays on Yao religion] (Nanning: Guangxi Yaozu yanjin xuehui, 1986). For an outline of Fei Xiaotong's work on the Yao and the relevance of the Yao to the study of minority unity and difference in the People's Republic, see Fei Xiaotong, preface to *Pancun Yaozu* [The Yao of Pan Village], ed. Hu Qiwang and Fan Honggui (Beijing: Minzu chubanshe, 1983), 1–16. I discuss Fei's views on the Yao question in Litzinger, *Other Chinas: The Yao and the Politics of National Belonging* (Durham: Duke University Press, 2000). For other ethnological work on the history of the Yao in the People's Republic, see Huang Yu and Huang Fangping, *Yaozu* [The Yao nationality] (Nanning: Minzu chubanshe, 1990); and Su Defu and Liu Yulian, *Chashan Yao yanjiu wenji* [Collected essays on the tea-mountain Yao] (Beijing: Zhongyang minzu xueyuan chubanshe, 1992).

2. The Central Nationalities Institute in Beijing—now known as the Central Nationalities University—sponsored my first visit to China in 1988 and my subsequent field research between 1990 and 1992 in the Jinxiu Yao Autonomous County in Guangxi. Funding for the research from 1990 to 1992 was provided by the Committee on Scholarly Exchange with the People's Republic of China and by a Fulbright grant. I wish to acknowledge here the warmth and intellectual camaraderie of Liu Yulian, Su Defu, Pan Chengqian, Huang Fangping, Huang Zhihui, Wang Hongman, and Su Xiaoxian.

3. For the best historical overview of ethnology and anthropology in China, see Greg Guldin, *The Saga of Anthropology in China: From Malinowski to Moscow to Mao* (New York: M. E. Sharpe, 1994). See also Litzinger for a discussion of the revitalization of ethnology and its relationship to the historical consciousness of socialism, pp. 90–98.

4. The reference here is to what has become known as the "culture fever" or *wen-hua re* movement. For an excellent discussion of this period, see Jing Wang, *High Culture Fever: Politics, Aesthetics, and Ideology in Deng's China* (Berkeley and Los Angeles: University of California Press, 1996). For a discussion of intellectuals during this period and their relationship to the state's cultural policy, see David Wu, "The Cultural Mission of the Chinese Intelligentsia: A Second Look at the Cultural Fever," in *From Beijing to Post Moresby: The Politics of National Identity in Cultural Policies*, ed. Virginia R. Dominguez and David H. Y. Wu (Newark, N.J.: Gordon and Breach, 1998), 247–62.

5. For a recent overview of the "invention of tradition" literature in anthropology, see Charles L. Briggs, "The Politics of Discursive Authority in Research on the 'Invention of Tradition,'" *Cultural Anthropology* 11, no. 4 (1996): 435–69.

6. Marilyn Ivy, *Discourses of the Vanishing: Modernity, Phantasm, Japan* (Chicago: University of Chicago Press, 1995).

7. Guarav Desai, "The Invention of Invention," *Cultural Critique* (spring 1993): 119–42.

8. Daniel Sherman and Irit Rogoff, *Museum Culture: Histories, Discourses, Spectacles* (Minneapolis: University of Minnesota Press, 1994); Allen Chun, "The Culture Industry as National Enterprise: The Politics of Heritage in Contemporary Taiwan," in *From Beijing to Post Moresby: The Politics of National Identity in Cultural Policies*, ed. Virginia R. Dominguez and David H. Y. Wu (Newark, N.J.: Gordon and Breach, 1998), 77–115.

9. Jean Comaroff and John Comaroff, *Modernity and Its Malcontents: Ritual and Power in Postcolonial Africa* (Chicago: University of Chicago Press, 1993).

10. For discussions of the question of postsocialism, see Arif Dirlik, "Postsocialism? Reflections on 'Socialism with Chinese Characteristics,'" in *Marxism and the Chinese Experience: Issues in Contemporary Chinese Socialism*, ed. Dirlik and Maurice Meisner (New York: M. E. Sharpe, 1989), 362–84; Katherine Verdery, *What Was Socialism, and What Comes Next?* (Princeton: Princeton University Press, 1996).

11. David Sutton, review of *Tradition and Modernity in the Mediterranean*, by Vassos Argyou (published on the Internet by H-NET, Society for the Anthropology of Europe [www.h-net.msu.edu/~sae/], July 1997).

12. R. Radhakrisnan, *Diasporic Mediations: Between Home and Location* (Minneapolis: University of Minnesota Press, 1996); Mark Rogers, "Beyond Authenticity: Conservation, Tourism, and the Politics of Representation in the Ecuadorian Amazon," *Identities* 3, nos. 1–2 (1996): 73–125; Jonathan Friedman, "The Politics of De-Authentication: Escaping from Identity, a Response to 'Beyond Authenticity' by Mark Rogers," *Identities* 3, nos. 1–2 (1996): 127–36.

13. Elizabeth Povinelli, "Settler Modernity and the Quest for an Indigenous Tradition," *Public Culture* 11, no. 1 (1999): 19–48.

14. Stuart Hall, "Negotiating Caribbean Identities," *New Left Review* 209 (1995): 3–14; quote is on p. 4.

15. Dru C. Gladney, "Representing Nationality in China: Refiguring Majority/Minority Identities," *Journal of Asian Studies* 53, no. 1 (1994): 92–123; Stevan Harrell, *Cultural Encounters on China's Ethnic Frontiers* (Seattle: University of Washington Press, 1995); Emily Chow, "Hegemony, Agency, and Re-presenting the Past: The Invention of Dongba Culture among the Naxi of Southwest China," in *Negotiating Ethnicities in China and Taiwan*, ed. Melissa Brown, China Research Monograph (Berkeley: Insti-

tute of East Asian Studies, University of California at Berkeley, 1996), 208–39; Andrew Parker et al., eds., *Nationalisms and Sexualities* (New York: Routledge, 1991).

16. See Esther Yau, "Is China the End of Hermeneutics? Or, Political and Cultural Usages of Non-Han Women in Mainland Chinese Films," *Discourse* 11 (1989): 115–36; Gladney, "Representing Nationality"; Gladney, "Tian Zhuangzhuang, the Fifth Generation, and Minorities Film in China," *Public Culture* 8, no. 1 (1995): 161–70; and Paul Clark, "Ethnic Minorities in Chinese Films: Cinema and the Exotic," *East-West Film Journal* 1, no. 2 (1987): 15–31. For an excellent discussion of the politics of gender and the body under Maoism, see Meng Yue, "Female Images and National Myth," in *Gender Politics in Modern China: Writing and Feminism*, ed. Tani E. Barlow (Durham: Duke University Press, 1993), 118–139. For a recent discussion of journalism and sexuality in post-Mao China, see Xu Xiaoqun, "The Discourse of Love, Marriage, and Sexuality in Post-Mao China: A Reading of Journalistic Literature on Women," *positions: east asia cultures critique* 4, no. 2 (1996): 381–415.

17. In addition to the previous chapter, see Schein, *Minority Rules: The Miao and Feminization in China's Cultural Politics* (Durham: Duke University Press, 1999).

18. See Lata Mani for a discussion of this phenomenon in Indian colonial history. Mani, "Contentious Traditions: The Debate on Sati in Colonial India," in *The Nature and Context of Minority Discourse*, ed. Abdul R. Jan Mohamed and D. Lloyd (New York: Oxford University Press, 1990), 319–56.

19. Outside of the China field, see Michael Kimmell and Michael A. Messner, eds., *Men's Lives* (New York: Macmillan, 1992).

20. Teresa de Lauretis, *Technologies of Gender: Essays on Theory, Film, and Fiction* (Bloomington: Indiana University Press, 1987), 1–3.

21. Gladney, "Representing Nationality," 94.

22. Tani Barlow, introduction to *Gender Politics in Modern China: Writing and Feminism*, ed. Barlow (Durham: Duke University Press, 1993), 1–12; Barlow, "Politics and Protocols of *Funu:* (Un)Making National Woman," in Christina Gilmartin, Gail Hershatter, Lisa Rofel, and Tyrene White, eds., *Engendering China: Women, Culture, and the State* (Cambridge: Harvard University Press, 1994), 339–59.

23. Gladney, "Representing Nationality," 93.

24. Perry Link et al., eds., *Unofficial China: Popular Culture and Thought in the People's Republic* (Boulder, Colo.: Westview Press, 1989).

25. Charles Tilley, "Performing Culture in the Global Village," *Critique of Anthropology* 17, no. 1 (1997): 67–89; see also Arjun Appadurai, "Disjuncture and Difference in the Global Cultural Economy," *Public Culture* 2 (1990):1–24.

26. Tilley, "Performing Culture," 74; see also Rogers, "Beyond Authenticity."

27. Ellen Strain, "Exotic Bodies, Distant Landscapes: Touristic Viewing and Popularized Anthropology in the Nineteenth Century," *Wide Angle* 18, no. 2 (April 1996): 71–100.

28. The "periphery" and the "frontier" continue to be dominant tropes in the study of China's ethnic minorities. See, for example, the title of Harrell's influential volume, *Cultural Encounters on China's Ethnic Frontiers*. In his introduction, Harrell correctly observes that China's "civilizing" projects (Confucian, Christian, Communist, etc.) have all used metaphors of education, history, and sex to represent ethnic

minority difference. Spatial metaphors of the remote, the periphery, and the frontier should also be included as important tropes in the civilizing imagination.

29. Laurie J. Sears, introduction to *Fantasizing the Feminine in Indonesia,* ed. L. Sears (Durham: Duke University Press, 1996), 1–46; see especially pp. 4–5.

30. Lisa Rofel, "*Yearnings:* Televisual Love and Melodramatic Politics in Contemporary China," *American Ethnologist* 21, no. 4 (1994): 700–22; Rofel, *Other Modernities: Gendered Yearnings in China after Socialism* (Berkeley and Los Angeles: University of California Press, 1999); Purnima Mankekar, "National Texts and Gendered Lives: An Ethnography of Television Viewers in India," *American Ethnologist* 20 (1993): 543–63.

31. Huang Yu and Huang Fangping, *Yaozu.* For a discussion of this material as it pertains to the politics of remembering and forgetting socialism, see Ralph Litzinger, "Memory Work: Reconstituting the Ethnic in Post-Mao China," *Cultural Anthropology* 13, no. 2 (1998): 224–55.

32. Perhaps the first time the ultraleftist mistakes of the Maoist period were publicly acknowledged and criticized in ethnological circles occurred at a huge ethnology studies meeting held in Guiyang, Guizhou, in October of 1980. The text of the opening speech, as well as other essays addressing the past and future of ethnology studies in China, is collected in the first edition of the journal *Minzuxue yanjiu* [Ethnological research]. See Qui Pu, "Minzuxue de xin kaiduan" [A new beginning for ethnology], *Minzuxue yanjiu* 1 (1981): 1–8.

33. I discuss the monitoring of household ritual through the Civilized Village Campaign in Litzinger, "The Politics of the Margin: Reimagining the State in Post-Mao China," in *Cultures of Insecurity: States, Communities and the Production of Danger,* ed. Jutta Weldes, Mark Laffey, Hugh Gusterson, and Raymond Duvall (Minneapolis: University of Minnesota Press, 1997). See also Anagnost's ground-breaking analysis of these campaigns and Dirlik's early report. Ann Anagnost, "Socialist Ethics and the Legal System," in *Popular Protest and Political Culture in Modern China: Learning from 1989,* ed. Jeffrey N. Wasserstrom and Elizabeth J. Perry (Boulder, Colo.: Westview Press, 1992), 177–205.

34. This point is further developed in Litzinger, "Memory Work." See as well Prasenjit Duara, "Knowledge and Power in the Discourse of Modernity: The Campaigns against Popular Religion in the Early Twentieth Century," *Journal of Asian Studies* 50, no. 1 (1991): 67–83; Comaroff and Comaroff, *Modernity and Its Malcontents.*

35. This point about how the Communist Party uses representations of popular ritual in order to represent its own image of itself to the population is taken from Anagnost's study of the politics of state representation in reform-era China. See Ann Anagnost, "The Politics of Ritual Displacement," in *Asian Visions of Authority: Religion and the Modern States of East and Southeast Asia,* ed. Charles F. Keyes, Laurel Kendall, and Helen Hardacre (Honolulu: University of Hawaii, 1994), 221–54. See also Anagnost, *National Past-Times: Narrative, Representation, and Power in Modern China* (Durham: Duke University Press, 1997).

36. See Schein's chapter for a description of such formalized toasts and photo sessions.

37. An exception is Stevan Harrell, "Jeeping against Maoism." *positions: east asia cultures critique* 3, no. 3 (1995): 728–58.

38. See, for example, Huang Yu and Huang Fangping, *Yaozu;* and Zhang Youjun, *Yaozu zongjino lunji.*

39. One post-Mao Communist-Party strategy to promote nationality unification *(minzu tuanjie)* is to encourage intermarriage among different ethnic minority groups. Gladney quotes the following policy statement on the importance of inter-marriage: "This serves as historical evidence of the fact that 'interracial' marriage adds to unity among nationalities. . . . the 'gang of four' totally neglected 'interracial' marriage. . . . In fact, 'interracial' marriage expands and strengthens economic and cultural exchanges among fraternal nationalities in our country. It is conducive to social development and pushes history forward." In Dru C. Gladney, *Muslim Chinese: Ethnic Nationalism in the People's Republic* (Cambridge: Council on East Asian Studies, Harvard University, and Harvard University Press, 1991), 208.

40. Stephen A. Tyler, "Post-modern Ethnography: From Document of the Occult to Occult Document," in *Writing Culture: The Poetics and Politics of Ethnography,* ed. James Clifford and George E. Marcus (Berkeley and Los Angeles: University of California Press, 1986), 122–40; quote is on p. 127.

41. Akhil Gupta and James Ferguson, *Anthropological Locations: Boundaries and Grounds of a Field Science* (Berkeley and Los Angeles: University of California Press, 1997).

42. Andrew P. Killick, "The Penetrating Intellect: On Being White, Straight, and Male in Korea," in *Taboo: Sex, Identity, and Erotic Subjectivity in Anthropological Fieldwork,* ed. Don Kulick and Margaret Willson (New York: Routledge, 1995), 76–106; quote is on p. 76.

43. Gladney, "Representing Nationality," 94. I am privileging Gladney's work here in large part because his article in the *Journal of Asian Studies* has enjoyed widespread attention in the China field and beyond. To the best of my knowledge, no one has yet to proffer a critical reading of this important essay. For different takes on these issues, one can consult Schein's chapter in this volume. Chow ("Hegemony, Agency, and Re-presenting the Past") and Sidney White have also taken up questions of gender and ethnicity. White, "State Discourses, Minority Policies, and the Politics of Identity in the Lijiang Naxi People's Autonomous County," in *Nationalism and Ethnoregional Identities in China,* ed. William Safran (London: Frank Cass, 1998), 9–27.

44. Gladney, "Representing Nationality," 95.

45. Rofel, *"Yearnings,"* 715.

# Afterword:
# Putting Gender at the Center

*Jeffrey N. Wasserstrom and Susan Brownell*

What would a book look like if it were not a text on gender *in* Chinese history but rather a text on Chinese history in which gender occupies a central and integral place? What if, instead of using history to explain gender, it used gender to explain history? Inspired by the chapters in this volume, we have sketched out in this afterword a gendered reading of a few of the main political stories of the twentieth century. In doing so, we have made it our goal to demonstrate how it might be possible to push the "engendering of Chinese history" even further than it has been pushed in the preceding pages and in the collections of essays on gender discussed in our introduction. We hope that when the possibilities for such interpretations are made clear, future researchers will want to explore them more deeply still. Taken together with the foundational scholarship by feminists and gender studies scholars that appeared between the 1970s and the end of the 1990s, *Chinese Femininities/Chinese Masculinities* might then stimulate further developments in the field.

One place to begin thematically is with the issue of national regeneration that has proved so central in recent times in China. What would happen if the topic of sexual politics were placed at the heart of one's analysis of this subject? An answer to this question might begin with a look back at texts produced just before the construction of China as a nation-state, as opposed to an empire, was undertaken—that is, at the end of the Qing period. Here, a natural focus would be the gendered aspects of Manchu-Han relations as presented in classic, early revolutionary works such as the famous call to arms by the radical martyr Zou Rong, *The Revolutionary Army*. This is because, in this 1903 nationalist tract, the revolution is presented in part as a means of avenging the Manchu rape of Han women and enslavement of Han men in the 1640s. Though seldom approached in this way, Zou's influential polemic—which was praised at the time by leading intellectual figures such as Zhang Binglin, and which has continued to be read by patriotic activists up to the present—clearly invites a feminist reading. The enduring impact of the work is linked to the author's martyrdom (Zou died in jail, imprisoned for his anti-Manchu writing) but also to the power and cultural resonances of his text.

Why exactly do we claim that Zou's polemic invites a feminist reading? We say this because of the gendered imagery and references to familial relations found throughout the text. Written when its precocious author was still in his twenties, *The Revolutionary Army* attacks earlier generations of Han fathers, sons, and brothers for having failed to prevent the "dogs" from the north from turning their daughters, mothers, and sisters into whores. Manchus are presented as sexually rapacious males who are driven exclusively by base desires to control and dominate, while Han women and men are presented as victims who should now rise up to avenge past wrongs and, through violence, regain control of their destinies.[1]

By utilizing models like those developed by Dru Gladney and others, including Louisa Schein and Ralph Litzinger in this volume, we might gain a deeper understanding of how ethnic distinction interlocks with gender in this work by Zou. In part, this interlocking in *The Revolutionary Army* and other related texts contributed to the "feminization" of the Han scholar. This emasculated male, and even more so his bound-footed wife, the victim of rape during the Manchu conquest and humiliation after that, would become symbols of and scapegoats for China's national humiliation and weakness.

Keeping in mind the arguments made by Schein and Litzinger in this volume, which draw upon earlier theoretical work by Michel Foucault and Edward Said, among others, we might move from analyzing Zou's work to examining related issues. How exactly, we might ask, were the Han literati active participants in the process of symbolic emasculation just described? And with this question in mind, we might look at similar developments that occurred in other times and places. After all, China's presumed status as the "sick man of East Asia" had parallels in other contexts, and bound feet had counterparts (e.g., the veil of Muslim women) as the symbol of "backwardness" and female oppression. Looking at contemporaneous discourses of nationalism and national humiliation in settings such as the Ottoman Empire (sometimes called the "sick man of Europe"), we could place in comparative perspective the ways that images of effeminate men and subjugated women fit into the Chinese discourse of frustrated modernity.

Of particular value here might be a work that looks at related issues in a still different setting. We are thinking of work on Jewish masculinity, which suggests that Jewish men embraced their "weakness" and feminization as a kind of resistance to or defiance of anti-Semitism.[2] In a more general sense, we might set distinctively entwined Chinese discourses of patriotism and gender against theoretical and comparative works. We might look, for example, at how Chinese themes do and do not correspond with those addressed in interdisciplinary, cross-national volumes, such as *Nationalisms and Sexualities,* that do not have much to say about China. Similarly, we might revisit forums in scholarly journals devoted to feminist assessments of nation-states, this time viewing nation-states as particular types of "imagined communities" that tend to be represented as families writ large, and noting that this, in turn, is always a gendered process. And, in all these forays outside Chinese studies, we might keep in mind Lydia Liu's oft-cited (and rightly so) essay on the role of patriotic symbol that the female body has played in Chinese novels: the violation of women's bodies in China, as elsewhere, is often treated as a metaphor for transgressions against national sovereignty.[3]

In the course of these various explorations, we would not want to forget Angela Zito's assertion that emperors in the mid- to late Qing attempted to present themselves as the perfect embodiment of the *Han* masculine ideals of filiality and literacy. Clearly, the processes of ethnic and gender distinction in the late Qing were complex and strategic and were made even more so by the ambivalent gender position of eunuchs, figures linked to the Manchu ruling house.[4] A fuller understanding of this complexity would provide a sounder foundation for understanding the Republican nation and nationalist ideology that emerged out of this period. Looking at issues of this sort would add a valuable dimension to exciting recent overviews of the Republican period's ideological dimensions—such as John Fitzgerald's *Awakening China*—which bring up in passing, but do not fully assess, the masculinist aspects of patriotic enterprises. Looking forward in time, the approach we have in mind would be a useful complement to work in progress by Paul Cohen that examines the trope of national humiliation as an enduring source of anxiety in the twentieth century and beyond. And it would be a useful complement as well to insightful recent discussions of real (in one case) and imagined (in the other) sporting events as showcases for national strength, written by Andrew Morris and Geremie Barmé, respectively.[5]

One motif in both late Qing and Republican versions of nationalism that remains powerful today is the theme of the suffering, self-sacrificing Chinese woman and the unfilial, or impotent, Chinese man who is unable to protect her. A number of scholars have traced this theme's role in specific events of the late Qing through the contemporary era. But there is still something of a split in the field when it comes to treating this issue, as well as others, in which gender and nationalism come together as topics. On the one side are the mostly male scholars who write conventional histories and political economies of nationalism, in which gender is an afterthought; on the other are the mostly female scholars who have described the engendered nature of nationalism mainly through literary theory and film criticism.

A deeper comprehension of the emotional forces involved in Chinese nationalism would be possible if these approaches were combined: we need historical and political scientific accounts of Chinese nationalism that give gender its rightfully central place. If the feminist theories are to reach their full potential, then they must move out of the realms of text and film and into the realm of mass demonstrations and everyday life as well.[6]

It is important, for example, for scholars working on popular movements to address the gendered dimensions of not only patterns of action—a theme taken up in the chapters by Emily Honig and by Elizabeth Perry and Nara Dillon in this volume—but also of terms used to galvanize support for demonstrations. Time and again, throughout the twentieth century, for instance, pamphlets and wall posters addressed the people of China as *tongbao,* a word sometimes translated as "brothers" but better rendered as "compatriots," but which literally means children of the same womb. And, time and again, reference was made to the need to defend to the *zuguo,* a term sometimes translated as "motherland" but more accurately rendered as "patrilineal homeland," since the *zu* is a descent group defined by male-to-male transmissions of power. What do these invocations of gendered categories mean, especially when taken together with other rhetorical devices that linked patriotism to communities defined in terms of men's or women's bodies and the fulfilling of particular types of familial roles? Do appeals to all Chinese as *tongbao*—a term that in private settings might refer mainly or only to the male children of a single mother but that in mass-movement settings expanded to also incorporate female children of the imagined motherland—complement or compete with the patrilineal vision of the *zuguo?* These are the kinds of questions that deserve closer scrutiny.

So, too, does the related question of how the language of *tongbao* and *zuguo* relates to an antagonistic gendered language turned against enemies of patriotic movements. What should we make, for example, of the frequent references during the May Fourth Movement of 1919 and May Thirtieth Movement of 1925 to traitors being *wangba* (turtles)? Is it relevant that this term has, among other unsavory meanings, the implication that one's mother sleeps around (turtles, according to Chinese folklore, do not know who fathered them)? Questions such as these deserve to be treated as more than just illustrative of literary or rhetorical phenomena, since it makes sense to assume that the persuasiveness of such imagery helped get people out onto the streets.[7]

One particularly interesting recent site for a case study of the kind of sexually charged and gender-inflected language we have been describing is the anti–United States and anti-NATO protests of 1999. The importance of gender in late-twentieth-century manifestations of Chinese nationalism is clearly evident in the demonstrations that erupted across China in May 1999, when—on the day before Mother's Day—three American bombs blasted into the Chinese embassy in Belgrade during NATO's air strikes against Yugoslavia. Twenty people were injured and three people were killed: a young married couple and a middle-aged woman, all journalists. The vehemence of the anti-U.S. sentiments expressed in mass demonstrations in cities across China took many China scholars by surprise. In the media and in public expressions of anger, such as letters to newspaper editors, big-character posters, placards, and Internet postings, much attention was devoted to the fact that President Clinton had deprived children of their mothers and mothers of their children on Mother's Day. The two deceased women got more publicity than the deceased man did, and the symbol of the victimized Chinese woman was much in evidence. The dominant television and front-page newspaper image was that of the distraught father of one of the female victims weeping over the bloodstained body of his daughter.

Overall, the television and photo images, combined with the media and popular rhetoric, seemed to portray the Chinese father as unable to protect his daughter from the brutal attack by the American president—whose voracious sexual appetite was already well-known because of his recent impeachment hearing. One poster at Beijing University, all in English, even accused Clinton of being a "bi-raper" because he had ravished Monica Lewinsky and then, unsatisfied, set out to rape the world. The double-filiality of this particular female victim of Western male violence was also stressed in at least some official propaganda, since a letter that her father wrote to Clinton was reproduced in some of the instant-history document collections issued when the protests subsided. In this letter, the father appealed to Clinton as a fellow father of a daughter and went into detail about how his own female child had shown her parents the greatest respect. The message was clear: she had made sacrifices to please and honor her parents before going on to make the supreme sacrifice of her life for the *zuguo*.[8]

In short, in the popular images of the anti-NATO protests the primary victims were typically women and the primary mourners were typically men. This was symbolically reinforced by the ceremony for returning the ashes of the dead to the homeland. The father of the fallen daughter and son-in-law, and the son of the fallen mother, went to Belgrade to retrieve the small caskets of ashes, and the men cradled the caskets in their arms as they walked down the steps of the jet at Capitol Airport and touched Chinese ground again. The grief of the mothers and daughters took place in the background, and when a video disk was issued to make footage of the protests and mourning rituals available for viewing at home, it was the father crying over his daughter's body that was emblazoned on the disk. All this makes sense if placed in the context of Chinese funeral traditions, which trace their roots back to the Qing code. As practiced in China today, traditional funerals in-

Figure 10. Demonstrators parade a phallic-looking missile labeled "Bring back our Compatriots!" near the embassy in Beijing during anti-NATO protests. Photo by Jeffrey Wasserstrom, 1999.

volve a gendered division of labor in which men are the primary, individual mourners and women engage in a collective, background lament.[9]

In sum, then, if we want to grasp where the strong anti-U.S. and anti-NATO sentiments were coming from in May 1999, then we must pay attention to the gendered images that provoked them *and* we must understand the gendered history that provided the context in which these images were interpreted. The anti-NATO demonstrations were but the most recent expression of a long tradition of Chinese nationalism in which gender has often occupied a central place, symbolically and practically, helping to galvanize people to take to the streets and shaping what they do and say once mobilized.

Another area of inquiry that awaits further exploration, which takes us away from the macro level of the nation-state and the uproar of street politics, is the role of gender in the formation of regional and local identities. Nationalist ideology is, of course, a constructed image of homogeneity that blankets multiple kinds of diversity. Many of the chapters in this volume focus on Han nationalist ideology, and this volume does not deal with the issue of gender and regional identity in any depth—largely because such work remains to be done. The typical treatment takes regional identity as the primary category and gender as, perhaps, an interesting illustration of regional difference—with the assumption being that regional differences are primarily generated by political and economic forces, not by gender practices.[10] But might it not be possible to place gender practices at the center of the formation of regional identities?

Helen Siu's research on marriage resistance in South China indicates that moves in this direction could prove fruitful. She shows how forms of marriage that are alternatives to the orthodox Confucian ideal have been used by different groups for different reasons in the Lingnan region of South China over the past centuries. In particular, upwardly mobile lineages used delayed-transfer marriage (in which the new wife was given a large dowry by her family and did not settle in to live with her husband for several years, if ever) as a sign of high status. Although wedding rituals of these lineages in other respects followed Confucian protocol, and the lineages used Confucian marriage customs to demonstrate their membership in the dominant Han polity and culture, Confucian authorities sometimes criticized the "bad custom" of delayed-transfer marriage and attempted to change it. Siu notes that in the mid- to late Qing, local marriage customs were creatively combined with Confucian practices, first by the elite families and then by the commoner households (but never by the Dan, the poor fisher families living in the sands).

Siu observes that women played an integral role in the historical evolution of mainstream regional culture, and that men and women actively contributed to, and were shaped by, regional culture.[11] Her detailed historical and ethnographic research creates a picture in which differences in gender practices are not simply tacked onto already existing local and regional identities but are in fact an integral part of the emergence of these identities in the first place. Gender is thus not an epiphenomenon accompanying political and economic processes but is a key player in its own right. Siu's edited book-in-progress, *Women and Regional Culture in South China: A Historical Narrative*, will provide more historical and ethnographic detail on this point. Moreover, such clarifications of gender in subnational identities should enhance our understanding of gender in national identity.

The need for more work on gender in local and regional identities within China is matched by a need for more work that places gender within the context of the larger regions of East Asia and Asia. Within sinology, gender studies seem to have developed in relative isolation from gender studies of the rest of East Asia and Asia. This relative isolation is evident in the fact that we have yet to see the publication of a book called *Gender in East Asia*. Certainly, much interesting work has been published on gender by other East Asianists, but it appears that, although sinologists read some of it, they seldom make explicit cross-cultural comparisons with it in their work.[12] There are significant cross-currents between gender in Japan, South Korea, Hong Kong, Taiwan, and mainland China that remain to be explored.

A gendered rethinking of the main political stories of the twentieth century in China would have to include the Cultural Revolution, a period whose excesses and madness have been a big question mark both for non-Chinese observers and for Chinese trying to make sense of their own experiences. One of the significant contributions of the chapters by Perry and Dillon and by Honig in this volume is their demonstration of the centrality of gender in revolutionary action and in the excesses of violence. These chapters give detailed descriptions of the roles played by socially marginal males trying to achieve what they felt was social justice, and by socially restricted females trying to prove their revolutionary worthiness by shattering the norms of propriety that bound them. The chapters suggest that, to the extent that these categories of people were more constrained by gendered social norms in normal life, they were more likely to engage in excesses when they finally broke free from those constraints. The chapters also show how the preexisting popular icons of gender transgression—male bandit-rebels and militia women—provided models for these young men and women. Considering the central role that gender and sexuality have played in many of the autobiographical accounts of the Cultural Revolution, it seems that a gendered history of the period could contribute quite a bit to our understanding of it.[13]

As China enters the twenty-first century, one narrative has just begun to fully unfold: the story of the market reforms and the growth of consumerism.[14] In one sense, the place of gender in this story has been easier to write because, unlike in the Maoist era, it was not erased; and unlike in the late Qing and early Republican eras, we sinologists are living through it, and the expressions of gender difference and the emergence of new forms of sexual inequality have been so striking that we can hardly avoid giving them their due. In another sense, however, we face new challenges because China's increasing linkages with global capital present problems that are increasingly similar to the ones experienced in the industrialized West—problems that we cannot solve or fully understand ourselves. This includes, for example, the connections between (capitalist) production and (human) reproduction, paid wage labor and unpaid household labor, wage earning and product-consumption, and so on—all of which involve complex relationships of gender to political economy. But these changes are not just political and economic. As the new millennium unfolds, it appears that, for better and also for worse, Chinese masculinity may be recovering its potency after a century of feelings of emasculation. Chinese men are inspired to flex their muscles in world politics, as well as at home by using newfound wealth to take mistresses, to allow their wives to stay at home, or to buy male tonics in the booming industry of male potency supplements.

These brief examples are designed to show that, when thinking about nationalist rhetoric or regional identities or protest movements or consumerism or a host of other topics, much can be learned from analyzing and contextualizing the sexual politics involved. We can all benefit from doing more to connect contemporary Chinese phenomena with the histories and cultures of masculinity and femininity outlined in this book. We hope that, if we have done nothing else, we have demonstrated the value of moving a concern with gender to the center of more discussions of both China's recent past and its present. We also hope we have shown that one must guard against simplification in such discussions. The subject of gender is too important to treat as an afterthought, too complex to treat superficially, and, as the contributors to the preceding pages have shown, too interesting to be discussed only in certain kinds of books or treated as the preserve of particular sorts of scholars.

## NOTES

1. Tsou Jung [Zou Rong], *The Revolutionary Army: A Chinese Nationalist Tract of 1903*, trans. and ed. John Lust (The Hague: Mouton, 1968). Although now out of print, this book is—conveniently for teaching purposes—available in libraries in a bilingual edition with copious explanatory notes by Lust.

2. Daniel Boyarin, *Unheroic Conduct: The Rise of Heterosexuality and the Invention of the Jewish Man*, Contraversions: Studies in Jewish Literature, Culture, and Society (Berkeley and Los Angeles: University of California Press, 1997); Sander Gilman, *The Jew's Body* (New York: Routledge, 1991).

3. See Andrew Parker et al., eds., *Nationalisms and Sexualities* (London: Routledge, 1991); Anne McClintock, "Family Feuds: Gender, Nationalism, and the Family," *Feminist Review* 44 (summer 1993): 61–80; Lydia Liu, "The Female Body and Nationalist Discourse: Manchuria in Xiao Hong's *Field of Life and Death*," in *Body, Subject, and Power in China*, ed. Angela Zito and Tani Barlow (Chicago: University of Chicago Press, 1994), 157–77.

4. Angela Zito, *Of Body and Brush: Grand Sacrifice as Text/Performance in Eighteenth-Century China* (Chicago: University of Chicago Press, 1997). In addition to works on eunuchs cited in the introduction, see Kam Louie, "The Macho Eunuch: The Politics of Masculinity in Jia Pingwa's 'Human Extremities,'" *Modern China* 17, no. 2 (April 1991): 163–87.

5. John Fitzgerald, *Awakening China: Politics, Culture, and Class in the Chinese Revolution* (Stanford: Stanford University Press, 1996), 132–39, 284–85, and passim; Paul Cohen's work on this subject has yet to appear in print; Andrew Morris, "Cultivating the National Body: A History of Physical Culture in Republican China" (Ph.D. diss., University of California at San Diego, 1998); Geremie Barmé, *In the Red: On Contemporary Chinese Culture* (New York: Columbia University Press, 1999), 91–93.

6. For a review of the relevant literature and a further commentary on these ideas, see Susan Brownell, "Gender and Nationalism in China at the Turn of the Millennium," in *China Briefing, 1997–1999*, ed. Tyrene White (Armonk, N.Y.: M. E. Sharpe, in cooperation with The Asian Society, 2000). For an edited collection that combines literary and film criticism with ethnography and social history, see Mayfair Mei-hui Yang, ed., *Spaces of Their Own: Women's Public Sphere in Transnational China*

(Minneapolis: University of Minnesota Press, 1999). Susan Brownell's earlier description of the gatherings that surrounded the women's volleyball team victories of the 1980s (see *Training the Body for China: Sports in the Moral Order of the People's Republic* [Chicago: University of Chicago Press, 1995], 80–92) is considerably less attentive to gender than the chapter she contributed to Mayfair Yang's volume ("Strong Women and Impotent Men: Sports, Gender, and Nationalism in Chinese Public Culture," *Spaces of Their Own: Women's Public Sphere in Transnational China* [Minneapolis: University of Minnesota Press, 1999], 207–31). The insights gained from Yang's conference and subsequent volume, as well as the sources cited in "Gender and Nationalism in China," provided the analytical inspiration to reexamine her initial account. For example, it was only in looking back at her slides that she noticed that the crowd that welcomed the team at Beijing University in 1985—an event that she herself attended—was predominantly male students.

7. The symbols and terms discussed above are examined—though, as close readers will discover, often with less attention to gendered meanings—in Jeffrey N. Wasserstrom, *Student Protests in Twentieth-Century China: The View from Shanghai* (Stanford: Stanford University Press, 1991), 220–27 and passim. See also the first photographic section in the book and note there the rendering of *tongbao* as "brothers," which now seems problematic to the author. See also the discussion of familial imagery and its nationalist dimensions in the 1989 student protests in Rudolf Wagner, "Political Institutions, Discourse, and Imagination in China at Tiananmen," in *Rethinking Third World Politics,* ed. James Manor (New York: Longman, 1991), 121–44, esp. 138–41; and Jeffrey N. Wasserstrom, postscript in *Popular Protest and Political Culture in Modern China,* ed. Wasserstrom and Elizabeth J. Perry, 2d ed. (Boulder, Colo.: Westview Press, 1994), 325–32.

8. See Jeffrey N. Wasserstrom, "Student Protests in Fin-de-Siècle China," *New Left Review* 237 (September-October 1999): 54–76; and Brownell, "Gender and Nationalism in China at the Turn of the Millennium."

9. Andrew Kipnis, *Producing Guanxi: Sentiment, Self, and Subculture in a North China Village* (Durham: Duke University Press, 1997), 101–3; William R. Jankowiak, *Sex, Death, and Hierarchy in a Chinese City: An Anthropological Account* (New York: Columbia University Press, 1993), 280; Emily Martin, "Gender and Ideological Differences in Representations of Life and Death," in *Death Ritual in Late Imperial and Modern China,* ed. James L. Watson and Evelyn S. Rawski (Berkeley and Los Angeles: University of California Press, 1988), 164–79.

10. An example is Ellen R. Judd, *Gender and Power in Rural North China* (Stanford: Stanford University Press, 1994).

11. Helen Siu, "Where Were the Women? Rethinking Marriage Resistance and Regional Culture in South China," *Late Imperial China* 11, no. 2 (December 1990): 32–62, 65; Helen Siu and Wing-hoi Chan, introduction to *Women and Regional Culture in South China: A Historical Narrative,* ed. Siu (manuscript).

12. In recent years, some of the works by anthropologists on gender in East Asian societies that cover issues similar to those covered here, have included Anne Allison, *Nightwork: Sexuality, Pleasure, and Corporate Masculinity in a Tokyo Hostess Club* (Chicago: University of Chicago Press, 1994); Matthews Hamabata, *Crested Kimono: Power and Love in the Japanese Business Family* (Ithaca, N.Y.: Cornell University Press,

1990); Dorinne Kondo, *Crafting Selves: Power, Gender, and Discourses of Identity in the Japanese Workplace* (Chicago: University of Chicago Press, 1990); Jennifer Robertson, *Takarazuka: Sexual Politics and Popular Culture in Modern Japan* (Berkeley and Los Angeles: University of California Press, 1998); and Laurel Kendall, *Getting Married in Korea: Of Gender, Morality, and Modernity* (Berkeley and Los Angeles: University of California Press, 1996). Equivalent recent works with a historical focus include Gail Lee Bernstein, ed., *Recreating Japanese Women* (Berkeley and Los Angeles: University of California Press, 1991); Gary Leupp, *Male Colors: The Construction of Homosexuality in Tokugawa Japan* (Berkeley and Los Angeles: University of California, 1996); and Jordan Sand, "House and Home in Meiji Japan, 1880s–1920s" (Ph.D. diss., Columbia University, 1995). One of the relatively rare collections to bring together works on related themes that deal with various parts of East Asia is *Modern Sex*, edited by Tani Barlow, a special issue of *positions: east asia cultures critique* 2, no. 3 (1995). This collection was also published in book form by Duke University Press in 1995.

13. In addition to works on the Cultural Revolution cited in the chapters above, see Xiaomei Chen, "Growing Up with Posters in the Maoist Era," in *Picturing Power in the People's Republic of China: Posters of the Cultural Revolution,* ed. Harriet Evans and Stephanie Donald (Lanham, Md.: Rowman and Littlefield, 1999), 101–22.

14. Two important recent books that look at aspects of this transformation, including their implications for intrafamilial hierarchies and/or gender relations, are James L. Watson, ed., *Golden Arches East: McDonald's in East Asia* (Stanford: Stanford University Press, 1997); and Deborah Davis, ed., *Consumer Revolution in Urban China* (Berkeley and Los Angeles: University of California Press, 1999).

# CONTRIBUTORS

SUSAN BROWNELL is Associate Professor of Anthropology at the University of Missouri, St. Louis. She is the author of *Training the Body for China: Sports in the Moral Order of the People's Republic* (1995) and several articles on gender and nationalism, including "Gender and Nationalism in China at the Turn of the Millennium," in *China Briefing 2000: The Continuing Transformation,* ed. Tyrene White (2000). She has given interviews on sports and beauty to NBC, the Discovery Channel, and the BBC and other international media. Her current research is on the body, gender, and nationalism in China as seen in practices such as cosmetic surgery and fashion modeling.

NANCY N. CHEN is Assistant Professor of Anthropology at the University of California at Santa Cruz. She is the author of *Breathing Spaces: Qigong, Psychiatry, and Body Politics of Contemporary China* (forthcoming) and coeditor of *China Urban: Ethnographies of Contemporary Culture and Market Socialism* (2001).

NARA DILLON is a Ph.D. candidate in Political Science at the University of California at Berkeley. She is currently writing a dissertation on charity and welfare in revolutionary Shanghai.

HARRIET EVANS is Senior Lecturer in Chinese Studies at the Centre for the Study of Democracy at the University of Westminster, where she is Coordinator of a new M.A. program in Contemporary Chinese Cultural Studies. She is the author of *Women and Sexuality in China* (1997) and coeditor of *Picturing Power in the People's Republic of China* (1999) and has published many articles on gender and sexuality in *Signs, New Formations,* and other journals. Her current work is on gender identities and the relationships between mothers and daughters in the People's Republic of China; and beauty, fashion, and the cultural production of gender in China.

CHARLOTTE FURTH is Professor of History at the University of Southern California. She is the author of many articles on concepts of pregnancy, childbirth, and sexuality in Ming-Qing China and, most recently, of *A Flourishing Yin: Gender in China's Medical History, 960–1665* (1999).

SUSAN L. GLOSSER is Associate Professor of History at Lewis and Clark College. She is author of *Saving the Nation: Chinese Visions of Family and State, 1915–1953* (2001). She also published "Milk for Health, Milk for Profit: Shanghai's Dairy Industry under Japanese Occupation," in *Inventing Nanjing Road: Commercial Culture in Shanghai, 1864–1949* (1999), and "The Business of Family: You Huaigao and the Commercialization of a May Fourth Ideal," in *Republican China* (April 1995). Her essay on women in occupied Shanghai, "'Women's Culture of Resistance'—an Ordinary Response to Extraordinary Circumstances," will appear in *Under the Shadow of the Rising Sun: Shanghai under Japanese Occupation* (forthcoming). Her current research topics include the Chinese dairy industry, Nationalist Party awards to chaste widows, and women in occupied Shanghai.

GAIL HERSHATTER is Professor of History at the University of California at Santa Cruz. Her books include *The Workers of Tianjin* (1986) and *Dangerous Pleasures: Prostitution and Modernity in Twentieth-Century Shanghai* (1997). She was also one of the coeditors of *Engendering China: Women, Culture, and the State* (1994) and a coauthor of *Personal Voices: Chinese Women in the 1980s* (1988).

EMILY HONIG is Professor of Women's Studies at the University of California at Santa Cruz. Her books include *Sisters and Strangers* (1986) and *Creating Chinese Ethnicity* (1992). A coauthor of *Personal Voices: Chinese Women in the 1980s* (1988), she is currently working on the gendered dimensions of the Cultural Revolution.

WILLIAM JANKOWIAK is Professor of Anthropology at the University of Nevada, Las Vegas. He is the author of *Sex, Death, and Hierarchy in a Chinese City: An Anthropological Account* (1993) and editor of *Romantic Passion: A Universal Experience?* (1995). In addition to numerous academic publications on Chinese society and cross-cultural topics, he has written for *The World and I* and *Natural History* and has given interviews to *Time, Newsweek, ABC Primetime,* and other popular media. His current research projects include an ethnography of a Mormon polygamous community and a restudy of Huhhot, Inner Mongolia.

THOMAS LAQUEUR is Professor of History at the University of California at Berkeley and is the author, most recently, of *Making Sex: Body and Gender from the Greeks to Freud* (1990). He writes regularly for the *London Review of Books,* the *New Republic,* and various professional journals on the cultural history of the body.

WENDY LARSON is Professor of Modern Chinese Literature at the University of Oregon. Her work includes *Literary Authority and the Modern Chinese Writer: Ambivalence and Autobiography* (1991), *Women and Writing in Modern China* (1998), a translation of Wang Meng's *Bolshevik Salute* (1989), and a coedited volume, *Inside Out: Modernism and Postmodernism in Chinese Literary Culture* (1993). She presently is working on a study of the Cultural Revolution and sexuality in New Era fiction and film.

RALPH LITZINGER is Associate Professor of Cultural Anthropology at Duke University. He is the author of *Other Chinas: The Yao and the Politics of National Belonging* (2000) and "Questions of Gender: Ethnic Minority Representation in Post-Mao China," *Bulletin of Concerned Asian Scholars* (October-December 2000), as well as other articles on the Yao and film criticism. His current research is on the environmental movement and nongovernmental organizations in China.

LYDIA H. LIU teaches jointly in the Departments of Comparative Literature and East Asian Languages at the University of California at Berkeley. She is the author of *Translingual Practice: Literature, National Culture, and Translated Modernity*

(1995) and editor of *Tokens of Exchange: The Problem of Translation in Global Circulations* (1999). She has published in the areas of popular televisual media, nineteenth-century translations of international law, and eighteenth-century English fiction and porcelain technology. Her new book, *Desire and Sovereign Thinking,* is forthcoming from the University of California Press.

SUSAN MANN is Professor of History at the University of California at Davis. She is the author of *Precious Records: Women in China's Long Eighteenth Century* (1997) and coeditor of *Under Confucian Eyes: Writings on Gender in Chinese History* (2001).

DAVID OWNBY is Associate Professor of History at the Université de Montréal. He is the author of *Brotherhoods and Secret Societies in Early and Mid-Qing China* (1996) and coeditor of *"Secret Societies" Reconsidered* (1993). He is currently working on popular religion and its intersection with local and national politics in the late imperial and contemporary eras.

ELIZABETH J. PERRY is Henry Rosovsky Professor of Government and Director of the Fairbank Center for East Asian Research at Harvard University. She is author of *Rebels and Revolutionaries in North China* (1980), coeditor of *Popular Protest and Political Culture in Modern China* (1992, 1994), author of *Shanghai on Strike: The Politics of Chinese Labor* (1993), and coauthor of *Proletarian Power: Shanghai in the Cultural Revolution* (1997). Currently she is working on a study of armed worker patrols in Republican and Communist China and coediting a volume on the changing meanings of citizenship in modern China.

LOUISA SCHEIN is Associate Professor of Anthropology at Rutgers University. She is the author of *Minority Rules: The Miao and the Feminine in China's Cultural Politics* (2000) and of numerous articles on the Miao, gender, and popular culture in China, including "The Consumption of Color and the Politics of White Skin in Post-Mao China," in *The Gender/Sexuality Reader: Culture, History, Political Economy,* ed. Roger N. Lancaster and Micaela di Leonardo (1997).

MATTHEW H. SOMMER teaches Chinese history at the University of Pennsylvania. The author of *Sex, Law, and Society in Late Imperial China* (2000), he has also published articles in journals such as *Modern China* and *Chūgoku: Shakai to Bunka.* He is currently working on a study of wife-selling, polyandry, and sex work as survival strategies among the poor in Qing dynasty China.

JANET M. THEISS is Assistant Professor of Chinese History at the University of Utah, and her research interests focus on late-imperial-Chinese gender and family history. She is currently working on a book titled *Dealing with Disgrace: Chastity and Statecraft in Mid–Qing China.*

JEFFREY N. WASSERSTROM is Associate Professor of History at Indiana University. He is the author of *Student Protests in Twentieth-Century China: The View from Shanghai* (1991), coeditor of *Popular Protest and Political Culture in Modern China* (1992, 1994), and coeditor of *Human Rights and Revolutions* (2000). His pieces on culture and politics have appeared in various academic journals, including the *Journal of Women's History* and *China Quarterly,* as well as popular publications such as the *Times Literary Supplement* (London) and the *Nation.*

# INDEX